Christmas 2009

Happy Holidays!
Enjoy the Show!

Sandy and Linda

STEVEN SUSKIN

The Sound of Broadway Music

A Book of Orchestrators and Orchestrations

OXFORD
UNIVERSITY PRESS
2009

OXFORD
UNIVERSITY PRESS

Oxford University Press, Inc., publishes works that further
Oxford University's objective of excellence
in research, scholarship, and education.

Oxford   New York
Auckland   Cape Town   Dar es Salaam   Hong Kong   Karachi
Kuala Lumpur   Madrid   Melbourne   Mexico City   Nairobi
New Delhi   Shanghai   Taipei   Toronto

With offices in
Argentina   Austria   Brazil   Chile   Czech Republic   France   Greece
Guatemala   Hungary   Italy   Japan   Poland   Portugal   Singapore
South Korea   Switzerland   Thailand   Turkey   Ukraine   Vietnam

Published by Oxford University Press, Inc.
198 Madison Avenue, New York, New York 10016

www.oup.com

Oxford is a registered trademark of Oxford University Press

Library of Congress Cataloging-in-Publication Data
Suskin, Steven.
The sound of Broadway music : a book of orchestrators
and orchestrations / Steven Suskin.
p.   cm.
Includes bibliographical references and index.
ISBN 978-0-19-530947-8
1. Instrumentation and orchestration—History.   2. Orchestrators.
3. Musicals—New York (State)—New York—History and criticism.   I. Title.
ML455.S87 2008
782.1′41374097471—dc22   2008005333

1   3   5   7   9   8   6   4   2

Printed in the United States of America
on acid-free paper

For my wife, Helen,
without whose love, encouragement, and patience
this book would have been a four-page article

for my children, Johanna and Charlie,
who make every day a joyous adventure

and for the heretofore anonymous orchestrators
whose names will nevermore be forgotten
by anyone who reads these pages

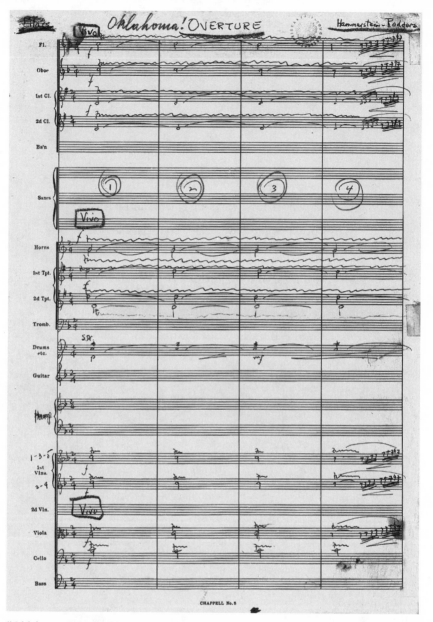

"Oklahoma! Overture" by Richard Rodgers and Oscar Hammerstein II. Orchestration by Robert Russell Bennett. Bennett labeled the overture as coming from *Lilacs*, short for the working title *Green Grow the Lilacs*. This was changed to *Away We Go!* by the time the show premiered in New Haven, and ultimately to *Oklahoma!* Copyright © 1943 by Williamson Music. Copyright renewed. International copyright secured. All rights reserved. Used by permission. From the Richard Rodgers Collection in the Music Division of the Library of Congress.

CONTENTS

The Sound of Broadway Music

"Standing on the Corner" from *The Most Happy Fella*. Music and lyrics by Frank Loesser. Orchestration by Don Walker. The melody is sung by a close-harmony quartet, with a trombone countermelody in the first two measures; the fill in bars three and four has solos switching from clarinet to English horn to flute (with a choke cymbal at the end). Used by permission of Frank Loesser Enterprises.

VERSE

On Orchestrators
and Orchestration

Theatre orchestration is the art of—well, *is* it a creative art? Or is it the work of skilled craftspeople? This question shall be addressed again and again over the course of this book. As shall the question: what precisely does the orchestrator do? And even trickier, I suppose, is: what does the orchestrator do that the composer doesn't?

Don Walker, orchestrator of *Carousel* and *Fiddler on the Roof*, gives us a somewhat basic answer:

> Orchestration is the clothing of a musical thought, whether original or not, in the colors of musical instruments and/or voices. The Composer creates the basic themes of a composition. The Arranger develops the basic themes into the desired form. The Orchestrator adjusts the arrangement to fit the size and composition of whatever orchestral combination has been selected.

Russell Bennett, orchestrator of *Show Boat* and *My Fair Lady*, puts it thus:

> You are engaged to work with a composer and put his melodies into shape for a performance in the theatre. Your task is to be a part of him—

the part that is missing. He may be capable of doing the whole score himself or he may not know a G clef from a gargoyle. Your job is to bring in whatever he doesn't, and make it feel like it belongs there.

Hans Spialek, orchestrator of *On Your Toes* and *Pal Joey*, draws a parallel to fine art:

> An artist, having an idea for a painting, draws first a sketch before putting the actual picture in all its contemplated color harmonies and combinations on canvas. Painting a musical picture follows the same procedure, with the exception that in musical theatre one man (the composer) furnishes the sketch from which another man (the arranger) paints the musical picture an audience actually hears. While the painter works either in oil, pastel or watercolors, the arranger uses the tone colors of the individual orchestra instruments.

Philip Lang, orchestrator of *Hello, Dolly!* and *Annie*, describes orchestration in terms of engineering:

> Like the construction manager, you get the right instrumentation; you understand the limits of the artisan and the technology; and you build something that lasts.

In an attempt to boil it down to the basics for the purposes of our discussion, I offer the following: the song is what they sing. The arrangement is how they sing it. The orchestration is how it sounds.

For a succinct view, we might turn to Ralph Burns, orchestrator of *Sweet Charity* and *Chicago*:

> Orchestrators are like good, high-priced whores. You're paid to make people look good. You may think of a better idea, but you try the best way that you can to do it their way and make them look good.

Writing the Score

As you sit in row E on the aisle, a song cascades across the footlights. The music and lyrics that you hear, naturally enough, were written by the composer and lyricist; perhaps not the names officially listed in the program, but that is not our concern. The words come directly from the lyricist, sung to a melody by the composer. You also hear, simultaneously, up to twenty-five (or more) musicians playing. Notes written by the composer? Well, not exactly.

Let us say that four violins and the oboe are playing the melody along with the singer; that the string bass and the bassoon are playing the bass line from the composer's original manuscript; and that the three remaining reed players, on clarinet, are playing the chord the composer wrote in between the top note (melody) and the bottom. That's ten musicians, playing five notes transcribed from the page the composer handed in.

There are another fifteen men and women on the payroll, however, and they are playing something. Notes indicated or suggested by the composer, supporting his melody, harmony, and rhythm? Yes, most usually. Notes *written* by the composer? Maybe so, but in many cases not. This question will be examined in due course, but it can be instantly understood that the omnipresent drummer spends most of his time pounding out sounds that—being without musical pitch—cannot be played on the piano and thus are almost never written on the composer's manuscript.

Glancing at our program, trying to make out the title page in the incandescence spilling over from the stage, we see—in big letters—music by so-and-so. The songs, yes, are by so-and-so, as is the melody being played by the first violins and oboe. But the trumpet part, and the horn part, and the clangs from the percussion section? Who chose the notes the other fifteen instruments are playing? And is it proper to consider these notes as being separate from the original song as written by the composer? When the singer holds a long note or takes a breath at the end of a phrase, the music necessarily continues; song sections need to be tied together, lest motion stop and boredom settle in. Who writes the phrases and counterphrases that fill the gaps? The composer? Well, maybe. But maybe not.

Much of this decoration evolves during the rehearsal period, with the dance arranger, vocal arranger, musical director, and rehearsal pianist coming up with little fills that find their way into the final orchestrated versions of the songs. Some of these touches are included in the composer's original manuscript, especially when he or she is someone who began their career paying the bills as a rehearsal pianist. Academically trained composers often have an intuitive grasp of composition; others, quite frankly, do not. Some Broadway songwriters, in truth, are hard put to come up with a lead sheet which need bear only melody, lyric, and chords; some orchestrators are quite satisfied with this, as it gives them far more freedom to write a creative arrangement. All of which is neither here nor there; durable melodies are built on inspiration, no training required. ("I'll let you know when Stravinsky has a hit," to quote Mr. Sondheim.)

The last stop in the creation of a song is the orchestrator's desk. Once the musical routine has been set, the orchestrator is called in to the rehearsal hall. He—virtually every Broadway orchestrator of the twentieth century whom I have identified was a man—is handed a copy of the music as played in rehearsal; he is seated for a runthrough or two of the staging of the number, performed by the cast, with tape machine running (since the advent of tape machines, anyway); he asks a few questions; and then he surreptitiously slips away. Who *was* that man, some of the younger chorus kids inevitably wonder.

Who was that man, indeed? Who were these guys? Musicians, all, most with backgrounds playing in small orchestras. Composers, some of them, although practical enough to realize that their livelihoods were going to come as craftsmen rather than as creators. That these men were hardworking and dedicated is a given, as the process of theatre orchestration was inevitably a grind. A highly lucrative grind, if they were in demand, but a grind nevertheless. The orchestrator was a key personage in the Broadway music department; but while he might well have been a musician, composer, and/or conductor by training, he worked in the shadows, making stealthy appearances at the rehearsal hall and only brief visits to the theatre.

In a world full of musicians—and in a city that inevitably collected many of the best of them—there was an infinite pool of capable music men. So why is it that the ranks of Broadway orchestrators were so severely limited? Success breeds success, naturally enough, and as we shall see, the assignment of orchestrators for Broadway's most important musicals for more than a quarter century was controlled by one man (with long-lasting implications). An intensive scan of the names included in the show listings of this book—more than 700 Broadway and non-Broadway musicals—leaves us with about 200 orchestrators in all. Of these, forty can be considered repeat contributors to the field. And if we consider people who served as a principal orchestrator on at least a dozen full-scale musicals, we come up with a surprisingly small group of twelve.

Before we proceed, let me point out that *The Sound of Broadway Music* concentrates on what might be considered the golden age of the Broadway musical. The discussion of Broadway orchestrators can be logically split into two eras: the acoustic age, with full orchestras and minimal use of electronic instruments; and the synthesized age, with plugged-in amplification and machinery replacing naturally produced sounds. The place to discuss the merits of one over the other is elsewhere, in another book altogether. For our purposes, it is enough to say that the orchestrators of *Show Boat, Carousel, My Fair Lady*, and even *Hello, Dolly!* were dealing with one palette of paints, while the orchestrators of *Dreamgirls, Sunday in the Park with George, Caroline or Change*, and *Spring Awakening* were dealing with another.

"Let's start at the very beginning," advises Sondheim's mentor Oscar Hammerstein; it is, indeed, "a very good place to start." For philosophical reasons, as well as unavoidable considerations of space, I have chosen to concentrate on the earlier, acoustic age. Examining the so-called golden age—generally defined as the days between *Oklahoma!* (1943) and *Fiddler on the Roof* (1964)—turned out to be far too limiting for our purposes. For that reason, I have enlarged my scope to include the full and complete careers of the orchestrators who were prominent during that fabled era. Thus, the musicals in this book span from Bennett's first show, in 1920, through the final show of Burns, which reached town (posthumously) in 2002.

Using the orchestration of a dozen full-scale musicals as our criteria, we come up with a group of twelve led—not surprisingly—by Russell Bennett and his close colleague Don Walker. They were joined, in terms of both shared shows and shared office space, by Hans Spialek and Ted Royal. These four men had most of the Broadway business tied up through the mid-1940s. Hershy Kay and Phil Lang came along during World War II; Kay was only an intermittent visitor, while Lang joined Bennett and Walker in Broadway's circle of busiest orchestrators. (The circle was so tight that five of the six were employed on one trouble-strewn musical, the 1946 hit *Annie Get Your Gun.*) Robert "Red" Ginzler, Irv Kostal, and Sid Ramin burst on the scene in the late 1950s, although the first two had been heavily ghosting throughout the decade. After a few attempts, Ralph Burns broke through in 1962. Larry Wilcox and Eddie Sauter—two less-familiar but excellent orchestrators who fit our twelve-show criterion—orchestrated their first complete scores just as the era was ending; they were fated to have only one hit musical between them. All twelve were active in 1962, although some only marginally so. By 1963, the number was down to ten; by 1968, it was reduced to eight (with the retirement or death of Bennett, Spialek, Royal, and Ginzler). Following the career-ending illnesses of Kay, Lang, and Walker, only Burns, Ramin, and Wilcox remained active past 1981, if only intermittently so.

Our concentration on the golden age inevitably excludes many important and fine orchestrators, who make only brief appearances in this book but are worthy of the same treatment as our chosen group. These include Harold Wheeler, Billy Byers, Michael Gibson, Michael Starobin, William David Brohn, and Don Sebesky. Most of the theatre credits of these men, through 1999, are included in a special section that follows the general show listings. Most prominent among this later group is Jonathan Tunick, who in terms of importance, longevity, and achievement ranks equally with Bennett and Walker. Tunick might be said to fit more in the earlier age, stylistically though not chronologically. His first Broadway shows, other than one short-lived intimate revue, came in 1968; this early, pre-Sondheim work is, for various reasons, included. Even so, the discussion of Tunick's full career would have necessitated bringing in just about every musical by everybody, exploding this book beyond manageable bounds. This omission has worked to my favor and the reader's as well, as Tunick—who knows more about orchestrations and orchestrators than anyone around—has actively guided me in my research in a manner that might have been unseemly were he among the book's subjects.

About This Book

Who were these orchestrators is a natural enough question, and one which will take up the first part of the book, "Men of Notes (and a Few Women, Too)." Biographical sketches have been compiled on the twelve above-mentioned gentlemen. Little has appeared in print about any of them, save Bennett. Three others, Walker, Spialek, and Kostal, left unfinished manuscripts; Ramin was happily available for extended interviews, about himself and the others. Each profile is accompanied by a list of productions on which the subject worked, serving as a cross-reference to the show listings which appear later in the book. These extended profiles are followed by a series of shorter sections about important music men and women of the period: dance arrangers, vocal arrangers, musical directors, and journeymen—rather than name-on-the-title-page—orchestrators. Information on some of these people is especially sketchy, but I have tried to at least acknowledge their contributions (which are, in some cases, substantial). While it is impractical to allocate the space that some certainly deserve, their careers are similarly cross-referenced.

Wherever possible, I have used the words of orchestrators, arrangers, and other show makers. It has been decided not to pepper each quote with a footnote identifying when and where it was said. A general guide to identifying the nature of the quotes can be found in the discussion of sources beginning on page 634. As a rule of thumb, most of the quotations from people who lived into the twenty-first century came from direct interviews. (As I was contemplating beginning this book, Ralph Burns and Luther Henderson both died—convincing me to start contacting everybody I could find then and there. The only key person I missed was Cy Coleman, who died the very day that I prepared a list of questions to ask him.) The quotations from Bennett, Walker, Spialek, and Kostal come from their memoirs, unless otherwise indicated. Many of the quoted passages from people who did not live into the twenty-first century were borrowed from a series of interviews that Lehman Engel conducted in the late 1970s. These invaluable first-person insights, originally gathered for a book that Engel never got around to writing, are used with the kind permission of his estate.

A book about Broadway orchestrators needs, necessarily, to address just what it is the orchestrator does. The second part, "The Art of Orchestration," follows the many steps that take the song from the piano bench to the orchestra pit. This encompasses not only the work of the orchestrator but the contributions of arrangers, musical directors, and even composers to the process. *The Sound of Broadway Music* is intended to be neither a how-to book for orchestrators nor a series of music-theory lessons. My aim is to explain the process—and there's a lot to explain—in a manner that is comprehensible to musicians and nonmusicians alike. If this causes some of the discussion to be overly simplistic for professional musicians, so be it; I have included enough inside information, I suspect, to keep even the most knowledgeable professional happy.

For those who feel that it is impossible to present an intensive musicological discussion on the art of orchestration without peppering the pages with musical examples, I wholeheartedly concur. This, though, is not that book. The vast majority of musical theatre fans—including several of the composers and creators whom I interviewed—do not read music. They will happily hum to you favorite numbers they have memorized from listening to cast albums, with reasonable fidelity to the arrangements; but they can not decipher the lines and marks on the manuscript paper. We have been able to incorporate a handful of orchestration pages into the book's design. I expect that, after reading "The Art of Orchestration," even those who do not read music will find these informative. Those in search of intensive musical examples, alas, will have to look elsewhere. (Bennett and Lang's dryly technical books on orchestration, which are mentioned in their place and listed in the bibliography, are filled with musical examples. These were apparently intended for working arrangers, though, and offer a rather mechanical discussion of the craft.)

The heart of the book, perhaps, is the show listings section. Who did what? That question has launched an intensive search for conclusive evidence of the authorship of the orchestrations of more than 700 musicals. The findings are not restricted to the information on orchestration; in the course of research, I stumbled across innumerable tales and anecdotes that were, for the most part, heretofore unrecorded. At least, they were unknown to me. Thus, the reader will learn not only who orchestrated what but have a vast store of "new" information about events from thirty, fifty, or seventy years ago. This makes for a voluminous tome, yes; but I determined that anything that contributes to our knowledge of the field should be included. Especially if it's juicy.

"Steam Heat" ("S-S-S-Steam Heat") from *The Pajama Game*. Music and lyrics by Richard Adler and Jerry Ross. Orchestration by Robert Ginzler (working on Don Walker's personalized paper). Ginzler crams in up to nine notes per measure. A revised two-bar intro has been visibly pasted in, replacing an earlier opening. The four-bar vamp is played by bass clarinet, trombones, the left hand of the piano, and the string bass. Used by permission of Richard Adler. From the Don Walker Collection in the Music Division of the Library of Congress.

REFRAIN

Men of Notes
(and a Few Women, Too)

SECTION I.
THE DREYFUS SYSTEM

Any discussion of Broadway's major orchestrators—the earliest and most influential ones, at least—is incomplete without first understanding the framework within which they thrived and the Machiavellian master sitting behind the rolltop desk who pulled the strings. And, if you will, the reeds and brass as well.

The names Harms, Chappell, and Dreyfus will be scattered through the pages of this book, and for good reason; Mr. Max, as he was known, in some ways controlled more than half of Broadway's musical output for the formative years of the modern era. Even after the end of his sixty-plus-year career, the system he created set the blueprint for the business of Broadway orchestration. Definitive information on Max Dreyfus is hard to come by, as he very assiduously remained in the background. A narrative has been pieced together, though, and it makes quite a story.

Back in the mid-1880s, a group of Jewish merchants in Jackson, Mississippi—that's right, Jewish merchants in Jackson, Mississippi—took up a collection to bring some boys over from their Alsatian homeland. Among the lads selected was thirteen-year-old go-getter Max Dreyfus of Kuppenheim, Germany, the son of a cattle dealer. (In the series of interviews that Lehman Engel conducted with various theatre people in 1978—portions of which are included in this book—Engel told both Bennett and Spialek that his grandfather, general-store proprietor Aaron Lehman, paid for Dreyfus's passage.)

Upon his arrival in 1888, Dreyfus's patrons put him to work as a traveling salesman, selling picture frames across the South. But young Max had a song in his heart, and by the mid-nineties he gravitated to Tin Pan Alley. Many American songwriters of the time were incapable of writing down their tunes, so Dreyfus found a living taking musical dictation and turning out song sheets—which is to say, arranging. Early on, he worked closely with Paul Dresser, author of such hits as "On the Banks of the Wabash" and "My Gal Sal." (Publishers Howley, Havilland, & Dresser issued a promotional magazine, *Every Month*. Dreyfus prepared sheet music for the publication, which was edited by Dresser's younger brother Theodore, an unsuccessful novelist who used the unadulterated family name, Dreiser.)

In the late nineties, Dreyfus got a staff job at the publishing house of Tom B. Harms. Harms first hit it big in 1892 with Harry Dacre's song "Daisy Bell," better known as "A Bicycle Built for Two." Tom Harms also started publishing songs from musical comedies, resulting in a notable success with "The Bowery" from the 1892 hit *A Trip to Chinatown*. Even so, T. B. Harms was dwarfed by the giant M. Witmark, home of Tin Pan Alley hits ("After the Ball" and "Sweet Adeline") and prestigious Broadway composers (led by the phenomenally successful Victor Herbert).

Most of Dreyfus's time was spent arranging and song plugging. During these years, he wrote a number of songs; these included "Cupid's Garden," a 1901 hit published under the pseudonym Max Eugene. (This instrumental intermezzo found new life thirty years later as incidental music in assorted early sound-era movies from Warner Bros., for reasons that will become apparent.) That same year, Dreyfus bought a 25% interest in Harms, bringing aboard his nonmusical younger brother Louis, who had also arrived via the Mississippi connection. By 1904, Harms had left the music business and sold his share to Max and Louis. (Mary Rodgers tells us that her father called them "the Dreyfei." She adds that the brothers were "killers," with Louis being more fun and jovial than the dour Max.) Soon thereafter, the brothers arranged a partnership with a successful London publisher; the new "T. B. Harms & Francis Day & Hunter" was thus able to magnify the impact of its songs, immediately rushing local hits to market on the other side of the Atlantic.

An aspiring nineteen-year-old songwriter wandered in one morning in 1904, much as Dreyfus had a decade earlier. Max hired Jerome Kern as a song plugger and part-time composer. Quickly recognizing his employee's talent, Dreyfus got Kern a stream of assignments interpolating songs into Broadway shows. These were often British imports that needed a little snap to compete in the American market; "How'd You Like to Spoon with Me," added to *The Earl and the Girl*, was a quick hit in 1905. By 1912, Kern was writing full scores; by 1914, he reached Broadway prominence with a series of intimate musicals written mostly with Guy Bolton and P. G. Wodehouse, known as the Princess Theatre shows (*Very Good Eddie, Leave It to Jane, Oh, Boy!* and more). All published by Dreyfus at T. B. Harms.

Kern's music was highly influential for the younger composers who came along just after World War I, beginning with George Gershwin, Vincent Youmans, and Richard Rodgers. Understandably, they aspired to join the house of Dreyfus. (Kern, perhaps unbeknown to the others, by this time had a partnership interest in T. B. Harms.) As the twenties roared along, Dreyfus added Cole Porter, Arthur Schwartz, and Vernon Duke as well. Victor Herbert (from Witmark), Rudolf Friml (from Schirmer), and Sigmund Romberg (from Schirmer, Witmark, and Feist), all jumped ship to join the Dreyfus bandwagon, reaping publishing bonanzas for Max like *Rose-Marie, The Desert Song,* and *The Student Prince.*

In 1920, Max and Louis Dreyfus were approached by the venerable English firm of Chappell Music to handle its U.S. interests. Louis took over management of Chappell's American branch, with Max remaining at the helm of T. B. Harms and the newly organized Harms, Inc. (T. B. Harms remained in business, apparently to keep ownership of Kern's catalog separate from the rest.) By 1926, the brothers had purchased Chappell outright.

With the advent of talking pictures in 1927, the Hollywood studios began investing heavily in movie musicals. Rather than licensing individual song hits for their films, they reasoned that they could more lucratively buy up publishers whole. Warner Bros., which pioneered the field with *The Jazz Singer*, was first in line; it snapped up Remick and Witmark in 1928. (The music-licensing branch of Witmark had spun off three years earlier, merging with its longtime competitor Arthur W. Tams to become Tams-Witmark.) The following year, Dreyfus sold Harms—but not T. B. Harms—to Warner Bros. for a reported $11 million. Just before the stock market crash.

Virtually simultaneously, Hollywood studios purchased many other major Tin Pan Alley publishers (including Feist and DeSylva, Brown & Henderson, but excluding Irving Berlin's self-named enterprise). With the field thus depleted, Warner's Harms—with Dreyfus in an advisory capacity—kept a strong Broadway presence. Between the lack of competition and the approach of the Depression, Harms had the field virtually to itself.

Dreyfus retained a close personal relationship with his stars: Gershwin, Rodgers,

Porter, Romberg, Harold Arlen, and more. (Bennett tells us that when the crash hit hard, the hard-nosed Max generously, though privately, used his newly gained millions to help keep his boys solvent.) So close was the relationship that, as soon as Dreyfus's five-year non-compete clause ran out in 1935, he rushed back into the fray, pulling his boys from Warner's Harms to the newly constituted Chappell, Inc. Max took a suite of offices at Rockefeller Center, while Louis went to London to handle the English branch.

This, apparently, had been Dreyfus's plan since selling Harms. Walker tells us that when he was hired as a staff orchestrator in 1934, he was given a one-year contract with Harms and a secret three-year contract with the successor firm. Walker gives us a firsthand view of his then-new boss:

> Mr. Dreyfus had a tentacle in nearly every worthwhile musical in New York. Rather small, looking like one of a thousand husbands taking the subway in the late afternoon from the garment center to upper Broadway, it wasn't until one was close up and could see his sharp, clever eyes that you could believe the scuttlebutt that he was a self-made millionaire. A shock of pure white hair added to his grandfatherly image, which usually turned out to have been less kind than foxy.

Vernon Duke's assessment was somewhat more colorful; he described Mr. Max as "a well-groomed Mahatma Gandhi."

The Arranging Room

What does all of this have to do with orchestrations and orchestrators? Everything, it turns out. Dreyfus was very much aware, from his earliest days in the music business, of the importance of providing composers with fast and proficient arrangements. Back in the pre-radio days, when a song's popularity was dependent on live performances, the major publishers were quick to provide band orchestrations of their songs. With Dreyfus going more and more into the Broadway field, he recognized the need for a somewhat different breed of arranger/orchestrator, capable of accommodating not only the musicians but singers, soloists, and dance directors. As early as 1911, Dreyfus had the innovative Frank Saddler doing theatre arrangements. The following year, Saddler did Kern's first complete musical, *The Red Petticoat*. Over the next seasons, the pair pioneered a new style of theatre orchestration in which the orchestration commented upon and enhanced the music.

The pre-1920 Harms stable included orchestrators Saddler, Maurice de Packh, Hilding Anderson, Charles L. Miller, and Stephen O. Jones. Upon Saddler's death in 1921, Dreyfus gave the others a chance at moving up to the all-important post as Kern's orchestrator. Dissatisfied with the results, he took Bennett—the star of his nontheatrical arranging department since 1919—and moved him into the chair of chief orchestrator. (Bennett recalls that Dreyfus joked, "We think it might be refreshing to have an arranger who speaks English.") Spialek joined the team in 1924, moving past the others into the second spot.

As Dreyfus cemented his hold on the Broadway musical, he devised a system in which he carefully kept Broadway's top orchestrators under exclusive contract. Walker joined the group in 1934, with Ted Royal coming along in 1936. The quartet would be supplemented, as needed, from a group of reliable standbys, including de Packh, Nathan Lang Van Cleave, Menotti Salta, Jack Mason, Joe Glover, and Robert Noeltner. (Another group of Harms/Chappell orchestrators of the twenties and thirties—Conrad Salinger, Alfred Newman, Max Steiner, Edward Powell, and David Raksin—gravitated to Hollywood, where it turned out there was far more money to be made.) Dreyfus also kept on staff a squad of full-time copyists, accustomed to the round-the-clock schedule needed to satisfy the demands of Broadway production.

Through the thirties and forties, Dreyfus had a virtual stranglehold on the Broadway musical, with almost all of the most successful songwriters (except Berlin) under contract. And the best and most knowledgeable theatrical orchestrators as well.

> WALKER: The trick was, Dreyfus had Russell Bennett, he had Hans Spialek, he had me and in another year or two he got a fellow named Ted Royal. So he got shows, because he had these arrangers and they were the only people who could really do theatre. And since he had us on this drawing account, he would give the show a little money, or else he would swallow some of the orchestration cost. But this is the way he got shows.
>
> One of the arrangers under contract would be assigned to a show as its supervising orchestrator. He would be primarily responsible for the correctness and readiness of the orchestrations. He had the right to call on any of the other "house" arrangers if he needed help and, if none of them were available, to hire "outside" assistance. As Actors' Equity increased its demands regarding rehearsal time and that precious preparation time grew shorter and shorter, it became almost impossible for one orchestrator to score an entire show himself. At Chappell in those days, there was almost always a show in the works, sometimes two or three at once. It was a great rarity for one man to write all the orchestrations of a production; it was common for them to have been scored by a group of three, four, five, etc., arrangers. It was a musical factory with a production line.

The general terms of the orchestrator contract gave Dreyfus first call on the orchestrator's services, with the requirement that he do up to five shows a year as assigned by Dreyfus. (Walker and Bennett regularly did far more than five shows, but they were guaranteed the income from at least five.) The contract stated, "You will personally do all the arranging of all shows assigned to you to the extent that it is physically possible for you to do so. In the event you require the assistance of another arranger, you shall retain such arranger at your own expense." This was not actually done at the orchestrator's expense, as the cost was passed on to the producer; it simply absolved Dreyfus of responsibility for any work that Bennett or Royal did on a Walker show (or vice versa).

This changed somewhat around 1943, when Bennett, Walker, and Royal agreed on a general policy of no longer collaborating on shows. In most cases thereafter, they would select a general assistant or two from the extended Chappell staff for each project, while still calling in their peers when necessary.

If a producer wanted to hire any of Max's songwriters, he had to give the publication rights to Dreyfus. If a composer wanted to work with Bennett or Spialek or Walker, he had to give the show to Dreyfus. Or make a cash arrangement. (Broadway's one major outside composer, the self-publishing Irving Berlin, apparently had to horse-trade to get Bennett when he wanted him.) Dreyfus also used his arrangers to keep the songwriters in line. If a composer chose to stray, he found himself cut off from his orchestrators. Youmans, one of Dreyfus's early stars, left in a huff in 1927; his career more or less fell apart, and he was forever after without Bennett and Spialek. Vernon Duke, another talented but testy composer, also severed his relationship with Dreyfus. Both Youmans and Duke found themselves working with the various imprints of the Robbins Music Corporation, where the orchestrations were overseen by Domenico Savino (who was several pegs below Russell Bennett).

Chappell's absolute grip on the field began to loosen in the mid-forties, as unaffiliated orchestrators began to enter the field (the most prominent of whom were Phil Lang and Hershy Kay). Spialek left in 1942, after an argument with Rodgers, but he remained an occasional contributor; Royal left in 1946, setting up as an independent orchestrator available to non-Chappell composers (like Frederick Loewe of *Brigadoon* and Frank Loesser of *Where's Charley?*). Around 1950, Walker and Bennett contemplated their own music preparation shop, separate from but in partnership with (and funded by) Chappell. Max did not take them up on this, however. Walker ended his exclusive contract in 1951; at the same time, Bennett took an extended leave to orchestrate Rodgers's TV series *Victory at Sea*. Chappell's dominance of Broadway orchestration was, finally, over. Bennett remained on contract for the rest of his career, turning out occasional shows even after the deaths of the Dreyfus brothers in the mid-sixties. But by this point, Broadway show tunes had been shunted out of the Billboard spotlight by the likes of Elvis Presley, the Beatles, and more.

Dollars and Cents

Conscientious readers of musical theatre biographies of the period are familiar with anecdotes about producers going to Max Dreyfus to get songwriters; Gershwin and Youmans, for example, got their first opportunities to write complete scores in this manner. This sounds backward to present-day ears: don't producers start with a script and score? No. If you were a novice producer, or merely a moderately successful producer with little clout, you could walk into Dreyfus's office and walk out with a talented young songwriting team. Harms/Chappell had a stable of writers eager to write musicals, which in those days were prime launching pads for prospective song hits. If you, the producer, took Mr. Max's suggestion, he would generally make you a money-saving proposition, advancing some or all of the upfront costs of orchestration and copying.

Orchestrations have always been relatively expensive. The thousands of dollars spent on scenery and costumes make a certain amount of sense, as you can physically see what the dollars are buying. Orchestration dollars, though, are invisible; the physical result is merely hundreds of pages of tattered paper. And the orchestration is only half the story; the copyists, collectively, usually earn an amount between 60% and 100% of the orchestrator. Copyists are paid by the line; each page of orchestral score might contain parts for twenty-five players. This comes to a considerable sum, compounded when new songs are added overnight during the tryout with everyone getting double-time at out-of-town rates.

Free orchestrations and parts (or even half-price orchestrations and parts), to be repaid after the show was open and safely running, make a substantial savings—especially to a producer scraping around for money. That's an offer that other publishers, without a theatrically knowledgeable staff of orchestrators and copyists already on salary, couldn't make. It was a win-win situation as far as the producers were concerned, as the song-plugging arm of Chappell automatically attempted to give the show an additional boost. While the relationship was technically between composer and publisher, most composers were more than glad to be invited into the home of Gershwin, Rodgers, Porter, and the rest. (Lerner & Loewe's first three shows were with small publishers. Following the success of *Brigadoon*, the team went to Chappell for the rest of their career, including the especially lucrative *My Fair Lady*, *Gigi*, and *Camelot*.)

More explicit information on precisely what strings Dreyfus pulled is hard to come by. A few Dreyfus memos have been found in which non-Chappell musicals are discussed. These present conditions for loaning out the orchestrator in question, or granting permission for the orchestrator to do such-and-such a show as long as the producer let Chappell publish the score.

One orchestration tally sheet has been located, for a negligible 1948 Shubert-Romberg operetta (*My Romance*, by name). The entire orchestration and copying cost came to $6,494, on what was perhaps an $180,000 investment. Chappell appears to have fronted all music costs, with the Shuberts reimbursing half the amount ($3,247) upon the Broadway opening. (If the show closed during its try-out, the payment was waived.) The balance was to be paid at the rate of $150 a week for twenty-eight weeks, if the show ran that long. It didn't, closing after thirteen. This presumably left Chappell with a paper loss of $2,250 or more, as weekly costs are often waived in losing weeks; if the show had never reached Broadway, Chappell would presumably have been out the full amount. As it works out, though, that kind of loss—$5,000 to $7,000, say, multiplied by five or six flop shows a season—was negligible compared to the potential gains.

While we're on the subject, this might be as good a place as any to touch upon the question of money. Theatrical orchestration has always been a lucrative trade, at least for orchestrators in demand. In the early fifties, $100 was a good weekly salary for a middle-class executive working in Manhattan. Broadway rates at the time were in the neighborhood of $5 or $6 a page. (The page rate was figured on the basis of four bars, or measures, a page; if the orchestrator fit eight bars on one score sheet, he got paid for two pages.) Thus, a moderate-sized song of, say, thirty pages was worth perhaps $150, and a fairly proficient orchestrator could turn out two of these a day—at a time when an office executive was fortunate to receive $100 a *week*.

Let us use *My Fair Lady* as an example. Bennett's invoices for the 1956 musical, at $5.70 a page, include: "I Could Have Danced All Night" (thirty-one pages, $176.70), "Wouldn't It Be Loverly" (thirty-three pages, $188.10), "Ascot Gavotte" (twenty-two, $125.40), and "Show Me" (thirty-nine, $222.30). Especially talky numbers, typically written in the faster-paced 2/4 tempo—which is to say, two beats per measure, rather than three (3/4) or four (4/4)—are correspondingly more lucrative: "Ordinary Man" (sixty, $342), "You Did It" (eighty-three, $473.10). Add to this a 25% premium for songs orchestrated out of town or on Sundays, which took the page rate up to $7.12. In addition, Bennett received an extra 25% of the total as the supervising orchestrator, whether the chart in question was by him or one of his ghosts. The most expensive chart in the show was "Get Me to the Church on Time." Phil Lang orchestrated the song during New York rehearsals, receiving $461.70 for the eighty-one pages. During the tryout, he received an additional $363.12 for the "wild street dance" and choral finale (fifty-one pages, at the out-of-town rate of $7.12). The combined "Church" charts, along with Bennett's 25% premium, cost $1,031. For what was probably three days' work altogether.

The total orchestration bill for *My Fair Lady*, split among three orchestrators, was $8,376. With Bennett's supervisor premium of $2,097, the total cost came to $10,473. Which illustrates another point: "I Could Have Danced All Night" ($176.70) might have been the hit of the show, but the figures show that about 10% of the orchestration cost was spent on the production number "Get Me to the Church" alone.

That a lengthy but undemanding number is worth more than a short but intricate song was addressed by musical director Elliot Lawrence:

> Orchestrators are paid by the page, at four bars a page. So for a dance number or a number in 2/4, there are a lot of pages, they make a lot of money. Ballads are very short, they work very hard on them. Red Ginzler said in every show, there's one number that you work four times harder on, you make nothing on it. In *Bye Bye Birdie*, it was "Talk to Me," a quartet that had a beautiful alto flute thing in it. He said, "I worked so hard on putting every note in the right place, that's the labor of love in this show." There's usually one you don't make any money on. If the number only has thirty-two bars, or sixty bars for a chorus and a half, that's eight or fifteen pages. You have a dance score that's this thick, and you make a thousand dollars.

The dollars have changed over the years, but the proportions remain the same. Under present-day terms, the typical page rate for a Broadway musical, including the obligatory 25% supervisory fee, runs between $65 and $85. (This plus a royalty, often at the 1/2% rate first negotiated by Walker in 1956, which—on a major success grossing over a million a week for each of two or three companies—can attain astronomical heights.) A typical-length number of 30 pages at $80/page, thus, comes to $2,400 for what might be four or five hours of work. Longer numbers—rapid-paced comedy songs or major production numbers— require more pages and more work; 100 pages or more are not unheard of. "Tradition" in *Fiddler on the Roof* is 60 pages; "The Small House of Uncle Thomas" in *The King and I* is 130 (!) pages; you do the math. And the orchestrator nowadays gets paid again for the road tour, London company, and cast albums. Highly lucrative, yes; that said, keep in mind that the number of Broadway orchestration jobs on an annual basis is minimal.

The Publisher's Slice

The first of many income strings from show tunes is the sheet music, which before the arrival of radio and recordings was by far the most lucrative. Under the age-old system, songwriters receive a fixed royalty per sheet sold; the rest goes to the publisher, covering the (minimal) costs and—in the case of a hit—accruing a (plentiful) profit. For recordings, all income is split, with 50% going to the songwriters—for the sake of simplicity, let us assume 25% to the composer and 25% to the lyricist—and the other 50% to the publisher. This is called a mechanical right, left over from the days when it applied not to Victrola records but to mechanical piano rolls. This per-copy mechanical payment extends to all playable media, including CDs and DVDs.

Broadway shows have always been a potential gold mine for songwriters, as performance royalties are the one area that is not shared with publishers. While a hit musical, thus, can generate an immediate fortune for the songwriters, there is far more money to be made elsewhere. Every time a song is performed publicly, in theory, the owners are compensated. A group of notable songwriters, Victor Herbert, Jerome Kern, and Irving Berlin among them, banded together in 1914 to form the American Society of Composers, Authors and Publishers (ASCAP). At the time, this meant collecting money from ballrooms, restaurants, cabarets, and other places that featured live music (excluding theatrical presentations). With the establishment of radio and television, the earning power of ASCAP— and its competitors, Broadcast Music, Inc. (BMI) and SESAC (formerly the Society of European Stage Authors and Composers)—increased. Money is not collected and distributed on an unwieldy play-by-play basis, of course; there is a complicated formula under which performances are surveyed, with credits accruing to the proper parties.

The proper parties are not merely the composer and lyricist; only 50% of the income goes to them. The other 50% goes to—yes, the friendly publisher. This, it turns out, can be far more than merely substantial. In 2004, the ASCAP income received by the estate of a popular Broadway composer—whose last hit show, and hit song, was in the mid-sixties—was $312,104. That is, the entire ASCAP earnings from his songs was about $1.25 million; his various lyricists, several dozen in all, split $312,104. His ten publishers—including, principally, Chappell—received $625,000. And that was only one composer, in one representative year.

And there's more. A potentially larger chunk of change comes from licensing songs—that is, allowing their use in motion pictures, television, and elsewhere. Every time a movie or sitcom episode includes a copyrighted song, the publishers charge a fee. This can range from reasonable to unreasonable; for triple-A songs in important uses—say, spotlighted in a big-budget film—the figure might be $30,000 or more. Furthermore, every time that movie or sitcom is broadcast—on TV or cable—a small cha-ching registers over at ASCAP. (Yes, whenever they rerun the episode of *I Love Lucy* wherein Lucy and Desi sit in the lobby of the Imperial Theatre during a performance of *The Most Happy Fella*, with selections from the original cast album playing in the background, Frank Loesser's heirs get another few crumbs.) When these movies or TV shows make it to DVD, there is yet another mechanical payment *per copy*. Should one of the songs be included on a million-selling CD of a soundtrack album, well—everybody gets paid again and again and again.

And that's not to mention commercial usage. For a major TV commercial campaign, one playing repeatedly in all U.S. markets, the fee can hit the $100,000 mark. Yes, that's for using *one song*. Or, if you have one of those titles that is irreplaceable, the sky is indeed the limit. Which helps explain why writers of Christmas songs are so flush. All of these monies get split: 50% to the writers, who dreamed up the song in the first place, and 50% to the publishers.

It should be noted that, in certain cases, Dreyfus allowed his songwriters to set up their own publishing companies within Harms/Chappell (and thus share the publisher's 50%): Rodgers & Hammerstein's Williamson, George & Ira Gershwin's New World, Porter's Buxton Hill, and more. It should also be pointed out that the vast sums earned by these songs, especially since the late 1980s (thanks in part to the CD/DVD revolution), would no doubt have astounded the songwriters and publishers themselves. The songwriters' estates and the publishers' corporate successors, though, take it in their stride (and their bank account).

Which brings us back to Max Dreyfus, lining up the publishing rights to every promising musical he could get his hands on (and using his orchestrators as bait). Yes, a hit-filled Broadway smash, like *South Pacific* or *Kiss Me, Kate*, contains multiple songs that keep on earning and earning. But the vast majority of Broadway musicals are failures; it follows that most Harms/Chappell musicals were unsuccessful. Let us look, as an example, at a long-forgotten failure from 1931, *Everybody's Welcome*. The show ran a few months at the Shubert and closed, most probably, at a total loss. Orchestrations came from a typical Harms five-man crew at the time, led by Spialek and Eddie Powell. Let us guess that the full orchestration and copying cost was no more than $3,000, and further assume that Harms never recovered a nickel of the $3,000.

I suspect that the Harms/Chappell losses weren't actually losses at all. Digging through some of Gershwin's quarterly royalty statements—the only such documents I was able to locate—I found invoices to him for three musicals, whereby he reimbursed Harms for what seems to be not only the orchestrations (at between $2 and $3 per page) and copyist parts (at between 25 and 40 cents per page) but piano arrangements, trips to the theatre or Gershwin's house for consultations, and even blank paper: $18.93 worth of paper for the 1926 musical *Tip-Toes*, for example. The total amount deducted from Gershwin's royalties was $1,684.33 for *Tip-Toes*, $4,096.91 for the 1928 musical *Rosalie* (split with co-composer Sigmund Romberg), and $3,226.44 for the 1930 "I Got Rhythm" musical, *Girl Crazy*. It is to be assumed that Dreyfus made similar charges to all his composers, in which case they—and not the publisher—footed the bill.

But let us assume that this was, at least in some cases, red ink on Dreyfus's books. In exchange for that $3,000 loss on *Everybody's Welcome*, Harms (and its successors) has earned 50% of everything that has come in—and continues to pour in—for one of the interpolated tunes, Herman Hupfeld's "As Time Goes By." I don't suppose there's an accountant around who could tabulate just how much that song has earned, every time someone "plays it again, Sam." One has to imagine that the publisher has pocketed well over a million dollars—simply because Max Dreyfus advanced the funds to orchestrate this long-forgotten musical. "As Time Goes By" itself was a simple job of fifty bars by Spialek. It made a negligible splash at the time; fame came about, presumably, because the higher-ups at Warner Bros. insisted that the producers of the film *Casablanca* use a song that was already owned by one of the Warner publishing companies. There are countless Harms/Chappell songs in the same money-earning category: "April in Paris," "Zing! Went the Strings of My Heart," "How High the Moon"—all prodigious earners, all from flop musicals with orchestrations courtesy of Max Dreyfus. Not to mention countless other flop-musical song hits like the Gershwins' "Mine," Rodgers and Hart's "With a Song in My Heart," Porter's "Begin the Beguine," Kern & Hammerstein's "All the Things You Are"—well, we needn't go on.

And the money still, today, streams in to the publishers (although copyright law provides certain windows of time when the authors' heirs can potentially wrest away publication rights). It's a fair bet that one or two of these titles, in themselves, have easily made up for all of the unearned orchestration and copying costs advanced by Harms/Chappell in the Dreyfus era. Max had a reputation as a brilliant and wily businessman; one suspects, though, that even he would be surprised at the value—sixty, seventy, eighty years later—of his copyrights.

The Harms/Chappell Shows

Just what kind of hold did Dreyfus have on Broadway? Max didn't publish every musical with every hit song, certainly, but it is safe to say that the majority of the shows in the thirties and forties were published by Harms/Chappell. An unscientific study of the thirties—a decade in which show production was depressed, certainly—demonstrates the stranglehold.

In 1930, Harms published 20 Broadway shows, with another 10 coming from seven other publishers. In both 1931 and 1932, the ratio was 15 for Harms to 6 from the others. In 1933, 1934, 1935, and 1936 combined, with Broadway production at its lowest level ever, Harms/Chappell published 43 musicals to only 8 from other publishers. In 1937, 1938, and 1939—with economic conditions starting to improve—Harms/Chappell published 27, to 16 by others. Through the entire decade, the tally was Harms/Chappell, 119; everybody else, 46. And that 46 is a not-quite-legitimate figure, as it includes quite a few slapped-together vanity productions that lasted less than a week. The total number of relatively successful musicals of the thirties *not* published by Harms/Chappell? Seven, including 4 revues (like *Hellzapoppin*, not especially noted for its songs) and only 3 musical comedies, 2 of them by Irving Berlin (*As Thousands Cheer* and *Face the Music*).

The imbalance was considerably less in the forties, as a new generation of songwriters entered the field. Leonard Bernstein, Jule Styne, Loewe, Harold Rome, and Loesser all came along with non-Chappell hit musicals. Even so, Dreyfus—with Rodgers, Porter, Arlen, Burton Lane, Arthur Schwartz, Kurt Weill, Hugh Martin, and others—retained Broadway's thoroughbred songwriting stable through the decade. (Styne, Loewe, and Rome, after their first Broadway hits, moved to Mr. Max.) The odd man out remained the self-publishing Berlin. His example was soon followed by Loesser, who set up his own Frank Music on the strength of the 1950 superhit *Guys and Dolls*. Loesser, unlike Berlin, quickly started signing up new Broadway songwriters in direct competition to Chappell, publishing such musical blockbusters as *The Pajama Game* and *The Music Man*.

As the century hit midpoint, the octogenarian Dreyfus seemed to cut down his involvement in the business. Chappell continued to publish the music of Max's boys, including shows like *My Fair Lady*, *The Sound of Music*, *Gypsy*, and *Funny Girl*. But the post-Loesser generation of composers who arrived in the late fifties and sixties—Jerry Bock, Stephen Sondheim, Charles Strouse, Cy Coleman, Jerry Herman, John Kander—signed with younger and more aggressive publishers.

Max Dreyfus died on May 12, 1964, at the age of ninety; Louis died on May 2, 1967, at the age of eighty-nine. Their widows sold Chappell to North American Philips in 1968 for a reported $25 million. As corporate merger followed corporate merger, Dreyfus's Harms and Chappell catalogs eventually joined forces as the music industry behemoth Warner/Chappell. And all for a song.

SECTION II.
TWELVE MAJOR ORCHESTRATORS

RUSSELL BENNETT

Born: June 15, 1894, Kansas City, Missouri
Died: August 18, 1981, New York, New York

Robert Russell Bennett—the so-called president of the Broadway orchestrators—resounds through the history of the American musical, seeming to go back almost to the *Mayflower*. Bennett did, in fact, go back to the *Mayflower*; his mother was a direct descendant of William Bradford, who came over on the first boat and later served as governor of the colony of Massachusetts. Paternally, Bennett came from the brass section; his father and three uncles were professional musicians, with papa Bennett on the trumpet. Bennett tells us in his autobiography that upon his birth on June 15, 1894, his mother named him after the writer James Russell Lowell. His father, just as definitely, insisted that he was named in honor of the comedian Sol Smith Russell. In light of the general confusion about his name—he was credited for much of his early career as Russell Bennett—Bennett points out that "Robert" was a family name but "Russell" was the name he was always called.

Bennett contracted polio at the age of five. This left him with a noticeable limp, although it did not prevent him from becoming a fearsome figure on the Broadway tennis and handball circuit. To help the boy's recovery, the family moved to grandfather Bennett's farm in rural Missouri. Given the musical nature of the family—his mother gave piano lessons—Bennett started piano and violin early on. (Family lore tells us that after hearing his mother play a Beethoven sonata, the three-year-old Bennett picked out the melody on the piano.) At nine, he took up the cornet. He recalls a day when he was playing a duet with his sister at the piano. When he played the notes printed on the sheet music, they came out a tone higher, so he instinctively transposed the part as he went along. An arranger was born. At ten, Bennett was playing cornet professionally with his father's band.

Following high school, Bennett moved back to Kansas City, where he studied with Carl Busch, conductor of the Kansas City Symphony. Bennett soon joined the symphony on the violin. Over these years, he played piano, trumpet, trombone, violin, and organ in dance bands, movie houses, and elsewhere.

I was only interested in the theatre because I played in the theatre to make a living. My father was a theatre musician, and two of his brothers were both playing in the theatre in Kansas City, so I just couldn't stay out of the theatre. I've never been desperately fond of it. It's not the be-all and end-all by any measure.

Bennett's composing career began in 1913, when two of his piano pieces were published in *Etude* magazine. In the summer of 1916, he moved to New York. Searching for a break as a playing musician, he stumbled upon a job copying music for the eminent music publisher G. Schirmer. Within a month, he found himself working with composer William Furst on the score for Cecil B. DeMille's *Joan the Woman*, starring Geraldine Farrar. (Silent films in those days were accompanied by live music; while a small town theatre might have one pianist thumping away, major engagements of major films in major cities employed full orchestras.) With Furst far behind deadline, Bennett was drafted to assist on the orchestration; he also played the piano accompaniment at a Washington preview and violin in the New York pit orchestra.

Within months, Bennett was working in the Broadway theatre. He had met violinist Maurice Nitke when the latter was touring in Kansas City. (Bennett describes Nitke as being crippled, which apparently forged a bond between the two.) In 1917, Nitke served as musical director for John and Lionel Barrymore's production of *Peter Ibbetson*. Bennett arranged the incidental music, as well as playing piano in the pit (and—since Lionel's character was a pianist—playing behind a flat while Barrymore pounded a prop piano).

Bennett's numerous odd jobs for Schirmer included assisting Winifred Eggerton Merrill on a 1918 book called *Musical Autograms*. (Merrill, an educator, was the first woman to receive a Ph.D. from Columbia University.) Autograms, which Merrill devised, took autographs of famous men—President Woodrow Wilson, Enrico Caruso, John Wanamaker—and reduced them to musical tones. That same year, Bennett enlisted in the army. Because of his physical condition, he was restricted to limited service, winding up in Kansas as a second lieutenant conducting the Seventieth Infantry Band.

Returning to New York after the war, Bennett helped Merrill to set up a shop which aimed to sell personalized autograms to society ladies. Nothing much came of the scheme, but in 1919 Bennett married Merrill's daughter Louise. Looking for a more productive way of earning a living, the returning soldier found no work available at Schirmer. He was advised, though, to stop in at T. B. Harms.

Harms's professional manager George Moody, like Bennett, hailed from a farm in the Midwest. He immediately assigned Bennett a stock arrangement. Unlike theatrical orchestrations, "stocks" were all-purpose charts that were sold to bands across the country. While they were scored for sixteen pieces or so, they were devised in such a manner that they could easily be adapted for any configuration. The song was "An Old Fashioned Garden," from the current revue *Hitchy-Koo of 1919*; the composer was a dilettante songwriter with one flop musical to his credit, another midwesterner (though not from a farm) named Cole Porter. Bennett pocketed $12 for "Old Fashioned Garden" and—to use his own words— "entered the golden age of the American musical." For the next few years, Bennett turned out numerous stocks of T. B. Harms show tunes like Gershwin's "Swanee" and Kern's "Look for the Silver Lining."

But these were merely auxiliary arrangements, coming after the songs had been introduced. Harms lived by its Broadway composers, so publisher Max Dreyfus always kept top orchestrators under contract; at the time, the stable included Frank Saddler, Maurice de Packh, and Stephen O. Jones. Saddler, perhaps the first important musical theatre orchestrator, broke away from the standard pit band sound to create clever and amusing arrangements contrived to fit the show at hand, especially in his collaborations with Jerome Kern on the Princess Theatre shows. But Saddler died in 1921. After trying out several other Harms arrangers, Dreyfus promoted Bennett to Saddler's desk.

Befitting his lack of experience in theatre, Bennett started with an unprepossessing show from second-tier songwriters (including a theretofore unsuccessful lyricist/librettist named Oscar Hammerstein II). *Daffy Dill* was negligible, with a two-month run in the fall of 1922, but Bennett was on Broadway to stay. The relationship with Hammerstein was to be important, as Oscar brought Russell along for virtually all of the high points of his celebrated career (including *Show Boat* and *Oklahoma!*). Bennett was a self-confessed musical snob and had little positive to say about the quality of any of the songwriters with whom he worked—except Hammerstein, whom he considered a great poet. ("Of course all the successful songwriters are poets and musicians in their souls," noted Bennett, "but why aren't we entitled to at least one or two Whitmans out of all that mass of talent?")

Prior to *Daffy Dill*, Bennett had already been on Broadway as a composer. Nitke, who played violin at Bennett's wedding, got Russell the incidental music assignment for three Barrymore productions, Lionel's *Macbeth* (1921), Ethel's *Romeo and Juliet* (1922), and John's legendary *Hamlet* (1922). The latter was scored for eight pieces, including Nitke's violin, plus a musical saw filling in for the ghost.

Daffy Dill was followed by the *Greenwich Village Follies of 1922* a month later. Early in 1923, Bennett, Hammerstein, and the latter's new collaborator, Vincent Youmans, had their first big hit, *Wildflower*. Bennett soon became Kern's orchestrator, with *The Stepping Stones* (1923) and *Sitting Pretty* (1924). This final show in the

Princess Theatre series (which did not actually play at the Princess) was a quick failure, but Bennett notes that "were I forced to choose the high spot in my theatrical career it would be hard to rule out eight weeks as a fourth at bridge with Bolton, Wodehouse and Kern." Once established, the Kern-Bennett relationship lasted until Kern's death in 1945, but it was not exactly a friendship: "I can easily see why people hated his insides, because Kern could be awful. He could really be as cruel as anybody has ever been. He was just as tough as he could be, and yet these lovely little things came out of him. Like Rodgers." When the Friml-Hammerstein operetta *Rose-Marie* was about to embark on its tryout, the tyrannical Kern demanded that Bennett be pulled off the show because he *might* need him in New York. As Kern was not only Max Dreyfus's most important composer but a partner in T. B. Harms as well, Russell stayed home and sent de Packh to finish up.

Bennett had quickly moved to the top of the Harms ladder, but what he really wanted to do was conduct opera. In 1926, at the age of thirty-one, he packed up his wife and five-year-old daughter and moved to Paris. Once there, he went to study with Nadia Boulanger, the legendary teacher (whose later American students included Marc Blitzstein, Aaron Copland, John Cage, Quincy Jones, and Charles Strouse). Boulanger found Bennett to be an exceptional musician and convinced him to change his focus to serious composition. At the same time, she virtually commanded the Guggenheim Foundation to present him with a fellowship, which it did in 1928.

Bennett's Paris sojourn was interrupted by a summons he couldn't refuse from Kern, for *Show Boat.* (He also picked up some additional theatre work at the time, both in New York and London—where he began his association with Richard Rodgers on the West End revue *One Dam Thing after Another.*) Bennett's studies included a five-month sojourn in Berlin, but by the summer of 1929 he was back on Broadway, working on Kern & Hammerstein's *Sweet Adeline.* Shows in the early thirties on which Bennett served as principal (or co-)orchestrator include *Girl Crazy, Of Thee I Sing, The Band Wagon, Music in the Air, Face the Music, Roberta, Anything Goes, Jubilee,* and *Red, Hot and Blue!*

Of general interest to readers, perhaps, is Bennett's opinion of his client and frequent tennis partner George Gershwin:

> As for George, you couldn't expect anything intellectual out of him at all. His mind didn't—he just didn't have an intellect. He had a talent where he'd sit down at the piano and the piano would play him, a lot of these things he'd look up and say, "Gee, that's great!" He didn't know where the things were coming from, he had no idea.

Bennett had already made occasional trips to Hollywood at the behest of his Broadway clients. In 1936, he moved west for three years. Film work included *Show Boat, I Dream Too Much, Swing Time,* and *High, Wide and Handsome* for Kern; *Shall We Dance* and *A Damsel in Distress* for Gershwin; and assorted nonmusicals under studio contract (including such hits as *Love Affair, Gunga Din,* and *Rebecca*). He returned to New York in the fall of 1939 to move into radio, although he first orchestrated Kern's final musical, *Very Warm for May,* and Berlin's *Louisiana Purchase.* He also provided additional charts for assorted Spialek and Walker musicals such as *Du Barry Was a Lady* and *Best Foot Forward.*

Radio station WOR offered Bennett a large orchestra and a weekly one-hour spot for *Russell Bennett's Notebook,* which remained on the air for sixteen months. Not only did Bennett get to conduct "serious" music, he found the time for a considerable amount of composing. He also included pieces written by Chappell Music colleagues, including Hans Spialek, Nathan Lang Van Cleave, Walter Paul, and even Dr. Albert Sirmay. (Sirmay, a transplanted Hungarian, was number two to Max Dreyfus at Chappell, as well as serving as the house's general editor. He also personally "took down" most of Porter's songs.)

Russell Bennett's Notebook was followed by *Music for an Hour.* In 1942, Spialek landed a CBS program—*Great Moments in Music*—and invited Bennett to join him. This radio activity gave Bennett limited time for Broadway until early 1943, when he undertook Hammerstein's first musical with Richard Rodgers, *Oklahoma!* At the same time, Bennett determined that he would henceforth be credited as Robert Russell Bennett, although almost nobody—before or after—ever called him anything but Russell.

Oklahoma! was followed by *Carmen Jones,* Hammerstein's Americanized resetting of Bizet's *Carmen.* (Contrary to general opinion, Bennett's work consisted chiefly of reducing Bizet's orchestration and revoicing the strings.) After two major 1944 musicals—Porter's *Mexican Hayride* and Arlen's *Bloomer Girl*—Bennett went back to radio in December for *Ford's Stars of the Future* (later known as *The Ford Show*). He returned to Broadway in January 1946 with a reorchestrated revival of *Show Boat* and an emergency fix on *Annie Get Your Gun* (see page 125). Over the next few years, Bennett worked on a string of classic musicals, including *Kiss Me, Kate, South Pacific,* and *The King and I.* He also collaborated on a few musicals with his friend Walker (who had contributed uncredited charts to the three shows just mentioned). The only success among the official Bennett/Walker shows was *Finian's Rainbow.*

In 1952, Bennett entered the world of television with one of his most important projects: *Victory at Sea.* This was a series of twenty-six half-hour documentaries broadcast during the 1952–1953 season, featuring footage from World War II.

Much has been said about the fact that Bennett provided thirteen hours' worth of music based on a mere twelve musical themes by Rodgers. Even so, Rodgers received full credit as composer while Bennett was content with an "arranged and conducted" credit. Bennett then returned to theatre, although he remained active with *Project 20*, a periodic series of NBC documentaries continuing until 1970 that was devised by members of the *Victory at Sea* team.

All through his Broadway years, Bennett made sporadic attempts to return to his career in "serious" music, but it appears that the money from Broadway was too tempting to ignore. Even so, Bennett wrote dozens of pieces, many of which were heard on *Russell Bennett's Notebook*. Works included *Abraham Lincoln* (1928), which was introduced by Stokowski and quickly forgotten; *Endymion*, an "operetta-ballet" (1932), which was quickly forgotten; the opera *Maria Malibran* (1935), which was presented at Juilliard and quickly forgotten; the Four Freedoms Symphony (1942); and Symphony in D for the Dodgers (1941), which was presented on the *Notebook*.

Bennett had always invited other orchestrators to assist on his shows; while he worked on more than 300 musicals, I can find only one "golden age" musical—*The Sound of Music* (1959)—that he scored by himself. (Bennett: "Rodgers told me that he liked the men that usually helped me—he liked them socially—but he wanted to get every bit requiring music ready in time for me to write every one without any assistance at all.") That takes in all of Bennett's shows for which invoices exist, from mid-1946 onward. He also single-handedly orchestrated Jerome Kern's *Music in the Air* (1932) and *Roberta* (1934) Most of Bennett's early shows are known to have had multiple orchestrators, although there are several Kern jobs that might belong on the list.

In earlier years, multiple orchestrators were the rule. When things grew hectic, Bennett, Spialek, Walker, and Royal often crossed over to each other's shows. Other ghosts very much in evidence on Bennett's shows were Harms/Chappell staffers Robert Noeltner, Jack Mason, and Walter Paul. By the time of *Oklahoma!* Bennett seems to have settled on one main assistant for each show, doing mostly utilities and dance charts; for key songs, he would occasionally bring in someone like Walker (as was the case on *South Pacific*, *Kiss Me, Kate*, and *The King and I*). Bennett's main assistant from *Out of This World* to *Flower Drum Song* was Joe Glover. You didn't think Bennett scored "Chop Suey" and "Fan Tan Fannie," did you?

When Glover was unavailable for *My Fair Lady*, Bennett enlisted Phil Lang. (Mason also was involved, writing utilities and one show-stopper, "With a Little Bit of Luck"). Lang wound up doing a significant portion of the last-minute work, as Bennett composed and conducted a one-hour TV special that aired the night before *My Fair Lady* opened. (This was *The Twisted Cross*, about the final days of Hitler, which Bennett had Noeltner orchestrate.) After *My Fair Lady* opened, Bennett saw fit to promote Lang to full co-orchestrator credit.

Lang reciprocated by offering Bennett full credit—for relatively little work— on three musicals. Bennett similarly invited Lang along for the *My Fair Lady* follow-up, *Camelot*. Bennett, sixty-six years old and with a long-term commitment to his TV work, chose not to attend the tryout; by the time the much-revised show reached Broadway, most of the orchestrations were by Lang. Bennett formed the same sort of equal-partnership-with-a-younger-orchestrator-willing-to-travel with Hershy Kay, but with diminishing returns. Post–*My Fair Lady* musicals by Bennett included *Bells Are Ringing, New Girl in Town, Redhead, Juno,* and *The Happiest Girl in the World*. Bennett received an Oscar for the 1956 film version of *Oklahoma!* and an Emmy for the 1962 *Project 20* television special, *He Is Risen*. There was no Tony Award for orchestration in Bennett's day; he was nominated for a special Tony in 1957, but lost. His heirs received an honorary Tony in 2008, in part due to the Lincoln Center Theater revival of *South Pacific* (which used his original or- chestrations to glorious effect).

As he neared his seventieth birthday in 1964, Bennett was all but ready to re- tire. He took on two additional musicals, *On a Clear Day You Can See Forever* (with Noeltner) and *Mata Hari* (with Spialek and others). Otherwise, his theatrical ac- tivity was restricted to Rodgers-produced 1966 New York State Theater revivals of *Annie Get Your Gun* and *Show Boat* —each with significant amounts of help. One of the last ghosts in Bennett's account book, for "Goodbye, My Lady Love" in *Show Boat*, is a beginner listed as "J. Tunik [*sic*]."

Bennett worked only sporadically thereafter. When he was offered Claibe Richardson's *The Grass Harp* in 1966, he turned it down as it was playing a re- gional tryout and he wasn't up to the necessary travel; he recommended Tunick instead, telling the producers "he can arrange music." When the much-revised show finally reached Broadway in 1971 and they were struggling with last- minute changes, Tunick suggested, "Why don't we ask Russell to do something, just for old time's sake?" And so he did the closing number, "Reach Out." His final Broadway work was on the entr'acte of the 1975 revue *Rodgers & Hart*. He lived on as revivals of his biggest hits—*Show Boat, Oklahoma! The King and I, My Fair Lady*—came and went. Russell Bennett died on August 18, 1981, at the age of eighty-seven.

In *The Broadway Sound*, Bennett drafted a set of important steps toward becom- ing a successful arranger of popular music:

1. Find a job with a publisher who has under contract a great "stable" of popu- lar composers and lyric-writers, such as Jerome Kern, Victor Herbert, Vincent

Youmans, George Gershwin, Cole Porter, Oscar Hammerstein II, Dorothy
Fields, Otto Harbach, and P. G. Wodehouse.

2. Either write fast or do without much sleep, or both.
3. Be sure your bosses can read music and also speak English.
4. Make sure also that the shows where the music is played and sung are big hits,
   wherever possible before the material gets to you.

These dictums Bennett was wise enough, and fortunate enough, to mostly follow.

Bennett was associated with the following musicals. He was principal orchestrator, or one of the principal orchestrators, on all except those marked with ♭:

♭All for Love
♭All the King's Horses
Allegro
America's Sweetheart
Annie Get Your Gun
Annie Get Your Gun (1966)
Anything Goes
♭Arms and the Girl
Around the World
♭At Home Abroad
The Band Wagon
♭Barefoot Boy with Cheek
Bells Are Ringing
♭Best Foot Forward
♭Billy Rose's Jumbo
Bloomer Girl
Blue Eyes
♭Bonanza Bound
♭Boys and Girls Together
♭Bright Lights of 1944
By the Beautiful Sea
Camelot
Carmen Jones
♭Carousel
The Cat and the Fiddle
♭The City Chap
♭Coco
Count Me In
♭Criss-Cross
♭Daffy Dill
Dance Me a Song

Dear Sir
Dream with Music
♭Du Barry Was a Lady
♭Earl Carroll's Sketch Book
Ever Green
Face the Music
♭Fifty Million Frenchmen
Finian's Rainbow
Flower Drum Song
♭Flying Colors
♭Fools Rush In
♭Gay Divorce
Gentlemen Unafraid
♭George White's Scandals of 1935
Girl Crazy
The Girl Who Came to Supper
♭Goldilocks
♭The Grass Harp
Great to Be Alive!
♭Greenwich Village Follies
   (Third Edition)
The Happiest Girl in the World
Happy Birthday
♭Heads Up!
Heaven on Earth
♭Hi Ya, Gentlemen!
♭Hitchy-Koo of 1920
Hold Your Horses
Hot-Cha!
If the Shoe Fits
In Gay New Orleans

Inside U.S.A.

Jackpot

Jennie

Jubilee

Juno

The King and I

Kiss Me, Kate

♭Lady Be Good

♭The Laugh Parade

♭Life Begins at 8:40

♭Life of the Party

♭Lollipop

♭Look Ma, I'm Dancin'!

♭Lorelei

Louisiana Lady

Louisiana Purchase

♭Lucky

♭Maggie

♭The Magnolia Lady

♭Make Mine Manhattan

♭Mary Jane McKane

Mata Hari

♭May Wine

Mexican Hayride

♭Miss Liberty

Music in the Air

Music in the Air (1951)

My Fair Lady

♭New Girl in Town

♭No, No, Nanette

Nymph Errant

Of Thee I Sing

Oklahoma!

On a Clear Day You Can See Forever

One Dam Thing after Another

♭One Touch of Venus

Out of This World

♭Paint Your Wagon

♭Panama Hattie

♭Parade

Pardon My English

Paris '90

♭Peg (1967)

Pipe Dream

Queen High

♭Rainbow

Red, Hot and Blue!

♭Redhead

Revenge with Music

Rhapsody

♭Roar of the Greasepaint

Roberta

♭Rodgers & Hart

Rose-Marie

Sally (1948)

♭Say When

♭Seven Lively Arts

♭Shangri-La

Show Boat

Show Boat (1946)

Show Boat (1966)

♭The Show Is On

♭Singin' the Blues

Sitting Pretty

♭Something for the Boys

♭Song of the Flame

The Sound of Music

South Pacific

The Stepping Stones

Sunny

Sweet Adeline

Sweethearts (1947)

♭Take a Chance

Texas, Li'l Darlin'

That's the Ticket!

♭13 Daughters

Three Sisters

♭Three to Make Ready

Three Wishes for Jamie

♭To Broadway with Love

♭Touch and Go

A Tree Grows in Brooklyn

Very Warm for May

♭Walk a Little Faster

We Take the Town

♭Wildflower

♭Ziegfeld Follies of 1924

♭Ziegfeld Follies of 1925

♭Ziegfeld Follies of 1936

♭Ziegfeld Follies of 1957

RALPH BURNS

Born: June 29, 1922, Newton, Massachusetts
Died: November 21, 2001, Los Angeles, California

There is little reason to even ponder the question of Broadway's greatest orchestrator. The old pro Russell Bennett, the versatile Don Walker, the Ginzler-Ramin-Kostal triumvirate, and the modern-day Jonathan Tunick all have their fans, as do Hans Spialek, Phil Lang, and even the not-to-be-overlooked Frank Saddler. In larger musical circles, though, theatre orchestration is merely an exotic niche. Only one of the Broadway regulars sits in with American music legends, the great Ralph Burns.

Burns's pedigree comes from his pre-Broadway work as a big band and jazz arranger. He brought his skill and jazz instincts to the theatre, coming along just after (and expanding upon) the work of the above-mentioned triumvirate. Ginzler-Ramin-Kostal (working in different combinations) changed the sound of Broadway music with *West Side Story* (1957), *Gypsy* (1959), and *Bye Bye Birdie* (1960), but all three effectively disappeared soon after their first credited jobs. Ginzler died in 1962, the same year Kostal decamped to Hollywood and Ramin returned to television. In that very same year, Burns established his name on Broadway—after six years of trying—with two musicals that were startlingly well orchestrated. One of these shows linked Burns with Bob Fosse, a combination that would prove to be mutually profitable and invigorating until Fosse's death in 1987, and even after.

Burns was born in 1922 in Newton, Massachusetts, within a few years and a few miles of Bernstein and Ramin. However, he came from the other side of the tracks and a broken family as well; he told Larry Blank that he "was born into a large Irish family, but raised in a large Italian family." From the age of seven, he was immersed in music. At twelve, he was playing piano in dance bands; at sixteen, he enrolled at the New England Conservatory of Music; and at eighteen he was professionally playing with Nick Jarret's band. (Burns noted years later that, when he played as a teenager at the same club as his friend Nat "King" Cole, he received the regular sideman rate of $35—while Cole received the "black" rate of $32.)

In 1943, Burns joined Woody Herman as pianist and arranger; with the growing popularity of Woody Herman's Thundering Herd, Burns soon gave up the keyboard for paper and ink. His charts from this period are legendary in jazz circles; these include the Frances Wayne recording of Arlen's "Happiness Is a Thing Called Joe," Herman's "Apple Honey," and Burns's own "Bijou" and "Summer Sequence." The latter was a three-part, twenty-minute piece that premiered at Carnegie Hall in 1946. A fourth section of this work, "Early Autumn," helped make a star of saxophonist Stan Getz and—with a Johnny Mercer lyric—became a pop standard.

As the touring bands started losing their audience in the late forties, Burns moved into the recording studio, writing charts for such singers as Carmen McRae, Tony Bennett, and Peggy Lee. He also tried to enter the Broadway field. His first show was the 1955 revue *Phoenix '55*. The Phoenix Theatre was what we would consider off-Broadway, but of notable caliber and with a decent-sized orchestra; two early Phoenix musicals transferred uptown, *The Golden Apple* and *Once Upon a Mattress*.

> Buster Davis called me. *Phoenix '55* had no violins—everybody thought of me as the "no violins arranger." They were nervous whether I could do it; I was backed up by one or two arrangers, I don't remember who. It was very hard for me to write. I was afraid of every note, especially with no strings. The melody had to be in the orchestration all the time; I had to make sure the orchestra didn't cover the singers. I would sweat over the notes.

Burns's first full-scale musical was the 1955 revue *Pleasure Dome*, although it is unknown whether his material was ever played; the show ran out of money and closed prior to its first performance at Washington's Shubert Theatre, but they might have gotten past the orchestra rehearsal. Jimmy McHugh and Harold Adamson's *Strip for Action* did reach the stage in 1956, but it succumbed after four weeks of its pre-Broadway tryout. In the spring of 1957, Burns contributed additional orchestrations to another short-lived Phoenix musical, *Livin' the Life* (out of *Tom Sawyer*). He finally reached Broadway later that year—for five weeks, anyway—with *Copper and Brass*. This was written by the songwriters of *Phoenix '55*, David Baker and David Craig, and starred Craig's wife, Nancy Walker. Burns: "David Baker said, 'You'll be perfect, we'll put a jazz band onstage.' They did, but nobody figured out how to coordinate them with the pit orchestra. We didn't have video monitors or anything. 'Don't worry,' they said, 'Ralph will figure it out.'" This was not an auspicious start and might well have been enough to send Burns back to the recording business for good; he had a chart-busting hit in 1960 with Ray Charles's Grammy-winning recording of "Georgia on My Mind."

How Burns wound up with the assignment to orchestrate Richard Rodgers's *No Strings* is unknown. Rodgers had used Russell Bennett, mostly, since *Oklahoma!* in 1943; *No Strings*—with its complement of onstage jazz-style musicians interwoven through the action—was clearly not a Bennett-type musical. Rodgers worked with musical director Peter Matz during the creation of the new show. As best can be determined, Matz must have sold Rodgers on Burns; Mary Rodgers, while she doesn't know the specifics, guesses that this was probably the case. At any rate, it was a masterful idea.

> I remember someone called and said, Richard Rodgers is interested in using you. I will never forget. Rodgers was demonstrating the score for Jerry Whyte [his production supervisor]. There were two pianos there. Dick said, "Ralph, would you help me a minute?" Because he is not the greatest pianist. I felt as if I wanted to say, it's all right—because I was the one who was supposed to be afraid. Rodgers didn't want to use Russell Bennett because he wanted it to be a show with no strings. It was his idea originally, I think. Peter Matz did one of the dance arrangements. I like to do the whole show myself. I am proud of the fact that I can do most of the stuff myself. Except dance arrangements, utilities. Rodgers gave me accompaniment with all the figures, but he was a little looser on the show because he wanted a different sound. He wanted me to follow exactly the piano parts, but I may have added.

No Strings used eight reeds (all playing sax, at times) and seven brass; that's fifteen combined, in a twenty-one-piece orchestra. This was a swing-band sound that had never been heard in musical theatre. Ralph Burns effectively arrived on Broadway in March 1962, and quickly moved into the upper echelon. His next assignment was also musically rambunctious, the Cy Coleman/Carolyn Leigh/Neil Simon/Bob Fosse *Little Me*. One wonders whether this show was first offered to Ginzler, as it came from the producers, director, and choreographer of *How to Succeed* and the composer of *Wildcat*, both of which were orchestrated by Ginzler. *Little Me* might also have logically gone to Irv Kostal, as star Sid Caesar was otherwise surrounded by his musical staff from *Your Show of Shows*. Ginzler had another show opening the same week, though, and Kostal was arranging and conducting a tour with Carol Burnett. Dance arranger Fred Werner recalls that he had the impression that Fosse fought for Ginzler—who had orchestrated his most famous dances at the time, "Steam Heat," "Whatever Lola Wants," and "A Secretary Is Not a Toy"—but that Cy Coleman and producer Cy Feuer wanted the authentic big band sound that Burns could bring. In any event, Ralph's saxes and brass (and xylophone) drove *Little Me*, and Broadway musical comedy had a new sound.

Burns's next assignment was indeed inherited from Ginzler, who died the week before *Hot Spot* went into rehearsal just after New Year's Day, 1963. Composer Mary Rodgers switched to co-orchestrators Burns (of *No Strings*) and Luther Henderson (who had worked on her father's *Flower Drum Song*). The Rodgers-Burns connection continued with a 1963 London production of *The Boys from Syracuse*. (The more successful off-Broadway revival of this show, produced seven months before London, was orchestrated by Larry Wilcox, who first worked with Burns on *No Strings*.) By 1964, Burns was in great demand with four musicals, including three major star vehicles: *Funny Girl* (Barbra Streisand), *Fade Out, Fade In* (Carol Burnett), and *Golden Boy* (Sammy Davis). Burns's other assignment was *Something More!* which was produced and directed, though not written, by Styne. Burns's shows in the next few years included *Do I Hear a Waltz?* (Rodgers), *Sweet Charity* (Coleman), *Breakfast at Tiffany's*, *Illya Darling*, and *Darling of the Day* (Styne).

The original cast albums of these shows display especially wonderful orchestrations, highlighted by the *Funny Girl* overture (which many rank with *Gypsy* as the best of the best) and including the phenomenally exciting sounds of *Sweet Charity* (and its "Big Spender"). However, at this point it must be said that substantial portions of these scores were ghosted. The partiturs for *Funny Girl* attest to the involvement of Wilcox, Henderson, and Jim Tyler. *Fade Out* has surprisingly little of Burns's work; he shared billing with Ray Ellis, but there are also charts by Wilcox, Tyler, Harry Zimmerman, and others. (This can be explained by the delays with *Funny Girl*, which underwent massive changes during its extended its tryout, culminating with the late-in-the-day arrival of demanding Jerry Robbins. Since Styne was producing *Fade Out*, he clearly—and wisely—allowed Burns to concentrate on the Streisand show.)

Something More! and *Illya Darling* include numerous contributions from Wilcox, *Do I Hear a Waltz?* and *Darling of the Day* from Wilcox and Tyler. The original scores of *Little Me*, *Golden Boy*, and *Sweet Charity* have not been located, leaving attributions to conjecture. It is known that Wilcox was present for *Little Me*—his first Broadway job was as one of the copyists on the show—and that he orchestrated parts of *Golden Boy* and *Charity*. It is also known that Tyler did one of the most striking charts in *Golden Boy*, "Night Song." The trouble was, Burns had a drinking problem. A severe one. This is in some ways beside the point, as the overall quality of the orchestrations on these shows is unquestionable.

Larry Blank was musical director of Burns's musical *They're Playing Our Song* and remained friendly with him thereafter:

> Ralph told me that he spent many years drunk. He was very open about his drinking. He told me that Larry ghosted on, at least, *Do I Hear a Waltz? Funny Girl*, and *Sweet Charity*. I heard this directly from Larry, too. During *Playing Our Song*, Ralph was clearly AA. From the time I met him in 1978 he never ever drank, and from what he said I would guess that he wasn't drinking by the time he did *No, No, Nanette* in 1970.

Even on the shows for which the scores have been located, the contributions of Burns and Wilcox are sometimes hard to separate. Burns had a somewhat unique—and all but indecipherable—handwriting, which overwhelms his scores. But on close examination, one can identify passages in Wilcox's more traditional (but equally messy) hand. Many of the *Illya Darling* scores, especially, seem to be joint efforts. In some cases, the charts start with Burns; he writes out the vocal line and lyric and often labels the instrumentation. But many of the lines are filled in by Wilcox, in some cases entirely so. One has to imagine that Ralph started these charts, but sometime around 4 a.m. dropped off and left it to Larry. Wilcox told Blank tales of writing through the night with Burns, with a bottle of scotch between them; when the bottle was empty, the charts were finished. Some of the *Illya* scores actually display bottle stains and cigarette burns.

To musicians like Elliot Lawrence (the former bandleader who served as musical director of *Golden Boy*) and jazz pianist-turned-composer Cy Coleman, Burns was a living legend. If his work habits were a little eccentric, so be it; he was a musician, after all.

> LAWRENCE: Ralph was drinking during *Golden Boy*. He wrote just as well drinking as otherwise. Except that it was very hard, difficult. We used to have production meetings after the performance, then go back to the hotel. I'd put a new song under his door, slide the paper through. Then Mattie Pincus, the copyist, would go over in the morning, at six o'clock. Ralph would slide the score back, under the door. Some days, we never even saw him.

When the final results sounded like *Golden Boy*, *Little Me*, and *Sweet Charity*, what does it matter how the charts were written? As for *Charity*, Blank relates that John Bowab, one of the producers, told him he would see Ralph, bombed, writing in the basement of the Palace. "And," Bowab added, "it sounded fabulous."

And then there's the curious case of "Night Song," Sammy Davis's opening number in *Golden Boy*. Burns told Larry Blank that he turned out several charts, but Sammy rejected them all. Finally, he threw up his hands and gave the song to Tyler, and that's the one that Davis accepted. (Tyler told Blank the same story.) In a discussion about whether composers of the period knew about ghost orchestrators, I asked Charles Strouse if he remembered Tyler and the multiple versions of "Night Song."

> STROUSE: Sammy's desire to be up front—to sing in one, to do a song that way— was in direct conflict with director number one, Peter Coe, and even director number two [Arthur Penn] to an extent. And certainly to me, but I didn't hold any sway with Sammy. "Night Song" ultimately came down to "Look, I'm going to do it my way!" He was running the show, and so the orchestration—which appears on the recording—is what Sammy wanted. I've gotten used to it. I think it's very good; I don't know, people like the song, so I shouldn't look a gift

horse. . . . I wrote the song with a great deal more finesse. It was a moment that had to do with a young man who was lost, sitting in Central Park. Like so many of us, he felt, would a girl ever like me? What's going to happen to me? Everybody seems to be going someplace. It was written with a lot of what I would call French sensibilities, tremolos. It was meant to be sung in a different style than Sammy wanted. I can't say we ever fought over it, but there was no question about who won. Sammy always won. If, as you say, that was maybe the third or fourth orchestration—well, that was a fair reflection of what was going on.

Given the documented need of so many hands, it is remarkable that the orchestrations of Burns's shows are so very good. Emile Charlap was Burns's copyist for much of his work in the theatre and recordings, beginning with *Little Me.* He pointed out that when Ralph was very busy, Wilcox, Al Cohn, and Billy Byers did a lot of writing for him. They were each very good orchestrators, and—as Charlap pointed out—they all learned to write in Ralph's style. Charlap makes the point with yet another story that relates to "Night Song":

Elliot Lawrence asked him for another new arrangement. He said, "Ralph, it's a good arrangement, but can you do something different?" But Ralph was very busy on something else. He had to leave, he saw Larry, he handed him the sketches and everything. "Write an arrangement on it, here's the sketch and the routine." Larry wrote the arrangement and brought it to Ralph, he took it to the rehearsal and they played it down. Elliot said, "What did you write the same arrangement for?"

From all descriptions, Burns was a soft-spoken gentleman, at least in public. Peter Howard: "Ralph, Larry, and I, we all lived at 853 Seventh Avenue [as did Michael Stewart]. That's how Ralph and I got so friendly, when he moved in. With Ralph's drinking, he hid it. He never let it show. He was always a gentleman, fastidious in his deportment, in his dress."

Charlap, however, told of many occasions when they would have to clean him, dress him, and drag him to recording sessions (at which point Burns was apparently able to keep control). "It was embarrassing as all hell," says Charlap. "There were a couple of cases he almost died."

One can find little evidence of Burns himself, other than his music. Little notes to his copyists, written in the margins of his scores, display a wry sense of humor, such as this note to the copyist of *Illya Darling* on page 20 of the score for the overture: "At this point shipyard noises and Illya's laugh etc. should come in if not before, as without them the audience will have left the theatre!!" Or this, from *No, No, Nanette*'s "Tea for Two": "I've been singing this song all night in my sleep and it's too repetitious. Vincent will probably write a new one in Boston to take its place!"

I have come across an enigmatic and outspoken 1966 interview from *Women's Wear Daily*. This piece quotes "the orchestrator for a current musical," one in which the best music is "an extended musical-dance sequence that works against a complicated and somewhat unusual meter." The musical in question almost has to be *Sweet Charity*, which opened two weeks before the article appeared and featured a show-stopping extended dance number as described, "There's Gotta Be Something Better than This." (The only other musicals of note to open within nine months of the article were *On a Clear Day* and *Man of La Mancha*, so one must conclude that this is Burns speaking.) The article quotes this unidentified orchestrator as saying, among other things, that "half of the show's music was garbage, despite its composer being very talented." Which seems to explain why composer Cy Coleman never used Burns again. But if you were the composer of *Little Me* and *Sweet Charity*, would you not want to sign Burns up for life?

Burns appears to have controlled his drinking problem by the time he orchestrated *Minnie's Boys* in the spring of 1970. (This followed a gap of more than two years, when he might have been off in the pop world—or he might have been controlling his addiction.) Stuart Ostrow, an ex-clarinetist who produced *Pippin* and worked on *Chicago*, indicates that he never saw any indication of less-than-professional behavior:

> Ralph came from Fosse. They were both geniuses in their own genre. I never had to doubt anything they suggested. I was a Ralph Burns fan because Woody Herman was my dream. Working with Ralph, I thought—maybe he'd tell me how to fix my embouchure! Ralph was cool when we did *Pippin*. I remember offering him a drink, and he said no. He didn't talk much, but he loved to write. He wasn't very sociable; it had to do with the drinking. It was a musician kind of thing.

Original scores for only three of Burns's post-1968 scores have been found, the 1971 revival of *No, No, Nanette*, the 1973 revival of *Irene*, and *Chicago*. Ralph received plenty of assistance on *Nanette* from Henderson, who was the show's dance arranger; but Luther's work is mostly on the orchestrations for the dances (although he did a few vocal numbers as well). *Irene* has some sections by Wilcox, as well as work by Tyler; but these are self-contained patches, indicating changes made during the long tryout tour when Burns was geographically unavailable. *Chicago* is entirely by Burns (with the exception of a ten-bar "new ending" by Michael Gibson).

Burns reunited with Fosse in 1969 for the film version of *Sweet Charity*, which was followed in short order by the 1971 film version of *Cabaret* (which won Burns his first Oscar) and the 1971 musical *Pippin*. Burns thereafter did all of Fosse's projects, including the musicals *Chicago*, *Dancin'*, and *Big Deal* and the films *Lenny* and *All That Jazz* (which won Burns his second Oscar). Other film credits ranged from *Annie* to *Urban Cowboy*, with *The Addams Family*, *New York, New York*, and three Mel Brooks films in the mix. When the Tony Awards finally added an orchestration category, Burns won for the 1999 Fosse revue, *Fosse*. Other musicals included John Kander and Fred Ebb's *The Act* and Marvin Hamlisch's *They're Playing Our Song*.

Burns's final show was the 2000 La Jolla tryout of *Thoroughly Modern Millie*. Ralph suffered a stroke in early 2001, which forced his retirement. He died of pneumonia on November 21, 2001. Orchestrator Doug Besterman, who had done *Fosse* with Burns, took over *Millie* when the show was retooled for Broadway in 2002. He saw to it, though, that Ralph received full co-orchestrator billing and shared the resulting Tony Award.

Although a significant amount of Burns's Broadway work was ghosted, there is no question about the overall results. And at least some Burns-scored moments of Broadway history don't have Ralph's name on them. Think of that the next time you hear the final grand refrain, with brass a-blaring, of "One" in *A Chorus Line*.

Burns was associated with the following musicals. He was principal orchestrator or one of the principal orchestrators on all except those marked with ♭:

The Act	Irene
Big Deal	Little Me
The Boys from Syracuse (London)	♭Livin' the Life
Breakfast at Tiffany's	Minnie's Boys
Bring Back Birdie	No, No, Nanette (1971)
Chicago	No Strings
♭A Chorus Line	♭Peter Pan (1979)
Copper and Brass	Phoenix '55
Dancin'	Pippin
Darling of the Day	Pleasure Dome
Do I Hear a Waltz?	St. Louis Woman (1998)
Fade Out, Fade In	Sheba
Fosse	♭Shinbone Alley
Funny Girl	Something More!
Golden Boy	Strip for Action
Hellzapoppin (1976)	Sweet Charity
Hot Spot	They're Playing Our Song
Ice-Travaganza	Thoroughly Modern Millie
Illya Darling	

ROBERT "RED" GINZLER

Born: July 20, 1910, Leechburg, Pennsylvania
Died: December 29, 1962, New York, New York

Red Ginzler was born in Leechburg, Pennsylvania, a small town thirty miles east of Pittsburgh. The fourth of four boys, Ginzler was shy, soft-spoken, and had a tendency to stammer. He was originally named Robert, after an Aunt Roberta; his grandfather objected to the boy being named for a woman, decreeing that he must be Seymour Robert Ginzler. Nobody other than his grandfather and mother called him Seymour, a name he detested; by the time he began his music career, he was Red (after his auburn hair). "Seymour" appears in various credits until *The Music Man*, in 1957, after which he was billed as Robert.

Ginzler's father was a not-very-successful entrepreneur. Following his parents' separation in the early twenties, Ginzler moved to the Detroit area with his mother. Although he did not come from a musical family, Ginzler picked up the trombone. Literally. He was transferred to a new high school which had a trombone but no trombone player. Ginzler taught himself to play, and this was to be his way out of his family and Detroit. With his older brothers training for careers as lawyers and doctors, the sixteen-year-old Red packed his trombone in 1926 and left home to join the Jean Goldkette band. While on the road, he roomed with cornetist Bix Beiderbecke, who was already at the height of his fame (and who was already in the process of drinking himself to death, which he accomplished in 1931 at the age of twenty-eight). When Goldkette disbanded in 1928, Ginzler—along with Bix and many of the others—moved over to the Paul Whiteman Orchestra.

While on tour in 1928, Ginzler played Casa Loma in Toronto. (Casa Loma—Canada's "majestic castle"—was built as a private playground by Sir Henry Pellatt, who made millions as the owner of the Toronto Electric Light Company. The scope of the building—with numerous wings, secret passages, and a five-acre garden—eventually sent him into bankruptcy. In 1927, the building was transformed into a luxury hotel, a venture that soon collapsed. The long-vacant castle lives on today as a tourist attraction; the name is best known—outside of Toronto, anyway—as the original home of Glen Gray and his Casa Loma Orchestra.)

Following the Toronto stint, Ginzler went back to New York. He was soon joined there by Ida Schulman, who had worked in the rental office at Casa Loma.

The two eighteen-year-olds were married at the beginning of 1929; as the birth of their first child neared, they moved back to Toronto to be with Ida's family. Ginzler spent the next decade there, playing in bands at the major hotels. He also joined the Toronto Symphony Orchestra in 1930, as first chair trombone. An apocryphal version of his hiring made the newspaper at the time: the conductor asked if Ginzler could play Ravel's *Bolero*. "I can play it lying down," he is recorded as having said, whereupon he lay down and played *Bolero*. The actual story, related by Ginzler to his daughters, is that he responded, "Not only can I play it, I can play it up a half-tone." He did so and got the job, at the age of nineteen. ·

During this period, Ginzler was also steadily employed with the CBC (Canadian Broadcasting Corporation) Orchestra, under Percy Faith. Sheila Ginzler Kieran, who was born in 1930, recalls that at one point there was a CBC children's program about a man with a magical musical instrument. That was her father, on his trombone. His first arrangements seem to have come in the early thirties, when he played for the Luigi Romanelli band at the King Edward Hotel. Romanelli was quite an operator, who booked a handful of groups across Canada under his name (albeit with other conductors on the podium). In 1931, Luigi asked the Ginzlers to call their second daughter Luigiana Mildred, offering to pay them for the honor. They instead named her Myra Louise, after Luigi, with Romanelli as her godfather.

Little more is known about this period, except that Ginzler appears to have done very well; Kieran recalls that her family had live-in help, which was highly uncommon in the late years of the Depression. It was also during this time that Ginzler found his first of several protégés. Trumpet player Robert Farnon (1917–2005) went on to earn a reputation as one of the world's finest musical arrangers, "the king of kings," per Sid Ramin. Ginzler and Farnon played together in hotel and radio orchestras and were lifelong friends.

Ginzler's Canadian period came to an abrupt end in 1940. Britain and Canada entered the Second World War in September 1939, with America choosing to remain neutral (until the Japanese attack on Pearl Harbor in December 1941). Under wartime conditions, foreigners became ineligible for employment at the CBC. With a major portion of his income cut off, Ginzler returned to New York in December 1940.

Details of the next seven years are few. In 1941, he played with Benny Goodman, albeit briefly. In 1942, he was pit trombonist for the Rodgers & Hart musical *By Jupiter*, presumably on the recommendation of Don Walker. (For a short period in 1930, Walker—at the time an out-of-work saxophonist-turned-conductor/arranger from New Jersey—led the orchestra at Toronto's Royal York, which had Ginzler and Farnon in the brass section.) Four months after *By Jupiter* opened, Walker did an innovative but short-lived musical about a dance band, *Beat the Band*, with music by Johnny Green (who had been musical director of *By Jupiter*). Ginzler played trombone and—during the show's nine-week run—took over as conductor. He then returned to *By Jupiter* and in April 1943 became conductor of the long-running hit.

The only other mention of Ginzler I found in this period was a notation on a Don Walker invoice, listing Ginzler as a copyist for the Fats Waller musical *Early to Bed*. It is quite possible that Ginzler did other copying, and his daughter Myra Kates recalls that he played trombone in other pit bands. As the 1940s continued, Ginzler apparently did some ghosting work for Don Walker; Ginzler's daughters remember him going along on the late 1947 Philadelphia tryout of the Hugh Martin/Jerome Robbins musical *Look Ma, I'm Dancin'!* The earliest Broadway charts by Ginzler that have been located are some minor numbers, also for Walker, in the 1949 Irving Berlin musical *Miss Liberty*.

By this time, though, Ginzler's professional life had changed radically. One of Ginzler's many clients during the forties was Boston society bandleader Ruby Newman. In 1946, local Boston arranger Sid Ramin—just out of the army— looked up Ginzler and sought advice. Two years later, Ramin suddenly found himself in New York with the offer of a weekly, one-hour television revue. Ramin invited Ginzler to join him, and their show—*The Texaco Star Theatre*—was an immediate success. Within a short time, the name was changed to *The Milton Berle Show*; Berle himself came to be known as Mr. Television. Ginzler found Berle to be "loud, vulgar and detestable"—he generally had that effect on people—but the show kept Ramin and Ginzler gainfully employed through June 1956.

Established with a top-rated television program, Ginzler turned to Broadway to pick up extra work. Around this time, Walker terminated his longtime agreement with Max Dreyfus at Chappell and set up business in a townhouse in Chelsea. Walker seems to have assigned Ginzler to be his general assistant. While no documentation of this arrangement has been found, Ginzler ghosted on at least two dozen Walker musicals during the fifties, occasionally with assistant orchestrator credit buried in the back of the program. (Ginzler was the first person Walker would call, according to Walker's daughter Ann Liebgold. Don and Red were very close; Liebgold recalls that when she was married—"on the Saturday after *Carnival in Flanders* began its tryout," which is how the families of top Broadway music men had to arrange their lives—Ginzler drove her and her parents to the wedding.) Ginzler, like Walker and unlike Ramin, was a very fast worker. He clearly was able to turn out mounds of additional pages, working around his Berle schedule.

The sound of Broadway music began to change markedly through the mid-fifties, mostly on Walker shows. Analysis of the charts, again and again, points to Ginzler. Among the most dynamic musical numbers of the period are the two dances with which Bob Fosse invaded Broadway: "Steam Heat" in *The Pajama Game* and "Whatever Lola Wants, Lola Gets" in *Damn Yankees.* To these can be added the production number "Conga" and "Ballet at the Village Vortex," both from *Wonderful Town*; all four were orchestrated by Ginzler. When asked why Walker would hand out such important numbers, Ramin answered, "Red was good at jazz. Don knew it would make his show sound better." Ginzler's other work in *Pajama Game* included "I'll Never Be Jealous Again" and "Seven-and-a-Half Cents"; in *Yankees,* "Heart" and "Two Lost Souls." (While many of the musical devices in these numbers were worked out by Fosse and dance arranger Roger Adams, Ginzler specialized in translating them to the orchestra. This can be heard especially well in Red's use of sandpaper blocks, cow bells, and a typewriter in a somewhat later Fosse number, "A Secretary Is Not a Toy" from *How to Succeed in Business Without Really Trying.*) As discussed in detail elsewhere, Ginzler did more than 40% of *Wonderful Town* (including "It's Love," "Christopher Street," and "One Hundred Easy Ways"). With or without credit, Broadway had an exceptionally inventive new orchestrator.

Other Walker shows to which Ginzler contributed include *Call Me Madam, Top Banana, Wish You Were Here, The Girl in Pink Tights* (on which Ginzler brought along his friend Farnon), *Silk Stockings,* and Frank Loesser's *The Most Happy Fella.* When Walker was hired as music director of TV's *Your Hit Parade* in 1957, he had Ginzler signed as his orchestrator. This job turned out to be short-lived, as Walker was ill suited to the chore. At the same time, Walker undertook *The Music Man,* with Ginzler providing a significant amount of the score.

Sid Ramin, meanwhile, had moved into a recording career at RCA. He had also made it to Broadway in 1957, with *West Side Story* (for his childhood pal Leonard Bernstein). In 1958, Ramin was assigned by RCA to orchestrate the original cast album of *Say, Darling,* a Jule Styne/Betty Comden/Adolph Green offering that had been performed on Broadway with two pianos and a small combo. Ramin invited Ginzler to collaborate (without credit). The *Say, Darling* album so impressed Styne that he hired these "new" orchestrators to do his next musical, *Gypsy.* This was not Ginzler's first Broadway orchestration credit, technically; that came on the short-lived 1958 musical *Oh Captain!* which listed Ginzler as the first of eight nonalphabetical orchestrators (including Joe Glover and Phil Lang).

Gypsy, as noted elsewhere, was a remarkable show with a remarkable score and a remarkable set of orchestrations. The musical opened in May 1959; thereafter,

Ginzler did three more shows in partnership with Ramin, *The Girls Against the Boys*, *Wildcat*, and Fosse's *The Conquering Hero*. Otherwise, he worked on his own, beginning in April 1960 with *Bye Bye Birdie*.

Ramin has described how he was the "idea man" during his partnership with Ginzler, and this is somewhat borne out by the shows for which the partiturs have been located (*Say, Darling, Gypsy*, and *Wildcat*). In many cases, the lead parts—that is, violin A and the first trumpet—are written by Ramin. He also fills in the strings and often the brass, on especially flashy sections. The rest of the instruments, including most of those remarkable woodwinds in *Gypsy*, are by Ginzler. There is no question that Ginzler wrote more, on a note-by-note basis; there is also no question that this had to do with the technical speed of Ginzler's writing. Ramin describes how in many cases he literally dictated figures, singing them as Ginzler put them on the manuscript page. It should also be factored into the discussion that *Gypsy* was, in effect, Ramin's first musical comedy; Ginzler had already worked on dozens of them, writing close to half of at least one major show (*Wonderful Town*). Based on a note-for-note basis, it seems odd that Ginzler received inferior billing for *Gypsy*. The billing read "orchestrations by Sid Ramin with Robert Ginzler"; Ginzler was in a type size almost half that of Ramin, and only Sid received a program bio. Ramin explains:

> On *West Side*, the billing read orchestrations by Leonard Bernstein, with me and Irv in smaller print. Since *Gypsy* was my show, I did the same thing, followed the precedent. I'm really sorry that I did that. Years later, Red said to me—and we were still great friends—he said, "There's been something in my craw that I must tell you. I always resented that billing: with, and the smaller size." I felt terrible. He was right, but at the time I did it because Lenny did that to me. When *Gypsy* was revived, long after Red died, I rectified that, changing the billing so it was equal.

This dovetails with Red's many years of writing important charts for Walker, with only occasional back-of-the-book credits. Did Ginzler resent his anonymity? Kieran says that it was in keeping with his shyness; if it bothered him, he never would have thought to mention it. However, Elliot Lawrence and John Morris—musical directors of two Ginzler shows each—both relayed their impression that he resented the lack of credit from Walker and, on *Gypsy*, from Ramin.

The situation changed with the arrival of *Bye Bye Birdie*. Ginzler got the job on Ramin's recommendation; despite Red's vast experience with Walker and *Gypsy*, his name at the time was all but unknown. *Birdie* composer Charles Strouse recalls that Ramin, in turning down the show, suggested Red: "Sid told me that he [Ginzler] had written a lot of great charts for Walker." *Birdie* positively sparkles, with a bubbly and inventive orchestration marked by Ginzler's distinctive writing for the flutes—four flutes!—and the rest of the wind section.

Birdie also got Ginzler a new protégé. Jonathan Tunick was a nineteen-year-old Juilliard student with no interest whatsoever in Broadway. Until he saw *Birdie*, that is. As it happens, Tunick's father had a lawyer named Ginzler: Red's older brother Walter. An introduction was arranged, and Tunick found a mentor. "Jonathan worshipped Red," said Ramin. "He looked like Red physically, and—rightfully so—he thought Red was the best. He would hang around our office when we were doing a show. He just adored Red."

Ginzler, working in near-anonymity through the fifties, was suddenly embraced by Broadway. *Birdie* was the first of ten Ginzler musicals from April 1960 through the end of 1962. Most important, perhaps, was Loesser's *How to Succeed in Business Without Really Trying*, with orchestrations that match the excitement and creativity of *Gypsy* and *Birdie*. Other shows of this period demonstrate Ginzler's skill in diverse styles. *Wildcat, Donnybrook! A Family Affair, All American, Bravo Giovanni*—listen to the cast albums of these musicals. The music might border on second-rate—most of it, anyway—but you'd never know it from the orchestrations. (Lawrence provided additional orchestrations, with credit, for *Birdie* and *How to Succeed.* The other scores that have been located reveal contributions from Walker, Ramin, Luther Henderson, and others.)

Nowhere to Go but Up opened at the Winter Garden on November 10, 1962. Ginzler went off to England, apparently working on some British project, details of which have been impossible to track down; he also visited his good friend Farnon, who for tax reasons had moved to Guernsey (one of the Channel Islands). Ginzler returned to New York to start work on the Judy Holliday vehicle *Hot Spot.* On the evening of December 29, 1962, four days before going into rehearsal, Ginzler suffered a massive heart attack and died at the age of fifty-two.

While Ginzler's career came to an abrupt end, Tunick—who was to have assisted Ginzler on *Hot Spot*—can be said to have inherited his mentor's style and standards, and carried them over into the new-style theatre orchestration he developed beginning with the Sondheim-Prince shows. Tunick's praise of Ginzler mirrors that of both Ramin and Farnon, both of whom continually expressed similar sentiments.

Tunick still keeps Ginzler's working tools. These include an illuminated magnifying loop, which explains those meticulously neat 15- or 22-note swoops in his wind and brass parts; and the mechanical numerical stamping machine used on such shows as *How to Succeed,* the better to number the bars of music. (Ginzler loved all things mechanical, although Tunick is convinced that this machine took more time to use than just writing in the bar numbers.) Tunick also inherited Ginzler's personalized score paper. These twenty-six-stave, eleven-by-fourteen sheets were relatively expensive, with as many as 1,000 pages needed per show. After two years of success under his own name, Ginzler finally broke down and ordered his own (matching Walker's score sheets). The paper seems to have arrived only in time for Ginzler's final show, *Nowhere to Go but Up*. People with a sense of historical continuity will be glad to learn that Tunick used the left-over Ginzler paper for *Company* and *Follies*.

The last words may as well come from Ginzler himself: "The more music you know, the more music you love."

Ginzler was associated with the following musicals. He was principal orchestrator or one of the principal orchestrators on all except those marked with ♭:

♭Agnes de Mille Dance Theatre	How to Succeed . . .
All American	♭Irma La Douce
♭Ankles Aweigh	♭Little Jesse James
♭Babes in Arms (1959)	♭Look Ma, I'm Dancin'!
♭Beat the Band	♭Maggie
♭Bless You All	♭Me and Juliet
Bravo Giovanni	♭Miss Liberty
♭By Jupiter	♭The Most Happy Fella
Bye Bye Birdie	♭The Music Man
♭Carnival in Flanders	Nowhere to Go but Up
The Conquering Hero	♭Of Thee I Sing (1952)
♭Curtain Going Up	♭Oh Captain!
♭Damn Yankees	♭On Your Toes (1954)
♭Dance Me a Song	♭The Pajama Game
Donnybrook!	♭Pal Joey (1952)
♭Early to Bed	♭Peter Pan (1954)
A Family Affair	Say, Darling
♭First Impressions	♭Silk Stockings
♭The Girl in Pink Tights	♭Top Banana
The Girls Against the Boys	♭Vintage '60
Gypsy	Wildcat
♭Happy Hunting	♭Wish You Were Here
♭Hazel Flagg	Wonderful Town
♭Hit the Trail	♭Ziegfeld Follies of 1943

HERSHY KAY

Born: November 17, 1919, Philadelphia, Pennsylvania
Died: December 2, 1981, Danbury, Connecticut

Hershy Kay was born in Philadelphia on November 17, 1919, the son of Russian immigrants. His father was a printer; his mother was a cousin to film director Sergei Eisenstein. (I have been told that Hershy was a nickname, due to his predilection for Hershey bars—although the name is spelled incorrectly—but as best I can tell, his given name was Hershel.) In 1935, he won a scholarship to the prestigious Curtis Institute of Music.

> I originally went to Curtis as a cellist, which I gave away in 1946 and haven't missed since. Actually I hate conducting, so I became an orchestrator. I decided to learn orchestrations strictly on my own, but I figured the best way to do it was to write small scores, have them played by the Curtis Symphony. I copied them out, since I was in no position to pay for a copyist, and so I wrote short pieces and had them orchestrated and I learned a great deal. In fact that's about the best way to learn orchestration, is to hear what you have done. I actually didn't graduate. I was thrown out twice—which is one of the things I pride myself on.

Kay left Curtis in 1939 and moved to New York. His first job was writing arrangements for the Brazilian soprano Elsie Houston. Rumored to be the mulatto granddaughter of Sam Houston of Texas, Elsie Houston was a surrealist singer known for her performances of "voodoo" music. A strange starting place for Hershy Kay, perhaps.

Kay took a job as a staff arranger at NBC in 1943. The following year he got a call from Leonard Bernstein, who had followed Kay at the Curtis Institute. The success of Bernstein's ballet *Fancy Free* had resulted in the commission of a new musical comedy; while Lenny had done his own orchestration for the ballet, he asked Kay to help out on the musical. As it turned out, *On the Town* came to town with four credited orchestrators. While the original scores have not been located, notations on the conformed score tell us that Kay did more than half of the show, including, notably, all of the "serious" ballet sequences. The comedy numbers were farmed out (mostly to Don Walker), as were some of the ballads. This anticipates Kay's later musical theatre career, where he specialized in "legit" shows with less of a feel for musical comedy.

On the Town brought with it an invigorating and exciting sound. It would be a full dozen years, though, before Kay would return to Broadway with another musical. Kay's one full score in the interim, *Shootin' Star*, closed during its tryout. (This was not about Annie Oakley but Billy the Kid; the two musicals tried out simultaneously, premiering back-to-back at the Shubert in New Haven in April 1946.) Kay is also credited as an additional orchestrator on the 1946 musicals *Beggar's Holiday* and *Sweet Bye and Bye*. In the meantime, Kay did orchestrations for three Broadway plays-with-music: *Dark of the Moon*; Kurt Weill's pageant *A Flag Is Born*; and the 1950 Jean Arthur production of *Peter Pan*, with six songs by Bernstein.

Kay firmly established himself in the ballet world during this period, starting with arrangements for Martha Graham and Pearl Primus in 1947. In 1951, he fashioned *The Thief Who Loved a Ghost* from themes by Carl Maria von Weber, for Ballet Theatre. A major success came later that year with *Cakewalk*, which Kay adapted from music by nineteenth-century American composer Louis Moreau Gottschalk. Other ballets followed, including—for choreographer George Balanchine—*Western Symphony* (1954), the Sousa-based *Stars and Stripes* (1958), and the Gershwin-based *Who Cares?* (1970).

Kay slowly worked his way back into musical theatre, starting with the 1954 Phoenix Theatre musical *The Golden Apple*. (The Phoenix was technically off-Broadway, but the award-winning show transferred to the Alvin Theatre, albeit unsuccessfully.) Composer Jerome Moross was one of the finest motion picture orchestrators of the day, but *Golden Apple* was an enormous undertaking in terms of both composition and orchestration. Kay—a serious orchestrator, as opposed to a commercial Broadway guy—seemed a likely prospect for the job. Moross and Kay shared the credit and the work, although after the fact Hershy reportedly sued Jerry over money. A second, less-successful Phoenix musical followed that fall, Earl Robinson's *Sandhog*.

Participation on *The Golden Apple* led to a similar assignment on Marc Blitzstein's 1955 musical *Reuben Reuben*. (The official credit read "orchestrations by Marc Blitzstein, assisted by Hershy Kay and Bill Stegmeyer," although choral director Abba Bogin recalls that Kay did most of the orchestration.) Blitzstein, an early mentor to Bernstein, no doubt took Hershy upon Lenny's recommendation. *Reuben Reuben*—with book, music, and lyrics (and orchestrations!) by Blitzstein— was unfinished when it began its tryout and collapsed after two weeks.

Kay finally returned to Broadway proper in 1956 with another call from Bernstein. Lenny had written a second Broadway musical three years earlier, *Wonderful Town*, but that was standard musical comedy fare with orchestrations from Walker (with Ginzler, Kostal, Ramin, and others). For *Candide*, Bernstein knew specifically what he wanted, and he hired Kay to work with him; the orchestrations were credited to Bernstein and Kay. While all the original partiturs are presumed to exist, most of them are presently jumbled together with numerous other versions of this much-revised musical; the process of separating, collating, weeding out alternate versions, and analyzing the handwriting would take a week or so, which—given the scope of this book—is about four days too long. I'll leave the song-by-song identification of *Candide* to someone with time to kill and a thesis to write. We know that Bernstein didn't write a note of *West Side Story*, despite his billing. But we also know that he carefully oversaw the work of his designated co-orchestrators, who did not begrudge Lenny the credit. I would guess that this is the case with *Candide*: the nine songs that have thus far been located, including the famous Overture, are pretty much by Kay, although presumably with page-by-page oversight by the composer. Whatever the case may be, the orchestrations for the 1956 version of *Candide* rank among the best heard on Broadway.

Candide, like *On the Town*, didn't earn Kay any immediate Broadway assignments. He did another Phoenix musical in 1957, the quickly forgotten *Livin' the Life*, and then went back to Balanchine. Blitzstein resurfaced in 1959 with his final musical, *Juno*. I expect that the unfinished tryout of *Reuben Reuben* convinced everyone, including the composer, to leave the orchestration to a full-time orchestrator. Russell Bennett signed on, but there was so much work to be done that Kay was brought in. The official credit went to Bennett, Blitzstein, and Kay, in that order. The music-heavy show was pretty evenly split between Bennett and Kay, with two charts by Blitzstein and three by the uncredited Lang.

Kay returned to the Phoenix for a fourth musical, *Once upon a Mattress*. This was not an altogether happy situation.

> MARY RODGERS: Hershy stopped in the middle. "I can't go any further," he said, "I have to go orchestrate something for George Balanchine." We said, "Well, why didn't you tell us about that?" Hershy said, "You didn't ask." He did just about half of the show. The biggest problem is that when I heard things that sounded wrong, I could say "There, that sounds wrong"—but I couldn't fix it, I didn't know how to repair it. There were all kinds of things that were not right.

Musical director Hal Hastings apparently had a hard time finding people to finish the show; I suppose the money was minimal, as this was an off-Broadway production. *Mattress* is officially credited to Kay, Arthur Beck, and Carroll Huxley. (Beck also did a considerable amount of *I Can Get It for You Wholesale* and some of *Cabaret*; Huxley did the sterling overture to *Take Me Along*.) *Mattress*, like *The Golden Apple*, moved uptown to the Alvin, with similarly unprofitable results.

Sixteen years had passed since *On the Town*. Despite—or perhaps due to—Kay's prominence in the world of ballet, he was still thought to be too specialized for Broadway musicals (unless they were composed by Bernstein). This finally began to change in 1961, when his work on *Candide*—a quick failure with a cast album that became a classic—started generating offers. Composer Jerry Herman made his Broadway debut with *Milk and Honey*, a contemporary musical with leading roles for two opera singers.

> HERMAN: I wanted as close to a classical sound as I could find, even though I was writing show music. Because of Robert Weede and Mimi Benzell—who were both opera stars—and some of the melodic lines, it was more operetta than musical comedy. I always admired Hershy's work; it turned out to be the right sound. I thought it gave the show a special sound, that none of my other shows had, almost semi-classical.

The musical comedy sections of *Milk and Honey* called for more contemporary scoring, so swing-band orchestrator Eddie Sauter was brought in to make his Broadway bow. Kay and Sauter shared equal billing, although Herman's recollection is that Kay did most of the show; again, the original scores—with the telltale handwriting—cannot be located. Bennett, meanwhile, followed *Juno* by inviting Kay to join him (with equal credit) on *The Happiest Girl in the World* and *We Take the Town.*

Harvey Schmidt and Tom Jones, of *The Fantasticks,* came to Broadway in 1963 with *110 in the Shade,* a musicalization of *The Rainmaker* for producer David Merrick.

> SCHMIDT: I had admired things of Hershy's. To me, anything western was Aaron Copland, who influenced western scores for the movies. Copland created the western sound. I wanted some of that feeling as a basis, and I was drawn to Hershy because he had done some things like that for City Ballet [including the 1954 ballet *Western Symphony*]. I was thrilled to be working with Hershy, and he loved that my piano parts were so complete. Hershy would insist, "I just put it down the way Harvey had it on the page."
>
> At the first orchestra reading—it was the first I'd ever had—they were playing the third piece, "Is It Really Me?" I thought everything was sounding great. Merrick stood up, he said, "I hate this! I hate this! I'm going to get Phil Lang to orchestrate this. I want to hear the melody." Richard Nash, the librettist, said, "David, if you feel that way, why don't we take this orchestration and then do one where Hershy has the band play along with the melody. Play them both, then decide which sounds the best." Everyone thought the original was preferable, because they weren't playing the melody. Ten or twelve of us all agreed. It was really a satisfying experience. Merrick wasn't happy if everyone was getting along too well.

Musical director Don Pippin tells a variation of the same story: "Merrick kept criticizing, saying, 'I want to hear the melody in the woodwinds.' I'm surprised Hershy didn't have a nervous breakdown." As for the instrumentation, Pippin tells us that Schmidt and Kay discussed it in advance: "Hershy said, 'Rather than violins, I'd like to use violas'—so he scored it for that. There were places I thought were too richly orchestrated, so we cut back. And we added violins for the tour."

Two months later, *Foxy*—another Merrick musical, with Pippin—was floundering on the road. Among the problems were Eddie Sauter's orchestrations; this was his first full musical and, according to Pippin, he hadn't yet learned how to write for theatre (although he would quickly become an expert). Merrick's number one music man, Lang, was otherwise occupied with *Hello, Dolly!* so Kay was called in. Hershy totally rewrote most of Eddie's charts, although Sauter retained sole credit.

Over the next years, Kay went through a string of flop musicals: *Cafe Crown, Kelly, Drat! The Cat!* and *I'm Solomon.* None of the partiturs have been located, but it is known that Bill Stegmeyer (of *Reuben Reuben*) assisted on both *110 in the Shade* and *Cafe Crown*, and there were several ghosts on *I'm Solomon.* Kay ended the decade with the Alan Jay Lerner/André Previn *Coco*, a poor musical that turned a profit due to the participation of Katharine Hepburn. It can only be assumed that Kay was handed the job by Lerner's longtime orchestrator Bennett, who was by this point retired. Bennett, in the end, came in during previews to replace three of Kay's scores. At least three other songs were ghosted as well, leaving one to wonder how much of the final show was by Kay.

Kay returned to Bernstein in 1971 for *Mass*, which he orchestrated with the composer and Tunick. Kay's next Broadway visit came in 1974 with his canny reconfiguration of *Candide*, cut down to thirteen pieces.

> HAL PRINCE: I asked Jonathan Tunick, because who else would I ask? He turned me down, but Hershy came in and he was spectacular. That was very important. I think Lenny wasn't as happy with the sound of that show. He was right, with reason. But the sound of that show was the sound of that production. When Lenny started to fiddle around with it for other productions, the show lost its balls again, all over again.

Kay was one of the three credited orchestrators—among a group of seven—on *A Chorus Line*, to which he contributed "And," "One," and "Sing." When Bernstein and Lerner joined together in 1976 for the misbegotten bicentennial celebration *1600 Pennsylvania Avenue*, Ramin (of *West Side Story*) got the call. He immediately suggested splitting the show with Kay. While the enterprise was an oversized catastrophe, the score is worthy and the orchestrations incredibly rich.

The happy experience with Hal Prince brought Kay the assignment of Cy Coleman's *On the Twentieth Century.* Coleman and Kay might not seem like an obvious pairing, but Hershy was the perfect choice for the operetta-style material. *On the Twentieth Century* might have Kay's finest set of Broadway orchestrations, along with the 1956 *Candide.* The scores, like those for many of Coleman's shows, have disappeared; it is assumed that most of the orchestration is by Kay, although it is known that Jim Tyler did at least one chart.

Kay had a reputation for being testy, as evidenced by this somewhat bitter discussion he had with Lehman Engel just after *Twentieth Century* opened:

> Cy's conception of operetta is I–V, and a diminished chord in between. I found the score basically very infantile. Cy, Betty and Adolph refused to make any cuts. When we actually talked about making cuts, they would end up adding something to the show. Cy never wanted to cut one note out of his music. Betty and Adolph never wanted to cut one word out of either their lyrics or book. In the last week they did make some cuts—and then replaced them, about three days before opening. I saw the show opening night, which is also the last time I am going to see the show. I can't take it that much. I don't understand how the critics went overboard. I think visually the show is wonderful, and that I would say is all due to Hal Prince and [set designer] Robin Wagner. The so-called sextet is really at most a duet, but with six people in it. You can call it a sextet, and let Cy feel that he was written a sextet.

If Kay was at the top of his craft with *Twentieth Century*, his work thereafter turned problematic. His next musical, four months later, was *Evita*, which was first produced in London in June 1978. The score is officially credited to Kay and Andrew Lloyd Webber; by the time the show reached Broadway in September 1979, much of the orchestration had been improved and revamped, apparently without Kay's participation. (According to Larry Blank, who conducted the Los Angeles company, this work was mostly done by René Wiegert, musical director of the Broadway production; specifically, he added another reed chair—doubling on English horn and oboe—and rewrote the cello parts.) Kay's other 1979 musical, the Alan Jay Lerner/Burton Lane *Carmelina*, also experienced problems in the orchestration area, and just about all other areas as well. Kay's charts were especially heavy on melody in the violins, with little imagination in evidence. Lane disliked the charts intently; when the show was recorded after the closing, he refused to use the Kay orchestrations and had new ones written by Phil Lang.

Kay's final assignment was the next Coleman musical, *Barnum* (1980). Fans of the show regularly heap praise on Kay for the orchestrations; as it turns out, his work was almost totally discarded prior to previews. Unbeknown to composer/producer Coleman, Kay had suffered a stroke at some point after *Twentieth Century* (which might explain some of the problems on *Evita* and *Carmelina*). "The orchestra rehearsal was a disaster," said librettist Mark Bramble. "We walked in, and everything sounded like 'Turkey in the Straw.'" Facing a tremendous rush—*Barnum* was opening cold in New York and about to start previews—emergency calls went out to just about every orchestrator in town (including Tyler, Lang, Michael Gibson, and Ramin). Kay nevertheless retained sole billing, but that was the end of his career. He died the following year, on December 2, 1981.

As for the personal side of Hershy Kay, let us report that composers Herman and Schmidt, who used Kay on their first Broadway musicals, were both highly complimentary (although neither turned to him again). So was Hal Prince, who was very happy with the reduced *Candide* and with *On the Twentieth Century*. Virtually everybody else to whom I spoke about Kay had only negative things to say; one of his peers, charitably, referred to him simply as "a real sourpuss."

In interviews, I gathered two balanced (and similar) views from the pit: Red Press, who played *Cafe Crown* and *Drat! The Cat!* said: "Hershy was a wonderful orchestrator and a very bitter little man. He was very caustic; very unhappy, I guess. But his charts were beautiful and inventive." Herb Harris was the drummer for *On the Town*—which he singled out as the most "fun" show he played in his career—and served as Bernstein's contractor on *Mass*, the reduced *Candide*, and *1600 Pennsylvania Avenue*: "Lenny used to think Hershy was a great orchestrator, but he wasn't the easiest person to work with. He had his problems psychologically, because of his height. He used to come in and create communications problems between people. But he was one hell of an orchestrator." To which those of us who listen again and again to *Candide*, *110 in the Shade*, or *On the Twentieth Century* can attest.

Kay was associated with the following musicals. He was principal orchestrator or one of the principal orchestrators on all except those marked with ♭:

♭Barnum	The Golden Apple	On the Twentieth Century
♭Beggar's Holiday	The Happiest Girl in the World	Once upon a Mattress
Cafe Crown	I'm Solomon	110 in the Shade
Candide	♭Jollyanna	Peter Pan (1950)
Candide (1974)	Juno	Reuben Reuben
Carmelina	Kelly	Sandhog
♭A Chorus Line	Livin' the Life	Shootin' Star
Coco	Love Match	1600 Pennsylvania Avenue
Dark of the Moon	Mass	♭Sweet Bye and Bye
Drat! The Cat!	Milk and Honey	We Take the Town
Evita	Music Is	♭The Yearling
♭A Flag Is Born	A Musical Jubilee	
Foxy	On the Town	

IRWIN "IRV" KOSTAL

Born: October 1, 1911, Chicago, Illinois
Died: November 23, 1994, Studio City, California

Irv Kostal was, in his own words, "smitten by a player piano" at the age of two and a half, and he spent the next eighty years immersed in music. "As soon as I could talk, I wanted a piano, but no matter how much I stomped my feet and bawled, my father said no." This was not a nurturing father; besides, Jerry Kostal had a bias against the piano. He had been expelled from the fifth grade, according to Irv, for pushing a piano out of a schoolhouse window; his first job, oddly enough, was moving pianos for the Kimball Piano Company. "He liked music, he just hated pianos."

Kostal was born October 1, 1911. His parents, children of immigrants, lived in what was called the Old Settlement, a Bohemian (Czech) enclave of Chicago. It was a rough upbringing. His father, who peddled firewood from house to house, was a quick-tempered strongman. As Kostal put it, "On weekends, he and my grandfather would often wind up in jail for demolishing a local bar."

The young Kostal took a different tack, burying his nose in books. He told of a vicious cycle of being beaten up by the neighborhood kids because he was carrying library books; of watching as the toughs destroyed said library books; and then getting beaten up again, by his father, when the bill came for the lost books.

When he was eleven, his father finally brought home a broken player piano—with the player mechanism missing—but for Kostal, it was enough. After three primitive lessons from a lady on the block, he was on his own. A self-taught musician, he was soon playing with small groups. His first stab at orchestration, he recalls, was a miserable failure for the simple reason that he wrote all of the parts in the same key. (The standard clarinet is pitched in B-flat—which is to say, one step lower than a C instrument like the flute. Thus, if you write the same G for the flute and the clarinet, the clarinet note comes out as an F.) The players explained the problem, and Kostal made the necessary adjustments. This served as his first and final lesson in orchestration.

At twelve, as he was graduating from grammar school, he joined a dance orchestra (at two bucks a gig). He also discovered the music of Wagner on the radio, specifically the prelude from *Tristan und Isolde*. He went to the library to borrow the score, looking under "V." (They said "Vagner," didn't they?) The librarian set him straight.

I found the miniature orchestral score, took it home and studied it. I saw that while parts of it could be played by one pianist, it really needed two. So I made a two-piano arrangement of the entire piece. Leonard Bernstein told me many years later he had done exactly the same thing. From this score, I learned about musical instruments I never knew existed: flutes, oboes, bassoon, French horn, harps.

Wagner influenced Kostal in another way: "My first name is really Ervin, but I figured if Vagner was really Wagner, I would become Irwin. In the Czech language there is no 'W' and because I was different from all my Bohemian relatives, this proved it. And that's why I changed my first name." Logical enough for a twelve-year-old.

In his memoirs, Kostal tells of a grammar school production of *Uncle Tom's Cabin*, in which he played a continuous musical background under the dialogue:

In a book on folk music, I found the melody, "Way Down upon the Swanee River"; and in a ragtime book by Max Kortlander I found a jazzy version of the tune. By taking away the rhythmic aspects and playing it in a minor key, I found lots of ways to play this song, making it fit the dramatics of the half-hour long story.

Kostal's description—devising an assortment of variations on "Swanee River" to match the action onstage—pretty much explains what a musical arranger does.

Kostal began playing in all kinds of musical groups:

The music libraries of these orchestras consisted of stock arrangements, which sold for as little as seventy-five cents. A lot of these arrangements were made by W. C. Polla and Jack Mason, and they were despised by the playing musicians. These arrangements were called "stocks." They were cleverly constructed so that any combination of musical instruments could find a way to play at least three-part harmony.

By the age of fourteen, Kostal was teaching ragtime for $22.50 a week. He was not the only high school student in the Chicago of the Roaring Twenties supplementing the family income with music. Kostal tells of a schoolmate who was found asleep one day in class. He explained to the teacher that he had been up all night, playing clarinet. "Tell me, Mr. Goodman," asked the teacher, "how much money did you make last night?" Young Benny answered, and the teacher said: "All right, you can go back to sleep."

During Kostal's final year in high school, his father got him a job driving a beer truck for Al Capone at $75 a week. Irv yelled: "You won't even let me drive your lousy old Ford, and now you expect me to drive a beer truck and get arrested?"

"We need the money and you'll do what you're told," said Pop Kostal.

"No, I won't. I screamed and lay down on the floor. He kicked me and beat me, but nothing he could do would make me obey him. He gave up in despair, and never let me forget how I had let down the entire family." As he had throughout his childhood, Kostal withdrew into music.

Kostal graduated from high school in 1929, not an especially good time to go on the job market. He spent the early Depression years taking whatever musical jobs he could get, playing in hotels, cafés, and funeral parlors (at $5 a throw). He did, indeed, spend a stretch working for Capone, as a pianist at the Coney Island Café, a mob hideout. All through these underemployed years, Kostal spent countless hours at the Chicago Public Library, studying orchestral scores of all types with the hope that the knowledge would ultimately pay off.

In 1934, Kostal went on the road with the Bobby Meeker Orchestra, a small-time big band. He describes the life of an on-the-cuff arranger:

> Part of my work was writing two arrangements a week. This I did without writing a complete score. In a rather ordinary-sized hotel room, I'd lay the parts on the floor, the three trumpets over here, the two trombones over there, and the woodwinds on the bed, with the rhythm section anywhere at all.

This type of training helps explain how Kostal, during his TV years, could turn out in the neighborhood of 700 pages a week—with the radio on. Marion Evans and Sid Ramin both report that Kostal was so fast that his copyists presented him with a hotel reception bell to ring every time he had a new page ready.

Kostal eventually tired of the road, and by 1938 he was back in Chicago—with no work:

> These were hard times, and I spent my time studying. At the public library, I went back to my original scheme and went alphabetically through the music of the masters. Bach, alphabetically as well as musically, came first. The inventions and the well-tempered clavichord [sic] were stumbling blocks of the first order. Then came Beethoven, Brahms, Debussy, Elgar, Frank, Gounod, on and on through the alphabet. Styles, generations, periods, meant nothing to me. I tried to absorb everything. By the time I came to Ravel, Tchaikovsky and Wagner, I knew quite a lot about music in a jumbled way.

Things began to change in 1943. Kostal got a job as pianist with the orchestra at Chicago's mob-backed Latin Quarter. When the bandleader was fired, the players—fearing that a new band would be brought in—reasoned that they might preserve their jobs if they could provide a conductor. Kostal was selected, the owners were pleased, and Irv finally had steady work. For a while, that is. The Latin Quarter soon changed to a policy of allowing the star attractions to bring in their own bandleaders, and Kostal was back on the bench. But in 1944, he was hired as an orchestrator for the NBC radio orchestra in Chicago. Accustomed to scoring for nine pieces, he suddenly had forty musicians—and, for the first time, a real string section. While at NBC, Kostal was invited back to the Latin Quarter, and other offers cascaded in:

> I was playing the piano and writing the arrangements for five radio
> shows a week, I was orchestrating for not only the Latin Quarter but also
> the Edgewater Beach Hotel, besides making as many arrangements for
> NBC as I could. Also maintaining my regular job as orchestra leader, six
> nights a week at the Latin Quarter. I never made an orchestral score for
> these nightclub shows, merely writing out the parts for each instrument,
> and sometimes I'd be finishing an arrangement while the band was still
> rehearsing. All this deadline writing prepared me for my future career as
> a television orchestrator.

But he ran into a brick wall. The Musicians' Union decreed that Kostal was doing too much work and ordered him to give up either radio or the nightclubs. ("Where's the rule that says I can't do as much work as I can get?" he demanded. "We just wrote one," said the all-powerful union—and it was unwise to dispute the union in Chicago.) This drastic cut in income, after so many lean years, impelled Kostal to leave town for the big time. A toss of the coin sent him east, rather than west, and in 1946 he moved to New York, where he had to start all over again.

Nobody wanted Chicago musicians, seeing them as either unsophisticated rubes or unwelcome competition. Kostal couldn't get arrested: "The only two people who treated me decently, without giving me any work, were two arrangers for the Milton Berle TV show, Red Ginzler and Sid Ramin. They at least talked to me, had coffee with me, and showed some interest in me." But no work.

Roy Shield, Kostal's contact at NBC Chicago, was transferred to New York. He finally got Kostal a job as staff pianist at the station, but the Chicago-based Kostal faced stern resistance and was fired after nine months. With prospects looking dim, Shield's secretary introduced Irv to a violinist named Sylvan Kirsner. Kirsner offered to introduce Kostal to a friend of his, Don Walker.

Walker was, as always, busy orchestrating musicals. Don also, throughout his career, wrote musical comedies of his own—with consistently unfavorable results. (Three musicals made it to Broadway briefly, *Allah Be Praised! Memphis Bound*, and *Courtin' Time*.) When Kostal arrived in New York, Walker and Jack Lawrence were writing *Wicked, Wicked City*, a never-to-be-produced musical about William F. Howe and Abraham Hummel, two shady Tenderloin era lawyers in little olde New York.

> They needed a pianist to play auditions for fund raising, and soon I was rehearsing with them and a friendship began to develop. I told Don I was really more interested in orchestration, but I would gladly rehearse and play the piano without remuneration if he'd use me as an orchestrator when he needed help. After looking over some of my scores, he promised to give me a chance the very next time he had an overcrowded schedule.

Television was just becoming a major force in American popular entertainment, and the folks at Admiral—a major manufacturer of television sets—decided to broadcast a weekly "Broadway" revue. Max Liebman, who had directed the successful 1948 revue *Make Mine Manhattan*, was signed as producer. Liebman had spent several years turning out variety shows at Tamiment, a summer resort in the Poconos, where he discovered newcomers like Danny Kaye, Imogene Coca, and Jerome Robbins. *The Admiral Broadway Revue* debuted on January 28, 1949, with a cast including Sid Caesar, Imogene Coca, Mary McCarty, and Marge and Gower Champion. Charles Sanford was the conductor, Don Walker the orchestrator—and Irv Kostal played the piano. Just before the first show went on the air, Kostal was informed that he was out of a job; the preferred pianist, who had been unavailable for the premiere, had been hired to take over beginning the second week.

> During the run of *The Admiral Broadway Revue*, Walker did most of the orchestrations, with me helping out to meet the deadlines. Don also handed me some of his Broadway assignments, just enough to keep me and my family from going hungry. Don told me that at first my arrangements scared the death out of him, until he realized it was because I drew such large notes, making the score look a lot busier than it really was. His handwriting was sheer pointillism, each note a fly speck while my notes were large and bold, and I had a tendency to make them bigger and bigger when the music became louder and louder, and smaller and smaller when a diminuendo was in progress.

The Max Liebman/Sid Caesar revue was an immediate hit, so much so that it was simultaneously broadcast on two opposing networks. Despite the show's success, it was not renewed when the season ended, going off the air after seventeen weeks.

In June 1949, Walker took on a second TV revue, *Fireball Fun for All*, starring Ole Olsen and Chic Johnson (of Broadway's long-running *Hellzapoppin*). With Don increasingly busy, Kostal provided more and more assistance for the television work. While Kostal had apparently ghosted on Broadway for Walker in 1949, his first verifiable assignment was on the revue *Dance Me a Song*, in January 1950.

> Don asked me if I'd be willing to work on a show that he had taken over from Russell Bennett, and now was too busy to continue working on. Besides, he felt that my acquaintance with jazz music might work to my advantage, as there were a lot of young people involved, and I might fit in with them a little better than he or Russell did. [The young people included top-billed dancer Joan McCracken and a small-time hoofer named Bob Fosse, who soon married McCracken. Within a few years, Fosse would be a major Broadway choreographer, and Kostal would score major dance numbers in Fosse's first two musicals, "Hernando's Hideaway" in *The Pajama Game* and the "Shoeless Joe" baseball ballet in *Damn Yankees*.]
>
> Looking at the scores by Russell and Don gave me my first idea of how to go about things in writing for the theatre. Russell's scores were great examples of four-part writing for strings, and Don's were very fine examples of what to do with the reeds and brass. There was no electric amplification in those days, no microphones and no individually de-signed theatrical sound system. The big problem was finding ways to make the music exciting and still let the audience understand the lyrics.
>
> The first thing I did was to do away with all the harmony singing. With the boys and girls dancing and running all over the stage, I felt it was absolutely necessary for all of them to sing the melody and let the orchestra play the harmonies. This way, no matter what dancers were closest to the audience, they'd be singing the tune, not some oddball har-mony part. Because the show was lively and the young people were good dancers doing very modern dancing for the time, I found it was possible to retain the original string and reed parts by Russell and Don, and add all kinds of jazzy brass fills to fit the dancing. My success with this show improved my relationship with Don, who now began to have more faith in me. *Dance Me a Song* closed after thirty-five performances. These were my first thirty-five steps up the ladder of success, though it didn't seem so at the time.

Kostal didn't receive credit for *Dance Me a Song*. Neither did Walker, for that matter, but Kostal finally made it to Broadway. Max Liebman, meanwhile, was still trying to get his revue back on the air.

> Max held another meeting in his office with the people from *The Admiral Broadway Revue*. He expressed deep faith in the talents of the people in the room, and assured all of us that there was a place on television for the kind of entertainment he visualized. In the room were Sid Caesar, Imogene Coca, Mel Brooks, Carl Reiner, Howard Morris, [writers] Neil Simon, Mel Tolkin, Lucy Kallen, [vocal arranger] Clay (Buck) Warnick, [musical director] Charles Sanford, plus Don Walker and me. Max said if we stayed in this room and talked to ourselves about how talented we all were, it would do no good at all. He advised us all to go out and tell everybody about what a great show we could do, and somebody just might give us the chance to do it. And that's what he was going to do.
>
> It worked—Liebman sold NBC the idea for doing a one-shot, ninety-minute revue, *Your Show of Shows*. He promised to make it the best thing he had done, and hoped we'd all pitch in and give it all we had. Don Walker and I walked out of this meeting together. And then Don pronounced the words that changed my whole life. "Irv," he said, "why don't you take this one over? I don't think there's much of a future in TV."

Your Show of Shows was an overnight success and was immediately converted to a weekly format. In all, Liebman and his cohorts did forty ninety-minute programs a season for the next four years. The show went off the air in June 1954, by which point Caesar had pretty much burned himself out. But we're still seeing plays and films about Liebman's merry band of writers, with Brooks and Simon eventually joined by Larry Gelbart, Woody Allen, and Michael Stewart.

> For the first show, I orchestrated 700 score pages in one week. From Monday to Friday I had not gone to bed, catnapping once in a while. I went from rehearsal to rehearsal, got the routines, and then made the arrangements. In two weeks' time, I made enough money to pay for my home. We went from very, very poor to very well off in one big hurry. I couldn't help thinking with a sense of satisfaction that only a year before, Sam Chotzinoff [head of NBC's music department] had fired me from a $300 a week job as staff pianist. Now I was making $7,000 a week from his company.

One can only wonder how Walker felt, especially since he underwent financial problems during this period. Even so, Walker remained proud of his protégé and

invited Irv to provide Broadway charts when he was available. With Kostal ensconced at *Your Show of Shows*, Walker took on Red Ginzler as his chief assistant
during this period. (Ginzler also had a weekly TV job, with Milton Berle, but Red
had Sid Ramin as a full-time partner, allowing him to make more time for
Walker.) *Wonderful Town*, the 1953 Bernstein-Comden-Green-Abbott musical, is
notable for a number of reasons; among them is the presence of Walker, Ginzler,
Ramin, and Kostal. Bobby Griffith and Harold Prince, the *Wonderful Town* stage
managers, graduated to producer status the following year. Kostal orchestrated
four of their seven musicals, and ghosted on two others; the only Griffith-Prince
show without Kostal contributions was *New Girl in Town*, from Bennett and Lang.

When *Your Show of Shows* disbanded, Sid Caesar and Max Liebman went their
separate ways. Kostal remained with Liebman for a three-year series of self-
proclaimed "NBC spectaculars," under the banner *Max Liebman Presents*. Many of
these were abridged versions of old musicals, ranging from Herbert and Strauss
to Rodgers and Weill. As an inveterate student of orchestration, Kostal pored over
the original materials, further enhancing his capabilities for the next stage of his
career.

Kostal also continued working for Walker, who was now entrusting him with
important numbers (rather than incidentals and reprises). Kostal's uncredited
credits during this period include "Pass That Football" from *Wonderful Town*, "Hey
There" from *The Pajama Game*, "Siberia" from *Silk Stockings*, and several bright spots
in *The Music Man*. In the spring of 1957, Bernstein invited his childhood pal Ramin
to orchestrate his upcoming musical.

> Sid told me quite frankly he didn't feel too sure of himself tackling a
> musical by Leonard Bernstein, and he didn't want to risk endangering his
> friendship with Lenny if the music became a little too classical. This
> would be something more than the run-of-the-mill Broadway show.
> There would be operatic sections as well as ballets, with Jerry Robbins
> doing the choreography. Sid, having a high regard for my musicianship,
> suggested to Lenny he would do the show if Lenny would agree to me
> working with him. "How do you feel about it?" Sid asked. "Let's do it,"
> was my immediate response.
>
> In the past while working with Red Ginzler on *The Milton Berle Show*,
> Sid had gotten into the habit of being the "idea man," while Red did
> much of the orchestration. With me, I told Sid he was going to have to
> sit down and write because we were loaded with information about what
> Lenny wanted and there was no need for another idea man. From the
> middle of May, Sid and I spent at least twelve hours a day working with
> Lenny on every song and dance routine in *West Side Story*, and as each item

was decided, Sid and I would go to my home and do the orchestrations. Working with Leonard Bernstein over a three-month period is an experience that no musicians besides Sid Ramin and myself have had the pleasure of sharing. Besides the educational aspects, his sheer joy of living was an inspiration in itself. Something was always happening, not always of musical value.

While Sid and I would be discussing the orchestration with Lenny, Stephen Sondheim would rush in, discuss a possible change of lyrics with Lenny, and hurriedly leave the room. Sid and I were never introduced to Steve Sondheim, but we got to know him by some sort of musical osmosis. After each visit by Steve, Lenny would complain, "There goes another of my lyrical contributions," until the day came when Steve came in with the latest changes and Lenny sat him down and said, "Steve, I am now going to take my name off the lyric credit. It's all yours." Steve was pleasantly shocked, but he did say, "Why?" Lenny answered, "Every line I have written has now been eliminated except one, 'Gee, Officer Krupke, krup you!' And I'll be damned if I'm going to take a lyric credit for that!"

Even though Sid and I did the orchestrations, there can be no doubt that we only fulfilled Lenny's intentions, based upon the detailed information we compiled from Lenny. He took keen delight in his own creativity and jumped for joy whenever Sid or I added a little originality of our own. He sometimes would look at one of our scores and say, "Who said orchestration couldn't be creative?" And he'd hug us warmly.

West Side Story coincided with Kostal's chores for Max Liebman (a relationship that ended in 1958). Kostal also moved into the recording field; notable early albums include two LPs with newly minted star Julie Andrews, *The Lass with the Delicate Air* (1957) and *Julie Andrews Sings* (1958). Kostal also states in his memoirs that, during this period, he continued ghostwriting for Walker and other Broadway orchestrators, specifically including Lang and Royal. If this statement is accurate, the likeliest shows are *Portofino*, *Whoop-Up*, or *Redhead* (Lang) and *Rumple* or *The Body Beautiful* (Royal). Early in 1959, Kostal went back to TV, as the arranger and conductor of *The Garry Moore Show*, a new and instantly popular program.

Plunged back into the high-stress atmosphere of weekly television, Kostal found time to orchestrate five musicals between 1959 and 1962: *Fiorello! Tenderloin* (from the *Fiorello!* team), *Sail Away*, and—teamed with Ramin—*Kwamina* and *A Funny Thing Happened on the Way to the Forum*. Simultaneously, Kostal and Ramin rescored *West Side Story* for the 1961 film version, earning Oscars in the process.

But Kostal's day job was with Garry Moore. (In fact, there's a clause in Irv's contract with Griffith and Prince for *Tenderloin* stating that "in no event will Mr.

Kostal be required to work on Thursdays or Fridays," the forty-eight-hour spread during which the weekly Moore show was orchestrated.) A wildly inventive new comedienne joined the cast in 1961; Kostal soon arranged and conducted her first LP, *Carol Burnett Remembers How They Stopped the Show*. When Julie Andrews appeared on the show in May 1961, Kostal paired her with Burnett in a duet of Frank Loesser's "Big D." Andrews and Burnett were obviously well matched, which led within the year to *Julie and Carol at Carnegie Hall*, which was televised as an Emmy-winning special and released as a bestselling LP. At the same time, Kostal worked with yet another unconventional superstar-to-be.

Barbra Streisand must have been 16 or 17 years old, and looked rough and tough, like a street urchin. She had been playing in small clubs like The Blue Angel, a spot where Carol Burnett used to work. Every guest on the Moore show had to do a cameo bit in the segment called "That Wonderful Year." [This was a section that featured vintage songs from a specific year.] Barbra was asked to sing "Happy Days Are Here Again." She was very upset by this selection; this being her debut on national TV, she felt this song was not the right one for her. We were sitting in a set that included what looked like a lectern, and with a little imagination could seem to be a bar.

Just prior to this time, Sid Ramin and I had done an album for RCA Victor in which we intentionally reversed the traditional tempos of the selected songs. The slow songs were played fast, and the fast songs were played slow. "Anything Goes," for instance, was done in a slow jazzy style. Having heard Barbra blast out with her big voice, I suggested she sing "Happy Days" sitting at a bar, doing it like a torch song, a broken-hearted woman who was not happy at all. In show biz talk, this kind of idea is sometimes called playing against the scene.

This version of "Happy Days" created quite a stir for Barbra and within a half year, on her next appearance on *The Garry Moore Show*, she had become much better known. It was no longer "where do I stand, how do I do this?" and her original meek self. She came to rehearsal much better dressed and not only sure of herself, but very demanding. I said to her then, as she stood next to me on the podium, "Barbra, if you do become a great star, you're going to be impossible to work with!" We proceeded smoothly.

When Barbra appeared on another TV show, Garry Moore was quite upset when she repeated "Happy Days Are Here Again" and it was widely reported as being her first performance on TV. On one of our shows, he made quite a speech about Barbra, and made sure that everybody was reminded of the true facts.

When Barbra recorded "Happy Days" [on her first solo LP, *The Barbra Streisand Album*, in 1963], Pete Matz called me in the middle of the recording date and asked if he could borrow my orchestral arrangement, and I sent it over to him. As far as I know, Barbra's original recording of the song uses my arrangement. The important thing to me is that it was my idea for Barbra to sing the song slowly. In the notes for her four-disc CD set *Just for the Record* [1991], Barbra refers to Ken Welch as the musical director of *The Garry Moore Show*, and how he suggested singing the song slowly, and how the musical director sat down at the piano and played the most beautiful chords, and I must be dreaming that I was the musical director, and . . . oh, well, what difference does it make?

The course of Kostal's career underwent another significant change in 1963, with a call from Hollywood. Walt Disney was preparing a movie musical based on the *Mary Poppins* stories, with songs from his in-house team of Richard M. and Robert B. Sherman.

Despite all the very talented orchestrators and conductors in Hollywood, the Sherman Brothers decided they wanted somebody who was active in the Broadway theatre. They visualized the movie in a more theatrical manner. With this thought in the back of their minds, they listened to recordings of Broadway musicals of the past five years. One of their favorite albums turned out to be *Fiorello!* and when they noticed my name on several other recordings, including two I had done with Julie Andrews and one with Carol Burnett, Dick and Bob campaigned very actively on my behalf.

But Walt Disney held back, and suggested that he'd rather have the man from *The Garry Moore Show*, who seemed to know exactly how to write for any year from 1880 on [as in the "That Wonderful Year" segment]. Because *Mary Poppins* was a period picture, Walt felt that this was the kind of person he'd prefer. The Shermans apparently had never seen *The Garry Moore Show*. They left Walt Disney's office disheartened, but when they watched our next broadcast they were amazed to see they were all talking about the same person. After my first session with Bob and Dick, they told me all this, and hoped I'd do their songs. But they warned me, "Don't tell Walt you won an Academy Award for *West Side Story*. He hated it!"

Having signed a contract to orchestrate *Fiddler on the Roof*, I knew I could not agree to do *Mary Poppins* if it had conflicting dates. In the past, I seemed to be able to meet all deadlines, but faced with a major movie and a possibly very important Broadway show, I didn't think I would be able to handle it unless the schedules had very generous separation.

I called Abe Newborn, the agent who was handling *Fiddler*, and asked him to ascertain the exact dates I would be needed. Instead, Abe charged into Hal Prince's office, demanded a brand new deal and Hal became so angry he literally threw Abe out of his office, and me along with him. Hal sent me a letter releasing me from my contract and swearing I would never work for him again. Why Abe Newborn did this, I'll never know. If I had found the dates conflicted, I would have stuck with *Fiddler*. After all, I was in a "can't lose" situation, as the passage of time proved. One thing I made sure of, and that was to cancel my arrangement with Abe Newborn, and never again to cancel a contract to which I have committed myself.

The success of *Mary Poppins* was followed by the even greater success of the 1965 film version of *The Sound of Music*, which won Kostal another Oscar. Richard Rodgers insisted on getting sole composing credit for Kostal's original contributions to the latter film, which included that grand crescendo leading into the title song. In exchange, Kostal negotiated a percentage of the soundtrack album—which turned out to be worth its weight in gold-leaf manuscript paper.

The combination of *West Side Story*, *Mary Poppins*, and *The Sound of Music* resulted in more movies (including *Half a Sixpence* and *Chitty Chitty Bang Bang*), keeping Irv virtually unavailable for theatre for the next decade. In his spare time, Kostal was able to fit in occasional musicals for Edwin Lester's Civic Light Opera, including Meredith Willson's *1491* and Lerner & Loewe's stage adaptation of *Gigi*. Kostal's later musicals included *Rex* for Rodgers and Harnick (of *Fiorello!*) and Jule Styne's West End musical *Bar Mitzvah Boy*. Kostal's final Broadway musicals were *Copperfield* and *Seven Brides for Seven Brothers*; his final major work was the 1983 opera *A Quiet Place*, which reunited him with his *West Side Story* collaborators Leonard Bernstein and Sid Ramin. Irwin Kostal died on November 23, 1994, of a heart attack, at the age of eighty-three.

Kostal was associated with the following musicals. He was principal orchestrator or one of the principal orchestrators on all except those marked with ♭:

♭Agnes de Mille Dance Theatre	♭Dance Me a Song
♭Ankles Aweigh	An Evening with Carol Burnett
Bar Mitzvah Boy	Fiorello!
♭Bless You All	1491
♭Carnival in Flanders	A Funny Thing Happened ...
Copperfield	Gigi
♭Curtain Going Up	♭Hazel Flagg
♭Damn Yankees	Kwamina

Lovely Ladies, Kind Gentlemen
Lute Song (1959)
Michael Todd's Peep Show
♭The Music Man
♭Of Thee I Sing (1952)
♭On Your Toes (1954)
♭The Pajama Game
♭Pal Joey (1952)
♭Perfectly Frank
Phil the Fluter

Rex
Sail Away
Seven Brides for Seven Brothers
♭Seventh Heaven
♭Shinbone Alley
♭Silk Stockings
Tenderloin
West Side Story
♭Wonderful Town
Zenda

PHILIP J. LANG

Born: April 17, 1911, Bronx, New York
Died: February 22, 1986, Branford, Connecticut

Phil Lang was raised in Oceanside, New York, a then-small Long Island town about an hour away from Manhattan. The son of a salesman, he was keenly interested in chemistry; after graduating high school in 1929, he went off to the Missouri School of Mines. Finishing up his studies in Missouri, he still needed one year of French to graduate. Lang had always enjoyed music playing drums through high school. "My father said, 'Go to a music school, you can get the year of French.'" And so it was that Lang, at Ithaca College in Rochester, New York, became an orchestrator. "I never left music. I loved it. And I realized that when we played, we were not good unless somebody brought in some music to play."

Rochester was, in those days, a frequent stop on the band circuit. Lang would often write unsolicited arrangements, hoping to somehow get his start. One story has Lang knocking on the door of Morton Gould's dressing room in 1932, offering to write orchestrations for him. Lang's son Roger finds the notion of his shy and retiring father knocking on doors to solicit business highly unlikely, and the anecdote presents some questions. Gould was indeed touring in 1932, but he was still a teenager. A piano prodigy, he started at the Institute of Musical Arts (now Juilliard) at the age of eight. The Depression forced him away from serious music. At seventeen, in 1930, he became the staff arranger at Radio City Music Hall, and in 1932 he had his own act on the vaudeville circuit. In any event, Gould and Lang met backstage in Rochester, forming what would be an enduring friendship.

When Lang moved to New York in 1934, he called Gould—who, at twenty-one, was conducting and arranging a weekly radio program on WOR. He occasionally assisted Gould, but otherwise work was hard to find. Roger Lang (who wasn't born at the time) remembers hearing stories about his reserved father rushing up to 3 a.m. meetings in Harlem, where he did dance band arrangements for McKinney's Cotton Pickers, Duke Ellington, and other groups. (Phil recalled, forty years later, that when he did charts for the Claude Hopkins Band at the Cotton Club, "Lena Horne was the first girl in the line.") Gould also introduced Lang to Russell Bennett, who handed him an occasional utility for a Broadway musical to write (although none of these charts have surfaced).

From 1942 through 1945, Lang served with the U.S. Maritime Service, stationed at the Manhattan Beach Training Station in Brooklyn. There, Chief Petty Officer Lang was placed in charge of a top-flight marching band. Lieutenant Jack Lawrence, the songwriter, was Lang's superior, in charge of welfare and morale; the lead trombone player was Nelson Riddle. In 1942, Lang made what seems to be his first Broadway contributions, with two charts for Irving Berlin's soldier show *This Is the Army.* He is also credited as co-orchestrator with Gould for a negligible one-week children's show at the Longacre, *Let Freedom Sing*, although it is unlikely that they had more than a handful of musicians.

Lang returned from the service just in time for his big break. Leonard Bernstein, Betty Comden, Adolph Green, George Abbott, and Jerome Robbins had joined in 1944 for a brash and refreshing musical comedy, *On the Town.* As the team prepared a follow-up offering, Bernstein opted out. Looking for another "serious" composer capable of writing both show tunes and jazz ballet, the group settled on Gould; his ballet *Interplay* had just been produced at the Met. *Billion Dollar Baby* opened just before Christmas 1945. "Morton didn't want any of those other Broadway orchestrators—he was a newcomer, we were both newcomers. We wanted to bring something new to the theatre." Gould, understandably, took billing as orchestrator; Lang and Allan Small were credited for additional orchestrations, although an examination of the original scores shows that they did all of the actual writing. One supposes that Gould gave his orchestrators detailed and specific instructions of his intentions (as was the case with Bernstein on *West Side Story*).

The ballet-heavy *Billion Dollar Baby* was a succès d'estime, although perhaps too brash and cynical for its time. It managed to immediately land Lang the biggest show of the season: Irving Berlin's *Annie Get Your Gun*, produced by Rodgers and Hammerstein. As discussed elsewhere in detail (see page 125), Berlin and company were distressed by the New Haven orchestra reading for *Annie.* Panic ensued, with Bennett, Spialek, Royal, and just about everyone else called in to replace the charts. Some of Lang's work remained in the show, but this had to be a very embarrassing—and highly visible—failure for a second-time Broadway orchestrator.

It should be noted, however, that in later years Lang was hired for shows by Berlin, Rodgers, and director Josh Logan. And he did Ethel Merman's final Broadway orchestrations, as well.

The *Annie* affair stalled Lang's Broadway progress. In 1947, he was hired for two shows, both Abbott musicals. *Barefoot Boy with Cheek* was quickly forgotten, while *High Button Shoes* (with choreographer Jerome Robbins) was a long-running hit. Lang was brought in by Royal in 1948 to write a few charts on another Abbott show, *Where's Charley?*; the work by brass-band specialist Lang presumably included "The New Ashmolean Marching Society and Students' Conservatory Band," which features some marvelously out-of-key contrapuntal writing. Lang didn't have another full Broadway assignment until 1950, when he did Gould's *Arms and the Girl.* Once again, Gould took lead credit; once again, Bennett came in to help.

For the next five years, Lang picked up about one show a year, presumably when the likely suspects were unavailable. These included Hugh Martin's *Make a Wish,* once more working with Allan Small; Cole Porter's *Can-Can;* Harold Rome's *Fanny;* and Albert Hague's *Plain and Fancy.* Lang also did some ghosting during these years, on shows including Royal's *Brigadoon,* Walker's *Two's Company,* and Bennett's *Pipe Dream.* He also taught summer courses at the University of Michigan and the University of Colorado; wrote a textbook, *Scoring for the Band* (1950); and spent five years (beginning in 1953) as the director of standard and educational music for the publisher E. H. Morris & Co.

Everything changed in early 1956. Bennett had a new show; his usual assistant at the time, Joe Glover, was off doing his first full musical on his own. The conductor of the new show, Franz Allers, apparently recommended Lang; the pair were good friends, from *Plain and Fancy.* (Roger Lang recalls that Allers was the only Broadway type who was a regular family visitor, with the Viennese conductor looking somewhat incongruous wearing shorts at backyard barbeques.) The new show turned out to be the blockbuster *My Fair Lady;* Bennett, after the opening, saw fit to promote the uncredited Lang to full co-orchestrator billing. One day, Lang was a struggling, anonymous arranger; the next, we are told, the milkman was leaving notes on Lang's doorstep in Freeport, asking for house seats. That's Broadway. By 1959, Lang was up to four full shows a season.

His shows covered a wide range of musical styles, including the raucous *Li'l Abner;* the calypso-flavored *Jamaica* (in which all of his charts for star Lena Horne were replaced during the tryout); the whip-cracking *Destry Rides Again;* the nostalgic *Take Me Along;* and the delicate but artful *Carnival.*

The general assumption is that Bennett and Lang collaborated on numerous shows; the reality, though, is that they shared only four assignments, the others being *New Girl in Town*, *Redhead*, and *Camelot*. (Lang did most of the first two and two-thirds of *Camelot*.) They also occasionally ghosted for each other, on shows like Bennett's *Bells Are Ringing* and *Juno* and Lang's *Goldilocks*.

If *My Fair Lady* gave Lang pedigree, much of his future work came via *Fanny*. Lang was surely not the first choice for the 1954 musical; composer-lyricist Harold Rome had been thrilled with Walker's work on his prior three shows, while director/co-producer Josh Logan might well have wanted Russell Bennett of *South Pacific*. (Logan, too, surely recalled Lang's problems eight years earlier on *Annie Get Your Gun*.) Lang nevertheless got the job, cementing a relationship with *Fanny*'s novice lead producer, a fellow named David Merrick. Nobody could have guessed that Merrick would become one of the most active Broadway producers ever; nor could Lang have known that *Fanny* would make him Merrick's orchestrator-of-choice, bringing fourteen jobs over the years—including the blockbuster *Hello, Dolly!*

Not that the relationship with Merrick was without difficulty. Merrick famously prided himself on being impetuous, bombastic, demanding, and unreasonable. But Lang had an easygoing nature; his philosophy seems to have been to smile and just keep writing. While other orchestrators could be prickly, outspoken, and protective of their charts, Lang seemed to give them whatever they asked for. Except, that is, his true opinion of the work.

> ROGER LANG: He was extremely soft-spoken. I never knew him to raise his voice. I think he was very collegial. Unlike a lot of the other people, he checked his ego at the door. He was very proud of what he did, but he sublimated himself to the job.
>
> DONALD PIPPIN: Phil's secret was that he never got involved in differences or conflicts with anyone on a show. "They might ask you your opinion," he told me, "but most of the time they don't want your opinion." Phil would do as he was told, he'd nod and smile. When everyone else was fighting or arguing, he just wouldn't get involved.

Tunick suggests that this might have been a lesson learned from the *Annie Get Your Gun* debacle; give them what they think they want, and always nod pleasantly.

Through his work with Merrick, Lang became the preferred orchestrator of both Gower Champion and Jerry Herman, which led to numerous other assignments. As the Broadway musical began to enter a more modern, pop-influenced era in the mid-sixties, and as Bennett and other "traditional" orchestrators disappeared from the scene, Lang became firmly established as the voice of old-fashioned musical comedy. While orchestrators like Burns and Tunick took pit orchestras in new directions, composers like Herman and Charles Strouse kept Lang busy with hits like *Mame* and *Applause*. Two of Lang's final musicals, scored in traditional Broadway style, were among the biggest hits of their time: Strouse's *Annie* (1977) and the Merrick-Champion *42nd Street* (1980). If Lang was not the most artful of Broadway orchestrators, he was perhaps the finest at constructing sturdy, workmanlike musicals with that traditional Broadway sound.

As his career slowed down, Lang continued to contribute uncredited charts; readers might be surprised to discover his name on "Dance Ten, Looks Three" from Marvin Hamlisch's *A Chorus Line* (1975) and "Join the Circus" from Cy Coleman's *Barnum* (1980). Lang developed intestinal cancer in the early eighties. When Jerry Herman returned to Broadway in 1983 with *La Cage aux Folles*, Lang—who had done everything of Jerry's since *Hello, Dolly!*—was physically unable to accept the assignment. Late in the process, Herman, conductor Don Pippin, and orchestrator Jim Tyler thought it fitting to invite Lang to do the show's theme song, "The Best of Times." He tried, but he simply couldn't do it. Phil Lang died on February 22, 1986, at the age of seventy-four.

Lang was associated with the following musicals. He was principal orchestrator or one of the principal orchestrators on all except those marked with ♭:

Ambassador	Camelot	Hello, Dolly!
Annie	Can-Can	High Button Shoes
♭Annie Get Your Gun	♭Carmelina	Hot September
Applause	Carnival	How Now, Dow Jones
Ari	Charlie and Algernon	I Do! I Do!
Arms and the Girl	♭A Chorus Line	I Had a Ball
Around the World in	Christine	I Remember Mama
Eighty Days	♭The Christmas Spectacular	It's Spring
Barbary Coast	Cyrano	Jamaica
Barefoot Boy with Cheek	Dear World	Jennie
♭Barnum	Destry Rides Again	♭Juno
♭Bells Are Ringing	Fanny	Kean
Ben Franklin in Paris	42nd Street	La Belle
Billion Dollar Baby	George M!	Let Freedom Sing
♭Bless You All	♭The Girl Who Came to Supper	Li'l Abner
Bonanza Bound	Goldilocks	Lorelei
♭Brigadoon	Good News	♭Lovely Ladies, Kind
♭Bring Back Birdie	The Grand Tour	Gentlemen
Calamity Jane	♭Hazel Flagg	Mack & Mabel

♭Maggie
Maggie Flynn
Make a Wish
Mame
♭Manhattan Showboat
Mardi Gras
♭Mata Hari
Meet Me in St. Louis
    (1960)
Mr. President
A Musical Jubilee
My Fair Lady
New Girl in Town
♭A New York Summer
♭Oh Captain!
One Night Stand

Peg (1967)
♭Peg (1983)
♭Pipe Dream
Plain and Fancy
Pleasures and Palaces
Portofino
Redhead
The Roar of the
    Greasepaint . . .
Rondelay
♭Sally
Saratoga
Shangri-La
Sherry!
Show Me Where the Good
    Times Are

Snow White and the Seven
    Dwarfs
♭Song of Norway
Subways Are for Sleeping
Sugar
♭Sugar Babies
Take Me Along
♭This Is the Army
♭Three Wishes for Jamie
To Broadway with Love
Tovarich
Two on the Aisle
♭Two's Company
♭Where's Charley?
Whoop-Up
♭Ziegfeld Follies of 1957

SID RAMIN

Born: January 19, 1922, Boston, Massachusetts

Sid Ramin started his musical training at the age of thirteen, studying with a precocious classmate. Lessons—at $1 per, plus a candy bar—weren't cheap, by Depression standards at least. But Sid's teacher, who was all of five months older, turned out to be one of the most influential musicians of the twentieth century. Ramin more than made up those $1 sessions when he orchestrated his mentor's *West Side Story*, although one doubts he ever recouped all those chocolate bars from Lenny Bernstein.

Ramin was born in Boston, where his father was a window dresser at the Jordan Marsh department store. Both parents were musical; his father played the violin, his mother piano. Sid was not much of an instrumentalist, though; he was that rare breed among orchestrators: an arranger who can't play an instrument.

> I became an orchestrator because I couldn't do anything else, and I love music. An orchestrator can write things that he'd never dare try to play, but you know it is going to be played by people who can play it, and if you have any common sense, once you know the ranges of instruments, you are not going to write something that is out of the range.

After attending the New England Conservatory of Music and Boston University, Ramin entered the army in 1940. His training got him assigned as an arranger, but he feels that it was in the service that he really learned how to orchestrate. With the army bands at his disposal, "I had a captive test tube. I could hear everything I wrote."

Ramin left the army in 1945 and moved the following year to New York to attend Columbia University. A disc jockey friend knew that the Three Suns, a group headed by Al Nevins on guitar, was looking for an orchestrator. Ramin got the job, the Three Suns got a recording contract with RCA, and Ramin started writing charts for the trio (who with success were assigned a full orchestra by the label).

He also picked up other jobs, including one for conductor Alan Roth at NBC, making transcriptions (recordings made specifically for circulation to affiliated stations around the country). In 1948, Roth was tapped to conduct *The Texaco Star Theatre*, which was moving from radio to TV. Roth hired Ramin as the arranger. Ramin invited Red Ginzler along as his collaborator, and the pair went to work on what was to be TV's first blockbuster, under the title *The Milton Berle Show*.

> Red Ginzler taught me so much, I cannot begin to tell you. I'm still using the devices that Red taught me. We had to turn out the show overnight. The cast met on a Sunday afternoon, when we took down the numbers. Red and I stayed up all night orchestrating. We had copyists in the office, and as we finished a page, they would hear the page being ripped off the score pad, and pick up the pages. Red was left-handed and I'm right-handed; when we got extremely behind, we would sometimes sit down at the same score pad and turn out pages, with about six copyists waiting. Monday morning, we wearily trekked over to NBC for the orchestra reading. We did that every week.

Ginzler's daughter Myra Kates recalled—fifty-five years after the fact—that she had to change her already-booked Sunday wedding to a Thursday, so her father could attend. Ginzler was a much faster writer, who apparently delighted in round-the-clock work. While Ramin contented himself with Berle and occasional recording work for RCA, Ginzler moonlighted on Broadway; as an unofficial assistant to Don Walker, Ginzler ghosted dozens of Broadway shows from 1948 to 1960. When Walker and Ginzler found themselves with three Broadway musicals opening within two weeks in early 1953, Ramin lent a hand. Sid's first Broadway chart, written with Ginzler, was "A Little More Heart" for Jule Styne's *Hazel Flagg*. With *Hazel* undergoing severe rewrites in Philadelphia and a second musical facing similar problems, neither Walker nor Ginzler could get to the tryout of the third show. Ramin, with almost no Broadway experience, was nevertheless designated to oversee *Wonderful Town*. He walked through the stage door of the Shubert in New Haven and bumped into the composer—Bernstein. "Lenny didn't know that I was going to show up, or that I was on the show, or even that I knew Don," said Ramin. "He was flabbergasted."

Ramin, who had thus far written only one complete orchestration for the show ("Swing"), oversaw the many fixes and changes until Ginzler arrived at the next stop in Boston. And then it was back to TV and the Berle show. In 1956, Ramin signed on as a staff arranger with RCA and was happily ensconced when Broadway beckoned once more.

> I remember very vividly—it was early in the morning. Lenny called and he said, "Would you like to do a Broadway show with me?" And I asked, "Isn't Hershy going to do it?" Because Hershy was his guy. He said, "No, I'd like to use you." I said, "Well, I'm busy at RCA. However, if I can work with somebody, would that be okay?" So he said, "If it's somebody that you like and you know can do the job." I said to Irv Kostal, "I have the chance to do a Broadway show, and I'm scared stiff of it. Would you do it with me?" He said, "Sure."

Kostal, with a strong legit background from years of studying operatic scores, was a perfect choice for a show that would necessarily mix musical styles. *West Side Story* gave Ramin and Kostal their first major Broadway credits, albeit in small print (with Bernstein taking first credit).

> Lenny had a lot to do with it, because we had what Lenny called "pre-orchestration meetings." We'd go over to Lenny's place at the Osborne. Lenny would play for us, and then sit down with us, and we would discuss what we would do, how we were going to orchestrate. Lenny really had pretty much of a general idea of who would play what. And then it was up to Irv and me to go back and put down on paper what Lenny had asked for. And then after we did that, we would have a post-orchestration meeting. We would walk in with our finished orchestration. He would look at it, take out his red pencil, and say, "Why did you guys do that?"
>
> "Because we wanted to add something," or sometimes we'd say, "Lenny, we thought maybe you meant that," and he'd say, "Well, maybe . . . okay." So he really was present at the pre-orchestration meetings and the post-orchestration meetings. He didn't actually physically put the notes down on paper. But he was present, and he literally proofread what we wrote.

Ramin also related the tale of "Something's Coming":

> Irv and I redid that over and over and over. Steve Sondheim didn't care for the orchestration. And we kept doing it over and over in Washington. Irv, in desperation, said, "Tell him to get Phil Lang." I went to Lenny. "Look, obviously we cannot do this properly, why don't you get Phil Lang?" Lenny said, "Aww, come on. You must be kidding!" And we went back to the original, and that's the one that they're using today, the very first orchestration Irv and I did for the song. That was both of us. Irv and I literally sat down next to each other and did our work together. We worked very very closely, which was better for me. I'm not sure if it was better for Irv, but it was certainly better for me.

West Side Story was not a typical Broadway orchestration, certainly, and Ramin did not consider the theatre a new career. He began to enjoy great success at RCA with a string of notable albums, including Abbe Lane's *The Lady in Red* and early stereo showpieces (in collaboration with Kostal) for Al Nevins.

In the spring of 1958, RCA decided to make a cast recording of the new Jule Styne/Betty Comden/Adolph Green show, *Say, Darling.* This was a play with songs, about the creation of a musical comedy (adapted from humorist Richard Bissell's fictionalized chronicle of the making of *The Pajama Game*). The show, in the theatre, was accompanied by two onstage pianos and a small combo. For the cast album, RCA requisitioned a full orchestration. Ramin, as staff arranger, received sole credit, although he is quick to point out that the job was done in close collaboration with Ginzler. "At the recording session, Betty & Adolph and Jule were in the control room, and they heard the overture. Jule loved it so much he feigned fainting. He fell down on his back in the control room, he just loved it so much. He had no idea that he was going to hear what he heard."

And that, Ramin believes, is how he (and Ginzler) landed the new Jule Styne/Stephen Sondheim/Jerome Robbins/Ethel Merman musical, *Gypsy.* While the orchestrators of *West Side Story* had their composer closely supervising their work, Ramin and Ginzler had a free hand with *Gypsy.* They came up with a very different sound than the typical Broadway musical of the time; one only has to compare the charts to those of the 1956 Styne-Robbins musical, *Bells Are Ringing. Bells,* a contemporary musical comedy, was graced with a traditional orchestration by no less than Russell Bennett (with contributions from Walker, Lang, Glover, and others). *Gypsy* was a period piece, taking place thirty years earlier; but out of the orchestra pit came a tornado of sound that literally brought chills to theatregoers in 1959, and still does fifty years later. This was not a predetermined choice on the part of Ramin and Ginzler; they were not looking to break rules and set a new standard, but rather to write in the manner that they were used to.

> We decided that having three or four trumpets was a heck of a lot better than only having two. Usually, theatre orchestras had only two. We had three, and three trombones, a big brass section. Whenever I hear *Gypsy*, as many times as I've heard it, I love to hear the brass riffs because it sort of makes me feel at home. And I think it added a quality to the theatre that maybe hadn't been there before. One of the biggest thrills any of us younger arrangers could ever have was to go to a ballroom, and hear someone like Les Brown and His Band of Renown. We would stand in front of the brass, and just bathe in the sound. That's what I did, and therefore when I had the opportunity to use some of those devices, I did. I think it's as simple as all that. Maybe it's called style.
>
> [As for Russell Bennett,] I only met him once or twice. I was flattered to meet him, but I don't think he could have done—or even would have wanted to do—a show like *Gypsy*. However, I'm not sure whether any of us jazzbos could have done the things he did, like *Oklahoma!* the way he did them.

That the sounds of *West Side Story* and *Gypsy* were distinctive was immediately noticed by composers and producers. Harold Prince: "Once you heard that sound, you wanted to hear that sound again."

Ramin joined Ginzler for a second show in 1959, the short-lived revue *The Girls Against the Boys* (top-lined by Bert Lahr and Nancy Walker). He remained at RCA, with a string of popular albums; continued his career in television, serving as music director of (and composer of the theme song for) *Candid Camera*; and moved into the lucrative field of advertising jingles. At the same time, Ramin and Kostal prepared the 1961 film version of *West Side Story*, for which they shared an Oscar. Ginzler, meanwhile, went out on his own as a Broadway orchestrator with *Bye Bye Birdie*. Late in 1960, Ramin and Ginzler undertook two musicals simultaneously, Cy Coleman's *Wildcat* and Bob Fosse's *The Conquering Hero*. They also committed to a third, which opened between the other two, Styne's *Do Re Mi*, but sensibly saw the wisdom of withdrawing.

> That was a bad time for me. Red and I went to Philadelphia, and somewhere along the line Red had to go cover *The Conquering Hero*. I was left alone with *Wildcat*. I got so used to working with somebody, and suddenly I was flying the plane solo. Things worked out okay, but I had a hard time.

Ginzler and Kostal, both, were exceptionally speedy writers, who could churn out pages by the hundreds. Ramin, however, could not. This was not a problem in the recording world, where he could lavish time on each chart. Broadway musicals were written in a time crunch, however, with the songs supplemented by underscoring, scene changes, utilities, dances, and more. "In a way, working with Red was almost a disservice in later years, because I got to depend on him so much. All the hard stuff I'd ask him about, and he always came up with a solution."

Ramin and Kostal's next show was Richard Adler's *Kwamina* (1961). In the spring of 1962, Ramin tried a musical on his own, Harold Rome's *I Can Get It for You Wholesale* (directed by Arthur Laurents, librettist of *West Side Story* and *Gypsy*). Working without Ginzler or Kostal, Ramin found himself swamped, and needed to call in a ghost, saxophonist-turned-orchestrator Arthur Beck. *Wholesale* was followed by *A Funny Thing Happened on the Way to the Forum*, which reunited Ramin and Kostal with Sondheim. This was a difficult show with endless changes, as described elsewhere.

Ramin undertook one more show on his own, composer/lyricist/talk show host Steve Allen's 1963 musical biography of Sophie Tucker. Again, Ramin needed help from Beck and others.

> *Sophie* was a troublesome show for me, schedule-wise. I had to give assignments to some people, and I don't even remember who, and I didn't even have time to look at the stuff before it went in the show. I was busy doing television and commercials. It was unfair to the show, and I'm ashamed of that. I remember there was an actor in that show, Phil Leeds. He saw me there one day, and he rather disdainfully said to me, "You're not giving the show any of your attention, and that's not fair." And it was the truth. I shouldn't have accepted the show, but I did. And I felt very badly about it; the fact that I say this after all these years shows how badly. Leeds wasn't talking about the quality of the work, I don't think. I just wasn't there. I was spoiled. I could make more in thirty seconds, with a commercial, than I could in a week with a musical.

Ramin continued in TV, with *The Patty Duke Show*. (You all know the song, composed by Ramin.) Even more lucrative was commercial work. One of Ramin's jingles, a Herb Alpert–style theme for the diet cola Tab, was expanded by producer Bob Crewe into a full-scale pop hit, "Music to Watch Girls By." Ramin had more or less withdrawn from the theatre.

> Strangely enough, I never really enjoyed the theatre. It was hard work. I never liked going out of town and working all night off bureau tops in hotel rooms, the way Don and Red were able to do. They could sit down at 5 a.m. in a hotel room, with pen and ink, on a makeshift desk, with

no piano, and write. I, on the other hand, needed a piano or I couldn't do it. I was spoiled, I guess. I began to do my commercials, and I did so well at that time, I was doing so many of them, and I was making so much money doing them, that I couldn't bring myself to leave it. And it wouldn't be fair to a show to do it. It's not that I wasn't working and I wanted to do something, I just was busy as hell.

Another phone call from Lenny brought Ramin back to Broadway in 1976 for *1600 Pennsylvania Avenue.* This time, Ramin invited Hershy Kay to collaborate on a score that was overloaded with music. Thereafter, Ramin made several visits to Broadway, working with collaborators on Marvin Hamlisch's *Smile* (1986), *Jerome Robbins' Broadway* (1989), and Jule Styne's *The Red Shoes* (1993). He also provided a sole chart, "Slap That Bass," for the Gershwin-derived *Crazy for You* (1992). Ramin has remained active into the twenty-first century, doing commissions and occasional recordings. Broadway, though, is a thing of the past. "I can't tell you how many shows call. I say, 'How many players?' They say, 'Twelve.' I turn them down. Not because I don't want to, I'm just not capable of thinking that way."

As the decades pass, virtually all of the hit musicals of Broadway's golden age have been revived. Changes are typically made, with the orchestrations inevitably undergoing revisions; even Bennett's *Oklahoma!* and Walker's *Fiddler on the Roof* have been "improved." Even so, *West Side Story* and *Gypsy* have remained relatively tamper-free, so far at least, which must be taken as a mark of the excellence of the once and forever revolutionary work by Ramin and his collaborators.

Ramin was associated with the following musicals. He was principal orchestrator or one of the principal orchestrators on all except those marked with ♭:

♭Barnum	♭Mass
The Conquering Hero	♭Nowhere to Go but Up
♭Crazy for You	The Red Shoes
♭A Family Affair	Say, Darling
A Funny Thing Happened . . .	1600 Pennsylvania Avenue
The Girls Against the Boys	Smile
Gypsy	Sophie
♭Hazel Flagg	♭Vintage '60
I Can Get It for You Wholesale	West Side Story
Jerome Robbins' Broadway	Wildcat
Kwamina	♭Wonderful Town

TED ROYAL

Born: September 6, 1904, Skedee, Northwest Territory (Oklahoma)
Died: March 27(?), 1981, Houston(?), Texas

Ted Royal Dewar was born September 6, 1904, in Skedee, Northwest Territory. This is present-day Oklahoma; it is unknown how large a town it was then, but the 2000 population was 102. By his teens, Royal had moved to Arkansas City, Kansas, a prairie town just north of the Oklahoma border. He graduated from high school in 1921, and after two years at the University of Kansas headed for the bandstand.

Royal is the most anonymous among the major Broadway orchestrators. His papers at the New York Public Library for the Performing Arts include an all-too-brief resume. Otherwise, I've been able to locate only one person who knew him more than tangentially, orchestrator Marion Evans. Royal's resume, starting in 1923, lists two years, minstrel shows (one-night stands, central and southern states); six months, tent shows (one-week stands, Oklahoma); six months, RKO vaudeville theatres, playing and arranging (Houston, Texas); four years, Publix Paramount (four shows a day, seven days a week); three years, sideman; one year, conductor, contractor, arranger; and six months, silent picture house (Queen Theatre, Houston). He also mentions that he played the Chicago and Oriental theatres, in Chicago, for Balaban & Katz.

By the early thirties, Royal was playing with the Ted Weems Orchestra, a small but popular dance band (which I suppose is referred to as "three years, sideman; one year, conductor, contractor, arranger"). Marion Evans: "The lead trumpet player was Vaughn Monroe; Royal played lead alto. Bob Noeltner for a long time played piano with them. They had a big hit on a shuffle rhythm thing called 'Heartaches' [recorded in August 1933]."

Royal apparently began arranging in 1934, for Wayne King and Weems. The following year, he went to New York, where he had his own radio show, the *Pompeiian Hour* (with vocalist Donald Novis). In 1936, Royal fronted an orchestra at the Jones Beach Café on the Mall, on Long Island. During this period, and for the rest of the decade, he did charts for Weems and for several other bandleaders, including Jimmy Dorsey, Isham Jones, Paul Whiteman, and Harry James.

Royal's theatre work seems to have begun in 1938, with two revues at Billy Rose's 4,000-seat Casa Manana in Fort Worth, Texas. In 1939, Rose hired Royal for his *Aquacade* spectacular at the New York World's Fair. Royal did about two-thirds of this mammoth extravaganza, which starred Olympic swimmer Eleanor Holm. (Rose divorced Fanny Brice to marry Holm, who at the same time divorced Art Jarrett—who had been the vocalist with Ted Weems.) Publisher Max Dreyfus just then needed a new man in his theatre-orchestrating department at Chappell Music. Royal got the job, joining Bennett, Spialek, and Walker. As the only one of the four with actual swing-band experience, Royal was apparently expected to handle the "hotter" material. Walker, however, seems to have proved more adept in this area, as evidenced by their contributions to *On the Town*: Royal provided the somewhat pallid "Lucky to Be Me," while Walker shook the rafters with "I Can Cook Too."

Royal's first Broadway assignments—at least, the first charts we can identify—were contributions to musicals orchestrated by Spialek; these include *George White's Scandals of 1939*, *Too Many Girls*, *Du Barry Was a Lady* (where he is said to have done "Friendship"), *Higher and Higher*, and *Pal Joey*. He was credited as co-orchestrator (with Bennett) of Porter's *Mexican Hayride* (1944) and as head orchestrator of Arlen's *St. Louis Woman* (1946). Royal estimated that, during his Chappell years, from 1939 to 1946, he contributed to about eighty musicals.

When asked who he studied with, Ted's pat answer was: "Nobody. I learned something on each job—that did it!" In the mid-1930s, though, Royal studied with orchestrator Joseph Schillinger. (Schillinger came up with a system of composition based on mathematical principles. While many musicians were highly critical, Schillinger's students included George Gershwin.) After Schillinger's death in 1943, Royal became a leading proponent and teacher of the system. Evans: "He did not have a background in classical music, so he embraced the Schillinger system. There were three great orchestrators in Hollywood, Conrad Salinger, Eddie Powell, and Herbert Spencer. They were friends of Ted's, and all three had studied with Schillinger." Royal taught a course in orchestration and arranging at Juilliard in the summers of 1945–1947. Evans, under the G.I. Bill, studied with Royal there in 1947; when Marion moved to New York in 1950, Ted started giving him work.

Royal left Chappell—and Max Dreyfus's guaranteed weekly stipend—to go out on his own in 1947. One suspects that Kurt Weill had something to do with it; Royal ghosted on Weill's *Lady in the Dark* (1941), *The Firebrand of Florence* (1945), and *Street Scene* (1947). This last, which was orchestrated in late 1946, seems to have been Royal's final Chappell show. Typically, Weill handed over the show's big swing number, "Moon-Faced, Starry Eyed." Maverick producer Cheryl Crawford had introduced Weill to Broadway in 1936 with *Johnny Johnson* and had also produced Weill's hit *One Touch of Venus.* Crawford was doing a new musical—a non-Chappell musical. Dreyfus was known to exact a payoff before loaning out one of his staff orchestrators. With Royal no longer under contract and with (presumably) a recommendation from Weill, Crawford hired Royal for *Brigadoon* (1947).

This was the first musical on which Royal received sole credit. It is the only set of Royal orchestrations that has remained in use; the charts have been recorded no less than four times, including two "complete" versions. The orchestrations exist in a conformed copy, prepared after the fact by a copyist; the originals, with their telltale handwriting, have not surfaced. A tally sheet—prepared by Royal before the show left on its tryout and thus necessarily incomplete—reveals the contributions of at least two ghosts, Lang and Noeltner. But most of the show is apparently by Royal. *Brigadoon*, which has one of Broadway's finer sets of orchestrations, represents Ted at his best. This might be a case where the composer deserves rather more credit than usual; Fritz Loewe was known to carefully oversee the musical aspects of his shows. Loewe's original piano-vocal arrangements not only include most of the figurations and fills; he actually dictates certain instruments, like the French horn on the countermelody between cadences of "From This Day On."

Brigadoon was a commercial and artistic hit, giving Royal stature that had evaded him at Chappell. Over the next eleven years, Royal was head orchestrator for roughly two dozen musicals. The most successful, by far, were Frank Loesser's first two shows. *Where's Charley?* (1948) was started by Royal. During the tryout, Lang and Spialek were called in; by the Broadway opening, the three shared equal billing. (With the charts missing, it's impossible to say—though not impossible to guess—who did what.) On *Guys and Dolls*, it was Royal who came in during the tryout. Most of the score was orchestrated by George Bassman before he was fired, with many changes and edits by Royal (who was granted equal billing).

Official credits notwithstanding, attributions for the musicals under Royal's name are especially difficult to determine. I've located a fair number of charts that Royal ghosted for other orchestrators, including *Annie Get Your Gun* (where his work included "There's No Business Like Show Business"). But of the many musicals for which Royal was head orchestrator, only one set of partiturs seems to have survived: *Paint Your Wagon*, his second and final Lerner & Loewe musical. This score was heavily ghosted (by Bennett, Spialek, Noeltner, and others), especially on the dances and ballets; this is somewhat understandable, due to the inordinate amount of music. All those Agnes de Mille ballets, you know. The songs, though, are mostly by Royal, and he did an admirable job.

Every other Royal musical, for reasons unknown, is missing. The likeliest explanation is that Royal kept the original scores in one place, and at some point in time they were destroyed or lost or abandoned. Royal's heirs donated a fair amount of material to the New York Public Library, including his band orchestrations. None of his theatre orchestrations are included, though.

Bennett and Walker continued as Broadway's two most in-demand orchestrators until about 1959. With Spialek all but finished on Broadway by 1950, and Lang just starting out, Royal seems to have filled the spot as the only established pro available to producers and composers who couldn't get Bennett or Walker. A string of shows followed, some rather interesting but most forgotten. These include *Flahooley, Seventeen, New Faces of 1952, The Boy Friend, House of Flowers, Mr. Wonderful, New Faces of '56, Rumple*, and *The Body Beautiful*.

Evans has described how he was part of a committee of contributors to Royal's musicals from 1951 to 1958. Among the names that recur, along with Evans, are Noeltner (the Chappell staff arranger, who played piano alongside Royal in the Ted Weems Orchestra), Charles L. Cooke, and Paul Weirick. In more than one case, the full team received credit for "additional orchestrations" in the staff listings of the program. Noeltner, who regularly ghosted for Bennett and specialized in dance orchestrations (including *Brigadoon's* "Come to Me, Bend to Me Ballet"), seems to have done many of the more "legit" things. Charlie Cooke, an old-timer who worked extensively with Eubie Blake, specialized in ragtime and provided many of the "hotter" numbers. (He received sole credit as orchestrator of the 1952 revival of Eubie Blake's *Shuffle Along* and co-orchestrator credit with Royal on *The Boy Friend*.) "Because I was very much younger and jazz-oriented," Evans said, "Ted would give me the things that he didn't feel comfortable with." These included the two exquisite Arlen art songs in *House of Flowers*, "A Sleepin' Bee" and "I Never Has Seen Snow." Evans also believes he was kept around because—unlike Royal and the others—during late-night crunches in hotel rooms, he was capable of composing introductions and transitions without a piano.

Evans describes a typical scene:

> At one point, we were doing *New Faces of 1952* and *Shuffle Along*. Ted set us up in a room at the Royalton Hotel. We had such a panic going on, so many people working, we had to get card tables and put them up. Ted would go out and buy a quart jar of peroxide and some camel-hair brushes. When you made a mistake, you'd paint over it, blot it, and wait. We were there sitting up all night, I was sharing a card table with Paul Weirick. Paul was on page fifty of something, he had been up for twenty-five hours straight. All of a sudden, the middle of the night, the phone rang. It was Paul's wife. When he got back, he looked at the table. He had bumped the peroxide all over the score. Fifty pages, the only thing

left was the drum part. Paul got his hat and got on the elevator. Never came back.

Royal orchestrated Jerry Bock's first two musicals, but it was a factory operation.

> BOCK: I did not have much to do with Ted Royal. I don't even remember a major conference with him on *Mr. Wonderful*. It's funny, in those days, we were so departmentalized in the writing of the show, we left the orchestration up to the specialist to do at his discretion. That was true of *The Body Beautiful* also. I do remember meeting with Ted occasionally, but never in the same kind of one-on-one that subsequently followed with Irv, Don, and Eddie Sauter.

The only people I found, aside from Evans and Bock, who remembered much about Royal were Sid Ramin and Elliot Lawrence, who came along at the end of Royal's career. Both had the same recollection: "I met him once," they said (individually, a month apart). "He was drunk."

This is explained to some extent by Evans: "Ted had a lot of interesting psychological problems, which sort of did him in. He was a very nice man, very intelligent. But he had been adopted as a child. He had a lot of problems trying to figure out who he was, where he came from. So he'd get drunk."

How much this affected Royal's work is unknown. Does the drinking problem explain the stable of ghosts he used? Possibly so. He seems to have had a great deal of trouble on his final important assignment, the 1956 Ethel Merman musical *Happy Hunting*. He presumably did the show with his usual ghosts, but this time major reinforcements were called in; while Royal retained his sole orchestration billing, a prominent title page credit was added, citing "additional orchestrations by Joe Glover, Don Walker, and Seymour Ginzler."

Royal did two quick flops during the 1957–1958 season, and that seems to have been the end of his Broadway career. Kostal describes giving Royal occasional TV work—unimportant endings and playoffs—in a tone that can only be described as pitying. Royal orchestrated and composed soundtracks for two compilations of silent film clips, *When Comedy Was King* (1960) and *Days of Thrills and Laughter* (1961), and he was credited on *New Faces of 1962* (receiving equal billing with four lesser-known, non-Broadway orchestrators). And that is the last reference to Royal I can find.

Royal's only child, a twenty-year-old daughter, was killed in 1961; as she left on her honeymoon, the car crashed on the Merritt Parkway in Connecticut. Evans suggests that this tragedy might well have finally sent Royal's drinking out of control. At any event, Royal became increasingly bitter.

By the early 1960s, Evans had become a major arranger in the recording field, with charts for the likes of Tony Bennett, Steve Lawrence, and Perry Como. Marion tells how Royal—who ten years earlier had been a father figure—started to come to his recording sessions, suggesting "improvements" and growing argumentative. By the early 1970s, Evans lost contact. Royal apparently spent an inordinate amount of time writing what he considered to be a major textbook on orchestration, expounding on the work of Schillinger. The manuscript, which survives in his papers, is unfinished and—to me—unfathomable.

Ted Royal reportedly died in 1981, although I can find no definitive record of his death. Even *Variety*—which twenty years earlier ran a squib about the death of Royal's daughter—neglected to run an obituary.

Royal was associated with the following musicals. He was principal orchestrator or one of the principal orchestrators on all except those marked with ♭:

♭All for Love
♭Allegro
Almost Crazy
♭Annie Get Your Gun
♭Are You with It?
Around the World
♭Artists and Models
As the Girls Go
♭Best Foot Forward
♭Billy Rose's Aquacade
♭Bloomer Girl
The Body Beautiful
The Boy Friend
Brigadoon
♭Bright Lights of 1944
Carib Song
♭A Connecticut Yankee (1943)
♭Dream with Music
♭Du Barry Was a Lady
♭Earl Carroll's Sketch Book
♭Early to Bed
♭The Firebrand of Florence
Flahooley

♭George White's Scandals of 1939
♭The Girl from Nantucket
Guys and Dolls
Happy Hunting
♭High Kickers of 1942
♭Higher and Higher
Hold It!
House of Flowers
♭I'd Rather Be Right
♭If the Shoe Fits
♭Jackpot
John Murray Anderson's Almanac
♭Jollyanna
♭Lady in the Dark
♭Let's Face It!
♭Life Begins at 8:40
♭Life of the Party
♭Louisiana Purchase
Make Mine Manhattan
♭Memphis Bound
Mexican Hayride
A Month of Sundays
Mr. Wonderful
♭My Dear Public (1942)

♭My Dear Public (1943)
Nellie Bly
New Faces of 1952
New Faces of '56
♭New Faces of 1962
♭On the Town
♭On Your Toes
Paint Your Wagon
♭Pal Joey
♭Panama Hattie
Rumple
St. Louis Woman
♭Seven Lively Arts
Seventeen
Shuffle Along
♭Sleepy Hollow
Small Wonder
♭Something for the Boys
♭Street Scene
Sweet Bye and Bye
♭Three to Make Ready
Tickets, Please!
♭Too Many Girls
♭A Tree Grows in Brooklyn
Where's Charley?
♭Ziegfeld Follies of 1943

EDDIE SAUTER

Born: December 2, 1914, Brooklyn, New York
Died: April 21, 1981, Nyack, New York

Like Ralph Burns, Eddie Sauter was a legendary band arranger long before he reached the Broadway stage. Born December 2, 1914, in Brooklyn, he switched from percussion to trumpet in his teens; at eighteen, he was playing with Archie Bleyer's Orchestra. After studying at Columbia University and Juilliard, he joined bandleader Red Norvo in 1935. Norvo led from the xylophone/marimba with his wife, Mildred Bailey, doing the vocals. Sauter (pronounced Saw-ter) soon put down his trumpet to write orchestrations full time. Norvo and Sauter combined for what was a new swing sound at the time, to considerable acclaim.

Norvo's group disbanded in 1939, at which point Sauter joined Benny Goodman. Sauter's intricate arrangements brought a new style to Goodman, along with such hits as Ravel's "Bolero," "Benny Rides Again," "The Man I Love," and "More than You Know." Sauter also did charts for Tommy Dorsey, Artie Shaw, and Woody Herman. After a bout with tuberculosis—which coincided with World War II—Sauter worked for Ray McKinley, writing yet more influential charts (and becoming one of the first band arrangers to be publicly credited). In 1952, Sauter and fellow arranger Bill Finegan (of Tommy Dorsey and Glenn Miller) decided to collaborate. They formed the Sauter-Finegan Orchestra and quickly began a highly influential if short-lived partnership. After several successful albums, the group took to the road, but the market for touring big bands was strangling, and Sauter-Finegan disbanded in 1955.

Sauter decided to get away from it all and took a job at a German radio station in Baden-Baden in 1957. After two years abroad, he returned to America. In 1961, Sauter joined with saxophonist Stan Getz for the LP *Focus*, which featured Getz improvising over Sauter's arrangements. The result was yet another jazz classic. More to the point, Hershy Kay (who had conducted the sessions) invited Sauter along as co-orchestrator of his next gig, Jerry Herman's first musical, *Milk and Honey*. This was a contemporary story set in modern-day Israel, with two middle-aged opera stars in the leads. While the partiturs are missing, Herman confirms that Kay did the legit sections while Sauter, logically enough, provided the more lively charts.

Sauter continued his theatre career with *Foxy*, which tried out in the Yukon Territory in 1962. When the intimate musical was retooled as a big, David Merrick production in early 1964, Sauter ran into trouble. Don Pippin was musical director.

> Eddie did not know how to orchestrate for the pit, at that point. He wrote for the rhythm section, but no full rich sound; it was just two thin woodwinds playing figures that normally you'd have brass on in a big theatre. Within a couple of years, with *Superman* and other shows, he had obviously learned what to do.

Most of Sauter's work on *Foxy* was discarded, with Kay coming in (without credit) to rewrite most of the show.

In 1965, Sauter did another job with Stan Getz, the jazz soundtrack for the Warren Beatty/Arthur Penn film *Mickey One*. He then returned to Broadway and was instantly revealed to be a musical theatre genius with altogether remarkable sets of orchestrations for two 1966 musicals, Charles Strouse's *It's a Bird . . . It's a Plane . . . It's Superman* and Jerry Bock's *The Apple Tree*. Producer (and former Loesser protégé) Stu Ostrow of *The Apple Tree* championed Sauter: "When Elliot Lawrence told me it was possible to get Eddie, I jumped. He was on the road doing one-night stands. I remember he said to me, 'Oh my God, I don't have to get on a train and go out for a one-nighter!'" As for Strouse and Bock, both marveled forty years later about the way Sauter interpreted and enlivened their work—and how modest he was about his contributions.

All but one of Sauter's musicals were unsuccessful, but his credits demonstrate a remarkable range: Bob Merrill's *Henry, Sweet Henry*, Lionel Bart's *La Strada*, Richard Rodgers's *Two by Two*, Alan Jay Lerner and John Barry's *Lolita, My Love*, Al Carmines's *Promenade*, and the Gertrude Berg–based *Molly*. Sauter is best remembered along Broadway for his one major hit, *1776*—which, again, is brilliantly orchestrated in unclassifiable style. "Eddie was somebody you just trusted," said producer Stuart Ostrow. "He was so talented, he never brought a bad chart in. So when he said, 'I hear something,' the best you could do was say, 'Go get it.'" Or, as Jonathan Tunick put it: "Eddie did these marvelous things, always theatrical, always effective. And completely unlike anybody else."

Sauter's final major shows came in 1980, the Robert Waldman/Alfred Uhry musical *Swing* (which closed during its tryout in Washington) and the Goodspeed revival of George M. Cohan's *Little Johnny Jones*. The latter toured and eventually reached Broadway, opening and closing on March 21, 1982. A year earlier, Eddie Sauter had died of a heart attack, on April 21, 1981.

Sauter was associated with the following musicals. He was principal orchestrator or one of the principal orchestrators on all except those marked with ♭:

The Apple Tree

♭Cyrano

♭Foxy

♭George M!

Georgy

Henry, Sweet Henry

It's a Bird . . . It's a Plane . . . It's Superman

La Strada

Little Johnny Jones

Lolita, My Love

Milk and Honey

Molly

Promenade

1776

Swing

Trixie True Teen Detective

Two by Two

HANS SPIALEK

Born: April 17, 1894, Vienna, Austria
Died: November 14, 1983, New York, New York

Out-of-town tryouts are famously hectic times. Backstage at a show in trouble can resemble a battleground. For the men of the orchestrating corps, it is a time of nonstop work as old numbers are fixed, new numbers are prepared, and any and all of them might be replaced before the copyist's ink dries. Producers and composers of bad shows with bad songs seem to think, all too often, that all they need are new orchestrations. Hectic and harrowing, yes, but not, I suppose, to Hans Spialek. When you've been wounded in battle, shuffled from prison camp to prison camp, transported to Siberia, and brought before a firing squad, you might well look at the goings-on in the Broadway wars as "just a show."

Spialek began his musical career at the age of twelve as a "singing boy" at the Vienna Imperial Opera. The musical and artistic director at the time was Gustav Mahler, no less; Spialek remembered him as a "short, funny-walking little man in a shriveled hat." (He also recalls that the vocal coach would refer to Mahler, in annoyance, as "that crazy Jew monkey." The forty-six-year-old Mahler, who in 1906 was writing his Eighth Symphony, was subject to continual anti-Semitic attacks at the time. He resigned from the Vienna Opera in 1907 and took over the conductor's chair at the Metropolitan Opera in New York in 1908.)

Spialek also got to stand onstage, in *La Boheme*, next to Caruso. "I just couldn't understand how anyone was able to sing so exquisitely and act at the same time seemingly as relaxed as if he were in his own home, and not performing in a huge opera house overcrowded with people who paid exorbitant prices to hear him." The kids were all thrilled by Caruso's voice, but made fun of the "excessively high heels" he wore.

When Spialek's voice changed, he was hired as a *claqueur*, which is to say a professional applauder. (That job description was phased out long, long ago, although if you ever sat in a theatre next to Charles Lowe when Carol Channing Lowe was onstage you'd know that it was not a forgotten art.) Spialek, as a teen, thus got to stand at the back of the house with the likes of Franz Lehar, "with his coquettish, uptwirled moustache, always elegant and giving the eye to every passing lady"; Emmerich Kalman, "looking like a banker or a stock broker, which he later became"; and Oscar Straus, "very tall with an aristocratic face and the characteristically aquiline nose of a medieval knight, suggesting a painting by Holbein if only imagination could dress him with the proper garments instead of the sloppy suits he wore."

Spialek next went to work as a movie house pianist, attending the Vienna Conservatory by day. In 1912, he formed his own band of four: "the Philharmonic Orchestra," he called it. Spialek's group eventually grew to sixteen, but in 1914, Austria entered World War I. Within months, Junior Officer Spialek was on the Russian Front. In September 1915, he was bayoneted, captured, and sent as a prisoner of war to Siberia. Spialek's bayoneted hand—sewn on the battlefield by an orderly with needle and thread, and without anesthesia—eventually healed. By 1917, Spialek was leading a prison camp orchestra of twenty-eight pieces.

The aftermath of the so-called October Revolution, in November 1917, set Spialek free, though stranded in Russia. He worked his way across the vast country, giving recitals in every small-town auditorium he could find, often playing for food. All the while, Spialek personally witnessed massacres carried out with gleeful cruelty and excessive (and, at times, pornographic) violence. At one point, in Samara in the fall of 1918, he was arrested by the invading Czechs as a Russian spy. He was moments away from execution—one of his four cellmates had been shot through the ears—when the Communist Army overran the prison. Then, it was back to work as a bandleader. One night in Nishny-Novgorod (Gorky), he was commandeered to lead the "Imperiale"—over and over again—at a speech by Trotsky, while he stared across the orchestra pit at the leader onstage. (Trotsky was received with boos and derogatory whistling from the audience—still possible in 1919!)

Escape from Russia entailed a long and dangerous trip arranged by smugglers. Spialek reached Romania in October 1920 and finally made it back to Vienna in January 1921. His reappearance startled his family, whose last information was that he had been executed in Samara by that firing squad.

Spialek published his first composition in 1923 in Berlin, a concert overture called "Volga Gypsies." He received an advance of one million marks, which due to rampant inflation was worth about $12; meeting his publisher in New York several years later, he was told that the piece had been selected not for its quality but because the publisher especially liked the neatness of the handwriting. (Having perused literally thousands of Broadway partiturs, I can attest that Spialek's charts are the most stylish of all.)

Spialek settled into a career as a conductor of small ensembles in Bucharest, Carlsbad, Hamburg, and elsewhere. (The only job he could get in snobbish Vienna was playing the piano in a bordello, which at least paid well.) An engagement in the Netherlands led to a tour of South America in 1923. He tells of a journey into the jungles of French Senegal, outside Dakar:

> In front of a hut we saw a little native girl squatted on the ground, churning and singing a tune, which definitely was neither native nor primitive music. Further on we encountered three girls. Two of them were sitting, humming the same melody and rhythmically clapping their hands while the third one was sort of improvising a dance. Neither my friend nor I knew the music, but memorized it. In fact, we sang it all the way going back.
>
> Arriving in Dakar, tired, thirsty, and hungry, we entered one of those outdoor cafés. Hardly five minutes after we sat down, we heard from a nearby house a scratchy phonograph playing the same tune we had heard in the woods. My friend jumped up and I saw him sprinting in the direction the music was coming from. After a few minutes he was back informing me that the phonograph belonged to a French officer, that the record was either American or English, and the title of the song was "Swanee."

Spialek expounds further on the point:

> I hate people who, deeming themselves no end sophisticated, dismiss popular music as something disgustingly inferior. The primitive South American girls sang and danced George Gershwin's "Swanee." Russia, from the Baltic all the way to Vladivostok, included into its limited list of patterned ballroom dances Irving Berlin's "Alexander's Ragtime Band," calling it "The Dance of the Bears." Austria adapted Jerome Kern's "They Didn't Believe Me" as a Viennese folk song.

As the South American tour ended, Spialek prepared to return to Austria; he had saved $360, enough to open a small movie house in Vienna. But the offer of a U.S. visa and the urging of his wife—who was seven months' pregnant—caused the Spialeks to switch boats. They arrived on January 13, 1924, in Brooklyn, where, being "a totally unknown young composer, an average pianist, a conductor of a small theatre who did not even know the language of the country," the services of Spialek were not exactly in demand. Through fate and luck, he was signed by Sol Hurok to accompany the Russian actor-singer Boris Borissoff. Spialek made his American (and Broadway) debut on February 10, 1924, at the Times Square Theatre. Borissoff quickly flopped and was sent home. Spialek was back where he started.

A chance meeting with violinist Maurice Nitke brought an introduction, on a paper napkin, to Russell Bennett. Bennett, who had only recently graduated to the theatre-arranging desk at Harms, had written incidental music for John Barrymore's record-breaking 1922 *Hamlet*, with Nitke serving as musical director. Spialek appeared the next day with a sample of his arrangements:

> Mr. Bennett, a very intellectual and distinguished-looking young man, was seated at the end of the front desk in the arranging room, bent over an orchestral score. Fascinated by the speed with which he filled one page after another, I didn't dare to address him. Very carefully I sneaked Nitke's note onto Bennett's desk. He took it, read it and without looking at me, handed it to a man who had just entered the room. This man, Charles Miller, then editor-in-chief of Harms, motioned me into the adjacent room, his office. Miller was small, his office was small with just room enough for a desk, a small upright piano and a couple of chairs. Next to the piano stood a big, corpulent man with a very jovial face netted by little multicolored veins. Miller spoke German, the large man tried to.
>
> I was spreading my neatly written scores on Mr. Miller's desk, with both men looking at them, when the stout one said, "Can you copy?" Although crestfallen and hurt—the same way a surgeon would be if asked can he put a band-aid on something—I did the right thing and said, "Yes." Mr. Miller led me to an empty desk, gave me music paper, a pen, and a score titled, "My Dream Girl" and said, "Let's see." Well, I sat down and started to copy, employing my best Sunday writing. After a while, the corpulent gentleman came into the room. Standing behind and watching me he asked, "Can you transpose?" Swallowing my pride again, I answered in the affirmative. Working fast, I finished the whole job by one in the afternoon, and obviously did well. I was told to come back the next day; that the composer, the same voluminous gentleman who watched me copying, a Mr. Victor Herbert, liked my work.

Herbert suffered a massive heart attack and died three weeks later as they finished work on *The Dream Girl*, which was produced posthumously in August 1924.

Spialek made $36 that first week as a copyist, at fifteen cents a page. The next week, he made only $17, being slightly preoccupied with the birth of his child

Alice (who has graciously granted permission to quote from her father's unpublished memoirs). The third week, he was sent to Long Branch, New Jersey, with the tryout of *Marjorie*. Stephen O. Jones was the orchestrator and the co-composer. He was also more interested in playing golf. Every day, he would disappear to the links. On the day of the opening, he called Spialek to his room at 5 a.m. Jones had forgotten to orchestrate one of the numbers of the show. They started to work, but Jones decided he must golf. "You can orchestrate that, yourself," he said, and left. Fortunately, it was a waltz, an exceedingly simple job for the Viennese Spialek. When *Marjorie* finally reached the Shubert, on August 11, 1924, Spialek broke into the ranks of Broadway orchestrators—because the other guy wanted to play golf. For the five days with *Marjorie*, at out-of-town rates, Spialek earned $126. He was more than happy to stay at Harms, copying up to 600 pages a week and—when the occasion arose—orchestrating a song or two along the way.

Spialek was well aware that his vast experience did not equip him for Broadway: "I first had to familiarize myself with the idiom of both American music and arrangements, greatly differing from those in Europe." At the time, Harms published (and provided orchestrations and copies for) the great majority of Broadway musicals. By the spring of 1926, Spialek was contributing at least one orchestration to just about every show that passed through the office; he also composed incidental music for several plays. In June, Spialek was assigned his first full show as orchestrator, the revue *Americana*, with an interpolated score from many songwriters, including the brothers Gershwin and Arthur Schwartz.

Spialek soon became one of the top orchestrators in the Harms stable; his importance was bolstered by Russell Bennett's decision to move to Paris for much of 1926 and 1927. In 1927 alone, Spialek calculated that he worked on some twenty-seven musicals, ranging from hits (like *Hit the Deck* and *Funny Face*) to forgotten stinkers (like *Allez-Oop* and *The Girl from Childs'*).

As the Depression hit, Bennett and Spialek held the top two positions in the Harms theatre department. While Bennett handled Kern and other gilt-edged composers, Spialek was assigned to many of the newcomers—including Cole Porter, who had his first hit show in 1928. Spialek tells of his experience on Porter's 1932 Fred Astaire musical, *Gay Divorce*.

> I had occasionally worked for Porter during the previous years [on *Paris, Fifty Million Frenchmen, The New Yorkers*, and other shows] but attending for nine weeks the preparatory stage of *Gay Divorce* gave me a chance to study the man closely. Cole Porter is one of the few composers of lighter music with a profound musical education. The expressions on his face— a modified version of the comedian Joe E. Brown—seemed to me constantly accentuating the language he spoke: a mixture of British, Yale and

Harvard, with a strong undercurrent of familiarity, I guess well-meant, but with an undeniable dash of snobbishness. (Porter conveyed once to me through the Harms errand-boy deluxe, Dr. Sirmay, his displeasure about my being too familiar with some of the principals in a show.) When something pleased him he was extremely nice, sent even telegrams of appreciation. But being dissatisfied, he clammed up, never spoke directly about the point in question to the one responsible for his ire. Even in cases where a quick, easy adjustment would have removed the cause of his uneasiness.

Gay Divorce was to me a wonderful show. The cast was not big, but an exceptionally good one (Fred Astaire, Claire Luce, Luella Gear, Eric Blore, Eric Rhodes). The principal song was "Night and Day." Sensing the greatness of that song, I was immeasurably proud of being its first arranger. The show opened to everybody's surprise only moderately successful on September 7, 1932, in Boston. It was there, at the beginning of the second week, that after eight successful years in the U.S. I suffered for the first time a heart-breaking defeat. Without being notified, my arrangement of "Night and Day" was dumped and the song was re-orchestrated by Russell Bennett. Now I knew what it felt like. Now I understood the misery and fears I saw so often before at replacements and failures. Now I fathomed the blinding, hysterical pangs that shook fragile Tamara, who I prevented the previous year from jumping down the empty elevator shaft at the Sylvania Hotel in Philadelphia after she was replaced during the dress rehearsal of The Gang's All Here. [Tamara, who within a few years was to introduce the Broadway standards "Smoke Gets in Your Eyes" and "I'll Be Seeing You," died in 1943, at age thirty-eight, on a USO plane that crashed in Portugal.]

Despite the replacement of "Night and Day," Spialek remained with the show. A couple of nights later, he stopped in at the Colonial, where the Shuberts were presenting a musicalization of Cyrano de Bergerac. Spialek watched the opening number, with Cyrano singing a Vagabond King–like number accompanied by sixteen shining knights in a diagonal line, building to two girls doing a tap routine. The song ended as the girls ricocheted into the belly of the comedian, in chef's garb. "Leaving the theatre in a hurry, I consoled myself with, 'and you are depressed over a rejected orchestration!'"

By 1936, the Broadway musical had all but dried up due to harsh economic conditions:

For more than two months, I found myself without a single assignment. Just as I began to worry, Max Dreyfus, the Almighty of Chappell & Co., called me into his sanctum and commissioned me to orchestrate the forthcoming Rodgers and Hart show, *On Your Toes.*

This came as a big surprise. Rodgers and Hart I had met before, working on the second edition of the *Garrick Gaieties* in 1926. To be perfectly frank, I didn't think much of Rodgers as a composer. I classified him then as a lucky example of the many college boys writing music for their campus shows. He even irritated me by his continuous nail-biting and wearing an almost never-changing mixture of dissatisfaction on his face. Lorenz Hart eluded me entirely as I still lived under another false illusion brought with me from Europe, putting the composer above everything and regarding the lyric writer as a necessary evil.

The day after my meeting with Dreyfus, Rodgers played his score for me. In the beginning I was a little scared: this wasn't just the run-of-the-mill musical with songs, songs and more songs, leaving it to the arranger to build them into ensembles, routines, ballets, finales, etc. Here I found, besides the necessary ballads and situation numbers, two full-bodied ballets; one in the classical vein ("The Princess Zenobia"), the other in the jazz idiom ("Slaughter on Tenth Avenue"). I listened and listened. The more I heard, the more I became enthused. Thanks to the inspiring material, my arranging job turned out a good one. But the greatest reward for my efforts came not from Rodgers, who in those days had seldom if ever anything encouraging to say to those working for him. My greatest reward came from Ray Bolger and Doris Carson, during the first orchestra reading. They sat on the stage and when the orchestra for the first time played their duet, "There's a Small Hotel," both started to cry. Asked why, Bolger said: "I can't help it, it sounds so beautiful."

"Slaughter on Tenth Avenue" is, in my humble opinion, the best piece of continuous music Rodgers ever wrote. I have had in the following years the never-ceasing pleasure of orchestrating this composition for the NBC Symphony, Paul Whiteman's recording, the Boston Pops, for publication, still later for the TV show given in honor of Rodgers's twenty-fifth anniversary as a composer.

On Your Toes, as a show, was at the beginning far from being perfect. Called in to cure its ills was the amazingly ingenious, non-drinking, non-smoking but never-tiring Rumba enthusiast, George Abbott. With little more than a few sizeable blue pencil strokes, Abbott steered *On Your Toes* into something.

I always regarded Rodgers and Hart as the ideal combination of composer and lyric writer, both immensely gifted, both incredibly fast in creating their tunes. But there the similarity ends. As persons they were as different as a sour grapefruit and a sweet apple. Rodgers seemed constantly discontented or nail-bitingly worried about something; Hart, always carefree and responsive in a warm, sympathetic way. Sure, Larry Hart drank—so what? I'd rather have that than offering somebody a drink and getting a request for Ovaltine. (Rodgers did just that during a very gay party after the opening of *Too Many Girls* in Boston.) Hart never failed in coming over to me, either during orchestra or dress rehearsals, patting me on the arm and saying, "Good boy."

In 1939, Spialek orchestrated Rodgers's ballet *Ghost Town*, which premiered at the Met. During the rehearsal, Rodgers—who was conducting—wanted to hear a section from the house, so he handed the baton to Spialek.

There I stood, the former singing kid from the Imperial Opera, the once-juvenile boy conductor in a small motion picture house in Vienna. There I stood, conducting in the world's most famous opera house. At the same spot, before the same conductor's desk, from where so many greats in musical history stood. These were two of the most precious minutes, probably the happiest one hundred and twenty seconds in my life. In comparison, even the most flattering reviews about my work for the ballet were just a fizzle.

Spialek had a tendency to speak his mind at inopportune moments; having already alienated the likes of Kern and Romberg, he proceeded to poison his relationship with his most important client.

After arranging six hit shows in a row for Rodgers, I made again one of my fatal, long-reaching mistakes. It happened after the orchestra reading of *Pal Joey*. Studying Rodgers's inscrutable face, I couldn't hold it any longer and asked him point-blank: "Tell me, Dick, is there anything wrong? Don't you like my work?" Rodgers: "Everything is fine. If it weren't, I wouldn't work with you." This incident, however insignificant, plus two newspaper writeups (one about *Pal Joey*, the other about *Ghost Town*) erroneously crediting me for some innovations which were entirely the composer's, brought my association with Rodgers to a regretful close. I subsequently worked occasionally for him, but an unbridgeable gap never ceased to exist. And, obviously, better men than I took over.

In 1942, Spialek was hired to serve as the arranger for the radio show *Great Moments in Music*, sponsored by the Celanese Corporation. This was an elaborate affair featuring abridged versions of musical comedies and operettas, with a sixty-four-piece orchestra selected from members of the NBC Symphony and the New York Philharmonic. Spialek invited Bennett to help him score the first episodes.

Sitting on jury duty at the time, I entrusted Mr. Bennett with the financial arrangement for our service. Russell Bennett may well be the world's greatest and certainly most equipped arranger, but his talents as a business man can best be described as pathetic. After my morning session in court, I got Russell on the phone. Learning from him the price he agreed on, I almost fainted. I contacted immediately the agency handling *Great Moments in Music*, met their representative at Toots Shor's bar and signed there an agreement for exactly three times the amount Bennett bargained for. Finding no other piece of paper, this agreement was drawn and signed on the blank inside of an empty matchbook cover, and subsequently held good for four-and-a-half years. Not realizing at the time that signing this little matchbook contract sealed my doom as far as the musical stage was concerned, I was happy and elated over my new assignment, looking forward to a luxurious future, free from any artistic as well as financial aggravations.

It is here that Spialek's memoirs end. His contract with Chappell—providing a weekly "drawing amount" against whatever theatre orchestrations he did—presumably ended with the beginning of the *Great Moments in Music* contract in 1942. He maintained an occasional presence on Broadway through the mid-fifties, receiving sole credit on four failed "European" musicals (three of which were adapted from classics): Emmerich Kalman's old-fashioned operetta *Marinka*, Arthur Sullivan's *Hollywood Pinafore*, Tchaikovsky's *Music in My Heart*, and Verdi's *My Darlin' Aida*. Spialek shared credit with two or three other orchestrators, usually including Bennett or Ted Royal, on another eight shows. Frank Loesser's *Where's Charley?* was Spialek's only post-1942 show to find success.

More interesting, perhaps, are the shows Spialek ghosted on during this period, usually at the behest of Bennett or Walker. I've positively identified almost twenty cases, including *Annie Get Your Gun*, *The King and I*, *Kiss Me, Kate*, *Paint Your Wagon*, and *Carousel* (which contains one of his finest charts, "When the Children Are Asleep," with a most felicitous opening section featuring a combination of harp and flute). Spialek's last Broadway orchestrations, so far as I can tell, were for Rodgers's *Pipe Dream*, Porter's *Silk Stockings*, and Coward's *The Girl Who Came to Supper*. He was invited back by Bennett in 1967 for one last show, which turned out to be Russell's final musical as well. Spialek—the World War I prisoner who, a half-century earlier, was moments away from a firing squad—provided a handful of charts for *Mata Hari*.

Hans returned to obscurity for another fifteen years, living in a modest apartment off Riverside Drive. Alice Gruber recalls that her father remained a cheerful, upbeat man, with a joke for everything. He saw every new movie that came out and reported on every fine meal that he ate. ("If ever you've gone hungry," he would say, "food is a marvelous thing.") He remained active into his eighties, living on his Local 802 pension and picking up occasional work as a copyist for City Ballet and other assorted odd jobs.

> LARRY BLANK: I was doing a cut-down version of the 1975 Rodgers & Hart revue that fizzled on Broadway, for a theatre in Chicago. I was working up at Associated Music, with Bob Haring as the head copyist. This little old European guy at the end of the table was copying, and called me over to check a note. He said, "Very interesting harp part!" And then he said, "I did the original." It was "It's Got to Be Love" from *On Your Toes*. Bob Haring told me he was an old-time, famous orchestrator who hadn't worked in years, and sometimes did some copying for him. And I suddenly realized—there was Hans Spialek!

Gruber remembers him calling her one day in the mid-1970s, marveling that he was doing a show with a song about "tits and ass," and another about gonorrhea. She took this to mean he was orchestrating, although it turns out that he was working as a copyist—on *A Chorus Line*. Larry Abel, that show's head copyist, remembered Spialek: "All the people he worked with, and for, had passed on. He did some copying for us. If you got him to do any work you were very fortunate; he was fast, exact and terrific. A very, very interesting man."

Spialek remained invisible professionally until 1983, when he returned to Broadway once more. George Abbott had agreed to direct a restored version of his 1938 hit with Rodgers & Hart, *The Boys from Syracuse*. The original scores were found and dusted off by musical director John Mauceri. Everyone assumed that Spialek was long gone, but an old-timer at the Rodgers office mentioned that he had seen "old Hans" at Russell Bennett's funeral. Spialek could not be found—the Musicians' Union had him listed, but without an address or phone. Somebody had the bright idea of calling 411, and there was Hans on West 86th Street. The bright and alert octogenarian left a message that Mauceri could "call him any day, from two in the afternoon till two in the morning."

Spialek began working on the scores; with his photographic memory and total recall, he had a firm hold on what was done originally (and what changes had been made after the fact to the original scores). At this point, the producer, Roger Stevens, decided not to do *The Boys from Syracuse*; he had just lost a fortune on *Oh, Brother!*—based on the same Shakespearean comedy—and refused to do another show with two sets of twins. Abbott agreed to substitute *On Your Toes*, and Mauceri and Spialek switched course.

Spialek hadn't worked in years, according to his daughter, but he was in fine shape, both physically (he was an avid swimmer) and mentally; Mauceri tells us that his "wit and wits were still there." John McGlinn worked closely with Spialek, comparing the original scores with the still-existing orchestra parts to determine just what was played in 1936. Little new orchestration was needed, but Spialek did the required revisions himself. (These included the final section of the "On Your Toes" production number.) McGlinn gives full credit to Mauceri for the rediscovery of Spialek and for convincing the producers that they must bring Hans in to supervise the restoration.

Spialek was hesitant about traveling to Washington for the tryout; the charts were almost fifty years old.

> MCGLINN: Hans was terrified that the orchestra would make fun of them. This was the first time anyone had revived a thirties show with real thirties orchestrations. Would they sound too old-fashioned, too ricky-ticky? At the first reading, I was sitting next to Hans; he was shaking like a leaf. We started with the overture. They played that opening fanfare—the "There's a Small Hotel" theme, with the cymbal crash, and they moved into "On Your Toes." The musicians were so excited, they almost stopped to applaud. Five minutes in, Hans was beaming like a racehorse. You could see by looking at him. He heard the charts, and he remembered how good he was.

The revival opened on March 6, 1983, to a favorable-to-mixed reception and a 500-performance run.

On Your Toes garnered Spialek a fair amount of publicity, including lengthy interviews in both the *New York Times* and the *Washington Post*; it also won Hans a Drama Desk Award for best orchestrations. The successful use of the 1936 charts was a key element in the movement to go back to original scores; since the *Toes* revival, we have heard original orchestrations on many recordings and in the now happily established field of concert stagings. (City Center Encores! has thus far performed Spialek's versions of *The Boys from Syracuse*, *Pal Joey*, and *Babes in Arms*.)

With the rediscovery of Hans Spialek and the corresponding press attention, National Endowment for the Humanities (NEH) grants were arranged to allow for the restoration of his other scores. Spialek finished *Anything Goes*, which McGlinn recorded for EMI, and had embarked on *Pal Joey* when he became unable to work. Both Gruber and McGlinn mentioned that Spialek was rushed to Boston to observe the tryout of *My One and Only*, the 1983 adaptation of the 1927 Gershwin musical *Funny Face*. The reclusive Ira Gershwin, in Beverly Hills, had been sent a tape of an early Boston preview and was appalled. He tracked down Hans and—according to McGlinn—said, "You've got to go to Boston and fix this thing." McGlinn took Spialek to Boston, where they attended a performance:

We had a meeting with the producers. Hans had worked on numerous shows with George; he started to explain how they could restore the Gershwin sound. After forty-five minutes, the producers stopped listening. You could see that they weren't going to fix anything. They were condescending, they treated him like a senile old man. They said, "Thank you very much" and left. Hans said to me, "Let's go back to New York."

On Spialek's eighty-ninth birthday, the company of *On Your Toes* gave him a grand surprise party, calling him onto the stage of the Virginia at curtain calls. ("I never would have believed that members of the Musicians' Union would play 'Happy Birthday' for me," he said to McGlinn.) Hans Spialek died of cancer seven months later, on November 14, 1983.

Spialek was associated with the following musicals. He was principal orchestrator or one of the principal orchestrators on all shows except those marked with ♭:

♭À La Carte
♭Agnes de Mille Dance
    Theatre
♭All for Love
♭All the King's Horses
American Jubilee
♭Americana (1926)
♭Americana (1928)
♭Annie Get Your Gun
Anything Goes
♭Are You with It?
♭Artists and Models
♭At Home Abroad
Babes in Arms
♭Ballyhoo of 1932
Best Foot Forward
Between the Devil
♭Billy Rose's Aquacade
♭Billy Rose's Jumbo
Boys and Girls Together
The Boys from Syracuse
♭Bright Lights of 1944
♭Calling All Stars
♭Carnival in Flanders
♭Carousel
♭Caviar

♭Count Me In
♭Criss-Cross
Dancing in the Streets
♭Dream with Music
Du Barry Was a Lady
East Wind
♭Everybody's Welcome
♭Fifty Million Frenchmen
♭Fine and Dandy
♭Flying Colors
♭Fools Rush In
♭Funny Face
♭The Gang's All Here
♭Garrick Gaieties (1926)
Gay Divorce
♭George White's Scandals
    of 1939
♭The Girl in Pink Tights
♭The Girl Who Came to
    Supper
Great Lady
♭Hello, Daddy!
♭Hi Ya, Gentlemen!
♭High Kickers of 1942
Higher and Higher
♭Hit the Trail

Hold It!
Hold on to Your Hats
Hollywood Pinafore
I Married an Angel
I'd Rather Be Right
♭If the Shoe Fits
♭The Illustrator's Show
♭Jackpot
♭John Henry
Keep off the Grass
♭The King and I
♭Kiss Me, Kate
♭La Belle Helene
♭Lady Fingers
♭The Laugh Parade
Let's Face It!
Life Begins at 8:40
♭Life of the Party
The Little Dog Laughed
Louisiana Lady
♭Lucky
Mamba's Daughters
Marinka
♭Marjorie
♭Mata Hari
♭Me and Juliet

♭Murder at the Vanities
Music in My Heart
My Darlin' Aida
♭My Dear Public (1942)
♭My Dear Public (1943)
♭Mystery Moon
♭New Faces
♭New Faces of 1936
♭The New Moon
♭The New Yorkers
♭A Night Out
♭Nina Rosa
♭Oh, Please!
On Your Toes
One for the Money
♭Paint Your Wagon

Pal Joey
♭Paris
♭Panama Hattie
♭Pipe Dream
♭Present Arms!
♭Red, Hot and Blue!
♭Right This Way
♭Rosalie
Set to Music
♭Seven Lively Arts
♭The Show Is On
♭Silk Stockings
Sing Out the News
Sleepy Hollow
Something for the Boys
Stars in Your Eyes

Streets of Paris
♭Take a Chance
♭This Is the Army
♭The Three Musketeers
♭Three to Make Ready
♭Thumbs Up!
Too Many Girls
Two for the Show
♭Venus in Silk
Virginia
♭Walk with Music
♭Where's Charley?
The White Horse Inn
You Never Know
♭Ziegfeld Follies of 1934
♭Ziegfeld Follies of 1936

DON WALKER

Born: October 28, 1907, Lambertville, New Jersey
Died: September 13, 1989, Trenton, New Jersey

Don Walker, the son of a small-town grocer, started on the piano when he was nine. He entered high school at the early age of ten; the school didn't have a drummer, so he took up the drums. The next year, the flute player left, so Walker learned the flute. The following semester, the cello player left; with no cello on hand, he taught himself to play the cello parts on a saxophone. When Walker graduated high school at fourteen, he was too young to go to a conservatory, so his parents sent him to business college.

While studying as an accounting major at the Wharton School of the University of Pennsylvania, he was playing tenor saxophone in Don Walker's Interfraternity Five (which, for some reason, had six men). There was quite a rivalry between the University of Pennsylvania and Penn State. The latter, to its credit, had Fred Waring and His Pennsylvanians, a jazz band featuring a collegiate glee club. Waring, who would later invent the kitchen blender he named for himself, achieved national acclaim courtesy of the Victrola with the 1925 hit "Collegiate." (The RCA studios were across the river from Philadelphia, in Camden, New Jersey.)

One fateful evening in 1927, the father of a girlfriend of Walker—a true blue Penn State man—heaped praise on Waring. "Yes, his vocals are great," said Don, "but the band arrangements aren't very good." "Oh you think so?" said the girl-friend. "Why don't you tell it to Waring?"

> WALKER: Waring came to Philadelphia. I went down to the Stanley Theatre, where he was appearing. I saw the doorman walk away, so I walked in and sat down. The band was onstage at the time. I sat there, and the band finished. Waring came over and said, "Who are you?" I said, "I go to the University of Pennsylvania, and I'm an arranger. I've made arrangements for a lot of bands around Philadelphia." He said, "When can I hear any of them?" I had been making arrangements for a band in a Chinese restaurant down the street, so I said, "Do you want to go to lunch with me tomorrow?" The next day we went to lunch. There was one chorus where the trumpet was playing, and he said, "Is that written or is he faking?" I said, "That's written." He says, "Come on back to the theatre with me." So we went back to the theatre and there was a stack of music. He pulled out two pieces of sheet music. He handed them to me and said, "We record a week from today, at RCA Victor in Camden. You do these two numbers. Go to Petey Buck, my arranger, and he'll give you the instrumentation and tell you how long it has to be and everything. You come over to Camden with these two orchestrations and we'll record them." So I went back and did the two orchestrations and copied them myself, as we had to do in those days, and I went over to Camden and they recorded both numbers. One of them turned out to be a hit, "Love Tale of Alsace-Lorraine."
>
> Fred Waring always was willing to listen to a young man; he'd make up his mind whether you had something or not, and he'd give you a break. I had done my thesis on insurance agency accounting. On the basis of the thesis, Penn Mutual offered me $35 a week. The same week, Waring offered me $125 a week to go with him, and I never looked back.

Walker continued writing for Waring and joined the band as a sax player after graduation in 1929. He soon put down his instrument to serve as arranger and assistant conductor, on tour and on Waring's *Old Gold* radio show. During a break— it was early in the Depression—Walker took a position in Toronto as conductor of the house orchestra at the Royal York Hotel. He soon returned to Waring and got his first taste of theatre when he orchestrated and conducted two University of Pennsylvania Mask & Wig shows, *Ruff-Neck* (1932) and *Out of the Blues* (1933). These experiences, as it turned out, gave Walker the tools he needed to take the swing-band sound to Broadway. He left Waring in 1933 and came to New York.

Walker saved a copy of a form letter he sent out to the most popular publishers: Witmark, Remick, Berlin, Robbins (but not including Harms):

> Dear Mr. So-and-so: I have recently settled permanently in New York City, coming here from Toronto, where I was programming director and

arranger for Fred Calley's Royal York Orchestra while they were on CBC. My first commercial arrangement, "Love Is Like That" (for Feist), is doing tremendously with the orchestras as the song moves in the hit class. I will be glad to do a commercial arrangement including the extra parts for $75, including a professional copying job. Remember the Don Walker slogan for commercial arrangements: Safe, Sane and Simple.

This offer didn't seem to have any takers, as New York was awash with out-of-work arrangers. But Walker soon caught another break:

> Waring's first trumpet was also working for Al Goodman, a Broadway conductor who had just gotten the radio program *Hit Parade* and needed orchestrations. I went and met him; he gave me two numbers to do. I walked into rehearsal; there was Tommy Dorsey, Benny Goodman, Artie Shaw!

Walker signed on as head arranger for Goodman's radio orchestra. Goodman was an important conductor of the day; he had been Al Jolson's musical director (and orchestrator) for *Big Boy*, in 1925, and still wielded great power on Broadway. In the meanwhile, fabled operetta composer Sigmund Romberg was approached to go on radio (for the Swift Ham Company). Romberg's Broadway career nose-dived in 1928, when he wrote his last of a string of hit operettas; he would continue to write Broadway operettas until his death in 1951, with eight out of nine being quick flops. In 1935, though, his music was still exceedingly popular, with a barrelful of golden standards from *The Student Prince*, *The New Moon*, and *The Desert Song*. For his radio show, Romberg wanted a newer, contemporary sound. "Al Goodman brought me to Romberg," Walker recalled, "I did the audition, and I was a sensation."

With the Swift show successfully launched, Romberg asked Walker to score his upcoming Broadway show. But first Romberg had a concert tour. The Broadway job was six months away, and Walker—with two small children—couldn't afford to wait. Romberg, looking for a way to keep Walker on board, went to see his publisher, Max Dreyfus. With business conditions slow and with a full complement of orchestrators on staff, Dreyfus demurred. (This despite the fact that Walker had already done some not inconsequential ghosting for Harms on two important Broadway revues, *Ziegfeld Follies of 1934* and *Life Begins at 8:40*.)

"But Max," said Rommy in his inimitable fashion, "you need Dan Vawker. He's the waif of the future."

> Max said, "How much money do you need a week?" I said I couldn't possibly live on less than $100 a week. And he said, "OK, you got it."

And it was a pretty good deal, because all he wanted back was his advance, he didn't want to run my business, so anything that came in over $100 I got.

Walker joined Harms in the fall of 1935. (As discussed elsewhere, Dreyfus moved his operation over to Chappell in 1936.) The deal at the time was that each orchestrator was assigned shows of his own, with the right to call on the other house orchestrators for assistance as needed. Walker's first show on his own was the Romberg-Hammerstein *May Wine*, which opened in December 1935. Bennett was called on for one minor chart and—his name being a sign of musical distinction along Broadway—was given full co-orchestrator credit with Walker.

Romberg was one thing. But the top man at Chappell in the mid-thirties was Cole Porter. (Kern, the Gershwins, and Rodgers & Hart spent much of the early Depression in Hollywood.) Walker was in Boston with another Romberg flop, *Forbidden Melody*, in October 1936 when he got a Friday morning emergency call. Porter's *Red, Hot and Blue!* starring Ethel Merman, Jimmy Durante, and Bob Hope, was opening on Broadway in two weeks. Merman had demanded a new opening number. Porter had just finished it; Merman had approved it; and it had to go in *that night*. Bennett and Spialek, the credited orchestrators on the musical, were off in other towns on other shows.

Typically, an orchestrator takes down the number—that is, listens to the performer sing it with a piano accompaniment. Merman was unavailable, so Walker worked blind. By four, it was in the hands of the copyists; at seven, the orchestra played it down at a pit rehearsal, for which Merman did not show up; and an hour or so later Ethel came on during the performance in her "pet pailletted gown" and sang "Down in the Depths (on the Ninetieth Floor)."

"Who did the chart?" Merman asked.

"*He* did," she was told.

"It's okay," she said.

Walker didn't receive credit, but his work was noticed. Several months later, NBC did a program featuring the music of *Red, Hot and Blue!* Dr. Frank Black, the musical director at NBC, was familiar with Walker's radio work for Romberg and hired him to do the arrangements. The results pleased Porter, who was listening on his sickbed following a crippling horseback-riding accident. Porter called Dreyfus, and Walker was assigned the next Porter show, *Leave It to Me!* (1938). Walker was in.

Walker quickly became known on Broadway for his jazzy, swing-influenced charts; while saxophones had been heard on Broadway before, Walker began to give them a more prominent position. When George Abbott and his silent partner Richard Rodgers decided to produce a "college" musical with a swing-band sound, they hired a new team of songwriters—Hugh Martin and Ralph Blane. Spialek, Rodgers's orchestrator since his return from Hollywood in 1935, was teamed with the "hot" Walker. We have never heard the original orchestrations for *Best Foot Forward* (1941) and are unlikely to, but it was apparently a first. Walker and Martin combined for a new-sounding pit orchestra, with three trumpets, three trombones, and five reeds, the latter all doubling on saxophone. (*The Boys from Syracuse*, the 1938 Rodgers-Abbott-Spialek hit, had two trumpets, one trombone, and four reeds, with three of them on sax.) Suddenly, an array of new, up-to-the-minute contemporary sounds could be heard from the orchestra pit.

In an apparently unpublished article, Walker wrote:

> [T]here is a fundamental difference between the music of *Best Foot Forward* and the music in every other show ever. Not only did Hugh Martin and Ralph Blane write a score as modern as a Bell Airacobra, but Archie Bleyer's orchestra is built on the plan of our top name bands. It's all new and hasn't been done before, yet only the critic in the *Christian Science Monitor* noticed it. Mr. Cole Porter noticed it, however. He thought the treatment of the orchestra in *Best Foot Forward* such an advance that he had no compunction in adopting the same type of set-up for *Let's Face It* (1941), which Mr. Spialek and myself have just finished orchestrating.

While *Best Foot Forward* was a beginning for Walker, it was the beginning of the end for Spialek. After using Spialek on nine consecutive Rodgers and Hart musicals—from *Jumbo* to *Pal Joey*—Rodgers switched to Walker. Walker would do nine jobs for Rodgers, including the final Rodgers and Hart show, *By Jupiter.* (Rodgers: "I will never be able to express myself adequately to you for the job you have done on the show. Not to you, at any rate, but believe me, I have told everybody within earshot." The lyricist sent a simple opening-night telegram: "A very good job—Larry Hart.") *Best Foot Forward* also cemented Walker as Abbott's favorite orchestrator, resulting in more than a dozen shows with Mr. A. (plus non-Abbott musicals like *Fiddler on the Roof* and *Cabaret*, for Abbott protégé Hal Prince).

Walker's earliest musicals came before the day of original cast recordings, but we can get a good sense of what he brought to the field by putting on our CD of *On the Town* (1944). Composer Leonard Bernstein's first show had four orchestrators, with Hershy Kay doing the ballets and a sizable amount of the rest. Walker was called in—presumably at director Abbott's request—for four comedy numbers. "Come Up to My Place" and "Carried Away" are fine examples of the genre, but Nancy Walker's showpiece "I Can Cook Too" sizzles—even now. (Walker had earlier scored Nancy Walker's star-making solos in *Best Foot Forward.*)

In 1945, Don co-wrote (with Clay Warnick) his second Broadway musical, the Bill Robinson vehicle *Memphis Bound* (out of *H.M.S. Pinafore*). As the show was about to go into rehearsal, Walker was summoned by Dreyfus: Bennett had mysteriously walked off his current show just as rehearsals started. Chappell was invoking the terms of Walker's contract, forcing him to postpone *Memphis Bound* so he could take over *Carousel.*

The selection of Walker made a certain amount of sense; he had done two of the last three Rodgers shows, as well as two Hammerstein-Romberg operettas. Still, jazz orchestrator Walker might have seemed a questionable choice for *Carousel*, a show whose already-set instrumentation included not even a single saxophone. But Walker outdid himself, with one of the best sets of orchestrations ever. One has to hedge the praise a bit, if only because four of the songs and much of the incidental underscoring were farmed out; these included the "Carrie and Mr. Snow Sequence" ("When the Children Are Asleep") by Spialek and what might be considered the theme song, "You'll Never Walk Alone," by Stephen Jones. The "Carousel Waltz," itself, was one of two numbers completed by Bennett; it was replaced, soon after the opening, with the now-standard version by Walker.

The ghosting was unavoidable. Walker came in a week late, with no preparation; the phenomenal success of *Oklahoma!* enabled Rodgers to insist on an unusually large, thirty-nine-piece orchestra (meaning more parts to write); and *Carousel* included two ground-breaking extended musical scenes, as well as a lengthy ballet. For Walker, the ballet was the killer, 131 pages. (For reference sake: this is the same number of pages as Bennett's *South Pacific* scores of "Some Enchanted Evening," "Bali Ha'i," "I'm Gonna Wash That Man Right Outta My Hair," "Bloody Mary," and "Younger than Springtime" *combined.*)

Carousel established, I suppose, that Walker could do anything—as orchestrator, that is. *Memphis Bound*, when it made its late arrival, ran a middling thirty-six performances. Walker's first musical as a composer, *Allah Be Praised!* had been a twenty-performance disaster in 1944; his third, *Courtin' Time*, played thirty-seven performances in 1951. That was the end of Walker's career as a composer of musicals, although he finished Romberg's final score, *The Girl in Pink Tights*, and composed a song for the ailing Porter in *Silk Stockings*. But Walker was firmly ensconced as Broadway's number two orchestrator, behind his colleague and officemate Bennett.

The nature of the Broadway orchestration business changed markedly with the aging of Max Dreyfus, resulting in Chappell loosening its hold on the field. Sometime around 1950, Walker and Bennett proposed to Dreyfus that he release them from their contracts and instead participate in an organization they called Orchestrations, Inc. This was to be "a permanent organization for the musical servicing of new musical theatrical productions, radio productions and television productions." Services would include the preparation and duplication of original piano manuscripts, orchestration, copying, and librarian service both during and after the show's run. A second branch of the business would lease and service stock productions ("frankly, in direct competition with Tams-Witmark, using new modern methods and offering many of the choicest properties of the last twenty years").

How far the Orchestrations, Inc., scheme got is unknown, although it was never adopted. What is clear is that while Bennett and Walker were to be equal partners, the scheme was surely hatched by the Wharton-trained Walker. With Dreyfus apparently opting out of participation, Walker terminated his exclusive deal with Chappell at the end of 1951 and set up his own variation of the Orchestrations, Inc., idea. Working with Mathilde Pincus—a violist-turned-copyist he imported from Philadelphia—Walker set up Chelsea Music, based in a brownstone at 349 West 22nd Street (in New York's Chelsea district). Rather than the usual method of working with one or two assistants on each show, Walker hit upon the idea of assembling a music factory of six or seven orchestrators willing to step in when needed. This allowed Walker to take as much work as he and his merry band could handle. Pincus assembled a coven of copyists too, and Chelsea Music Service quickly became Broadway's preferred music preparation house, with Mattie reigning for twenty-five years as one of the most beloved behind-the-scenes players. Chelsea Music more or less fit the description of Orchestrations, Inc., except in one area; it did not serve as a licensing house. Walker had other ideas on the subject, which he soon brought to fruition.

In 1951, Don created new orchestrations for a revival of *Pal Joey*, which opened only twelve years after the original production. (Rodgers later had Walker replace Spialek's orchestrations for revivals of *On Your Toes* in 1954 and *Babes in Arms* in 1959, as he felt that the original charts were too tame for contemporary tastes.) The *Pal Joey* materials provided by the licensing house Tams-Witmark were incomplete and in disarray. Reasoning that blockbusters *Oklahoma!* and *South Pacific* were soon to hit the licensing market, Walker took his idea to start a competing house to Rodgers. The composer keenly embraced the notion, realizing the bounteous financial benefits. (Hammerstein, at the same time, saw it as a place to employ his black-sheep brother Reggie.) On reflection, though, Rodgers wondered, why give Walker a cut of the business? Thus was born what became the Rodgers & Hammerstein Library, without the participation of Don Walker.

Walker nevertheless plowed ahead. A new licensing house needed, first and foremost, product; why not invite in a composer who could bring along his own shows? And so it was that Frank Loesser, with the blockbuster *Guys and Dolls* in his pocket, joined Walker to form Music Theatre Inc. in 1955. Don was president, with Frank as vice president and Allen Whitehead as secretary; the initial catalog was headed by Loesser's *Guys and Dolls* and *Where's Charley?* along with Rome's *Wish You Were Here*, Romberg and Walker's *The Girl in Pink Tights*, and Styne's *High Button Shoes* and *Gentlemen Prefer Blondes*. Within a year, these were joined by the Frank-published *Kismet* and *The Pajama Game*. By 1957, Loesser—who preferred to personally control his several businesses—bought out Walker. (Wishing the new corporate entity to have a similar identity, Loesser changed Music Theatre Inc. to Music Theatre International.)

But we stray from Walker-the-orchestrator. With Chelsea established and footing office costs, Walker apparently determined to take on every show that came his way. He was abetted in this, unintentionally so, by his friend Bennett, who took a hiatus from Broadway. The massive documentary TV series *Victory at Sea*— along with other film and TV work—allowed Bennett time for only one new musical between March 1951 and April 1954. With Spialek all but unusable (though available for ghosting) and Royal apparently displaying increasing signs of alcoholism, this left the field to Walker—who racked up fifteen musicals over the period of Bennett's absence. Over the 1951–1952 through 1954–1955 seasons, Walker orchestrated two dozen musicals.

There was a drawback, alas. It had always been common for orchestrators, running out of time as the out-of-town tryout approached, to call in uncredited ghosts for a song or four. Walker himself had filled in for Bennett on *South Pacific* ("Carefully Taught") and *The King and I* ("Shall We Dance"); on *Kiss Me, Kate*, which was an extreme case, Walker did ten charts without credit. (Bennett carefully prorated all record album reuse fees on *Kate*, sending along checks for Walker's share.)

But twenty-four shows in four seasons is something else. At the beginning of this period, Walker drafted Red Ginzler as a general assistant. Ginzler was no youngster; by this point, he was co-orchestrating TV's *Milton Berle Show*, but like Walker he was a quick writer with a tremendous capacity for work. The pair had first met when Don conducted the orchestra at the Royal York Hotel in Toronto, with Ginzler on trombone. Red played in two early forties Walker musicals, moving up to conductor in each case, and by 1947 he was starting to ghost orchestrations for Walker. Within a few years, he was entrusted with more and more important charts, like "Steam Heat" (in *The Pajama Game*) and "Whatever Lola Wants" (in *Damn Yankees*).

The 1953 musical *Wonderful Town* makes an interesting case. This was a high-profile star-vehicle for one of Walker's most important clients, George Abbott, and thus worthy of his best efforts. Once schedules were worked out, though, *Wonderful Town* proved to be Walker's third show to open on Broadway within fourteen days! The first, *Hazel Flagg*—from another important client, Jule Styne—started poorly in Philadelphia and needed a load of new songs and a corresponding pile of last-minute, rush orchestrations. Walker was stuck in Philadelphia when he should have been in New York orchestrating *Maggie*, a musicalization of *What Every Woman Knows*. As work began on *Wonderful Town*, *Maggie* was starting *its* troubled tryout, and Styne was still turning out new songs for *Hazel*. When all was said and done and written, the breakdown was: *Hazel Flagg*, nine orchestrators, with Walker doing approximately 45%. *Maggie*, seven orchestrators, with Walker doing approximately 31%. *Wonderful Town*, eight orchestrators, with Walker doing only 14% (to Ginzler's 44%).

This activity had several consequences, both favorable and non-. With Chappell no longer underwriting the orchestrations, the Musicians' Union rules provided that each musical have a "supervising orchestrator," who was to receive an additional 25% on top of the orchestration bills. (If the supervisor wrote the entire show himself, he received, in effect, 125% of the page rate.) Set up a factory that allows you to orchestrate six shows a year and your supervisory fees on the work of your assistants will more than make up for the charts you could have written yourself if you had the time. And there must have been a mercenary nature at work, here; why else would Walker accept vanity productions that were sure to be hooted off the stage, such as *Buttrio Square* (1952) and *Hit the Trail* (1954)?

The second consequence was that—given the Broadway hiatus of Bennett—the demand for Walker grew and grew. When he did the aforementioned *Hit the Trail*, a vanity production from a one-time-only lyricist-producer, Walker demanded and received a royalty of ½% of the gross; this at a time when neither orchestrators, designers, nor even choreographers received a percentage royalty.

The *Hit the Trail* stipend was irrelevant, as the show hit the dirt within a week. But the royalty remained in the air. Walker received his ½% from *Silk Stockings*, a moderate success, and from the following year's *The Most Happy Fella*. The deal provided that the producers could recoup his full initial fee before paying the royalty. (As *The Most Happy Fella* had more music than any show Broadway had ever heard, the orchestration bill came to $21,371—as compared to, say, that season's *My Fair Lady* at just under $11,000.) But a precedent is a precedent; Walker's ½% became his standard deal, and without recoupment of the fee. Walker's royalty on his next show broke the bank—or, more properly, fixed the bank. (Walker's avocation of growing gladioli had turned into a business. A disastrous flood in the Delaware Valley in August 1955 put Walker and his partners literally underwater.) The royalty for *The Music Man* was ½%, plus a similar slice of the road companies. Those seventy-six trombones proved to be a blockbuster for the investors, and for Walker.

Let us add, for the record, that *The Music Man* was a music-factory operation, with six contributors. While Walker didn't have two other shows in production at the time, he had just signed a three-year deal as musical director of the TV program *Your Hit Parade*. (Walker had started his New York career twenty-four years earlier, writing for the radio version.) Walker's theatrestyle was too subtle for the needs of TV, however, and the relationship was severed after a few months, with Walker receiving a $17,500 buyout.

There were adverse effects from all that music-factory activity. Following that four-year, twenty-four-show stretch, Walker did only one show in 1956, two in 1957, none in 1958, and one in 1959. The reason seems twofold. First, while the extent of the ghosting was apparently not evident to the composers, it can't have escaped their notice that Walker was not always physically present. Jule Styne, for example, in 1948 had promised that "no one shall ever touch a note of my music but Don Walker."

> KOSTAL: Don Walker called me the night before the orchestra rehearsal for *Hazel Flagg* and asked me to do a big production number in the show ["Big Parade Ballet"]. He handed me a description of the music in this fashion: "8 bars Salvation Army orchestra style, 16 bars ragtime, 8 bars hillbilly, 32 bars can-can, and so on, with a note underneath: 'Please use the songs from the show.'" When you're involved in a show, you get to hear the songs night after night, and when you're called upon to orchestrate them in various styles, it's not so difficult. When you've never heard them before, it's almost impossible. First, you have to rummage through the lead sheets, pound them out on the piano, and then make immediate decisions as to which songs to use where. And then orchestrate them, modulating into various keys, and they need it in the morning. When Jule heard the orchestration, he walked over to Don and told him that it was the best he had ever done. Don meekly said, "Thanks," with me sitting right next to him. Red Ginzler endeared himself to me when he yelled out, "Irv made that arrangement."

Styne switched to Bennett for his next musical, *Bells Are Ringing*, but was faced with the same multi-orchestrator situation (with Walker himself among the ghosts). For *Gypsy*, he used Ramin and Ginzler, who did the entire show themselves. Richard Adler, of the Walker-orchestrated, Kostal-ghosted musicals *The Pajama Game* and *Damn Yankees*, used Ramin and Kostal on his next musical; even Loesser (of *Most Happy Fella*, *The Music Man* and *Greenwillow*) switched to Ginzler, for *How to Succeed*.

Most curious, perhaps, was the case of Robert Griffith and Hal Prince, who had started their producing careers with *Pajama Game* and *Damn Yankees*. The novice producers had a long history with George Abbott, from whom they evidently inherited Walker. After Griffith's death in 1961, Prince used Walker on such musicals as *She Loves Me*, *Fiddler on the Roof*, and *Cabaret*; but Don hadn't done any of the five Prince musicals between *Damn Yankees* and *She Loves Me*. When I asked Prince for the reason, he was momentarily stumped. Until I brought up that royalty.

In 1954, nobody other than the authors, directors, and producers received a percentage royalty. Period. Not the designers, not the orchestrator; even the choreographer usually settled for a flat weekly stipend. Walker got his foot in the door, however, and pried the door open. Through the rest of the decade, no other orchestrator got the royalty. Yes, Bennett, Lang, Ginzler, and Kostal got more work than Walker. But Don was still happily collecting his *Music Man* money.

Prince wouldn't pay. Even today, he is proud of the fact that he produced *Damn Yankees* for $162,000. Both *Damn Yankees* and *New Girl in Town* had severe trouble on the road, which they managed to overcome. *New Girl* (orchestrated by Lang and Bennett) ultimately squeaked by to show a moderate profit. Research the cumulative gross, calculate a ½% orchestration royalty, and deduct it from the net profit; would this tip the show into the flop column? I leave it to you. Prince greatly admired Walker, mind you. But Walker didn't get any more work from Prince until 1963, by which point the brotherhood of orchestrators (excluding only Bennett) had banded together, and Prince—along with other producers— had been forced into paying the royalty that Walker wrought.

At any rate, Walker's early fifties period of factory orchestration—followed by a period of relative idleness—had a decided effect on his future work. *Carousel* and *The Most Happy Fella*—perhaps his two finest jobs until that time—pointed the way. In 1960, Walker orchestrated Loesser's *Greenwillow*. A failure and a disappointment, yes, but Walker provided a warm, pastoral setting. In the following year came another forgotten flop, Arthur Schwartz and Howard Dietz's *The Gay Life*. A musicalization of Arthur Schnitzler's *Anatol*, about a Viennese Don Juan, the score had its ups and downs (including some radiant ballads from Schwartz). But the instrumentation bears examination.

Walker built his score around the cimbalom, which is sort of a xylophone with strings (instead of metal bars), played with mallets, a mainstay of old-time Hungarian tearooms. Walker placed the cimbalom where the harp might usually be; what would otherwise have been the piano chair was split between accordion and celesta. There were four reeds and seven brass (three trumpets, one trombone, three horns), along with string bass and one drummer. Otherwise, there were just violins; while the precise number is unknown, it appears that Walker used twelve (with, in places, four separate solo violin lines). While *The Gay Life* is all but forgotten, the orchestration—from the opening cimbalom cadenza in the overture—is suffused with unusual, vibrant colors. Earlier shows had flirted with "exotic" instruments, but this is the first case I can find where the stranger became the featured guest.

The *Gay Life* orchestration bore dividends two years later with a second sacher torte of a musical, *She Loves Me* from Jerry Bock & Sheldon Harnick (and Prince). This show was fated to a run of only eight months, not long enough to make it into the hit column. Even so, I rank it as one of the finest scores of the decade without question—and, for that matter, high on the all-time best score list. The same goes for the orchestration. As with *The Gay Life*, Walker settled on an instrument that evokes the time and place—in this case, an accordion—and mated it with solo gypsy violins and pristine trumpets. Listening to *She Loves Me*, you feel like the music and the lyrics and the orchestration, all, sprang from the very same mind—a playfully spry mind, at that, unafraid to allow an unabashedly sentimental (and human) streak to break through. The first act contains a song about a musical candy box, which pretty much describes the orchestration, all right.

Walker's expert handling of these two Broadway/Viennese musicals might well be attributable, in part, to his years with the Hungarian-born Romberg (who spent his formative years in Vienna). *Fiddler on the Roof*—from the songwriters and producer of *She Loves Me*—was something else. As excellent as the *She Loves Me* charts were, Walker of Bucks County was not the first choice for this musical of the *shtetl*. As it turned out, Walker gave the show a strong sense of period and—again—made a key contribution to the overall effectiveness of the supremely effective piece.

Ghosting, or rather the lack of it, might well have played an added factor in the impact of these later scores. Walker continued to have an assistant or two, an unavoidable necessity in dealing with out-of-town changes; but unlike on the fifties shows, Walker generally did most of the important musical numbers himself. The later ghosts were usually relegated to dance music and underscoring; these helpers included Arnold Goland and Jim Tyler.

Walker started to slow down in the late sixties; after almost forty years of music, with the continued strain of work-through-the-night emergencies, the grand success of *Fiddler on the Roof*—and ½% of the gross of each first-class production in America and abroad—enabled Walker to temper his activities. "From being a specialist in musical theatre I now have become still more specialized," he wrote in 1968, "restricting myself to productions that have a need for, and offer me the opportunity to create, a musical ambience supporting the story and the time and place of the play." The most unique of these, perhaps, was *Cabaret* (1966).

JOHN KANDER: In both *Cabaret* and *Zorbà*, Don and I developed a philosophy of what the orchestration should be. In *Cabaret*, there were two orchestras, an orchestra which played standard music for interpersonal songs, and an orchestra for the presentation numbers that took place in the cabaret. In *Zorbà*, there were also two orchestras—an ethnic orchestra and a musical theatre orchestra. The first four violinists, the first two stands, could also play the mandolin, so we could get them to take us to a plectrum sound [plucked banjo, mandolin]. There was a concept—we tried to, at a moment's notice, be able to add as much plectrum sound as we could. That was when I began to participate a lot more in orchestration.

Other musicals of this period are mostly forgotten, and perhaps deservedly so, but Walker turned out some fine work. *Anya*, an Abbott adaptation of the play *Anastasia*, gave the solo part to the pit pianist—a concerto-style piano part, suitably so in that the score was adapted from themes by Rachmaninoff. *70, Girls, 70* was also built around a pianist; in this case, Dorothea Freitag—an accomplished dance arranger who appeared as one of the septuagenarian retirement-home residents—was built into the plot with an onstage piano. This might sound odd, but it worked wonderfully in context. Kander and Ebb even gave her a showpiece called "Hit It, Lorraine," in which the cast serenaded her while she fiendishly tickled the ivories as—if I remember correctly—her piano revolved on a turntable like an out-of-control carousel. *70, Girls, 70* was at the forefront of a new and unhappy trend, with a tiny orchestra of only thirteen players (including three trombones). Which Walker made sound perfectly fine, as it happened.

The Rothschilds, from Bock and Harnick of *She Loves Me* and *Fiddler*, displayed a similar sense of period. The score and the show, though, were far less successful. Before that came *Her First Roman*, from Bernard Shaw's *Caesar and Cleopatra*. In this case, Walker and the composer chose to evoke a musical image of Shavian rather than Egyptian times, because—as Don pointed out—nobody knows what kind of instruments they played back in 51 B.C. While the show was an ignominious failure, Walker provided an interesting description of his instrumentation:

> We decided on a nine-man brass section of three trumpets, three trombones, and three French horns ("for Rome") and a six-man woodwind section, two percussionists, and a harp ("for Egypt"). Plus the necessary string bass. This totaled 19, and only six more musicians were allowed. Inevitably, we were led to the completely unorthodox device of using nothing but resonant celli—five, to be exact. That's our string section. And the 25th man? Hold your hats. In search of strange and exotic colors, we chose a Rocksichord—a complexly electronic piano-harpsichord developed for, and dearly loved by, many rock 'n' roll combos. One might say we took their most dangerous weapon and adapted it to peaceful purposes.

The results, which received a posthumous unearthing for a studio cast album in 1993, are immensely pleasing. The charts, that is, not the songs. Other late Walker shows included the long-running *Shenandoah* and a half-week *Angel*, two musicals from a team aspiring to *Carousel* but falling considerably short. Walker did a professionally atmospheric job on both. The former reflects its Civil War period with a featured harmonica chair, while the latter—based on Thomas Wolfe's *Look Homeward Angel*—includes moody and suitably Joplinesque piano writing.

There were also three considerably grander failures. Failures on the parts of others, that is; don't blame the orchestrator. The unlikely team of Andrew Lloyd Webber and Alan Ayckbourn ran aground in 1975 with *Jeeves*, an "outsized turkey" (to quote Lloyd Webber). Rather than shutter the thing on the road, they imported Walker to London—and shuttered *in* town. The following year, the even more unlikely team of David Merrick and Stephen Schwartz put their heads together on *The Baker's Wife*—more or less a Gallic setting of the Italianate *The Most Happy Fella*, without the heart or the art. When the underbaked mess foundered in Los Angeles, they fired the orchestrator and called in—who else?—the veteran Walker. Don provided new orchestrations in time for the Boston opening, but even so the show closed before reaching Broadway.

Walker's final musical came in 1981. *The Little Prince and the Aviator*, it was called. Based on you know what, with a score by John Barry and Don Black, the show disappeared after two weeks of previews at the Alvin. Walker sat out the rest of his time in his beloved Bucks County, with winters in Florida. His health deteriorated as the decade progressed, so much so that when Kander & Ebb and Prince revised *Cabaret* in 1987, Walker was unable to participate. (Musical supervisor Don Pippin: "We could tell that Don's focus was going, early Alzheimer's. He wasn't even sure how many flats were in the key of F. It just broke our hearts.") Don Walker died on September 13, 1989, in Trenton, New Jersey.

This seems as good a time as any to talk about Walker's crusty demeanor.

> HAROLD PRINCE: One of the things that's interesting about Don Walker is that I loved him—we all loved him—but it was hard to love him. He was grim. He was a grim presence, but he was so good. He would walk down that aisle for the orchestra call, and you'd say, "Oh, God, I hope it's better than he thinks it is."

This description was typical. Don's personality didn't bother people like George Abbott or Richard Rodgers, both of whom were frosty in their own right. And many Broadway people were in awe of Walker's reputation and thrilled to have him. But to others, he was forbidding.

Kander and Ebb's first show was *Flora, the Red Menace*, the 1965 musical that marked the end of the Abbott-Prince era. Kander's prior credits are instructive: replacement pit pianist for *West Side Story* (Ramin and Kostal); dance arranger for *Gypsy* (Ramin and Ginzler); dance arranger for *Irma La Douce* (Ginzler); composer of *A Family Affair* (Ginzler, with ghosting by Walker and one number by Ramin). Ginzler died in 1962, and Prince teamed Kander with Walker for what would be five consecutive musicals—until *Chicago*, which was orchestrated by Fosse favorite Ralph Burns.

> KANDER: Don Walker was a very major guy. He was brilliant, really brilliant. But in the first shows that we did together, I would come in and sometimes be surprised about what he was doing—I wasn't always courageous about saying that.... By surprises I mean bad surprises, where I go in and find they've changed the harmonic structure and so forth. There are a lot of good surprises, textures, orchestral textures, a funny solo here and there. But not rewriting me—or if he did, he would get together and say, I think this would be better if ... When *Cabaret* started, I got a little more comfortable with Don.

Walker was a major Broadway presence for more than forty years. Along the way, he orchestrated new musicals by virtually all of the major composers of the time: Romberg, Porter, Berlin, Rodgers, Schwartz, Duke, Lane, Rome, Styne, Bernstein, Loesser, Meredith Willson, Bock, Sondheim, and Kander (plus Andrew Lloyd Webber and Stephen Schwartz). *Carousel, Gentlemen Prefer Blondes, Call Me Madam, The Pajama Game, The Most Happy Fella, The Music Man, She Loves Me, Fiddler on the Roof, Cabaret*—Don Walker's credits speak for themselves.

Let's allow the last word to Hal Prince: "I remember once going out for coffee with George Abbott after rehearsal and saying, 'Jesus, does Don hate this show?' There was a lot of that. The truth is, that was his personality. He was stern and serious. And he was brilliant."

Walker was associated with the following musicals. He was principal orchestrator or one of the principal orchestrators on all except those marked with ♭:

Agnes de Mille Dance Theatre	Ankles Aweigh	Babes in Arms (1959)
♭Alive and Kicking	♭Annie Get Your Gun	Baker Street
♭All for Love	Anya	The Baker's Wife
Allah Be Praised!	Anyone Can Whistle	Beat the Band
Angel	♭Are You with It?	The Beauty Part
Angela	♭Artists and Models	♭Bells Are Ringing
	♭At Home Abroad	Best Foot Forward

Bless You All
♭Boys and Girls Together
♭Bravo Giovanni
Buttrio Square
By Jupiter
Cabaret
Call Me Madam
The Carefree Heart
Carnival in Flanders
Carousel
♭Caviar
A Connecticut Yankee
   (1943)
♭Count Me In
Courtin' Time
Curtain Going Up
Damn Yankees
♭Dance Me a Song
The Duchess Misbehaves
♭Earl Carroll's Sketch
   Book
Early to Bed
♭A Family Affair
Fiddler on the Roof
Finian's Rainbow
♭Fiorello!
First Impressions
Flora, the Red Menace
Forbidden Melody
The Gay Life
Gentlemen Prefer Blondes
♭George White's Scandals
   of 1939
The Girl in Pink Tights
Great to Be Alive!
Greenwillow
Hans Christian Andersen
♭Happy Hunting
The Happy Time
Hazel Flagg
Heaven on Earth
Hellzapoppin (1967)
Her First Roman

Here's Love
♭Hi Ya, Gentlemen!
♭High Kickers of 1942
♭Higher and Higher
Hit the Trail
Hold on to Your Hats
Hooray for What!
♭I'd Rather Be Right
♭Inside U.S.A.
♭It's a Bird . . . It's a
   Plane . . . It's Superman
Jeeves
Keep Off the Grass
♭The King and I
♭Kiss Me, Kate
♭La Belle Helene
Leave It to Me!
Let's Face It!
♭Life Begins at 8:40
Little Jesse James
The Little Prince and the
   Aviator
Look Ma, I'm Dancin'!
Lorelei
Maggie
May Wine
Me and Juliet
Memphis Bound
Miss Liberty
Mistress of the Inn
The Most Happy Fella
The Music Man
♭My Dear Public (1942)
My Romance
Nice Goin'
♭Nowhere to Go but Up
Of Thee I Sing (1952)
♭On the Town
On Your Toes (1954)
The Pajama Game
Pal Joey (1952)
Panama Hattie
Park Avenue

♭Peter Pan (1954)
♭Pipe Dream
Polonaise
♭Red, Hot and Blue!
♭Rex
The Rothschilds
♭Seven Lively Arts
70, Girls, 70
She Loves Me
Shenandoah
Silk Stockings
Something for the Boys
♭Song of Norway
♭South Pacific
♭Spring in Brazil
Stars in Your Eyes
Sunny River
That's the Ticket!
♭This Is the Army
A Thousand Clowns
♭Three Waltzes
A Time for Singing
♭Too Many Girls
Top Banana
Touch and Go
Two for the Show
Two's Company
The Unsinkable Molly
   Brown
Up in Central Park
♭The Vamp
♭Walk with Music
What Makes Sammy Run?
Windy City
Wish You Were Here
Wonderful Town
Xmas in Las Vegas
♭You Never Know
♭Ziegfeld Follies of 1934
♭Ziegfeld Follies of 1936
Ziegfeld Follies of 1943
Zorbà

LARRY WILCOX

Born: March 19, 1935, Loveland, Colorado
Died: November 24, 1993, New York, New York

Larry Wilcox came to New York in 1955, after studying at Colorado Teachers College in Greeley (now the University of Northern Colorado). He majored in music theory but dropped out "because they weren't teaching me anything."

> FRED WERNER: Larry and I grew up together. He was a sax player. I had a little band, we were using stocks. I wanted to expand the band, so Larry said, "I'm an arranger." So he started out trying to do Stan Kenton stuff, listening to records, copying them off charts. I moved to New York, Larry came six months later, trying to work as a sax player. He started doing charts for singers, record dates.

After years of struggle, Wilcox took a job in 1962 as assistant copyist on the Ralph Burns musical *Little Me.* Whether he orchestrated any songs on this show is unknown, but he immediately began ghosting for Burns, contributing charts to *Funny Girl, Golden Boy, Do I Hear a Waltz? Sweet Charity, Darling of the Day,* and more. His first credited orchestration jobs—both Burns-related—were the road reduction of *No Strings* and the 1963 off-Broadway revival of *The Boys from Syracuse.* After two out-of-town flops, Wilcox reached Broadway in 1965 with *The Yearling* (on which he replaced Hershy Kay). Other shows followed, including Duke Ellington's *Pousse Café,* James Van Heusen and Sammy Cahn's *Walking Happy,* and Styne and Cahn's *Look to the Lilies.*

Unfortunately, Wilcox was—like Burns—a serious alcoholic. While this did not seem to interfere with the quality of his writing, it often made him obstreperous. His big break came when he took over *Seesaw* (without credit) during its Detroit tryout, rewriting the orchestrations to order for replacement director Michael Bennett. This resulted in the assignment of Bennett's next musical, *A Chorus Line*—until composer Marvin Hamlisch found Wilcox drunk at the bar of a Chinese restaurant.

Wilcox continued, however, to do excellent work on infrequent musicals, including *Merlin, Singin' in the Rain,* Tom Jones and Harvey Schmidt's *Colette,* and the Royal Shakespeare Company's version of *The Wizard of Oz.* Wilcox suffered a heart attack in 1993 at the age of fifty-eight.

Wilcox was associated with the following musicals. He was principal orchestrator or one of the principal orchestrators on all except those marked with ♭:

♭Annie 2

Ballad for a Firing Squad

The Boys from Syracuse (1963)

♭Breakfast at Tiffany's

♭A Chorus Line

Colette

Cool Off!

♭Darling of the Day

♭Do I Hear a Waltz?

The Education of H*Y*M*A*N K*A*P*L*A*N

♭Fade Out, Fade In

♭Funny Girl

♭Golden Boy

♭Illya Darling

♭Irene (1973)

Jokers

♭Lolita, My Love

Look to the Lilies

Merlin

A Mother's Kisses

♭A New York Summer

♭Nine

♭Peg (1983)

Peg (1984)

Pousse Café

Royal Flush

Seesaw

♭Sherry!

Singin' in the Rain

♭Skyscraper

♭Something More!

♭Sweet Charity

The Three Musketeers (1984)

Walking Happy

The Wizard of Oz

The Yearling

SECTION III.
GHOSTS AND OTHER HELPERS

Before we move on to biographical sketches of other music personnel, a few words on the practice of bringing in additional orchestrators is in order. A quick perusal of the show listings will point to a surprising and somewhat uncomfortable fact: a considerable amount of what we hear in a Broadway musical—including virtually all of Broadway's classic musicals—is not orchestrated by the orchestrator of record. In the course of my research, partiturs and other documentary evidence of authorship have been located for approximately 550 musicals. The number that were conclusively written in one hand—and one hand only—is 14. That statement bears repetition. I have found only 14 Broadway musicals that can be proven to have been completely orchestrated by one person: *Gigi* (Kostal), *The Grand Tour* (Lang), *Johnny Johnson* (Weill), *Music in the Air* (Bennett), *One Night Stand* (Lang), *Pleasures and Palaces* (Lang), *Rex* (Kostal), *Roberta* (Bennett), *1776* (Sauter), *70, Girls, 70* (Walker), *The Sound of Music* (Bennett), *Sugar* (Lang), *Tenderloin* (Kostal), and *Two by Two* (Sauter). Of these, only two—*The Sound of Music* and *Tender-*

loin—were produced between the golden years of *Oklahoma!* (1943) and *Fiddler on the Roof* (1964). Less help was needed from the mid-sixties on due to the slackened production pace, which meant that the supervising orchestrator was less likely to be off working on another show when changes were needed; and due to changes in the Actors' Equity rehearsal rules, which made putting in new numbers overnight prohibitively expensive.

There are another 6 musicals in which virtually everything—save for inconsequential fixes, new endings, or minor utilities—are by the man whose name is on the title page: *Chicago* (Burns), *Fiorello!* (Kostal), *Greenwillow* (Walker), *One Touch of Venus* (Weill), *Promises, Promises* (Tunick), and *Singin' in the Rain* (Wilcox). Of these, only 3 fell within that golden period. There are presumably more musicals that belong in these two categories among the numerous shows for which neither partiturs nor other evidence has been located. But the key statistic, here, is 14 out of 571, which works out to a shade over 2%. Add in the 6 virtually complete jobs and you come up to just over 3%. Only 1 in 28 musicals within this group, which contains most (though not all) of Broadway's golden musicals, was orchestrated by one person.

While we're compiling lists, we might as well add a somewhat broader category of musicals that are *mostly* by the orchestrator of record, which is to say that he provided about 85% or more. It is impractical to make precise calculations, save in cases where invoices provide exact figures, but I have estimated that another 38 musicals—within our 571 for which definitive information has been located—belong in this "mostly" group: *Allegro* (Bennett), *Anya* (Walker), *Anyone Can Whistle* (Walker), *Baker Street* (Walker), *The Baker's Wife* (Walker), *Band Wagon* (Bennett), *Cabaret* (Walker), *Carmelina* (Kay), *Dear World* (Lang), *Do I Hear a Waltz?* (Burns), *A Family Affair* (Ginzler), *Fanny* (Lang), *Fiddler on the Roof* (Walker), *Flora, the Red Menace* (Walker), *The Gay Life* (Walker), *The Happy Time* (Walker), *How to Succeed* (Ginzler), *Irene* (1973 revival, Burns), *It's a Bird . . . It's a Plane . . . It's Superman* (Sauter), *Knickerbocker Holiday* (Weill), *La Cage aux Folles* (Tyler), *La Strada* (Sauter), *Lady in the Dark* (Weill), *Look to the Lilies* (Wilcox), *Lost in the Stars* (Weill), *Mame* (Lang), *Me and Juliet* (Walker), *The Most Happy Fella* (Walker), *Music Is* (Kay), *Oklahoma!* (Bennett), *She Loves Me* (Walker), *Show Boat* (Bennett), *South Pacific* (Bennett), *Street Scene* (Weill), *Take Me Along* (Lang), *The Unsinkable Molly Brown* (Walker), *What Makes Sammy Run?* (Walker), and *Zorbà* (Walker). Combining the "solely," "virtually," and "mostly" categories, we come up with 57 musicals—which is to say about 10%, one in ten—which we can say were orchestrated mostly (or totally) by one person.

This does not take into account the other musicals—a shade over 150—for which we are unable to find attributions and which might theoretically have a sole orchestrator; but the ratio presumably holds. (Incomplete records suggest that

Walker was most likely the sole orchestrator on at least 3 additional musicals, *Gentlemen Prefer Blondes*, *The Rothschilds*, and *Shenandoah*.) This lack of one-man musicals is a rather stark finding, and one that I did not expect to find. But there it is. Nine out of 10 musicals prove to be group efforts, and the number orchestrated single-handedly is infinitesimal.

One might have assumed that Bennett, Walker, and Lang—Broadway's most active orchestrators of the modern era, by far—turned out more shows on their own. They wrote score pages by the tens of thousands, but each employed a small squad of assistants (many of whom were shared among them). Ghosts, they were called. On examination, we find that not only these gentlemen but Spialek, Royal, Ginzler, Ramin, Kay, and Burns also used ghosts. And all of them—including Bennett, Walker, and Lang—ghosted for the others.

Surprising though it may be, the system on reflection is perfectly practical. At base is the very same reason that the more capable Broadway composers did not orchestrate their own shows: time. Keys, arrangements, and dance routines cannot be set until the director, musical director, and choreographer have had time to devise them, set them, and teach them. While everybody involved has plenty to do during the first two weeks of rehearsal, the orchestrator sits and waits. The first finished numbers start to trickle in during the third week or so. By the fourth week, the trickle has become a steady stream, after which comes the torrent. Broadway orchestrators are accustomed to working through the night when the crunch comes; most are remarkably fast writers, which is one of the prime requisites of the job. But there are times when there is simply too much work to handle.

It can be seen that the orchestrator is in some ways at the mercy of the musical director (who is ultimately responsible for setting the routine) and the choreographer. The longer it takes them to hand over completed numbers, the more backed up the orchestrator becomes. It can also be seen that a show that opens its out-of-town tryout or preview period in good shape allows the orchestrator to take a nap or two. When a show is in trouble on the road, demands for new orchestrations—new songs, new dances, new routines for old songs—come fast and furious.

The situation changed somewhat in the seventies, by which point Actors' Equity rules increased the cost—and restricted the hours—of rehearsal time; thus, it was impractical for new numbers to be written, rehearsed, and ready for performance the next day. This meant that the orchestrator didn't have changes continually piling on his shoulders that had to be ready for the copyists by 5 a.m. Fast writers like Walker, Kostal, or Lang could manage seventy or eighty pages a day when necessary. This allowed them to personally score at least some of their later shows. But in the old days, most of Broadway's orchestrators—having gone through this madness once or twice—came up with a working structure that could deal with the exigencies. Which is to say, the use, and sometimes the whole-sale use, of ghosts.

Back to Chappell

The orchestration system at Harms/Chappell, with three or four top orchestra-tors under exclusive contract, has already been discussed. The widespread ghost-ing in the later era was in some ways an offshoot of the Chappell system. When a new musical was put on the schedule, Chappell would assign one of its theatre specialists to the show. (I have found some reference to these assignments being doled out by Bennett himself, although the decision could be dictated by pub-lisher Dreyfus or by the demands of his more important composers.)

The employment contract at Chappell stated that you pretty much had to ac-cept any assignments that came along, with a little room to wriggle out of some-thing you didn't feel comfortable doing. Once assigned a show, you were supposed to personally write as much as you could handle—after which point you were to call on the other staff orchestrators for help. Similarly, the staff orchestrators were required to pitch in, when available. Since additional assignments translated into additional money, this was not seen as hardship but opportunity.

Bennett, Spialek, Walker, and Royal—the Chappell foursome from roughly the mid-thirties through the mid-forties—were a collegial team, sharing a small, two-desk office in the RKO building at Rockefeller Center. (Walker, who lived in Bucks County, commandeered one desk; the others, who lived in town and usu-ally worked at home, shared the other.) A glance at the credits for the Porter mu-sicals of the era, for example, will usually find the involvement of two, three, or all four of them. Chappell had staff orchestrators in its nontheatre departments as well. When things got busy, these men were called; in the hitherto anonymous Bob Noeltner, Jack Mason, and Walter Paul will become familiar names to read-ers of this book. One Chappell musical, Cole Porter's 1944 revue *Seven Lively Arts*, had charts from Bennett, Spialek, Royal, Walker, Noeltner, and others. For that matter, Irving Berlin's *Annie Get Your Gun*—also in 1946—had orchestrations by Lang, Bennett, Royal, Noeltner, Spialek, Paul, and Walker. But *Annie* was a special case, as we will see, in part because it was written by a non-Chappell composer—but produced by Chappell's own Richard Rodgers.

By the mid-forties, the Chappell operation began to change. Spialek went off contract in 1942, Royal in 1946, and neither were permanently replaced. Bennett and Walker carried on; at midcentury, the pair actively collaborated on a series of shows. But when things got busy, they regularly called in outside ghosts (including the departed Spialek). Relatively few partiturs from before 1950 have been located, which makes discussion of early ghosts a little sketchy. Even so, we can address the use of ghosts in broad categories.

Ghosts with Different Hats

The Assistant

Let us start with the words of Bennett, from *Instrumentally Speaking*:

> How much help will you need in meeting your deadline? You proceed as though you can put every note of the score on paper in time for the out-of-town opening, and sometimes you can. Sometimes (more often) you can't, so you must sit down with the composer and your conductor and discuss the available dependable arrangers who could take over some of the numbers, go on the road with you if necessary, and take away some of your worries. There are never a great many to whom you can entrust this responsibility. Finding one of them with time to help you is the next question. Needless to say, it is worth a lot of hard work for you not to have to call in any help at all.

Before moving on, let me question Bennett's assertion that the composers were in on the discussion. Maybe so in some cases, but in the course of researching this book, I specifically asked all of the composers I interviewed if they were aware of ghosting on their shows. Sondheim, Bock, Herman, Schmidt, Hugh Martin, Richard Adler, Kander, and Strouse were all generally unaware; Kander and Strouse added that they were indeed consulted on their later shows, once they were more established. Producer Hal Prince addressed the question: "We knew about the ghosts, sometimes, but we didn't care. The head orchestrator knew that the buck stopped with him, so he'd better be sure everything's fine. I'd say to the orchestrator, 'You do what's best for the score. I trust you.'"

Yes, many or most shows required help, especially during the final days prior to the orchestra reading. When the time came, you couldn't just call Don or Hans to hop on over; during the busy years of musical theatre production, there might be three or four major musicals simultaneously in production (and in different cities). One of the strengths of the Chappell stable was that one staff orchestrator could usually be found to cover another—which is why Bennett, Spialek, Walker, and Royal often wound up contributing to the same show. For illuminating examples of this, see Walker's discussion of "Down in the Depths" (page 102) and Spialek's tale of "Night and Day" (page 92).

In the post-Chappell era, with everyone working as a free agent on his own and without a bullpen available to bail you out, it was a safe precaution to line up a dedicated assistant for each show. Doing so meant guaranteeing these orchestrators some work; when you took them out of town, the union insisted on a daily minimum (by virtue of the fact that, by leaving New York, they were unavailable for other work). Thus, backup orchestrators would be set to work on utilities, underscoring, scene changes, bows, and the like.

Bennett used Menotti Salta on two of the (few) forties musicals for which the partiturs have been found—namely, *Oklahoma!* and *Allegro*—and presumably on other musicals. In the late forties, he switched to Joe Glover for almost a decade. Bennett also frequently called in Noeltner, apparently from the late thirties onward; Noeltner was Russell's sole assistant on his final musical to reach Broadway, *On a Clear Day You Can See Forever.*

Walker set up Ginzler as general assistant starting in 1948 or so, although it soon became evident that Ginzler was too good to waste on incidentals. Thenceforth, Walker split the important numbers with Red; other songs would go to Kostal or Glover, while incidentals and utilities were regularly farmed out to Mason, Paul, and Spialek. (In one of our interviews, Elliot Lawrence mentioned that he was impressed by the orchestrations of *Wonderful Town* when that show was revived in 2003: "I said to Jonathan Tunick, 'It says Don Walker. Don couldn't do that.' Jonathan said, 'He didn't.'") By the early sixties, Walker was frequently working with Arnold Goland (*Flora, the Red Menace, Fiddler on the Roof*) and Jim Tyler (*Cabaret, The Happy Time*).

Royal had a somewhat different method, using a group of four or five assistants (including Noeltner) with different specialties. Lang seemed to frequently use Mason (*Fanny, Goldilocks*) in the fifties and Jack Andrews (*Hello, Dolly! Dear World*) in the sixties. Ralph Burns used Larry Wilcox on many of his shows (*Funny Girl, Sweet Charity, Darling of the Day*), with Tyler making limited contributions to a number of Burns musicals as well.

When new songs (as opposed to incidentals and fixes) came in, the supervising orchestrator might of necessity assign some to his assistant—of necessity, or sometimes just out of lack of interest. If you were Russell Bennett and they handed you "Chop Suey" (from *Flower Drum Song*), wouldn't you ask the other guy to do it? We should also point out a common tendency on multipart numbers (i.e., song [solo or duet], dance, vocal ending). These often emerged from the rehearsal hall in separate sections. The orchestrator of record might well do the verse and first refrain, but by the time the rest of the number was ready for orchestration, he would be busy with new numbers—and thus hand over the excess to an assistant.

Help from Friends

In any number of cases, the general assistants became overloaded or were deemed not up to important assignments. So even when there was a full assistant on contract, the orchestrator might call in one of his peers. Bennett had minor assistants, but he handed important assignments (like "Carefully Taught" in *South Pacific*, "Shall We Dance" in *The King and I*, and a full third of *Kiss Me, Kate*) across the adjoining desk to Walker. Walker, for that matter, called in Bennett for the "Mlle. Scandale Ballet" in *Look Ma, I'm Dancin'!* This, presumably, because Walker learned a lesson on *Carousel*; that show's excellent, 525-bar second act ballet took Don so much time that he was forced to call in Spialek and others to work on major songs that he would have preferred orchestrating himself. Bennett specialized in ballets, so why not use him—and get excellent orchestrations in the process?

One of Bennett's primary strengths was his overtures; while rare is the orchestrator who wants somebody else represented in the overture, Lang called Bennett for *Roar of the Greasepaint* (with especially felicitous results). Bennett called Lang for songs in *Juno*, while Lang called Bennett for *Goldilocks*; also on *Goldilocks*: composer Leroy Anderson, Mason, and Noeltner. *Bells Are Ringing* was something of a mess, apparently due to the opposing temperaments of Bennett, director Robbins, and composer Styne. In this case, Bennett gave Glover (his general assistant on the show) minor songs like "Drop That Name," but assigned others to Lang and Walker. Noeltner was there, as well. Walker, as mentioned, had Ginzler on perhaps two dozen shows from 1948 through 1960. After Ginzler became a star orchestrator in his own right, he invited Walker in to finish up at least three musicals. This included a considerable amount of work on Kander's first musical, *A Family Affair*. Walker subsequently orchestrated Kander's second, third, fourth, fifth, and sixth—but the composer, in our interview, did not recall that Walker had worked on the first.

Pairing Up

As time went on, Bennett in particular found that it was easier and less stressful to simply split shows with an equal partner. In the late forties, when activity at Chappell was dying down, Bennett and Walker shared a handful of shows. These mostly turned out to be failures, unrecorded and quickly forgotten.

Some years later, on *My Fair Lady*, Bennett saw fit to promote his uncredited assistant, Lang, and give him full co-orchestrator billing. Even with the assistance of Lang, the show was too much to handle. In came Mason, who was not only given utilities but entrusted with two major numbers, "With a Little Bit of Luck" and "Say a Prayer for Me Tonight" (which was ultimately cut). The pleasant experience on *My Fair Lady* resulted in Bennett and Lang splitting four musicals, including *Redhead* and *Camelot*, with equal billing. Bennett formed the same type of arrangement with Kay on musicals including *Juno* and *The Happiest Girl in the World*. Russell was, of course, considerably older than his colleagues—he turned sixty-five in 1959—and on several of the split musicals, the arrangement seemed to be predicated on the understanding that he could stay in New York while the junior partner accompanied the out-of-town tryout. And not just because of age; Bennett at this point was heavily involved with the NBC documentary series *Project 20*.

Influential two-man orchestrating teams were formed by Walker protégés Ginzler, Kostal, and Ramin. Ginzler and Kostal were extremely fast writers—a skill honed writing weekly live broadcasts for, respectively, Milton Berle and Sid Caesar. Ramin, though, was a slow writer, not temperamentally suited to the round-the-clock world of Broadway. Sid was far more personable, which resulted in offers of two musicals which turned out to be major: *West Side Story* and *Gypsy*. In both cases, Sid wisely insisted on splitting the shows, the first with Irv and the second with Red. In the next few years, Ramin teamed with them on shows such as *Wildcat* and *A Funny Thing Happened on the Way to the Forum*. Kostal and Ginzler (who never worked together and apparently had a respectful but wary relationship) were also orchestrating shows on their own, such as Irv's *Fiorello!* and Red's *Bye Bye Birdie*; neither of them, in truth, needed a co-orchestrator. When Kostal and Ginzler became unavailable to partner with him, Ramin mostly phased out of Broadway although he was to make occasional reappearances.

Four-handed teams came about naturally when the music staff contained a second person capable of orchestrating. Dance arranger Luther Henderson orchestrated many of the dance numbers on his shows, including dance-heavy musicals such as *Hallelujah, Baby!* and *No, No, Nanette*. Being a full-fledged orchestrator himself, Henderson was often assigned full songs (such as the title number of *Hallelujah, Baby!* and "I'm All I've Got" in *Bravo Giovanni*). Laurence Rosenthal orchestrated the ballets he composed for *The Music Man*, *Goldilocks*, and *Take Me Along*. Music director Elliot Lawrence—a former big band bandleader/orchestrator—regularly provided orchestrations for his shows, with "additional scoring by" billing. While this was usually a case of providing incidentals and tryout fixes in the absence of the orchestrator of record (on such shows as *How to Succeed* and *The Apple Tree*), he more than proved his skill in his first musical—*Bye Bye Birdie*—with an exceptional chart for "English Teacher."

Uninvited Guests

Sometimes the calls for ghosts were hostile acts, forced upon the orchestrator by composers, producers, conductors, or even stars. Such cases are hard to track down, but Burns told of one case where he and Wilcox wrote three or four charts for the star's opening number, which said star continually rejected. Ralph finally gave the number to Tyler, who turned out something that the star liked. Composer Charles Strouse didn't like it, but Sammy Davis did; Tyler's "Night Song" went into *Golden Boy*.

Lang's charts for Lena Horne in *Jamaica* were all thrown out during the try-out—even her sections of the ensemble numbers—and replaced with superior ones by MGM orchestrator Lennie Hayton (and not simply because he happened to be married to Horne). Lang, a friendly and popular man, seemed to strike a distinct chord (nonmusical) among his brethren. I've come across at least two instances in which orchestrators, frustrated by the demands of their employers, said—specifically—"if you don't like it, why don't you call in Phil Lang?" ("Awww, c'mon," responded Lenny Bernstein of *West Side Story*.") Conversely, producer David Merrick—when he didn't get what he wanted from his orchestrator—was known to threaten to call in Lang, who gladly worked for Merrick on a dozen musicals, despite finding him to be generally abominable.

Even more hostile were occasions when the orchestrator was actually fired or simply sent home. This happened to the best of them, mind you, even Bennett and Walker. Bennett's problem on *Finian's Rainbow* wasn't the quality of his work, but friction with one of the powers that be (apparently Yip Harburg). Walker was called to Philadelphia, with Bennett very happy to leave. The extent of Walker's contributions is unknown, but he was given full co-orchestrator credit. Not too soon thereafter, Don was surprised to find himself similarly supplanted by Glover on *Call Me Madam*. Reasons again are unknown, although one supposes that only Merman or Berlin could have pulled the plug. Royal was separated from the next Merman musical, *Happy Hunting*, replaced by Ginzler, Glover, and—Walker. Lang was replaced on his second musical, the 1946 *Annie Get Your Gun*; a quarter of a century later, he was also removed from *Lovely Ladies, Kind Gentlemen* (retaining sole credit) in favor of Kostal. Eddie Sauter retained sole credit on *Foxy* (where he was replaced by Kay), but none on *Cyrano* (where he was replaced by Lang). Kay retained full credit on *Barnum*, even though his work was almost completely replaced (by Lang, Tyler, Ramin, and others). Wilcox, meanwhile, completely rescored *Seesaw* (without credit) for Michael Bennett but was fired from Bennett's next musical, *A Chorus Line*.

Mind you, our knowledge of ghosted scores and terminated orchestrators is limited to the shows for which partiturs or telltale invoices have been found. Hearsay also provides hints, but I find it wisest to take such hints as suggestion rather than fact. The true authorship of the other shows included in this book—those without partiturs or other corroborating evidence—is anybody's guess.

A Word from a Ghost

Kostal discussed his days as a frequent ghost for Don Walker:

> Ghostwriting did not bother me. When orchestrators like Russell, Don, Ted, and Phil signed up to do the orchestrations for a Broadway show, they sometimes ran out of time. While writing the script, songs, planning the scenery, costumes, and lighting may take as long as two years to execute, once a show goes into rehearsal, the orchestrator usually has six weeks to arrange the music. The first two weeks of rehearsal are chaotic indeed, what with meetings, changes, choreographers setting routines, so very little can be orchestrated. Facing an unalterable deadline, the orchestrator may need help to finish the job on time. Ghostwriting demands that you be invisible. As far as the credits are concerned, the arrangements were by Don Walker. This never bothered me, as for one thing Don was very grateful, and the financial rewards were substantial. Sometimes I made as much as $1500 within a twelve-hour time span, usually from ten at night until ten the next morning. Staying up all night is an absolute necessity when you're trying to meet a Broadway show premiere. In my early years in New York, when money was a problem for me, Don Walker's help to me, not only monetarily, but from a learning standpoint, was a godsend. When I became active in TV, I continued ghostwriting. I bounced back and forth between the theatre, TV, and recordings, sometimes doing all three at the same time.

Broadway's Most Ghosted Musical

The typical Broadway musical has one chart for each song, with inevitable fixes and changes. Occasionally, a chart is thrown out and replaced, and on rare occasions—usually when there is a hard-to-please star present—we might find three charts for the same song. And then, there's the tortured saga of *Annie Get Your Gun*, with as many as five different orchestrations for some songs. The story starts a year earlier, with *Carousel*.

BENNETT: Rodgers & Hammerstein were mad as hornets at me several times, but they never contacted me; I heard about it behind their backs. During the war, I had a radio show on which I was getting $2,000 a week. Well, that was money in those days, and you didn't turn that down to orchestrate a Broadway show. So I told Dick the situation, saying I didn't know you were going to do this show, etc. I did a couple of numbers—the "Carousel Waltz" and "Mister Snow"—even before they went into rehearsal. They turned to Don Walker, and he did a fine job. But Rodgers turned his back on me, and decided he was going to get somebody else.

The next musical produced by Rodgers & Hammerstein was *Annie Get Your Gun*, with a score by Irving Berlin. Rodgers, who was in charge of the music department, ruled out Bennett—and Walker as well. (Walker had a dispute with Rodgers following the opening of *Carousel*. Don wanted credit on the initial pressing of the cast album; Rodgers gave the conductor billing, but refused Walker.) Rodgers was still so angry at Bennett—this according to John Fearnley, a long-time Rodgers & Hammerstein associate and casting director—that he said, "I am going out on the highways and byways, and I'll find the first orchestrator. And this is the guy I am gonna hire."

Phil Lang was the one. He had just arrived on Broadway with his first musical, *Billion Dollar Baby*, composed by his longtime friend and client Morton Gould and staged by Abbott and Robbins. He had actually done two charts for Berlin's 1942 soldier show, *This Is the Army*, but as one of twenty contributing orchestrators, it is unlikely that the composer had any personal contact with Lang.

LANG: A couple of weeks after the opening, Dr. Sirmay [the number two man at Chappell] called me in and grilled me. He called again a week later, set up a meeting to talk to Dick Rodgers about *Annie Get Your Gun*. I had gone from no place to *Annie* for a simple reason. Dick went to see *Billion Dollar Baby*. There was a ballet, the gangster's funeral. I gave it a colored-band treatment, high clarinets, wailing sounds—novel in those days. That impressed Dick, and on that basis I got the show.

All went smoothly until the orchestra rehearsal in New Haven. The composer didn't like the orchestrations; the star didn't like them. This was not some low-profile musical where a few patches were possible; this was Irving Berlin and Ethel Merman, with Rodgers and Hammerstein's names above the title.

BENNETT: Dick didn't like to call me at this particular time, so he had Max Dreyfus call and ask if I'd go to New Haven to see what the trouble was with the orchestrations. Phil did a very good job, but he treated the vocals the way you would for radio or recording, where you don't have the tune in the pit. They weren't prepared for that at the orchestra reading; they wanted to hear the tune, too. So they decided it wasn't a good orchestration. It's not true; it was a very good orchestration. But I pitched in and knew exactly what they wanted, and I did seven numbers over. They came around and said, "Oh, you saved our lives," and I wanted to say, "I didn't save anybody's life." But that's as near to an argument I ever had with Rodgers & Hammerstein. When the next show came along, Dick said, "We're doing *Allegro* in September, will that be notice enough?"

Bennett's account, recalled thirty years later, is somewhat oversimplified. Lang appears to have done most of the initial charts, with some help on utilities and incidentals. When *Annie* went into crisis mode, not only Bennett but every available Chappell orchestrator was called on to pitch in: Royal, Spialek, Noeltner, Walker, and several others. Bennett went to work on some important numbers, but there are cases where Phil wrote a second version, which proved unsatisfactory; Hans wrote a third, which still didn't solve the problem; and Bennett finally found time to do a final chart. This compares to happier cases—like "There's No Business Like Show Business"—where Royal's replacement chart was quickly accepted.

An anecdote concerning this song, relayed by Jule Styne:

> The three fellas are trying to sell her to come join this shooting show, this circus. They are trying to sell her, so they sing "there's no business like show business." So when Ethel hears the song, she says—"Wait a minute, how do I sing it? I want that song." So Dorothy Fields says, "It's very easy, Ethel. After they sing one chorus, you say—"you mean: There's no business like show business?"

There are as many as five different orchestrations extant for some of the songs—which indicates that this was more than just a question of adding the melody to Lang's original charts. In all, seventy-nine scores survive for twenty-one musical numbers; this compares to shows like *Kiss Me, Kate* (from four orchestrators) or *South Pacific* (from two), with only one chart per song. On reflection, we find that *Miss Liberty, Mr. President*, and apparently *Call Me Madam* also had multiple charts. Perhaps Mr. Berlin was somewhat difficult to please?

SECTION IV.
VALUED MEMBERS
OF THE MUSIC DEPARTMENT

Space constraints prohibit including extended biographical information about the many other orchestrators, arrangers, and musical directors who have made their mark upon Broadway. Many of them, though, have done too much influential work to be overlooked. There follows apologetically brief biographical information on thirty-four additional music makers, accompanied by a list of their musicals.

ROGER ADAMS

Born: September 11, 1917, Maidenhead, England
Died: September 6, 1999, Doylestown, Pennsylvania
Dance Arranger

Roger Adams, son of twenties musical comedy star Odette Myrtil, was one of Broadway's first and most important jazz dance arrangers. He served in the Special Services branch of the army from 1942 to 1946, composing incidental music for a series of military shows. After several years as a nightclub pianist/arranger in Hawaii and on the West Coast, he was dance arranger on the 1952 musical *Three Wishes for Jamie.* This was the first of ten shows over seven seasons, including Bob Fosse's first four musicals (*The Pajama Game, Damn Yankees, New Girl in Town,* and *Redhead*) and the first film he choreographed, *My Sister Eileen.* After a gap of several years, Adams returned for four mid-sixties musicals, three of them for Onna White (including *Mame*). After a suicide attempt during the tryout of *A Mother's Kisses*, Adams left the business and spent many years running his mother's restaurant, Chez Odette, in Bucks County Playhouse, Pennsylvania.

Adams was associated with the following musicals, as dance arranger.

Ankles Aweigh	Illya Darling	Once upon a Mattress
Ben Franklin in Paris	Mame	The Pajama Game
Buttrio Square	Mata Hari	Peter Pan (1954)
Carnival in Flanders	Me and Juliet	Redhead
Damn Yankees	A Mother's Kisses	Strip for Action
Happy Hunting	New Girl in Town	Three Wishes for Jamie

FRANZ ALLERS

Born: August 6, 1905, Carlsbad, Bohemia (Czech Republic)
Died: January 26, 1995, Las Vegas, Nevada
Musical Director

After attending the Academy of Music in Prague, Franz Allers moved to Berlin at the age of eighteen and eventually worked his way into the violin section of the Berlin Philharmonic. He started conducting at opera houses in 1926, with stints at the Wagner Festivals in Bayreuth and Paris. He spent most of the thirties conducting opera in Czechoslovakia and came to America in 1939 as conductor of the Ballet Russe. A subbing assignment for fellow émigré Maurice Abravanel on the 1945 musical *The Day before Spring* brought him to the attention of the show's composer, Fritz Loewe. Allers became conductor for all of the subsequent Lerner & Loewe musicals, including *Brigadoon*, *My Fair Lady* (Tony Award), and *Camelot* (Tony Award). Following Loewe's retirement and an unhappy experience on the 1963 pre-Broadway tryout of *Hot Spot*—Judy Holliday found him autocratic and demanded his replacement—Allers left theatre for opera house. He periodically returned, though, for limited-engagement revivals produced by Richard Rodgers under the auspices of Music Theater of Lincoln Center.

Allers was associated with the following musicals, as musical director.

Annie Get Your Gun (1966)	My Darlin' Aida	Show Boat (1966)
Brigadoon	My Fair Lady	To Broadway with Love
Camelot	Paint Your Wagon	
Happy as Larry	Plain and Fancy	

JACK ANDREWS

Born: 1915?
Died: 1993? Florida?
Orchestrator

Little information can be found about Jack Andrews. Someone who worked with him in 1950 estimated that he was born sometime around 1915, and someone else remembered that he died in Florida "shortly after Milton Rosenstock" (who died in 1992); we are also told that he was "very tall." Andrews spent sixteen years (including most of the fifties) working on Perry Como's various TV programs as a full-time staff orchestrator. He also did charts for Benny Goodman, Tommy Dorsey, Mel Tormé, and Tony Bennett. The first evidence of his work on Broadway is on *The Girl Who Came to Supper* in 1963, by which point he was probably nearing fifty. This was followed by ghosting jobs for Phil Lang; partiturs have been located for four musicals (including *Hello, Dolly!* and *Mame*), and he is said to have participated on other Lang shows of the time (including *I Had a Ball* and *Maggie Flynn*). Andrews was principal orchestrator on three musicals, *Golden Rain-*

bow (co-orchestrator), *A Mother's Kisses*, and *Jimmy*. The latter two are known to have been ghosted, and none of the partiturs for these shows has been located—which means that there are very few Andrews charts that can be positively identified other than the *Supper* charts (including "The Coconut Girl" and "Curt, Clear and Concise") and minor charts for Jerry Herman musicals.

Andrews was associated with the following musicals. # indicates shows on which he was principal orchestrator or one of the principal orchestrators.

Applause	#Golden Rainbow	#A Mother's Kisses
Cafe Crown	Hello, Dolly!	Sherry!
Dear World	#Jimmy	
The Girl Who Came to Supper	Mame	

DAVID BAKER

Born: June 6, 1926, Portland, Maine
Died: July 16, 1988, Fire Island, New York
Dance Arranger, Composer

David Baker left Juilliard in 1944 to serve in the navy. Following the war, he returned to Juilliard. His first Broadway jobs were as pit pianist for *Gentlemen Prefer Blondes* and rehearsal pianist for *Alive and Kicking*. He was pianist for Nancy Walker's nightclub act in 1950 and began providing dance arrangements with the 1951 musical *A Month of Sundays* (which starred Nancy Walker and closed during its tryout). Other early shows included the 1952 revival of *Of Thee I Sing* and the Bette Davis/Jerome Robbins revue *Two's Company*. He collaborated on several projects with lyricist David Craig (Walker's husband); the pair contributed songs to off-Broadway revues and wrote two full musicals, *Phoenix '55* and *Copper and Brass*. Baker also composed the 1969 Ray Bolger/Agnes de Mille musical, *Come Summer*. Dance arrangement credits included Kander & Ebb's first two musicals, *Flora, the Red Menace* and *Cabaret*, and Richard Rodgers's *Rex*.

Baker was associated with the following musicals, in most cases as dance arranger. ♮ indicates productions outside our area of discussion, with dates and credits in the supplementary List of Additional Shows.

Cabaret

Come Summer

Copper and Brass

Do Re Mi

Flora, the Red Menace

A Month of Sundays

Of Thee I Sing (1952)

Phoenix '55

♮The Prince of Grand Street

Rex

Two's Company

The Yearling

JAY BLACKTON

Born: March 25, 1909, New York
Died: January 8, 1994, Los Angeles, California
Musical Director, Vocal Arranger, Orchestrator

Jacob Schwartzdorf developed polio when he was nine months old, and his father—a shopkeeper—died three months later. As a child, he took up the violin; his mother had him change to piano at the age of nine, so he "wouldn't have to earn his living standing up." She enrolled him as a scholarship student in what became the Brooklyn Music School Settlement. After graduating in 1927, he went to the Institute of Musical Art (which later changed its name to Juilliard). On another scholarship, he went to Berlin to study opera. He returned to Juilliard to teach students—including Risë Stevens and Ray Middleton—about opera. While he was playing singer auditions, he was noticed by the producers of the St. Louis Municipal Opera; they hired him as assistant conductor in 1937, promoting him to head conductor in 1940. One of the visiting shows trying out at the Muny was the Kern-Hammerstein musical *Gentlemen Unafraid.* Hammerstein recognized Blackton as a fine conductor, and—Blackton's physical handicap notwithstanding—brought him east in 1941 to conduct *Sunny River.* The show was a quick failure, but Hammerstein gave him his next musical: *Oklahoma!* (While he was conducting a radio show during the run of *Oklahoma!* the advertising agency asked him "for a more euphonious name"; hence Schwartzdorf—German for "black town"—became Blackton.) Blackton next did the Rodgers and Hammerstein production of the Irving Berlin/Dorothy Fields/Josh Logan *Annie Get Your Gun,* after which Blackton had a dispute with Rodgers and the relationship was severed. He remained Berlin's conductor on his subsequent musicals (including *Call Me Madam*) and worked on Logan's *Wish You Were Here,* Merman's *Happy Hunting,* and Fields's *Redhead.* Blackton returned to Rodgers in the seventies for the composer's final ill-fated musicals—*Two by Two, Rex,* and *I Remember Mama*—and ended his career with the 1979 revival of *Oklahoma!*

Blackton was associated with the following musicals, in most cases as musical director.

Annie Get Your Gun	I Remember Mama	Sherry!
At the Grand	Inside U.S.A.	Snow White and the Seven
By the Beautiful Sea	Jamaica	Dwarfs
Call Me Madam	Let It Ride!	Sunny River
Carnival in Flanders	Miss Liberty	A Time for Singing
Christine	Miss Moffat	A Tree Grows in Brooklyn
Gentlemen Unafraid	Mr. President	Two by Two
George M!	New Faces of '56	The Utter Glory of
The Girl Who Came to Supper	Oh Captain!	Morrisey Hall
Gone with the Wind	Oklahoma!	Wish You Were Here
Happy Hunting	Redhead	
Hazel Flagg	Rex	

PEMBROKE DAVENPORT

Born: July 3, 1911, Dallas, Texas
Died: January 27, 1985, Henderson, Nevada
Musical Director, Vocal Arranger

Pembroke Davenport started his career as a pianist, appearing in Dallas as a teenaged soloist with the Palace Theatre Symphony. He moved to New York in the early thirties and served as the in-house composer at Radio City Music Hall for several years. His first Broadway credits were as vocal arranger on the revues *All in Fun* and *Sons o' Fun* and on the 1946 revival of *Show Boat*. His first conducting stint was as replacement on Cole Porter's *Seven Lively Arts*, followed by musical director jobs on *Look Ma, I'm Dancin'!* and his big break, Porter's *Kiss Me, Kate*. On his fourth Porter show, he made the mistake of insulting the composer; he was immediately fired during the tryout of *Can-Can*. While he continued to work on Broadway for another decade, his subsequent jobs were on lesser musicals, such as *Hazel Flagg*, *Kean*, and *I Had a Ball*. (The latter show was directed by his son-in-law, Lloyd Richards—who was summarily fired during the tryout.) He also served as replacement conductor on a number of Merrick musicals, including *Fanny* and *110 in the Shade*.

Davenport was associated with the following musicals, in most cases as musical director.

All in Fun
Arabian Nights
Can-Can
Carib Song
Hazel Flagg
I Had a Ball
Kean

Kiss Me, Kate
La Belle
Look Ma, I'm Dancin'!
Out of This World
Paradise Island
Sally (1948)
Shootin' Star

Show Boat (1946)
Sons o' Fun
Sweethearts (1947)
13 Daughters
Zenda

BUSTER DAVIS

Born: July 4, 1918, Johnstown, Pennsylvania
Died: July 1987, Massachusetts
Musical Director, Vocal Arranger

While this section of the book mostly includes only brief sketches, Davis's auto-biographical account—in a 1978 interview with Lehman Engel—is far too entertaining to overlook:

Well, I came from Johnstown, Pa., very wet, and naturally, I wanted to get away from Johnstown, Pa. I went to Princeton. My major accomplishment was that I played the soubrette and I did, I think, the only strip tease ever in the Triangle Show. I had no idea of doing anything in music. I wanted to act or write. At Princeton, I won a MGM college contest—$75 a week at MGM as junior writer—but I didn't go. Instead I went to work as a copywriter at McCann Erickson; I looked so young people thought I was an office boy. After six months at McCann, I said to my parents, "Well, I did what you said, and now I am going to do what I want to do." The reason I went into the theatre, quite frankly, is because I fell in love with a chorus boy in a Broadway musical. If I had gone on working in an advertising agency I would have had no time to see him, because when he was free I was working and when he was working I was free. So it wouldn't have worked. I was absolutely bananas over this foolish little boy. I decided the only solution for me was to use my piano playing, so I got a job at Tony's, and at Spivey's Roof. So that brought me into the theatre. Then I got to know gypsies, other dancers, and then I decided why not try the theatre? Fred Kelly, Gene's brother, was doing *Sweet Bye and Bye* [1946]. This was his first chance to choreograph, away from his brother. He asked me to write the dance music. I did it. It closed in Philly, but I had the taste for it. Then I heard Hugh Martin was looking for an assistant. This was 1947, on *Barefoot Boy with Cheek*. The first of three in a row with George Abbott. When working with Hugh, he did the arrangements. I mostly wrote out the parts and coached the singers. Hugh was called in during the Philadelphia tryout of *High Button Shoes*. Then, they needed someone to fill in at the piano. Why not me? Then the guy left altogether, and I became assistant conductor.

You don't need to know everything to be a Broadway conductor. The one or two things you must have are rapport with the stage and the ability to conduct vocals, to feel and breathe with the singers. If somebody asks me, "Do you want the oboe to sound like this or that?" I just say, "Ask the oboist." The whole thing is to keep the stage and the pit together—and really to be more with the stage, than the orchestra. The orchestra can get along, but you have a lot of amateur musicians up on that stage. They might be stars, but they may not know C from D. And they may have faulty rhythm, which the orchestra doesn't have. So you have to know what they are doing and stay with them. I never take my eye off the stage. On both *As the Girls Go* and *Top Banana*, Hugh got into arguments and left the shows so I took over. On *John Murray Anderson's Almanac* [1953], Murray Anderson insisted on hiring an old-time conductor, John McManus. He was too old, couldn't do it. So they asked me to take over. I didn't know anything about conducting, so I said to the drummer— "Help me, this is new to me." The drummer gave me notes after every performance, and that's how I learned to conduct.

When Martin stopped doing vocal arrangements in the mid-fifties, Davis took over the Jule Styne account, working on such shows as *Bells Are Ringing*, *Funny Girl*, and *Fade Out, Fade In*. He became Styne's musical director as well, starting with *Hallelujah, Baby!* His biggest success was the hit 1971 revival of *No, No, Nanette*. This led to a major fiasco in 1975, the five-performance flop *Doctor Jazz*; Davis served not only as musical director and vocal arranger but as composer, lyricist, and librettist as well. Four more musicals followed, all of which failed.

Davis was associated with the following musicals, in most cases as musical director or vocal arranger. ♮ indicates productions outside our area of discussion, with dates and credits in the supplementary List of Additional Shows.

As the Girls Go	Do Re Mi	Funny Girl
Barefoot Boy with Cheek	Doctor Jazz	Half a Sixpence
Bells Are Ringing	Fade Out, Fade In	Hallelujah, Baby!
Darling of the Day	First Impressions	Happy New Year

Hazel Flagg
Heaven on Earth
John Murray Anderson's
    Almanac
Look Ma, I'm Dancin'!
Look to the Lilies
Lorelei

Make a Wish
Nellie Bly
No, No, Nanette (1971)
Phoenix '55
Pleasure Dome
Rodgers & Hart
Smile

Something More!
♮Something's Afoot
Strip for Action
Sweet Bye and Bye
That's the Ticket!
Top Banana

FREDERICK DVONCH

Born: July 18, 1912, Chicago, Illinois
Died: November 18, 1976, New York, New York
Musical Director, Vocal Arranger

Frederick Dvonch grew up in the same poor Chicago neighborhood as his class-mate Irv Kostal. A violinist, he won several awards and scholarships (including the Paganini scholarship at Chicago Musical College, the Ditson Award, and a Mac-Dowell Young Artist prize). He began his professional career as a symphonic con-ductor of several radio orchestras on the Mutual Network. He entered the the-atre as conductor of the touring company of Hammerstein's 1946 revival of *Show Boat*, moving over to *Carousel* for its 1949 return engagement at City Center (which transferred to the Majestic). After serving as musical director of *Arms and the Girl*, Dvonch did the London production of *Carousel* (with the principals from City Center) and then the original Broadway production of *The King and I*. Begin-ning in 1955, he spent three seasons with the City Center Light Opera Company. He went back to Rodgers for *The Sound of Music* and *Do I Hear a Waltz?*—after which he seems to have lost favor. By 1976, he was a pit violinist and the associ-ate conductor of the long-running *Pippin*. His conducting was apparently unsuit-able; the story goes that he received one last chance, with producer Stu Ostrow in the house, listening. Dvonch suffered a stroke at the podium and died that night.

Dvonch was associated with the following musicals as musical director.

Arms and the Girl
Do I Hear a Waltz?

First Impressions
The King and I

Rumple
The Sound of Music

LEHMAN ENGEL

Born: September 14, 1910, Jackson, Mississippi
Died: August 29, 1982, New York, New York
Musical Director, Vocal Arranger

A pianist, Lehman Engel left Mississippi to study at the University of Cincinnati and then headed to Juilliard in 1929 on a scholarship. He began his Broadway career as a composer of incidental music for a dozen plays, beginning with the 1934 production of Sean O'Casey's *Within the Gates* and T. S. Eliot's 1936 *Murder in the Cathedral*. He also wrote music for a series of productions for Orson Welles and John Houseman's Mercury Theatre. He made his debut as a musical director in 1936 with Kurt Weill's *Johnny Johnson*. Engel also taught composition; this resulted in his first traditional musical comedy, *The Little Dog Laughed* (written by one of his students, Harold Rome). Following wartime service conducting a symphonic orchestra in the navy, Engel returned to Broadway with Rome's hit revue *Call Me Mister*. After a few more incidental music jobs, he switched permanently to the podium in 1950 with Gian Carlo Menotti's Broadway opera *The Consul* (for which Engel won a Tony Award). Dozens of musicals followed; these included several by Rome (including *Fanny*, *Destry Rides Again*, and *I Can Get It for You Wholesale*), *Wonderful Town* (for which he received another Tony), *Li'l Abner*, *Jamaica*, and *Take Me Along*. In 1961, Engel began a series of workshops for musical theatre composers and lyricists in conjunction with BMI (Broadcast Music Inc., the competitor to ASCAP). By the late sixties, he had tired of the nightly grind, and thereafter devoted much of his time to the workshop and a series of well-received books on musical theatre. Herb Harris, who played *Call Me Mister*, *Wonderful Town*, *Fanny*, *Li'l Abner*, and other shows, was Engel's "first" drummer: "Lehman didn't have the greatest stick [for leading musicians], but the casts loved him. They loved him, and he got the performance from them."

Engel was associated with the following musicals, in most cases as musical director and/or vocal arranger. ♮ indicates productions outside our area of discussion, with dates and credits in the supplementary List of Additional Shows.

Alive and Kicking	Call Me Mister	Goldilocks
Bajour	♮ The Consul	I Can Get It for You Wholesale
♮ The Beast in Me	Destry Rides Again	Illya Darling
Bless You All	Do Re Mi	Jamaica
Bonanza Bound	Fanny	Johnny Johnson

♮La Grosse Valise A Month of Sundays Take Me Along
The Liar Music! Music! That's the Ticket!
Li'l Abner A Musical Jubilee What Makes Sammy Run?
The Little Dog Laughed Shangri-La Wonderful Town

MARION EVANS

Born: May 1, 1926, Goodwater, Alabama
Orchestrator

Marion Evans started as a trumpet player, although he studied engineering in college and was something of a math wizard. Following his wartime service, he began his arranging career with Tex Beneke (who led the Glenn Miller Band after Miller's death). In 1947, Evans studied at Juilliard with Ted Royal. Royal invited him to ghost on numerous shows, including *New Faces of 1952*, *House of Flowers*, and *Mr. Wonderful*. At the same time, Evans carved out a highly successful recording career, working with the likes of Tony Bennett, Steve Lawrence & Eydie Gorme, Sammy Davis, and Perry Como. While amassing sixty-five gold records and two Grammy Awards, Evans continued to work in his favored field of mathematics. He came up with one of the early computer programs for stock picking; he made so much money for some of his singers that they all went to him for investments. So, he left music to concentrate on the far more lucrative money management business. Completely off-topic is a story Evans tells:

> I got to know a lot of people on Wall Street; I used to tell them that Alan Greenspan was a musician. He was at Juilliard when I was there, a clarinet major, and he played in the Henry Jerome Band at the Edison Hotel. After he became chairman of the Fed, *Time* had his picture on the cover, and inside they had a picture of him with the Edison Hotel band. One of the guys said, "I don't understand something. Why did Greenspan give up the music business, to become an economist?" "Very simple," I told him, "you should have heard him play the clarinet."

Evans was associated with the following musicals as an orchestrator.

Almost Crazy Mr. Wonderful Shuffle Along (1952)
The Boy Friend New Faces of 1952 What Makes Sammy Run?
House of Flowers Paint Your Wagon
John Murray Anderson's Almanac

DOROTHEA FREITAG

Born: December 2, 1914, Baltimore, Maryland
Died: December 29, 2001, Michigan
Dance Arranger, Vocal Arranger

The daughter of a musician and a dancer, Freitag attended the Curtis Institute and the Peabody Conservatory; she also studied two years with Nadia Boulanger. Freitag made her theatre debut in 1946 with arrangements for the pre-Broadway tryout of *Windy City*. She served as pianist on a number of musicals, including *Lend an Ear*, *Courtin' Time*, and *Phoenix '55*. She was musical director of the 1957 two-piano revue *Mask and Gown* and several off-Broadway musicals, including the 1960 two-piano revival of *Oh, Kay!* She was co-composer and arranger of the 1962 ballet *District Storyville* and worked with its choreographer, Donald McKayle, on such musicals as *Kicks & Co.*, *Golden Boy*, *I'm Solomon*, and *Raisin*. She also worked with Kander and Ebb on *Zorbà* and *70, Girls, 70* (in which she played a prominent on-stage role). Offstage, life was tragic: Freitag's estranged son, Charles Yukl, committed a grisly murder in 1966. After being paroled under questionable circumstances, he committed a second murder in 1974.

Freitag was associated with the following musicals, in most cases as dance arranger. ♮ indicates productions outside our area of discussion, with dates and credits in the supplementary List of Additional Shows.

Dear World	I'm Solomon	70, Girls, 70
Gantry	Kicks & Co.	Tovarich
Golden Boy	♮King of Hearts	Windy City
Home Again, Home Again	Lend an Ear	Zorbà
	♮Raisin	

JOE GLOVER

Born: February 6, 1903, Westhampton Beach, New York
Died: August 1969, Los Angeles, California
Orchestrator

Of the many Broadway ghosts who never broke through to prominence, Glover probably did more important charts than any of his colleagues (including such familiar titles as "You're Just in Love" from *Call Me Madam,* "Wrong Note Rag" from *Wonderful Town,* "Small Talk" from *The Pajama Game,* and "The Man I Used to Be" from *Pipe Dream*). Glover preceded Walker at the University of Pennsylvania—he was four years older than Don—and began his career as a playing musician and studio arranger in Hollywood. His earliest verifiable Broadway job was ghosting for Walker on the 1937 Arlen musical *Hooray for What!* (The Walker Collection contains a brief 1943 letter from Glover in California: "Coming back to New York. What do you think?") He was credited as one of many orchestrators on such forties musicals as *Follow the Girls, Sadie Thompson,* and *If the Shoe Fits*; he also received first credit on the 1945 musical *Are You with It?* in a nonalphabetical list that included Spialek, Royal, Walker, and Paul. He was a frequent ghost for Walker, beginning on *Carousel,* and Bennett's main assistant on several musicals (including *Out of This World, Bells Are Ringing,* and *Flower Drum Song*). Glover's one major show as principal orchestrator was *A Tree Grows in Brooklyn*; he moved up when Bennett became unavailable. Other shows on his own included *The Amazing Adele* (which closed out of town) and *13 Daughters.* A prickly personality who thought he was every bit as good an orchestrator as his peers, he tended to pick fights and alienate his colleagues. In 1955, Glover reported Walker to the union over a money dispute, hastening his own downfall. He moved to California and more or less disappeared. Kostal told Larry Blank that, one day in the mid-sixties, he called for a piano tuner. In walked Joe Glover, and that's the last anyone seems to have heard of him.

Glover was associated with the following musicals. # indicates shows on which he was principal orchestrator or one of the principal orchestrators.

The Amazing Adele

Ankles Aweigh

Arabian Nights

Are You with It?

Bells Are Ringing

By the Beautiful Sea

Call Me Madam

Carousel

Damn Yankees

Fanny

Flower Drum Song

Follow the Girls

Happy Hunting

Hazel Flagg

Hit the Trail

Hooray for What!

If the Shoe Fits

The Littlest Revue

Livin' the Life

Maggie

Meet the People 1955

Miss Liberty

New Faces of '56

Oh Captain!

Out of This World

The Pajama Game

Paradise Island

Pipe Dream

Sadie Thompson

13 Daughters

A Tree Grows in
  Brooklyn

Wonderful Town

Ziegfeld Follies of 1957

MAX GOBERMAN

Born: 1911, Philadelphia, Pennsylvania
Died: December 31, 1962, Vienna, Austria
Musical Director

Max Goberman began his career in ballet; the earliest credit I can find is as assistant conductor on the 1939 Ballet Russe tour of Australia. His first Broadway job is notable, as music director for a program of three works from the Ballet Theatre repertoire at the Majestic for a month beginning February 11, 1941. The program included "Three Virgins and a Devil," a five-person Agnes de Mille ballet with the ladies of the title performed by Lucia Chase, Annabelle Lyon, and de Mille; the Devil by Eugene Loring; and "A Youth" by Jerome Robbins. Among the dancers in the other two ballets were Robbins, Maria Karnilova, Donald Saddler, Anthony Tudor, Anton Dolin, and Nora Kaye. Goberman's Ballet Theatre work presumably resulted in his being hired for his first musical in 1944, Robbins and Bernstein's *On the Town*. He followed this with Robbins's *Billion Dollar Baby*, Balanchine's *Where's Charley?* and Robbins and Bernstein's *West Side Story*. Even so, he was apparently problematic as a theatre conductor.

> KOSTAL: Max had been a schoolmate of Lenny's at Harvard. Near the end of our tryout in Washington, I was riding in a cab with Bobby Griffith, Lenny and Jerry Robbins, when Lenny complained, "Where did we get this terrible conductor? He not only hates me, he hates my music." Jerry answered, "We thought you liked him. After all, he was our conductor of *On the Town.*" Lenny said, "I was twenty-five years old at the time, and I wasn't all that sure of myself. But I couldn't stand him even then."

Kostal also relates the following:

> Max really detested *West Side.* Originally the curtain came down at 11:10, and Max found if he hurried the music along a little, he could catch the 11:15 train to get home. Then, he speeded up the tempo and managed to catch the 11:05 train. Over a half year, he continued speeding up the tempos until he managed to catch the 10:45. This meant the cast was running around like crazy, and they became very adept at climbing up the 10-foot-high metal fence in the rumble scene. When Lenny happened to walk in on a performance, and saw and heard what was going on, he really blew his stack.

In 1960, Goberman undertook the recording of the 104 symphonies of Haydn. He got through 40 of them with the Vienna State Opera Orchestra, and then he died suddenly on December 31, 1962 at the age of fifty-one.

Goberman was associated with the following musicals as musical director.

Billion Dollar Baby	A Tree Grows in Brooklyn
Milk and Honey	West Side Story
On the Town	Where's Charley?
Polonaise	

HERBERT GREENE

Born: June 16, 1921, Brooklyn, New York
Died: September 25, 1985, New York, New York
Musical Director, Vocal Arranger, Orchestrator

After training as an opera singer, Herbert Greene got his first Broadway job in 1944 in the chorus of *On the Town*; his bit parts included the "3rd Workman" ("Six o'clock, will ya!"). He insistently bugged conductor Max Goberman until he was given a chance to conduct a matinee; he did well, and thereafter periodically filled in for Goberman on both *On the Town* and *Billion Dollar Baby*. His first major credit was as vocal arranger of *Guys and Dolls*. He served as musical director and/or vocal arranger on a string of shows, including *Silk Stockings*, *The Most Happy Fella*, *The Music Man* (on which he also served as associate producer), *The Unsinkable Molly Brown*, and *Anyone Can Whistle*. Stu Ostrow, who worked with him on *The Most Happy Fella* and *The Music Man*: "Herbie was a masterful conductor, and a strict disciplinarian—I've never heard choruses sound as good. He knew how to make them sound like Fred Waring or Robert Shaw. He used to talk about the 'clarity of utterance.'" Unfortunately, Greene's overbearing personality and tendency to alter tempos served to end his Broadway conducting career after only a dozen years.

> ABBA BOGIN: He couldn't play piano, couldn't read a full score, but he managed. In his own way, he was very talented—but he was so obnoxious that after a while, people didn't want to work with him. He was so stubborn about his own ways, he would just move ahead and wouldn't care what the singer was doing. In *Most Happy Fella*, he wouldn't give Jo [Sullivan] time to breathe. She would scream about him to Frank [Loesser]. It got so Frank wouldn't use him on *Greenwillow*.

Greene made a brief return to Broadway in 1981, as a replacement on *42nd Street* (upon the recommendation of leading lady Tammy Grimes, his Molly Brown). Producer David Merrick thought it was a great coup to get him, but Greene was almost immediately let go due to his autocratic manner. Even so, he is the only Broadway conductor who has been memorialized for all time in a show tune, the verse to the title song of *The Most Happy Fella*, courtesy of Frank Loesser. Before he alienated Loesser.

Greene was associated with the following musicals, in most cases as musical director and/or vocal arranger.

Anyone Can Whistle	The Most Happy Fella	Silk Stockings
Bells Are Ringing	The Music Man	Small Wonder
The Gay Life	Nowhere to Go but Up	Two on the Aisle
Guys and Dolls	On the Town	The Unsinkable Molly Brown
Happy as Larry	Saratoga	Where's Charley?

HAL HASTINGS

Born: December 19, 1916, New York, New York
Died: May 30, 1973, Larchmont, New York
Musical Director, Vocal Arranger

After attending New York University and the University of Denver, Hal Hastings got his start in early television. He served as assistant conductor of *Sleepy Hollow* (1948) and as dance music arranger of the revue *Tickets, Please!* His first major credits were as musical director of two Don Walker musicals, *Top Banana* and *Carnival in Flanders.* Walker, apparently, secured Hastings the job on *The Pajama Game*, the initial production of Bobby Griffith and Hal Prince. (Prince was assistant stage manager of *Tickets, Please!* but in our interview didn't recall Hastings on that show.) Hastings did all but two of the Prince-produced musicals until his death in 1973; these included *Damn Yankees, Fiorello! A Funny Thing Happened on the Way to the Forum, She Loves Me, Cabaret, Company,* and *Follies* (during which a certain amount of conflict arose). Hastings died of a heart attack three months into the run of *A Little Night Music.*

Hastings was associated with the following musicals, in most cases as musical director. ♮ indicates productions outside our area of discussion, with dates and credits in the supplementary List of Additional Shows.

Anya
Baker Street
Cabaret
Carnival in Flanders
♮Company
Damn Yankees
Fiorello!
Flora, the Red Menace
♮Follies

A Funny Thing
    Happened . . .
It's a Bird . . . It's a Plane . . .
    It's Superman
La Strada
♮A Little Night Music
New Girl in Town
Once upon a Mattress
The Pajama Game

♮The Selling of the
    President
She Loves Me
Sleepy Hollow
Tenderloin
Tickets, Please!
Top Banana
Zorbà

LUTHER HENDERSON

Born: March 14, 1919, Kansas City, Missouri
Died: July 29, 2003, New York, New York
Orchestrator, Dance Arranger

Luther Henderson came from a family of teachers. When he was four, they moved from Kansas City to Harlem, where Duke Ellington was a neighbor. Henderson started early on the piano; one of his strongest memories was going at twelve to see the great, seventy-two-year-old Polish pianist Ignaz Paderewski play at Madison Square Garden—yes, Paderewski at Madison Square Garden! Four years later, he saw *Porgy and Bess* "and I thought to myself, well, that's it." He graduated from Juilliard in 1942, then went into the navy, where he served as an arranger at the Great Lakes Naval Station. Following the war, he became an arranger for Ellington, handling the "concerto grosso things"; Ellington regularly referred to Henderson as his "classical arm." Henderson made his Broadway debut as one of several orchestrators working under Billy Strayhorn on Ellington's 1946 musical, *Beggar's Holiday*. He also did orchestrations for Benny Goodman, Count Basie, and Louis Armstrong; spent three years as musical director, accompanist, and arranger for Lena Horne; and ghosted a few charts on the 1951 Phil Silvers musical *Top Banana*. Henderson's first important Broadway job came in 1958, when he was hired as dance arranger for Rodgers and Hammerstein's *Flower Drum Song* at the behest of choreographer Carol Haney (with whom he'd worked on TV). His continued association with Silvers, for whom he'd served as musical director of two TV specials, resulted in a last-minute replacement job as the full orchestrator of the 1960 Jule Styne musical *Do Re Mi*. The orchestrations, while effective, were so inefficiently done that they came in at more than double the price of similar musicals; Henderson didn't get another shot at a full-scale musical until 1976. In the meantime, though, he served as dance arranger for numerous musicals, including Haney's *Bravo Giovanni* and *Funny Girl*, Styne's *Hallelujah, Baby!* and the wildly successful 1971 revival of *No, No, Nanette*. In many cases, he provided orchestrations for his arrangements as well as helping out with nondance numbers. Henderson finally achieved Broadway prominence as orchestrator and arranger of the multicompany hit *Ain't Misbehavin'* (1978) and—somewhat later—as adapter, orchestrator, and additional composer of *Jelly's Last Jam* (1992).

Henderson was associated with the following musicals, in most cases as orchestrator or dance arranger. ♯ indicates shows on which he was principal orchestrator or one of the principal orchestrators. ♮ indicates productions outside our area of discussion, with dates and credits in the supplementary List of Additional Shows.

♯Ain't Misbehavin'	Golden Rainbow	♮♯Play On!
Beggar's Holiday	Good News (1974)	Purlie
♮Black and Blue	Hallelujah, Baby!	♯Rodgers & Hart
Bravo Giovanni	♯Happy New Year	St. Louis Woman (1998)
Coco	High Spirits	♯So Long, 174th Street
♯Do Re Mi	♯Hot Spot	Top Banana
♯Doctor Jazz	I Had a Ball	♯Wild and Wonderful
♮♯The First	♮♯Jelly's Last Jam	
Flower Drum Song	No, No, Nanette (1971)	
Funny Girl	Perfectly Frank	

PETER HOWARD

Born: July 29, 1927, Miami, Florida
Died: April 18, 2008, Englewood, New Jersey
Musical Director, Dance Arranger, Vocal Arranger

Peter Howard started his career as a pianist. A Juilliard graduate, he made his Broadway debut as composer (under his birth name, Peter Howard Weiss) of the ballet "Prodigal Daughter" in the 1949 revue *All for Love*. (Fifty-odd years later, he remained honored that it was orchestrated by the great Russell Bennett.) After several years as a nightclub pianist, he went to work in 1955 as assistant conductor to Franz Allers on *Plain and Fancy*, followed by *My Fair Lady* (on which he helped to train that famed singer, Rex Harrison). After a couple of out-of-town conducting stints and the assistant conductor job on *The Sound of Music*, his friend

Mike Stewart got him an audition with Gower Champion, who hired Howard as dance arranger on *Carnival*. This resulted in a string of musicals with both Champion and producer David Merrick—including *Hello, Dolly!* on which he also became conductor shortly after the opening. Among his numerous shows (as musical director, dance arranger, and/or vocal arranger) were *Subways Are for Sleeping, I Can Get It for You Wholesale, 1776, Chicago, Annie, Barnum,* and *Baby.*

Howard was associated with the following musicals, in most cases as musical director and/or dance arranger. ♮ indicates productions outside our area of discussion, with dates and credits in the supplementary List of Additional Shows.

All for Love	♮Dance a Little Closer	Oh Captain!
The Amazing Adele	The Grand Tour	Plain and Fancy
Annie	Hello, Dolly!	Prettybelle
♮Annie 2	Her First Roman	Roar of the Greasepaint . . .
Ari	Here's Love	Say, Darling
Babes in Arms (1959)	How Now, Dow Jones	1776
♮Baby	I Can Get It for You	The Sound of Music
Barnum	Wholesale	Subways Are for Sleeping
Carnival	La Strada	Swing
Chicago	Minnie's Boys	♮The Tap Dance Kid
Crazy for You	My Fair Lady	The Wizard of Oz

ELLIOT LAWRENCE

Born: February 14, 1926, Philadelphia, Pennsylvania
Musical Director, Orchestrator

Elliot Lawrence already wanted to be a conductor at the age of four. At twelve, he formed a fifteen-piece radio band, which was featured on *The Horn & Hardart Children's Hour* in Philadelphia. By nineteen, he had his own program, *Listen to Lawrence;* his orchestra was critically acclaimed as "the greatest studio band in the country." He moved into television in the fifties, as the musical director of numerous shows. While preparing a historic 1959 Ed Sullivan telecast from Russia, dancing star Gower Champion invited Lawrence to join him for his upcoming Broadway show, *Bye Bye Birdie.* This was followed in short order by *How to Succeed in Business Without Really Trying* (Tony Award), *Here's Love, Golden Boy,* and other shows. An accomplished arranger, he provided occasional orchestrations for his musicals (with "additional scoring" credit); among his charts are "English Teacher" and "Honestly Sincere" from *Birdie* and "Make Way" from *The Apple Tree*. Lawrence left Broadway for the TV and advertising worlds following *Sugar*, but he has remained in the theatre world as musical director of the Tony Awards telecast since 1967.

Lawrence was associated with the following musicals, in most cases as musical director. He was one of the principal orchestrators on the shows marked with ♯.

The Apple Tree	Golden Boy	How to Succeed ...	♯Prettybelle
Bye Bye Birdie	Golden Rainbow	La Strada	1776
Georgy	Here's Love	♯Music! Music!	Sugar

STANLEY LEBOWSKY

Born: November 26, 1926, Minneapolis, Minnesota
Died: October 19, 1986, New York, New York
Musical Director, Vocal Arranger

Stanley Lebowsky was playing in a band in Long Beach in the fall of 1950 when he saw an ad for a fringe musical in Los Angeles that was looking for a conductor. He took the show—*I Love Lydia*, a Livingston & Evans retelling of *The Rivals*. This led to a job as pianist and assistant conductor of the national company of *Guys and Dolls*, which was being staffed out of California. Producers Feuer & Martin moved Lebowsky up to musical director and kept him on the road for much of the decade with national companies of *Can-Can* and *The Boy Friend*. In 1958, Feuer finally brought Stan to Broadway for *Whoop-Up*. That show's choreographer, Onna White, took him along on her musicals *Irma La Douce* and *Half a Sixpence*; the dance arranger of *Irma*, John Kander, used Stan for his first musical, *A Family Affair*, as well as for *Chicago*—on the original cast album of which he can be heard giving the downbeat—and *The Act*. Other musicals included *Tovarich*, *Breakfast at Tiffany's*, *Pippin*, and *Me and My Gal*. He also served as music supervisor for *Cats* and *Singin' in the Rain*. Lebowsky composed one Broadway musical, the 1970 Robert Shaw/Rita Moreno vehicle *Gantry* (directed and choreographed by Onna White).

Lebowsky was associated with the following musicals, in most cases as musical director.

The Act	A Family Affair	Manhattan Showboat
Ari	Gantry	Pippin
Breakfast at Tiffany's	Half a Sixpence	Singin' in the Rain
Chicago	Home Again, Home Again	Tovarich
The Christmas Spectacular	Irma La Douce	Whoop-Up

HUGH MARTIN

Born: August 11, 1914, Birmingham, Alabama
Vocal Arranger, Composer, Lyricist

Growing up in the provincial southern town of Birmingham, Hugh Martin fell under the lure of Gershwin and Kern as a teen. In 1933, he formed a quartet with three girls; the Blue Shadows made a smashing debut as the live stage attraction accompanying the first-run showing of the 1933 film *42nd Street* at the ornate Alabama Theatre. After gaining experience as a radio singer on the local affiliate, Martin stormed New York and in 1936 found a spot as a member of the Kay Thompson Rhythm Singers. Harold Arlen heard them on the radio and wrote Thompson and her singers (including Martin and Oklahoma-born Ralph Blane) into *Hooray for What!* Thompson was fired during the tryout, but Martin made it to Broadway. As related elsewhere (see page 187), he challenged Richard Rodgers to give him a chance to write a contemporary vocal arrangement for Broadway; this resulted in the galvanizing show-stopper "Sing for Your Supper" in *The Boys from Syracuse*. Martin went on to similar assignments on Rodgers's *Too Many Girls*, Berlin's *Louisiana Purchase*, and Duke's *Cabin in the Sky*. Casting about for new songwriting talent, Rodgers and George Abbott hired Martin and Blane to write the 1941 musical *Best Foot Forward*. The film version of that show transplanted Martin to Hollywood, where he found a home in the movies. He made numerous return visits back east into the sixties, as Broadway's preeminent vocal arranger (on such shows as *Gentlemen Prefer Blondes*) and as composer-lyricist of such shows as *Look Ma, I'm Dancin'! Make a Wish,* and *High Spirits.*

Martin was associated with the following musicals, in most cases as vocal arranger.

As the Girls Go	The Boys from Syracuse	Good News (1974)
Barefoot Boy with Cheek	Cabin in the Sky	Hazel Flagg
Beat the Band	Du Barry Was a Lady	Heaven on Earth
Best Foot Forward	Gentlemen Prefer Blondes	Hi Ya, Gentlemen!

High Button Shoes	Make a Wish	Streets of Paris
High Spirits	Meet Me in St. Louis (1960)	Sugar Babies
Hooray for What!	Meet Me in St. Louis (1989)	Too Many Girls
The Lady Comes Across	Mr. Wonderful	Top Banana
Look Ma, I'm Dancin'!	My Dear Public (1942)	Walk with Music
Lorelei	One for the Money	Ziegfeld Follies of 1956
Louisiana Purchase	Pal Joey	

JACK MASON

Born: January 18, 1906, Cleveland, Ohio
Died: December 28, 1965, New York, New York
Orchestrator

Jack Mason started out as chief arranger at Famous Music from 1930 to 1933, after which he moved to Harms/Chappell. He was known as "king of the stocks," stocks being the standard arrangements that were prepared and sold for use by bands. (The more popular jazz, swing, and big bands used in-house orchestrators. Other groups used the stocks, which were written in such a manner that they could be easily adapted to bands of different sizes.) The stocks were, of necessity, somewhat basic; Kostal mentions that he was embarrassed when Mason—whose relatively generic charts he disparaged in his bandleader days—approached him for work in the fifties. Even so, Mason frequently filled in with utilities and incidentals for Broadway musicals by the likes of Walker, Bennett, and Lang. His most familiar chart—and one of the few important songs of his that has been identified—is "A Little Bit of Luck" from *My Fair Lady*; he also did well over half of the excellent overture to *Wonderful Town*. He served as the main assistant to Lang on *Fanny* and, I suspect, other musicals of the fifties. His last show that has been located was *Goldilocks* in 1958.

Mason was associated with the following musicals as an orchestrator.

Best Foot Forward	The Girl in Pink Tights	Me and Juliet
Can-Can	Goldilocks	My Fair Lady
Carnival in Flanders	Hazel Flagg	Pipe Dream
Fanny	Maggie	Wonderful Town

PETER MATZ

Born: November 6, 1928, Pittsburgh, Pennsylvania
Died: August 9, 2002, Los Angeles, California
Dance Arranger, Conductor

Peter Matz majored in chemical engineering at UCLA, playing his way through college. After studying in Paris, he moved to New York, where he got a job as rehearsal pianist on Harold Arlen's *House of Flowers*. Arlen was impressed by Matz's musicianship and invited him to contribute dance arrangements for the show. He also recommended Matz to Marlene Dietrich, who was in need of an accompanist; Dietrich just as quickly sent Matz to Noël Coward, for his legendary 1955 concerts at the Desert Inn in Las Vegas. Matz served as arranger and conductor for the resulting, bestselling Coward LP, and for two recordings by Arlen. He returned to Broadway as dance arranger for several shows, including Arlen's *Jamaica*, and as musical director for Coward's *Sail Away* and Rodgers's *No Strings*. Long and profitable relationships with Barbra Streisand (beginning in 1963) and Carol Burnett (beginning in 1967) left him little time for Broadway, but over the years he did orchestrate several musicals, including Jule Styne's *Hallelujah, Baby!* and Tommy Tune's *Grand Hotel* and *The Best Little Whorehouse Goes Public*.

Matz was associated with the following musicals. ♯ indicates shows on which he was principal orchestrator or one of the principal orchestrators. ♮ indicates productions outside our area of discussion, with dates and credits in the supplementary List of Additional Shows.

The Amazing Adele
♮Anna Karenina
♯Beg, Borrow or Steal
♮The Best Little Whorehouse Goes Public
The Boys from Syracuse (1963)
♮Grand Hotel: The Musical
♯Hallelujah, Baby!
House of Flowers

Jamaica
Look to the Lilies
A New York Summer
No Strings
Sail Away
Vintage '60
Whoop-Up

JOHN MORRIS

Born: October 18, 1926, Elizabeth, New Jersey
Dance Arranger

John Morris started out as a teenaged concert pianist. While on tour, he realized that he didn't enjoy the pressure of performing. He became a theatre accompanist instead, which led to jobs as rehearsal pianist and arranger. He began his Broadway career as assistant conductor of the 1952 revival of *Of Thee I Sing*, which was followed by dance arrangements for *Carnival in Flanders* and *Peter Pan* (1954). He also served as assistant conductor on the latter and "played" Tinkerbell on the legendary telecast. Other early shows included *Phoenix '55, Bells Are Ringing*, and *Shinbone Alley* (on which he worked with first-time librettist Mel Brooks). His excellent work as dance arranger (and associate conductor) on *Bye Bye Birdie* resulted in the musical direction/dance arrangement assignments on *Wildcat* and *All American*. The latter reunited him with Brooks, who enlisted him to compose additional music and conduct the score for the 1968 movie *The Producers*. (Morris points out that the delicious twelve-minute opening sequence was orchestrated by Burns, while the "Springtime for Hitler" production number was orchestrated by Lang.) Morris continued with Brooks for twenty-five years, composing music for such films as *Blazing Saddles, Young Frankenstein*, and *The Elephant Man*, as well as numerous non-Brooks films. Along the way, he found time for the occasional Broadway dance music gig, including a notable job on *Mack & Mabel*. He also composed one Broadway musical, *A Time for Singing*.

Morris was associated with the following musicals, in most cases as dance arranger. ♮ indicates productions outside our area of discussion, with dates and credits in the supplementary List of Additional Shows.

All American	Hot Spot	Peter Pan (1954)
Baker Street	Ice-Travaganza	Phoenix '55
Bells Are Ringing	Kwamina	Pipe Dream
Bye Bye Birdie	Lolita, My Love	Shangri-La
Carnival in Flanders	Look to the Lilies	Sherry!
Copper and Brass	Mack & Mabel	Shinbone Alley
Dear World	A Month of Sundays	A Time for Singing
First Impressions	♮Nash at Nine	Wildcat
The Girls Against the Boys	Of Thee I Sing (1952)	

ROBERT H. NOELTNER

Born: November 2, 1908?
Died: July 20, 1994?
Orchestrator

Robert H. Noeltner is perhaps the most anonymous orchestrator of our group. Marion Evans tells us that Bob was playing piano with the Ted Weems Orchestra in the thirties, with Ted Royal on alto sax. By the late forties, Noeltner had joined Chappell. He was apparently an all-around hand, arranging as well as assisting editor in chief Albert Sirmay. Noeltner was frequently called on by Bennett and Royal as a ghost. His most important charts that have been identified are "I Got the Sun in the Morning" from *Annie Get Your Gun* and, from *Brigadoon*, the "Come to Me, Bend to Me" ballet and "Sword Dance" (a section of which seems to have been used, intact, as the instrumental opening that takes the place of an overture). He also appears to have done important ballets for the Cole Porter musicals *Out of This World* and *Can-Can*. In addition to his orchestrations, Noeltner served as the editor of numerous published vocal scores, making piano reductions (suitable for rehearsal and for piano-only accompaniment) for an impressive assortment of musicals. These include Sondheim's early musicals (*Gypsy, A Funny Thing Happened on the Way to the Forum, Anyone Can Whistle, Do I Hear a Waltz? Company, Follies*) and other important shows (*110 in the Shade, Hello, Dolly! Funny Girl, Fiddler on the Roof, Cabaret, A Chorus Line*).

Noeltner was associated with the following musicals as an orchestrator.

Annie Get Your Gun	Early to Bed	Paint Your Wagon
Bells Are Ringing	Flahooley	Pipe Dream
Best Foot Forward	Goldilocks	Seven Lively Arts
The Body Beautiful	New Faces of 1952	Ziegfeld Follies of 1943
Brigadoon	On a Clear Day You Can See	Ziegfeld Follies of 1957
Can-Can	Forever	

WALTER PAUL

Born: 1901? France?
Died: ?
Orchestrator

Walter Paul was one of the staff orchestrators at Harms/Chappell. Bennett tells us that his real name was Walter Paul Dauzet; that he was born in France; and that he had been a classmate of musical comedy star Jack Whiting at the University of Pennsylvania. (Whiting introduced Paul to Bennett, who brought him in to the Harms stable.) Paul contributed charts to at least a dozen Chappell-related musicals; most of the partiturs which have been located have been for incidentals and utilities (which occasionally made their way into overtures), although occasionally he did full numbers as well. His most recognizable chart is the version of "Were Thine That Special Face" used in the overture to the original cast album of *Kiss Me, Kate* (which is actually the show's Entr'acte).

Paul was associated with the following musicals as an orchestrator.

Agnes de Mille Dance Theatre	Hazel Flagg	Life Begins at 8:40
Annie Get Your Gun	Higher and Higher	Maggie
Are You with It?	Hooray for What!	The Pajama Game
The Boys from Syracuse	I'd Rather Be Right	St. Louis Woman
Curtain Going Up	If the Shoe Fits	Something for the Boys
Du Barry Was a Lady	The King and I	This Is the Army
Follow the Girls	Kiss Me, Kate	Three to Make Ready
The Girl in Pink Tights	Let's Face It!	Too Many Girls

MATHILDE PINCUS

Born: 1917? Philadelphia, Pennsylvania
Died: March 6, 1988, Dania, Florida
Music-Preparation Supervisor

A pit viola player in Philadelphia, Mathilde Pincus occasionally helped out as a copyist on pre-Broadway tryouts. Don Walker came to know her from his trips to Philly; when he left Chappell (with its built-in copying staff) in 1951, he convinced Pincus to move to New York. The pair established Chelsea Music, initially in a brownstone on West 22nd Street. Matty, as she was known, soon became indispensable to orchestrators (including Walker, Burns, and Tunick) and composers (including Styne, Sondheim, and Kander). Kander, who worked with her on most of his musicals until her death, called her "the Jewish mother of all copyists; instead of chicken soup, she would give you pencils and special kinds of paper." Late in her career, Pincus estimated that she had worked on more than 150 shows. A complete listing is impossible to compile, but highlights include

Wonderful Town, The Pajama Game, The Music Man, Fiorello!, A Funny Thing Happened on the Way to the Forum, Funny Girl, Fiddler on the Roof, Cabaret, 1776, Company, Follies, Pippin, Chicago, Sweeney Todd, Dreamgirls, Evita, Les Misèrables, Into the Woods, and *The Phantom of the Opera.* The Broadway community did not see fit to consider orchestrators worthy of Tony Awards until 1997, but Matty received a special Tony in 1976 for "outstanding service to the Broadway musical theatre."

DONALD PIPPIN

Born: November 25, 1926, Macon, Georgia
Musical Director, Vocal Arranger

Pippin began his career as musical director at the Lambertville Music Circus, an indoor arena in Lambertville, New Jersey. His first Broadway job came during the tryout of *Ankles Aweigh*; when dance arranger Roger Adams became unavailable, Pippin was called in to do the "Code Dance" (for uncredited choreographer Jerome Robbins). Pippin next served as rehearsal pianist for *The Amazing Adele,* which closed out of town. (The other rehearsal pianists were newcomers John Kander and Peter Matz.) His first Broadway job was as pianist and assistant to conductor Stan Lebowsky on *Irma La Douce.* Pippin served as musical director for the Las Vegas company; because it was one of the first Broadway musicals to play in that city, producer David Merrick was more involved than usual. Pippin pleaded for Merrick's upcoming import, *Oliver!* and successfully landed the job (with Merrick sneering, "You better be as good as you think you are"). Pippin picked up a Tony Award and two more Merrick musicals, *110 in the Shade* and *Foxy.* He then went with the troubled *Ben Franklin in Paris.* When ghost songwriter Jerry Herman joined the show in Philadelphia, Pippin took one of his contributions (a ballad named "To Be Alone with You") and turned it into a major vocal arrangement ("A Balloon Is Ascending"). This turned out to be fortuitous, as Herman liked Pippin and his work; their shows together included *Mame, Dear World, Mack & Mabel,* and *La Cage aux Folles.* Other Pippin musicals included *Applause, Seesaw, Woman of the Year,* and *A Chorus Line.*

Pippin was associated with the following musicals, in most cases as musical director and/or vocal arranger. ♮ indicates productions outside our area of discussion, with dates and credits in the supplementary List of Additional Shows.

The Amazing Adele
Ankles Aweigh
♮A Broadway Musical
Applause
Ben Franklin in Paris
A Chorus Line
The Christmas Spectacular
Dear World
Foxy

The Grand Tour
Irma La Douce
It's Spring
♮Jerry's Girls
La Cage aux Folles
Mack & Mabel
Mame
Manhattan Showboat
A New York Summer

Oliver!
110 in the Shade
The Red Shoes
Seesaw
Snow White and the Seven
   Dwarfs
♮Teddy and Alice
Woman of the Year

GENEVIEVE PITOT

Born: May 20, 1901, New Orleans, Louisiana
Died: October 4, 1980, New Orleans, Louisiana
Dance Arranger

Genevieve Pitot was second only to Trude Rittman among dance arrangers of the forties and fifties. She met choreographer Helen Tamiris in about 1929 and worked with her for almost two decades in ballet and Works Progress Administration (WPA) projects before coming to Broadway. (Pitot actually has two early obscure dance-on-Broadway composing credits: a *Candide* with Charles Weidman and José Limon, which played for a week at the Booth in 1933; and something called *Adelante* with Tamiris in the cast, which played Daly's 63rd Street Theatre for two weeks in 1939.) Composer Arthur Schwartz wanted to write his own ballets for the 1948 Beatrice Lillie revue *Inside U.S.A.*, but when he failed to attend rehearsals, Tamiris called in Pitot. Her work immediately resulted in a string of shows for choreographers Hanya Holm (*Kiss Me, Kate, Out of This World*), Jerome Robbins (*Miss Liberty, Call Me Madam*), and Michael Kidd (*Can-Can, Li'l Abner*). She worked fairly steadily on Broadway into the mid-sixties, at which point the age of the ballet-influenced musical was over.

Pitot was associated with the following musicals as dance arranger.

The Body Beautiful
By the Beautiful Sea
Call Me Madam
Can-Can
Cool Off!

Destry Rides Again
Drat! The Cat!
The Girl Who Came to Supper
Great to Be Alive!
Here's Where I Belong

Inside U.S.A.
Kiss Me, Kate
La Belle
Li'l Abner
Livin' the Life

Milk and Honey	Saratoga	Touch and Go
Miss Liberty	Shangri-La	Two on the Aisle
Out of This World	Sophie	Two's Company

TRUDE RITTMAN

Born: September 24, 1908, Mannheim, Germany
Died: February 22, 2005, Lexington, Massachusetts
Dance Arranger, Vocal Arranger

After fleeing Nazi Germany in 1933, avant-garde composer Trude (pronounced "Trudy," short for Gertrude) Rittman settled in America in 1937 and became music director of George Balanchine's short-lived touring company, Ballet Caravan. Agnes de Mille found Rittman in the rehearsal hall, brought her in as rehearsal pianist for Kurt Weill's *One Touch of Venus* (1943), and enlisted her to work on her subsequent musicals (including *Bloomer Girl*, *Carousel*, and *Brigadoon*). Rittman was quickly hired for non–de Mille shows as well, including *South Pacific*, *The King and I* (for which she composed the ballet "Small House of Uncle Thomas"), *My Fair Lady*, and *The Sound of Music* (for which she devised the extended vocal sequence for "Do-Re-Mi"). Rittman retired in the mid-seventies and lived until 2005, when she died at the age of ninety-six.

Rittman was associated with the following musicals, in most cases as dance arranger.

Agnes de Mille Dance	Darling of the Day	A Musical Jubilee
Theatre	Fanny	My Darlin' Aida
All American	Finian's Rainbow	My Fair Lady
Allegro	Gentlemen Prefer Blondes	New Faces of 1952
Ambassador	Gigi	On a Clear Day ...
At the Grand	The Girl in Pink Tights	Out of This World
Billion Dollar Baby	Gone with the Wind	Paint Your Wagon
Bloomer Girl	Hot Spot	Peter Pan (1950)
Bonanza Bound	Jennie	Peter Pan (1954)
Brigadoon	Juno	Sadie Thompson
Camelot	The King and I	Seventh Heaven
Carousel	Look Ma, I'm Dancin'!	The Sound of Music
Christine	Maggie Flynn	Two by Two
Come Summer	Miss Liberty	Wish You Were Here

MILTON ROSENSTOCK

Born: June 9, 1917, New Haven, Connecticut
Died: April 24, 1992, New York, New York
Musical Director, Vocal Arranger

A clarinetist by training, Milton Rosenstock received a New York Philharmonic scholarship as a teenager; attended Juilliard on a conducting fellowship; and at twenty-one was named conductor of the Brooklyn Symphony Orchestra. In 1941, he was hired by Balanchine to tour as conductor of Ballet Caravan. Before he started work, he was drafted and assigned to conduct the military band at Camp Upton, New Jersey.

> One day, the guy who conducted the shows left. I went over to help, but I didn't know anything about theatre. I had never listened to any kind of pop music because I wanted to keep my head pure. I didn't even know what a refrain was, what the verse was. They did big variety shows twice a week, and I got real good at it. Ezra Stone, the director, was at the head of it. Irving Berlin came by with *This Is the Army.* My job was to put the orchestra together and assemble the chorus. Lyn Murray was supposed to be the conductor, but at the last minute Lyn was rejected from the service. They were going crazy, what the hell to do without a conductor? So I did it.

After the war, Rosenstock—now proficient in both theatrical and serious music—was hired to conduct the tour of *On the Town,* and then as the replacement on *Billion Dollar Baby.* He became part of the tight-knit Robbins-Comden-Green group. Robbins took him along for *High Button Shoes,* which cemented a relationship with Jule Styne that extended through *Gentlemen Prefer Blondes, Bells Are Ringing, Gypsy,* and *Funny Girl.* Other major musicals included *Finian's Rainbow* and *Can-Can.* By the seventies, he was the grand veteran of Broadway and worked on a string of high-profile revivals.

Rosenstock was associated with the following musicals, in most cases as musical director. ♮ indicates productions outside our area of discussion, with dates and credits in the supplementary List of Additional Shows.

Barefoot Boy with Cheek	Come Summer	Funny Girl
Bells Are Ringing	Curtain Going Up	Gentlemen Prefer Blondes
Can-Can	Finian's Rainbow	Gypsy

High Button Shoes
Hot September
Hot Spot
Jimmy
Look to the Lilies

Lorelei
Make a Wish
♮Nash at Nine
Stop the World—I Want
　to Get Off

Subways Are for Sleeping
This Is the Army
Two's Company
The Vamp

MENOTTI SALTA

Born: July 23, 1893, Perugia, Italy
Died: July 1974, Italy?
Orchestrator

The Italian-born Salta moved to New York in 1927, when he was in his mid-thirties. He is said to have worked as a theatrical arranger for the next twenty years, although few partiturs by him have been found. He worked extensively in radio, including a ten-year stint at NBC, and served as the conductor at Radio City Music Hall. He worked at Chappell and with Bennett during the thirties and forties. Most of the charts that have surfaced are either continuations of longer numbers (such as "Sing for Your Supper" from *The Boys from Syracuse*) or incidentals. His most important number that has been positively identified is the "Many a New Day Dance" from *Oklahoma!*

Salta was associated with the following musicals. ♯ indicates shows on which he was one of the principal orchestrators.

Allegro
Annie Get Your Gun
Anything Goes

The Boys from Syracuse
Oklahoma!
♯St. Louis Woman

♯Toplitzky of Notre Dame
You Never Know

WILLIAM STEGMEYER

Born: October 8, 1916
Died: August 19, 1968, Michigan
Orchestrator

A big band musician, Stegmeyer played clarinet with Glenn Miller and Bob Crosby in the late thirties and arranged for Billie Holiday and others in the late forties. Through most of the fifties, he was a staff arranger on the TV show *Your Hit Parade*. He is credited on a mere handful of musicals, starting in 1955 with Marc Blitzstein's *Reuben Reuben* (working with Hershy Kay). He also assisted Kay on *110 in the Shade* and *Cafe Crown*. Other musicals included *Do Re Mi* and *The Girl Who Came to Supper*. His one musical as sole credited orchestrator was *A Joyful Noise*, which he did two years before his death.

Stegmeyer was associated with the following musicals as an orchestrator.

Cafe Crown	A Joyful Noise	Ziegfeld Follies of 1957
Do Re Mi	110 in the Shade	
The Girl Who Came to Supper	Reuben Reuben	

JIM TYLER

Born: January 7, 1929, Louisville, Kentucky
Died: March 5, 2005, Middletown, New York
Orchestrator

Kentucky native Jim Tyler came to New York in the early fifties, following service in the armed forces in Korea. Early work in recording and television (on such shows as *The Bell Telephone Hour* and *Kraft Music Hall*) led to a Broadway career as a journeyman ghost; he steadily contributed charts to musicals orchestrated by Burns, Walker, and others. These included *Funny Girl*, *Golden Boy*, *Cabaret*, *Barnum*, *On the Twentieth Century*, and more. He was principal orchestrator on a half-dozen musicals, most notably *Half a Sixpence*, *Celebration*, and *La Cage aux Folles*.

Tyler was associated with the following musicals. ♯ indicates shows on which he was principal orchestrator or one of the principal orchestrators. ♮ indicates productions outside our area of discussion, with dates and credits in the supplementary List of Additional Shows.

Barnum	Darling of the Day	Golden Boy
Bring Back Birdie	Do I Hear a Waltz?	Grind
Cabaret	Fade Out, Fade In	♯Half a Sixpence
♯Celebration	Fiddler on the Roof	Hallelujah, Baby!
The Christmas Spectacular	Funny Girl	The Happy Time
Colette	♯Gantry	Her First Roman

♯Home Again, Home Again
♮♯Honky Tonk Nights
Irene (1973)
It's a Bird ... It's a Plane ...
   It's Superman
♮♯Jerry's Girls
♮King of Hearts

♯La Cage aux Folles
The Little Prince and the
   Aviator
Meet Me in St. Louis
   (1989)
Music Is
♯Oh, Brother!

On the Twentieth Century
♮Onward Victoria
♮♯Over Here!
Rodgers & Hart
♮♯Teddy and Alice
Zorbà

BETTY WALBERG

Born: July 11, 1921, Hebron, Nebraska
Died: October 3, 1990, Santa Barbara, California
Dance Arranger

After graduating from Bennington College in Vermont, Walberg served as a pianist at the American Dance Festival in 1948 and became a frequent rehearsal pianist for Martha Graham, Hanya Holm, and others. She came to Broadway courtesy of choreographer Anna Sokolow and served as musical director of the 1953 Tennessee Williams play *Camino Real* and as arranger for the 1955 play *Red Roses for Me*. Walberg was credited as "dance coordinator" for *West Side Story* (which presumably means she sat in the rehearsals with Robbins, playing the music composed by Bernstein). She served as company pianist with Robbins's troupe Ballet USA, established in 1958, and appeared with the troupe for its Broadway engagements (including as the onstage performer in the comic ballet *The Concert*). She continued with Robbins on *Gypsy*, where she came in to supplement the original dance arranger, John Kander. (Sondheim: "My recollection is that on *Gypsy*, Johnny did the underscore and Betty did the dance. She was extremely close to Jerry Robbins; they were like thumb and forefinger.") Other Robbins-related duties included serving as musical coordinator for *Oh Dad, Poor Dad, Mama's Hung You in the Closet and I'm Feeling So Sad*, and as dance arranger for *Fiddler on the Roof*. Post-Robbins shows included *Anyone Can Whistle* (Sondheim: "She was terrific") and *On a Clear Day You Can See Forever*.

Walberg was associated with the following musicals as dance arranger.

Anyone Can Whistle
Fiddler on the Roof
A Funny Thing Happened ...

Gypsy
It's a Bird ... It's a Plane ...
   It's Superman

Kelly
On a Clear Day ...

SECTION V.
ASSESSING ORCHESTRATORS

Activity Log

For more than a half-century, Broadway's most active and most well-known orches-trators—or, I should say, the orchestrators with the most well-known shows—were unquestionably Bennett, Walker, and Lang. While Bennett worked on more than the others—perhaps as many as 200 from 1922 through 1975—much of this activity was in the early Harms/Chappell period, when orchestration was by committee. Walker worked on fewer shows, but seems to have done more as a principal orchestrator than anyone else in Broadway history. (For our purposes, this includes shows split between two orchestrators.) With partiturs and invoices missing on so many musicals, it is impossible to compile accurate statistics; even so, of the 550 musicals for which I have found definitive proof of authorship, Walker was principal orchestrator on about 93; Bennett clocks in at around 70.

Lang worked on less than half as many musicals as Bennett, but he was usu-ally the principal orchestrator on his shows; his total is 70, which—given the in-exact nature of this count—can be considered a tie. (The odds are that those undiscovered partiturs include evidence that might edge Lang past the 75 mark.) Spialek is difficult to gauge; his name is on over 125 early shows in the multiple-orchestrator period, but little definitive evidence survives. What does exist implies that he was principal orchestrator—or, more usually, the most heavily represented of six or more orchestrators—on about 40 musicals. The only others to top 25 are Burns (with 31), Royal (with 30), and Kay (with 27). Kostal and Wilcox have 18, by my count, with Ginzler, Ramin, and Sauter each at 14. Quantity, needless to say, doesn't signify quality. The Kostal-Ramin-Ginzler group turned out such orchestrally striking shows as *West Side Story, Gypsy, Fiorello! Bye Bye Birdie*, and *A Funny Thing Happened on the Way to the Forum*; the three men combined, though, were responsible for fewer shows than Spialek alone. Ginzler—whom Ramin, Tunick, and others rank high among their peers—was a principal orchestrator on only a dozen musicals over the three-and-a-half-year period between his emergence from the shadows and his early death. Adding in the numerous ghosted charts that have been documented, Ginzler can be said to have spent ten years on Broadway, con-tributing to about 50 shows.

Present-day orchestrators cannot hope to join the top three, given today's rel-atively low production pace. Tunick, who has been the most active orchestrator of the modern era, is fast approaching the 50 mark. (While his Broadway career wasn't fully launched until *Promises, Promises* in 1968, Tunick had one credit in 1960—which means that, should he still be at work in 2011, he will surpass Bennett as Broadway's longest running orchestrator.) The late Michael Gibson was credited with about twenty musicals, a total that William David Brohn will presumably exceed. The only other orchestrators I can find with at least a dozen shows as principal orchestrator are Luther Henderson, Michael Starobin, and Harold Wheeler, with Doug Besterman, Don Sebesky, and Bruce Coughlin fast approaching that mark. Where Frank Saddler and Victor Herbert fit in is hard to say, as evidence from the pre-1920 period is minimal.

Comparative Orchestrators

All orchestrators are not created equal. It is safe to say that some are better than others—but assessing their skill is not the purpose of this book. Rather, let us say that expert orchestrators have different styles: different styles, different methods, different goals, and different philosophies. As Ramin notes elsewhere in these pages, *Gypsy* would have been a very different-sounding show if Russell Bennett had orchestrated it. (Bennett, indeed, orchestrated composer Jule Styne's prior musical, *Bells Are Ringing*—which sounds worlds away from the world of *Gypsy*.) Ramin adds in the same breath, though, that he doesn't know what he would have made of *Oklahoma!*

Comparative orchestration is something that might be best left in the hands or, rather, the ears of the listener. It is logical to assume that anyone who has gotten this far in *The Sound of Broadway Music* has at least a passing acquaintance with the work of Bennett, Walker, Lang, Ginzler, Burns, and the others—if not by name, then by show. The reader is presumably familiar with the orchestral sounds—the very different orchestral sounds—of *The King and I*, *Fiddler on the Roof*, *Hello, Dolly! Bye Bye Birdie*, and *Chicago*. It is unprofitable to even begin to try to compare the orchestrations of these shows. The list of Broadway's major orchestrators includes the quintet above as well as Kostal, Ramin, Kay, and Sauter. And, of course, Tunick, Gibson, Starobin, Wheeler, Brohn, Byers, and other more recent practitioners. Any three or five of them might be on your list of favorites, and let me assure you—your list of favorites is perfectly valid.

That said, comparisons were freely expressed in many of the interviews undertaken in the course of this project. Opinions are, in the end, merely that; but opinions from peers and co-workers provide at least a point of comparison and an idea of how these people were perceived in their own times. That is worth a few pages, though this is not a scientific survey with a verifiable margin of error. Rather, these observations are based on the musings of a group of respected and accomplished music and theatre professionals in their seventies, eighties, and nineties, looking back over as much as fifty years.

In talks with Sid Ramin, Elliot Lawrence, and Marion Evans—each of whom were working back in the days of Bennett, Spialek, Royal, and the others—we came up with the notion of "generic" orchestrators. These were men who would often simply take the rehearsal-piano part and distribute the notes among the instruments in a formulaic fashion; they would "take the chords right off the lead sheet" of a song, while their more adventurous brethren would alter the chords and thereby make them more interesting to hear (and more interesting to play). Part of the job description of an orchestrator—as opposed to an arranger—is, indeed, to take the notes and distribute them; but this can be accomplished with flair, or note by rote.

Consider a piece of sheet music, suitable for an average nonprofessional to play on the piano. You can orchestrate this by simply giving the low notes to bass and bassoon, the melody to violins and trumpets, and the chords in between to cello and clarinet. Conversely, you can find interesting instrumental combinations, vary the rhythmic pattern, and add more artful ornamentation than the piano-friendly fills that exist on the page. Some orchestrators take the beat, for example, and simply split it up into oom-pahs from the string bass and the low strings, combined with whatever reeds are available. More adventurous orchestrators might build on some combination coming out of the percussion section, perhaps in tandem with a vamp from the bass clarinet. As an example, consider the arpeggiated bassoon in "What's the Use?" from *Candide*. This could have been assigned to the bass and middle strings just as easily—but not nearly as deliciously.

This difference in treatment can be found easily enough by looking at reed fills. Take a simple figure, five notes up followed by a similar run down. Lang, almost always, would just give the figure to two clarinets, or a clarinet and a flute (if the second player already had the flute in hand), and be done with it. Ginzler, though, might vary the instruments; flute goes up, clarinet goes down. In comedy numbers, this would be a flute/oboe combination or clarinet/English horn. A little touch like this does not make an enormous difference, but it does provide color; the ear might not pick it up, exactly, but it is an extra hint of flavor. Provide a dozen hints of flavor per song, and you have the difference between *Bye Bye Birdie* and *Destry Rides Again*.

For the orchestrator, it is much easier to simply write the figure for one instrument and use the musical equivalent of ditto marks on the other line and to then repeat the figure as is, each time the fill is used. Making slight changes—repeating the figure but changing the English horn to the bass clarinet, say—keeps the orchestrator engaged, on his toes, musically speaking. As for the musician, it is easy to play the same figure, again and again, and far more relaxing to keep the quick changes of instrument to a minimum. But lines and lines full of repeated passages quickly lead to boredom; boredom, over the course of eight performances a week, leads to a lack of orchestral sparkle.

The so-called generic orchestrators—Lang, Spialek, Royal, and Glover were most frequently mentioned—were all more than merely proficient; it came up repeatedly in the interviews that all of the major Broadway orchestrators, and most of the ghosts as well, needed to be highly capable in order to survive under the high-pressure conditions of a tryout. With respect to Lang, Spialek, and Royal, one could easily go through their collective charts and find any number of wonderful orchestrations. All too often, though, faced with mountains of pages to finish, they seemed glad to take the easy way out.

Peer Ratings

Most of the comments on our orchestrators—from other orchestrators, arrangers, musical directors, composers, and producers of the period—were favorable, with some carping here and there. Everybody loved Bennett—he and Lang were apparently the "favorite old uncle" figures of the Broadway musical—but some pointed out that his work began to sound old-fashioned as he moved toward old age. (He was born in 1894 and remained active until 1967.) *Bells Are Ringing* and *Flower Drum Song*, two contemporary musicals that took place in big-city America in 1956 and 1958, respectively, could both use a little more life; it's no wonder that Richard Rodgers moved from Bennett to Burns for his jazz-oriented *No Strings*.

Walker, too, was mostly praised. There was a period in the fifties when he took on too many shows, with a resultant falling-off in originality; but he adjusted his outlook and developed a new, later style by restricting his output to projects that called for the creation of their own instrumental soundscapes (like *Fiddler on the Roof* and *Cabaret*). Over the course of his forty-eight years on Broadway, Walker orchestrated *Carousel*, *The Most Happy Fella*, and *She Loves Me*, and I don't see how anybody can argue with the quality of that trio.

Spialek was old-fashioned, by 1940 or so anyway, and relatively nonadventurous. The considerably younger Walker was paired with Spialek on a few important shows; Don quickly won over clients like Rodgers, who found that Walker was "hot" and Spialek was not. Royal was a workhorse but thought by many to be merely serviceable; of his relatively few recorded musicals, only one—*Briga-doon*—has orchestrations that are up to the Bennett-Walker caliber. Kay was strong on legit shows and perhaps the best candidate for such jobs as *Candide* and *On the Twentieth Century*. He was deemed less effective on contemporary musicals, though, and several interviewees offered that his orchestrations were only as vibrant as the rehearsal scores he was handed. The work of Ginzler, Kostal, Ramin, Burns, Sauter, and Wilcox was universally praised.

Let it be clear that the praise applied only to musicianship. Bennett was well liked and respected by all, despite the fact that his memoirs reveal that he looked down on the music and the people of Broadway as musically inferior. (Bennett considered Oscar Hammerstein to be a true poet, but nobody else he came across backstage was up to his standards, at least in private.) Walker had a dour person-ality and could act imperiously, as reported by three of his young clients (Sond-heim, Kander, and Hugh Martin); Sondheim suggested that Don's lack of suc-cess as a composer made him jealous of the younger songwriters to whom he was assigned. Spialek had a sharp personality, with a tendency to say the wrong thing to the wrong person at the wrong time; in his memoirs, he reveals how he alien-ated Kern, Romberg, Rodgers, and others. Kostal, too, was sharp-tongued, but the quality of his work—and his occasional collaboration with the sweet-mannered Ramin—kept him in demand. Sauter was difficult as well; he was one of those geniuses who did remarkable work but bristled at criticism or input, especially from composers, producers, or directors.

Alcohol was a major issue with three of our orchestrators. Royal drank increas-ingly frequently over the years, until he seems to have pretty much vanished from view. Burns and his close associate Wilcox were both highly skilled orchestrators, despite their liquor problems. The shy Burns was apparently a gentlemanly drunk, with a sweet disposition; Wilcox was the opposite, with a tendency to be wither-ingly caustic. Burns tempered his alcoholism around 1970 and thrived; Wilcox—who during the sixties seemed to be the one who cleaned up and finished jobs for Burns—grew increasingly out of control, self-sabotaging his career.

And then, there's Phil Lang.

The Trouble with Phil

Over the course of his long career, Lang was arguably Broadway's most successful orchestrator. Financially, at least. Lang generally worked for scale, unlike the other major orchestrators (except Bennett) and when royalties became the norm accepted a cut-rate ¼%. This was half of what Walker demanded and received, but Walker had only one massive long-running hit, *Fiddler on the Roof.* Lang had three: *Hello, Dolly! Annie,* and *42nd Street.* (Lang was co-orchestrator of *My Fair Lady,* too, but in those days he did not receive a royalty.) Financial success aside, Lang did some admirable work; his charts for *Camelot* alone are perhaps as good as Broadway orchestration gets. Other shows that stand out among his seventy-odd scores include the rambunctious *Li'l Abner,* the artfully delicate *Carnival,* and the exuberant *Mame.*

But much of Lang's work tended toward the generic. Just about everyone with whom I spoke liked Lang, personally; he was described, again and again, as something akin to your favorite uncle. (A couple of people who worked with him in later years said that, with age, he looked like a Chinese uncle.) But he was also the only one of our orchestrators who was repeatedly criticized in my interviews with his peers. I have reluctantly decided to include these discussions in this book; they are an accurate representation of what I heard, and thus I've concluded that inclusion is warranted.

Lang came to be looked on as the inheritor of the mantle of Russell Bennett, due in part to their collaboration on two Lerner and Loewe musicals. (The impression that Lang and Bennett worked together frequently is inaccurate; their collaboration was restricted to only five shows.) But Bennett was an intensively trained, serious composer with an endlessly inventive mind; Lang was a skilled craftsman. Producer Stu Ostrow, who was thrilled to be able to hire Bennett for his first musical, *We Take the Town,* offered a comparison: "Bennett did Copland. Phil didn't do Copland; Russell's range was enormous, Phil's was limited. I thought Phil was corny."

Lang did have several staunch supporters among our interviewees, chief among them frequent collaborators Don Pippin and Peter Howard and happy customers Jerry Herman and Charles Strouse. Herman called Phil's style "straight down the middle-of-the-road Broadway." Stephen Sondheim, curiously enough, offered that "Lang was great," adding, "*Make a Wish* is the only LP I bought two copies of." (I, too, confess to buying a second copy of the *Make a Wish* LP; the first—one of those early green-labeled platters from RCA—wore out.) Praise from Sondheim is high praise indeed; still, he never chose to work with Lang.

Sid Ramin offered even-handed praise, with qualifications.

> RAMIN: Phil was a wonderful arranger; he used to do a lot of stuff for Morton Gould, very rough stuff to do. But it seems to me that—and I don't say this in a disparaging way—he was a generic arranger. It was a matter of style and temperament. His shows are all very professionally done, but they're not exciting.

John Morris, who worked with Lang on *Dear World* and *Mack & Mabel,* agreed: "Phil was a good orchestrator. I never thought that he had any wide-ranging technique, or desire to be known as a classical or pop orchestrator. I can't say he was wonderful; he was just a good workaday show orchestrator." Walker, who for many years was perhaps Lang's closest direct competitor, called Lang "an excellent and competent orchestrator, who does his best to carry out the ideas and direction of the composer and lyricist." Excellent, yes, but one suspects that "competent," in this context, was not a compliment.

The overall criticism, mostly, was that Lang's work was not adventurous; the word "generic" was frequently joined by "formulaic" and even "hack." This can best be illustrated by an experience I had back in 1974 on the opening night of *Mack & Mabel*. In a song called "Big Time," the strings and reeds played an especially flashy phrase. I thought—well, I've heard that before. ("BUM-pa-dum-pa / BUM pa-DUMMMM, pa-DA" it went, the best I can describe it without littering these pages with musical notation.) I'd heard it in two other musicals by the composer of *Mack & Mabel*, yes, but also in shows by Jule Styne, Arthur Schwartz, and even Anthony Newley. And who knows how many others? While the *Mack & Mabel* program promised music by Jerry Herman, this familiar musical theme— something that can best be described as "inverted icicles" or "syncopated stalactites," take your pick —was surely not something that Jerry Herman thought up. This *was* music, or a succession of musical notes, by any definition. It *was* emanating from Jerry Herman's pit in the Majestic Theatre, but it was demonstrably not written by Jerry Herman. Rather, it was a shortcut used by the orchestrator in an attempt to boost the excitement that wasn't happening on the stage.

A minor point, yes. But an unsophisticated theatregoer might well have thought: it says "music by Jerry Herman," so why is this stretch of song in *Mack & Mabel* identical to something I remember hearing on the original cast albums of *Subways Are for Sleeping* ("Ride Through the Night") and *The Roar of the Greasepaint* ("A Wonderful Day Like Today")? And *Mame, Jennie, Maggie Flynn,* and who knows how many other musicals that have gone unrecorded. It would seem a crime of orchestration to dress up one composer's music so that it sounds precisely like someone else's. Red Press, who played the Reed I chair in *Subways* and *Jennie*, remembers going through passages at the orchestra reading for *Mame* and saying to himself, "Hey, I played this in another show!" And not just in relation to those inverted icicles.

Opinions from the Pit

Elliot Lawrence:

> You can tell about orchestrations by talking to musicians who played the scores. They'll say, "What a pleasure; it's fun to play for two and a half hours. Everything's on the right place on your instrument." With Phil,

the guys would say they were worn out by the time they got through the night: "The way he writes, nothing is completely right on my instrument." On a Ralph Burns show, year after year, it's a pleasure to come in and play the show. *Birdie*, too; it was not only fun to play, but it is all in the right place to play. I hated to conduct Phil's scores. I didn't like his stuff at all, ever. When something says loud, it's supposed to be loud; always the trumpets in a certain way, that's the way he always wrote.

I dutifully tracked down three top pit musicians from the period, asking them what it was like to play the charts of our various orchestrators.

PRESS: With Phil, everything is dull all the time. With Ralph Burns, it's always interesting—even if you're playing a harmony part, he gives you leading tones from one to another and shows you how to get there. Playing in *Pippin* or *Chicago*, every person in the orchestra has a moment where they have something to play, where they can express themselves, where they can be heard. Nobody sits there all night sucking on their horn. If you're sitting there and it makes no difference what you're doing, it makes you tend to not care. *Mame* had terrible, terrible orchestrations to play. I remember, he wrote a little alto solo for me. It was in the wrong register, but there it was on the alto.

Joe Soldo played reeds in Lang's *Jamaica*, as well as in musicals by Ginzler, Burns, and Sauter:

You could tell immediately the difference between Red or Ralph, and someone like Phil. The saxes were voiced just right. I especially loved the way Red and Ralph wrote for bass clarinet. Phil wrote it like it was a tuba part; it didn't make any sense. The way Red and Ralph wrote, the harmonies were so much greater. On *How to Succeed*, the charts were excellent and a lot of fun to play. Red was a master—all of the parts are voiced just right. I remember when we read through "I Believe in You." Red came over and said, "Try to make a schmear on the flutes." Don or Phil would never think of that.

Herb Harris, who played drums in several Lang shows (including *Bonanza Bound, Fanny, Li'l Abner,* and *Goldilocks*), was less critical: "Phil was a simpler kind of orchestrator. He was very basic, but he didn't have the imagination. He wasn't up to a lot of the orchestrators; solid, but not creative in the sense that the others were."

Lawrence ascribed part of the "wrong place on the instrument" problem to the arrangements that Lang was handed to orchestrate: "Phil would write whatever the arranger gave him. Even if everything was in the wrong place for the wrong instrument, he would score it."

John Franceschina recalls a conversation with Ernie Bright, a veteran reed player, back in the late sixties. Bright said that he never had to worry about sight reading on Lang shows; he knew exactly what to expect. He added that he "rarely put in a new reed for one of Phil's shows since the part sounded just as good on a worn-out reed as a clean one!" (This was, perhaps, an exaggeration—but a perfect expression of the attitude of so many pit musicians.) Bright, who played the Broadway productions of *Oklahoma! South Pacific*, and *My Fair Lady*, had a similar complaint about Bennett shows; the reed parts were often repetitious and uninteresting. Franceschina added, "I don't recall musicians ever complaining about a Walker chart—and that's a pretty big feat!"

The complaints about Lang were exacerbated by the work of Lang's favorite copyist, Tom Brown. Even fans of Lang—like Don Pippin and Peter Howard—complained about Brown's parts, which were hard to read and full of wrong notes. Musicians generally play in extended phrases, so a good copyist is careful to either complete the phrase on one page or start it on the next. Brown paid no attention to this, nor did he use any of the tricks that make it simple to read and play music. Whenever Brown's name came up, it was in the context of "the worst copying in New York." Lang certainly heard the complaints, but for some reason he remained loyal to Brown for over twenty years.

The most outspoken viewpoint came from someone who frequently worked with Lang: "Phil was the notorious 'nothing' orchestrator, as most musicians feel. My theory is that he wrote so bland and so uninventively that it let the vocals come out plainly, and the lyricist[s] heard [their] lyrics so they thought the orchestration was good." This sounds a little strong to me, but it's from an accomplished pit musician who knows what he's talking about. While undoubtedly harsh, it is merely a variation on the other criticisms I heard.

While it seems like everybody is picking on poor Phil Lang, this is an accurate representation of what I heard. I asked everyone I interviewed for comments, positive or otherwise, on the various orchestrators with whom they had worked. Lang was mentioned again and again, more than Bennett, Walker, and the others combined—and most often in a negative light; this from people who almost universally expressed great personal fondness for him. Even so, I think I'll go listen to *Mack & Mabel*, *Li'l Abner*, and maybe even *Whoop-Up*.

Orchestrating *Mame* by Philip J. Lang

While Phil Lang is the only one of our orchestrators to bring forth such mixed opinions, he also seems to have been the most likable (perhaps tied in this by Russell Bennett). Right on cue, here comes Lang with the most illuminating overview of the process of orchestrating a Broadway musical that I've found in print. Well, it's the only such piece, but still. The following, written by Lang, was included in a long-out-of-print book called *Season In, Season Out,* a diary of the 1965–1966 season by Jack Gaver. Through the courtesy of Roger Lang, it is included here in its entirety.

> The music department of a Broadway show consists of the composer and lyricist (sometimes they are one and the same as in the cases of Jerry Herman or Bob Merrill); the orchestra conductor (sometimes also the choral arranger); the dance arranger; one or more rehearsal pianists; and the orchestrator. This group, having familiarized themselves with the script and music, may have many meetings prior to the first rehearsal.
>
> The purpose of these meetings is to establish the basic music style of the show. The period and locale of the action of the play are discussed in terms of music treatment. Obviously a song for *My Fair Lady* would not get the same musical treatment as one for *Mame.* The periods of these plays are many years apart and the locale of one is London; the other, Beekman Place, New York City. Essentially we are trying to do in music what the sets, costumes, and lighting accomplish in establishing period, locale, style, and mood. For example, a musical set in 1890–1900 would require a study of the songs of the Gay Nineties. The Roaring Twenties are immediately typified in songs like "Forty-Second Street" and "Tip Toe Through the Tulips," and the big bands of Glenn Miller and Benny Goodman are the unmistakable sound of the 1930s.
>
> Having established the style desired, the members of the musical department begin their separate functions. The conductor attends all try-outs, selects singers, and begins the choral arrangements. The dance arranger sketches his treatment of the composer's music for the approval of the choreographer. When the cast, singers, and dancers are assembled, the pianists rehearse them, separately and in groups, in the music they are to work with in the show.
>
> The first function of the orchestrator is to set the instrumentation of the orchestra. Within the producer's budget, he decides what and how many instruments are to comprise this group. The style of the show dictates his choice. For a classical musical, he will select symphonic instruments such as strings, harp, oboes, bassoons, etc. For a contemporary sound, he will lean toward saxophones, a guitar, and more brass instruments.
>
> The locale of the action also has a strong bearing on his selection. The time period might be the same for two plays, but whether they were set in New York, Paris, or Spain would have a great bearing on the instruments he chooses. *Fanny* included a concertina and mandolin, as re-

search revealed that they were the then predominant instruments in French seaport towns. *Can-Can* featured an accordion for the "streets of Paris" sound. A "tack" piano (mechanically treated for a "tinny" sound) was used in *Destry Rides Again* to suggest the atmosphere of a Western saloon and dance hall.

The orchestrator confers with the composer in the instrumentation of the orchestra, but he is rarely overruled, as he is painting the orchestral music and has the right to select his instrumental colors.

By now the production is fully cast and rehearsals have begun. As the director blocks each musical number, the orchestrator is called to the theatre. The number is performed for him, onstage, with piano accompaniment. He will want to know how the performer moves onstage (in relation to the foot microphones); a description of the costume and a clarification of the mood. He may request that the number be performed many times as he asks questions. His visits to the theatre will be frequent, perhaps every few days, getting routines on more vocals, production numbers, and finally—because they involve many members of the cast—the dance routines.

For the latter, the dance arranger will have a sketch of the music he has prepared for the choreographer. As the dance is performed, many other additional desires of the choreographer, such as lifts, groupings of dancers, counter-rhythm passages, are noted and incorporated into the sketch. At the end of the usual five-week rehearsal period, all the music of the show will have been performed and discussed with the orchestrator.

The craft of orchestration requires a complete familiarization with orchestral instruments, a feeling for the music at hand, and a theatrical experience to equate the music with the dramatic action. The orchestrator usually has a facility on the piano and may play many instruments, not necessarily well, but well enough to write intelligently for them. He dips into his orchestral colors (instruments) much the same as a painter makes selections from his palette.

Some instruments are strong, loud, and intense, such as trumpet, trombone, drums, etc. Others, such as strings, clarinet, and harp, are soft, tender, and capable of subtle shadings of dynamics. Within this oversimplification, the qualities can be reversed. The soft, tender strings can be written to produce a hard, strident sound, and the usually commanding brass instruments have a variety of mutes to temper their tone to a brittle chatter or a velvet glow.

The orchestrator has numerous devices at his command, for example, harmony and rhythm. A gay song identified with a performer, such as the title song of *Mame*, can undergo a harmonic change suggesting that the performer is unhappy or angry. Inversely, a sad song can be given a bright harmonization, sprightly rhythms with chattering flutes and harp runs, to illustrate a sudden lift of spirits in the character under-scored. Remember, the melody is never changed—its setting is altered. With the devices at his command, the orchestrator can create almost any mood desired.

Specifically, he does his work on what is called a "score page." This is a large sheet of paper with a musical staff for each instrument of the orchestra. Each score page usually consists of four measures of music, and he writes every note for each instrument, with all directions of tempi and dynamics. The copyist extracts a part for each instrument off this score page. The score is used by the conductor in working with the orchestra. It enables him to see what each player is playing.

The orchestrator, conductor, and composer usually leave two days before the company for the out-of-town theatre, where the orchestra is assembled and the music played. The cast then joins the orchestra for what is called the company reading, and the entire score is performed. This gives all concerned a chance to evaluate the orchestrator's work and occasionally suggest changes, a passage too loud here, a confusing rhythm there, etc. If the orchestrator has done his work well, the changes will be few and minor. If not, he is in for some sleepless nights, as the opening is usually but a few days away.

The theatre orchestrator is basically an accompanist and is largely concerned with providing a proper setting for the music and the performer. Similar to music for the films, most of it should be felt, rather than heard. If you are not conscious of the orchestra, the orchestrations are right; but if the orchestra demands your attention, it is exceeding its function and distracting or detracting from overall enjoyment of the show. The action must be supported, the mood underlined, tension heightened and climaxes underlined. However, the lyrics must be heard. In today's musicals, lyrics are an integral part of the book and delineate characters. Unless they are heard, a part of the action may be missed or a character lost.

While Lang's methods and goals (and results) were perhaps different from those of some of his peers, this is a concise and accurate description of the orchestration process.

"Don't Rain on My Parade" from *Funny Girl*. Music by Jule Styne, lyrics by Bob Merrill. Orchestration by Ralph Burns. Burns crams eight busy measures onto one score sheet (labeling it pages 8 and 9, as he got paid per four-measure page). The vocal line—without lyric—corresponds to the beginning of the refrain ("Don't tell me not to live ... "). Note the driving, three-note rhythm played through most of the sample, and the accented fill in the last two measures from trumpets, trombones, and French horn (abbreviated "f.h."). Used by permission of Jule Styne Enterprises. From the Music Division of the Library of Congress.

BRIDGE

The Art of Orchestration

SECTION I.
FROM SONG TO STAGE

Almost two hundred pages later, we find ourselves back with the same questions. What, precisely, does the orchestrator do? And what does he do that the composer doesn't?

The Composer and the Orchestrator (Should Be Friends)

The good orchestrator considers his job description to include supporting and enhancing the efforts of the composer wherever necessary, using musical language that echoes the original composition. Or at least sounds like it does. The relationship between orchestrator and composer is extremely close although somewhat one-sided—and there's the rub. The composer is the creative one, without whom there is nothing; but the "sweetest sounds" that emanate from the orchestra pit are sometimes several times removed from the composer's original manuscript.

The lyricist writes the lyrics and the singers sing them, and the audience hears the lyricist's words. The librettist writes the lines and the actors say them, and the audience hears the librettist's words. The composer's notes, however, are not so easily translatable; a considerable amount of work must be done before the music— even if it is *great* music—reaches the ears of the audience. This work is comprised of two somewhat interlocking stages, arrangement and orchestration. While some Broadway composers are excellent arrangers, orchestration is something few composers are capable of.

If the song is good, the composer deserves the praise. If the song *sounds* good—well, here comes that tricky question again. The melody played by the oboe and violins is incredibly lovely, but who devised that soaring countermelody played by the French horns? There is no reason that a man who can sit down and write "Some Enchanted Evening" need be self-conscious if he didn't devise the cello countermelody which fills in the second measure, while Ezio Pinza is holding his whole note. There is no question about the musicality and genius (if we wish to use that word) of Richard Rodgers. He had his pick of Broadway's finest orchestrators, choosing to work extensively with Spialek, Walker, and Bennett. Yet we find direct evidence of Rodgers turning on them all, including one episode during which he was so mad at Bennett that he more or less pulled his next orchestrator from the nearest street corner, an impetuous decision that ended with Bennett being hurriedly (and expensively) rushed in to salvage that particular show.

For every composer insecurely looking over the shoulder of his orchestrator, there is another who acknowledges and marvels over the work of his valued collaborator. In the course of my research, I spoke with just about every major Broadway composer of the 1940–1970 era who was still available to talk. Some saw their orchestrators as allies and collaborators. The two Jerrys, for example.

JERRY HERMAN: Phil Lang really captured me. I recognized it the day of the first orchestra reading for *Hello, Dolly!* I knew I had found a soulmate. Like the rhythm section of "Put on Your Sunday Clothes." I said, "I patterned this after the sound of horse's hooves on cobblestones, that's what I'm looking for." That's all I had to say. The first time I heard it, I walked over and gave him a hug because he had translated what was in my brains to those instruments. We got to the point where I would say, do it like you did in a certain passage of one of our shows. He'd just shake his head "yes," and it came out exactly like I envisioned it.

JERRY BOCK: When we opened *The Apple Tree*, I went over to Eddie Sauter with reverence and appreciation, and complimented him beyond measure on his contribution. Eddie, in his rather remarkable demure way, said everything he did was inherent in the piano-vocal score that was given to him. Now, that is modesty beyond belief! What he claimed was, he did my figures, but he converted and translated them into such a magical reincarnation of the piano-vocal score that it simply took off on its own. It was for me an extraordinary experience, an orchestrator translating the music.

Other composers, when questioned, responded with a litany of "that was my figure," "I wrote that countermelody," "I'm sure that fill was in my original piano part," etc., until I just stopped that line of questioning. I had several conversations like this with composers whom you might think had no reason to be defensive. (I quite obviously did not speak with Richard Rodgers, who died in 1979, but here's this from his daughter, Mary: "Daddy was peeved when Russell kept getting credit for the little, complicated things he put into the manuscripts. He bruised very easily, and was very unforgiving when Russell got too much praise.") I would guess this was not evasive self-deception on their part; after forty or fifty years of repeatedly hearing cast recordings and viewing numerous revivals, they might well believe that they wrote it all themselves. These same composers were the ones who invariably said, when I brought up a specific show, "remind me, who did the orchestrations on that?"—as if their orchestrators were so many interchangeable mechanics.

Let us turn back to Spialek, orchestrator of the great Rodgers & Hart musicals of the late 1930s until he was unceremoniously dropped by the composer. This was due, in part, to a newspaper review praising Spialek's contribution to Rodgers's 1939 ballet *Ghost Town*, which was presented at the Met by the Ballet Russe. Imagine! A composer incapable of orchestrating his own ballet!! The breakup severely affected Spialek's Broadway career, and he retained an understandable bitterness toward Rodgers. *On Your Toes* was revived in 1983, with Spialek supervising the reconstruction of his original orchestrations. He suddenly found himself, for the first time in his eighty-eight years, in the Broadway spotlight. When an interviewer commiserated about the lack of credit accorded orchestrators for their integral contribution to the shows, Spialek shot him down. "Don't you believe it," he said. "This was such wonderful music, the orchestrations wouldn't matter."

An Ancient Model

Lurking behind the composer-orchestrator question is the outdated yet persistent idea that "real" composers, really, ought to be capable of writing their own orchestrations. This can be dismissed, out of hand, as inapplicable and impractical to musical theatre of the twentieth century. It comes up so often, however, that it bears examination.

Composers of symphonic music and opera traditionally wrote their own orchestrations. The practice continued as opera moved to light opera and operetta. Sir Arthur Sullivan often (though not always) wrote his own for the classic series written from 1875 to 1889 with W. S. Gilbert. Franz Lehar, the composer of *The Merry Widow* and other Viennese operettas that swept across the West End and Broadway from 1902 through 1934, wrote his own orchestrations. Victor Herbert (active 1894 through 1924), the Irish-American composer of *The Red Mill* and *Naughty Marietta*, was the first in a string of innovative Broadway orchestrators—although his scores inevitably underwent last-minute rewriting by musical associates.

But Broadway musical comedy is a far different animal. Opera and even operetta are more focused on the score; the composer is the king, and the music is the thing. The composer would follow his muse, more or less conforming to standard vocal ranges, and would write his orchestrations as part of the creative process. By the time the cast and the rehearsals came along, the music was set and fully orchestrated. While changes were sometimes made during the production period—star singers can be temperamental, it seems—they were the exception rather than the rule, and the composer usually had time to score the new pages himself.

Broadway musicals, on the other hand, are—as they say—not written but rewritten. The music and lyrics are combined into a preliminary rehearsal script, but everything is subject to development along the way. Changes creep in, even before the cast is signed. As rehearsals proceed, songs are custom fit to the talents and abilities (and inabilities) of the performers. The libretto is typically the source of all problems, at least in the eyes of the songwriters. Script changes are common; major changes inevitably require changes to the score. And then there are the dances. In a very few cases, ballet music is written in advance, by the composer. Mostly, though, dance routines are worked out during rehearsals, with the dance arranger always a few steps behind the choreographer.

What this means, practically speaking, is that the job of the orchestrator cannot begin until the musical numbers are set, with exact routines and keys. Broadway musicals since 1940 generally start rehearsals five or six weeks prior to the first performance. The first finished numbers usually come along at the end of the second week of rehearsal, leaving a mere three weeks for most of the show to be orchestrated. (After which, the charts must be copied into separate parts for each musician and rehearsed prior to the first preview.) From the point that the first finished number is handed over, it becomes a game of catch-up, with additional routines handed to the orchestrator every day or so. The treadmill continues until the out-of-town opening; then, after a brief pause to breathe and absorb the tryout reviews, changes and rewrites start in earnest.

It is a general assumption—an accurate one—that most Broadway composers are incapable of orchestrating their scores. This is very much beside the point. An opera can, and perhaps should be, composer-orchestrated. In the musical theatre, there is simply no time for a composer—even a capable one!—to orchestrate his score. Broadway orchestrators need be versatile and resourceful, and also quick.

As deadlines loom, orchestration becomes a cramped and lonely work-through-the-night occupation; sixteen-hour days (and more) are the norm. In the three-week period during which much of the orchestration is done, the composer's time and energy are more properly concentrated on rehearsals.

The properly equipped composer can, indeed, do it himself. Kurt Weill is Broadway's exceptional exception to the rule. Weill began his career in Germany, where he regularly orchestrated his musicals and operas. When he arrived on Broadway in 1938, he saw no reason not to continue the practice. (Given Weill's ever-precarious financial condition—he was forced to abandon everything when he fled Germany—he apparently needed the not-inconsequential orchestrator fees.) At least some of his associates theorized that the high-stress, round-the-clock chore of orchestrating *Street Scene* (1947), *Love Life* (1948), and *Lost in the Stars* (1949) contributed to Weill's fatal heart attack soon after the opening of the latter.

Leonard Bernstein was unquestionably capable of orchestrating his scores, although he rarely did so (despite the credit on the title page). A few Broadway operas were orchestrated by their composers, including Gershwin's *Porgy and Bess* and presumably the assorted works of Gian Carlo Menotti. Walker, over the course of his career, wrote three (unsuccessful) Broadway musicals; Bennett wrote one. In these cases, they naturally served as their own orchestrators (albeit with assistance). But orchestration is not a skill in the typical Broadway composer's composer bench, and there is no reason that it should be. Even so, the finished orchestration remains—or, at least, should remain—a direct product of the composer's creation.

BENNETT: The vast majority of Broadway's tune writers didn't know their ankles from their uncles when it came to the orchestrations, and that's how we all got to a certain importance. There was probably never a tune writer in the world so simple-minded that he didn't have many ideas as to how the orchestra should sound playing his music, but the craft of putting the sounds on a piece of paper and having a bunch of musicians sound that way is something else.

The original inspiration, normally, comes through the original composer. Nearly all show composers carry around a conviction that everything in their score is their own creation, whether they write it down or not, and they are a lot nearer right than you might think. No matter how rich or poor a composer's idiom may be, a sensitive arrangement of his music is pretty well bound 'round by what the tune writer does.

Irving Berlin, working with the arranger, would sometimes stop at a chord and say, "Is that the right harmony?" We would say, "It's probably not the one you want. How about this?" We would strike a chord and he would say, "No, that's not it," or his face would light up and he'd say, "That's it!" Which means that his inner ear was way ahead of his fingers on the black keys of the piano. The right harmony, as he called it, was a part of the original inspiration, whether he could play it for you or not.

SECTION II.
THE ARRANGEMENT

The Song

It all starts with the song, which can be described—in words borrowed from Walker—as a musical idea developed into a complete and stable form.

This volume is not intended as a technical primer in orchestration, nor for that matter as a treatise on music theory; *The Sound of Broadway Music* discusses the work and careers of the major orchestrators of a certain period of the Broadway musical, along with the shows that they orchestrated. While these pages are presumably packed with information that will be of keen interest to professional musicians, my goal is to keep the discussion comprehensible to nonmusicians. Page after page of musical diagrams embedded in the text would only scare away many readers, so the choice has been made to proceed without any such examples. While there is theoretically a place for a complete and concise text on theatrical orchestration, this book is not intended as such.

How do you describe the writing of music without staffs and staves? Not as precisely as some might wish. Let us discuss the song, for example. A set of musical examples could present a clear and precise discussion of melody, rhythm, and harmony; clear and precise to people who read music, that is. In the case of this book, we will refer, as necessary, to examples we feel that average musical theatre fans are familiar with, and presumably have on their CD shelves. It is a given that the brows of the majority of people in America today would furrow if I asked them to reference the Overture to *Gypsy*. It is my supposition, however, that readers of these pages already know the Overture to *Gypsy*.

To illustrate the song, I refer not to a show tune but to a fragment of melody introduced in 1938 in a long-forgotten movie short. Hoagy Carmichael and Frank Loesser are two of America's top songwriters, but I don't suppose either expected their initial collaboration to become one of only two songs that can be played on the piano by people who can't play on the piano. If you know "Chopsticks," odds are that you know Hoagy and Frank's "Heart and Soul." The main strain, that is; has anybody out there ever heard the bridge? Be that as it may, "Heart and Soul" is second only to "Chopsticks" as a four-handed piano duet, and I will assume that everybody knows how it goes.

The melody (or tune) is played by the right hand of Player 1, who sits on the right side of the bench. "Heart and Soul / I fell in love with you" go Loesser's words. The melody of a song customarily comes from the highest notes being played on the piano at any given moment; this is not a rule by any means, but the notes in the two octaves above middle C usually make for clearer listening than the other ranges, while the fingers on the right hand—in this world of right-handed people—are the stronger.

The bass line (or foundation) is played by the left hand of Player 2, on the left side of the bench. In the standard four-handed duet, this is a one-fingered part; the player pounds out two syncopated Cs, two As, two Ds, and two Gs. These are the lowest notes being played at any given time, providing a firm ground for the listener's ear.

The accompaniment (or rhythm/harmony) is played by the right hand of Player 2. A chord, simply put, is a group of three or more musical notes, usually (but not necessarily) in a pleasing combination. Here, the lowest note of the chord is being played by the left hand of Player 2. The accompaniment fills in the middle, echoing the syncopated notes of the rhythm. Musical accompaniment tends to boil down to oom-pah, oom-pah; or, in the case of the waltz, oom-pah-pah. Viola players, especially, have been earning their rosin by playing the offbeats for years. But let's not jump ahead of ourselves.

The left hand of Player 2 keeps us on the beat, the right hand of Player 2 fills in the chords that were in the composer's mind, and the right hand of Player 1 gets the cushy part: the melody. In the case of "Heart and Soul," Player 1 sometimes uses the left hand to double the melody, playing the same notes an octave lower in order to make sure the tune gets over to the customers.

Our friend the composer, when writing a song, usually starts by devising a distinctive phrase of melody. The corresponding rhythm suggests itself somewhat naturally. In cases where the lyricist submits a completed lyric to the composer—as was the norm with the team of Hammerstein & Rodgers—it can be seen that the composer's rhythm might often be indicated by the lyricist's rhyme scheme. The composer who works at the piano typically writes in sections, going over and over a passage until he finds the combination that sounds right. With the top fingers of the right hand constantly repeating the same melodic phrase in search of what comes next, the other fingers of the fairly competent piano-playing composer typically find accompanying chords that fit. Happily, the perfect chord for the situation will often propel the top fingers into the next phrase of an inspired melody.

By the time the melody is finished, the composer usually has a pretty good idea of the rhythm and harmonies he or she has in mind. That is not to say that the composer can necessarily write down what she hears. As Bennett told us, Irving Berlin didn't know how to write it or describe it (or sing it)—but he knew it when he heard it. Frank Loesser, the lyricist of "Heart and Soul," converted himself into a rather exceptional composer; *The Most Happy Fella*, Broadway's most musical musical, is awash with lush harmonies. But talking to three of his musical assistants, we discover that Frank, like Irving, knew it when he heard it. And there was often a lot of yelling along the way.

Abba Bogin helped "take down" *The Most Happy Fella* and *Greenwillow*: "Basically, Frank was a guy who knew what he wanted, but he very often was not able technically to put it down the way he wanted it. When you played it back, he would listen and say 'That's not what I wrote, that's not what I want.' You would keep changing, until it was right."

Here again, we find ourselves in the discussion we had just moments ago. Berlin pounded out his songs in a fairly rudimentary manner, on a tricked-up, pentatonic pianner. Jerome Kern was far more capable, per Bennett: "Kern liked to improvise everything at the piano and then write it down, or have one of us write it down for him. He was very conscious of the basses and the harmonies under his tune. By the time he was satisfied with them, they were very hard to improve."

Jerry Herman composed his scores on the piano and would play them for assistants, who took them down and filled them in. Harvey Schmidt, too, couldn't notate his music; but anyone who has heard recordings of him at the piano will know that his orchestrators generally set precisely what he played. Schmidt told me that his first Broadway musical, *110 in the Shade*, was taken down by a pianist named Herb Schutz (just then playing *A Funny Thing Happened on the Way to the Forum*). A few days later, Herman told me, Schutz took down *his* first musical, *Milk and Honey*. (Don Pippin, musical director for *110 in the Shade* and many Herman shows, commented on the amount of arrangement provided by the composers: "Harvey, who didn't write down music, played much more orchestrally complete. Jerry, at the piano, could give you a feeling of the style he wanted. Phil or I would translate that into reality.")

Other composers have been even less musically adept. It is no secret that Richard Adler (winner of two Tony Awards for best score) and Bob Merrill (nominated for three) composed their melodies in their heads, demonstrating them on toy xylophones. Was Adler, Merrill, Berlin or Herman less of a musician than Leonard Bernstein? Or less of musicians than the fourth-string violinist sawing away in the pit of one of their musicals? Perhaps, depending on your definition. But the songwriters in question never claimed they were musicians. They've each got numerous swell songs to their credit, and the royalties to prove it.

Old-time orchestrators used to classify songwriters in one of two groups: the composers and the hummers. The orchestrators had a freer hand with the hummers, who were often happy for any help the orchestrators provided. But as Spialek points out: "a good song just played on a Jew's harp is still good. A bad song remains bad even if masterfully orchestrated and played by the 110-piece NBC orchestra under Toscanini."

Bennett expands on this:

> Those of us whose lot it has been to carry a thousand or more songs and dances to the orchestra have learned a lesson that keeps hovering over this entire monologue: the one thing an orchestration cannot furnish is *the music*. When Vincent Youmans composed the melody of "Tea for Two," he couldn't have written four measures of orchestration of anything, and yet what he did do is still the main and indispensable part of the hundreds of arrangements that followed. In other words, the music, however great or small, is what there is to say. The orchestration is how you say it.

It is safe to say that the composer does, indeed, compose the songs. He or she can't write, nor describe, a D♭ vii°; but the odds are that this is the sound he or she had in mind, at least vaguely, during the creation. We stray, though. Take the melody, add the bass line, and fill in the accompaniment (defining the rhythm and sketching the harmony). Put these together, and you've got your basic song, ready for treatment.

The Demonstration

Once a composer has written a song, he must demonstrate it. The lyricist needs to hear it repeatedly, of course, in order to write the words. If the words were written first, the lyricist still needs to hear it to evaluate how the words are set; the writers at this point might well choose to alter lyric or music for a better fit. Once the composer and lyricist (or the composer/lyricist) are satisfied, the song needs to be played for the librettist, the director, the producer, the choreographer, and on down the line. Typically, there are auditions for backers and theatre owners, publishers and record companies. Most keyboard-adept composers play their music again and again and again, often with the lyricist singing along. This culminates in what might be the most important demonstration, on the first day of rehearsals. The cast sits around a rehearsal hall with newly printed scripts in hand, reading their newly minted lines out loud. As the songs come along, everybody turns politely to the composer and lyricist.

And so they sing the new show tunes. But you don't get the version precisely as it will be sung onstage. You get, well, the melody (and lyric), accompanied by our old friends the rhythm and harmony. If there is a duet included in the number, the composer and lyricist might well give it a try, but this will no doubt be a user-friendly version, unless the composer and lyricist have vocal ranges that approximate those of the singers who will be performing the roles. Any dance sections included in the song will not be played, because they will at this point not have been devised. As for the actual notes the composer plays, these are restricted by the pianistic ability of the composer. All of this assumes the presence of a musically literate composer. When working with what the professionals call a hummer, the basic melody-rhythm-harmony parts inevitably bear the handprints of the pianist, musical director, vocal arranger, or *someone.*

This is the song in its presumably finished state, with the cast making a typically enthusiastic audience. (You can almost hear the wheels spinning in the cast's brains, secretly comparing the quality of their songs to everyone else's.) Over the first few days of rehearsal, private time is scheduled for the singers to meet with the musical director, and sometimes the composer, to start learning their songs. They work from a rehearsal copy of the song, which often tracks with what the composer demonstrated albeit with a more complicated piano part.

The Key

First things first. What key should the song be placed in? Back in opera days, the composer usually had a good idea of the key in which he intended his song to be sung. In the musical theatre world, though, shows are cast with—ideally—the best performer for the job, or at least the best performer available who will work for the money. While vocal ranges and styles are taken into account in the audition process, the exact key to be used is usually altered to suit the performer. Different keys have different natures, musically speaking; some keys are more ideal for evoking certain moods than others. And we should reiterate that, while the key may be altered, a change in range can be fatal; the role of Sweeney Todd can theoretically be altered so that it can be sung by a high tenor, but I don't think I want to hear it. Even so, the primary desire of the composer is that the singer can produce the notes, with the lyricist looking for the intelligible enunciation of the words. One step up, or a half-step down, can make the number that much better. It is up to the musical director and the vocal arranger (if any) to achieve this, sometimes with the composer in the room. As far as orchestration is concerned, nothing can be started until the key is set.

Some songs are easier to sing than others. "Just in Time," from *Bells Are Ringing*, was written for leading man Sydney (son of Charles) Chaplin, who had a treacherously narrow singing range; Jule Styne purposely devised a tune that repeated the same notes over and over again. Shortly thereafter, Styne wrote "Some

People" for Ethel Merman, with a range of an octave and a half, and "Don't Rain on My Parade" for Barbra Streisand, with a range of—well, who's counting?

A relevant story, in passing, from Styne:

> I told Betty and Adolph, "You know, Vincent Youmans is the greatest songwriter, and he used to write on a sequence on three or four notes," and I demonstrated with "Tea for Two" and "Time on My Hands." And I said, "I am going to write one with all half-steps, nothing but half-steps, all the way through." Betty said, "Well, won't it become monotonous?" Adolph said, "With the same half-step?" I said "It won't become monotonous because I will keep it harmonically attractive." That song became "Just in Time."

When your song spans more than an octave, you've got to place it where the singer can hit the notes. (When your song spans half an octave with an actor who can't sing, the correct key can be even more crucial.) When working with a woman, you've also got to deal with the chest voice and the head voice; simply put, there is a break where the vocal production audibly changes, and the trick is to avoid musical phrases traversing this gap as much as possible. "Glitter and Be Gay," from *Candide*, spans from B below middle C to the E♭ above the treble clef—a range of two and a half octaves. It is safe to say that when Barbara Cook stood in the rehearsal room back in 1956, they were careful to set the key in the best of all possible ranges, where she could ring out those high E♭s. Lower "Glitter and Be Gay" too much, though, and you lose the glitter.

Doesn't the composer dictate the key, you might ask? Kurt Weill did, probably; but the Broadway rehearsal period is all about making the material work to its best effect. In *Sondheim on Music: Minor Details and Major Decisions*, a 1997 series of interviews between the composer and Mark Eden Horowitz, Sondheim explained his choice of keys quite simply: he writes a song in a key that he can sing, knowing that he is going to need to demonstrate it over and over again before it finally reaches the rehearsal hall. When Sondheim prepared his manuscript for "The Worst Pies in London," he chose a key in which he himself could get through it at the piano. It was presumably not his intention, nor desire, that Angela Lansbury necessarily sing it in his range. In more legit musicals, Sondheim aside, keys (let alone registers) are sometimes indeed chosen because of the sound of their tonality. And yes, some composers will be very touchy about alteration of their "artistically" selected key.

There follows the story of a key, which might be illuminating—especially in that the song became a classic, launching a first-time-on-Broadway ingenue from Weatherford, Texas, to overnight stardom.

WALKER: Mary Martin was obsessed by the mistaken belief that her orchestration of "My Heart Belongs to Daddy" had been prepared for June Knight and hurriedly adjusted when June was replaced [during the 1938 tryout of Cole Porter's *Leave It to Me!*]. Such was not the case. The number had not been ready, and the orchestration was written especially for Mary. "Daddy" has the rather large range of an octave and a third. It is a stiff challenge to its interpreter because important lyrics lie both at the top and at the bottom of its compass; there is no place to cheat or slough off, every word has to be bravely projected. The key was crucial in determining audibility in the far reaches of the auditorium.

In Mary's case the key of B♭ minor was as low as she could go and still be heard and understood in the rear of the balcony. Near the end of the refrain, where at a thrilling moment the minor key suddenly becomes major, Mary had to reach a high D♮ . . . three times! [at "so I WANT TO WARN you, laddie"]. After a breath and a pickup, again that high D♮ had to be hit three more times! Then came the rapid descent to the final low B♭. When Mary went after those high D♮s no one, including Mary, knew exactly what would happen. One performance she would reach the Ds in her "chest" voice, the next night shift into "head." There were even times when she gave her audience a dollop of both. No wonder she wanted to lower the key.

This was a suggestive song from a naïve young girl, complete with a mock striptease. The very tentativeness visible on Martin's face (and on the faces of her four backup dancers, who were wondering if she'd make it) as she reached the climax apparently added much to the humor of the moment; nobody, including the composer, *cared* if Mary's voice cracked. Except Mary. She fought to have the key lowered, but the powers that be said it was impossible. Blaming it on the orchestrator. "From that time on," said Walker, "whenever I encountered Mary, the thermometer seemed to drop suddenly."

Duets have a different key problem: how do you find a key that works for both the boy and the girl? Enter the arranger's best friend, the modulation. The girl will sing her refrain; there will be a stretch of music, often with a few words of dialogue or a bit of staging or dance, and then the orchestra might innocently play a chord progression that leads us to the boy's key.

"Lovely," from *A Funny Thing Happened on the Way to the Forum*, gives us six bars of underscoring. (During this, the boy asks the girl to say his name, which she has already forgotten.) A mellow musical phrase is repeated on different tones, allowing the arranger to surreptitiously slip into a new key for the boy. "Sixteen Going on Seventeen," from *The Sound of Music*, follows the boy's refrain with a seventeen-bar soft-shoe dance break. The last four bars repeat the same figure four times, from different tones, resolving naturally enough into the girl's key. "Tonight," from *West Side Story*, works in reverse; in order to accommodate the not-especially-strong singers who originated the roles—they needed to sing high and soft at the end of the number—the key was lowered in stages, starting in B♭, moving to A, and ending in A♭.

Setting the Routine

The song, as written and demonstrated, is usually a straightforward affair; it starts, it continues, it ends. (Even at this early stage, there might be a written-in modulation or two.) Onstage, any number of things can happen. There could be dialogue incorporated into the number, either at the beginning or during the song; there could be blocking—a performer crossing from one part of the stage to another, someone moving to pick up a prop, a bit of a costume change—that needs extra music. Many numbers, especially in post-1960 musicals, incorporate dance, movement, and even scenic movement.

The basic material of the song, thus, is reordered into a routine. Verse–refrain–dance–refrain makes a fairly reasonable, if generic, routine. Let us consider a standard love duet, "People Will Say We're in Love," from *Oklahoma!* (1943). The song was written as a simple verse and refrain for the girl, followed by a verse and refrain for the boy. As performed in the original production, it starts with a leisurely four-chord progression. Laurey starts her verse with a question ("why do they think up stories?"). Curly sings the second line of the verse with his own question, about the neighbors gossiping; this is as if to say, the soprano is doing the first part but don't forget I'm here. Laurey sings the rest of the verse and the whole of the first refrain. Lyricist Hammerstein gives Curly a spoken gag line during the refrain ("who laughs at yer jokes?"), keeping him in the picture; but the first half of the routine is almost all Laurey. After a simple two-bar ending, Curly launches into his verse and refrain. This is a direct duplicate, with no change in key (or orchestration) other than Laurey joining Curly for the final six words—the title phrase—of the refrain.

That is the end of the initial presentation of the song as written. After applause, the number continues. While the orchestra plays, the villainous Jud enters; Curly asks Laurey to rescind her acceptance of Jud's invitation to the box social; Laurey insists that she will go with Jud; Curly exits to visit Jud in the smokehouse; Laurey watches him exit, starting to cry. All of this is accompanied by the orchestra playing the first sixteen bars of the refrain (the A section). Laurey picks up the lyric for the second A section, but doesn't get all the way through; she breaks down after thirteen bars, at which point Aunt Eller gives her a hanky. During the B section, Laurey runs off, still crying. The song (and the scene) ends with Aunt

Eller lookin' at the serious romantic tribulations of the young 'uns, humming the last bars of the melody as the orchestra builds to a grand finish.

Rodgers and Hammerstein, sitting at their respective worktables, wrote what we hear before the break for applause. The rest—a partially sung combination of song, dialogue, and action—was presumably worked out by director Rouben Mamoulian and musical director Jay Blackton in the rehearsal room. While nominally one piece, the scene was orchestrated in two sections, by two different orchestrators. Bennett did the important, earlier section—which is really only a verse and a refrain, repeated without orchestral changes. The latter half was handed off to an assistant, which allowed Bennett to concentrate on the next song that came out of the rehearsal hall.

"I'll Know," from *Guys and Dolls* (1950), makes another typical example. This number has a verse, once again split between the soprano Sarah—who will own the first half of the song—and her suitor. Sky Masterson's part of the verse is sarcastic, about a Scarsdale Galahad, which sets up the difference between the doll and the guy. The verse is connected to the refrain by a two-bar link, with a brief exchange of dialogue ("You certainly have him all figured out"). Sarah's refrain ends with a modulation directly into a lower key for Sky, who takes up his verse and refrain. Once again, the two come together at the end, with a brief coda in two-part harmony.

But it's not always so simple. "Some People," from *Gypsy* (1959), begins with Rose barking out a couple of short lines of dialogue between orchestral stings, launching immediately into the refrain. There is then an interlude, the "I Had a Dream" motif that will recur elsewhere in the score. This section dissolves into a two-line interchange of dialogue ("you ain't getting 88 cents from me, Rose") between the star and her father, over a repeated one-bar vamp carried over from the end of the interlude. There is then what might be termed a grand, four-bar windup, as the father exits and Rose prepares for battle. The song continues with a new, eight-bar section ("goodbye to blueberry pie"), a repeat of the previously heard stop-time section ("all the socials I had to go to"), and then a final statement of the main theme. Midway through, the tag begins ("They can stay and rot!"), after which the lyric halts while the music continues. Rose crosses to the mantel, snatches her father's gold plaque (for hocking), and returns center—a process which takes eight bars of music—before she finally sings her last three words ("but not Rose").

Jule Styne presumably turned in the song straight through, in whatever key he happened to choose; as a longtime vocal coach—he taught Shirley Temple, which was no picnic—he might well have chosen a key that he knew would work for Merman (another former client of his). As it is, Styne tailored the song to Merman's style; the bridge features ten-beat notes for her to hold ("but IIIIIII—at least got-ta TRYYYY") followed by that section in syncopated stop-time. The dialogue might well have been written into the original song, although the under-scoring and timing was presumably worked out during rehearsal. (You can almost hear Jerry Robbins saying, "All right. Pop, you exit here. Ethel, go pick up the bag. And you"—turning to the dance arranger, who happened to be John Kander— "I need some beats.")

The business at the end is deliciously contrived, presumably by the lyricist or librettist. (From the script: "She starts out, takes the plaque from the wall, dumps it in her purse, then finishes her song.") But it all came together in the rehearsal hall. It might be noted that this business wasn't all that new; in the prior Styne-Robbins musical, *Bells Are Ringing*, the leading lady had the same type of trick end-ing with a full-stage cross for her eleven o'clock song, "I'm Going Back."

Vocal Arrangement

Anytime someone is singing, the notes in themselves constitute a vocal arrange-ment of the song. The simplest vocal of all is the melody, as handed over by the composer. This is more likely to be the case with a solo. One person sings it as the composer wrote it, transposed perhaps to a more suitable key. Bring in an-other singer, or two, or twelve, and the vocal part often needs to be adjusted.

A few composers specialize in multivoice vocals; the majority, though, simply write their songs and send them in. The adaptation to specific performers is usu-ally the province of the musical director, who works things out in the rehearsal hall. Broadway developed a tradition of grand vocal arrangements, with twelve or sixteen singers coming on—after the stars have introduced the song—and enter-taining the customers with refrain after refrain. The operettas of the twenties, es-pecially, were known for their stout-hearted choruses; the Shuberts built their em-pire on all those boys ringing the rafters with drinking songs, fighting songs, and more. But these were relatively simple vocals: The melody magnified by num-bers—all those tenors, say—with simple harmonies provided by the rest. The sit-uation changed abruptly, and not with a chorus of fifty but with three skinny girls. Well, two skinny girls and one of the Kate Smith school.

Hugh Martin was a backup singer for arranger Kay Thompson in the Harold Arlen/Yip Harburg musical *Hooray for What!* (1937). When Thompson was fired during the tryout, Martin remained with the show, which was a moderate hit. The swing band sound was just then beginning to invade the Broadway orchestra pit, and about time. But why were Broadway vocals so behind the times? Martin wondered. With the brash assurance of youth, he sent a letter posing that question to Broadway's most active composer at the time, Richard Rodgers. Rather than simply dropping the letter into the circular file from whence no answer emerges, Rodgers summoned Martin to the stage door of his then-rehearsing *The Boys from Syracuse* (1938). Hugh was given a song manuscript and told, more or less, "Prove it."

The song, "Sing for Your Supper," was a tuneful ditty for the show's three female leads. Martin took the simple sixteen-bar verse and split it in three. Adriana (the neglected wife) got the first line and held her note while Luciana (the ingenue) sang her line; they continued to hold their notes as Luce (the butterball comedienne) sang her line, after which they sang the fourth in three-part harmony. The next three lines were similarly divided, with the verse ending on yet another set of three-part chords.

The first refrain was sung straight through by Adriana. With a simple two-measure progression, Martin modulated from G♭ to C for Luce's second, swingier refrain. (This refrain starts on an E, as opposed to Adriana's, which began four and a half tones higher on B♭. And if you should find these Cs and G♭s hieroglyphical, dear reader, no matter; simply note that Martin changed key at will, to build the excitement and accommodate his vocalists.) The fills, here, are taken up by Adriana and Luciana. Hart's lyric tells us that "songbirds always eat if their song is sweet to hear"—that's all Martin needs to hear. That same two-bar modulation takes us up to D♭ for the third refrain—but only for the first eight bars, sung by all three girls. Martin almost immediately swings into D. All three girls sing the next eight bars, and then hand off the melody lines for the bridge. The next four bars they sing together, launching into a wild twenty-two-bar tag that includes songbird solos for each and winds up with a big band rideout. Martin devised this, he tells us, at the request of orchestrator Spialek, who had no big band experience. Martin also tells us that Rodgers used to call Hans "the bouncing Czech."

This was not only a vocal arrangement, with vocal notes augmenting the melody, nor merely an elaborate routine, building numerous vocal and instrumental refrains from the original song. This was a full treatment, with the arranger given free rein to improvise upon the melody (as in the scat sections), modify the tempo, and actually—after the initial statement of the material—alter the composer's rhythm.

"Sing for Your Supper," itself, is a perfectly nifty song. In the context of the show, the Martin arrangement makes it soar in a way that a straight rendition couldn't. Comparing the notes in the arrangement to the notes in the original song, you find that the basic melody, rhythm, and harmony remain the work of

Rodgers. Much of what the girls sing, though—all that songbird trilling, plus two of the three parts in the harmony sections—is Martin. The rhythm has been subverted, or sparked, here and there, giving the song an authentic big band treatment; Rodgers's harmonies have not so much been changed as expanded with "modern" colors. The tag is presumably all Martin, including the melodic phrase and lyric ("You don't have to buy even a crumb of bread, it's said") and the trio's trilling. Due credit seems to go to Martin; however, he would be the first to say that it is all Rodgers. What Martin did was take the song, embellish it, swing it, and expand it; but to coin a Porter phrase, he remained true to it, darling, in his fashion. Martin's work is all dressing, of a dazzling variety. Remove the music of Rodgers, though, and there is nothing.

What Martin wrought was a smashing show-stopper. While vocal arrangements in earlier musicals had stopped the show—bravura operetta duets and all those male choruses in *The Desert Song*, *The Student Prince*, and others—here were three women swinging the auditorium into delirium. Broadway immediately took note. Martin was quickly assigned similar numbers by Rodgers, Berlin, Porter, and Duke, and in 1940—just two years after "Sing for Your Supper"—Martin was hired by Rodgers and George Abbott (producer-director of *The Boys from Syracuse*) to write a musical of his own, *Best Foot Forward*.

Let it be added that all of the composers mentioned above welcomed Martin's changes and alterations to their songs—save Berlin of *Louisiana Purchase*.

MARTIN: "That's not bad," Berlin commented, "but there are lyrics in there that I didn't write." I was surprised. "They're not part of your song, Mr. Berlin. They're part of the arrangement. And very insignificant; usually just a transition or a modulation to get back to the song itself." Berlin said, "Listen to me, my young friend. When people come to the Imperial Theatre to buy tickets for this show, what does the marquee tell them about who wrote the lyrics?" Irving Berlin, of course. "Then those customers are entitled to hear lyrics by Irving Berlin, not Hugh Martin." I was chagrined. None of my other heroes had suggested anything like that; they had accepted my lyrics without a murmur. But of course, I did as he asked. He wrote the necessary lyrics, and they fit the music perfectly. In fact, they were better than the ones I had written—which really bugged me.

Martin had an unusual career, combining work as a songwriter (five musical comedies, plus MGM's 1945 Judy Garland vehicle, *Meet Me in St. Louis*), vocal arranger (at MGM and on Broadway), and accompanist (including Garland's legendary 1951 appearance at the Palace). Sandwiched between these chores was a series of Broadway vocal arrangement jobs in the late forties and early fifties.

Martin's vocal arrangements during this spell are easily among the best Broadway has heard. *Gentlemen Prefer Blondes* (1949) might have the finest set of any Broadway musical, ever. (A live performance tape of the post-Broadway tour offers evidence that the audience actually disrupted the show to applaud the chorus.) We shall never hear such luscious vocal arrangements on Broadway again, and for good reason; Martin had sixteen real singers, while choreographer Agnes de Mille had twenty-four dancers who could dance. The body count was supplemented by six showgirls who, well, did neither. An ensemble of forty-six, as opposed to later full-scale musicals like *My Fair Lady* (1956), with thirty-six; *How to Succeed in Business Without Really Trying* (1961), with twenty-four; and the budgetarily challenged *Pippin* (1972), which made do with ten Fosse bodies doing all the ensemble singing and dancin'. Martin, in most of his musicals, had sixteen singers, enough for double quartets of both men and women. Gone are the days.

The all-time most famous Broadway vocal arrangement, perhaps, is the "O-K-L-A-H-O-M-A" chant from *Oklahoma!* The case bears examination, in that it helps to demonstrate just what a difference an arrangement can make. It is common knowledge that the show (under the title *Away We Go!*) opened poorly in New Haven, and that it was fixed and renamed in Boston. "Oklahoma," a paean to the Sooner State—the musical is set in 1907, at the time the former Oklahoma Territory achieved statehood—started out as a grand affair in the eleven o'clock slot. The song was introduced by leading man Alfred Drake, followed by an apparently breathtaking display of athletically acrobatic de Mille dancing from Marc Platt and Eric Victor. The number, we are told, was excellent, but it simply wasn't landing—perhaps because it came at the tail end of the evening, the musical comedy witching hour when audiences are willing to be roused but don't want to sit back and watch another production number. (Director Rouben Mamoulian: "I said, 'We are repeating ourselves. What we need here is a rousing choral number, not a dance number.' Agnes could have killed me.")

At a matinee late in the Boston run, the creators hit upon the problem and decided to try "Oklahoma" without the dance. Alfred sang his verse and chorus; the full company repeated the chorus, all on the melody; and that was it. This seemed to work better, so Rodgers called Bennett—who was already back in Manhattan—and asked him to patch together a quick vocal arrangement. The dance was retired; Victor, who unlike Platt was not featured in the first act ballet, packed his lasso and went home.

Bennett thought through the night and entrained for Boston the next morning. By the time he reached Old Saybrook, Connecticut, he had his eight-part vocal pretty much down on paper—including that cannily devised "spelling lesson" tag which sixty-odd years later still never fails to get the audience roaring.

Arriving at the Colonial, Bennett handed the arrangement to conductor Jay Blackton (at the time, Jacob Schwartzdorf). Blackton taught it to the company by rote—there were no copies other than Bennett's handwritten original—while Rodgers, Hammerstein, director Mamoulian, and choreographer de Mille stood by. (The latter was indeed fuming, realizing that her big showpiece was in the process of being ousted in favor of a bunch of singers clumsily stepping down to the footlights.) As soon as the parts were learned, Mamoulian staged the number. Bennett, meanwhile, did a rush orchestration—music copyists at his side, working page by page—and the song made Broadway history.

The number was infinitely more effective with the vocal arrangement than without; the vocal arrangement contained significant new material, in the form of that exhilarating tag; and everybody went home ecstatically happy, especially the audience. The vocal arrangement was devised—and that O-K-L-A-H-O-M-A chant written—by Bennett, yes; but that spelling lesson would have been meaningless without the music by Rodgers (and Hammerstein's use of the state's name as the song title).

An arrangement story that is very much beside the point but too amusing to overlook comes from Kostal's Hollywood adventures with *Mary Poppins*:

> In "Just a Spoonful of Sugar," Julie [Andrews] goes to a window and sees two birds in a nest, and while she sings, the birds whistle. Their whistling is part of the song. When I came home, I told my wife, Sylvia, about this lovely scene and she remarked, "both birds shouldn't sing. Only the male sings." The next time I saw Walt Disney I told him what Sylvia had said. Walt's answer was direct and to the point: "Go home and tell your wife that in Disney movies, all birds sing."

This brief discussion of vocal arrangements has only peripherally touched on the vocal arrangers themselves. They are duly credited in the show listings, and many have been discussed—at least briefly—in the biographical section. It seems fitting, though, to run them together through a paragraph. Martin, who more or less originated the craft of vocal arrangement on Broadway, was a singer-turned-composer. He was assisted on numerous shows by Buster Davis, who took over the Jule Styne account and was responsible for many vocals from the 1950s into the 1970s. Inevitably, Buster moved up to the conductor's podium, despite—as he admitted—no training in the field. (It should be added that the musical directors of old were erstwhile symphonic conductors, trained in the classics. Beginning in the 1950s, a new breed of Broadway-trained conductors were developed out of the ranks of rehearsal pianists and, yes, vocal arrangers.) Herbert Greene, too, started in the chorus—of *On The Town*—and worked his way to vocal arranging and conducting. Jay Blackton, Milton Rosenstock, and Lehman Engel, on the other hand, were trained conductors who displayed special ability with vocals. The last of the expert conductor/vocal arrangers was Donald Pippin, who came along in the early sixties. The prevalence of strong Broadway vocals diminished along with the size of the singing chorus.

Composer Vocals

A good vocal arrangement, though, remains just that. A composer writing chorally—an inventive composer, that is—can come up with something that is not only vocally adventuresome but, with the help of the lyricist, integrated with the action of the show.

Bernstein and Sondheim's so-called "Tonight Quintet" from *West Side Story*, for example. (The number is officially called "Tonight," with the classic duet version of the song entitled "Balcony Scene.") Three of the leads (Tony, Maria, and Anita) each have their own sections, while two others (Riff and Bernardo) sing backed by their gangs of Jets and Sharks. This is not a mere choral embellishment of a song; the "Quintet" drives the plot forward into the next scene, "The Rumble," which ends the first act and forces the action of the second.

Writers of integrated musicals began to see their singers as characters in their own right. Take a specialty number like Jerry Bock's "Politics and Poker," from *Fiorello!* This is a song for one of the main characters, Ben, and five unnamed political hacks (First Cardplayer, Second Cardplayer, etc.). The singers are not graced with character names, but they are nevertheless specifically voiced. (One of them is indeed named, but solely for a laugh. With everybody trying to come up with "some qualified Republican who's willing to lose," one sings, "How about Ed Peterson?" Ed, the high tenor of the group, shouts him down with "You idiot, that's me!") The song is constructed on the lines and jokes that are built into the lyric; this is not merely a number for star and chorus. *Fiorello!* had a second song for the same group, "Little Tin Box," which indeed included some barbershop-like writing and was very much a showpiece for six characters as opposed to a choral ensemble. This last was, perhaps, inspired by a similar item from a then-running show from the same producers, "Gee, Officer Krupke," from *West Side Story.*

While *The Sound of Broadway Music* has chosen to concentrate on the pre-*Company* era, it would be remiss not to acknowledge how Sondheim has contributed to the change. He has again and again constructed musical scenes using his entire cast not as ensemble but as characters, in multipart vocals such as "A Weekend in the

Country," from *A Little Night Music*, and "Sunday," from *Sunday in the Park with George*. Most remarkable, perhaps, is "Simple," a seven-section, thirteen-minute, cacophonous whirlwind from the 1964 musical *Anyone Can Whistle*.

A Sondheim or a Bock, when faced with something like "Do-Re-Mi," from *The Sound of Music*, might well have written the whole thing himself. Rodgers did not. He provided the song we all know and presumably love, but Trude Rittman—a somewhat anonymous arranger who created some of Broadway's most effective musical moments of the forties and fifties—provided the extended scene between Maria and the children. According to assistant conductor Peter Howard, the heart of the number—in which Maria assigns a musical tone to each child, like so many Swiss bell ringers—was devised in rehearsal by Rittman (who was credited for choral arrangements) and choreographer Joe Layton. The fourteen-note tune and lyric—"when you know the notes to sing . . . "—were provided by Rodgers and Hammerstein; the rest, apparently, came from Rittman. Howard: "Rodgers allowed her to do whatever she liked. When we started doing the staging of it, Joe took over. He asked Trude for certain parts to be repeated, certain embellishments."

By this time, the era of calling in arrangers for this sort of extended number (as opposed to mere choral embroidery) was ending. Charles Strouse's "Telephone Hour," from *Bye Bye Birdie* (1960) is a chorus number, but it is written as a string of small solos, duets, and boys-against-the-girls. This is not a song that a clever arranger can assemble from an original tune by the composer; this is a concerted number, with the lyric steeped in plot information, which only the songwriter can devise.

As musicals became more integrated, they called for greater specificity in the construction of vocals. The days when a chorus would traipse in and take over are long gone—or are they? While Sondheim changed (almost) everything, Jerry Herman's choral numbers—through *Dolly*, *Mame*, and *La Cage aux Folles*—continued to be built by arrangers (usually Don Pippin) upon the same effective patterns. As long as there are enough voices to sing them, a good rousing old-fashioned vocal arrangement still has an effect.

Dance Arrangement

If vocal arrangements more or less follow the general pattern set by the composer, dance arrangements are considerably further removed. And with good reason. The songs are written, ideally, before the show goes into rehearsal. Dance music cannot be devised until the choreographer and dancers are hired and in the rehearsal hall. Most, though not all, dance music is derived from the songs written for the score. It is not impossible for the composer to sit at the piano beside the choreographer and devise the dances. Time, conditions, and circumstances being what they are, though, the composer almost always hands over the chore—and is more than glad to do so. Kander: "The reason a composer, for the most part, is not his own dance arranger is that it's a full-time job. You would be spending all day long with the choreographer."

Some dance arrangements are merely interludes within vocal numbers, which can be relatively simple to devise. More complicated dances and production numbers are something else again. The choreographer and dance arranger often sketch these numbers thematically; work them in sections, with the dancers; and then, once the ideas formulate, assemble the pieces. Some dance arrangers improvise on the spot, using themes from the composer's tunes; others simply play the equivalent of "dummy" tunes, accommodating the choreographer's tempos and the dancers' accented beats. They then go home, after hours, and jigsaw the songs from the show into the preordained beats. (Dance arranger Roger Adams told fellow arranger Johnny Morris that, at one point during rehearsals of *Me and Juliet*, Rodgers came over to him and said, "Let's have less of you and more of me.")

This is exacting work. A song might well have been composed in an hour or two; the vocal routine, as well, can be set in a one-hour session with the singers. The corresponding dance arrangement, however, can take twelve or fifteen hours' worth of rehearsal time over the span of a week, during which the arranger/piano player sits there repeating that old five–six–seven–eight. It is no wonder that most composers—even those who fret and fuss over just about every aspect of production—rarely bother with the dance arrangements.

> CHARLES STROUSE: Sometimes, and I think most of the times, the noncomposer of the show is better than the composer for doing dance music. In dance music, you have to be kind of a slave to the choreographer. The choreographer, while they're working, wants a step that goes "ta-TUMP, ta-TUMP." So you sit at the piano, there's a lot of tension, a lot of people waiting around, and so you play "ta-TUMP." He says, "That's it!" They rehearse to it, and that becomes the thing. You, as the arranger, wish in a way that you didn't write "ta-TUMP"— but by the time you get to the "ta-TUMP" all the dancers are singing it, and everyone's doing it. So you let it go. In my opinion, most of the dance music is bad. It's like improvisation; but it's not, exactly. You're listening to a lot of creativity from the choreographer, you're listening to dancers saying, "Oh, yeah," and then everybody's out there doing it. And that's it.

While most composers gave the dance arranger free rein, others—perhaps self-conscious about the way the rest of the show was going—were territorial. Such was the case of Arthur Schwartz vs. Genevieve Pitot on *By the Beautiful Sea*, as related by choreographer Donald Saddler:

> There was a marvelous dance in the first act, a slow adagio. Peter Gennaro and Maria Karnilova were the lead dancers. At the orchestra reading in New Haven, all the musicians applauded Pitot. Arthur Schwartz was furious—particularly because they had all cheered, "Bravo, Pitot." He complained to me, "She has taken my music and changed it!" In all the revues he had done, they had just taken the songs and repeated them for the dances. Arthur was furious. "By the time we get to New York," he told me, "every note that woman has written will be out."

Saddler went on to praise his favorite dance arranger:

> Pitot was just a genius. She was from New Orleans, she knew jazz so wonderfully. Anything that you wanted to do, it was all right with her— as long as you told her when you were going to go for the ending. She would say, "Now this isn't what it's going to be like. But I'll play this now, while you're choreographing." The next day, she'd come in with something she wrote that fit exactly. The only thing, she'd always ask, "Now are you going for the ending? I have to start building." She was a great inspiration for me. I'd get up and demonstrate a step, she caught it all.

Before he got his first Broadway composing job, John Kander had two very different dance-arranging assignments. A replacement pit pianist on *West Side*, he was invited to work on the next Robbins musical, *Gypsy*.

> KANDER: The music was all based on vaudeville; the dance arrangements were basically extensions of the songs as they would be performed in a vaudeville situation, according to Jerry Robbins's staging. In the next musical I did, *Irma La Douce*, there were long sections of the "Freedom of the Seas Ballet" where the choreographer wanted to go off and do a whole other thing, which sometimes didn't relate to the song. So what I did to that was a much more creative kind of thing. It wasn't taken from the composer; it was Onna White saying, "John, play some penguin music."

This last show was an import of a London adaptation of a Parisian musical. Which is to say that the composer—Piaf collaborator Marguerite Monnot— was across the sea from the rehearsal room, and none the wiser.

> SAMUEL "BIFF" LIFF: *Gentlemen Prefer Blondes* was the first time I realized how complex an aspect the dance part of it was, and how important the dance arranger was to the show. As assistant stage manager, I was with Agnes de Mille most of

the time, and so I was very familiar with how she worked together with the dance arranger. Agnes had Trude Rittman, and Trude was with her all the time. The music was developed using the themes. The dance arranger is taking somebody else's music and working it in, all during the rehearsal. Changing the music! Agnes did *Oklahoma!* and *Carousel*, and it's amazing to me that Dick Rodgers allowed her to adapt his music. The same thing happened with *My Fair Lady*. Trude and Fritz Loewe had a very close relationship; he let her write the dance music herself. Or, think of Gower Champion and Peter Howard. They would sit in the room while Gower was doing a number, and finally he would turn to Peter and say, "This is what I want to hear."

The relationship between choreographer and dance arranger is close, far closer than the relationship between choreographer and composer. Choreographers are not necessarily the most verbal individuals; they tend to speak in beats and accents, rather than descriptive adjectives. The successful dance arranger is one who can translate what the choreographer wants; while the composer typically staffs his shows, the choreographer usually has the choice of dance arranger written into his or her contract. Agnes de Mille—after *Oklahoma!*—found the aforementioned Trude Rittman working for Balanchine's company, Ballet Caravan. She brought her in on *One Touch of Venus*, and used her on subsequent shows. (Rodgers and Loewe were so impressed with Rittman that they continued to use her, even on non–de Mille shows.) When they had a choice, Michael Kidd worked with Genevieve Pitot; Jerome Robbins with Betty Walberg; Bob Fosse with Roger Adams; and Gower Champion with Peter Howard.

Some composers—a very few—created at least some of their dance arrangements. Kurt Weill is generally assumed to have written everything that came to Broadway under his name, although he didn't write the ballet and major dances in at least one—and possibly both—of his dance-heavy musicals. Leonard Bernstein wrote the ballet music for *On the Town* and *West Side Story*, his two dance shows (but not for all his musicals).

SADDLER: Bernstein came into *Wonderful Town* late, when they changed the composer. The last dance was "Ballet at the Village Vortex." He said to me, "I'm behind so I'm going to give you the tempo. Then you just go ahead and do what you want. But keep track of the number of beats that you're going to use." We finished the number, he came in and watched. Every once in a while I saw him jot down something. At the orchestra run-through, it just fit like a glove. There were moments when a girl would be lifted up, then slither down. It was all in the music.

One of Broadway's legendary ballets (and there aren't many) was Jule Styne and Jerome Robbins's "Bathing Beauty Ballet," in the 1947 musical *High Button Shoes*. Musical director Milton Rosenstock told Lehman Engel about the creation:

Jule kept calling guys in. I said, "No, this is your show." Then I told Robbins, "Look, this guy pisses melodies. You just sit down, he will give you fifteen songs in about twenty minutes. All you have to do is edit it. Tell him to make it a little longer, a little shorter." So the ballet music actually was Jule doing it, but Jerry saying, "I need something, okay, like that," and they went through the whole ballet.

The program includes the credit "Ballet music by Mr. Styne. Assistant to Mr. Styne, Jess Meeker." We can take this to mean that Styne pounded away at the piano for twenty minutes; Meeker took down the tunes; and the actual ballet was painstakingly routined in the rehearsal hall by Robbins, with Meeker slavishly chained to the piano. (Genevieve Pitot is in some places credited for this ballet, but she apparently did not personally claim involvement. The attribution is almost certainly erroneous.)

The first important Broadway ballet was "Slaughter on Tenth Avenue," from *On Your Toes*, which Richard Rodgers—working with choreographer George Balanchine—apparently composed himself. (If it seems like we keep returning to Rodgers, there is a reason: he was arguably the most successful, the most popular, and the most influential composer on Broadway for at least a quarter-century. He was also one of the most powerful producers; as already seen, he played the central role in the remarkable tale of the orchestration of *Annie Get Your Gun*, a musical that he didn't even write!)

It is unknown who wrote the ballets in the other Rodgers-Hart-Balanchine musicals, but Rodgers definitely did not write the ballets (or dance music) for any of the Rodgers and Hammerstein shows. Why wouldn't the composer of "Slaughter on Tenth Avenue" choose to write the ballets for *Oklahoma!* and *Carousel*? Bruce Pomahac asked Rittman, who worked on four Rodgers shows. Her response was something to the effect that there was no way that Rodgers would have wanted to sit, day after day, in a small rehearsal room alone with Agnes de Mille.

DE MILLE: Dick would give us a song and say, expand this to two or three minutes. Someone like Trude Rittman actually composed—not an accompaniment—she composed the ballets, in collaboration with the choreographer. And we don't get any of the shares. . . . The end of the first act of *Oklahoma!* originally had a circus dream, with Aunt Eller on a surrey of diamonds and gold, with beautiful white horses, and Laurey on a trapeze. I said to Oscar, "Girls don't dream like this." He said, "They don't?" Finally, I came up with a new version, "Laurey Makes Up Her Mind." I wrote out a scenario, handed it to Dick. He said, "I will read it later." I asked him for music. He said, "You've got the songs, what else do you want?" I would say, "I'm going to use this piece of this song"; he'd say, "fine."

They had no music for the end of the dream ballet, but Rodgers refused to write any. De Mille finally staged the end without music, set to chords played by dance arranger Morgan "Buddy" Lewis (who four years earlier had composed the jazz classic "How High the Moon"). The first act ends with the dream villain breaking the hero's back; for safety reasons, stage fights in dances are carefully timed to beats. De Mille presented the ballet to Rodgers & Hammerstein; Rodgers liked the music, telling de Mille they should just keep the chords at the end. Bennett took it under silent protest—"Dick has really gone out of his mind," de Mille quotes him as saying—and filled in the chords with old-time movie-melodrama music. And that's the way the ballet remains: a wonderfully constructed string of themes from *Oklahoma!* ending with the sort of music Bennett used to improvise as a teenaged accompanist for silent movies in Kansas City.

> RITTMAN: The composer usually has a certain wish as to what should happen to his songs. Some of them—not everybody, but some of them—would have a certain vision of what he would like to do. Rodgers cared only that his song didn't disappear. But then, after the second show, he had made a carte blanche to me and said, "do." On *The Sound of Music*, Rodgers just said, "Go and do. Don't ask me questions."
>
> The principal on which I have always worked was that one should not notice where I would take up the pen and where the composer would leave off. In other words, the style of the show must be one. But it isn't always easy because on each show that one does, each composer has a slightly different style. But my endeavor was always to maintain the style of the composer in order not to interrupt the flow of a show.

In separate conversations, dance arranger Peter Howard and composer Jerry Herman both brought up "Dancing," the extended production number in *Hello, Dolly!* (The original cast album offers a truncated version. A live recording of the Broadway production demonstrates how the number builds, builds, builds, and then finally flickers out gently, to a rousing audience response.)

> HOWARD: When I got it, all it was, was Jerry playing it simply. "Oom-CHA-CHA, oom-CHA-CHA." Gower said, "I want something a little different." There was a piece of my own music I had written just then called "Make Love to Me," sort of a jazz waltz. That rhythm worked perfectly for "Dancing."
>
> HERMAN: If you look at "Dancing," it never varies from that tune. It varies in rhythm, varies in style, but never varies in the melody. Peter was just perfect for the dance music, because he knew how to keep the melody going. That's the secret of my whole career: keep the melody going.

Given the presence of a strong director/choreographer, dance arrangements can come about without the composer's input. For example, the "Hot Honey Rag" in

Chicago. Howard: "Fosse wanted a ragtime piece for Gwen and Chita to do at the end of the show. John hadn't written anything for them. Bobby kept asking, so I said, 'Why don't we take one of the songs and rag it?' And that's what we did."

Howard also tells of the opening number for *Here's Love*, which he devised with choreographer Michael Kidd:

> It was called the "Big Clown Balloons," but of course you never did get to see the balloons. All you saw was the strings, and Kidd didn't want to make it a typical parade, a Macy's parade. He just couldn't. So he got the idea of instruments. Everybody would represent a different instrument. Little girls on point were violins. For the xylophone, we used two of the kids on a big xylophone, tap dancing. And there were trombones, and trumpets. Everything. And then it culminated with an actual onstage band. That was that. For the music, I took the main theme of "Big Clown Balloons," and I did everything I could. Every type of rhythm I had to use—Dixieland, a classical pizzicato, sax kind of figures—and I turned it inside out and upside down and backwards and forwards to get variations on the theme. Meredith Willson wanted his music used as much as possible.
>
> What I did with Michael a lot, it was all homework. I'd get ideas and I'd bring them into the studio and we'd try things out. The same thing for the dream ballet, too, the little girl's dream in the second act where all of the toys came to life. I incorporated different songs from the show, and treated them entirely differently than in their original form, so it sounded quite good.

Elliot Lawrence agreed: "Peter laid it out, it was completely Michael Kidd's idea. A wonderful opening number, but the show wasn't any good after that."

For another view of the process, composer Charles Strouse discusses "This Is the Life" from *Golden Boy* (dance arrangement by Dorothea Freitag).

> STROUSE: I remember watching the number and saying, "I ain't doing this right, because that's not the way I hear it." But it was like playing choreographic piano. Suddenly there were two powerhouses, Sammy Davis and Billy Daniels, they were doing it in rehearsal, suddenly they were going like this, snapping their fingers. That wasn't exactly the way I had intended. I had had a whole thing with a canon, you know, very spiffy and—it just got lost in rehearsals, it was taken over by Sammy, and then before you know it the whole company is going "yeah" and you know, that was that.
>
> Arrangements can be swayed by a very powerful personality like Sammy Davis, or Ethel Merman. I'm sure if you played something for Ethel Merman and she wasn't really close to you, she would say, "No, I want —" and she'd go "clear the decks," with finger snaps.

Production Number

And then there's the big production number, a combination of song, vocal arrangement, and dance arrangement. "Mame"—which Jerry Herman himself thinks "outshone" the "Hello, Dolly" number—serves as a good example. After a gentle, two-bar vamp, the song is delivered smoothly and calmly by the chorus singing the melody in unison. The two-bar end cadence modulates up a half-step, from B♭ to B major, and the song becomes—briefly—a solo for the heroine's future husband. (The role of Beauregard Jackson Pickett Burnside is negligible; he was the nominal love interest, but he only got to sing sixteen bars before falling from an offstage mountain top.) The male chorus returns for the next eight bars, after which the women join in, again in unison. (On the partitur, Phil Lang wrote, "Add girls. Yeah!") The refrain ends with a brief solo from one of the assembled old biddies.

A two-bar cadence takes us up another half-step to C, with a countermelody in stop-time ("hush my mouth"). Fourteen bars—or nearly half the refrain—in, we go back to the unison chorus singing the unembellished melody. There follows a six-bar transition, built on an ascending scale, into an eighteen-bar dance section, led by the trombones and the trumpets. (This section was originally thirty-six bars long, but the latter half was deleted.)

The last four bars of this contain another modulation, into G, for another dance section using a new musical phrase in galop tempo. (The scene includes a foxhunt.) Another sixteen bars of dance, another two-bar modulation (to A♭), another fourteen bars of the galop music, and then a grand four-bar choral transition into the "sell chorus" (which is to say, the final, all-stops-out rendition of the song). Midway through, they throw in yet one more modulation—the sixth, by my count—to A major. Pippin: "I love modulations. Thank God, Jerry Herman does, too."

This is a cannily assembled number, and highly effective. Choral refrain, principal-led refrain, stop-time refrain, dance refrain, dance variation refrain, repeated dance variation refrain, final refrain. Seven sections, 242 bars of music, all derived from the 36-bar song by Jerry Herman.

Herman and musical director/vocal arranger Pippin initially sketched out ideas for the number on the beach in St. Thomas, but the actual routine was built in the rehearsal hall.

HERMAN: There was a great deal contributed by [choreographer] Onna White, a great deal of [director] Gene Saks saying, "I'd like to insert dialogue here, music under dialogue, return to the melody." [Dance arranger] Roger Adams was also perfect, because he kept the melody going. It was a true collaboration. But I had the right people.

Don Pippin continues the story.

> PIPPIN: At the ending, I wasn't satisfied. So I started doing sequential chord structures. Oh, that sounded so good! We ran it through, then we ran it again. Bea Arthur had tears in her eyes; she said it was the most exciting ending of a number she ever heard in her life. Onna White, though, had a strange look on her face when she heard it. "How many f**king times can you kneel in a number?" she asked. Bea said, "Have them kneel one section at a time." For the orchestration, it was one of the strangest numbers to build because it was too long. "Phil, can you think of something to do on this last chorus? What can we do?" And he came back with the brass pyramids; they lift the number. It's corny, but effective!

An extended number of a very different stripe is "Tradition," the opening sequence of *Fiddler on the Roof* (1964). The song begins with the eight-bar "fiddler" theme (the daughter's melody), which is then repeated against a clarinet countermelody (the papa's melody). Violin and clarinet continue for another sixteen bars of underscoring during Tevye's opening speech. The speech ends ("That I can tell you in one word—Tradition!") with a vamp that allows the ensemble to enter. "Tradition," they sing, in an eight-bar fragment, followed by an eight-bar dance incidental (led by the trumpets). Tevye has a speech over twelve bars, plus vamp. Then, after a three-bar tutti, comes the song proper, or what there is of it. Eight bars for the papas, followed by the "Tradition" fragment; a two-bar connection into the eight-bar "mamas" section, followed again by "Tradition"; then the sons, then the daughters.

They then all sing their parts contrapuntally, four groups competing over the course of eight bars before finally falling together for a restatement of the "Tradition" fragment. There follows an extended, musically underscored dialogue section, in which Tevye introduces villagers Yente (the matchmaker), Reb Nahum (the beggar), and the Rabbi, with brief exchanges (and jokes) for each. After another eight bars of choral singing ("dai dai dai dai," etc.), Tevye continues his dialogue, a section with the Russians and then another working into the "horse! mule!" argument. As the entire village explodes in argument, they return to a full-voiced rendition of the eight-bar "Tradition" fragment. The roar quickly dies down, leaving Tevye to finish his narration to sixteen final bars of music, composed of the "son" fragment followed by the "fiddler" theme.

The "fiddler" (daughter) theme, the "Tradition" fragment, the papas, mamas, and sons: five sections of 8 bars each. These 40 measures are woven, extended, and repeated into the 240-bar whole, one of the most brilliant seven-minute opening numbers in musical theatre history. The 40 bars were written by composer Jerry Bock; so, one must suppose, was some of the underscoring. The contrapuntal section must have been worked out in the rehearsal hall; the same can be said for the underscoring necessary to incorporate the dialogue vignettes (which appear to have been rewritten and shortened during the tryout) and the extra beats needed to bring on and move about the four groups of characters. So here we have a complete musical scene, written by the songwriters but molded into form by committee: musical director/vocal arranger Milton Greene, dance arranger Betty Walberg, and the ever-demanding Jerry Robbins.

> BOCK: If the musical theatre is to be considered an art form—unlike the poem or the painting or the novel, it must be the art of collaboration, where each and every member of this creative group makes a contribution. When it works, the sum is far greater than the individual.

SECTION III. OVERTURE

Curtain Up

Overture comes from the French word *ouverture*, which means opening. The overture dates more or less to the seventeenth century, when it was originally used in opera. Such openings were also used for plays; some of these early theatre overtures, in fact, have led far more far popular lives than the plays themselves (like Beethoven's "Egmont" and "Coriolan"). Over time, composers came to use the term to describe independent concert works similar to but on a smaller scale than symphonies (including Mendelssohn's "Hebrides" and Tchaikovsky's "1812"). The medley-type overture came into fashion in the nineteenth century; a look at the works of Gilbert & Sullivan shows the theatrical song-medley overture in full swing.

The Broadway overture is one of the glories of the American musical theatre. Or is it? Enthusiasts armed with CDs of their favorite musicals point with pride to the overtures, a pride which—to some extent—might be misplaced. Through repeated hearings, these overtures have grown on us. It should be pointed out, though, that these were openings in the most rudimentary terms. Back in the pre-1943 era of not so well-integrated musicals, shows often began with undistinguished choruses of little import to the proceedings, which were intended merely to hold the stage while the latecomers filed in. If the opening chorus was in a sense a mere time-filler, what of the overture that proceeded the opening chorus?

Overtures might indeed sound glorious on cast albums, but in the theatre they are usually interfered with by the entrance of latecomers and—perhaps more annoyingly—the chatter of theatregoers, who don't realize that this is part of the show. (This seems to have gotten worse, rather than better, over the years.) One result of this has been the move toward omitting the overture entirely. This can be traced to the era of the director-choreographer. In the old days, the composer was king, relatively speaking; here was a chance to plug the songs, without the interference of singers or dancers (or lyrics). The director-choreographer, though, had a different viewpoint. What do these four minutes of music have to do with the show? That is, the overall experience of the show? When, in actuality, *does* the musical—*my* musical, sez the director—begin?

If you are Jerome Robbins directing *West Side Story*, there is no question where you want the starting point. Even with a musical heavyweight like Bernstein on hand, there was no overture. (An overture was added when the show, which had closed prematurely, returned to Broadway in 1960—and for the unlikeliest of reasons: Bernstein wanted to conduct an overture at the grand reopening. So Ramin and Kostal patched together existing sections of the "Quintet," "Somewhere," and "Mambo" from "Dance at the Gym." This overture remains available for use, but is performed only intermittently.) Robbins allowed an overture—to which we will return—for *Gypsy*, his next musical, but not for his final musical. *Fiddler on the Roof* opened with two actors—the star and the fiddler/dancer, the latter scratching out the show's predominant musical theme—with the song ("Tradition," discussed above) eventually building into as grand an opening number as you might want. But the audience's attention was focused on the two actors from the very moment the lights went down, not on the fellow in the tuxedo standing in the pit.

Between *West Side* and *Fiddler*, Gower Champion—who joined Robbins in the director-choreographer spotlight—opened *Carnival* with a lone actor playing the show's predominant theme, this time on a squeeze-box (accordion), with the number eventually building into a grand opening ("Direct from Vienna"). Champion's next musical, the one about that exasperating matchmaker, arguably did call for a rousing, tuneful overture. Champion nevertheless cut it during the tryout, preferring that the audience start the experience of the show with the chorus calling on Dolly.

The deleted *Hello, Dolly!* overture, sketched by Peter Howard and orchestrated by Lang, was included in the published vocal score. By the time Pearl Bailey went into the show in 1968, Champion wasn't around to object. A new overture, which can be heard on the Bailey cast album, was written by studio arranger Glenn Osser; this might have been commissioned by RCA solely for the recording, or it might have been used in the show as well. Herman disliked it, and when he supervised the Houston Grand Opera production, which visited Broadway in 1978, he asked Lang for a new overture. This version appears on the 1995 revival cast album (starring Carol Channing), which was recorded during the tryout. This proved to be unsatisfactory as well. For the Broadway opening of the 1995 production, yet another overture—routined by Don Pippin and orchestrated by Larry Blank—was prepared. This is now the officially sanctioned overture, although for economic reasons it has not yet been incorporated into the parts available for rental.

Robbins and Champion are long gone, but overtures have fallen further out of fashion over the decades. Going back to the days of Bennett, Walker, Lang, et al., though, they were very much in fashion. Virtually all Broadway overtures were of the song-medley variety, with almost no exceptions. The "almost," in this case, includes less than a handful of concert-style overtures. Leonard Bernstein's Overture to *Candide*, indeed, has had a far more popular life than the musical for which it was written—or, at least, the original version of said musical. (The piece does include a section of at least one tune, "O Happy We.") Another case is the "Carousel Waltz," which is not technically an overture in theatre terms, as it is played during pantomime (as opposed to dance) with the curtain up and a stageful of actors. The off-Broadway musical *The Fantasticks*, too, has a totally separate overture. While writing the show, the authors attended a Carlo Goldoni play, which sparked the idea of a group of strolling commedia dell'arte players setting up their stage.

As the sixties progressed, more and more musicals began to omit overtures. It is perhaps surprising that the great traditionalist Richard Rodgers moved decidedly into the anti-overture camp. *Carousel*, as mentioned, has no overture per se. Many of Rodgers's later musicals—*The Sound of Music, No Strings, Rex*—did without an overture as well. So much for getting in an extra plug for your songs.

Many of the early song-medley overtures are, arguably, less than distinguished. The so-called utilities, the arrangements devised to be plugged in for scene changes, incidentals, and other gaps calling for musical accompaniment, were regularly used in overtures. (Utilities will be discussed later, in their place.) Into the 1970s, it was typical for a show to go on the road with what was called a "temporary overture." This generally consisted of a string of utilities of the presumed-to-be hit songs, with some usually undistinguished bridgework connecting the songs (and camouflaging severe key changes). When the show approached the Broadway opening—assuming that there was still some money left in the budget—an all-stops-out "New York overture" was usually prepared.

The New York overture for *Oklahoma!* makes a straightforward example. Bennett begins with a four-bar trill, notable because it includes a trill from the trumpets. (Hershy Kay must have liked this, because he began the overture to *110 in the Shade* in the same manner.) The trill is followed by four bars of fiddling, then an eight-bar vamp. This leads into fourteen lively bars of "The Farmer and the Cowman," capped with six bars of bridgework. Another tremolo takes us into a slow (andante) seven bars' worth of "Pore Jud Is Daid." The tempo then picks up with a four-bar lead-in to "Many a New Day." This is a jaunty thirty-two-bar section, which slows down for the final four. A long and slightly forlorn note marks what might be deemed the end of the first section and the beginning of the second. Next come forty bars of "Out of My Dreams," in what might well be a utility arrangement. There is an eight-bar ending, marked "animato"; four bars of highly dramatic bridgework (which I think we heard before in Bennett's overture to *Show Boat*, leading from "Make Believe" to "Can't Help Lovin' Dat Man"); and a two-bar vamp, in cut-time, leading to forty-six bars' worth of the hoped-to-be big-ballad hit, "People Will Say We're in Love." This, again, might as well be a utility arrangement. The section ends with two rather grand bars of a deceptive ending, which leads into a rousing teaser of an eight-bar intro to "Oklahoma." Bennett gives us fifty-eight bars' worth, capped by a slowed-down version of the pre-"Oklahoma" teaser and a final orchestral chord and sting.

There you have a standard Russell Bennett overture. While utilities and borrowed sections were the norm in many overtures of the time, Bennett's overtures generally sounded fresh, dramatic, and creative. He did seem to specialize in overtures. Back before he started orchestrating for Broadway, he was already arranging the "piano selections" that Harms regularly published for its major shows (which were, more or less, song-medley overtures for piano) and full-band medley arrangements for nontheatrical use. He continued this throughout his career, arranging and orchestrating song selections for concert orchestra for numerous shows, including some (*Funny Girl, Do I Hear a Waltz?*) with which he wasn't otherwise involved.

Bennett displayed a favorite device in many of his overtures. He would grind to a stop about two-thirds of the way through; then, usually after a fermata (hold), he would launch into a grand refrain of the expected-to-be hit song and continue through the end. This can be seen, for example, in *Oklahoma!* (leading from "Out of My Dreams" into "People Will Say We're in Love"); in *Finian's Rainbow* (leading from "Old Devil Moon" through a brief "Something Sort of Grandish" picking up with a flourish leading into "That Great Come-and-Get-It Day"); and in *Bells Are Ringing* (following "Hello, Hello There," with a chime leading into "The Party's Over").

Bennett's account book shows that the temporary overture would usually be orchestrated in the days between the out-of-town orchestra reading and the out-of-town opening. (Many of his temporary overtures are invoiced on the day of the New Haven opening.) The New York overture—in cases where there *was* a complete, new New York overture—was often prepared a week before the Broadway opening, at which point songs deleted during the tryout would be removed.

The King and I makes an interesting case. Bennett finished his overture—clearly intended to be the permanent one—the night before the New Haven opening on February 26, 1951. The show moved to Boston from March 5 through March 24. Bennett arrived on March 18 to orchestrate three last-minute additions, "Getting to Know You," "Western People Funny," and "I Have Dreamed." Several songs were deleted, including "He Was Tall" (the second song Bennett orchestrated for the show). This was featured in the original overture, coming just after "Whistle a Happy Tune" (which, incidentally, was the first song Bennett orchestrated). Listeners familiar with the overture are aware that things stop rather abruptly at this point (in the vocal score, after the ninth bar of section 6 on page 8). Out went "He Was Tall."

Bennett did not reorchestrate "I Have Dreamed" for the overture. At the second statement of the refrain, following Tuptim's singing of the verse, he added the melody line for the brass, in red ink. Going back to the partitur for the overture, he crossed out a bar in the middle of the "Happy Tune" tag; inserted a five-bar bridge, which changed the tempo and altered the key from D major to F major; and wrote, "copy 'I Have Dreamed' from #4, with red revisions." This was followed by another two-bar bridge in 6/8, modulating to E♭ major and the "Hello, Young Lovers" section of the original overture.

Other orchestrators seemed content to simply string together utilities for overtures. These included Spialek, Royal, and even Walker (through the fifties, at which point he began to lavish infinitely more care on his shows). Our exact knowledge of this is somewhat limited by our inability to find partiturs of many of these shows; even where partiturs have been found for the overtures, it is sometimes impossible to identify when an interpolated chart is copied from a utility or written specifically for the overture.

The Spialek overtures for which partiturs have been found—including *On Your Toes*, *The Boys from Syracuse*, *Too Many Girls*, and *Du Barry Was a Lady*—consist of openings, endings, and connective bridgework interspersed with utility versions of the songs orchestrated by various hands. (Half of these came from Walter Paul, who seemed to specialize in this sort of writing.) The only Royal overture that has been located is *Paint Your Wagon*—in which the opening and bridgework are mostly by Spialek, with the song sections (possibly utilities) by Royal. The "I Talk to the Trees" section, apparently much revised, is labeled in Ted's hand: "Trees–Overture, 17th Version." The only surviving partiturs for *House of Flowers* are Royal utilities for "I Never Has Seen Snow" and "A Sleepin' Bee," neither of which he orchestrated in their song versions. The utilities can be heard, precisely as written, in the overture.

Walker's overtures are harder to assess, as his fifties musicals were usually team efforts from a factory of as many as six or more orchestrators. *Wonderful Town*'s is written mostly by Jack Mason, with one transition by Walker and the final section by Joe Glover (using material from his song version of "Wrong Note Rag"). *Silk Stockings* is mostly by Walker, with the insertion of Ginzler's "All of You" (perhaps a utility?) and Kostal's "Silk Stockings" (not a utility). *Hazel Flagg* appears to be assembled of utilities, with bridgework by Mason. Let it be added, though, that Walker orchestrated the overture (and almost the entire score) for *The Most Happy Fella*, his most important show of this period, by himself.

And let's not overlook Bennett. He was sole orchestrator of the overtures for his six Rodgers shows (including *Oklahoma! South Pacific*, and *The King and I*), but we find that *By the Beautiful Sea* does, specifically, call for the use of utilities (for "Alone Too Long," "By the Beautiful Sea," and "More Love than Your Love"). So does the overture for *Kiss Me, Kate*—that is, the Overture (beginning with "Why Can't You Behave?") that is heard on the original cast album, which is actually the Entr'acte. On the partitur, Bennett instructs the copyist to use Paul's utility of "Were Thine That Special Face"—which is a beguiling beguine version, with some lovely interior countermelodies.

And Then Came *Gypsy*

The sound of Broadway overtures—as well as so much more—changed almost overnight with *Gypsy*, orchestrated by Ramin and Ginzler. The very opening was startling, especially compared with the shows that preceded it.

A brass fanfare, over a cymbal roll, starts things out for seven bars. The orchestrators take the somewhat tricky rhythm offered by Styne's triplets (the "I had a dream" theme) and explode it into an eight-bar section, switching from the opening cut-time to 6/8, 5/8, and then 2/4; the reeds and strings play staccato eighth-notes, while the trumpets come back in with a pyramid built on "I had a dream." Then comes an abrasive downward scale from the brass, a howling wind whistle, and we're off to the races with the first tune ("Everything's Coming Up Roses"). All of the above happens in eighteen bars, which are packed with blaring brass and variegated rhythms.

"Roses" is not given a commonplace utility treatment; the melody is punctuated by xylophone glissandos and some high violins playing half-note triplets.

The bridge is filled with exciting trumpet scales. A calming period—marked "l'istesso tempo"—takes us into a somewhat standard reading of "You'll Never Get Away from Me," with trumpets teasing at the end of the first two sections and taking over for the melody in the final eight. There is then a somewhat abrupt timpani roll, followed by a majestic nine-bar transition (interrupted by a piccolo gliss) into "Small World." Again, this tune appears to be somewhat standard, but the fills include a bravura eleven-note fill by the reeds; a pizzicato pluck for the strings; and some colorfully harmonized "living strings" in the bridge. This devolves into two measures of blaring brass triplets, leading into an astounding sixteen-bar section of raucous strip music. Back in 1959, this trumpet solo pretty much tore the roof off the theatre, and it continues to do so a half-century later. It ends with a three-octave descending scale of triplets, leading into a march-time introduction to "Mr. Goldstone," with piccolos flying. The section leads back into a restatement of the opening "I Had a Dream" trumpet pyramid, followed by a highly syncopated presto section leading to another brisk, scale section—two octaves up, two octaves down, with a horn solo marked "Whoop, whoop, whoop" on the score—and a final, tremulous chord.

Compare this to any Bennett, Walker, Royal, or Lang overture. Ramin and Ginzler took off the gloves, rolled up their sleeves, oxygenated their reeds, and threw raw meat to the brass section. We all have grown accustomed to the *Gypsy* overture, to the extent that it's hard to place it in context. The reader looking for a break might want to listen to a few of the overtures from preceding seasons: *My Fair Lady, Li'l Abner, Bells Are Ringing, New Girl in Town, Goldilocks, Flower Drum Song, Redhead,* and *Destry Rides Again.* These are the overtures that the theatregoers entering the Broadway Theatre had most recently heard. *Gypsy* was, musically, a new sound altogether. Hal Prince: "*Gypsy* sounded different from the downbeat; the overture sounded like nothing I ever heard before. It remains one of the best overtures I've ever heard; it's there with *Porgy and Bess.*"

Routining the Overture

The natural assumption is that overtures are composed by composers. Not orchestrated by them, of course, but sketched or routined. One can easily imagine composers sitting there thinking, I'll start with a big fanfare, see, then go into *insert name of surefire uptempo song hit*, then do a nice little bridge into *insert name of surefire ballad hit*, and on.

It is virtually impossible to prove that this was not the case; however, every piece of evidence that has been found indicates that the composer rarely had much to do with the overture. Yes, the composer sometimes provided a list of songs to be used. This usually came in early, for use in assembling the temporary overtures for the tryout—which invariably included surefire favorites that were ig-nominiously cut on the road.

The full extent of the composer's involvement could be explained by looking at the handwriting on existing sketches for overtures. Unfortunately, no such doc-uments have been located. This is something of an answer in itself. While some shows offer scanty documentation, voluminous amounts of material can be found on others. There are cases where I have examined five or eight cartons' worth of materials, not only partiturs and pit parts but piano-vocal rehearsal copies, con-ductor copies, and composer manuscripts. It is to be assumed that if a composer's sketch of the overture existed, it would be included.

What have appeared, in not very many cases, are simple lists of songs to be used in the overture. These are often written on the back of the last page of a partitur of another number, which is why they have survived: a quick rundown in the orchestrator's hand, perhaps dictated by the composer or musical direc-tor. While these notes have usually consisted only of song titles, a more exten-sive rundown has been found for one show. A negligible show at that, and long forgotten; *Heaven on Earth* it was called, a quick 1948 flop orchestrated by Ben-nett and Walker (in the brief period when they worked as a team). Still, it clearly illustrates how this overture was assembled, in this case a temporary overture for a show that turned out to be all too temporary. Bennett's partitur begins with a fourteen-bar introduction. He then instructs the copyist as follows: "'Coffee' utility: cut out intro and both endings. 'So Near' util: intro is good. Cut from 3 to the 17th bar of 4. 'Heaven on Earth' util: Intro good. Make hold over last beat before ending. Both endings out." Bennett then wrote a fourteen-bar end-ing. This overture represented a bargain for the producers, as Bennett only charged them for the opening and closing; the utilities were already paid for. It came to $49.50, and worth every penny.

But in most of the cases I have been able to verify, the overtures were routined by either orchestrator, musical director, or dance arranger. Bennett, as already noted, specialized in this area. His many overtures are sterling, including such rousers as *Show Boat, Oklahoma! South Pacific, The King and I, My Fair Lady*, and *On a Clear Day. Camelot* is not his—it's by Lang—but the overture for Lang's musical *Roar of the Greasepaint* is by Bennett.

Otherwise, the only information I can find on the subject comes from people who are remembering events of long ago. Don Pippin tells us that he routined the overtures for most of his shows, specifically including *Ben Franklin in Paris, Mame, Dear World, Applause*, and *Mack & Mabel*. Exceptions were *110 in the Shade*, which was routined by dance arranger Billy Goldenberg, and two routined by the composers, Cy Coleman of *Seesaw* and John Kander of *Woman of the Year.*

Pippin tells an interesting story about working with Lang on *Mame*:

> I did a complete concert sketch of the overture, like a small orchestration. Originally, I wrote this complicated ending, with tempo changes switching from 5/4 to 6/4, very complicated. At the orchestra reading, the overture was magnificent. But when we got to the ending, it sounded like factory whistles going off. It was horrendous, it sounded awful. I stopped. We did it again. It sounded awful. We went to lunch; I was so despondent. "The end of the overture is a mess, isn't it?" I asked. Phil said, "Yes." "Can you fix it?" I asked. "I already have," Phil said. "I knew it wouldn't work." "Why didn't you tell me?" I asked. "Don," he said, "if I'd told you, you would never learn." He did it the way I wrote it so I could hear how wrong it was! He had the new ending—a practical version of what I wrote—already written and copied. We played it after lunch; the orchestra cheered. I learned by hearing it. It says a lot about Phil's character.

Peter Howard says that in his experience it very much depended on who else was involved with the show. Trained composers like Styne or Loewe were more likely to be interested in the overture than people like Meredith Willson or Jerry Herman, who were glad to leave it in an arranger's hands. Howard says that he did *Subways Are for Sleeping*, but with the very close participation of Styne. Jule would give him specific ideas—some of which, Howard says, were excellent. Peter would sketch out an overture, play it for Styne, and be given more ideas and changes. After four versions, they arrived at the overture we know. Howard says that he did most of *I Can Get It for You Wholesale* and *Here's Love* himself, as well as *Chicago. Annie* was routined by Howard together with composer Strouse, *Minnie's Boys* by orchestrator Ralph Burns.

Elliot Lawrence recalls that Red Ginzler did *How to Succeed*, with Frank Loesser dictating which tunes he wanted spotted. He also remembers that Styne did not sketch, but was very much interested in, the overture to *Sugar*; the final version is labeled "Overture (Jule)." Jerry Bock says that his overtures were presented at the orchestra readings, coming—as far as he could tell—from the orchestrator. (Bock did report that on the original cast album of *Fiorello!* he himself is operating the police siren that begins the recording.)

Another telltale piece of paper has shown up, a typed memo from Walker to himself regarding *Bless You All*, Harold Rome's 1950 revue: "LE [Lehman Engel] suggests the following utilities for the overture: Big introduction (20 bars). 1. 'A Rose Is a Rose.' 2. 'Love Letter to Manhattan.' 3. 'Bless You All.'" Walker goes on to list Engel's suggestions for the Entr'acte and Exit music as well. The memo is dated November 2, one week before the orchestra reading in New Haven.

This is, alas, not a whole lot of information on the question. However, the lack of vestigial evidence indicates that overtures, indeed, are rarely sketched by composers. As Lawrence pointed out, in the old days—with multiple tryouts and quick turnaround times—the composers were usually off struggling with new songs when the time came to routine the overture.

Yes, some composers clearly—or at least presumably—did their own overtures, such as Bernstein's *Candide* and *1600 Pennsylvania Avenue* (although not *On the Town* or *Wonderful Town*). We do have proof of one overture by Stephen Sondheim.

> KOSTAL: Steve insisted on sketching his own overture for *A Funny Thing*. His idea was not without merit. He composed a brilliant piece of work, using large blocks of sound, trying to make it sound Roman, and sometimes Grecian, writing the kind of music that might have been played 2,000 years ago. He thought a very serious piece of music would contrast with the comedy of the show, and get things started with a novel approach. When George Abbott heard the orchestra play this very ambitious overture, he blamed me and asked what the hell I thought I was doing.

Out went Sondheim's overture (orchestrated by Ramin). In went "Overture #2," dated three days after the New Haven opening, quickly orchestrated by Kostal. Following the Washington opening, the final overture—"Overture New 4/15/62"—was routined and orchestrated by Kostal and Ramin. All three sets of partiturs survive.

This takes us back, more or less, to Ramin and Ginzler's *Gypsy*.

> RAMIN: I didn't realize that you're not supposed to write the overture until the show is set. Because it was literally my first show, after *West Side*. I said to Red, we better start at the top. So we did the overture, and brought it to Jule. He said, "How could you do an overture! You don't know what tunes are going to be taken out of the show, you don't know what new tunes are going to be added! How could you do the overture! And look how long this overture is!!" But he looked at it, and he liked it. Very, very much. And the overture stayed exactly as it was written. Except Jule said, "It's much too long, you got to cut it." He thumbed through the score, then said, "from here to there." I said, "Well, wait a second, Jule. How are we going to get from here to there?" He said, "Put a timpani roll in." I said, "Okay."

Thus, the "Cow Song" ("Caroline") was cut from its spot after "You'll Never Get Away from Me" (at bar 146 of the published vocal score). It was replaced—as Styne suggested—with a mere four-beat timpani roll. And that's what we still hear today.

SECTION IV.
MEET THE COLORS

Before the orchestrator can begin to assign the composer's notes to the instruments, the makeup of the pit band must be determined. Spialek, at the beginning of our discussion, compared orchestration to painting. If orchestration is indeed the combination of colors into harmonies and dissonances, instrumentation can be seen as the selection of the fifteen or twenty tubes of paint with which to work. Paint can be blended in any variety of colors, yes; but it can be seen that there is a difference in the palettes of Van Eyck and Van Gogh, and, further, that Van Gogh's sun-drenched Arlesienne fantasies differ from his indoor, brown-and-muddy potato eaters. So, too, is the difference between Walker's *Carousel* and *Fiddler on the Roof*, or Lang's *Li'l Abner* and *Carnival*.

There are any number of instruments available to the orchestrator, but Broadway is a world of traditions. Traditions waiting to be subverted, yes, but musicals of our time—at least until the advent of rock bands and synthesizers—more or less used the same starting point. Bennett elaborated on this in 1975 in *Instrumentally Speaking*, and his description is presented here in abridged version:

> Around the beginning of the twentieth century a "full" orchestra was referred to as "fifteen and piano." They seldom had a piano in the pit unless the band was much smaller, but the part was there for the use of the conductor. The parts furnished were Violin I, Violin II, Viola, Cello, Bass, Flute, Oboe, Clarinets I and II, Bassoon, Horns I and II, Trumpets I and II, Trombone, and Drums. No matter how this adds up they called it "fifteen and piano."
>
> Nearly all popular music was oom-pah (bass and after-beat) or, in case of a waltz, oom-pah-pah (bass and two after-beats). An arrangement of a song was: a loud introduction, a vamp (soft, with oom-pahs), a soft verse, a soft chorus (refrain), and a loud chorus made by repeating the same arrangement with the brass and drums added and the first violin up an octave. The first violin played the tune throughout, the second violin and the viola played after-beats (the pahs), the cello had some kind of sustained counter-melody or doubled the bass, who played the ooms. The flute and the two clarinets did "noodles," the oboe played the melody, and the bassoon either played in unison with the cello or played ooms and sometimes oom-pahs. The horns were mostly concerned with pahs, but also might reinforce a cello counter-melody; the first trumpet played the melody (on the repeat), the second trumpet found thirds and

sixths under the first and the trombone doubled the bass, helped the trumpets to make a triad, or played the tune an octave under the top trumpet. The drums did oom-pahs and kept the whole thing from dying, just about as they do now. This basic set-up has never quite disappeared. With a little study you can still see kinship with it in any of its descendants.

To get to a Broadway-sized orchestra of twenty-five, one could simply take these sixteen parts and augment the strings to include four players on violin I, three on violin II, four violas, and two cellos. As for Bennett's discourse on oom-pahs and noodles, it may be taken as an accurate description of the utility arrangements which peppered Broadway musicals into the 1960s.

> MARION EVANS: Max Dreyfus came up with the idea of doing utility arrangements. He's the one who invented that, because it saved a lot of money. They would pick a dozen top songs from the show. When you got ready to go into production, the first thing you did was write one chorus of each song for the entire orchestra, self-sufficient for each section. You could later circle the brass, or the strings, cutting out whatever sections you wanted and leaving the others to play, whatever. They would basically start with these orchestrations. The conductor would say, "Okay, first eight bars, brass play the melody, then lay out, then let's transpose this up a third. Then somebody would come in and say, "We're throwing that song out."

> LEHMAN ENGEL: Utilities were fully scored so that at the discretion of the conductor, he could do this section for strings only, or this section for brass only, or this section for reeds only. And those were used often for changing scenery, and then they got patched together with modulations for what was laughably called the temporary overture or the temporary entr'acte.

You can find any number of instrumental combinations in a Broadway orchestra pit, but the choices were remarkably similar into the mid-1950s. Let us start by breaking the pit into four pieces: reeds (flute, clarinet, oboe, bassoon, saxes); brass (trumpet, trombone, French horn); strings (from violin to bass); and the so-called rhythm section, which includes everything else (piano, harp, guitar, accordion, percussion).

Twenty players, traditionally, get you something along the lines of four reeds, with principal assignments of flute, oboe, clarinet I, and either clarinet II or bassoon; five brass, with two trumpets along with two horns and one trombone (or the reverse); seven strings, with four violins, one viola, one cello, and one bass; and four others, say piano, harp, guitar or other plectrum (plucked) instrument, and percussion.

Twenty-five players would allow a fifth reed; a third trumpet, along with two trombones and two horns; and perhaps a total of ten or more strings. (Six violins, two violas, two cellos, and one bass make a reasonable lineup.) As mentioned above, many musicals—especially in the golden age—happily exceeded the minimum, especially if there was a big star or a gilt-edged composer in the mix. *Carousel*, from the songwriters of the superhit *Oklahoma!* had thirty-nine (including twenty-two strings); Frank Loesser's *The Most Happy Fella* had thirty-six. We can be certain that this wasn't unprecedented, although it is often impossible to pin down the number of pieces originally used.

Different shows, of course, have different needs. A legit musical, such as those mentioned in the above paragraph, call for well-padded string sections and, inevitably, a harp. A more contemporary dance musical, such as *Gypsy* or anything with the name Fosse connected to it, might well have twelve players in the reed and brass sections combined, along with two percussionists; this is necessarily balanced by a depletion of the strings. (*Gypsy*, for one, made up for the extra power by omitting the viola section altogether—which was a common choice in musicals with a nonlegit sound.) But even within the same genre, the timbre of the music and the specificity of the setting can pose different demands, as in two of Bennett's musicals for Rodgers and Hammerstein. The thirty-piece *South Pacific* (1949) used five reed, nine brass, and fourteen strings. (The other two pieces were harp and drums.) For *The King and I* (1951), Bennett chose to add two additional reeds as well as a second drummer. While the *King and I* orchestra was only one piece smaller than *South Pacific*, the strings were reduced from fourteen to ten.

The Instruments

It is imagined that most readers of these pages have a certain familiarity with the instruments of the pit orchestra, but it seems in order to present at least a sketchy overview of the components. As we shall occasionally be referring to various colors or sounds, let us try to give some generalized examples. Trained musicians are welcome to skip ahead.

Reeds

The flute is perhaps the most agile instrument in the orchestra. The ease of using its keypad and the method of "tonguing" individual notes allow rapid scales and trills (representative flute parts: the four-flute filigree of "Put on a Happy Face," from *Bye Bye Birdie*, or the opening of "The Sweetest Sounds," from *No Strings*). When the orchestrator needs more than an occasional high note from the flute, he turns to the piccolo, which is basically a little flute playing an octave higher; *piccolo*, in Italian, means—simply—"little." The tiniest reed instrument, yes; but set the entire symphony orchestra playing and—due to sonics—you will still hear that piccolo up top (representative piccolo part: the soft-shoe interlude of "Sixteen Going on Seventeen," from *The Sound of Music*). When the orchestrator wants strong lower notes, he turns to the mellow alto flute (representative alto flute part: the countermelody at the beginning of "Talk to Me," from *Bye Bye Birdie*). There are six flutes in all, although only three find their way into the orchestra pit. As is the case with virtually all of these instrumental families, the shorter the air passage, the higher the pitch. This applies across the orchestra: piccolo-flute-alto flute; trumpet-trombone-tuba; and even violin-cello-bass.

The oboe, while smaller and quieter than most of the instruments, has a tendency to stand out with a tone that is at turns tender or melancholy (representative oboe part: the countermelody at "Oh, what a melancholy choice this is" in "Far from the Home I Love," from *Fiddler on the Roof*). The lower neighbor is the alto oboe, which is more familiarly known as the English horn. This instrument is neither English nor a horn. The name apparently stems from the instrument's angled mouthpiece, as opposed to the straight one of the oboe; somebody along the line confused the French word *anglé* (angled horn) for *anglais* (English). Don't bother to call for a nationalized horn in England, by the way; "horn" will get you a French horn while "cor anglais" is the English. At any rate, the English horn bears the same relation to the oboe as the alto flute does to the flute. The English horn has a somewhat mellower sound, caused by its pear-shaped bell (representative English horn parts: the countermelody to the opening section of "Glitter and Be Gay" from *Candide*, or the four-bar introduction to "Sabbath Prayer" from *Fiddler on the Roof*).

The bassoon is what we might call the bass oboe. It shares the range of the cello, and often accompanies the string bass (representative bassoon part: the fill after "the French don't care what they do, actually, as long as they pronounce it properly" in "Why Can't the English?" from *My Fair Lady*). There are several other oboe family members, including an actual bass oboe; little used in the theatre, it falls between the bassoon and the English horn. The contrabassoon is an octave lower than the bassoon, but rarely found in the orchestra pit. Falling somewhere between the oboe and English horn is the oboe d'amour, so called for its relatively sweet tone. Bennett used it in the original production of *Oklahoma!* but the parts were soon switched to oboe—presumably due to a dearth of musicians who played the instrument. Or, practically speaking, owned one. (Pit musicians are required to provide their instruments, with a few understandable exceptions.)

The clarinet—which is how we generally refer to the B♭ clarinet—is perhaps the most valuable instrument to the orchestrator, as it has a wide range of uses (representative clarinet part: the solo accompanying David's refrain in "The Sweetest Sounds," from *No Strings*). There are three distinct registers; the fingering sequence results in an awkward jump, or bridge, between registers. For this reason, the orchestrator needs to consider the key when formulating the clarinet part. Don Walker had a standing rule: when writing a vocal background, never place the clarinets above the bridge because—in Walker's opinion, anyway—it interfered with the singer. (There is high-register writing for the "Speedy Valenti" section of the verse to "Swing" from *Wonderful Town*, but it does not conflict with the vocal.) Other family members include a high, E♭ clarinet (representative E♭ clarinet part: the Gershwinesque fills in "Poor Baby," from *Company*); an alto clarinet; and even a basement-level contrabass clarinet. The most frequent clarinet cousin used on Broadway is the bass clarinet. It is a counterpart to the bassoon without that instrument's reediness, and it can provide a liberal dose of humor (representative bass clarinet part: the moody accompaniment throughout most of "I'm Still Here," from *Follies*).

Saxophones serve a special purpose in the pit, as they are both reed instruments (by definition) and brass instruments (by material). This places their sound somewhere in between the two, allowing them to blend well with either family. There are three saxes commonly found in the pit band. Commonest are the alto (representative part: solo fills throughout "The Music That Makes Me Dance," from *Funny Girl*); the mid-range tenor (representative part: the long solo in the dance section of "The Music and the Mirror," from *A Chorus Line*); and, usually serving as the bottom voice of the sax section, the baritone (representative part: the bass line of "Who's That Girl?" from *Applause*). There is also a bass sax, rarely used in the pit but a favorite of Burns (representative part: the countermelody at "Hi, ya, Hugo, are ya stupid" and elsewhere in "The Telephone Hour," from *Bye Bye Birdie*). A higher sax, the soprano, is an occasional visitor to the orchestra pit (representative part: the solo at the beginning of the Prelude to *Follies*).

Brass

The brass section is relatively svelte. The trumpet is the leader of the band; nothing approximates the power and excitement of a trumpet at full blast (as in the culminating sections of the overtures to *Gypsy* and *Funny Girl*). Though not the most difficult instrument to play, a barrage of high notes can wear out the lips in a manner that is not generally an issue with other musicians. Broadway musicians work for union scale, with overrides for doubles and other special duties. The first trumpet has long received a special bonus; at present, this chair has a separate, higher union scale than the other instruments. The cornet is similar to the trumpet, with a somewhat more lyrical tone, but is rarely found in the Broadway pit. (The solo in "Cornet Man," from *Funny Girl*, is not a cornet but a trumpet—played on Broadway and on the original cast album by Dick Perry, from *Gypsy*.) A third, lower member of the trumpet family is the flugelhorn, which is somewhat warmer in the alto range (representative flugelhorn part: the introductory vamp to "You'll Think of Someone," from *Promises, Promises*). When the budget does not allow a French horn section, the orchestrator can approximate the sound by doubling his trumpeters on flugelhorn.

The trombone is also a valuable asset, able to play the bass line in its low register while capable of soaring solos in its upper range (representative trombone part: accompaniment and fills in "Love Makes the World Go," from *No Strings*). The trombone has a lower brother with a crisp sound, the bass trombone (representative bass trombone part: the foundation line in "Deep Down Inside," from *Little Me*). The trombonist occasionally doubles on two siblings. The baritone, or euphonium, has valves—rather than the trombone's slide—and offers a mellower sound. The tuba is another valve instrument, perhaps the loudest and lowest member of the pit orchestra (representative tuba part: the bass line in "All That Jazz," from *Chicago*). While the tuba fits in nicely with the trombone—they use similar mouthpieces, though different in size—it was originally a string bass double (as discussed below). The French horn is a hidden treasure of the pit, capable of great beauty with the ability to cut through a couple of dozen other instruments and soar. It is generally included with the brass family, as it is made from brass and uses a somewhat similar mouthpiece; in sound, though, it blends especially well with the reeds (representative horn part: the "Most Happy Fella" theme in the overture to *The Most Happy Fella*). The horn can also be especially arresting: Jule Styne's overtures for *Gypsy* and *Funny Girl* both stop in their tracks for horn solos, just before "Small World" in the first and before "People" in the second.

Strings

The string players, royalty of the symphonic orchestra, have somewhat lost their franchise in the Broadway pit, crowded out by increasing brass and reed contingents. The violin, the soprano of the family, is both the most expressive and most dynamic (representative violin part: the opening of the Prologue, from *Fiddler on the Roof*). The viola, the alto of the group, is a valuable supporting player capable of helping to fill in the middle. Violins generally outweigh violas, three or four to one. A few musicals (including Ramin and Kostal's *A Funny Thing Happened on the*

Way to the Forum and Kay's *110 in the Shade*) have seen fit to use violas but no violins, which sets the violas playing uncharacteristic parts (representative viola part: the solo at the opening of Finale act II /reprise of "I'll Marry the Next Man," from *Fiorello!*). More usually, orchestrators sacrificed the violas, picking up extra chairs for reeds and brass (as on *West Side Story, Bye Bye Birdie*, and *How to Succeed*). The cello is the baritone of the strings, marked by a sonorous beauty (representative cello part: "Later," from *A Little Night Music*). The double bass, or string bass, serves an altogether different purpose than its brethren. The bass is there to establish the foundation, sounding the low note (as the lower left hand does in our "Heart and Soul" example). No matter who else is playing, and no matter how loudly, the bass holds its own (representative string bass part: pizzicato foundation line in "Loads of Love," from *No Strings*). For these reasons, it is frequently present in musicals that otherwise include no strings—including *No Strings.*

In musicals with large string components, the violins are usually split into two, three, or sometimes four groups (denoted A, B, C, D). In these cases, the A chair has the important material; the others, typically, fill in the harmony except in cases where the melody warrants violins in force. With respect to violins, let us point out that two is *not* better than one. Due to the slight variation in sound caused by the vibration of the strings, two violins playing in unison tend to sound out of tune. A solo violin sounds perfectly fine; otherwise, three (or more) are needed on a single note.

Rhythm Section

Finally, we come to what is usually referred to under the catchall phrase "rhythm section." The drums are key. Broadway musicals typically had one percussionist until the incursion of jazz dance choreographers (Jerome Robbins, Michael Kidd, Bob Fosse). Modern show dances are built on offbeat accents, which the dancers—characteristically ranged across the stage—need to hear; in the old days, one drummer banging out the beat had been enough. Ramin: "Dancers want what they heard in the rehearsal hall. And that's what they need you to give them, not the notes."

The percussion component can be divided into two sections: instruments with indefinite pitch (snare drum, bass drum, cymbal) and instruments with definite pitch (timpani, xylophone, chimes). The needs for each musical vary and can mount up to quite an assemblage of instruments along with the necessary sticks and brushes to play them. Typically found in the percussion section are drums (snare, bass, tom-tom, bongo, timpani); cymbals (hi-hat, hand, suspended, finger, tam-tam, gong); xylophone, vibraphone, marimba, glockenspiel, chimes, bells;

and miscellanea (wood blocks, temple blocks, triangle, castanets, maracas, slap-stick, whistles, and more). Although the percussionists play numerous instru-ments, these are not considered doubles. Drum solos are infrequent, although they occasionally have important spots (such as the trap-set solo at the culmina-tion of the multipart "Simple" in *Anyone Can Whistle*, or the pitched drums as the Jets and Sharks flee the stage—leaving the dead bodies of Riff and Bernardo be-hind—at the end of the "Rumble" in *West Side Story*). Mallet instruments, how-ever, are frequently spotlighted, such as the xylophone that is prominent in the overture to *Funny Girl* (including a solo just after the "People" section); the marimba that is prominent in the overture to *La Cage aux Folles*, and the vibraphone that takes the lead in "Cool" in *West Side Story*. The celesta—basically an upright glockenspiel, with a piano keyboard—is technically a percussion instrument, al-though usually doubled by the pianist. (Noncomplicated celesta parts being rel-atively easy to play, the instrument has also been doubled by whoever might be available: sometimes percussionists, sometimes accordionists, and, in the case of *Pacific Overtures*, it was played by one of the trombonists.) The results are bright and somewhat heavenly. The invisible Tinker Bell in *Peter Pan* is played on a celesta as is the candy-box song in *She Loves Me*. Tchaikovsky's "Dance of the Sugar Plum Fairy," from *The Nutcracker*, is perhaps most readily identifiable.

Lest one wonders whether producers ever notice what's going on down in the pit, Herb Harris—one of the great Broadway percussionists, who went on to be-come contractor on such musicals as *Hair* and *A Chorus Line*—offers this:

> When *Fanny* was winding down, Lehman Engel—who was the conduc-tor—asked me to leave with him to do *Li'l Abner*. Merrick, who produced *Fanny*, came to me and said, "Look, Herb, I want the St. James in the fall, and *Li'l Abner*'s going in there. If you promise to throw *Li'l Abner* off on opening night—and you can do it, I've watched you play and you can louse up the show by playing just a little bit wrong, get everybody con-fused onstage. If you throw it off so the show really doesn't get off the ground, I'll give you $1,500." I said, "David, in the first place $1,500 is chicken feed and, secondly, you know I would get there and it would be impossible to do that." Oh well, I thought, he has a wry sense of humor, hasn't he? Six years later, I was married to Rae Allen, and Rae was doing *Oliver!* as standby to Georgia Brown. We were at a party and she intro-duced me to David and he said, "Yeah, I remember him. He's the kid who turned down fifteen hundred bucks."

There remains a handful of frequently used instruments that—like the mallet instruments in the percussion section—are distinguished by their ability to sound numerous notes simultaneously (as opposed to one note at a time). Should an or-chestrator wish to have a four-note chord played across two or three octaves, he might well assign nine string players—more than one-third of the twenty-five-piece orchestra—to the task. One piano player, however, can play all nine of those notes, freeing the strings for other assignments. It goes without saying that nine notes on the piano will not sound anything like nine notes from the string section; if it is a warm musical quality you want, you won't get it from the keyboard. How-ever, assign four strings (in strategic positions) to the chord, supplemented by piano, and you might get a reasonable substitute. Throw in a guitar, with one player reinforcing six of the notes, and you have an even stronger string sound while re-serving half of your nine-chair string section for other duties. With a string com-ponent of only six, nine-note chords can only come with outside assistance.

The sound of the piano is familiar to most of us, but it has long been rele-gated to secondary status in the rhythm section of the pit. There was a spell in the 1920s when producers Aarons & Freedley featured the popular two-piano team of Phil Ohman & Victor Arden in seven musicals (five by Gershwin, two by Rodgers). Twin pianos still occasionally turn up, as in *I Do! I Do!* and the 1971 revival of *No, No, Nanette.* There have been a number of musicals in which the plot includes characters who play the piano, such as *On Your Toes, They're Playing Our Song,* and *70, Girls, 70;* in Jerome Kern's 1931 musical *The Cat and the Fiddle*—which wove a romance between a classical composer and an American pop songwriter—Bennett used three pianos. Occasional musicals have made use of the piano con-certo sound, both in authentic operettas, like Rachmaninoff's *Anya,* and elsewhere, like Loesser's *How to Succeed,* in which the composer—in a mock Romantic frenzy—inserted Grieg's Piano Concerto in A Minor into "Rosemary." (This was not played in the theatre as grandly as it sounds on the original cast album. *How to Succeed* was scored without a piano; one of the violinists, proficient on the key-board, played the passage—ten bars in all—on a cut-down, five-octave cabaret piano.) From time to time, some orchestrators have seen fit to include exciting piano writing (Walker's *Cabaret* and *Shenandoah,* for example). But for the most part, especially during the so-called golden age of Broadway musicals, the pit pi-anist was relegated to playing chords, offbeats, and fills.

Keyboard instruments can give you ten notes; guitars and their relations can give you six; and the forty-five-stringed harp can give you—well, more than all your violins and violas combined. The harp has always been the great lady of the orchestra, capable of filling the theatre—or King Solomon's temple, I suppose—with the warmest of tones (representative harp parts: the accompaniment for "You'll Never Walk Alone," from *Carousel,* or the verse to "Do-Re-Mi" from *The Sound of Music*—which consists of one note, played in octaves, 128 times! while the low strings play the melody). The harp is not the most versatile of instruments, nor the most contemporary, and it is easily the most unwieldy; these factors have conspired to limit its usage in post–Rodgers and Hammerstein musicals. But for Bennett and Spialek, especially, the harp was much preferred to the piano as it could "fill up the sound" in the theatre with its overtones, unlike the piano, which has a dampened effect. The piano also brings with it the sound of a rehearsal hall, although this was apparently more objectionable to musical ears sixty years ago than it is today.

Another aspect of the harp is technical. It is constructed diatonically, with seven notes to the octave; think of a piano without any black keys. The harp can be tuned to any key, through the use of a series of foot pedals—professional harpists need be expert at shifting those pedals—but it can only play in the chosen key, without any accidentals (raised or lowered sharps and flats). In the Cole Porter musical *Out of This World* (1950), which took place on harp-happy Mount Olympus, the ever-resourceful Bennett found a solution to this problem: two harps in simultaneous action, tuned differently where warranted. This provides *Out of This World* with what might be the most ambitious harp writing on Broadway.

As the pit orchestra size has diminished, the harp became more and more of a luxury. (Harps, like the mallet instruments in the percussion section, offer sound more decorative than rhythmic; we nevertheless include them in the so-called rhythm section, as they don't fit elsewhere.)

The guitar, like the piano, has a contemporary sound associated with either folk or rock music, take your pick, and therefore in noncontemporary musicals it was often hidden by the "real" strings. Beginning around 1960, the guitar began to achieve more importance (representative guitar part: "Edelweiss" from *The Sound of Music*). Musicals from Latin or Mediterranean climes often feature the guitar or its cousin, the mandolin, and where would *Man of La Mancha* be without flamenco? And where, for that matter, would Phil Lang and Jerry Herman be without the banjo? But most of the time, the guitar's use is utilitarian. Lang, for example, used the guitar in *Take Me Along, Carnival, Hello, Dolly! Dear World*, and *Mack & Mabel*—shows set in very different times and places. Ginzler prominently spotlighted the electronically amplified guitar in *Bye Bye Birdie*, where it can be heard playing the underlying vamp to "The Telephone Hour." (The instrument was heard on Broadway as early as 1954, when Ginzler used it in "Steam Heat" from *The Pajama Game*.) Following the invasion of *Hair* (1968), electric guitars of all sorts have been frequently found in orchestra pits, blasting (literally) away. Other guitar doubles include the banjo (representative part: the introduction to the "That's How Young I Feel" section of the Overture to *Mame*) and the mandolin (representative part: under the melody of "Anatevka" in *Fiddler on the Roof*).

Occasional Instruments

Orchestrators, by and large, are content to work within the instrumentation available. Bennett expressed the notion that part of the challenge, to him, was to make a new—that is, show-specific—sound using the same old instruments; this was, indeed, what made Bennett unparalleled for much of his career. In the 1950s, the Broadway sound began to change with the incursion of reed doubles and the more prominent placing of saxophones (with the increasing reed and brass personnel serving to cut the string contingent). Bennett, Lang, and Hershy Kay continued to favor the style to which they were accustomed, while Walker, Ginzler, Kostal, and Burns forged ahead with new combinations. Much of Lang's success through the 1970s stemmed from his being virtually the only orchestrator who still wrote in the old-fashioned Broadway style, which—even in the age of Sondheim—was still desired on shows like *Annie* (1977) and *42nd Street* (1980).

Occasionally, the time and locale of a show called for special instruments not ordinarily found in the pit, bringing with them an exotic sound. Walker's Viennese-flavored *The Gay Life* eschewed piano and harp altogether, replacing them with cimbalom and accordion. (The cimbalom, commonly found in Hungarian tea rooms, is something like a xylophone with metallic strings.) Burns's *Illya Darling* and Walker's *Zorbà*, both set in contemporary Greece, featured onstage bouzouki bands. They added visual authenticity to the show, although they didn't mix especially well with the Local 802 players in the pit. (The rarity of these players in New York caused difficulties, as they typically could not read music, would not take direction in English, and could easily surpass the weekly Broadway pay scale by playing a wedding or two. And substitutes who could play, and sight-read, the parts were impossible to find.) Walker's *Shenandoah* had a harmonica chair, played by the celebrated Richard Hayman. (The pit pianist, as it happened, was Don Pippin, who was recuperating from the back-to-back bloodbaths of *Seesaw* and *Mack & Mabel* by taking a break before embarking on *A Chorus Line.*) In the percussion section, composer Harold Arlen specified an array of Caribbean sounds—starting with the steel drum—for Royal's *House of Flowers* and Lang's *Jamaica.* Tunick's *Pacific Overtures* featured a pair of onstage Japanese musicians, one playing an unfamiliar percussion set and the other on the three-stringed, guitar-like shamisen.

Tunick was also responsible for bringing the sound of the sixties recording studio into the pit—not out of desire but necessity, as Burt Bacharach's *Promises, Promises* (1968) called for replicating the composer's pop hits (complete with "pit singers"). While sound amplification was already commonplace on Broadway, the use of electronic instruments and offstage voices necessitated a portable sound-mixing board at the back of the orchestra section. Tunick brought this same setup along to his next major assignment, Sondheim's contemporary *Company*. While most of Tunick's shows have featured more traditional instrumentations (*Follies, A Little Night Music*), the Broadway pit—for nonrock musicals, even—was permanently transformed.

Of course, there had been a time when the saxophone sounded exotic; the accordion, too, was unusual when first introduced in the pit (in the early 1930s?). What seemed jarring to some ears, and reeked of lower forms of entertainment to others, nevertheless had the ability to provide synthetic stand-ins for the sounds of other instruments. Walker, especially, found the accordion a helpful solution for creating depth and filling in the lower tones when he started to cut back on strings; Tunick points out that Walker used the accordion in the same manner that the synthesizer is used today (representative accordion part: the countermelody to "Far from the Home I Love" from *Fiddler on the Roof*). The accordion has been prominently featured in several shows, including *Fiddler, She Loves Me*, and *Carnival.*

Starting in the fifties, orchestrators began using electronic pianos of various sorts. Walker used a small Allen organ on at least two shows, *The Rothschilds* and *Shenandoah. Shenandoah*, in fact, rented *The Rothschilds'* organ from Manny Azenberg—who, as one of the general managers, had inherited it—for $50 a month. As a producer of Bill Finn's musical *Falsettoland*, I might as well add that we borrowed our keyboard from *Annie 2*, which had just "closed for repairs" in Washington.

West Side Story ushered in what might be called the split orchestra. The jazzy dances of "Cool" and "The Jet Song" called for a certain type of instrumentation; the operatic "A Boy Like That" and the elegiac "Somewhere" called for something else entirely. This situation also existed in *Tenderloin*, an 1890s tale pitting polite, religious society with the rough and salacious underworld. In this case, Irv Kostal—one of the *West Side* orchestrators—used creative doubling, with the organ and guitar/mandolin for the do-gooders and the piano and banjo for the lowlife denizens. Other split shows included *Cabaret* and the aforementioned *Zorbà*, two Kander and Ebb musicals orchestrated by Walker; the former had frisky nightclub numbers contrasted with more genteel book songs, while the latter juggled ethnically Greek sections with more traditional musical theatre. *On a Clear Day You Can See Forever* jumped the centuries, which Bennett achieved mostly by using a harpsichord. This type of situation comes up occasionally; it is up to the orchestrator to either make an effort to contrast the two styles, or simply plunge ahead in the same old manner. As in *Can-Can*, set in Montmartre in the Offenbachian gay nineties, which Lang outfitted with a guitar.

Then, there are the instruments that are not really instruments. Beginning around 1960, a few orchestrators began thinking out of the (band) box. The best examples, perhaps, are in *How to Succeed in Business Without Really Trying* (1961). Faced with "I Believe in You," in which the staging calls for the singer to use an electric shaver, Ginzler came up with a novel solution: kazoos. Actually, kazoos accompanied by trumpets, French horn, and violins instructed to "play sharp." This effect not only recreated the hum of electric shavers; the eerily nonmusical sound startled and then delighted the audience, building on the sight gag in the staging. Elsewhere in the show, Ginzler followed choreographer Fosse's lead—in "A Secretary Is Not a Toy"—by accompanying the sexy walk of a girl dancer with an actual typewriter. He capped the secretary's walk with a cowbell; during the boy's dance break, he also used sandpaper. Ginzler had done something similar seven years earlier in Fosse's first legendary dance number, "Steam Heat" (in *The Pajama Game*). Following an unprecedented dance section accompanied by no musicians at all—solely the actors shuffling their feet, clapping their hands, and clucking their tongues—Ginzler added the clanging of a plumber's steam pipe to the mix. He also used the sound of an anvil in the gym-workout number "Physical Fitness," in *All American* (1962).

Other notable cases are the cash register that Ramin brought in for "The Sound of Money" in *I Can Get It for You Wholesale* (1962) and the mallet on a strip of leather Wilcox devised for the shoemaker's duet "How Do You Talk to a Girl," in *Walking Happy* (1966). For that matter, Don Walker experimented with several sounds for "The Music of Home," in *Greenwillow* (1960), including a tea kettle singing "a-way-a-wee." This was accomplished by having two piccolos playing a note and its upper neighbor (creating a discord), while the violins played harmonics (with an eerily shimmering sound). Walker also illustrated the lyric "the neighbor's choppin' axe ringin' on a maple" by telling the drummer to hit the wooden side of the pit railing with a metal stick. Walker, Ginzler, Ramin, Wilcox, Kostal, and Burns all started thinking outside the traditional. Thus, a police siren at the top of the overture to Kostal's *Fiorello!* as well as the four pistol shots that began Ginzler's Prohibition era *Nowhere to Go but Up*.

In sum, the orchestrator—with input from the musical director and perhaps the composer—chooses his instruments, both traditional and unconventional; determines his doubles, according to his musical needs, the available players, and budgetary considerations; and uses whatever devices he can devise to remind the audience, whenever possible, where the characters are and what the composer intends the sound of the show to be.

Doubling (and More)

You cannot, understandably, get the same sound from a pit orchestra of twenty-five as you can from—take your pick—a symphony orchestra, a Hollywood sound-stage orchestra, a recording studio orchestra . . . Ten strings, out of a total of twenty-five pieces, will never sound like forty strings. Broadway orchestrators long ago figured out how to use reeds to give the impression of more strings; for a start, you can split your violins into two sections, enhancing the top part with flute or oboe. Viola chords can be supported by clarinets; the cello can be strengthened with bassoon or French horn; the cello–French horn combination, actually, gives a warm and romantic sound. The string bass is frequently accompanied by bassoon or bass clarinet. As the reeds and brass expanded, the resulting smaller string sections were of necessity bolstered by other voices. The trick is to let the violins and cellos ring out, with the reeds playing in a supportive manner. You can just as easily do the reverse, spotlighting the reed instruments with strings in support.

While the volume of a twenty-five-person pit can't be enhanced without the use of amplification and synthesizers, the colors can be expanded by doubling. Simply put, this is the practice of one musician switching off between two or more instruments. Any flute player can logically be expected to play the piccolo, which is more or less a miniature flute sounding an octave higher. There are simple doubles and more complicated ones. Before we continue, let us point out that pit musicians work almost exclusively for union scale; each double brings an additional amount. At present-day dollars, Broadway scale (at January 1, 2008) was $1,501. The first double earns you an additional eighth, which—with compulsory vacation pay—works out to about $300. Each additional double is paid an additional sixteenth. Thus, a flutist who also plays piccolo, clarinet, bass clarinet, and tenor sax will earn five-sixteenths over scale, or about $2,200 (with vacation). These add-ons mount up, but they allow the orchestrator the use of extra instruments without costing the producer $1,500 per.

Strings rarely double, with the exception of the bass, which traditionally doubled the tuba. The reasoning was logical; the tuba, while cumbersome, was portable, allowing it to play those bass notes when strolling (or marching) musicians were called for. The tuba is used sparingly in the orchestra pit, taking the place of the bass in especially brassy numbers (such as "A Little Bit of Luck," in *My Fair Lady*). Rather than having an unoccupied tuba player sitting on payroll all night, Broadway cultivated bass players who could play the tuba. As the trombone contingent gradually expanded from one to three players, it became more practical to hand the tuba to the second or third trombone, who could easily adapt to the tuba's mouthpiece. Look at the scores of many classic musicals, like *My Fair Lady* and *Hello, Dolly!* and you'll find the bass/tuba double still on the page—which can prove problematic when they revive these shows. Even more challenging is the tuba doubling with guitar, which Bennett saw fit to use on *Show Boat*.

Brass players have several customary doubles. The trumpets might be assigned the cornet or the flugelhorn; all three use a similar mouthpiece. The trombones double on bass trombone or—as discussed above—the tuba. Both trombone and trumpet occasionally double on the baritone (euphonium) as well. The French horn is in a musical world of its own, with a different mouthpiece, playing style, and personality—and thus usually not a doubling instrument. (When City Center Encores! revived *Damn Yankees* in the summer of 2008, they found that the second of three trumpet parts was written to double as a French horn—which none of the trumpeters were able to play.)

The piano often doubles on the celestial celesta, the full-bodied organ, or—since about 1960—the electric piano and synthesizer. The conductor of smaller-sized pit orchestras occasionally serves as pianist as well, beginning as far as I can tell with Peter Matz on *No Strings* in 1962. Stepping back to yesteryear, I found an interesting partitur from a show called *Piccadilly to Broadway*, a 1920 debacle which overtook George Gershwin early in his career. This chart, by the innovative Frank Saddler, predates the period discussed in this book; it merits attention, however, calling for both a grand piano and an upright.

The accordion, depending on the amount of use, can be a chair of its own or a piano double; this player might also double on concertina. The percussionist plays the required set of instruments, but these are not considered doubles. The harpist, like the French horn, is in her own world. The guitarist has a number of doubles, ranging from the common (banjo, electric guitar) to the obscure (lute, balalaika, you name it). The mandolin is usually a guitar double, but in some cases it is handed to a violinist as the two instruments share a similar string system.

The reed section is where things become complex. The reeds are just as frequently called winds or woodwinds; none of these terms fit, exactly. The flute does not use a reed, nor is it made of wood any more (although it was long ago). The saxophone has never been made out of wood. If the use of wind is the criteria, then why shouldn't the trumpet and trombone be included? Even so, "winds," "woodwinds," and "reeds" are used interchangeably. Most of the orchestra scores I've perused label the parts reed I, reed II, and on, so for the purposes of this book we will stick to the term reeds.

The reed itself is a piece of cane which, when it vibrates, makes a noise; think of a blade of grass and move on from there. The clarinet and saxophone families use a single reed; the oboe, bassoon, and their relations are double-reed instruments, using two reeds tied together back to back. Single- and double-reeds require different playing techniques, but in both cases the sound is made by breath blowing over the single reed or between the double reeds. The flute, on the other hand, is sounded by blowing across a flat hole in the instrument. You can practice this by blowing across the rim of a glass soda bottle, if you can find a glass soda bottle.

Reed doubles are assigned, to some extent, along family lines. The clarinet (or the B♭ clarinet, as it is officially named) has a three-octave range; the opening schmear of "Rhapsody in Blue" pretty much covers the terrain. But you wouldn't want your clarinet to dwell on those low notes, which can sound somber; thus, somewhere along the line, they invented the alto clarinet, which is half an octave lower. Similarly, there is the bass clarinet, which sounds an octave below the regular (treble) clarinet and is often used to supplement the low strings. (The larger size of the instrument means a longer path for the air, creating a lower sound.) While the alto clarinet is infrequently used, the pit clarinetist will frequently double on bass clarinet. The flute player will similarly switch off with piccolo and alto flute; the oboe will periodically pick up the English horn. In each case, the mouthpiece and fingerings are similar within the family. The double-reeded bassoon player, oddly enough, is likely to play clarinet and bass clarinet—but not oboe or English horn, the other double reeds.

A symphonic orchestra might use ten brass (three trumpets, three trombones, four horns) and twelve reeds (flute, clarinet, oboe, and bassoon, times three). The full-sized Broadway pit orchestra, from the mid-1950s on, might include nine brass and only five reeds. Heavy reed doubling was of little help in battling the brass contingent. Still, it at least allowed the orchestrator to choose a symphonic-sized trio of—say—clarinets at any given moment; or, alternatively, to go with all the colors (though not in groups of three). Ginzler, in "Put on a Happy Face" from Bye Bye Birdie, used a startlingly unconventional four flutes.

For many decades, the typical pit orchestra featured one flute, two clarinets, and one oboe, with a bassoon sometimes thrown in as well. Matters were complicated, and eventually subverted, by the intervention of the saxophone. This is a combination of brass and pads played with a clarinet-like single-reed mouthpiece. (Unlike the rest of our traditional instruments, which developed over the centuries, this one was invented in 1840 in France by a monsieur named Adolphe Sax.) The saxophone—which by design sounds like a combination of reed (wind) and brass—was long restricted to marching bands. In the early twentieth century, it gained popularity in dance bands, and by the roaring twenties was a mainstay of dance music. The hot musicals of Gershwin and Youmans brought the sax into the orchestra pit, as a double usually played by the (similarly single-reed) clarinet. Soon most reed players in nonlegit musicals needed to be capable of playing at least one of the members of the sax family, of which the most theatrically popular are the alto, tenor, baritone, and sometimes soprano. Moving into the mid-1950s, the sax component somewhat took over. The professional clarinetist could still play nonswinging shows, like *My Fair Lady* or *The Most Happy Fella*, but the live-lier scores—like *Wonderful Town* or *Li'l Abner*—needed reed players who were more than merely proficient on sax.

> RED PRESS: The orchestrations were different; they were swing scores, with con-temporary playing. They needed jazz-oriented orchestras. The older shows were principally legit, with flute, clarinet, and oboe, sometimes with doubling on sax-ophone. Once you got into things like *Gypsy* and *West Side*, they brought in sax as a basic instrument. You needed real sax players who could double on the other reeds. The older players couldn't play the style, and they couldn't play all the instruments. In the original *Gypsy*, one of the chairs played flute, piccolo, clarinet, bass clarinet, tenor sax, and bass saxophone. Once this style came in, a lot of the younger orchestrators demanded it, and it became more predominant. When we did *Bye Bye Birdie* at Encores! in 2004, there were some guys I couldn't hire. Think of "Put on a Happy Face"; some guys can't play eighth-notes that way, they don't have the feel. A lot of string players still can't play that kind of show, in the same way that a lot of fine musicians won't sound good in a rock show. They don't have the feel.
>
> When I got out of the army, I went on the road and made a living for years. But little by little the swing band business dried up. I was a saxophone player, but I knew that I had to become a good flutist or I couldn't make a living in New York. It depended on learning the doubles. The radio stations, with their sixty-five-piece orchestras, dried up; a lot of those wonderful players simply weren't equipped to do Broadway because they weren't doublers. They could play sax and clarinet, but that wasn't enough. If you learned all the instru-ments—well, it's fifty years later and some of us are still working.
>
> Another change that came in was that you started to get better musicians in the pit. The union had gotten a better contract; if you could get a pit job, you were in seventh heaven. So the band guys—the orchestrators and conductors who came from the bands—brought in their favorite musicians, much to the consternation of the old-time contractors. Look at the pit of *Gypsy*: Jimmy Crawford, the drummer, and the bass player (I forget his name) were from the Ellington band; the pianist was Frank Signorelli from Paul Whiteman; the trumpeter, Dick Perry, and I were from Tommy Dorsey.

An earlier view of the practicalities of doubling came from Morris Stonzek, a longtime contractor who spanned from Flo Ziegfeld to David Merrick:

> Some doublers are very good on flute and not so good on clarinet. So you would write the first chair for the first flute and second clarinet. The clarinet would play very good clarinet but lousy flute, so you'd write him the second chair. And the bassoonists usually were not very good saxo-phone players, so you gave him a baritone sax to play, which was not as

important as the alto and tenor; and the tenors would usually be oboe doubles, because the embouchure would not be that much affected by changing from tenor sax (which has a looser embouchure) to an oboe (which has a very tight embouchure). In the theatre, I usually knew the men because I'd worked with them either on recordings or radio shows, so I had a very good idea of who could play what and what fitted the show. When I did Billy Rose's *Seven Lively Arts* in 1944, we had a Stravinsky ballet specially written for Alicia Markova and Anton Dolin; we had a big opera finale; and the rest was a Cole Porter score. So the men had to be able to play symphonic music, ballet music, opera music, and pop music. That was the most difficult show I ever had. But for normal shows, I knew pretty well who was around and who was available at the time. Certain shows needed an exceptional jazz trumpet player; other shows didn't.

A Tale of Two Reed Sections

Let us look at the reed components of two hit 1949 musicals, one legit and one swing. Rodgers and Hammerstein's *South Pacific* (orchestrated by Bennett) was a contemporary, romantic love story with tragic overtones. There were five reeds: flute (doubling on piccolo), oboe (doubling on English horn), two clarinets, and bassoon.

Compare this to the five chairs on Jule Styne's *Gentlemen Prefer Blondes* (orchestrated by Walker), a fondly satiric look back at the roaring twenties with an emphasis on the hot music of the time. Reed I: alto sax/clarinet/flute II (and "jazz clarinet"); reed II: alto sax/clarinet; reed III: tenor sax/clarinet/bass clarinet (and "jazz tenor sax"); reed IV: tenor sax/flute I/piccolo; reed V: baritone sax/alto sax/clarinet/bass clarinet. (The "jazz clarinet" and "jazz tenor" were listed in Walker's hand along with the doubles, indicating that the players were to receive extra payments for their solos. Walker, a great fan of Dixieland, inserted an impressive Dixieland section in the "Mamie Is Mimi" dance.)

This lineup allowed Walker—who started his career playing sax in roaring twenties bands—to use up to five saxophones or four clarinets at any given moment, with two bass clarinets on call as well. At the same time, this is the earliest Broadway orchestra I can find without an oboe—the acknowledged center of the pit orchestra—or bassoon. Walker covered what would have been the former's functions with a tenor sax, while the bass clarinet filled in for the latter. A loss in texture, yes; but the upside was the ability to set five saxes a-wailing. Doubles per chair are customarily listed in order of dominance; flute/clarinet/tenor would indicate that the part was written for a flute player who also played the other in-

struments. *Gentlemen Prefer Blondes* is the earliest case I've found that cast sax players—first and foremost—who could double.

In Walker's papers, I found an illuminating statement on doubling for a four-
reed show. (The show—a 1981 miscue called *The Little Prince and the Aviator*—
closed during previews for a number of reasons, none involving orchestration.)
The reed section consisted of four chairs: flute/alto flute/clarinet/tenor sax/so-
prano sax; oboe/English horn/flute/clarinet/alto sax; clarinet/E♭ clarinet/bass
clarinet/alto sax/soprano sax/flute; bassoon/baritone sax/soprano sax/clarinet.
Walker explained his "objectives of woodwind doubling": 1) a legit woodwind
quartet; 2) 3 flutes and bassoon; 3) complete clarinet sound—3 clarinets and
bass clarinet; 4) sax quartet; 5) 3 soprano saxes; and 6) dynamite woodwind 4-
octave unison of piccolo, E-b clarinet, oboe, bassoon. This nineteen-person orchestra also included four brass (two trumpets, one trombone, one French horn),
seven strings (four violins, one viola, one cello, one bass), keyboard, harp, and two
percussion.

Another notable case of doubling came from Burns on *No Strings*, which—as
advertised—had no violins, violas, or cellos. Ralph used eight reeds—a Broadway record, apparently—with their combined thirty-two doubles allowing him to
have, at any given time, as many as eight saxes, eight clarinets, seven flutes, or four
bass clarinets. This was combined with seven brass (four trumpets and three
trombones); the band was completed by harp, string bass, guitar, and two percussion. All this plus a sparingly used piano, played by the conductor.

Doubling, as we see, allows the orchestrator to have considerably more colors
at his disposal. The *Gentlemen Prefer Blondes* orchestra had twenty-six musicians
playing forty instruments. More specifically, eighteen musicians played one instrument each; the other eight played twenty-two (including the customary doubles of piano/celesta, guitar/banjo, and string bass/tuba).

How do eight musicians play twenty-two instruments in the course of one
show—or, possibly, one musical number? And how does one reed player play four
or five? For that matter, how do they find room to keep them all at hand, in a small
and crowded pit? (By cramming them into every available cranny.) This is a question of careful planning on the part of the orchestrator. Typically, some sections
of the number—solo parts, be they in the melody, countermelody, or fill—will cry
out for a specific color. The orchestrator will make sure he has the instrument(s)
he wants available at these points, working backward and forward from there.

These changes of instruments— "go to picc"—are written into the partitur
by the orchestrator, for transfer to the individual part books. Different instruments take different amounts of time for the switch; larger instruments—bassoon, baritone sax—take longer to be lifted than the switch from flute to piccolo.

(Players of the smaller reeds, in especially busy numbers, sometimes seem to be juggling; a flute player with a clarinet clutched between his knees and a piccolo tucked under his left arm is not an uncommon sight.) The wise orchestrator must keep careful track of his assignments. Lang, at some quick changes, would indicate which notes were more important, allowing the player some leeway. Burns, on one partitur, tells his trombones to switch mutes "from bucket to open FAST! Sorry—you wanted to go on the road and see America!" And then there's Kostal's note to the flutist at the climax of the fugue in *West Side Story*'s "Cool," where he provides a mere five beats (at quick-time) to change instruments: "Grab ze piccolo!" Kostal writes.

Carefully contrived instrument switches can become nightmares when musical numbers—especially dance or production numbers—are altered during the tryout. It is almost a given that, whenever cuts are made, doubling musicians inevitably find themselves playing this measure on one instrument and the next on another. This also applies to difficult-to-play passages. The wise orchestrator always leaves rest time for the trumpets between sections with the highest notes, and not only out of thoughtfulness; when the trumpeter misses crucial high notes because his lips are shot, it's the orchestrator who looks bad. Cuts and patches always seem to splice together sections which increase the difficulty of the playing.

Doubling aside, there are any number of methods of making different musical sounds on the same instrument. The use of mutes, the most striking of which is perhaps the wah-wah mute used in the brass section, is common. (Fielding complaints from the waiting room in "On the Side of the Angels" from *Fiorello!* the Jewish clerk sings, "that bench is crowded / it's a regular wailing wall." "WAA-WAA-WAA-WAA-WAA," Kostal's trumpets respond in a descending scale; the part is marked "not too much!") The brass instruments have several mutes, which are placed in the bell of the instrument and thus either muffle or enhance the sound. The most familiar is the straight mute, which—well, which mutes the sound. Dance bands contributed the cup mute (which sounds smooth and mellow, as in the trombone prominent through "I've Got Your Number" from *Little Me*), the Harmon (which sounds crisply brassy, as in "If He Walked into My Life" from *Mame*), and the plunger mute (which wails, as in the trombone at the opening of "Pass That Football" from *Wonderful Town*). The French horn has a straight mute as well, although this instrument is usually played with a natural mute—namely the right fist of the player. The reeds occasionally use the solotone mute (which provides the period sound of the twenties and thirties). Strings have mutes as well, small combs that clamp to the bridge which lessen the vibrations and thus the sound. There is no way to mute a flute or a double reed other than to instruct the musician to play softer.

Each instrument can create a variety of sounds. The strings are a perfect example. They are most regularly played with a bow (arco), which gives them a smooth sound. Occasionally, they are plucked by the fingers (pizzicato), which gives them a pinched and percussive sound (representative pizzicato section: the melody accompanying the vocal countermelody ["isn't this the height of nonchalance"] in "You Are Woman," from *Funny Girl*). At times, the string player is instructed to use what are called harmonics, producing an eerie sound by adding overtones. More familiar is the tremolo, which adds tension by moving the fingers back and forth on the string (representative tremolo section: the violins at "around the corner" in the bridge to "Something's Coming," from *West Side Story*). Tremolos of a different sort are commonly assigned to timp and piano. Portamento, from the Italian word for "carry," is a manner of gliding through the tones from one note to another (representative portamento section: the emotional violin fills in "Don't Cry," from *The Most Happy Fella*).

The trumpeter can create many different sounds, even without mechanical alteration. One need only contrast the clear, pure Salvation Army trumpet in "Follow the Fold," from *Guys and Dolls*, with the burlesque growl in the "strip" section of the overture to *Gypsy*. Another more obscure sample can be found in the overture to *Tenderloin*, in which there is a pristine trumpet solo labeled "band in the park style." (This was intended to be played on a cornet, but the orchestrator and musical director decided to use their doubles allowance elsewhere.) The sound of these three trumpet solos is different, by design; the orchestrator will often indicate what he wants with a few well-chosen words, and the player—under the direction of the conductor—takes it from there.

The *Gypsy* solo, marked "burlesque strip style," makes an interesting case. The first chair trumpet was a fine player with legit training, but he apparently had never been in a burlesque house. When they ran through the number at the orchestra reading, the solo sounded too polite. They asked the second chair trumpet to give it a try. Dick Perry, who like Red Press was an alumnus of Tommy Dorsey's Orchestra, knew what to do and how to do it. (Perry quickly became Broadway's most sought-after trumpeter, with his playing preserved on the cast albums of not only *Gypsy* but *Do Re Mi*, *Subways Are for Sleeping*, *I Can Get It for You Wholesale*, *Funny Girl*, and *42nd Street*. He was also lead trumpet on Sinatra's recording of Kander & Ebb's "New York, New York.") To quote an old saying around the orchestra pit, "as the first trumpet goes, so goes the show."

Play the *Gypsy* solo in the Salvation Army style of *Guys and Dolls* and it will sound wrong; for that matter, play "Follow the Fold" burlesque-style and the audience will infer that the missionaries are not quite kosher. The point is, a trumpet—or any instrument—can sound different depending on the manner in which it is being played. This is perhaps the most valuable skill of the orchestrator; not only deciding that this section should be played by the clarinet, but dictating how that clarinet should sound. Sweet, pure, weepy, salacious, you name it.

As can be seen, orchestration is not only a question of which instrument should play what. How the instrument is played, and the combination of instruments at any given time, is what makes an orchestration flavorful rather than generic. Contrast three sections from two numbers of *Candide*, all featuring a bassoon. In the verse to "What's the Use?" Hershy Kay backs the singer with a bassoon playing arpeggiated chords (in 3/4 time, with the bass downbeat), while the flute accompanies the melody. The second verse, with a male rather than a female singer, puts a clarinet on the melody. In the interlude to "Bon Voyage" ("I'm so rich that my life is an utter bore"), Kay gives the bassoon a scale-like passage while the melody is played by the oboe. Three very different effects, each driven by the bassoon but with a different reed instrument up top.

While we don't wish to keep harping on *Tenderloin*—a relatively obscure musical which readers might not have on their CD shelf—Irv Kostal created a striking sound for a song called "My Gentle Young Johnny." The orchestration (in 3/4 time) consists mainly of the bass line—an eighth-note pickup, leading to a half-note, offset by a half-note accompaniment on the second beat of each measure; the singer is joined on the melody by an alto flute. Part of what makes the piece so striking is that the cellos have been split; one plays the bass line, joined by the bass clarinet and the string bass. The accompanying half-note is played by the other cello, combined with violas, guitar, harp, vibraphone, and two alto flutes.

This combination was born, in part, of necessity; with only two cellos and four reeds (one of which must be on the melody), the choices are limited. Kostal could have put both cellos on the foundation, but he wanted the cello on the bass line. In fact, he wrote in a third cello part on the partitur, with a notation that it was to be used for the recording—the only such case I noticed on the thousands examined. In effect, you get a cello on both the beat and the offbeat, with the tones overlapping. On a number like this, in the midst of a busy musical, the orchestrator will typically think, okay, let's give the brass a rest here. But Kostal is atypical. As the bridge of the song builds to a climax, he gives the trumpets and trombones two notes. That's it; instead of sitting doing their crossword, the brass section has to pay attention and count. But it's called for by the song. At the same spot, he also gives the vibraphone five-note chords—which means the fellow must use five mallets spaced between ten fingers.

Composer Jerry Bock, in our discussions, singled out this number:

> The orchestration to "My Gentle Young Johnny" was so sensitive to what we had in mind, I never imagined it could be translated as delicately and as sensitively from the piano copy. There was a remarkable chamber music sound that so supported the emotion, and was yet another example of Irv's mastery and sensitivity to what he heard.

SECTION V.
THEN COMES THE ORCHESTRATOR

Setting the Instrumentation

The instrumentation is set by the orchestrator, right? Well, no. The composer often exerts influence in this area, and not without reason. So does the musical director, who will be entrusted with the nightly task of getting the score to sound like the composer and orchestrator intend. The musical contractor—something like the casting director and paymaster for the musicians—can weigh in with demands of his or her own. And then, there's the producer.

Playing by the Numbers

Before we get to the actual instrumentation of Broadway musicals, we must first discuss the size of the pit orchestra. Orchestra size, not surprisingly, is a function of economics combined with union-negotiated minimums. Shows with larger budgets, from pedigreed songwriters, often expand the number; but the union minimum is always the starting place of the discussion, and sometimes the end of the discussion as well.

Broadway theatres are customarily placed into three categories. The largest of these, the so-called musical houses, have upward of 1,400 seats. These include the most desirable theatres, including the Shubert, Imperial, Majestic, Winter Garden, and St. James. The Broadway, with 1,700-odd seats, was long the largest, although newer houses of recent decades have pushed past the 1,800 mark.

The "swing houses" are an intermediate group, so called because their 1,200–1,400 capacity made them suitable for either a small musical or a large nonmusical (usually with a star). There were traditionally only a few houses in this category, led by the Alvin (Simon), 46th Street (Rodgers), Martin Beck (Hirschfeld), and Broadhurst.

Finally, there are the dramatic houses. These range between 700 and 1,100 seats, with a few smaller houses added over the years; the Booth, Music Box, Barrymore, O'Neill, and Plymouth (Jacobs) are among the most popular. Economics long made them all but impractical for any except the smallest musicals.

For most of the period from about 1940 into the 1980s, union minimums were roughly as follows: for a musical house, twenty-five or twenty-six players; for a swing house, twenty or twenty-one players; for a dramatic house, twelve players.

The relationship between seating capacity and suitability for musical production no longer applies, due to the emergence of superhit musicals which run ten years or more. A theatre like the Winter Garden, which housed a full fifteen musicals (plus a dozen nonmusical attractions) in the 1950s, was off the booking market for eighteen years thanks to *Cats*; *Phantom of the Opera* has passed the two-decade mark at the Majestic; *Les Misérables* took the Imperial for twelve and a half years, after three and a half at the Broadway; and the list goes on.

What this has done, along with entertaining millions of theatregoers and employing thousands of theatre workers, is deplete the housing stock. Broadway's biggest musicals have been forced to go into swing houses and are lucky to get them. Inevitably, full-scale musicals like *Jekyll & Hyde* and the 2006 revival of *A Chorus Line* now find themselves in so-called dramatic houses. With ticket prices pushing past the $125 mark, this has become economically feasible. Two recent intimate musicals, in fact, managed to be lucrative money makers in Broadway's tiniest houses, *Avenue Q* at the 796-seat Golden (with six musicians) and *The 25th Annual Putnam County Spelling Bee* at the 684-seat Circle in the Square (with five musicians). But most of the shows discussed in this book go back to the earlier era, when all but a very few musicals were produced in musical houses (with at least twenty-five musicians) or swing houses (with at least twenty).

The house minimum, logically enough, is the minimum number of musicians required to be employed in a given house. Bring a musical into a twenty-five-player house and you are obligated to pay twenty-five musicians. This does not mean that a tenant will necessarily employ that number. Flush producers looking to keep their composers happy can be prevailed upon to, and into the 1970s often did, hire more musicians than required. A special provision known as the "cuts list" allowed shows to cut down to the minimum when finances demand. Given the complexity of creating a balanced orchestration, it is almost impossible to pull a reed or brass player out of the mix; thus, the axe usually fell, when it fell, on the violas and violins. (The musicians in question, and the union, had to be advised before the opening that their chairs were subject to eventual termination.) A few months or a year into the run, a musical might not sound as bright or lush as when it opened—not with six violins cut to four and the viola and cello sections both losing one or two players. Orchestrators scored these shows accordingly, keeping the "cut list" chairs expendable.

There have been occasional cases where a show chose to employ fewer musicians than required. Two examples from the 1970s attracted significant attention. When Hal Prince booked his revised version of *Candide* into the Broadway Theatre in 1974, the environmental reconfiguration of the house halved the seating capacity from about 1,800 to 900. This new *Candide* was orchestrated for thirteen pieces, with the musicians spotted throughout the arena. The Musicians' Union, to the dismay of producer Prince, insisted that the Broadway had a twenty-five-player minimum regardless of the number of seats used. Prince waged battle, but was unsuccessful. *Candide* enjoyed an award-laden run of 740 performances, but nevertheless closed at a loss. Calculate the salary and benefits for twelve musicians for ninety-two weeks; I suspect the figure will more than exceed the amount of the loss. Meanwhile, a dozen musicians streamed in every Thursday night to collect their paychecks for not playing. *A Chorus Line* (1975)—like *Candide*, a direct transfer from a small nonprofit theatre—was also devised for a smaller orchestra than the minimum. Rather than rejigger the orchestra, the producers decided to play the show as originally devised. Seventeen musicians played, eight sat out—for the fifteen-year run.

Musician minimums have long been seen by many as unfair. There is no minimum for actors, singers, or dancers, for example; each show, rather obviously, has its own requirements. But the orchestra minimums were set up in negotiations between the producers and the Musicians' Union, and that is what the producers had to live with. (In recent negotiations, the minimums have been reduced. In 2008, the minimum for the six largest houses is nineteen.) Let it be added that a considerable number of nonplaying musicians—popularly referred to as walkers, as they walk in to pick up their checks and then leave—were not card-carrying musicians but relatives or colleagues of the producers and managers, who were slipped into union membership with the collusion of officials. Let us also add that, in the dark days of the 1980s, at least some company managers, conductors, and musical contractors regularly tried to assign walker jobs to bona fide union members who were unable to work due to terminal illness.

Weighing Choices

The first question, thus, is: how many musicians? The major factor is the house minimum, so that the final decision is usually delayed until the show has booked a theatre for its Broadway engagement. Through the mid-seventies, this meant twenty-five or twenty-six for a musical house, or twenty or twenty-one for a swing house. In cases where a show began its tryout without a Broadway booking, budget-conscious producers would usually start with twenty and add more depending on where they found a home. It is relatively simple to add five or six pieces if you're paying for the extra musicians anyway; removing five pieces from a well-orchestrated twenty-five-piece orchestration, though, is problematic. Nothing ever prevented a producer from employing more musicians than the union demands, but this is certainly not the norm. As production costs began to rise, and as long-running shows began to tie up the larger houses, the question of orchestra size became even more problematic. A full-scale musical in a 1,100-seat theatre needs to make numerous financial adjustments due to the smaller potential capacity; the number of musicians is, perhaps, first on the list of variables.

With the house minimum as either a base (in the case of plush budgets) or a cap (in the case of the opposite), the number of musicians is determined. The decision makers split the orchestra into the already-discussed four sections: reeds, brass, strings, and rhythm/catchall (keyboard, percussion, guitar, and special needs). A 1956 musical like *My Fair Lady* demanded more strings than, say, a 1956 musical like *Li'l Abner*; *Abner*, on the other hand, called for more sax and brass.

Elliot Lawrence fills us in on the process:

> Instrumentation is usually between the musical director, the orchestrator, and the composer, taking into account the economics—how do you divide what they're going to give you? You look at the score. You need six brass, whatever; then you figure out what you're going to do with the rest. Often the composer will say he's got some vague notion, like I hear French horns; or Jule would say he wants a big brass section. Originally, the orchestrators never had more than two trumpets and one trombone; that was the brass. Four reeds, two trumpets, trombone, also a French horn occasionally. The more modern arrangers—Red, Irv, Ralph, Eddie—wanted enough so that they could make a chord. In the old days, in the brass section, you could only write basically triads. You can't have big full chords with sixths, ninths, thirteenths added; you'd have to have more players. We were all used to that, those who came from recordings and dance bands. That's how it came gradually into the theatre. The old orchestrators, they didn't really want to do what we were doing in the bands. They were so set on saying, "No, we want a flute player, clarinetist, a bassoon player; but if these guys can double on saxophone, fine, we might want a sax here or there." They didn't want to do what we did in the bands, everybody with multiple doubles. I don't know why, but

they insisted on staying with the old tried and true. They had always heard it that way, and that's the way it stayed.

As for the composers, they come in four classes, orchestration-wise: the composer who knows it all; the composer who thinks he knows it all; the composer who knows he doesn't know it all, but has constructive ideas; and the fellow who hands in the music and lets the professionals do the job. Leonard Bernstein is a pretty good example of the fellow who knows what he wants and needs; John Kander and Jerry Bock are examples of the constructive composer who looks at his orchestrator as a key ally. Jerry Herman admits that he was glad to leave it to Phil Lang. As for the composers who think they know it all, they shall remain nameless here. For the orchestrator, these fellows are merely an occupational hazard. Ramin tells about one famously egotistical composer who called to offer a job, saying "I'd like the score to sound like *West Side Story*." Ramin: "I had to hold myself back, and not say, 'if you write music like *West Side Story*, it will sound like *West Side Story*.'"

Many are the stories of the "hummers." Perhaps they'll come running over at the orchestra rehearsal, screaming that the trombones are playing much too loudly in a number in which no trombones are playing. Or they'll sidle over to the orchestrator at the rear of the house during a brilliantly received preview and compliment him on the French horn part, in a show without French horns. In cases such as this, most orchestrators simply nod and say okay.

The musical director is another source of input on the instrumentation question. A knowledgeable musical director can be incredibly helpful, while an obstructive one can be a nuisance. The musical director is a constant presence all through rehearsals; the orchestrator, working in the shadows as it were, has far less access to the songwriters than the musical director does. What's more, the orchestrator has only peripheral contact with the director, choreographer, and producers. One of the skills of a good musical director is knowledge of potential pit musicians: who is the right player for the job, who can be relied on to play the show conscientiously, and more. With this comes the ability to dictate personnel to the orchestrator and producer. (Walker's contract with producers usually gave him the right of approval of musical director, although in practice this was usually preordained.)

Musical directors play a key part in the production process; many of them serve as vocal arrangers as well. They are duly noted in the show listings, and many have been included in the biographical section of this book. Even so, it seems proper to mention—in alphabetical order—at least some of Broadway's most important musical directors of the 1940–1970 period, along with some of the creators with whom they were closely associated: Franz Allers (Loewe), Jay Blackton (Rodgers, Berlin), Lehman Engel (Merrick, Rome), Hal Hastings (Prince), Peter Howard (Merrick, Champion), Elliot Lawrence (Champion), Stanley Lebowsky (Kander), Don Pippin (Herman), Milton Rosenstock (Styne).

House Musicians

The question of housemen added another hurdle for orchestrators into the early sixties. The Musicians' Union contract at the time provided that theatre owners were virtually required to hire four musicians as permanent employees for the season, paying them every week the theatre was open. Even if it was booked with a nonmusical. The theatre owner could choose not to hire house musicians, in which case it became a "penalty" house—the penalty being that the minimum for any musician necessary at that theatre was 50% higher than scale. Thus, a musical like *The Boy Friend*, which played at the small Royale (now the Jacobs), used twelve musicians but paid for the equivalent of eighteen.

Most theatre owners chose to hire housemen, who inevitably were chosen for reasons other than musical acumen. Nepotism, and worse, prevailed. Four house musicians who couldn't play effectively lowered your twenty-five-person orchestra to twenty-one. (Harnick: "On *The Body Beautiful*, I remember that Ted Royal said that due to the union rules, we needed to hire more violins than we wanted. Because only four could play.") The power of the union being what it was, the orchestrators and contractors—all union men—couldn't exactly squawk. So almost everybody simply lived with it.

Irv Kostal tells what happened when the producers of *West Side Story* arranged their New York booking:

> One of the first things Lenny, Sid, and I did was to visit the Winter Garden Theatre to study the acoustics and also to hear the orchestra we might have to use. At that time, the Musicians' Union insisted that each theatre designate four housemen, who had to play any show booked in that theatre. When Lenny heard the housemen at the Winter Garden, he groaned in despair. In particular, he could not stand the two cellists in the orchestra. He immediately dubbed them "the Shuberts." Then he asked us if we could hear the violists. We said no.
>
> At our next meeting, Lenny asked us how we felt about eliminating the violes from the orchestra. Sid and I had many times used all kinds of dif-

ferent instrumentations, and we readily agreed to a two-part string section, celli and violins. Now Lenny said, "What are we going to do about
the two Shuberts?" Between us, we decided to have two very good cellists
play the difficult parts, and use the two mediocre players only on the loud
parts, the tuttis, and, of course, the more simple parts, the potatoes
(whole notes). That's how major decisions are made! We could never mention any of this because, according to union rules, one musician is as good
as another and it's a punishable offense to infer otherwise. And other lies!

And so, great and long-lasting decisions were made. Kostal's anecdote, from his
unpublished memoir, was too good not to look for firsthand verification.

> RAMIN: Sometimes politics were involved. On *West Side* we had to use the house
> players, the cellists, and they weren't so hot. Lenny had a wonderful sense of
> humor, and on our scores we had cellos A and cellos B, and the second line we
> marked "Shuberts," because the Shuberts had two cellists who were so bad but
> they were there. We had to use them, but we made sure that they didn't play any
> important stuff. We didn't use the viola—the house contractor—out of desper-
> ation. We didn't have that many strings, and we thought that a cello really could
> do practically anything a viola could do, and even better. So we didn't miss the
> viole at all. I thought it was very good. I did that on *Gypsy*, too. On *Forum*, we
> didn't even use violins, but that was a different story. That was just wanting to
> be different. I hadn't used viole on *West Side* or *Gypsy*, so I thought let's use four
> viole and no violins. For the tour and stock, someone added violins.

West Side was not the first musical to omit violas; many "dance" shows did without them. It was unheard of, though, to do a legit musical—one with symphonic
aspirations, no less—without them. Let it be added that both *Wonderful Town* and
West Side, two musicals calling for extensive reed doubling to provide all of the necessary colors, both had a nondoubling reed chair. The reason? Bernstein had a
friend—Sandy Sharaff—who played bassoon (very well), but only bassoon.

The subject of the missing violas came up in discussion with Stephen Sondheim,
the lyricist of *West Side*. When I mentioned the reason, he was surprised: "I never
heard that. But it's very funny." With respect to the question of composer input on
instrumentation, I mentioned Ramin's explanation of the lack of violins on *Forum*.

> SONDHEIM: That's news to me. It was up to them. They came to me with their plan,
> I doubt if I questioned it. When they suggested the instrumentation, it had to
> do with the size of the orchestra. The score was hardly lyrical or soaring. It was
> not a violin score.
> KOSTAL: At first the violists found it difficult to be playing such important parts,
> but when they got the idea, it was a very pleasing effect. . . . Sid and I were both

quite amused when Goddard Lieberson, recording expert, complimented us after he had seen the show, telling us the violins had "never sounded better." We didn't have the nerve to tell him there weren't any.

Other Interference

Ramin refers to the house contractor at the Winter Garden, a violist so poor that the instrument was excluded from *West Side Story*. Broadway musicals have two contractors. The show contractor is, in some ways, a casting director for musicians; with input from the musical director and orchestrator, he lines up and hires the players. He is also in charge of rehearsals, equipment rentals, personnel problems, and whatever needs may arise. The house contractor is of far less importance, especially since the end of the house musician system (when the presence of the house contractor and his musically suspect cronies could seriously cripple an orchestrator). Most of the pit musicians, while selected by the production, are employed by the theatre; the house contractor's main functions nowadays is to oversee the musicians and prepare the payroll.

Modern-era show contractors, including Red Press, Mel Rodnon, Herb Harris, John Miller, and John Monaco, are especially adept at catering to the needs of their clients. In an earlier era, a small group of men had the business pretty much tied up. Morris Stonzek began as a cellist on the *Ziegfeld Follies of 1921* and ended his career with the 1971 revival of *No, No, Nanette*. He became Ziegfeld's contractor, playing and contracting such shows as *Show Boat*; he also served as first chair cellist and contractor for the original production of George Gershwin's *Porgy and Bess*. Stonzek continued his career with such shows as *Kiss Me, Kate*, *Wonderful Town*, and all of David Merrick's musicals in the fifties and sixties. Sol Gusikoff had a somewhat parallel career, contracting most of the musicals of Rodgers & Hammerstein and Lerner & Loewe.

One name kept coming up in conversation, with rolled eyes. Henry Topper was contractor for producers Cy Feuer & Ernest Martin, who had an unprecedented five consecutive hits in the early fifties (including *Guys and Dolls* and *Can-Can*). Elliot Lawrence recalls a pair of meetings on *How to Succeed*:

> I go in with Frank Loesser, and he was very strong, and he said, "Now look, Elliot, in my contract I have all approvals. The first thing I want you to do is go to Cy Feuer." Cy's uncle, Henry Topper, was a saxophone player, he played sax on all Cy shows.
> "I don't want him in the orchestra," Frank said. I said, "I know who he is, I don't want him either." Frank said, "Okay, you go. *You* say *you*

don't want him, I'll back you up—and I got approval." So I went to Feuer, and said, "I don't want your uncle, he's not good enough. The parts are too hard for him to play." Cy got apoplectic. He did a 360 around me, screaming. But in the end, Cy's uncle didn't play the show. That's one of the reasons orchestras sounded better on the later shows than they sounded originally. There were many political reasons, the connections between the union and the housemen, having a friend who has a brother, please put him in the orchestra. The politics of the theatre has changed a lot; "please put this guy on," that's all gone.

Copyist Emile Charlap worked frequently with Ralph Burns on shows, including *Little Me.*

CHARLAP: Cy Feuer's uncle was a saxophone player who couldn't play anything, Henry Topper. They would assign him ten doubles, but give him nothing important to play. One time I told Ralph that Topper was copying parts from the other reed books and playing along. Ralph went up to the conductor's stand and said, "Anybody writing music in the books that I didn't tell him to write, I'm gonna murder him." Topper came over to me, really gave me a bad time. Cy Feuer had told me when he hired me, "I have a guy you're going to hate his guts, but he works for me and I tell him what to do."

Red Press also mentions Topper in connection with a show where the theatre had a twenty-five-player minimum:

They scored it for twenty-four men, and they added Henry Topper as the twenty-fifth player. Whenever there were unison parts, they had Topper play along on tenor sax or bass clarinet. Topper sat behind me; he was such a bad player that from listening in front of him, I never knew what instrument he was playing.

Words from the Composer

It goes without saying that the composer can have a strong measure of input on the orchestration. While some composers are knowledgeable in that area, many—especially in the pre-1970 era—were more of a hindrance than a help. Phil Lang discussed this in his interview with Lehman Engel.

LANG: If a songwriter is too specific about what he wants, he is probably impeding a lot of help that he might get. The less you give me, the more comfortable

I am. I think I know more about the theatre than most of the composers. *Pleasures and Palaces* was the most distressing experience I have had. Frank Loesser gave me a complete sketch—three or four staves, with instruments and all. Frank insisted he have exactly what he wanted, even if it sounded horrendous. It was the worst straitjacket I have ever seen in my life.

Bob Merrill used to give me the tune over the phone, on the xylophone; and he'd tell me what he is looking for, what rhythms he would like me to explore. When we did *Carnival*, though, Bob said, "Phil I want one thing: I don't want the melody in the orchestration." I said, okay. When orchestrating, I cued the melody in. [That is, he had the melody written on the parts in small notes, meaning they should not be played unless the conductor specifically cued the musician to play them.] We had the reading, Bob said to me, "Phil, there's something wrong." "I know something's wrong," I said, "and I'm glad you know it, too." So I said to the conductor, "Saul, have the guys play the cues."

A composer who knows how he wants his music to sound, and how it should sound, is something else again. Sondheim, for the most part, falls in this category. So did Frederick Loewe and so does Burt Bacharach. *Promises, Promises* is a perfect example of a show in which the composer knew exactly what he wanted to hear. Tunick told John Franceschina that every time he attempted to add something to the orchestration that Bacharach hadn't written, Bacharach had him cut it out.

On rare occasions, the creators left the music people on their own, which, with the right combination, could work wonders. In the case of *Li'l Abner*, the result was one of Phil Lang's most colorful sets of charts:

Nobody was around; Johnny Mercer [lyricist], Gene de Paul [composer], the producers. Michael Kidd and Lehman Engel did the whole show. Nobody ever bothered us, nobody ever consulted. They just didn't show up. Johnny Mercer came to hear the orchestra reading. He stayed about twenty minutes, and then went to play golf.

An exception to the rule is Vernon Duke, whom Bennett admiringly singled out for his "modern" compositions. But Bennett had great difficulty orchestrating his music:

Duke put more things into chords than you can possibly get out of a theatre orchestra. You never had a chance to sit down and say "one lovely chord of four flutes would be just ideal"—you don't *have* four flutes. So you have two flutes and two clarinets; that's not a very good substitute, but it's the best you can do.

And of course, there is nothing more supremely helpful to an orchestrator than specific direction from a composer who knows what he wants—and how to describe it. Stephen Sondheim, for one, is noted for providing his orchestrators with virtually complete arrangements.

> SONDHEIM: It's something I've always done, because I majored in music in college. I'm classically trained; I was writing piano sonatas. My teacher, Milton Babbitt, used to say that I thought orchestrally, meaning that I thought in terms of counterpoint. I think of myself as thinking of the piano: I can't pretend that I hear clarinets and horns, but I hear the two different lines. Some of the songs I write are very easy for Jonathan Tunick. Others are so pianistically written, that he goes through hell. A classic example being "Another Hundred People." I wrote it as a piano toccata.

Sondheim does not determine which combinations of instruments play which combinations of notes; but as part of the writing process he hears, in his head, almost every note that is to be played—and his musical training enables him to put down, on paper, a highly detailed sketch for his orchestrator to work from.

Input from the Top

It is safe to say that the interrelated trio of George Abbott, Jerome Robbins, and Hal Prince were Broadway's most important, influential, and successful directors of the period upon which we are concentrating. (Abbott began directing innovative musicals in 1936, and Prince has continued to do so into the twenty-first century.) How much influence did they have on the musical departments of their musicals?

> PRINCE: George Abbott didn't know as much as I know about music, which means he didn't know a helluva lot. He was the same kind of guy as me. I think it's pretty, I don't think it's pretty, I love it a lot, I don't think it works on the stage. The truth is, songs did not interest him. Pretty songs interested him, pretty rhythms; he loved to dance. That's one of the things that came into it. But actually saying, "That's a well-made song"? No, as a matter of fact, if you want to go back to *The Pajama Game*, there was a song called "Her Is." And I almost jumped out the window at 630 Fifth Avenue, because I thought it was such a lousy piece of material. The thing about Adler and Ross was that they were incredibly talented, and inventive, and great theatre writers. On the other hand, there is a huge variance of quality between one song and another. Some of them are just dazzling, and some are very ordinary. They were always theatrical, that's what those guys knew how to do. So you got a good song, and one that wasn't so good. George didn't know why I was having a fit over that song. And the song worked in the show, no question, with Stanley Prager and Carol Haney. But the

point is, George didn't care. Because he was less interested. And also because he wasn't absolutely hounded by a family like mine, that was so musical.

Adler and Ross, those guys had a very strong sense of what orchestration should be, because they depended so on the orchestration. They wrote swell scores, but they weren't Leonard Bernstein. And they knew what should happen onstage with their numbers, almost as much as anyone I ever knew. Kander and Ebb knew some of that, too; but Jerry and Richard could sit there and show you the number the way it was going to be on stage. "Hey There" with the microphone, dictating into the thing; "Steam Heat." Adler and Ross knew, they knew—it was amazing—they knew what the song was going to be on that stage. They staged their numbers as they wrote them. They knew what the number had to be, in order for it to work on stage.

An interesting though not disinterested viewpoint on Abbott was expressed by his most frequent orchestrator, Walker.

KOSTAL: Don Walker told me that Mr. Abbott was responsible for slowing down any progress in the development of the Broadway theatre because of his ability to make the old "shtick" work. Mr. Abbott had prolonged the life of the Broadway musical as it had existed from the early twenties by his sheer ability to cut, alter, and reverse scenes; his ability to cast the right performer for the right part; and his sure knowledge of what would or wouldn't work.

The most influential director-choreographer of all was Jerome Robbins, and he was famously difficult with his orchestrators (and everybody else, for that matter). A tale of *West Side Story*, related by Sondheim:

Jerry took over the orchestra during the dress rehearsal for "Somewhere," and proceeded to circle the instruments. "Now I want those out of there . . . " [Rather than erasing or crossing out the notes, offending passages are circled. This indicates that they shouldn't be played, allowing the passages to be easily restored later, if desired.] He thought that Lenny had made it too lush. I remember, I was sitting next to Lenny in the back of the house. Jerry hadn't objected at the two orchestra readings. But hearing it in the theatre with his dancers onstage, Jerry went running down the aisle, changing the orchestration. I went, "Oh my God, I can't wait to write home about this." Then I looked over, and Lenny is gone. Where is he? Not in the house. I went out in the lobby of the theatre. He wasn't there. Then I had a hunch. I went down the street, to the nearest bar. There he was, in a double booth, with five shots of scotch lined up in front of him. For all I know it was two, but I think it was five. Nobody could face Jerry Robbins down, so he went to the bar.

It was the ballet part of "Somewhere," with the singing and what follows. Jerry circled the parts, and that's what they still play in the show.

Robbins came in to help fix the Abbott musical *A Funny Thing Happened on the Way to the Forum.*

KOSTAL: At the beginning of the show, Jerry devised some very comical bits for Zero Mostel. The routine came right out of burlesque. With the curtain closed, the lights would hit the stage, and one of Zero's legs would protrude from between the split in the curtains. Then he did a pratfall, followed by a lot of very funny bits. When we viewed this for orchestration, Jerry said to me, "Let's not be obvious. Don't be vulgar. Play against the scene, be delicate," and so on. He suggested a harp glissando when Zero's leg came into view, and a triangle played softly when Zero did the pratfall. Well, Jerry was the boss, so I obeyed his suggestions faithfully. At the same time, knowing Zero as well as I did and having had enough trouble with George Abbott, who always came to me when things went wrong, I cross-cued the burlesque musical cues that usually accompanied such activities on the stage. [Which is to say, he wrote alternate parts into the scores, to be cued from the podium as required.]

When we rehearsed this opening scene with the orchestra, Jerry Robbins was sitting between George and me. When Zero's leg came into view, a flute played a little run accompanied by a harp glissando, and when Zero did the pratfall, the triangle was struck delicately by our percussionist. Abbott turned to me in disgust. He really gave me a talking-to: had I never seen a burlesque show, what was I thinking of, and so on. Jerry sank lower and lower into his chair. Unperturbed, I yelled across the orchestra seats to Hal Hastings, "Hal, play the cues." I had already discussed this with Hal, and he knew what was coming.

This time, when Zero stuck his leg through the curtains, he was accompanied by a very raucous trombone glissando, and when Zero did the pratfall, there was a great big hit on the timpani with a special "boing" sound effect, and so on. Mr. Abbott said to me afterward, "That's more like it!" When we were alone, Jerry said to me, "Don't tell anybody, but I liked it. But you know my reputation . . . "

Robbins's final—and perhaps most influential—musical was *Fiddler on the Roof.*

BOCK: With Robbins, you had someone who was a vital contributor to what things should sound like. I remember at orchestra rehearsals for *Fiddler,* Robbins' habit was always to cut, cut, cut. Everything was too loud—he wanted to bring it down to as simple a sound as possible. Since Don had worked with Robbins before, he knew this was going to happen. He knew that, at one point, Robbins would say, "Too much brass. Too many woodwinds and brass; it's overbearing." So Don confessed to me that he had written the score so that if it had to be played by a quartet, it would still sustain. And that was a result of preparing for the possibility that Jerry might dislodge most of the orchestration. No matter how far he went, Don felt that he had backed up that possibility by scoring the whole show for, ultimately, a quartet of instruments.

HARNICK: At the first reading, Robbins was hands-on. Every song, he would say too many trumpets, take out the violins. After the reading, Jerry Bock went to Don to commiserate. Don wasn't upset at all. "I've worked with him before. He loved it."

A couple of months after *Forum* opened, Kostal went on the road as conductor/orchestrator arranger for *An Evening with Carol Burnett*, an offshoot of the TV special *Julie and Carol at Carnegie Hall*. (Julie Andrews wasn't available for the already-booked tour, so Burnett fulfilled the booking without her.)

KOSTAL: Jerry Robbins saw the show in Detroit and came to see me afterwards. He complimented me on my orchestrations for the dance numbers, and asked me why I had never done as good a job for him. I explained to him that Ernie Flatt, the choreographer, told me to orchestrate any way I wanted to, and he would make the dance fit the orchestration. Jerry said, "I'll have to try that, sometime." I reminded him, when he set a ballet to classical music, he set his dance routines to preconceived music and orchestrations. Popular music choreographers feel free to set their dance routines any way they like, and then demand that the orchestrator spoil the melodies by asking for cymbal crashes, arpeggios, flourishes by the instrumentalists, all in the wrong places.

The Score Sheet

With the routines set, the instrumentation determined, and the key musicians contracted (allowing the assignment of reed doubles), the orchestrator is ready to go to work. The songs finally start to arrive from the rehearsal hall, and the orchestrator sits down with his score sheet. He stares at the blank page, with the rehearsal piano-vocal copy and perhaps a tape recording of the number as performed for him earlier that day in the rehearsal hall. Musical ideas begin to percolate, at least hopefully they do.

Before he does anything, though, he must engage in the mundane task of preparing the pages. This is something that can now be done handily by computer software. Orchestrators are split on the wisdom of working without pen and ink, as the computer tends to make it too easy to copy and paste patterns rather than decide what, ideally, the English horn might be playing here. The time that it takes to manually prepare pages, as more than one orchestrator has told me, tends to get them into the rhythm (literally) of the number. At any rate, this book concentrates on the pre-computer era of orchestration.

Score pages come in a variety of sizes and types. The standard size for Broadway shows is seventeen inches long by eleven and a half inches wide, which is as large as is practical to turn on a conductor's podium. The page is separated into two dozen or so horizontal staves. Each staff is the traditional five lines, with space above and below for notes higher and lower. Most instruments are written on one line, although two-handed instruments—piano, organ, synthesizer, harp, accordion—naturally need two lines, as does the percussion in some cases. At the same time, two trumpets or four violins might be included on one staff. The ever-busy reeds (flutes, clarinets, oboes, saxophones, etc.) need one line for each player. There will also be a separate line or lines (as necessary) for the vocal part; a musical performed without a piano will occasionally have a piano part written in nonetheless, to be extracted for use at rehearsals.

Full scores are arranged by instrumental sections. The reeds are generally written on the top; having the four or five lines together allows the orchestrator to see his entire section, which is especially helpful when writing block chords. Broadway orchestrators usually follow reeds with brass (trumpets, trombones, French horns). In each of these sections, the highest instrument—flute or piccolo, trumpet, violin—is typically on the top staff within the group. What is often referred to as the rhythm section—percussion, piano/keyboard, harp, guitar—is usually next, followed by the strings (violin, viola, cello, bass) at the bottom. The vocal lines are fit in wherever practical.

The orchestrator has several choices of scoring paper. The above-referenced standard size is preferred. Ralph Burns, though, sometimes used an oversized sheet of canary yellow, the favored format for swing band writers. (This paper, printed horizontally, generally allows eight or more bars of music to a sheet, rather than Broadway's standard four; however, it is impractical to turn these pages in the pit.) Hershy Kay often used twenty-seven-stave paper, in pastel green, while the unaffiliated Lang usually wrote on the cheapest paper he could pick up at the corner music store.

Basic scoring paper is plain, nothing but staves on a page. Paper with suggested instruments printed in the margin is also commonly available. The instrumentation on the page rarely matches the arrangement at hand, but a few pen scratches—changing harp to guit., or the first horn line to Trb III—can save an enormous amount of busywork. Calculate, if you will, labeling twenty lines with instrument names on 900 pages' worth of score. And this is *before* you can start work.

Chappell, the music publisher that had an almost monopolistic hold on the Broadway musical industry through the 1940s, provided orchestrators with a choice of prelabeled papers. Many of the scores by Bennett, Spialek, Walker, and Royal (and their ghosts) are on paper imprinted "Chappell Musical Comedy Score," "Chappell No. 4," "Chappell No. 5," and the like. These each had slightly different line labelings (harp, piano, guitar, multiple horn or sax lines, etc.). The orchestrator would select the page blank that was closest to his needs, but inevitably penciled in at least a few changes to conform to the chosen instrumentation.

Paper also came with or without bar lines. If you were writing a standard song in standard time, four vertical bar lines to a page worked fine; if your uptempo tune allowed eight bars, you would simply draw on the additional lines. Again, Broadway orchestration was inevitably done in a bleary-eyed rush; after a while, every saved pencil stroke was a saved pencil stroke.

Things changed somewhat when Chappell phased out of the orchestration business in the early 1950s. Bennett alone remained at Chappell, using its score sheets. Walker and copyist Mathilde Pincus started their own music preparation company, Chelsea Music, and began working in the more easily reproducible format called Deshon (borrowed from the world of blueprints). This was transparent paper of onion-skin consistency, although considerably stronger than standard onion skin. The bar lines were printed on the reverse, so they would not erase when the orchestrator made the inevitable changes. The Deshon process allowed alterations with relative ease. As Chelsea became the music preparation firm of choice for other orchestrators, Deshon came into more general use.

Walker prepared his own personalized scoring paper, with his name in bold letters at the bottom of the page. (Scoring paper was relatively costly in those days, with personalization only adding to the expense. But Walker, at Chelsea, had his own printing equipment.) Burns, also, sometimes worked on personalized paper. But the name on the page didn't necessarily mean that Don or Ralph orchestrated the song; the many ghosts on a Walker show usually worked on Walker paper. I have found occasional orchestrations for Walker shows with Don's name razor-bladed off the bottom. I also came across at least one Bennett show written on Walker paper; Russell obviously ran out and borrowed from Don. Ginzler, once he established himself with a string of important shows, finally went ahead and ordered his own personalized paper. He used it on only one show, apparently, after which he had a heart attack and died.

For what it is worth, let me note that I've found only two cases in which the title of the show was printed on the scoring blanks: *Jumbo*, which is emblazoned with "Paul Whiteman's JUMBO Orchestra," and "*The Grand Tour*, Orch. by Philip J. Lang."

A page of orchestration, in union terms, is defined as four bars of music. Orchestrators are paid by the page; the page rate is calculated on four-bar segments, regardless of how many bars are crammed on the actual page. Thus one scoring sheet, with eight bars on it, is paid as two pages; one sheet that directs the copyist to repeat twelve bars from earlier pages earns the orchestrator three times the page rate. (On the final sheet of a partitur, one occasionally finds a pencil calculation of the number of bars divided by four.)

Some Broadway conductors work from the full score, which allows them to see—at any given moment—what each of the musicians is supposed to be playing. As time has progressed, more conductors work from the P/C, or piano-conductor score. This is a reduction of the arrangement to three or four lines. All of the solos and main fills are transposed and written in, so that the piano player could play just about everything important by him- or herself. These arrangements are used extensively for general rehearsals, for which no musicians are employed other than the rehearsal pianist and/or the musical director. The published vocal scores, suitable for piano-only accompaniment in amateur productions, are more or less edited versions of the P/Cs.

Solos and other distinctive parts on P/Cs are labeled by instrument, allowing the conductor to visually cue the trumpet or cymbal when necessary. Unlike the four-bar-per-page full orchestration, the P/C might contain as many as eighteen bars per page. Bound as a book, with page facing page, this allows the conductor to see as many as thirty-six bars at a time, which is much less unwieldy than the four-bar pages of the full score. This results in far fewer page turns, which can be an issue when you are waving a baton and visually following the movement onstage.

SECTION VI.
THE ORCHESTRATION

The art of theatrical orchestration is a cumbersome subject, in part because the techniques—as well as the needs and the possibilities—are limitless. The first thing that should be said is that, in theatrical presentations, even musical comedies or musical dramas, music is only one of many contributing elements. The music of the composer, as well as the work of the orchestrator, must almost always share the stage with other elements (although I can think of some composers who might well dispute this). This is not the case in the symphonic world, and opera has customarily bowed low to the all-powerful fellow who writes the tunes. But, as Walker took pains to point out, the first function of music in the theatre must be to "aid and enrich what is happening on the stage." The aim of any theatrical production is to attract and hold the interest of the audience. Music is a main ingredient, yes, and sometimes *the* main ingredient, but if the story and characters don't grab the theatregoer, the production is unlikely to succeed.

Musical theatre, as we have heard countless times, is a collaboration, not only of composer, lyricist, and librettist but also director, choreographer, producer, designer, arranger, conductor, and often even the performing talent.

> WALKER: A theatrical composer, in addition to being aware of and respectful towards the story, must be sensitive to all physical movement on the stage and, where appropriate, underline it. Since the final result onstage is everything, it matters not how it was achieved. This often is too much for a pure musician to accept.

Walker's papers include the outline for a course he taught at New York's Hunter College in the fall of 1957. This outline raises many provocative points, without necessarily providing the answers; Walker didn't need notes on what to say, just a roadmap of what to include. In recent discussions, Jonathan Tunick addressed many of the same issues. A good deal of information in this section is derived from Walker's notes, supplemented by Tunick's observations and by clarifications from Larry Blank.

The Four Classes

The music to be orchestrated can be separated into four distinct classes, which Walker called "story," "dance," "variety," and "concert." Each serves a specific purpose, calling for distinctly different handling. Complicating matters is the fact that a single musical number might well combine all four classes. But first, let's separate them.

STORY: This class tells us what is happening, using music and lyrics in place of dialogue. This is the most frequent type of number found in traditional musical comedy or musical drama.

> WALKER: The words of the songs, since they are "telling" the main purpose of the entertainment, are the most important element. The music's main function is to enlarge the meaning of the words, establish the right mood for the character and the thought, and make it possible for the audience to hear the words clearly.

This class also includes music that underscores dialogue. The purpose here is to color the mood and add emphasis, but the ruling element is the dialogue, which must at all costs remain clearly intelligible over the music.

DANCE: This class can tell a story by choreographic means, or merely entertain us with more or less formal patterns of physical movement.

> WALKER: The musician must still concede that the main part of the entertainment is on the stage, and that music only exists to help the dance. The functions of the music are to mark a rhythm to which dancers can perform their steps; to create an atmosphere, with or without the aid of scenery and lighting; to point up and accent various movements of the choreography; and, in dances with a story-line (no matter how tenuous), to aid and explain the wordless plot, generally by proper use of leit-motifs and character or symbol-linked themes.

VARIETY: A sort of catchall class, from music hall to revue, in which the music may be the accompaniment to a song, the motivation of a dance, or just the unnoticed accompaniment to a dog act. The main characteristic of this class is that there is no overall story (and the song makes no dramatic contribution to the plot). The function of the music is still to enhance the entertainment, but the importance of the words varies; often, this class is close to concert.

CONCERT: This is a class in which the orchestra entertains on strictly musical terms. No singing, no talking, no dancing; this is the closest we get to "pure" music. The showcase in this class is, of course, the overture. Other examples are entr'actes, change music, and bows.

The lyricist has traditionally taken a back seat to the composer in the modern musical theatre—not in the case of Rodgers & Hammerstein or Lerner & Loewe perhaps, but more often than not. (Look at the opening night reviews of *West Side Story* and *Gypsy*, if you will; the poor lyricist was largely ignored.) To the orchestrator, though, the words are the key. They must be audible, at least when the character is presenting information that the creators want us to hear. By the time you get to the third refrain of a big production number, the words might well be irrelevant—which in effect moves the number into either the dance or variety class. But the orchestrator, in vocal numbers, must always work around the words.

Musical sections with lyrics, quite obviously, call for different treatment than the same music performed without lyrics. One need only look so far as the overture to *South Pacific*, which ends with a grand "concert" presentation of "Some Enchanted Evening," brass a-blazing. When Emile de Becque sings it at the end of the first scene, though, the melody barely emerges from the orchestra pit. The singer provides the full force of the melody, with a bit of support from the strings.

In the dance class, the orchestrator is called upon to create mood or excitement in the ears, minds, and hearts of the audience. At the same time, the dancers need their beats and rhythms. Choreography is based on counts and cues; it's not enough to instruct your dancers to enter when they sing this phrase or that, as there are no phrases being sung. We needn't get into a discussion of sound production and aural frequencies, but it will be readily comprehended that all instruments, sitting in the pit, are not equally audible to a dancer standing in the upstage wing. The orchestrator is not merely charged to make beautiful sounds and let the melody sing out; he needs to provide the onstage dancers with what they need to hear at the specific moments they need to hear it. (By the seventies, backstage sound monitors came into use, somewhat alleviating this problem. Until then, though, the beats had to come from the pit.) At the risk of making an overly broad generalization, one can hear how "dance shows"—specifically those of jazz-oriented choreographers like Jack Cole, Jerry Robbins, and Bob Fosse—altered Broadway pit instrumentation. Two percussionists, the better to hear the beat, became the norm in place of one; the brass section grew from three or four to six or seven, making tricky rhythms and hot syncopation far more audible not only to audiences but to the dancers. Saxophones, which can be a whole lot louder than clarinets and flutes, began to dominate the reed sections. All of this, mind you, at the expense of strings.

The variety class was somewhat diminished in the later days of the well-made musical, as the once-prevalent Broadway revues moved to TV and elsewhere; lyrics with no content relevant to the entertainment at large fell out of favor. This class has not disappeared altogether. There was indeed a dog act in the 1991 Tony winner *The Will Rogers Follies*; and the advent of jukebox musicals, shoe-horning existing lyrics of famous songs into plots and the mouths of characters that don't necessarily correspond, has provided spots where the orchestrators (and the creators) might well choose *not* to protect the integrity of the words.

The concert class frees the orchestrator of many of these constraints; the overture exists, after all, to give us the music pure and simple. Or so it seems. The overtures to *My Fair Lady*, *Candide*, and *Gypsy* are all quite wonderful models and can be said to work equally well in the concert hall, apart from the performance. If the orchestrator is not constrained by the necessity of protecting the lyrics or supporting the dancers, there are nevertheless stylistic constraints. Set the overture to *My Fair Lady* in the musical style of the overture to *Gypsy*—with over-the-top brass and chromatic reeds—and audiences would be jarred when Henry Higgins started singing "Why Can't the English?" Begin *Fiddler on the Roof* in the style of *West Side Story*'s "Jet Song," with all those vibraphone solos, and I expect that "Tradition" might puzzle us all.

The combination of styles within a given score is fairly obvious; *Gypsy*, for one, has story ("Some People"), dance ("All I Need Is the Girl"), variety (in the newsboy and farmboy acts, as well as the "Let Me Entertain You" burlesque montage), and of course that concert overture. But orchestrators are frequently called on to mix classes within specific numbers. Just about any song and dance, of course, combines story and dance; these can be straight combinations, such as "Sixteen Going on Seventeen" or "Put on a Happy Face"; specialty combinations, such as "Whatever Lola Wants" or "America"; or songs with ballets, such as "Out of My Dreams" or "Luck Be a Lady." The orchestrator not only needs to identify the proper class, but needs to understand the orchestral function at each section of the number.

Readers can identify mixed-use numbers on their own, but as an example let us use "Hernando's Hideaway" from *The Pajama Game.* This begins with story, giving us a lyric that advances the plot. ("You'll get my heart, you'll get my soul—but not my key," sings the comedienne to the hero. She wears, on a chain around her neck, the key to the cooked accounting books; our hero is determined to unlock their secrets.) This part of the number ends with a quick blackout, accompanied by a fanfare and a short concert section, with several dancers doing a crossover while the set is changed upstage. (They go from the office, to the street entrance of the nightclub, to the Hernando interior.) The number continues with a novelty dance section, performed mostly in the dark, with the dancers striking matches (which adds an unusual percussive sound to the orchestration). The final section of the song is a full-ensemble refrain, which can be considered the variety class.

The Three Layers

Early in our discussion, we divided the song—using "Heart and Soul" as an example—into simple components. At this point, let us look at the parts of the song from the viewpoint of the orchestration. This book cannot hope to be a how-to guide for would-be orchestrators; that is not within the expertise of the author nor would it meet the needs of most readers, and there is too much other ground to be covered. A brief consideration and understanding of these layers, though, can hopefully give us a look at—to adapt a line from Cole Porter—"what is this thing called orchestration?"

Accompaniment

At the bottom of every orchestration—both figuratively and audibly—lies the foundation, or bass line. This is the note upon which the orchestration is built; in the Broadway musical, it usually comes from the string bass. Due to the sonic nature of the orchestra pit, this is often played pizzicato (with the strings plucked, rather than bowed). The foundation can be constant or merely on the first beat of each measure; while the overall rhythm comes from other portions of the accompaniment, the foundation defines the beat and keeps everyone—musicians, singers, dancers, and even audience members—together.

The string bass is neither the loudest nor the most distinctive instrument in the orchestra, but it has proven to be the sturdiest provider of the bass line. It is occasionally joined by other low-register instruments, such as cello, harp, piano, trombone, or bassoon. When present, a tuba is often used for the bass line; as discussed elsewhere, the string bass player often doubled on tuba into the sixties. (In *My Fair Lady*, the same musician provides the foundation line for "I Could Have Danced All Night" [on the string bass] and "With a Little Bit of Luck" [on the tuba].) In more modern Broadway musicals, especially with a strong dance component, the bass clarinet and occasionally the baritone sax are frequently called upon to provide the bass line, either with or without the string bass.

Built over the bass line is the supporting structure. This provides the body of the orchestration, both rhythmic and harmonic. In the familiar oom-pah-pah format, the support provides the pahs (to the ooms of the bass line); that is, the support gives us the rhythmic impulse and movement, as opposed to the actual beat. Harmonically, the supporting layer provides the middle; if the foundation is the bass line and the melody is more or less the top, it is the support that provides the inner notes that define the chords.

Given that most instruments have a wide range, just about all of them can be used in support. Often present are the strings en masse (or with the exception of the first violins, which are more commonly used for the melody); the rhythm section (percussion, piano, harp, guitar); the horn(s), trombone(s), and trumpets, except for the higher reaches of the latter; and the reeds, again except for the higher ranges of the clarinet and flute (and the piccolo altogether). The instruments in support are usually used together in pairs—two horns, two clarinets, two trombones—because they can make two notes of a chord, with the "missing" part of the chord often in the melody. Two parts of the chord, plus the melody note from the singer, are enough to define the harmony.

The supporting section at any given time will usually comprise the bulk of the players—at least it did in the days of the twenty-odd-piece pit orchestra. Over the years, accordions, electric keyboards, and synthesizers have come along to fill in the support in lieu of various "real" instruments. The supporting instruments, by definition, are intended to blend in with the rest; distinctive musical lines are reserved for the other layers. In the story (vocal) class, low reeds—including saxes—are often used to strengthen the string sections; in dance sections, this can be the other way around, with the sax sound predominating. In all cases, the supporting structure provides not only the notes in between, but the body of the harmony.

Melody

The melody, so beloved to composers the world over, is the most important—and trickiest—aspect of the orchestration. Do they, or don't they? Double the melody, that is. When someone is singing, do we want to hear only the vocalist on the melody? If the singer is strong and with an attractive voice, you might get one answer; if the singer is average (or worse), or pitch challenged, the wise orchestrator might choose another method of handling this.

It should be pointed out that vocal numbers are orchestrated taking into consideration the strengths and weaknesses of the actor who originates the role. A case in point is Gertrude Lawrence, who optioned the underlying material for *The King and I* for herself and enlisted Rodgers and Hammerstein to write it. Lawrence had what might be called a wandering voice, which was strong enough but not necessarily accurate. The story goes that Noël Coward was standing at the back of the house with his friend Rodgers at an early performance in New Haven. On the final phrase of "Hello, Young Lovers"— at "I had a love of my own"—the orchestra swelled, altogether drowning out Sir Noël's lifelong pal Gertie. Glancing sideways, Coward said, "Wise choice, Dick." Anna has been played over the years by many fine singers—Barbara Cook, Risë Stevens, Constance Towers, and Donna Murphy among them—but Bennett's orchestral swell remains.

While numbers might infrequently be transposed or reorchestrated for incoming stars, the original orchestration in most cases remains. On the other hand, when the orchestrator starts with a strong singer, he will often cue in the vocal for the violin or clarinet—which is to say, write it on the parts in extra-small notes, so that future conductors can have it played if warranted.

The melody line tended to be doubled, in most cases, into the fifties. At this point, a new breed of orchestrators—trained in recordings (where the vocalist was king and frequently independent of the melody) or big bands (where it was preferable to have the instrumental soloist unrestrained)—started to avoid the actual melody line. Even so, there remains a strong melodic layer in the orchestration. The melody is often indicated by blocking or etching.

A blocked melody will be accompanied by related notes, either in chordal fashion (enforcing the melody with a fuller sound) or in other manners (for example, in thirds). Imagine the main pillars of the melody expressed in chords, and then remove the note that the singer is singing; the rest of the chord blocks, or "circles," the melody. An etched melody, on the other hand, gives an outline of the melody line. Take those same chords and play them only on the beats, while the vocalist sings the eighth-notes in between; in this manner, the orchestra is giving us the main parts of the melody, without covering the vocalist. Blocking and etching serve several purposes; among other things, they help to keep the singer on pitch and, yes, reinforce the melody for the customers.

A severe case of etching comes in stop-time sections, like the "get yourself some new orchestrations" section of "Some People." Ten bars, forty-four notes sung by the singer. The orchestrator (Ginzler in this section of the number) gives us a mere six chords from the pit, which etch the melody and provide enough harmonic and rhythmic support to get the singer—Ethel Merman, originally—through.

In instrumental numbers, and nonvocal sections of vocal numbers, the melody line will of necessity emanate from the pit. When there is no question of obscuring the lyric, the orchestrator has a relatively free hand; one need look no further than all those high trumpets sprinkled throughout overtures.

Decoration

The decoration, or the counterpoint, is the "extra" material that adds flavor and color to the orchestration. The decoration might come from only one instrument, with twenty others busily making music. Even so, the decoration—often contrasting with whatever else is going on—stands out, both by nature and design. Decoration often comes in one of two forms, commentary and fills.

Commentary, in a vocal number, is often tied directly to the lyric. Is there something about a phrase that can be illustrated? How much space is available to do so? Comedic comment usually comes from so-called funny instruments: reeds, saxes, trombones. For example, listen to the fluttery flutes commenting on the phrase "tits and ass" in Lang's "Dance Ten, Looks Three," from *A Chorus Line.* Burns's "I'm the Greatest Star," from *Funny Girl,* abounds with comedy fills by flute, clarinet, and trumpet as the character (B. Streisand) displays her comic versatility. Robert Farnon's "You've Got to Be a Little Crazy," from *The Girl in Pink Tights,* is a cacophony of "crazy" reeds and raps on wood blocks, temple blocks, and more. In "An Orthodox Fool" from *No Strings,* as the character sings, "I descend the escalator when it's going up," Burns gives the xylophone a brisk, descending scale in direct counterpoint to the escalator; to cap it off, he finishes the phrase with a contrary bassoon going upward.

Romantic comment is less literal but very much noticeable. "I Could Have Danced All Night," from *My Fair Lady,* is filigreed by Bennett with high eighth-notes from flute and clarinet. "And as if it isn't bad enough a violin starts to play" sings the lovelorn heroine in the first act finale of *She Loves Me,* "Dear Friend." Walker, logically yet effectively, counters with a solo violin. Romantic numbers, in their second or third refrains, will frequently bring in the strings, the better to swell the emotion. The instrumental possibilities for commentary are limitless, although for obvious reasons the instrument(s) providing decoration should be in a different register than the voice.

Fills are more rhythmic in nature, keeping pace and building excitement by literally filling in the gaps when the melody is at rest. Examples abound: from Bennett alone, we have the melodic echoes (from the hills?) in "The Sound of Music," the mysteriously shimmering strings (from the hills?) in "Bali Ha'i," and the quizzical bassoon cementing Henry Higgins's joke ("the French don't care what they do as long as they pronounce it properly") in "Why Can't the English?" The latter is a comic fill, as is Walker's use of squeaky reeds commenting on the sidewalk-Casanova quartet "Standing on the Corner," watching all those girls go by in *The Most Happy Fella*. As for excitement, one need look no further than Ramin and Ginzler's use of trumpet fills in the overtures of *Gypsy* and *Wildcat*.

A bravura sample of decoration comes from Red Ginzler in "Together" from *Gypsy*. The first two A sections, in A–A–B–A coda ("Wherever we go, whatever we do"), prominently feature a high eighth-note fill from the flutes; the B ("Wherever I go, I know he goes") is supported by a rising scale of whole notes (a "thumb-line") from the cellos; and the final A ("Through thick and through thin") has a clarinet countermelody that unequivocally breaks Don Walker's rule that no such thing should ever compete with the singer.

As important, and enlivening, as fills are, they are not to be overused. In comedy numbers, especially, there is a place for jokes to be heard; put in a fill and you'll kill the laugh that the songwriters no doubt struggled to create. Observe how Lang handles the cash register jokes in "So Long Dearie," from *Hello, Dolly!* (Lang told Larry Blank that, to him, "the lyric is the most important thing—because that's where the fills come from.") Or consider the tag to "Spanish Rose," from *Bye Bye Birdie*. Ginzler underplays the final joke ("not Yiddish") with a mere tweet from the flute; more notes and the audience might follow the music rather than let the joke land.

The decoration is the area in which the orchestrator is most likely to add his own creations. The most artful fills, perhaps, are those that are derived from the melody, like Bennett's echo fills in such numbers as "Some Enchanted Evening" and "The Sound of Music." They are, indeed, counterpoint: musical phrases that run counter to the melody and the general supporting structure. However, the orchestrator does well to heed one of Irv Kostal's rules: *Never write an obbligato that tries to be better than the song written by the songwriters.*

The passage leading to the stop-time section of "Some People," mentioned above, is worth taking a brief look at as well. "I had a dream," Rose sings, holding the final note for two and a half bars of the four-bar section. The cellos play the melody along with the singer, two octaves lower so as not to conflict with her range. What to do while she's holding that note? Ginzler and Ramin (working together here) build a pyramid: the trumpets play "I have a dream" in the second measure, one octave up; the oboe in the third, another octave up; the flutes in the fourth, yet another octave up. The singer then continues with "a wonderful dream, Poppa"—with the notes of "wonderful dream, Pop-" echoed by the flute. More technically speaking, the cellos hold the orchestra together with their sustained note, which is followed by a canon forming a pyramid of sound, serving to tie "I have a dream" with—four bars later—"a wonderful dream."

Slightly off the subject, but interesting nonetheless, is this account from Styne:

> One day I played this chord progression. Steve [Sondheim] said, "Wait a minute, what was that? Play that again." He says, "That's the background for something." All of a sudden, one day, he comes in and says, "Get that background out. I want you to write a slow theme on top of that background because that slow theme—I got a page of dialogue from Arthur [Laurents]—I am going to musicalize it." It was "I had a dream . . ."

Decoration, commentary, and fills are routinely included in the piano arrangements worked out by composer, music director, and dance/vocal arranger; but fills on piano arrangements are conceived to be played on the piano. Walker, Ginzler, Burns, and others routinely wrote reed fills crammed with notes, as the various padded instruments are capable of flying up and down the chromatic scale. Someone working on a piano, though, is likely to write only what can be played with the top fingers of the right hand, not only in terms of intervals and ranges, but in technical terms as well. (Try playing the melody, the accompaniment, and at the same time a seventeen-note run.) Some orchestrators—Burns, Sauter, Ginzler, Kostal—tended to fit in delicious countermelodies for sax or trombone, a direct result of years writing for or playing with the big bands. For that matter—and this applies not only to decoration but to all aspects of orchestration— the reed and string instruments can hold notes for extended periods of time, with the ability to get louder and softer and louder again, and end with a staccato sting.

> MARION EVANS: One of the problems with the piano players when they write arrangements, they're not used to the sustaining quality of instruments, so they tend to write a lot of notes. I was originally a trumpet player. I might write, for the brass, a whole note, getting louder and louder. A piano player can't do that on the piano; they'd write repeated notes.

It is something of an accepted maxim that piano players can't orchestrate; they are simply tied to the keyboard, unable to provide those flights of instrumental virtuosity that bring life to orchestrations. This makes perfect sense, yes, although Ralph Burns is the exception that disproves the rule. But we wander from the point at hand.

SECTION VII.
PUTTING IT TOGETHER

The accompaniment, melody, and decoration join together, sometimes inseparably, to create the overall effect; in special cases, some of the layers are missing altogether (by design) from an orchestration. Let us now attempt to illuminate the discussion by examining twelve specific orchestrations, which have been selected not only for general interest but on the assumption that readers most probably have the relevant original cast albums on their CD shelf. Or should, anyway.

It might be helpful for these descriptions of orchestration to be read with the relevant track playing in the background. Or not. If after one paragraph of the following, your eyes glaze over, you are hereby excused. No quiz shall be given, and you may proceed to page 281.

Two by Russell Bennett

"The Sound of Music" (Richard Rodgers/Oscar Hammerstein II)
from The Sound of Music

The song begins with a sprightly seven-bar introduction from the reeds and harp, with trills from the strings. This ends with an A (in the key of D) held by the violins and violas, giving the singer her first note. The first eight bars of the verse ("My day in the hills") is virtually a cappella, with the only accompaniment coming from the two clarinets playing along in thirds. At "deep in the dark green shadows," Bennett adds the English horn, bassoon, violas, and cellos on the melody (with some harmony), while the harp plays eighth-note octaves (on A) for the remaining ten bars of the verse, seventy-two of them. We end with another violin tremolo on A, taking us into the refrain.

The left hand of the harp provides the quarter-note foundation for the first two A sections, of A, A2, B, A3, C. ("A2" represents a section in which the first four bars are identical to those of the "A," but the last four are different.) Harmony, in the form of whole and half-notes, comes from the strings, lower reeds, and horns. The distinctive part of the orchestration is a simple but effective echo fill for one flute plus the right hand of the harp; with capital letters used to indicate the fill, this goes "The hills are a- (HILLS ARE ALIVE) with the sound of mus- (HILLS ARE ALIVE)." The first A section ends with an anthem-like cadence of chords (on beats one, two, and four), after which we go back to the harp foundation with the flute fills for A2.

In the bridge ("my heart wants to beat"), we change to oom-pahs, with the harp joined by the bass for the ooms; the violins, violas, guitar, and right hand of the harp play the pahs. This is accompanied by a pair of conflicting half-note lines, with half of the cellos and one clarinet going up while the other cellos and clarinet descend. This is repeated for the second half of the bridge, with the addition of an eighth-note countermelody from flute and English horn (reflecting the lyric, about a brook that trips and falls). Accompaniment turns prayer-like for the final four bars of the bridge ("to sing through the night"), with the horn added to the mix. The melody is etched here, with violins, flute, and English horn accompanying the singer for "a lark who is learning to pray."

A harp gliss takes us back to the A3 section; once again, foundation comes from the harp, with flute (and right hand of the harp) on the fills, now strengthened by the addition of the English horn. Another anthem-like cadence takes us to the C ("my heart will be blessed"), where Bennett maintains the one-two-four rhythm played by the strings, reeds, and the three horns. He closes with one last echo fill from the flute, countered by an arpeggiated ladder figure from cellos, harp, and bassoon.

"I Could Have Danced All Night" (Frederick Loewe / Alan Jay Lerner) from My Fair Lady

Bennett builds his orchestration on eighth-notes, most distinctively in the reeds but elsewhere as well. The pickup phrase of the melody—"I could have"—consists of three eighth-notes; the bridge is constructed upon a similar eighth-note phrase ("I'll never," "what made it") while the second, fourth, and eighth measures of the brief verse have eighth-note clusters (on the phrases "couldn't go to," "try to set it," and "couldn't sleep to-"). This seems to have given Bennett his cue; the orchestration is driven by sprightly eighth-notes. (The song can be, and has been, performed out of the context of the show, but it has a very different effect; the eighth-notes can be seen as an extension of Eliza's heightened heartbeat.) In the same manner, the upward progression of Loewe's eighth-notes seem to have suggested to Bennett the widespread use of scale-like progressions.

The verse ("sleep, sleep, I couldn't sleep tonight") has the strings playing eight staccato notes to the bar, while the reeds etch the melody; the first fill is provided by the harp, playing a downward scale progression of, yes, eighth-notes. The verse ends with an ascending scale of quarter-notes ("not for all the jewels in the crown"), which is played by reeds and strings while the bass belatedly enters, after eight bars. Another downward scale fill, from harp, cello, and bassoon, leads to the refrain. The pizzicato bass provides the bass line; the harp fills out the accompaniment with oom-pahs; and the other strings, plus bassoon, play the melody. The flavor comes from the flute and two clarinets, playing a bubbly decoration that fills in the spaces between "I could have danced" and "all night." At the cadences after "begged for more" and "never done before," Bennett adds pace by syncopating the decoration. The reed bubbles stop for the verse ("I'll never know"), although the accompaniment is taken up by the violins, in four-part harmony, with descending scales of eighth-notes; the melody here switches to bassoon, horns, violas, and cellos. This section is supported by muted brass, with the trumpets on the offbeats, and has fills (as before) by the flute and clarinets. Everybody plays the three tenuto (held) notes—"I on-ly"—that lead back to the final section of the refrain. Here, as before, the melody comes from strings and bassoon (with oboe added), while the high reeds play those bubbles. The trumpets dominate the end, with a scale-like fill after "danced, danced, danced" and some spicy eighth-notes, accompanied by strings, leading to the four-bar interlude—with the harp playing the melody (housemaids: "it's after three, now," etc.) over a held note in the strings—that takes us forward.

The second refrain is a contrapuntal duet, with Eliza on the melody and the maids singing—what else?—eighth-note fragments. The bass plays the bass line; the harp and drummer, heretofore absent, fill in the rhythm; the harmony comes from violins (playing whole-note chords) and horns (on oom-pahs). Eliza's melody is played by the first trumpet, while the maids' countermelody is played by the flute, one clarinet, and the bassoon. The fills from the first refrain are gone, the countermelody taking their place. The bridge, sung by Eliza only, has the melody in full force from all of the strings (except the bass) and one clarinet. Harp and brass provide the rhythmic accompaniment, while the horns enhance the harmony with a leisurely descending scale. A lovely countermelody comes from the oboe, echoing the melody. (If oboes used words, it might sound like, Eliza: "I'll never know" [oboe: "I'll never know"] E: "what made it so" [o: "what made it so"] E: "ex-ci-ting" [o: "aah-aah"].) In the second part of the bridge, the same countermelody comes from the flute. The end of the refrain is as before, with the first trumpet (now pianissimo) on melody and three reeds on countermelody.

Another brief interlude, with just about everybody playing the melody, leads to the grand final refrain, once again a star solo as the maids have been sent off to the chorus room. The melody comes from half of the violin section plus cellos, with the other strings and harp providing accompaniment. The clarinets have a subdued countermelody, echoing the lyric, while the flute and oboe have more eighth-note fills. The bridge is even stronger than before, with strings, trumpet, and bassoon on melody; the bass, harp, and horns provide the oom-pahs; while the four high reeds provide decoration (mostly in the form of descending eighth-note scales). The trombones come in, while the singer holds "exciting," with a nice chromatic scale of descending quarter-notes. With the song so well established, the lyrical content fully comprehended, and the audience in love with the whole thing, Bennett ends it with just about everyone—except bass, timpani, and bassoon, which play the offbeats—belting out the melody.

Two by Don Walker

"If I Loved You" (Richard Rodgers / Oscar Hammerstein II)
from Carousel

This song is the centerpiece of the extended, eleven-minute "Bench Scene"; we will examine here only the "If I Loved You" section. One refrain is sung by the heroine, the other by the hero, with significantly different orchestral treatments. Julie's version is spare: harp and strings, with reeds on the fills. There is no brass (other than a very limited horn part) and no percussion. The bass line is provided by the two string basses (almost entirely pizzicato); the left hand of the harpist joins the basses for the downbeat, as well as playing a treble-clef chord on the third beat of each measure. The harp is also the dominant feature of the rhythm, giving the song movement with arpeggiated triads—one note at a time—throughout. The violins contribute to the support with a six-part whole-note chord in each measure, played with a tremolo. The melody is doubled by violas and cellos, playing two and three registers lower than the soprano is singing. This simple and effective orchestration is enhanced only occasionally by the reeds. As for decoration, Walker ends each phrase of the A section with a descending fill from the high reeds, mimicking the words "time and again I would." (Walker recalled Dr. Albert Sirmay—the musical editor and number-two man at Chappell—"coming to me, amazed, complimenting me on the way I used that figure as a fill between phrases. He called them 'two of the best bars in the whole piece.'") In the bridge, there is a solo clarinet countermelody at "longin' to tell you," complemented over the next two measures by the rest of the reeds plus horns (which play a contrasting descending figure). The refrain builds to a climax at "never, never, to KNOW," with the "time and again" fill supported by the horns.

The bench scene continues through several sections, in which Billy Bigelow—initially skeptical of Julie's theoretical description of love—eventually falls under her spell. His refrain calls for something stronger; while Julie was tentative, Billy is in effect declaring his love despite himself. The foundation remains with the basses plus the left hand of the harp, but the rest of the treatment is remarkably expanded. The arpeggiated chords, which the harpist had played one note at a time, are now six-fingered chords. What's more, the low reeds (two clarinets and bassoon) play these notes as well; the other three reeds (two flutes and oboe) fill in the harmony with half-note chords on the third beat of each measure. As for the melody, Walker increases the intensity by giving it to the entire string section (except the two basses), which in the case of the original production of *Carousel* numbered twenty players. This might have overpowered one skinny soprano, but with John Raitt onstage, the effect was positively rapturous. (This is what Walker referred to as "the Puccini effect": sell that melody!) The fills, too, have been expanded; now we have all six reeds, with increased dynamics. At the bridge, there is another change: the strings join the harp arpeggios; the low reeds join in support; while the flute and oboe double the melody. By the end of the bridge, all pretense of make-believe has vanished. Walker fills the return to the main strain with an ascending scale for flute, bassoon, and strings, accompanied by a harp glissando and—for good show—the tuba and timpani. For the grand climax, once again at "never, never, to KNOW," tuba and timp are joined by the three trombones. After all that drama, the song ends on a quiet note, with the harp dominating as at the very beginning of Julie's refrain.

"Ya Got Trouble" (Meredith Willson) from The Music Man

This number was presumably orchestrated pretty much as written by composer Meredith Willson, with little room for arrangement. The foundation line of the song, even played on the piano, clearly indicates low strings; the most distinctive part of the arrangement is the use of so-called slams—slap-like accents—as punctuation. These, again, don't leave much room for creative orchestration. Even so, Walker found ways to add orchestral color into the support and especially the decoration.

The opening twenty bars are mostly foundation (bass and two cellos) and slams (reeds and brass), with violin support from "the hours I spend" onward. At "but just as I say" the cellos join the accompaniment, leaving the bass on its own the rest of the way through. At this same point, Walker gives the clarinets a mel-low harmonic line, with similar support from the strings at "medicinal wine." All of this, mind you, is accompanied by slams. There is a bass clarinet fill at "Dan Patch" and a step-like passage for the reeds accompanying the "one, two, three, four, five, six, pockets of the table." (The partiturs reveal that after "P and that stands for pool," there is a twelve-bar section for the chorus—presumably in-tended to give the star a breath. Bob Preston, apparently, didn't need this, so the section was cut.) The number continues as before with a small clarinet counter-melody (at "noontime, suppertime"), a "growl and plunger effect" (at "beef-steak pounded"), and more clarinets at the "empty cistern." A second choral pas-sage was deleted (after the second "P and that stands for pool").

The third section ("now I know all you folks are the right kind-a' parents") begins as before. New colors are added with reed trills at "cigarette fiends" and "sneaky" trombones when the boys cover up their telltale breath with Sen-Sen. (If you must know, these were the Tic-Tacs of the day, strong-flavored little pellets that served as "breath perfume.") At the "libertine men and scarlet women," Walker adds a nine-bar ragtime countermelody for the five reeds, starting a few bars before Willson specifies ragtime in the lyric. The soloist-plus-chorus section ("oh, we got trouble") features reeds and cellos accompanying the bass on the beat, brass and piano on the offbeat, and the violins with a high trill. The section ends with a few slams, after which there is an extended speech ("mothers of River City"), with the chorus repeating the word "trouble." Two slams from reeds, brass, and percussion (rim shot) lead into a repeat of the "oh, we got trouble" section. The extension ("terrible, terrible trouble") has some syncopated support from the reeds. The end of the vocal is bolstered by the trombones, and this basically underorchestrated number ends up with trumpets, and everyone, blaring.

Two by Phil Lang

"We Need a Little Christmas" (Jerry Herman) from Mame

Lang starts with a four-bar introduction, played in unison by oboe, one clarinet, bells, and the right hand of the harp (on a single note). The bass line is played by the bass and third trombone, with support from cellos and harp, on whole notes, while violins, violas, and guitar play on the offbeats. The melody in this section is doubled by the alto sax. There is no decoration until the fill at the end of the first eight (just before the title phrase), played by oboe, brass, and strings. The B section ("for we need . . . ") uses a similar foundation and support, with four reeds on the melody and two-note decorative fills coming from flute and bassoon. The final four bars of this section ("it hasn't snowed a single flurry") are a cappella, except for strings (for pitch) on the first notes of the first and third measures. The second refrain continues with the bass and third trombone, with support coming from the cellos. The melody comes from the second clarinet now, doubling the singer. The decoration is split; flute, oboe, and bassoon do a fill after each line of lyric. The violins, violas, harp, and bells play a two-bar descending scale—which the bells give a Christmas-y feel—under "climb down the chimney," followed by six bars of offbeat support; this is then repeated for the second half of the section ("slice up the fruitcake"). The decoration at the end of the section is as before, although somewhat fuller. The B section ("for we've grown a little leaner") has the solo trumpet on melody this time, with the reeds switching to a high decoration (and the piccolo giving it a marching band feeling); there is also a somewhat booming descending scale from two trombones and the bass accompanying "grown a little older." This refrain ends with a two-bar modulation from the brass, guitar, and bass.

The A section of the next refrain is instrumental, with melody from the piccolo and Christmas-bell-like half-notes from the violins, viola, and bells; the pizzicato bass, meanwhile, keeps plugging away. The bass finally gets a rest at the B, when the vocal picks up ("for we need a little Christmas"). Here, trombones play the foundation while the sound is dominated by sleigh bells ringing out quarter-notes. These are accompanied by reeds and strings etching the melody. This section ends with the a capella section, modulating once again. The third refrain is as before, this time with the melody doubled by cello (for the first eight bars) and flute (for the second eight). The beat is provided by the bass for this A section, switching to the three trombones for the B (at "for we need"); the reason becomes apparent twelve bars in, by which point the bass player has put down his bass and picked up his tuba. The number continues as a march-like instrumental, marked by the piccolo.

"If He Walked into My Life" (Jerry Herman) from Mame

"Where's that boy with the bugle?" goes the verse, the lyric crystallizing a main point of the plot. Little Patrick, the boy with the bugle, grows up and—inevitably—grows away from his Auntie Mame; the artwork of the musical, in fact, featured a distinctly deco leading lady—a glamorized version of original star Angela Lansbury?—holding a bugle to her lips. Lang builds this orchestration on bugle call fills; played not by a bugle, actually, but by a trumpet with a Harmon mute (which gives a crisp, brassy sound).

The intro begins, fittingly enough, with the eighth-note figure that will start the refrain ("did he need a stronger hand?"), first from the bassoon, then from one of the three clarinets that will play all but the final seven-bar tag of the song. The rubato (loose tempo) verse is accompanied by half- and whole-note chords from reeds and harp, with two fills from the trumpet (the first coming directly after the word "bugle"). Midway, there's a modulation, accompanied by a gliss from the harp; the remainder of the verse has the strings join in on the chords.

At the cadence into the refrain (after "why did I ever buy him those damn long pants"), the low strings, reeds, and brass play on the beat, the higher components on the offbeat; this continues for two measures only. Mame sings the "stronger hand" pickup alone, after which the accompaniment turns rhythmic. The bass plays pizzicato notes on one and three, while the other strings etch the melody with whole- and half-note chords; the harp plucks on the offbeats; and the trumpet continues with those fills. As the melody moves to eighth-notes ("was I soft or was I tough"), the reeds join in on the etching. At the B section ("at the moment when he needed me"), the harp and cello add movement with arpeggiated eighth-notes; at the end of the phrase ("would I be there when he called, if he walked into my life today"), the melody is etched by the trumpeters (on flugelhorn) and violinists. The two-bar cadence, again, offsets the low instruments with the high, this time with an appearance by the timp. In the second A section, Lang temporarily retires the trumpet and gives the sweet ("dolce") fills to the English horn; otherwise, the accompaniment is the same, strings and harp joined by reeds. After "and forget the child," he reinstates the arpeggiated chords from harp and cello. The section ends as before, with the pairing of flugelhorns and violins.

The interlude ("should I blame the times I pampered him") is built as before, with the melody etched by strings and reeds while the cello and bassoon provide movement. The cadence ("before I lost him") builds with violins playing the melody high, brass playing a triplet fanfare, and harp offering another gliss. In the final statement of the A, Lang adds tension by giving offbeat trills to the clarinets and strings; this time, the English horn (eventually joined by flugelhorns) plays the melody along with the singer. The cadence ("not enough of me") builds once again, this time with brass triplets, after which Lang cuts back down to strings and harp accompaniment with a simple fill from the bells (after "what went wrong along the way"). He then broadens the accompaniment for the tag, with tattoos from the brass, a high variation on the melody from strings and reeds ("if that boy with the bugle"), and a brassy ending built on the bugle call fills from the verse. While this chart sounds more than satisfactory on the original cast album, with Angela Lansbury singing it, it was only partially successful, according to musical director Pippin: "We had four different arrangements, we kept trying to avoid a studio/commercial presentation of the song. The last was definitely the best, but I never felt it really landed. It never made you really sit on the edge of the seat."

This arrangement illustrates the traits that left many of Lang's peers less than enthusiastic about his methods: the orchestration is simple and sturdy, effective but not especially flavorful. Worth noting is Lang's practice of doubling just about everything. Harp plays along with cellos, high strings with clarinets, low strings with bassoon. This is seen as something of a safety clause. If you've got a weak cello section, you'll at least hear it from the harp; if the violins don't support the melody, the flugelhorn certainly will. This allows the score to be played by smaller groups without rewriting, as in utility and stock arrangements. Lang was very much cognizant of this, as he was often hired to simplify charts of his own (and others') shows for use by touring and stock & amateur groups. The advantage is that every strain in the arrangement is likely to be heard; the disadvantage is that you don't get the distinct flavoring of solo voices. Walker, Ginzler, Kostal, Burns, and even Bennett delighted in subtle touches here and there, delicate or brusque solos that "almost jump off the page" (as the arrangers say). Lang constructed his scores in the same manner, but with many of these mini-solos padded by an extra instrument (or three). Nothing gets lost, but there are relatively few touches of imaginative fancy.

Two by Irv Kostal

"Everybody Ought to Have a Maid" (Stephen Sondheim)
from A Funny Thing Happened on the Way to the Forum

The form is unconventional, giving a hint of what would come in the future from composer Sondheim: section A ("everybody ought to have a maid"), A ("everybody ought . . . "), B ("oh, oh, wouldn't she be delicious"), A ("everybody ought . . . "), C ("fluttering up the stairway"), B ("oh, oh . . . "), A ("everybody ought . . . "), C ("skittering down the hallway"). The arrangement is distinctive for the contrapuntal vamp in the bass—two contrapuntal vamps, actually.

The foundation line, again, comes from our good friend the string bass playing pizzicato, accompanied by the third cello (of three) and the left hand of the piano, with the drummer also marking out the beat; the offbeats are provided by the violas along with the right hand of the piano. (Forum's unconventional string section called for three violas, three cellos, and one bass; look ma, no violins!) The rhythmic support is dominated by the vamps. The first, accompanying the A section, is played by two cellos. This song was performed by four character comedians with gravelly (or worse) voices. Thus, the melody is doubled; when the star, Pseudolus, sings, it's with two low reeds (bass clarinet and bassoon); when the others sing, it's with two higher reeds (flute and clarinet). Pseudolus sometimes sings the first line of the melody, at other times the "echo" (or canon). In all cases, Kostal gives him the lower reeds instead of taking the easy way by simply repeating the orchestration. The decoration comes after "around the house," a jumpy descending passage, sounding somewhat like a cartoon pebble falling down a flight of stairs. This is played by the xylophone with five of the six reeds (omitting only the lowly bass clarinet, which comes in at the bottom on the final four notes).

Next comes the contrasting B section. The foundation remains as it was, but the support features a different vamp that is somewhat more mysterious than the jaunty one at the opening. This is played by violas, accompanied by one clarinet; the offbeats go to the cellos with low reeds. The melody, here, is only hinted at by the flute; the decoration comes briefly, with a trill from oboe, flute, and piccolo on the last note of the first phrase ("wearing a GOWN"). The opening A is repeated verbatim until the orchestra reaches the E, an eight-bar stop-time coda (which was orchestrated by Ramin). This consists of single-note stings in the first five bars, followed by two bars of triplets and a final two-note sting. The whole number repeats in an encore, this time extended by a gloriously corny eight-bar playoff (also by Ramin). There then follows a second encore, the same as the first.

"When Did I Fall in Love?" (Jerry Bock/Sheldon Harnick)
from Fiorello!

Kostal also gives us "When Did I Fall in Love?" which is among the most exquisite and understated orchestrations in the Broadway bandbox. Here, psychology comes into play. The singer is not the loyal secretary-in-love-with-her-boss heroine; rather, it's Thea, the beautiful blonde he marries in the first act. In this song, which opens the second, Thea is bemused to find herself romantically involved with her husband; "I never once pretended that I loved him," she admits, wondering "when did it start—this change of heart?"

The verse is split into two distinct parts. The first is built on a bubbly flute solo, in 6/8 time, which has something of a young-man-marching-through-Congress feel (the lyric refers to her husband, then a first-term congressman). The flute solo is picked up here and there, canonically, by violins, alto flute, and bass clarinet, with the bassoon playing contrariwise. After twenty bars, we move into a rubato mood ("out of the house ten seconds, and I miss him"), just strings and piano, no reeds (other than three half-note chords from the flutes).

Kostal sneaks into the A–B–A–C refrain with a simple passage, marked "slowly and tenderly (dolcissimo)." This has bass and piano playing a half-note (marked "let ring"), with violins finishing the phrase with an ascending two-note figure; at the same time, violas and cellos play a three-note descending figure. Thus, we have the first group playing up, on one, two, and three, while the other group plays down on two, three, and four, a combination that is at once restful and restive. This measure is repeated before the vocal starts, and continues throughout the A section (with variations, and at times accompanied by high reeds on the upward figure while the low reeds descend). Blessed with a strong singer, Kostal avoids the melody for most of the song.

For the B section, Kostal uses chords, initially from violas, cellos, and piano. The partiturs reveal that he initially wrote a harp part, which was ultimately not used in the show. (The harp here is circled—signifying that it was not to be copied—and pretty much was transferred into the piano part.) The lyric at the end of the B section refers to a crashing chord, and this is seemingly the key to the orchestration. For four measures ("where was the blinding flash? where was the crashing chord?"), the singer builds and builds from pianissimo to fortissimo while the orchestration swells, featuring a rhapsodic piano solo. As Thea returns to her calmly wondered "when did I fall in love?" and the A section, though, Kostal goes back to that gentle upward-downward figure. He brings in the brass for the crescendo (just after "not that it mattered at all") leading into the C section but quickly restrains the orchestra; Thea, though emotional, can't quite express her love for Fiorello.

The interlude ("when did respect first become affection?") is extremely delicate: a whole-note chord tied over several measures from the strings (and, in places, the reeds) while the celesta plays key tone quarter-notes in octaves, forty times in succession! Again, Kostal has so far totally eschewed any melody in the orchestration; the chords and these subtle figures do the job, supporting the singer on what seems to be a cloudlike foundation. Kostal does briefly etch the melody with alto flute, oboe, and viola in the second part of the interlude ("what a strange and beautiful touch"), while the piano plays more rhapsodic chords (lifted verbatim from the vanished harp part).

As the A section returns, Kostal reintroduces the upward-downward figure, but not so gently. Composer Bock has modulated to a warmer key, as Thea is finally beginning to break through her emotional wall. Kostal accommodates him by having the high reeds and trumpets join the ascending violins while bassoon and trombones join violas and cellos. The rhapsodic piano in the B section is countered by a high violin solo, and the "crashing chord" crescendo—which the first time through was muted—here has full and unstoppered brass. Kostal pulls back again for the final A, but gives up all restraint for the final C ("I'm where I want to be . . . "); Thea is in love all right, and Kostal—for the only time in the song—lets the violins play along with the melody for the last eight bars. The final ending builds to sforzando, with a run of high eighth-notes from flutes, trumpets, and violins. The discord in the penultimate measure of the piano part bears a note to copyist Mathilde Pincus: "dissonance OK, I.K."

In recent discussions, both songwriters praised Kostal's orchestration. Harnick: "I thought what he added to what Jerry Bock had written, how he realized the intent and implications in Jerry's music, was brilliant." The only problem with this altogether stunning show tune from the Messrs. Bock and Harnick is dramaturgical; when the skinny blonde songbird finishes her big ballad by chirping that she's gonna love her man "until the end of my life," it's blatantly clear that she won't make it past 10:15.

Two by Ralph Burns

"Don't Rain on My Parade" (Jule Styne/Bob Merrill) from Funny Girl

The form for this rouser, which brings down the first act curtain, is highly unconventional, perhaps fittingly so in that it was coming from the composer of "Rose's Turn" (albeit working without structural assistance from the lyricist of "Rose's Turn"). To wit: A ("don't tell me not to live"), A ("don't tell me not to fly"), B ("I'll march my band out"), A ("rose of sheer perfection"), C ("I gotta fly once"), A ("get ready for me, love, 'cause I'm a winner"), D ("I'm gonna live and live now"), B ("I'll march my band out"), A2 (coda, "get ready for me, love"). The twenty-six-bar verse, included in the partiturs, was deleted; in the theatre, this song took off from the first measure.

The rhythm of the A section is built on a six-note progression of chords over two measures. (This is, in cut-time, two dotted quarter-notes followed by a quarter: [rest] "don't tell me not to" / [rest] "live, just sit and putter.") The three-note chords—from reeds, brass, piano, guitar, and strings—rise chromatically in the first bar, fall in the second; the foundation line is cemented by the string bass playing pizzicato. Fills come, in a similar syncopated manner, from trumpets and trombones.

The B section keeps the bass playing the beat, now in quarter-notes; the harmony is from strings and horn, now playing mostly half-notes; and the rhythm is filled in by piano, guitar, and percussion. Reeds play an unobtrusive countermelody that syncopates the rhythm, while brass punctuates it all with brief fills. The third A ends with a grand fill from trumpets along with excitement-generating tremolos from strings. The C features a descending line of half-notes from strings and bassoon, with a syncopated rhythm (etching the melody) from reeds and percussion. The next A ("get ready for me, love") is as before, with a reed and brass fill leading into the next section.

The D is built on the same syncopated rhythm as the A. (Or the reverse. This D predates *Funny Girl*, having been used as the interlude to "A Man with a Plan," a song cut from Styne's 1961 musical *Subways Are for Sleeping*.) Here, though, the melody corresponds directly to the rhythm, with three syllables ("I'm gon-na / live and live / now") per measure. Styne alters the rhythm like a train on a broken track (two bars in 2/2, followed by one in 1/2; this theme is repeated twice, raised a step, repeated twice, then raised another step and repeated twice). Everybody plays the rhythm, with full-orchestra glissandos filling the empty half of the 1/2 measure. The D ends with a much slower four-bar, 4/4 section ("hey Mr. Arnstein, here I am") built on grand chords followed by a jazzy, two-bar trumpet fill. This is followed by one more B section, somewhat grander than before; and finally the A-based coda with a pull-out-the-stops Hollywood orchestration, befitting the end of the cyclonic number and the end of the first act.

"The Music That Makes Me Dance" (Jule Styne/Bob Merrill)
from Funny Girl

Making an interesting contrast to "Don't Rain on My Parade" is "The Music That Makes Me Dance," another Streisand tour de force from the same show. Both orchestrations are built on chords that provide harmonic etching, but with remarkably different effect. "The Music That Makes Me Dance," to begin with, is as placid as "Parade" is strident and forceful.

This introspective ballad from *Funny Girl*—the eleven o'clock song and the star's *tenth* major number of the evening—is scored with noticeably greater restraint than the rest of the show. It begins in rehearsal mode, with the character sitting at her makeup table. The verse, thus, is accompanied solely by harmonic support, with the piano playing mostly half-note chords. (On the cast recording, and presumably during Streisand's run, this was changed to an improvisatory piano accompaniment.) The partiturs also cue chords for reeds, guitar, and strings, indicating that Burns thought that the director—Jerry Robbins by the time this verse was added—might want something more than just piano. (The partitur also includes an earlier verse, with very different music and lyrics. This pre-Robbins verse has a much fuller orchestration than the rest of the song, with reeds and French horn throughout, fills by violins and celesta, and a grand lead-in to the refrain with fortissimo brass, timpani, and even a triangle.)

The refrain is built on those half-note chords from the reeds and strings, with a rising inner line from—initially—the first cello. The rhythm is provided by the bass, playing pizzicato. The decoration is sparse but tremendously effective, in the guise of a half-dozen fills and a brief countermelody (at "he'll sleep and he'll rise") from the alto sax. These are marked "quasi Johnny Hodges" (Hodges was a Duke Ellington musician known for his sexy solos). There is also a two-bar trumpet fill ("quasi Bobby Hackett") after "need less of myself and need more him." As for the melody, it is etched in those half-notes that just about everyone is playing, but the notes are provided by the singer. This is not only because Ms. Streisand didn't need any help, but to allow her to freely act her way through the number by phrasing all those triplets at will.

Two by Red Ginzler

"I Believe in You" (Frank Loesser) from How to Succeed in Business Without Really Trying

This chart reflects the playful nature of the show, a tongue-in-cheek satire of Madison Avenue. The verse begins in what we might call a percolating-coffee commercial style. A vamp is played by bass, electric guitar, and bass clarinet to the rhythm of a brush on a cymbal. The male chorus—washing up in the executive washroom—plot, in a subdued tone, that they've "gotta stop that man." For fill, Ginzler uses four reeds (including two piccolos), muted trumpets, and vibes. The sixteen-bar preliminary verse is followed by the verse proper, with the hero singing a hymn to himself in the mirror. The first eight bars ("now there you are") are devotional, with chords from strings and reeds, each phrase etched by a celestial chord from harp and bells. A harp gliss takes us into a slightly swinging section ("it may embarrass you to hear me say it") with rhythm from bass, electric guitar, and cymbal and with support from reeds. The phrase "say it I must" is echoed by trumpets with tight mutes, changing the coffee commercial sound to an even more contemporary after-shave commercial sound.

The refrain is purposely schizophrenic. Ginzler has taken the conflicting moods of Loesser's lyric and divided them into three alternating parts: after-shave commercial, rhapsodically earnest, and rapturously devotional. He begins in the commercial mode for four bars ("you have the cool clear eyes of a seeker of wisdom and . . . "), with rhythm from bass, guitar, and brush on snare; the tight-cupped trumpets provide those same echoes from the end of the verse, here accompanied by reeds (four flutes plus English horn). This leads into four rhapsodic bars, in which the singer holds the word "truth" while the strings play a broad legato theme with pulsating chords from trombones and horn. These two four-bar sections are repeated ("upturned chin . . . impetuous youth"). The next eight ("Oh I believe in you, I believe in you") is marked "religioso," featuring strings, trombones, and horn (with the melody etched by the first chair cello). The over-all section ends with a chord from the string/low brass group, perked by harp. The twenty-four-bar A section is repeated more or less intact, with the addition of vibes on the echoes (in the after-shave portion) and the English horn on the broad string countermelody (in the rhapsody).

The bridge ("and when my faith in my fellow man") can be described as rap-turously rhapsodic. A grand scale of sixteenth-notes from the violins takes us into a new key. The harp leads the section with eighth-note arpeggios; cellos play quarter-note pyramids; violins play octaves (developing into a high counter-melody); the reeds mostly fill in the harmony, while the flute doubles the melody. Ginzler heightens the end of the bridge with trombone chords and (after "I take heart") pure, unmuted trumpets. Then it's back to the twenty-four-bar A section (as played the second time, with vibes and English horn).

The Pulitzer-winning *How to Succeed* was marked by jokes on top of jokes on top of jokes, coming not only from lyricist Loesser and librettist Abe Burrows but from director (Burrows), choreographer (Fosse), and even the designers. Ginzler kept right up with them. "I Believe in You, Part II" continues with a four-bar reiteration of the opening vamp (with the men singing "gotta stop that man, gotta stop that man"). We go back to the refrain, except that now the hero—J. Pierpont Finch—is shaving in the mirror. Thus, Ginzler gives the melody to electric razors! Not electric razors exactly, as they would prove impractical. (To begin with, the stagehand union would have no doubt demanded an electrician in the pit.) Instead, we have a novel combination: kazoos from the five reed players, accompanied by trumpets, French horn, and violins with instructions for alter-nating chairs to play "one in tune and one sharp." This accompanied by rhythm from bass, guitar, and brush on snare, with echo fills from trombones.

The men, meanwhile, sing a countermelody ("big wheel . . . boiling hot with front office fever"). This takes up the first sixteen bars of the A section, leading back to the rapturously devotional section ("oh, I believe in you") with the horn on melody and the men (for the first time in harmony) singing a countermelody ("don't let him be such a hero"). A repeat of the A section by Finch has been deleted, with an abrupt cut to the coda. "Stop that man, gotta stop him," sing the men as Finch sings—repeatedly to himself in the mirror—"you." Bass, cellos, guitar, and even timpani pound out the beat, reeds and trombones play the choral countermelody, and violins give us octave glissandos and wildly trill away.

"Put on a Happy Face" (Charles Strouse/Lee Adams)
from Bye Bye Birdie

Strouse's bright song and dance is a simple thirty-two bars, in four eight-bar sections: A section ("gray skies are gonna clear up"), B ("take off the gloomy mask of tragedy"), A ("pick out a pleasant outlook"), C ("spread sunshine all over the place"). This is followed by a second refrain containing a taste of big band sound, then two additional dance refrains with the orchestrator pulling out all the instrumental stops.

The number is built on a sprightly two-bar vamp that merits examination. The bass provides the foundation line (pizzicato quarter-notes on one and three, in cut-time); cellos provide support (four half-notes), along with drums (with brush on cymbal) and guitar chords on two and four; the melody is played by four flutes plus xylophone. (The distinctive four-flute sound was unheard of on Broadway, presumably inspired by the recordings of the Sauter-Finegan band.) Decoration comes from the six-person trumpet/trombone contingent, with a final note played with "very tight cup mutes" and labeled "doit!" (Not "do it," but a sound similar to "loit-" as in loiter. This is accomplished by squeezing the lips into the mouthpiece, resulting in a comic effect.) This vamp is repeated five times on the partitur, although it was played considerably longer in performance.

The underlying accompaniment—bass on the beat; cellos, cymbal, guitar on support—continues into the A section, with the melody coming totally from the male soloist. (The song was performed by the star, Dick Van Dyke, originally, with two "sad girl" dancers.) High decorative fills are played by flutes and xylophone. In the B section, violins (in three parts) and cellos (in two) play a sweet descending line of half-notes in support, while the others continue with their functions; brass spices the fills in the fourth (after "it's not your style") and eighth measures (after "decided to smile"). The second A repeats the orchestration from the first; the C has fuller support, with two high trombones providing a descending scale of half-notes. The decoration here is one of those reed figures for which Ginzler was noted, with the four flutes playing an eighteen-note run of triplets— eight up, twelve down—on "all over the place, just . . . " This in direct opposition to one of Walker's cardinal rules: no bravura decoration whatsoever allowed during the vocal (as opposed to during the rests). All through the first refrain, the melody has been supplied solely by the singer.

The first A section of the second refrain gives the first and third lines ("gray skies are gonna clear up" and "brush off the clouds and cheer up") over to dance (Dick follows the girl for two bars, as she crosses away), with the melody played by brass and vibes; the second and fourth lines, the title phrase, are sung as before. Bass, guitar, and drums continue to provide accompaniment, with the decoration highlighted by a brisk eleven-note fill from the flutes. The B section is basically the same as before, with sweetened support in the latter half from violins, cellos, and trombones. This support is continued through the second A, with the C repeated from the first refrain. The transition to the dance begins with the opening vamp played two times, followed by a descending scale of quarter-notes from reeds, vibes, and strings.

While we haven't been concentrating on dance orchestrations in these pages, Ginzler's treatment is remarkable enough to make us want to look at the dance refrains. The accompaniment continues from bass, guitar, and drums, but the rest is very different, attributable to the collaboration between dance arranger John Morris (who shifts rhythms and styles from phrase to phrase) and Ginzler (who dizzyingly shifts the melody line from player to player). The extended vamp continues with a descending line, as Van Dyke goes into a penguin step.

"Gray skies"—or what would be "gray skies" if the lyric were being sung—continues as in the second refrain, with blaring brass (he does a jazzy, though clumsy, step). The answering title phrase is totally different, marked "delicato!": four flutes playing staccato, violins playing pizzicato, and—suddenly, out of nowhere—a harp playing in thirds, accompanied by bells (she swiftly walks away, with him following). "Brush off" goes back to the brass; the second title phrase is once again delicato. (After another jazzy step, the same swift walk—although this time she follows him.) The first part of the B section moves into "light swing" (a cross-step) with the melody from high trombones and a seven-note run from the trumpets as fill. The timpani—another new sound—ends the B (she steps on his toe) with four machinery-like bars (he comes at her in mock anger). The second A continues in the delicato style, with reeds, violins, and the (newly added) xylophone playing the melody discordantly while the bassoon—yet another new color—and cellos play eighth-note scales. "Gray skies are gonna clear up," with its ascending melody, is countered by a descending scale from bassoon and cellos; "put on a happy face," with a descending melody, has an ascending accompaniment. (They do a silent movie–like step, with the tall man leaning over the short girl.) The C starts with three bars of syncopated swing from the brass (they do a "Marge & Gower" step, in this first musical directed and choreographed by Gower Champion himself), only to go back to delicato for the rest of the third refrain. (As the reeds twitter, he tickles her, then does a laughing, stair-climbing step as he crosses away.) This leads us back to that opening vamp, at which point he finds another sad girl.

The fourth refrain begins with the previously heard swinging brass for "gray skies"; switches to sweet strings and flutes for the title phrase; goes delicato (with bells and pizzicato violins) for "brush off"; then returns to swing for the final two bars of the A. (All the while, the three of them do a full-stage dance.) The B section goes to an even fuller swing, with Ginzler now finally retiring the flutes and other reeds in favor of a saxophone blast (two alto, two tenor, and a baritone). For decoration, we have a thirteen-note schmear from three trumpets and three trombones. The next two bars (which, if there were a lyric, would be "you'll look so good . . . ") revert to only eight players: the bass on the bottom, drums and guitar on support, and five saxes on melody. The section ends with the brass joining the sax for a syncopated variation of the "decided to smile" line. This treatment continues through the second A until midway through the C section ("spread sunshine"). At this point, Ginzler writes "smoother," with brass playing the title phrase over bass, drums, and guitar. No reeds for these three bars; as it turns out, Ginzler has them doing a quick change back to flutes and piccolos for the reemergence of the vamp. (The second girl exits, leaving the star and the first sad girl back where they started.) After several repeats of the vamp, there is an ascending five-note scale from the brass (he turns to leave and starts off) after which—yes, boys, grab those saxes!—we have an eleven-note run from the saxes, accompanied by a glissando from the brass (he bangs his face into a luggage truck), leading to a big band finish as the girl—finally—laughs.

From Ginzler to Tunick

The young Jonathan Tunick, twenty-two and already working as an arranger, sneered at the Broadway musical as being hopelessly square. One day in 1960, his father got some house seats from his lawyer and took Jonathan to see *Bye Bye Birdie.* Tunick was stunned; if a Broadway pit orchestra could sound like this, then Broadway was where he wanted to be. Touches like those four flutes—the very four flutes in "Put on a Happy Face"—got him. His father asked, "Oh, do you want me to ask Arthur" (his lawyer, Arthur Ginzler) "to introduce you to his brother?"

Red Ginzler took Tunick under his proverbial wing and let him observe what he was doing. Ramin: "Jonathan worshipped Red—he looked like Red physically, and he thought Red was the king. Rightfully so. He hung around our office when we were doing a show, and he just adored Red." In the fall of 1962, Ginzler invited Tunick to assist him on his next musical, *Hot Spot.* Just as the show was about to go into rehearsals, Ginzler died of a heart attack. Tunick struggled for Broadway work over the next five years—Bennett was one of the few people to give him a chance, ghosting on the 1966 revival of *Show Boat*—but after *Promises, Promises* (1968), *Company* (1970), and *Follies* (1971), he was firmly established as a successor to Bennett and Walker. Stylistically, though, he was heir to the brilliant, inventive, and all-but-unknown Ginzler.

While the work of Tunick and the orchestrators who followed him is outside the general compass of this book, I take the prerogative to make an exception. Through the course of my research, I was invited by Jack Viertel to sit in on orchestra readings for musicals in the City Center Encores! series. The studio is the best place to hear orchestrations; you get to hear the orchestrations without distractions, the conductor carefully examines complicated passages, and you usually get to hear each chart two or three times. And there is no competition from those pesky singers—which means that everybody, including the musical director, can concentrate solely on the music.

Everything sounds good in these readings. Sitting in Carroll Studios for the rehearsal of the Encores! *Follies* in 2007, one chart ("I'm Still Here") sounded especially phenomenal, so good, in fact, that the orchestra—after working their way through it—stopped to applaud. It was my good fortune to have Jonathan sitting next to me, munching a turkey sandwich. While conductor Eric Stern went over some fine points with the players, I was able to ask Jonathan about fine points in his orchestration. The chart is not only excellent and worthy of study; it clearly illustrates what an orchestrator can do. Hence, I include it here, where it doesn't exactly belong. Bennett, Walker, and Ginzler, I feel, won't mind.

"I'm Still Here" is a powerhouse character study. The singer, a survivor, cycles through moods of rueful nostalgia, determination, frustration, anger, resentment, and finally sheer, gutsy tenacity. This is all in Sondheim's lyrics, yes, and in the hands of an expert actress, the song is a simmering tour de force. But look, I say, at the orchestration. Sitting in the rehearsal hall, the above-mentioned emotions—nostalgia, frustration, resentment, tenacity, and the others—were very definitely present, without anyone singing the lyric. Five refrains, with Tunick's shifting orchestral treatment, built to a pressure cooker.

The song is written in a typically Sondheimesque form, which is to say, unusual. I will map out the form, not because it is important in itself—Sondheim is never restrained by form—but because it will help to clarify the stages of the orchestration. After a two-bar vamp comes refrain 1 (there is no verse). This is in four sections: A ("Good times and bum times"), B ("I've stuffed the dailies"), A ("I've slept in shanties"), C ("I've stood on breadlines"). The first three are eight bars each; the twelve-bar C starts with the first two bars of the B before working its way into a new direction. The shortened refrain 2 (which is not included in the version on the 1971 original cast album) begins with A ("I've been through Gandhi"), then jumps directly to a modified C ("I got through 'Abie's Irish Rose'"). This follows the initial C for the first half, but the final six bars are altered to build to interlude 1 ("I've gotten through Herbert and J. Edgar Hoover"). This is a simple eight bars, followed by four bars' worth of the opening vamp.

Refrain 3 follows the pattern of refrain 2, to a point, with A ("I've been through Reno") followed by yet another altered C ("Been called a pinko Commie tool"); still twelve bars, but with a different resolution. Refrain 4 follows suit, with A ("Black sable one day") followed by the fourth version of C ("First you're another sloe-eyed vamp"). As previously, the first four bars are similar, with variations in the rest. Interlude 2 ("I've gotten through 'Hey, Lady, aren't you whoo-zis?'") is identical to the first except for the final cadence, with a grand modulation from E♭ to E major. Refrain 5 follows the prior pattern of A ("Good times and bum times," with the lyricist repeating the first line of the song for emphasis in the new key) to C ("I've run the gamut"); for the first time, the C is cut to eight bars. This takes us into a twelve-bar coda ("Lord knows, at least I've been there—and I'm here").

Now, let's see what Tunick does with it. To begin, he builds almost the entire orchestration on the bass clarinet, featuring an arpeggiated chord of four eighth-notes with the last tied to a half-note (and thus held throughout the measure). From the opening vamp, the bass clarinet plays almost constantly, with the exception of the first eight bars of each C section. This continues until the end of interlude 2, at which point the bass clarinet function is taken over by bass sax. The vamp consists of the bass clarinet's arpeggiated chord, joined by first trumpet and celesta playing a figure of three eighth-notes.

The arpeggiated figure is clearly from the composer's piano part; this is a vamp that you would sit at the keyboard and play with the left hand. Any orchestrator would need to translate this to another instrument (unless he, lazily, just left it with the piano). Tunick, cannily, chooses the bass clarinet, with embellishment from the clarinets above: the sound of the dance bands of the thirties and early forties, Benny Goodman, Glenn Miller, and all. This is when Carlotta—the gal who's "still here"—was in her element. While the 1971 musical *Follies* takes place "at the present time," the reed writing takes Carlotta back to the days when she was still in her prime. This is a subtle touch; while few theatregoers would have actually picked up on it, many of those over forty would have been subconsciously transported back in time with the character.

The bass clarinet—along with a pizzicato note on the first bar of each measure from the bass and some light melodic etching from the four clarinets—provides the accompaniment for the first A–B. Cup-muted trombones play a mellow fill at each "I'm still here"; trumpet and celesta return for the two-bar cadence into the second A ("shanties"), at which point bass and guitar fill in the rhythm. At the C ("breadlines"), the trombones temporarily take over for the bass clarinet while the strings sweeten it with whole-note chords. The trombones have a substantial fill at "nowhere near," as the bass clarinet returns (with clarinets). At the end of the refrain, the drummer comes in as the trombones throw down their mutes for the cadence into the next section. Refrain 2 ("Gandhi") is marked by this trombone figure (two quarter-notes followed by a dotted eighth and sixteenth—bah bah DA-DA), the first of several methods Tunick uses to increase the drive of the song. After "Abie's Irish Rose," he gives the reeds a figure marked "1950s Ellington." The emotion is then momentarily pulled back down for "heebie jeebies," with the refrain ending with the trombones commenting on "Brenda Frazier," joined by the trumpets for the cadence into the next section.

Interlude 1 ("J. Edgar Hoover") continues with bass clarinet and trombones, with high strings playing whole and half-notes; if we want to divide the song into emotional levels, the strings here take us from the starting position to level 2. The section ends with the full reed and brass section commenting on the lyric ("anything else is a laugh"), after which Tunick pulls all the way back down again to his opening vamp; the character is trying to keep an even keel as she dictates her memoirs, although the emotional pressure cooker cannot be controlled indefinitely. After the repeated vamp, we are back to refrain 3 ("Reno"); the accompaniment starts out the same as before, although with an added undercurrent of emotion provided by chords from the strings. By the C ("pinko"), the stakes are higher; the trombones play their countermelody up an octave, with the strings also making the jump. The refrain ends as before, the brass driving onward—and this time they will not let up. Refrain 4 ("black sable") has the bass, guitar, and drums pounding out quarter-notes while the trombones have their rhythmic tattoo, the strings have high whole notes, the trumpets come in on the fills, and the bass clarinet keeps playing along. The trombone tattoo and those high string notes take us to level 3. Interlude 2 ("Hey, lady") is the same as before, except the first violins have leapt an octave to an eerily high G three octaves over middle C—which puts us on level 4. Tunick pulls out all the stops for the modulation on the final bar (after "whatever happened to her"), with the introduction of a full complement of saxophones and the brass playing a dotted eighth-note figure topped by a flare—which takes us to the climactic level 5. Everybody plays for refrain 5 ("Good times and bum times"), with a strong quarter-note beat ("drive hard," he instructs the drummer). At C ("gamut," which is rhymed with "dammit"), there is a countermelody in close harmony for the saxes. The coda is sparked (after "Lord knows at least I've been there") by a fill of brass and sax triplets. "And I'm here"—bass, trombones, drums, and guitar pound out the beat, with fill by the reeds; "Look who's here"—same; and then the final "I'm still here," with the trumpets capping things by taking the fill up an octave to high C.

Tunick's work, brilliant as it is, would be nothing without the music and lyrics from Mr. Sondheim; lavish this expert handling on a mundane song by mundane writers and you'd wind up with something, well, mundane. Let us further point out that the arrangement—the routine, the countermelodies, that modulation—are all surely the work of the composer, not the orchestrator. Tunick's job was to dress the work in instrumental sounds: the mellow trombones, the crisp trumpets, the clarinet quartet, and that ever-present bass clarinet, which provides exactly the right textural skeleton. The combination approaches the sublime, as on so many of the Sondheim-Tunick joint adventures; the in-theatre sound of the orchestras of *A Little Night Music*, *Sweeney Todd*, and the others is just about as rich as it gets.

SECTION VIII.
SWEENEY IN THE PIT WITH STEVE

We have discussed orchestration at length, and virtually all readers of these pages have experienced the sound of theatre music from a seat in the auditorium. But what is it like to watch—or, rather, hear—the orchestrations, in performance, from the pit?

Over the course of more than thirty years working in and around the Broadway theatre, it never occurred to me to do so. But as I was starting to research this book, Larry Blank said: "You're coming down to see the Sondheim Festival, right?" (This was the remarkable mounting by the Kennedy Center of six full-scale productions in the summer of 2002. Larry was musical director for *Sweeney Todd*.) "Why don't you sit in on *Sweeney*?" I thought: Well, of course.

Here follows an account which I wrote at the time, although I was unable to find any suitable place to print it. I trust that it will be of interest here; please pardon me as I switch to the present tense, and join me as the events of that singular evening unfold.

> I duly journey to Washington on a steamy June Thursday. Upon arrival, I discover that my catbird seat has been usurped; turns out that, over the course of more than fifty years in the theatre, it never occurred to Stephen Sondheim to sit in the pit either. But now it has, tonight is the night, and I am out in the (ninety-four-degree) cold.
>
> "But Sondheim can't do that," I say. "I asked first." Well, no, I don't say that. I just say: "Oh."
>
> "We can squeeze in a stool between the trumpets and trombones, if you don't mind." The way Larry says it, it sounds *loud*. But here I am at

Kennedy Center, it's hot and steamy outside, and I realize that the pit is precisely where I want to be.

I take my place fifteen minutes before curtain. When you walk to the front row and look down into the pit, you notice right off that it isn't laid out in even rows with neat aisles; it's more like the closet you use for storage after all your storage closets are full. One item is placed smack dab against the next; the walls and door and gravity conspire, hopefully, to keep it all from spilling out like the hard-boiled eggs in the stateroom in *A Night at the Opera*.

The pit is packed with an awful lot of stuff. Chairs for the musicians, of course. Music stands, with attached music-stand lights. Microphone stands, with attached microphones. Instrument stands, on which players who double on more than one instrument park their excess clarinets and saxophones and tubas. Instrument cases, briefcases, backpacks, pocket-books, magazines, newspapers, water bottles. The floor is coiled with ca-bles, linking microphones to the soundman, stand lights to the electri-cian. Then there are the larger, less portable items, which in the case of *Sweeney* include one electric organ, one celesta, one harp, one string bass, and a cartload of percussion equipment, including timpani, xylophone, chimes, bells, vibes, a gong, and two glockenspiels.

And let's not forget the musicians. Tall musicians, small musicians, thin and stout and all kinds. Broadway musicals are usually scored for anywhere from six to thirty players, depending on economics, pit size, and union requirements. Sometimes, they even take into account the needs and desires of the composer. *Sweeney Todd* at the Kennedy Center is played by twenty-six men and women. So there we were: twenty-six musicians, thirty-six instruments (plus assorted drums & things), and one conductor. Plus two interlopers from New York, Stephen Sond-heim and me.

Sondheim's comfy cushioned chair with padded back awaits in the civilized alley on the stage-right side of the pit between piano and harp. I'm twenty feet away, with two trumpets directly to my left; three trom-bones, diagonally, to my right; and my shoulder blade nestled against the curve of the big bass drum. (Larry never mentioned that drum.) I'm an item of curiosity. The musicians nod pleasantly, on their best behavior; if somebody has wedged an extra stool into their crowded midst, they figure they better not take any chances. Especially when the guy is hold-ing a legal pad and jotting notes.

Ringed in front of me are the five reeds, with fourteen instruments among them; each has a primary assignment, but the job calls for them to switch off frequently. (In some sections, Jonathan Tunick has scored *Sweeney* for four clarinets at once.) Sitting at my right knee is reed I, the principal flute and piccolo player; at my left knee, separating me from Larry, is reed IV, who switches between oboe and English horn.

Both are especially personable. Reed IV's first words to me are, "did you bring ear plugs?" No, I thought I was going to be sitting over by the harp. Reed I says that it gets a little loud, maybe Beverly has some extra ear plugs. I don't know who Beverly is; as I'm now shoehorned into place, with the percussionists blocking access, there's no way out. Reed III, the lead clarinet, says not to worry: "just cover up when you see me do this." He clamps his hands tight over his ears, wincing.

The pre-show pit is fairly busy, with people practicing tricky passages; I suppose they are going over sections they had trouble with the night before. At 7:28—two minutes before the announced curtain time—a red cue light strung to the conductor's podium flashes on. Everyone snaps to attention. A friendly-faced fellow with well-trimmed beard who looks somewhat like Nathan Lane without the wince approaches the podium, violin in hand. This is the head violinist, otherwise known as the concertmaster.

"Por favore," he says, nodding to reed IV. Her oboe at the ready, she plays an A. The concertmaster plays an A, adjusting his pitch to match the oboe. Satisfied, he nods to the right half of the pit. Reeds and brass play, matching the tone. When they finish, he turns to the strings—six violins, two violas, two cellos, and one double bass—and gives them another A. He then takes his seat, to the immediate left of the podium.

Out comes Larry, dressed in his best conductor garb. In the symphony hall, the conductor gets a grand entrance *mit* spotlight. In a theatrical orchestra pit, the poor guy threads his way through the near-dark, weaving among the seated musicians and the standing microphones, stepping on toes and electric cables, trying not to look foolish as he knocks over a music stand or two.

At 7:30, with the house lights still on and the audience filing in, Larry cues the piano player, who begins playing hymn-like organ music on the synthesizer crammed in next to the piano. (*Sweeney Todd* has no overture.) Trumpet II, the dour fellow directly to my left, pulls a book out of his knapsack—*The Sum of All Favors* by Tom Clancy—and opens it to his bookmark. He's on page 208.

Larry adjusts his headset, exchanges a word or two with the stage manager, then turns to glance at the sold-out house. He swivels back to his little band of men and women. "You all look much too happy," says he. This *Sweeney*, still in previews, has been very well received; even jaded musicians can feel part of something special.

At 7:33, I notice a flashing movement way across the crowded pit, gray hair, gray beard bobbing above the seated heads. The composer quietly takes his seat (that is—*my* seat!). Nobody seems to notice his presence, other than Larry; the keyboard player, David Gursky—who is about to embark on three hours of *Sweeney* with Stephen Sondheim (i.e., God) at his elbow, thank you very much—and me.

The mood is still casual. "So where did you decide to go?" asks trumpet I of trumpet II, forcing the latter to grumpily put down his Clancy. Reed IV cleans her glasses. The trombones, meanwhile, seem to be discussing the union pension fund. Reed III blows hot air into the mouthpiece of his clarinet.

With the house lights on, I survey my domain. I am just in front of the stage overhang; the trombones are under the deck, not a place I'd recommend for a claustrophobic. The top of my head is three feet below stage level; by craning my neck, I can see the upper reaches of the proscenium arch. The rail separating the pit from the auditorium cuts off my view of most of the orchestra seats, although I can see the people in the far left of the first three rows. I have a clear shot of the upper reaches of the balcony. I can also look into the boxes ringing the rear wall of the theatre, including the presidential box, situated dead center. I was once in there with Reagan, Nancy, Burt Reynolds, Dom DeLuise, and Joe Theismann, not my type of crowd (except for maybe Dom DeLuise). But that's another story.

At 7:36, the red cue light flashes once more. Larry signals the keyboard player, who abruptly switches to a prescribed section that leads into the prologue. The house lights start to dim. The buzz of the audience dies out, and there is that momentary air of extreme expectation peculiar to live theatre. A sudden chill hits the pit, a physical wave of cold air. Is this from the excited knowledge of what lies in store? Or is it from the closing of the lobby doors, giving renewed power to the air conditioning?

Larry rises from his stool, picks up his baton, and raises his arms. A moment before, he had been jovial and sun-burn red, joking with the musicians; now he is grim, murderous determination, the color drained from his face. His left hand darts like an arrow, and we hear the piercing blast of a steam whistle. The reeds play a woody accompaniment as "The Ballad of Sweeney Todd" begins. The stage lights come up, presumably; I can't see the stage, but there is a round of applause that must be for the set. "Attend the tale of Sweeney Todd," a baritone sings, somewhere above me.

I feel like I'm in a wood of woodwinds, rippling. Things move quickly, too quickly; I follow the oboe part on reed IV's stand for a moment. Trumpet I, a chair away from me, is tacet (which means he has a page full of rests). He stands against the orchestra rail, looking at (part of) the stage. I try, but I'm too close to the overhang and can't see anything.

There is a discordant chirping in the twelfth measure. Look fast. My eyes dart to the stand in front of me; reed I is preparing to play his flute; what I heard must have been the piccolo.

The second stanza of the opening song has an eerily discordant overlay of reeds and strings. Before I can discern who is playing what, we move into a choir-like section, heavy with brass. "Swing your razor high, Sweeney," thunders the chorus.

A familiar, forgotten odor hits me, from my days in the trumpet section of the high school band. Piston lubricant, the oil you use to keep the valves gliding smoothly, that's what it is. Mixed with excess moisture escaping from the trumpets and trombones; in other words, spit. Reed IV, by my left knee, is on the English horn. Her shoulder is tensed, oboe tucked under her arm for a quick switch. And then, an explosion. The chorus is singing the word "moralize," but that's not what I hear; it's the big bass drum against my spine. I don't hear it; I *feel* it, the timbre vibrating through me.

We quickly move into a different musical section altogether. ("Inconspicuous Sweeney was," goes the lyric.) Larry now has three-quarters of his attention on the stage. I can't see the singers, but they are in full harmony and impressively strong. Real singers, not the dancer-singers you find in musical comedy. The chorus enters a sibilant patch—"Sweeney was smooth, Sweeney was subtle"—until the soprano sound approximates the discordant chirping of the piccolo and that steam whistle.

Something is imminent, I can sense. I look up at the ceiling of the auditorium, eerily blocked in yellow-white light. On the roof of the Eisenhower Theatre, I see the silhouette of a man, a tall, thin man. As the shadow moves forward, the house erupts in a round of entrance applause. "Attend the tale of Sweeney Todd," a brutal baritone commands, breaking through the ovation. Brian Stokes Mitchell. The trombones play mournful quarter-notes. "What happened then—well, that's the play, and he wouldn't want us to give it away," he sings. Moments later, I'm in a thicket of reeds and trumpets and trombones, ending with four blaring beats on the timpani that cut right through me. The lights black out and the audience explodes with the first ovation of the night. A moment's rest for me, but the harp and woodwinds have already started to play the rather more rhapsodic introduction to the next number.

The show continues with a scene between Todd and the sailor Anthony. Their song is interrupted by the half-crazed Beggar Woman (who, as we will learn, is Todd's long-lost wife). Out comes a passage of off-kilter chords so striking that I spin around to identify them. It's the three trombones, the notes of the chords alternating between them. In the distance, I see Sondheim on his feet; he, too, is searching for the sound.

Todd tells us—to music that will recur throughout the evening—that "there was a barber and his wife." It's a haunting passage, in variable tempo on its first appearance. Larry stands like a surgeon, or maybe a diamond cutter cutting a priceless gem. He pushes, he prods, he follows Stokes, he holds back ever so tentatively.

The scene ends with a wild dash of music, leading into a vamp as the lights come up on "The Worst Pies in London." The audience explodes again, the entrance hand for Christine Baranski, no doubt. She is worthy of the ovation, as we soon learn; her song is punctuated by enormous laughs from the house. (At one point, reed I—the slight, gentle flutist, temporarily at rest—mouths the words along with Baranski, simply for his own amusement.) What Baranski is doing, I can't tell; I stick my head up into the black void, but cannot see her. This song is quite a workout for the performer—who is kneading dough onstage, punctuating her number—and for the pit, which matches her jab for jab. It is followed by a restatement of "The Barber and His Wife"—a richly woody one, with oboe, flute, and harp luxuriantly combining. The scene ends with a memory section ("Poor Thing") that grows faster and faster until the orchestra goes wild and Todd yells, "Will no one have mercy!" Larry—who entered the pit only thirty minutes before, resplendent in fresh tuxedo with red carnation in lapel—is wilted and sweaty.

At 8:25, Anthony sings "Johanna." Sondheim has been criticized throughout his career for writing cold, unemotional music, but this is a fallacy; "Johanna" is sheer beauty in music. The harp and strings take the lead, interwoven with a luxuriant flute solo. Listening to this setting— no, enveloped in its warmth—it suddenly hits me: five years ago, I named my daughter Johanna. Now I realize why. (My wife thinks we chose it because it was her grandmother's name.)

Next comes a scene out of comic operetta, closer in style to Bernstein's *Candide* than Sondheim's *Sweeney*. The tension lets up for the first time. The pit seems as bright as a sandy beach—the stage must be fully lit— and everyone is having a jolly old time playing "funny" music. As the barber Pirelli flamboyantly shaves a chorister, reed II gleefully plays comic runs on his clarinet. I make a note to find out what they use for the sound of the razor. (The percussionist happily demonstrates this for me during intermission, rubbing a hair brush—his own dog's hair brush—against the cardboard core of a roll of paper towels covered with sandpaper.)

The villainous Judge Turpin sings a second, altogether different song called "Johanna." The setting is intense, with bassoon playing against strings for an unsettling sound. In come brass and timpani for impassioned sections, in which Judge Turpin whips himself in self-flagellation. ("Deliver me from this hot red devil with your soft white cool virgin palms," he whimpers.) Sondheim is on his feet again, caught in the passion of the trumpets. I have a nodding acquaintance with Sondheim; I've seen him in various public settings over the years, often at theatre, the last time in the customs line at JFK. Here is revealed a different Sondheim, a private Sondheim, peering across the void in rapt concentration at the unexpected discovery of a new and visceral element in something he wrote twenty-five years ago.

Next comes another lull in the tension, a comic scene in which Pirelli—the mock-Italianate barber—visits Todd and has his throat slit. The orchestra holds an endless chord as Pirelli dies a long, bloody death. Rather than simply cutting the musicians off with his baton, Larry chokes—hand clutching his throat—and finally collapses across the podium, effectively ending the chord.

There comes a brief interlude of dialogue. Baranski gets an enormous laugh, including from me, with the line "well, that's a different matter." (You had to be there.) Sondheim has his hands stretched up against the roof of the pit in a reverse push-up, with a big beaming smile.

Now arrives the main event. The final twenty-minute stretch of the first act of *Sweeney Todd* is among the most amazing scenes in musical theatre history. There is a discernible change of atmosphere in the pit; thirty bodies visibly tense for the onslaught, like the offensive line on fourth-and-inches in overtime in the mud with a wild-card slot at stake.

8:45: Judge Turpin—upon whom Todd is determined to exact revenge—walks into the demon barber's lair, baring his neck to the razor. Before Todd can dispatch the villain, of course, he must sing. "Pretty Women" go the words, a lushly beautiful counterpoint duet for Todd and Turpin (with mood enhancement from French horn and bassoon).

As the song climaxes, Turpin narrowly escapes the razor and flees to his dressing room. "I had him," Todd cries, "his throat was bare beneath my hand, and he'll never come again!" This is the part where reed II, the head clarinet, sticks his fingers in his ears. And no wonder. There is a series of charges from the two trumpets (to my left) and the three trombones (to my right), buoyed by timpani (by my shoulder) and bass drum (in my ear). And the steam whistle, for good measure. This song is called "Epiphany," as the audience watches Todd go—to use a technical term—bonkers. I had my own epiphany here, too, forcibly blasted from my backless stool.

"They all deserve to die," Todd sings, to a straggling, piercing, offbeat accompaniment that brings to mind the first bubbles as the pot starts to boil. And I hear tom-toms—not restless natives, but the sound of an exploding heartbeat, catching me unaware from behind the far side of the bass drum. "I'm alive at last!" Todd sings. The house erupts once more. Stokes has been absolutely magnificent. I time the applause: a full ninety seconds, and that's a long time. But as anyone familiar with *Sweeney Todd* knows, there's more to come.

Mrs. Lovett, the meat pie madam, has a solution that merges Todd's body-disposal problem with her need for what she refers to as "fresh supplies." ("You know me, bright ideas just pop into my head," she explains.) Planting my heels on the rung of my stool and maintaining my balance by gripping the ceiling of the understage, I make one of my periodic attempts at viewing the stage.

"Business needs a lift," Baranski sings—and suddenly her pig-tailed head pops into view; she is on the edge of the apron, directly above me, and has apparently just raised herself on tiptoes to accompany her words. I realize that I can, indeed, see the action, at least whatever action takes place in the slice of airspace above my perch. Which is precisely where this number is staged. I keep watching, and here is Stokes, wildly swinging his razors as he tells us of "man devouring man." A bead of sweat drips down the blade and flies—well, toward me, in the pit. It dissolves on the way down, like a snowflake.

I turn to the audience, or at least the people in the three rows that I can see. Smiles break out on the individual faces like one of those time-lapse documentaries of tulips in bloom, as they "get" it and decide that it is perfectly acceptable to get into the swing with this pair of cannibalistic serial killers.

The music turns into a demonic waltz as Lovett offers Todd a bite of an imaginary meat pie. "Have a little priest," she sings. As Todd tastes the meat pie, he says—what else?—"Heavenly!" The house roars, and Sondheim has achieved what might well have seemed impossible. Within one continuous scene, a glorious male duet rhapsodizing on the wonders of "Pretty Women," an attempted murder, climax into a viciously mesmerizing mad scene, topped by a stunningly loquacious, punningly mad, rollicking *valse macabre*.

That's the end of the first act. We file out of the pit, in reverse order—last in, first out—as if we've just emerged from victorious battle. Larry, I suppose, escapes to the conductor's suite to dunk his head in cold water and get a clean shirt; the musicians congregate in the dark and cool understage, where they share a birthday cake for one of the viola players baked by another of the viola players. Sondheim is nowhere to be seen.

After seventeen minutes, we return to our perches. Act 2 features more of the same. The opening romp of a production number about meat pies, "God, That's Good," with the reeds whistling away and the trombones pouncing on the offbeat; the second act reprise of Anthony's "Johanna," with bassoon and French horn combining for a (temporarily) soothing effect; Baranski rocking the premises with "By the Sea." (At some point along the way I look over and find Sondheim back at his haunt; he seems far more relaxed than during the first act.) Along comes a lullaby; "nothing's gonna harm you, not while I'm around" go the words. *Piu mosso espressivo* it is marked on reed IV's part, and that's what it is. The harp and cellos lull us peacefully, joined by the movingly expressive French horn and oboe. The first refrain is sung by the half-witted boy, Tobias; when the murderous Mrs. Lovett sings her section, the sweet flute joins her but the violins play eerily off-pitch. Tunick's orchestration clearly informs us of the lyric's false promise; within twenty minutes, Lovett will be baking in the oven, marked with a "T."

Todd discovers that he has just unwittingly murdered his Beggar Woman/wife. I look at the trumpet part: "Big Cue!" it says. I suppose this message is there as a not so subtle reminder. The trumpets have spent a fair amount of the evening underutilized; trumpet II is the only person I've seen in the pit with the time to read. He closes Tom Clancy at page 247, to be continued tomorrow night.

Larry gives us the big cue, and we're off into one final rollicking waltz. "Life is for the alive, my dear," Todd sings as he dances Lovett into the bakehouse oven. "The Ballad of Sweeney Todd" comes back once more— its sixth appearance of the evening. Two dozen voices fill the hall with the full-throated vocal, and *Sweeney Todd* ends.

The standing ovation sweeps across the footlights, but we get it first. Even before it reaches the stage, it pours into the pit like an ocean wave lapping against the high tide mark on the shore. Then, the curtain calls are over. House lights on. The cast goes down to the showers, the audience goes up the aisles. Sondheim, beaming, gets up, nods to Larry, and leaves.

Everybody leaves; everybody except the orchestra, which plays the exit music. But it is a lighthearted group of musicians playing now: the drama is over, the tension is gone, the spell is broken. It is now merely music. Larry gives the final cutoff, the music ends with a crisp button from the brass, and we file out of the pit.

"Everybody Ought to Have a Maid" from *A Funny Thing Happened on the Way to the Forum*. Words and music by Stephen Sondheim. Orchestration by Irwin Kostal. Note the vamp in the intro (bars B and C) from clarinets, bass clarinet, trombone, and cello. The two-part duet is written on the voice line (without lyric). Senex is doubled by flute and clarinet; Pseudolus—two octaves lower—by bass clarinet and bassoon. Copyright © 1962 (renewed), Burthen Music Company, Inc. All rights administered by Chappell & Co., Inc. All rights reserved. Used by permission of Alfred Publishing Co., Inc.

FINAL REFRAIN

What's the Score?

SECTION I.
ABOUT THE LISTINGS

Where Have All the Partiturs Gone?

For as far back as we can determine, the completed partiturs were the property of the songwriters. (Paid for by the producers, yes, although in some cases Chappell advanced all or some of the cost as an inducement for the publishing rights.) At some point in time, this was written into the standard minimum basic agreement of the Dramatists Guild. Correspondingly, a provision was made that allowed the producers to deduct a minimal amount from the weekly royalties as reimbursement for as much as half of the orchestration cost. (Given the size of the weekly reimbursement, the producer recovered this amount only on the most successful, long-running hits. In 1975, when orchestrations might cost between $10,000 and $15,000, the Dramatists Guild charge was $100 per week.)

In theory, once the Broadway production closed, the producer would send the partiturs to the composer. But there were other places the partiturs went along the way. New sets of orchestra parts were needed for touring companies; while sometimes they would simply copy the Broadway parts, the partiturs were more practical when they started making alterations in keys, routines, songs, and instrumentation. The originals might be shipped off for foreign (mostly UK) productions, and most of them made a stop at the stock & amateur licensing house. In some cases, the partiturs were sent to Hollywood, not necessarily for reuse, as a movie orchestra is likely to use different personnel than a stage orchestra, but for consultation. (Walker sued the producers of the film versions of *Damn Yankees* and *Fiddler on the Roof*, cases in which the studios used numerous ideas from the Broadway charts but had another arranger create "new" orchestrations without paying for reuse.) The partiturs also might make a trip to the recording studio, especially in cases where shows were recorded after they closed.

So, the short answer to the question "where have all the partiturs gone?" seems to be, ask the composer. Which is what I did. Sondheim, Strouse, Kander, Bock, Hugh Martin, Richard Adler, and Mary Rodgers all said something along the lines of, did you ask so-and-so? (So-and-so, if still alive, more often than not had no idea.) Only one composer I interviewed, Jerry Herman, actually had the partiturs in his possession. Or at least some of them. His biggest hit, *Hello, Dolly!*—which he thought he had—is not presently in his warehouse, nor is *Mack & Mabel*. But *Mame* is, in its entirety, along with *Dear World* and others.

Several composers did retain their partiturs, at least for some musicals. Richard Rodgers, Irving Berlin, Frank Loesser, and Jule Styne each maintained offices and therefore had a permanent place to store materials. Kurt Weill (who self-orchestrated his musicals) and Leonard Bernstein, too, kept just about every scrap of relevant music. But these were the exceptions. The Rodgers, Berlin, and Bernstein estates sent many of their scores to the Library of Congress, gifts which help to make the LOC the largest repository for Broadway partiturs. Weill's scores were donated to Yale.

The Styne estate, on the other hand, still maintains an office that includes a room full of partiturs, pit parts, and song manuscripts. But the omissions in the collection illustrate the fate of the typical Broadway partitur. Styne's office has the materials from eight of his sixteen major musicals. The missing scores include *Gypsy, Gentlemen Prefer Blondes, High Button Shoes, Bells Are Ringing,* and *Funny Girl*—which is to say, the hits. Nobody, seemingly, ever asked to borrow *Darling of the Day, Look to the Lilies,* or *Hallelujah, Baby!* The partiturs for the popular shows, though, were apparently sent out one time too many.

Gypsy makes a good example. Following the closing of the original production, the music trunks from the theatre went to producer David Merrick's storage facility at Walton's Warehouse on West 46th Street. In 1970, Merrick donated most of his existing parts and partiturs (including *Fanny, Oliver! Breakfast at Tiffany's*) to the Library of Congress. Styne, though, insisted (rightfully so) that the *Gypsy* partiturs and pit parts were his property, and demanded their return. The LOC sent them back to Styne's old office, on the second floor of the Mark Hellinger Theatre, in 1974. The pit parts are still in the possession of the now-transplanted Styne office, but the partiturs have long since vanished.

Most fortunately, orchestrator Sid Ramin kept a copy of the *Gypsy* partiturs, which he sent to Columbia University (along with his copies of *West Side Story, A Funny Thing Happened on the Way to the Forum,* and *I Can Get It for You Wholesale*). So *Gypsy* is not lost. *Funny Girl* was last seen intact at Tams-Witmark, where the show was prepared for licensing. At some point in time, Tams donated a significant amount of important material to the LOC, including *My Fair Lady, Camelot,* and about two-thirds of the *Funny Girl* scores. Orchestrations for many cut songs from *Funny Girl* remain at Tams; the rest of the scores are missing. Of *Gentlemen Prefer Blondes, High Button Shoes,* and *Bells Are Ringing,* not a trace has turned up. We know about the actual orchestrators of the latter show only because Bennett kept a register of the invoices.

Partiturs for many shows were at some time held at the licensing houses for safekeeping. Music Theatre International (MTI) still has partiturs from some musicals of the fifties and sixties, including such shows as *How to Succeed in Business Without Really Trying, The Music Man,* and *The Apple Tree.* Tams-Witmark has considerably more (including *Bye Bye Birdie, Cabaret,* and *Wonderful Town*), although in most cases these are second-rank musicals (*Jamaica, Illya Darling, Promises, Promises*). The original partiturs of all of the Rodgers &Hammerstein musicals (save one) are at the Library of Congress, but the Rodgers & Hammerstein Organization still has many of the musicals that Rodgers wrote without Hammerstein (including *The Boys from Syracuse* and *Do I Hear a Waltz?*), an assortment of other partiturs (including *Carmen Jones*). These, plus copies of the scores sent to Washington. Samuel French, which represents a considerable number of fifties musicals (including *Peter Pan, The Boy Friend,* and *Plain and Fancy*), can find no trace of any of partiturs whatsoever. Not one! The French musical materials have been shifted from warehouse to warehouse over the years, and the fear is that the partiturs were lost—literally—in the shuffle. Or worse, thrown out for space considerations.

Numerous partiturs wound up in the warehouses of Chappell Music. These included the famous trove of materials found in Secaucus, New Jersey, in 1982, which was rich in Kern, Gershwin, and other early Harms/Chappell composers. These were sent to the Library of Congress, as were a group of partiturs and pit parts from Chappell musicals of more recent vintage, including *Fade Out, Fade In* and *Something More!*

One other sizable group of important materials exists. Walker apparently returned partiturs of the shows he orchestrated to the composers, when requested;

everything that wasn't requested remained in storage at Chelsea Music, the music preparation firm he and Mathilde Pincus established in 1952, and eventually made it to his home in New Hope, Pennsylvania. The Walker Collection, at the Library of Congress, now has partiturs for such musicals as *The Pajama Game*, *Damn Yankees*, *The Girl in Pink Tights*, and *Zorbà*, as well as lesser shows like *Allah Be Praised!*

As can be discerned from the paragraphs above, the Music Division of the Library of Congress has the most extensive collection of partiturs extant, both in importance and quantity (more than fifty complete shows relevant to our study, plus a considerable number of Kern, Herbert, and Romberg musicals). Based on the research done for this book, it is safe to say that the LOC partitur collection is well preserved, under pristine (and well-funded) conditions with an especially knowledgeable caretaker in the person of Mark Eden Horowitz.

The Performing Arts Research Collection of the New York Public Library has a relatively smaller collection of partiturs, including several from shows controlled by Billy Rose (including *Jumbo* and *Foxy*); some minor and long-forgotten shows (such as Jay Goreny's *Heaven on Earth*, *Touch and Go*); and two important Jerry Bock musicals, *Fiorello!* and *Tenderloin*. The Irving Gilmore Library at Yale has the Kurt Weill collection of partiturs; a few shows by Eddie Sauter (including *1776* and *It's Superman*); and several other musicals (e.g., *Goldilocks*, *Bless You All*). The Butler Library at Columbia University has a handful of important partiturs, namely the above-mentioned Ramin collection plus Jerome Moross's *The Golden Apple*. Add in the approximately fifty scores at MTI, Tams, and R&H combined; add in another twenty or so that have been located in the hands of composers, estates, or private individuals; and we've got about 150 full sets of partiturs for shows discussed in this book, along with bits and pieces of other shows.

Missing in Action

It is safe to say that the partiturs for Broadway's most important musicals, by and large, are safely preserved. But the ranks of the missing include some not-inconsequential titles, beginning with *Fiddler on the Roof* and *Hello, Dolly!* (In some cases, orchestrator attributions can nevertheless be made thanks to invoices or other documentary records which survive.) A brief listing of scores by major composers for which the original partiturs have not as yet been located includes (Arlen) *Bloomer Girl*, *St. Louis Woman*, *House of Flowers*, *Saratoga*; (Berlin) *Call Me Madam*; (Bernstein) *On the Town*; (Bock) *Fiddler on the Roof*, *Mr. Wonderful*, *The Rothschilds*; (Coleman) *Little Me*, *On the Twentieth Century*, *Seesaw*, *Sweet Charity*; (Herman)

Hello, Dolly! Mack & Mabel, Milk and Honey; (Kander) *Flora, the Red Menace, The Happy Time*; (Lane) *Finian's Rainbow*; (Loesser) *Where's Charley?* (Loewe) *Brigadoon*; (Porter) *Can-Can, Out of This World*; (Rodgers) *Babes in Arms, By Jupiter, Pal Joey*; (Rome) *Destry Rides Again, Wish You Were Here*; (Schmidt) *I Do! I Do! 110 in the Shade*; (Strouse) *All American, Golden Boy*; (Styne) *Bells Are Ringing, Gentlemen Prefer Blondes, Hazel Flagg, High Button Shoes, Subways Are for Sleeping.*

Also missing—or let us say, presently unlocated—are a wide assortment of musicals by other composers, including *Anya, Baker Street, The Boy Friend, A Chorus Line, Coco, Donnybrook! Flahooley, The Grass Harp, Happy Hunting, Henry, Sweet Henry, Here's Love, High Spirits, I Had a Ball, Kismet, Kwamina, Li'l Abner, Look Ma, I'm Dancin'! Maggie Flynn, Minnie's Boys, New Girl in Town, Oh Captain! Once upon a Mattress, Peter Pan, Pippin, Plain and Fancy, Redhead, Regina, Skyscraper, Song of Norway, Top Banana, Up in Central Park, Walking Happy*, and *What Makes Sammy Run?*

It is to be imagined that at least some of these are still carefully (or not so carefully) preserved in cartons somewhere, either in warehouses, in unprocessed donations to research collections, or maybe even in somebody's attic. With any luck, some important scores are still in existence, just waiting to be found.

What the Partiturs Reveal (and Don't Reveal)

The original partiturs, should they exist, are the most precise record of the orchestrations used when the show opened on Broadway. The original pit parts, should they exist, are the most precise record of the orchestrations used when the show opened on Broadway. The original cast album, should one exist, is the most precise record of the orchestrations used when the show opened on Broadway. Three competing claims; the correct answer lies somewhere in between.

The partiturs are, theoretically, the documents of record. However, changes to the orchestration can begin before the ink is dry. The orchestra reading is merely a tryout, if you will; the composer might well hear things that surprise him or her. The same can go for the director (should the show have a strong director) or the star (ditto). Or the producer, who typically knows little about such things but is paying the bills. Even without such changes, it is not uncommon for the reading to reveal incorrect notes—either in the partiturs or in the copying—and sections that need to be altered for technical reasons.

Throughout the reading, various changes and fixes are discussed; sometimes, the orchestrator or head copyist takes note; other times, changes are written in by the musicians themselves. All such changes, theoretically, make their way back to the original partiturs, keeping them an accurate record of what is being played.

In practice, though, these changes are not necessarily registered. Once the show is in tryouts or previews, additional changes and fixes can be frequent: new endings, new beginnings, new dance routines and transpositions. These might be hurriedly dictated to the musicians in the half-hour before the next performance and hand-written into the parts. Ideally, all of this is reflected on the partiturs, but the orchestra pit is not an ideal world. So, the original partiturs might not reflect what is actually being played.

We speak of the "original" partiturs, but the fact is that duplicate copies of the partiturs are made early on; as the number is played down in the orchestra reading, there might be sets in the hands of the orchestrator (who probably has the original), the musical director, and the head copyist. Let us suppose that all of the changes and alterations are carefully transcribed—but on which copy? More important, which of these copies has survived the years? In some cases, I have discovered multiple copies, some stored together but others in separate locales. (Leonard Bernstein's copies of *West Side Story*, with handwritten changes, are at the Library of Congress; Sid Ramin's copies, with handwritten changes, are at Columbia University. Many of the handwritten changes—the earliest ones, anyway—are in the same hand, written by the head copyist in green ink. But then there are other changes; Bernstein's copies seem to reflect alterations made following the original production, which naturally don't appear in the Columbia copies.) In most cases, though, I only located one set of partiturs, sometimes the originals, on the onion skin–like Deshon paper or on the older, Chappell Music manuscript paper, and sometimes reproduced copies, with or without corrections and edits. Are there other, more accurate sets of partiturs for these shows stored away somewhere? Or were the "good" copies lost, leaving us with uncorrected proofs?

The pit parts, on the other hand, do tell us precisely what was played in the pit, which seems to be authoritative. And I suppose that the pit parts *are* an authoritative record when we're dealing with a show that quickly folded and was never performed again. But in the old days—which is to say, back when a standard hit might run two or three years, and before modern technology made reproductions feasible and cost-effective—the pit parts would be used on Broadway and then, perhaps, sent out for touring or other productions. All along the way, musical changes were made; dance routines might have been simplified, replacement singers might have needed different keys, weak singers might have needed additional instruments beefing up their melodies, the number of musicians might have been reduced (necessitating the spreading around of the solos of the departed player), and more. When significant, these changes came in on new, clean parts; often, though, they were simply dictated from the pit and written in by the musicians. The individual books, too, often attracted graffiti over the course of time. So, yes, the pit parts tell us what was played—but, more precisely, what was played *at the end of the run* (or, in some cases, the end of the tour). And when we say the "books," we are talking about one book per stand, which might come to a total of fifteen or twenty books for a full-scale musical. (Some chairs generally share one book: the first and second trumpet, for example, or the multiple players in the string section.) Orchestrations can be reconstructed from pit parts only by transcribing each line from each part onto new score pages; it is not atypical for at least some books to be missing.

The original cast album was recorded—at least, in the old days—on the Sunday following the Broadway opening, when everything was fresh and new. (And the stars were generally exhausted and vocally worn out, but that's another story.) What better time to lay down, for posterity, precisely what was heard on opening night? Once again, though, it ain't necessarily so. In the first place, numbers were frequently edited for recording; a song in the theatre doesn't necessarily start and end the way you might want it to on a record. (This was especially so in the days when tracks from original cast albums received radio play.) Back before the advent of the long-playing album, songs were quite obviously restricted by the track time of a 78 rpm disc. This continued even after LPs came along in the late forties, as a significant segment of the market still used, and bought, 78s. Hence, the original cast albums of the great Rodgers & Hammerstein musicals—which are our best record of how shows like *Oklahoma!* and *Carousel* originally sounded—necessarily presented abridged versions of the longer songs. (*Carousel*'s "Soliloquy," as well as the famous opening waltz, were both Solomonically separated into two parts, split across the front and flip side of a single platter.)

Even without the question of time restrictions, it can be seen why a seven-minute production number might be cut down to size; refrain after refrain of dance music, which accompany all sorts of wonders in the theatre, can seem mighty redundant when you're sitting in your living room. In the course of plowing through thousands of partiturs, I found quite a few additional pages—and sometimes entire scores—marked "recording version."

If you were the composer of a show that was a massive hit, wouldn't you—when the recording session rolled around—insist on adding in those extra instruments that the cost-cutting producer wouldn't let you have in the pit? Of course you would. Thus, we can frequently hear instruments on the cast albums that were not used in the theatre. This usually means beefed-up strings, but there are cases where a mysterious piano or harp might make an appearance. Let us add one more word to our lexicon, "ringers." Into the sixties, there was more money to be made playing for recordings than in the theatre pit. Top musicians who weren't available for eight-times-a-week gigs were frequently brought in for the recording sessions, or perhaps just for the overture. The songwriters, the producers, and the record labels wanted the cast albums to sound as good as possible—and the musical directors took a personal interest in making themselves look, and sound, good.

Cast albums can be especially misleading in terms of tempo. How close is the recorded tempo to what was heard in the theatre? There are any number of reasons for this, ranging from practicality to LP disc space to the desires of the songwriters and record producers. This can be illustrated by a story John McGlinn tells regarding his excellent 1991 studio recording of *Brigadoon*. In preparation, he tracked down the ailing Agnes de Mille in hopes of restoring the original tempos. She saw no reason to do so (although she expressed that the recording "will make Trude very happy"), and instructed McGlinn to "just conduct it the way your heart tells you."

> DE MILLE: Think of it like this. Have you ever seen *Swan Lake*? Do you have any recordings of *Swan Lake*? Have you ever compared those tempos? [Yes, McGlinn admitted, the ballets seem to be slower on stage than on recordings.] When you're making a recording, people are listening to the music. When you're conducting a ballet—and this is true whether you're talking about *Appalachian Spring*, *The Firebird*, or *Sleeping Beauty*—people are watching the ballet. When you're conducting in the studio, it's you and the orchestra. When you're conducting in the pit, it's you, the dancers, and Sir Isaac Newton.

Which is to say, original cast recordings often present dance music at an increased speed that the dancers could never maintain in performance.

From the Rental Houses

Of course, there are always the rental scores. Broadway's more popular musicals are performed hundreds and hundreds of times a year, if not more, by road companies, stock companies, and nonprofessionals across the land (and other lands as well). The orchestrations that they play clearly exist, and can be easily examined. In most cases, the conductor works from a reduced score; partiturs, generally, do not accompany these rentals (although some of the houses have been compiling them of late). But even so, if we want to hear what the score sounds like, can't we just go to a performance, hopefully one with a full and proficient orchestra?

Well, no. These second-generation scores were usually prepared shortly after the Broadway openings, when the rental houses had full access to the original scores (sometimes borrowing the pit parts by day and sending them back over to the theatre by night). But the Broadway orchestrations were rarely copied as is.

The complications began with the reeds. Broadway doublers could be expected to play any combination of instruments; the reed I chair on *Bye Bye Birdie*, for example, played alto sax, clarinet, bass clarinet, flute, G flute, and piccolo. Outside of New York, one couldn't expect to find people who could play these instruments proficiently, if at all. And this doesn't just apply to stock & amateur productions; one couldn't necessarily find professional musicians in touring cities who could play these chairs as written. This was not a case of preparing for inadequate players across the country. Most of the major towns had good players—including symphony musicians, very much available off-season to play in the pit and in some cases more talented than the standard Broadway musician. But few of them ever had the occasion, or the need, to cross the line from clarinet to flute to sax. Thus, the parts were reconfigured, usually upon the formation of the first national tour, and eventually used for stock & amateur productions. Unfortunately, Broadway revivals tend to use these readily available rental parts as well.

Let's look more closely at *Bye Bye Birdie*, why don't we? Joe Soldo played the reed I chair, with the six instruments listed above. The reed I on tour played four: alto sax, clarinet, flute, and piccolo. Reed II dropped from alto sax/clarinet/bass clarinet/flute/piccolo to alto sax/clarinet. Reed III went from tenor sax/clarinet/flute to tenor sax/clarinet; reed IV went from tenor sax/clarinet/oboe/English horn to baritone sax/clarinet/bass clarinet. Last, but most interestingly, reed V went from baritone sax/clarinet/flute/bassoon to—nothing. That's right, not only were the reed doubles reduced, the chairs were as well. Gone was all of Red Ginzler's remarkable four-flute writing, as Tams reduced Ginzler's instrumentation to one solitary flute. Missing altogether were oboe, bassoon, and English horn. Ginzler had the ability at any given moment to put his five players on any of twenty-two instruments; the road and rental version had four on eleven. When *Birdie* was performed at City Center Encores! in 2004, the orchestrations sounded spectacularly vibrant. As well they should have; this was the first and only time that Ginzler's charts were played since the original production closed in 1961.

The same can be said for *A Funny Thing Happened on the Way to the Forum*. The rental house saw fit to add violins, which Ramin and Kostal chose to specifically omit from the original orchestration; Tams reasoned that the show would be playing in many theatres with existing house orchestras that included, and automatically paid for, violins. So violin parts were added—not by Ramin and Kostal, but by an anonymous staffer—resulting in a reduction of three players in the reed/brass component. What did the violins play? Parts borrowed from other instruments, thus throwing off the original balance.

These reductions were usually made by in-house arrangers, without the agreement, participation, or knowledge of the original orchestrators. (The orchestra-

tions are the property of the songwriters; while orchestrators are nowadays entitled to payment for certain additional uses, they have no right of consultation.)
The exception to this nonparticipation rule was Phil Lang, who frequently
worked on the reduction of his own (and other people's) scores for Tams-
Witmark. We do know that Walker (probably with assistants) did the reduction
of *Wonderful Town*; his collection includes two invoices to Tams, from the fall of
1954. One calls for him to "rearrange and revoice woodwind parts for stock productions. Eliminate flute, piccolo, oboe, English horn, bassoon and baritone sax
doubles. Of 678 pages, 484 require approximately three parts changed per page."
The second invoice was to "voice and rearrange brass parts. Eliminate Trumpet
IV and Trombone III. Of 678 pages, approximately 492 require change."

This was not simply a matter of indiscriminate tampering, mind you; the goal
was to have the music sound as good as possible, which required scaling back to
the realities of the orchestras that would play it. Thus, the new scores accommo-
dated reed players who couldn't handle the original array of instruments;
reconfigured the strings so that theatres wouldn't be stuck paying for unused
house musicians; and almost always added a piano part. (The less accomplished
the string section, the more important it is that there be a piano player to hold
things together.) The unfortunate aspect of this is that when first-class, full-scale
productions of these musicals are mounted, the producers almost always choose
to go with the readily available rental parts, rather than dusting off and recon-
structing the original Broadway parts. In most cases, I contend, few people realize that there is a difference.

All of which takes us back to the partiturs. Not the most accurate, unimpeach-
ably precise guide to what was heard in the theatre when the show was new and
alive and at its peak, perhaps, but as close as we are likely to come. What can be
said, with certainty, is that the partiturs tell us precisely what the orchestrator had
in mind—and in his inner ear—when he sat down facing that blank score page.

Deciphering the Listings

The show listings include 717 productions, mostly musicals and revues, with the
occasional play or arena attraction added in. If one of our twelve orchestrators
did it, it is here. Notable musicals from other orchestrators are included as well.

(There is also a less detailed section that includes 142 shows that opened
through 1999 by the later generation of orchestrators—Tunick, Gibson, Starobin, Wheeler, and more—so that readers can find out who orchestrated *Follies*,
Dreamgirls, or the like. Non-American musicals—such as *Les Misèrables*—are ex-

cluded, unless they had the participation of American orchestrators or arrangements; so are small-sized off-Broadway shows—such as *The Fantasticks*—which were performed with only a handful of instruments, without full orchestrations.)

Each listing might contain, literally, dozens and dozens of pieces of information. I have endeavored to fit these facts into a format that is as concise and unwieldy as possible. Before heading into the listings, it will be helpful to offer an explanation of just what this information represents and from whence it comes.

Shows

These are listed in alphabetical order.

Orchestrators

No, the songwriters do not come first—at least, not in this book! In cases where I've found evidence of additional orchestrators, they are listed, more or less in order of importance of contribution. ("With" signifies orchestrators who were only peripherally involved, with relatively minor contributions.) Assistants are listed in parentheses, except for those who are known to have received full program credit.

For the purposes of quick summary, I have labeled cases where the orchestrator did the show entirely alone with "orchestrations (totally) by"; cases where the orchestrator did practically everything, other than a few bars' worth of changes or edits, are labeled "orchestrations (virtually totally) by." Cases where I estimate that the orchestrator of record did at least 85% of the show are labeled "orchestrations (mostly) by."

The many shows for which no information is available are labeled "orchestrations credited to" rather than "orchestrations by"; I have found at least a few major musicals where the orchestrator retained sole billing despite being replaced, and there are likely more among the shows for which partiturs or invoices have not been located.

Statistics

The date of the official opening is followed by the theatre and number of performances. I have also added information on pre-Broadway tryout engagements, if available; these dates give a better idea of the period during which the orchestrator was working on the show. (By cross-checking this information with the chronological show index, one can understand how one man might have been working on two or more musicals simultaneously, in different towns—hence the need for all those additional orchestrators.) In the case of shows that closed during tryouts, the closing date (if known) is given as well.

Let me add a word about the accuracy of these statistics, which have been previously recorded in numerous reference books, on the Internet, and elsewhere. The uncomfortable fact is that different sources give us different dates and figures. One little error or typo in one reference book, alas, is just as likely to be picked up and repeated as is a correct figure. I have used the sources that I consider to be most accurate; even so, just how crucial is it in the greater scheme of things whether a certain show played 654 performances rather than 645? The dates of out-of-town tryouts are necessarily approximate, as these were not widely recorded. I have pulled dates from various sources, although vintage ads, programs, and even the theatre's records—should they exist—are not necessarily accurate as to the date of the premiere. (It was not uncommon for the opening to be delayed a day or two, especially in the first city.) The purpose of listing this out-of-town information is to give an idea of the orchestrator's activity, workwise and geographic; a not-especially-accurate date, or in many cases no date, will still suffice.

Credits

While full show information might be preferable, space considerations have restricted us to a few relevant credits. These include, primarily, the songwriters and the music staff (musical director, vocal and dance arrangers, and other music people). There follows a string of people under the heading "other participants." These include selected producers, directors, choreographers, librettists, and significant performers; in general terms, these are people who might have been in the position, at some point in their careers, to have a say in the selection of the orchestrator.

Materials

This gives the location of the partiturs and other documentary evidence that have been examined for the purposes of identifying authorship.

Songs

Every attempt has been made to identify the actual orchestrators of as many musical numbers as possible. The information for each show is listed in two parts: first, an orchestrator-by-orchestrator listing of songs which were orchestrated solely in one hand. (In cases where the main orchestrator did most of the show, I have simply stated "the orchestrations are by Walker [or whoever], with the following exceptions.")

There then follows a section labeled "Other Scores." This includes musical numbers that were orchestrated by multiple hands and numbers for which alternate orchestrations exist. Basically speaking, this section includes songs for which the authorship requires an explanation. In the cases of a few musicals—most notably the all-important *West Side Story* and *Gypsy*—many numbers are combined scores, with frequent changes of hand. Due to the more than usual interest in these two musicals, they are chronicled to an extent that may be incomprehensible to some readers. You are welcome to skip ahead. The task of identifying the partiturs rates a discussion in itself, which will follow presently.

Instrumentation

The instrumentation is listed, where known. Oddly, this is often a mystery; how many musicians were used is a question that can be all but impossible to determine at this late date. The partiturs give a clear and definitive picture of certain elements. The number of reed lines is self-evident, although the precise doubles can only be determined by paging through the entire score (should it exist) and making a list. Trumpets and trombones are plainly numbered; the French horns might not be, but by looking at the score one can determine whether there were one, two, or three. (The horn part is usually written on a single stave; full orchestra chords—found at the end of a loud number, perhaps—will usually answer the question, as an orchestrator with two or three horns will give them a two- or three-note chord.) Percussionists usually have a line each, although on busy shows a single drummer might need two lines. (The drummer might play several instruments at once, using separate hands, a foot pedal or two, and perhaps a whistle.) It is not always apparent whether there were one or two men standing in the back, but this can often be determined by considering precisely what array of sounds are being made at a given moment.

A harp line or a guitar line will either be present or not; the same can be said for accordion and just about any kind of keyboard instrument except piano. The piano is problematic; shows that are orchestrated without piano often have a piano part written in, to be used as the piano-conductor score. (This is used for rehearsals when no other musicians are present—even if the show didn't use a pianist in performance.) A bit of observation will determine whether the piano part on the partiturs is for performance or rehearsal. A piano part that switches to celesta or organ, for example, is obviously intended to be played in performance. If the partiturs have a very full piano part, indicating just about every strand and solo, this is probably meant to be extracted for a piano-conductor score. Phil Lang, for one, frequently included a P/C line on his partiturs; in fact, he sometimes seemed to write the P/C part first, and then assign the parts to the various instruments.

That leaves us with the strings. The violins can be written on one, two, or three staves, depending on how many players and how many parts. (There are usually two violinists per stand. A show with violin parts marked A, B, C, D, and E would probably have nine or ten violinists, although some would likely be cut after the opening.) The viola, cello, and bass usually have a single stave each; as with the horns, by examining grand climaxes, one can sometimes identify the number of players. When we're lucky, one of the orchestrators noted the string components on the first page of one of the charts. This happened most frequently when it was a ghost; working quickly on a project with which he was not familiar, he might reasonably notate the exact number available on the margins.

Instrumentation information is compiled from partiturs and whatever other documents we could find. Walker customarily had Mathilde Pincus type up copies of the instrumentation list (on onion skin) for distribution to ghosts. Copies of some of these are in the Walker Collection, and they helpfully provide authoritative information—except in cases where the initially proposed instrumentation might have been altered by the time the songs were orchestrated.

Original(?) Partiturs

Traditionally, the original partiturs are kept in a locker at the theatre during the run of the show. These are accompanied by the partiturs for the cut material and the corresponding pit parts. (During the tryout, it is not unheard of for cut material to be reinstated. Once the show has opened, changes occasionally occur: altered keys to accommodate stars, for example. The parts will remain at the theatre, in case they are needed for future replacements or understudies.)

Once the show closes, the entire trunk of partiturs and pit parts is sent off—usually to the producer (if other companies are in the works), the music prep house (ditto), the composer (if he has a place to store them), or the publisher. The material is typically divided into two folders: one with the partiturs for the complete show as played in New York, the other with deleted and obsolete material. These two packets of material are what I found—for about a quarter of the shows, anyway.

In a very few cases, there was plenty more. *Carousel* has about eleven cartons' worth: partiturs, pit parts, piano-vocal arrangements from the rehearsal period, scripts both official and preliminary, chorus books, and more. The treasures were conductor Joseph Littau's rehearsal score, which included taped-in pieces of fold-out changes, and a fascinating four-page carbon of Hammerstein's preliminary "Liliom Outline." Many cartons' worth of material, alas, is no guarantee that the partiturs exist. The Rodgers & Hammerstein Organization has seven cartons of *No Strings* material, with partiturs of deleted songs and a complete ten-piece orchestration by Wilcox for the bus & truck tour. Ralph Burns's remarkable partiturs for Broadway, though, are missing.

The "Liliom" outline, which illustrates Hammerstein's developing thoughts on the musical, merits a tangential paragraph. In this early sketch, Hammerstein uses the original character names from Molnar's play and offers no hint at the transplanted locale. Among the developments was a second suitor for the Carrie character, a "romantic and unreliable" fellow with a guitar called Dwight. The opening waltz pantomime is present, as is the notion that what became the extended "Bench Scene" ("If I Loved You") should "drift from dialogue into singing, eventually developing into major refrain." Also present is a proposed song called "Bustin' Out All Over" ("The sap is runnin', the buds are poppin', I'm full o' ginger and my gal's full o' beans") for the Mill Owner and chorus; a duet for the Carrie and Snow characters called "Put Your Faith in Sardines and Me"; and a comedy quartet for Julie, Carrie, Nettie, and Mullins, which Oscar describes simply with the note "form of *Desert Song* number." (He also puts in a trio for Carrie and her two suitors, which he describes as the "Marchbanks Song, as in 'Candida.'") Most remarkably, buried in the description of the climactic ballet in which Liliom/Billy dreams of his daughter, Hammerstein writes, "The child is a young woman. Bambi!" While little is known yet of what *Carousel* would come to be—with no hint of the transplantation to New England—the authors have already decided to build in a ballet for Bambi Linn, who was just then a teenager playing a small dance role in *Oklahoma!*

But we stray from the partiturs. Once these two valuable packets of partiturs go into storage, they ideally remain together undisturbed until they are sent off to some archives (or, alas, the dumpster). With hit shows, though, the partiturs were necessarily used and consulted for additional productions, revivals, and the like. Which means they were periodically pulled off the shelf, for shipping hither and thither. Were they returned? Usually, but not necessarily. *No Strings*, I suppose, must have gone off for use in the London production, never—apparently—to return. (I wrote this paragraph at 6:30 one morning. At 11:00 that very same day, browsing through a folder of correspondence at the Rodgers & Hammerstein warehouse concerning the 1963 production of *The Boys from Syracuse*, I found a notation that the *No Strings* partiturs were sent to London on November 20, 1963. Have they been seen since?) Irving Berlin's *Call Me Madam* seems to have met the same fate; the packet of deleted scores is carefully preserved in the Berlin Collection at the Library of Congress, but the songs in the show are lost.

The problem is well illustrated by two Jerry Herman shows. *Dear World* sits happily complete in the composer's storage locker, partiturs, pit parts, and more;

but I don't suppose anybody ever borrowed *Dear World* until I took it home with me for study. *Hello, Dolly!* sits on shelves diagonally across. One stack of partiturs contains deleted material, including the original overture and numerous songs that were cut in Detroit; another consists of "new" scores that later went into the show, including transposed versions orchestrated by Lang for Mary Martin (of the international company) and Ethel Merman (who was the final Dolly in the Broadway company). This material includes the partiturs for two songs that were added to the show for Merman, "World, Take Me Back"—which has an especially rousing pull-out-the-stops orchestration—and "Love, Look in My Window." The partiturs for the original Broadway production itself? Missing, every single chart. Somebody borrowed them, no doubt—for the 1976 Houston Grand Opera production, perhaps? Or maybe the music department at 20th Century Fox used them for consultation during the making of the 1969 film version? It's hard to imagine that anyone would throw out the partiturs for *Hello, Dolly!* They are presumably sitting around somewhere, and one hopes that they will make their way back to Mr. Herman.

When the original partiturs cannot be found, copies serve our purpose almost equally well. (More than half of the partiturs I located were copies, not originals.) As mentioned above, several sets were usually made: for the musical director, the head copyist, and sometimes even the composer. Hopefully, these were kept up to date with changes. The likeliest to have survived, perhaps, is the conductor's score (that is, in cases where the conductor used a full score, rather than a simplified four-stave piano-conductor score). The advantage of the conductor's full score is that it represents the show as played at the theatre. The disadvantage is that it represents the show as played at the theatre—without any of the deleted material, and usually marked and revised to reflect changes made during the run of the show (and thus corresponding to the show as it was when it closed, not when it opened). Still, the conductor's full score is a perfectly legitimate substitute for the original partiturs; in many important cases—including *She Loves Me*, *Bye Bye Birdie*, and *Cabaret*—this is all that I have been able to locate.

Identifying the Orchestrators

All right. The partiturs for some show or other have been found, 700 to 1,200 manuscript pages in a not-so-neat, out-of-order pile. Usually dusty with age or crumbling, affixed with rusted paper clips, dotted with yellowed scraps of fifty-year-old tape, or perhaps printed on thick paper using some ancient and nearly unreadable photocopy process. Now what?

Some of the partiturs are signed, which makes identification simple. Or, rather, simpler. Spialek always wrote "H. Sp." on the first page; Lang scrawled his name, in an all but unidentifiable hieroglyphic, at the end. Royal occasionally wrote his name or "T. R." on the first page. Other orchestrators sometimes signed their charts—adding their union card number—when ghosting; this might have had more to do with payment than credit. A signed partitur might be seen as instantly authenticated, but no. Many charts are joint efforts, switching hands here and there. Lengthy numbers with dance sections often switch orchestrators; it is not uncommon for the opening lead-in—or the final ending—to be altered during the tryout, by which point the person who did the original number is off in another town. (I found some Spialek charts and numerous Lang charts that were missing the signature, as Hans's first page or Phil's last page had been replaced.) Thus, to positively identify a chart—signed or unsigned—you must go through it, page by page. For starters.

While Spialek and Lang almost always signed their work, most of the other major orchestrators never did. I found several signed charts by Burns and Kostal and some by more frequent ghosts (Glover, Henderson, Noeltner, Tyler), but none whatsoever by Bennett, Walker, Ginzler, Burns, or others. (As I was doing my final edits on this book, I found two early Bennett charts for Youmans which were signed, in effect, "VY/RB" and "VY/Rus.") Even so, the handwriting itself can be seen as a signature. Spialek's charts are instantly recognizable, as they are written in an ornate, Old World hand. Bennett is Old World, too, although more classic than stylish. Walker wrote with an easy-on-the-eyes modern flair, circa the mid-twentieth century. Ginzler's charts look altogether different; his notes resemble chicken tracks in the snow. (Unlike most of his peers, Ginzler wrote in pencil—and for a practical reason. He was left-handed; writing left to right, his sleeve would drag across the page and smudge the ink.)

Lang, meanwhile, led the group in indecipherable handwriting. He had company, though. Royal's hand is often messy and artless. Kostal has a clumsy hand; as he himself mentioned, he had a tendency to write big notes in loud sections and small notes when the music became quiet. Kay, Ramin, and Wilcox usually seem rushed. Matching Lang in difficulty, but more readily identifiable, is Burns, whose notes often seem to be slanting backward.

Personalized score paper, with the orchestrator's name printed on the page, is helpful but unreliable. The one Broadway orchestrator who regularly used personalized paper—following his years at Chappell, when he used Chappell paper, that is—was Walker. But he supplied his personalized paper to his ghosts, and his score sheets can occasionally be found on non-Walker shows. (Bennett scored *By the Beautiful Sea* on Don's paper, and for reasons unknown Larry Wilcox used some on *Funny Girl*—probably just cadging blanks off Mathilde Pincus's desk at Chelsea Music.) Burns sometimes used personalized paper, but it was similarly available to his assistants. Ralph also sometimes had loyal copyists who wrote or stamped his name on the first page of all of the partiturs from his shows, regardless of who actually did the orchestration.

In some cases, the problem of identification was compounded by joint scores. Not simply where the orchestrators switched off—eight bars here, ten bars there—but where they actually both wrote on the same page. This happened frequently on the first collaborations of Ramin and Ginzler (*Gypsy*, *Wildcat*), where Ramin, who specialized in strings and trumpets, might write those lines, while Ginzler, who was tops in reeds and the rhythm section, would do the rest. This occurred with some frequency during Burns's alcoholic years, when it appears that Wilcox filled in whatever Ralph didn't get around to.

Signed partiturs are helpful, but they only tell part of the story. For that matter, even positive identification of the handwriting on an existing chart does not prove who orchestrated that song in the show. I have found any number of cases where there are two, three, or even five different orchestrations for one number; in these cases, one, two, or four of them were rejected. Which one was used in the show? If I'm familiar with the Broadway orchestration, I can often tell; if the original pit parts exist, and if they have been maintained in their original folders, one can place the pages side by side and determine whose orchestration is in the parts. (One can also check partiturs against the cast album, but cautiously, as it was not uncommon to prepare special charts for the recording session.) Over the course of time, some ghosts claimed that they orchestrated this number or that. This identification is invalid, though; the ghosts rarely bothered to see the shows they were working on. They might understandably remember that they orchestrated this song or that, and were paid for it; this doesn't mean that theirs wasn't one of those rejected charts. Invoices, similarly, can provide inexact information. For example, Bennett's ledger spells out each chart he orchestrated for *Finian's Rainbow*. But then Walker came in and replaced five or six charts, titles unknown—which means that some of the listings in Bennett's ledger are misleading. He orchestrated those songs, yes, but his versions were cut in Philly. The best we can do is attempt to be as precise as possible.

A Trip to the Library

When I decided to make my first exploratory trip to the Library of Congress to begin research, I was not quite sure what I was looking for or what I would find. I had very few tools to work with. On my own bookshelves, I had a couple of scores by Kay and one—"Who Can I Turn To?" from *The Roar of the Greasepaint*—by Lang. At least, the latter was the chart used on Broadway, and the show was orchestrated by Lang; it turns out, however, that this was *not* Phil's orchestration, although it took a fair amount of time to realize that. Larry Blank faxed me a few pages of *A Funny Thing Happened on the Way to the Forum*, with handwriting samples of Kostal and Ramin. He also told me that Kostal had positively identified—both in conversation and in his unpublished memoir—some charts he had ghosted, namely, "Hey There" (from *The Pajama Game*) and "Heart" (from *Damn Yankees*). The LOC had the partiturs from these two musicals, so I reasoned that these—plus the orchestration invoices in the Walker Collection—would be a perfect place to start.

The Personal/Business Papers section of the Walker Collection—twenty-five storage boxes, containing as many as twenty folders apiece—includes the invoices from neither *The Pajama Game* nor *Damn Yankees*, as it happens. Picking four boxes at random, I did come upon *The Music Man*—which revealed a jumble of six different orchestrators! Plus a post-opening demand for credit from one of the assistants. I then turned to the partiturs from my two chosen shows. Identification of Walker's hand, which I had never seen before, was fairly obvious. More than half of the pages of these two shows were in the same hand; and besides, the stylish flair *looked* like it must be Don Walker.

However, the authorship of the rest of the partiturs for the two musicals was nonverifiable. *The Music Man* had prepared me for what to expect, perhaps; but *The Pajama Game* kept switching from one hand to another, not only in separate songs but in the same songs. I laid out in front of me the two "definite" Kostal charts, "Hey There" and "Heart." The first was in a clumsy, heavy hand, with the slant childishly switching from left to right. The other was carefully printed, with uniformly small notes that looked like chicken tracks in the snow. Two totally different hands. I checked these against my barely decipherable faxed Kostal samples from *Forum*, which didn't look much like either. I noticed that "Hey There" was in the same hand as "Hernando's Hideaway" and *Damn Yankees'* "Shoeless Joe" Baseball Ballet; "Heart" was the same as "Steam Heat" and "Whatever Lola Wants." "Who's Got the Pain?"—another one of the dance numbers with which Bob Fosse set his style—was in the hand I had already determined to be Walker.

My time at the LOC on this trip was limited; I returned to New York with pages of notes from the Walker invoices, and questions as to whether definitive handwriting identification would be possible at all. On my second trip, I took a look at the *West Side Story* scores, which—again—were a jumble of hands, including a good deal of green ink in yet another hand. (These turned out to be Ramin and Kostal, with revisions—in green ink—by Sid, Irv, or head copyist Arnold

Arnstein.) After several hours of despair, I stored *West Side* away and turned to the next set of invoices, for the unimportant and forgotten *The Girl in Pink Tights*. This was a 1954 musical featuring music by Romberg (who died in 1951), "developed" and orchestrated by Walker. The invoices bore witness to the presence of Ginzler, Spialek, Walter Paul, Jack Mason, and the great recording arranger Robert Farnon.

As I dutifully transcribed the bills, it hit me in a flash; this being a Walker musical, the partiturs might be somewhere in the building. In theory, shouldn't the names on the invoices directly correspond to the handwriting on the partiturs? I called for the scores, which took an hour or so to make their way from the sub-basement of the James Madison Building; while waiting, I noted my favorite orchestrations in the show, namely, the ballad "Lost in Loveliness"; a concerted number called "Up in the Elevated Railway"; and an eccentric comedy quartet called "You've Got to Be a Little Crazy." And then, there it was: my Rosetta stone, orchestration-wise.

Walker's hand, on about two-thirds of the scores, proved to be the one I had guessed: strong, handsome, and with flair. There was a significant amount of material in the chicken-scratch hand of "Steam Heat," and "Heart," positively identified in the invoices as that of Ginzler. Spialek's chart, for a ballet, was clearly signed "H. Sp." Paul looked somewhat like Walker, with the same flair; some of the notes and letters, though, were markedly different. Mason was rather messy; he did a lot of the utilities, which I would come to learn was his specialty.

The overture proved a bad place to start, as it switched from hand to hand. (There were multiple invoices for this, listing the number of pages but not identifying the precise sections.) Once past the overture, though, everything seemed to match perfectly. More to the point, I realized that Walker, Spialek, and Ginzler were easily recognizable. I learned something else that would become a recurring refrain: two of the three favorite numbers I had listed turned out to be by Ginzler. "Lost in Loveliness" was his, while "Up in the Elevated Railway" was a collaboration between him and Farnon. "You've Got to Be a Little Crazy," a breezy chart full of novel effects, was by Farnon.

Midway through *Pink Tights*, as I saw the puzzle being solved, I called for the partiturs of another Walker show with full invoices, Cole Porter's *Silk Stockings*. After a late lunch break in the upstairs cafeteria overlooking downtown Washington, I successfully tested my hypothesis. The score, again, was two-thirds Walker, with about a quarter by Ginzler. One partitur was written in the Old World style of "H. Sp."; and there, to my delighted relief, was that clumsy, slanting "Hernando's Hideaway" hand. Kostal provided several *Silk Stockings* charts, including the delightful novelty "Siberia." The overture was mostly by Walker, but thumbing through I found that the pages containing the title song-section of the overture were written in that now-familiar hand. Written on the top was the legend "scored by I. Kostal."

From there on, identification became easier, though not easy. By this point, I had realized the wisdom of keeping a digital camera handy. Copying materials, especially in libraries, can be impossible; most places, though, allowed me to photograph handwriting samples. By photographing multiple samples of each orchestrator's hand and printing them out into a little cheat book (which ultimately grew to 200 or so samples), I could bring everything I'd learned along with me. The trick, whenever I came upon an unrecognized hand, was to try to determine who it *might* be, and then check the evidence. This did not always work, so I photographed numerous unidentified hands as well. By the time I finished researching this book, many of the unknowns had been identified in one manner or another: a signed partitur from some show, perhaps, or a note to the copyists from Bennett or Spialek instructing them to insert pages 5–14 of so-and-so's chart into the overture.

A Typical Tale of Identification

Annie Get Your Gun, as related elsewhere, underwent a salvage job involving no fewer than ten orchestrators. As I went through four boxes of original partiturs—almost eighty different charts—I initially separated out the clearly identifiable charts from Lang, Bennett, Royal, Spialek, and others. This left me with several mysterious hands. One unknown orchestrator, in particular—who used small and precise treble clefs that, when placed next to a cut-time symbol, looked almost like dollars and cents—contributed several *Annie* charts of negligible importance. The last of his charts that I came to, happily enough, was signed; unfortunately, the name was illegible. But it was clear that the first name began with an M and had between six and eight letters, while the last was a shorter name beginning with an S, F, P, or similar letter.

A half-year later, when examining the partiturs for *Oklahoma!* I came across another score by that mysterious hand. (This fellow's chart for the "Many a New Day" ballet was labeled "Many a New York Dance.") He was the only ghost on the show, which was mostly by Bennett. I took some photos and moved on to *Allegro*—and there he was again. When I transcribed my notes and collated the digital samples, I recognized something familiar about those clef signs; browsing through my sheaf of handwriting samples, I came across the ones from *Annie Get Your Gun*.

Was this the same orchestrator, the fellow with the scrawled name? MP? MS?

The hands looked similar, and it made sense in that all three—*Oklahoma! Annie*, and *Allegro*—were Bennett musicals from the same period. But who was the orchestrator? Something about those initials seemed familiar; I had already compiled a working version of the show listing section, and I vaguely recalled a name of this sort in the credits for one of the missing Duke or Arlen musicals of the forties. Paging through the listings, I found it: *St. Louis Woman*, with orchestrations credited to Ted Royal, Allan Small, Menotti Salta, and Walter Paul. Menotti Salta, that must be. Checking the signature on my photograph, it certainly looked like it.

How likely was it that Bennett, working on an unquestionably important job like *Oklahoma!* (in that it was the successor to his Hammerstein-Kern musicals *Show Boat* and *Music in the Air*), would choose someone like Salta when he had full access to officemates Walker, Spialek, and Royal? The answer became apparent some time later. I had originally planned to start the show listings chronologically, with *Oklahoma!* Eventually, I reasoned that, since I was discussing the careers of Bennett, Walker, and Spialek, I needed to examine their prior work. As I did, I found evidence of several more Salta charts, a few of which were duly (and legibly) signed. What's more, they were on shows like *The Boys from Syracuse*, *Anything Goes*, and *You Never Know*—musicals by Rodgers and the equally important Porter, orchestrated by Bennett and Spialek. Clearly, Salta was one of the circle; just as clearly, his participation on *Oklahoma!* made perfect sense. Examining a Salta-signed *Syracuse* chart at the Rodgers & Hammerstein Organization, I was able to perform a side-by-side comparison with the unsigned *Oklahoma!* charts. This was definitely the same hand. One more mystery solved.

Logical Connections

Certain people often worked together, which provided hints. Walker, in different time periods, was assisted by Ginzler, Kostal, Spialek, Paul, Jim Tyler, and others. Bennett frequently invited in Walker, Glover, Bob Noeltner, and others. Burns often had Wilcox, Tyler, and Luther Henderson on tap. Royal, as well, had his own stable of assistants.

But the search for logical pairings was a danger in itself. On my first examination of *My Fair Lady*, I was easily able to differentiate the messy Lang from the elegant Bennett. Several of Lang's charts were not quite as indecipherable as others; was this because he was less rushed that day? Or perhaps writing with a different pen? The answer came when I compared my findings to Bennett's ledger: those in-between charts weren't by Lang at all, they were by Jack Mason. On my next trip to Washington, I checked the specified partiturs—including "A Little Bit of Luck"—for verification, comparing them to *The Girl in Pink Tights* samples of Mason (whose hand falls somewhere on the messy scale between Lang and Royal). Yes, Bennett's ledger was precisely correct. Without my knowledge of *My Fair Lady*, would I have readily identified Mason's contributions to Lang's *Fanny* and *Goldilocks*? Hopefully.

Over the course of time and thousands of pages, I became pretty good at recognizing the various hands. Are all the identifications in this book incontrovertibly correct? Of course not. Due to various considerations, I had more time to examine some scores than others; in some cases, I was permitted to view only one partitur at a time, which made extensive comparison of hands impossible. Further, originals in especially fragile condition were not conducive to the sort of shifting, shuffling, and spreading around the table that can be necessary when there are four or five different hands to sort out. In cases where hands switch off in the middle of a number, it is almost impossible to catch every bar. With so much evidence missing, much of this attribution is subject to interpretation and guesswork. But I venture to say that it is very close; and whenever possible, I went back to double-check identifications that—on reflection—seemed curious or questionable.

It was immediately apparent when I first started thinking about this book that before I could discuss the work of a given orchestrator, I would have to identify who did what. I bow to no man in my admiration for the work of Don Walker, who has *Carousel*, *The Most Happy Fella*, *The Music Man*, *She Loves Me*, and *Fiddler on the Roof* to his credit. "You'll Never Walk Alone," "When the Children Are Asleep," "Swing," "One Hundred Easy Ways," "Hey There," "Hernando's Hideaway," "Steam Heat," "Heart," "Whatever Lola Wants," "Goodnight My Someone," and "Anyone Can Whistle" are among the thousands of songs credited to him—but he didn't orchestrate a single one of these titles. Discuss the work of Don Walker with "Steam Heat" included, and you have described an orchestration that he didn't—and perhaps couldn't—have written.

To those who wonder how closely the head orchestrator supervised his ghosts, the answer seems to be: not much, especially when the ghost was an experienced pro. Under the typical working conditions—with so much to be done in so little time—any instructions tended to be necessarily sketchy. (Irv Kostal's instructions from Walker for a ballet in *Hazel Flagg*: "8 bars Salvation Army orchestra style, 16 bars ragtime, 8 bars hillbilly, 32 bars can-can and so on," with a note underneath: "Please use the songs from the show.")

The first section of this book has discussed who was who; the show listing section helps to clarify who, specifically, did what.

SECTION II. THE LISTINGS

À LA CARTE

Orchestrations uncredited. (Orchestrations by Hans Spialek, Hilding Anderson, Maurice de Packh, Charles Grant, Louis Katzman, and Stephen O. Jones.)

Opened August 17, 1927, Martin Beck, 45 performances. Tryout: unknown.

A revue. Music and lyrics by various writers (including Louis Alter and Herman Hupfeld). Musical direction by Milton Schwarzwald.

THE ACT

Orchestrations credited to Ralph **Burns**. (Additional orchestrators, if any, unknown.)

Opened October 29, 1977, Majestic, 233 performances. Tryout: (as *In Person*) July, Chicago (Shubert); (as *Shine It On*) July 19, San Francisco (Orpheum); September, Los Angeles.

Music by John Kander, lyrics by Fred Ebb. Musical direction by Stanley Lebowsky. Vocal arrangements by Earl Brown. Dance arrangements by Ronald Melrose.

Other participants: Feuer & Martin (producers); Martin Scorsese (original director); Gower Champion (replacement director, uncredited); George Furth (librettist); Liza Minnelli (star).

AGNES DE MILLE DANCE THEATRE (1953 TOUR)

Orchestrations by Don **Walker**. (Additional orchestrations by Hans **Spialek**, Walter Paul, and Robert **Ginzler**, with Maurice Gardner and Irwin **Kostal**.)

Opened: October 14, 1953, Washington, D.C. (Constitution Hall). Tryout: October 9, New Hope, Pennsylvania (Bucks County Playhouse).

Music by various composers (including Frederick Loewe and Harold Arlen). Musical direction by Francis Jaroscky. Musical arrangements by Trude Rittman. Other participants: Sol Hurok (producer); James Mitchell (star); Gemze DeLappe (star).

Invoices indicate: Walker (32%), Spialek (24%), Paul (18%), Ginzler (10%).

This touring production included recreated numbers from several de Mille musicals, including *Bloomer Girl*, *Brigadoon*, and *Paint Your Wagon* (but none from the Rodgers & Hammerstein shows). The break-in engagement was at the Bucks County Playhouse, which at the time was operated by Don Walker.

AIN'T MISBEHAVIN'

Orchestrations credited to Luther Henderson. (Additional orchestrators, if any, unknown.)

Opened May 9, 1978, Longacre, 1,604 performances. Tryout: February 8, Manhattan Theatre Club (off-Broadway).

Music by Thomas "Fats" Waller, lyrics by various writers. Musical direction and arrangements by Luther Henderson. Vocal arrangements by William Elliott. Other participants: Nell Carter (star), Luther Henderson (pianist).

ALIVE AND KICKING

Orchestrations credited to George Bassman. (Additional orchestrations by Don **Walker** and others.)

Opened January 17, 1950, Winter Garden, 46 performances. Tryout: December 12, 1949, Boston (Shubert); January 10, 1950, Hershey, Pennsylvania (Hershey Community Theatre); elsewhere.

A revue. Music by Hal Borne, Irma Jurist, and Sammy Fain, lyrics by Paul Francis Webster and Ray Golden. Special music and lyrics by Harold Rome. Musical direction and vocal arrangements by Lehman Engel. Conducted by Irving Actman. Dance arrangements by Billy Kyle. Other participants: Jack Cole (choreographer, featured dancer); Joseph Stein (sketch writer); Michael Stuart [Stewart] (sketch writer); Gwen Verdon (dancer).

Walker's invoice is at the Library of Congress. Base page rate: $5.80.

Walker: "One Word Led to Another."

ALL AMERICAN

Orchestrations credited to Robert **Ginzler**. (Additional orchestrators, if any, unknown.)

Opened March 19, 1962, Winter Garden, 80 performances. Tryout: February, Philadelphia (Erlanger).

Music by Charles Strouse, lyrics by Lee Adams. Based on the novel *Professor Fodorski* by Robert Lewis Taylor. Musical direction and dance arrangements by John Morris. Musical continuity by Trude Rittman. Other participants: Joshua Logan (director); Mel Brooks (librettist); Ray Bolger (star).

ALL FOR LOVE

Orchestrations credited to Ted **Royal**, Don **Walker**, Russell **Bennett**, and Hans **Spialek**. (Additional orchestrators, if any, unknown.)

Opened January 22, 1949, Mark Hellinger, 121 performances. Tryout: none.

A revue. Music and lyrics by Allan Roberts and Lester Lee. Musical direction by Clay Warnick. "Prodigal Daughter" ballet composed by Peter Howard Weiss (aka Peter Howard). Other participants: Paul and Grace Hartman (stars).

Walker's invoices are in the Walker Collection at the Library of Congress. Bennett's invoices are preserved in his ledger. Base page rate: $5.

Walker: "Buy Bond Clothes" ("It's a Living"), "Choreographer's Dance," Entr'acte, "My Heart's in the Middle of July" (song, specialty, and dance), Overture, "What Fools These Mortals Be," "Why Can't It Happen Again?"

Bennett: "Benjamin B. O'Dell" (song and dance), "Money Clip," "Prodigal Daughter" (ballet).

ALL IN FUN

Orchestrations credited to Charles L. Cooke and Hilding Anderson. (Additional orchestrators, if any, unknown.)

Opened December 27, 1940, Majestic, 3 performances. Tryout: unknown.

A revue. Music and lyrics by Baldwin Bergersen, June Sillman (Carroll), John Rox, and others. Musical direction by Ray Kavanaugh. Vocal arrangements by Pembroke Davenport. Other participants: Leonard Sillman (producer); Bill Robinson (star).

ALL IN LOVE

Orchestrations credited to Jonathan Tunick.

Opened November 10, 1961, Martinique (off-Broadway), 141 performances.

Music by Jacques Urbont, lyrics and book by Bruce Geller. Based on the play *The Rivals* by Richard Brinsley Sheridan. Musical direction and vocal arrangements by Jacques Urbont. Dance arrangements by Anne Sternberg.

ALL THE KING'S HORSES

Orchestrations uncredited. (Orchestrations by Russell **Bennett**, Hans **Spialek**, and others.)

Opened January 30, 1934, Shubert, 120 performances. Tryout: January 5, New Haven (Shubert); elsewhere.

Music by Edward A. Horan, lyrics and book by Fred Herendeen. Based on the play *Carlo Rocco* by Lawrence Clarke and Max Gierberg. Musical direction by Oscar Bradley.

ALLAH BE PRAISED!

Orchestrations credited to Don **Walker**. (Additional orchestrators, if any, unknown.)

Opened April 20, 1944, Adelphi, 20 performances. Tryout: March 2, Philadelphia (Forrest); March 29, Boston (Shubert).

Music by Don Walker and Baldwin Bergersen, lyrics and book by George Marion, Jr.

Musical direction by Ving Merlin. Vocal arrangements by Don Walker. Other participant: Jack Cole (choreographer).

The partiturs are in the Walker Collection at the Library of Congress (unexamined). Walker's invoices are at the Library of Congress.

Allah Be Praised! was produced by department store magnate Alfred I. Bloomingdale. Play doctor Cy Howard was summoned to Philadelphia for aid. His advice: "close the show, and keep the store open Sundays." The show was capitalized at $128,900. It closed with a staggering loss of $173,446. (*Oklahoma!* [1943] came in under $100,000.)

As an illustration of relative costs, Walker's total orchestration fee for *Allah Be Praised!* was $4,539—more than the fees of both the director ($3,000) and choreographer ($1,187) combined.

Walker's correspondence includes a letter to the Armed Forces Induction Center, requesting an extension of his induction date until after the opening of *Allah Be Praised!* "a considerable production involving an investment of $100,000." In any event, Walker was rejected due to "disposia" (which my eye doctor neighbor tells me is an obsolete term for what is more or less double vision).

THANKS AND WISHES   From Doretta Morrow (featured actress) to Walker: "Your most amusing wire did my old dejected heart good! Thank you for remembering our helacious opening. Allah be thanked it's over."

ALLEGRO

Orchestrations (mostly) by Russell **Bennett**. (Additional orchestrations by Menotti Salta, with Ted **Royal**.)

Opened October 10, 1947, Majestic, 315 performances. Tryout: September 1, New Haven (Shubert); September 8, Boston (Colonial).

Music by Richard Rodgers, lyrics and book by Oscar Hammerstein II. Musical direction by Salvatore Dell'Isola. Choral direction by Crane Calder. Dance arrangements by Trude Rittman. Other participants: Theatre Guild (producer); Agnes de Mille (director, choreographer).

The partiturs are in the Rodgers Collection at the Library of Congress, with copies at the offices of the Rodgers & Hammerstein Organization. Invoices are preserved in Bennett's ledger. Base page rate: $5.

The orchestrations are by Bennett, with the following exceptions:

Salta: utilities ("The Gentleman Is a Dope," "So Far," "Wildcats," "You Are Never Away").

Royal: utility ("It's a Darn Fine Campus").

Agnes de Mille reports that, walking away from a frustrating production meeting with Theatre Guild producers Lawrence Langner and the blue-haired Theresa Helburn, Oscar and Dick made up this parody lyric about Terry Helburn to the tune of their opening number, "Joseph Taylor, Jr.": "Her brain is fuzzy / Her hair is blue / She'll change her mind / She often do / She's all of that and looney too / But Lawrence Langner's—loonier."

Instr.: 5 reed, 9 brass (3 tpt, 2 tb, 1 tuba, 3 hrn), 14 strings (7 vln, 3 vla, 2 c, 2 b), piano, perc = 30 total.

ALMOST CRAZY

Orchestrations credited to Ted **Royal**. (Additional orchestrations by Marion Evans and others.)

Opened June 20, 1955, Longacre, 16 performances. Tryout: unknown.

A revue. Music and lyrics by Portia Nelson, Raymond Taylor, and James Shelton. Musical direction by Al Rickey. Other participant: Kay Medford (featured).

THE AMAZING ADELE

Orchestrations credited to Joe Glover. (Additional orchestrators, if any, unknown.)

Tryout: December 26, 1955, Philadelphia (Shubert). Closed January 21, 1956, Boston (Shubert).

Music and lyrics by Albert Selden. Additional lyrics by Sheldon Harnick. Based on the play by Pierre Barrillet and Pierre Gredy. Musical direction by Saul Schechtman. Assistant musical director, Peter Howard. Vocal and dance arrangements by Peter Matz. Musical continuity by Donald Pippin. Other participants: Albert Selden and Morton Gottlieb (producers); Herbert Ross (choreographer, "entire production supervised by"); Anita Loos (librettist); Tammy Grimes (star); Johnny Desmond (star).

The music department of this forgotten show, which closed during its tryout, included newcomers Peter Matz, Peter Howard, Donald Pippin, and rehearsal pianist John Kander.

AMBASSADOR

Orchestrations credited to Philip J. **Lang**. (Additional orchestrators, if any, unknown.)
Opened November 19, 1972, Lunt-Fontanne, 9 performances. Tryout: Philadelphia.
Music by Don Gohman, lyrics by Hal Hackady. Based on the novel by Henry James. Musical direction and vocal arrangements by Herbert Grossman. Dance arrangements by Trude Rittman. Other participant: Howard Keel (star).

AMERICAN JUBILEE

Orchestrations credited to Hans **Spialek**. (Additional orchestrators unknown.)
Opened May 12, 1940, Flushing, New York (New York World's Fair). Closed October 12, Flushing.
Music by Arthur Schwartz, lyrics and book by Oscar Hammerstein II. Musical direction by Don Voorhees. Vocal arrangements by Ken Christie.

AMERICANA (1926 EDITION)

Orchestrations uncredited. (Orchestrations by Hans **Spialek** and others.)
Opened July 26, 1926, Belmont, 224 performances. Tryout: July 12, Long Branch, New Jersey (Broadway).
A revue. Music and lyrics by George Gershwin, Ira Gershwin, Arthur Schwartz, B. G. De-Sylva, and others. Musical direction by Gene Salzer. Other participant: J. P. McEvoy (producer, sketches).

AMERICANA (1928 EDITION, "THE NEW AMERICANA")

Orchestrations uncredited. (Orchestrations by Hans **Spialek** and others.)
Opened October 30, 1928, Lew Fields, 12 performances. Tryout: unknown.
A revue. Music by Roger Wolfe Kahn and others, lyrics by Irving Caesar and others. Musical direction by Gene Salzer. Other participant: J. P. McEvoy (producer, sketches).

AMERICANA (1932 EDITION, "NEW AMERICANA")

Orchestrations uncredited. (Orchestrations by Conrad Salinger and others.)
Opened October 5, 1932, Shubert, 77 performances. Tryout: unknown.

A revue. Music by Jay Gorney, Harold Arlen, Richard Myers, Vernon Duke, Burton Lane, and others, lyrics by E. Y. Harburg. Musical direction by Jay Gorney. Other participant: J. P. McEvoy (producer, sketches).

AMERICA'S SWEETHEART

Orchestrations credited to Russell **Bennett**. (Additional orchestrators unknown.)

Opened February 10, 1931, Broadhurst, 135 performances. Tryout: January 19, Pittsburgh (Shubert); January 26, Washington, D.C. (National); February 2, Newark, New Jersey (Shubert).

Music by Richard Rodgers, lyrics by Lorenz Hart. Musical direction by Alfred Newman. Other participants: Monty Woolley (director); Herbert Fields (librettist).

ANGEL

Orchestrations (mostly) by Don **Walker**. (Additional orchestrations by Arnold Goland and William Cox.)

Opened May 10, 1978, Minskoff, 5 performances. Tryout: Glen Cove, New York (Northstage Theatre Restaurant).

Music by Gary Geld, lyrics by Peter Udell. Based on the novel *Look Homeward, Angel* by Thomas Wolfe. Musical direction and dance arrangements by William Cox. Other participant: Fred Gwynne (star).

Invoices are in the Walker Collection at the Library of Congress. Base page rate: $11.15. Orchestrations are mostly by Walker, with minor incidentals and fixes by Arnold Goland and musical director William Cox.

ANGELA

Orchestrations credited to Don **Walker**.

Opened October 30, 1969, Music Box, 4 performances. Tryout: October 8, New Haven (Shubert); elsewhere.

A comedy by Sumner Arthur Long. Incidental music composed by Don Walker. "Angela Knows Best" by Don Walker and Arnold Goland. Other participant: Geraldine Page (star).

The partiturs are at the Library of Congress.

ANKLES AWEIGH

Orchestrations by Don **Walker**. Assistant to Don Walker, Seymour (Red) **Ginzler**. (Orchestrations mostly by Walker and Ginzler, with Joe Glover and Irwin **Kostal**.)

Opened April 18, 1955, Mark Hellinger, 176 performances. Tryout: March 23, New Haven (Shubert); March 29, Boston (Shubert).

Music by Sammy Fain, lyrics by Dan Shapiro. Musical direction by Salvatore Dell'Isola. Vocal arrangements by Don Walker. Dance music devised by Roger Adams. Additional dance arrangements by Donald Pippin. Other participant: Jerome Robbins (replacement choreographer, uncredited).

Invoices are in the Walker Collection at the Library of Congress. Base page rate: $5.87. Invoices indicate: Walker (56%), Ginzler (29%), Glover (11%).

Walker: "Italy" (and vocal arr.), "La Festa" (song, tarantella, and chase), "Old Fashioned Mothers," Opening Dance, "Ready Cash" (and vocal arr.), "The Villain Always Gets It."

Ginzler: "Code Dance" (dance arr.: Pippin), "An Eleven O'Clock Song," Finale Act II (vocal arr.: Walker), "Headin' for the Bottom Blues," "Honeymoon" (vocal arr.: Walker), various utilities.

Glover: "His and Hers" (see below), "Nothing at All" (vocal arr.: Walker), "Nothing Can Replace a Man" (vocal arr.: Glover), "Skip the Build Up," "Song of Montefino," various utilities.

Kostal: "Kiss Me and Kill Me with Love."

Other scores:

"Here's to Dear Old Us" is by Walker and Ginzler.

"His and Hers" (vocal arr.: Glover) is mostly by Glover, with 2 pages by Walker.

Overture and Entr'acte are compilations of utilities, with bridgework by Ginzler.

"Walk Like a Sailor": "Part A" (Jane and men) and "Part B" (Jane solo) are by Walker; "Part C" (dance and ensemble) is by Ginzler.

Walker's contract included a weekly royalty of $100 for "special services." Walker had a complex relationship with producer Harold Hoyt, who at the time was a business partner of Walker's and served as Walker's agent. As part of the deal, Walker also contracted for "vocal orchestrations" at full orchestration rates. These were farmed out, as indicated above.

The Walker Collection includes a letter to the producers of *Ankles*, offering the names of potential conductors (with the proviso that union rules don't allow him to recommend one over the other). Don lists fifteen names of people who asked him for the job, an astounding group, including Pembroke Davenport, Frederick Dvonch, Max Meth, Jay Blackton, Oscar Kosarin, Buster Davis, Irving Actman, Robert Ginzler, and Salvatore Dell'Isola of *South Pacific* (who got the job, perhaps because he was first on the list).

THANKS AND WISHES   From Jule Styne to Walker: "I'll be digging every eighth-note. Good luck."

From Walker to Chorus: "You have all been so wonderful and cooperative, the finest singing group I have ever heard. Thanks for singing so sweetly, beyond the call of duty, especially Sandy and Patty."

From Walker to costume designer Miles White: "In our next show let's tape the mouths of the singers and install individual microphones, then we'll both be happy."

Instr.: 6 reed (including 6 sax and 3 fl), 7 brass (4 tpt, 3 tb), 9 strings (6 vln, 1 vla, 1 c, 1 b), piano, guitar, perc = 25 total.

ANNIE

Orchestrations credited to Philip J. **Lang**. (Additional orchestrators, if any, unknown.)

Opened April 21, 1977, Alvin, 2,377 performances. Tryout: March 5, Washington, D.C. (Eisenhower).

Music by Charles Strouse, lyrics by Martin Charnin. Based on the comic strip *Little Orphan Annie* by Harold Gray. Musical direction and dance arrangements by Peter Howard. Other participants: Mike Nichols (co-producer); Martin Charnin (director); Peter Gennaro (choreographer); Thomas Meehan (co-librettist); Dorothy Loudon (star).

The partiturs are in the Philip J. Lang Collection at Ithaca College (unexamined).

ANNIE GET YOUR GUN

Orchestrations credited to Philip J. **Lang**, Russell **Bennett**, and Ted **Royal**. (Orchestrations mostly by Lang, Bennett, Royal, and Robert Noeltner, with Menotti Salta, Hans **Spialek**, Walter Paul, Sherman Bunker, Jr., R. C. Williams, and Don **Walker**.)

Opened May 16, 1946, Imperial, 1,147 performances. Tryout: March 28, New Haven (Shubert); April 2, Boston (Shubert); April 30, Philadelphia (Shubert).

Music and lyrics by Irving Berlin. Suggested by events in the life of Annie Oakley.

Musical direction by Jay Blackton. Vocal arrangements by Joe Moon. Piano arrangements by Helmy Kresa. Other participants: Richard Rodgers and Oscar Hammerstein II (producers); Joshua Logan (director); Herbert & Dorothy Fields (librettists); Ethel Merman (star).

The partiturs are in the Berlin Collection at the Library of Congress.

    Lang: "Anything You Can Do" (with fixes by Bennett, see below), "Ceremonial Chant," "Circus Dance," "Colonel Buffalo Bill," "Doin' What Comes Naturally" (with fixes by Bennett, see below), "I'll Share It All with You" (see below), "Moonshine Lullaby," "Who Do You Love, I Hope?" (see below), "You Can't Get a Man with a Gun" (with fixes by Bennett, see below).

    Bennett: "The Girl That I Marry" (see below), "I Got Lost in His Arms" (see below), "My Defenses Are Down" (see below), Overture.

    Noeltner: "I Got the Sun in the Morning" (see below).

    Royal: "There's No Business Like Show Business" (see below).

    Salta: "Funeral March," "The Girl That I Marry" (incidental, see below), utilities ("Colonel Buffalo Bill Utility #1," "You Can't Get a Man with a Gun").

    Bunker: utilities ("Colonel Buffalo Bill Utility #2," "There's No Business Like Show Business").

    Other scores:

    "Anything You Can Do" is by Lang, with Bennett writing in instruments to play along with the melody line in numerous places (offering support at such places as "Yes I can, yes I can, yes I can").

    Entr'acte—a string of utilities—is missing, except "Coda" (20 bars) by Jay Blackton.

    "The Girl That I Marry" is by Bennett, replacing versions #1 and #2 (by Lang) and #3 (by Spialek); reprise is by Bennett, replacing Lang's original version; "Girl That I Marry Opening" and "Incidental" are by Salta; "Girl That I Marry Ballroom Scene" is by Royal.

    "I Got Lost in His Arms" is by Bennett, replacing Lang's original version; "Scene Change" is by Lang; "Lost in His Arms Waltz Insert" is by Walker.

"I Got the Sun in the Morning" is by Noeltner, replacing original version by Lang; "New 5th Chorus" is by Royal; "Scene Change" is by Lang; utility is by Royal.

"I'll Share It All with You": there are two complete versions by Lang. There are also two dance scores, one by Lang and one, which was probably used in the show, by Walker. There is also an early waltz version by Spialek.

"I'm a Bad Bad Man" is by Bennett, with the verse by R. C. Williams. There is also an earlier version by Lang and an interim version combining Lang's verse and dance with a refrain by Spialek. There are also additional dance scores and openings by Lang and Royal.

"I'm an Indian, Too" is by Paul; "Drum Dance (specialty)" and "Fanfare" are by Lang.

"My Defenses Are Down New" is by Bennett, replacing a version by Paul.

"There's No Business Like Show Business New" is by Royal, replacing a version by Lang; reprise is by Lang (with the first 6 pages replaced by Bennett); dance is mostly by Lang, with 24 pasted-in measures by Walker ("2nd Chorus of F Strain").

"They Say It's Wonderful": song is by Bennett, with the continuation of the number (Frank and Annie's embrace, dialogue, and vocal finish) in other hands. This replaces the original chart by Lang; reprise is by Lang. There are two utilities, by Lang and Royal. A partial score marked "in C, for Watson" (apparently Milton Watson, who replaced Ray Middleton for the last six months of the run) is by Noeltner.

"Who Do You Love, I Hope?": there are two complete versions by Lang. There is also a 16-page dance by Walker.

"You Can't Get a Man with a Gun" is by Lang (with violin rewrites and new reed lines written in by Bennett); "Introduction" (heard on the original cast album) is by Royal.

There are as many as five different orchestrations for some songs; seventy-nine scores survive, for twenty-one musical numbers. (The norm is one chart per song, with two versions on occasion and very rarely three.) Unlike in similar circumstances on other shows, few of the scores are dated, so the order in which the charts were written is not always clear. The final section of Bennett's Overture, where the band plays "They Say It's Wonderful," is marked: "The Works."

Instr.: 5 reed, 6 brass (3 tpt, 2 tb, 1 hrn), ? strings (vln, vla, c, b), piano, perc.

(See pages 125–27.)

ANNIE GET YOUR GUN (1966 REVIVAL)

Orchestrations by Russell **Bennett**. (Additional orchestrations by Ruth Anderson.)

Opened May 31, 1966, New York State, 47 performances (with a return engagement of 77 performances at the Broadway).

Musical direction by Franz Allers. Dance arrangements by Richard de Benedictis. Other participants: Music Theater of Lincoln Center, Richard Rodgers (producers); Ethel Merman (star); Jerry Orbach (featured).

The partiturs are at the offices of the Rodgers & Hammerstein Organization. Bennett's invoice is preserved in his journal. Base page rate: $7.05.

Bennett: "Annie's Indian Dance," "Birds and Bees," "Chant" (sections I and II), "Doin' What Comes Naturally," Exit March, Finale act I, "I'm a Bad, Bad Man" (dance),

"Old Fashioned Wedding," "There's No Business Like Show Business" (song, encore, and reprise), "You Can't Get a Man with a Gun" (song and encore).

Anderson: "Anything You Can Do," "Colonel Buffalo Bill" (and utility), Entr'acte, Finale, "The Girl That I Marry," "I Got Lost in His Arms," "I'm a Bad, Bad Man," "I'm an Indian, Too," "Moonshine Lullaby," "My Defenses Are Down," Overture, "There's No Business Like Show Business" ("Ensemble" and utility).

Other scores:

"I Got the Sun in the Morning": first 19 pages are by Anderson, followed by 33 by Bennett.

"They Say It's Wonderful": first refrain is by Anderson, the rest (beginning with Frank's verse) is by Bennett.

Ruth Anderson, who did about half of this *Annie* as well as half of the following year's *Show Boat*, is the only woman orchestrator I have found evidence of in the course of this project. A student of Nadia Boulanger, she also assisted Bennett on his television work at NBC. Jonathan Tunick (who provided one chart for the 1966 *Show Boat*) believes that she was the wife of conductor Paul Anderson, who worked on the Music Theater of Lincoln Center shows and had especially close ties to the Rodgers family.

Instr.: 6 reed, 7 brass (3 tpt, 3 tb, Ihrn), ? strings (vln, 4? vla, 3 c, 2 b), harp, guitar, 2 perc.

ANNIE 2: MISS HANNIGAN'S REVENGE

Orchestrations credited to Michael Starobin. (Additional orchestrations by Larry **Wilcox** and possibly others.)

Tryout: January 4, 1990, Washington, D.C. (Opera House). Closed January 20, Washington, D.C.

Music by Charles Strouse, lyrics by Martin Charnin. Based on the comic strip *Little Orphan Annie* by Harold Gray. Musical direction and dance arrangements by Peter Howard. Other participants: Martin Charnin (director); Danny Daniels (choreographer); Thomas Meehan (co-librettist); Dorothy Loudon (star).

ANYA

Orchestrations (mostly) by Don **Walker**. (Additional orchestrators, if any, unknown.)

Opened November 29, 1965, Ziegfeld, 16 performances. Tryout: unknown.

Music and lyrics by Robert Wright & George Forrest, based on themes of Sergei Rachmaninoff. Based on the play *Anastasia* by Marcelle Maurette and Guy Bolton. Musical direction by Harold Hastings. Other participants: George Abbott (producer, co-librettist), Hanya Holm (choreographer), Constance Towers (star), Lillian Gish (star).

Walker's pocket notebook is at the Library of Congress. Base page rate: $10.

Walker's personal notes, kept for billing purposes, indicate that he did most of the score himself. Two numbers, "A Quiet Land" and "That Prelude!" are unlisted and thus probably by others (most likely Arnold Goland or Jim Tyler).

THANKS AND WISHES   From Abbott to Walker: "Thanks for your note. It seems that the demand for operetta is not as vigorous as I had hoped."

ANYONE CAN WHISTLE

Orchestrations (mostly) by Don **Walker**. (Additional orchestrations by Arnold Goland and Herbert Greene.)

Opened April 4, 1964, Majestic, 9 performances. Tryout: March 2, Philadelphia (Forrest).

Music and lyrics by Stephen Sondheim. Musical direction and vocal arrangements by Herbert Greene. Dance arrangements by Betty Walberg. Other participants: Kermit Bloomgarden (producer); Arthur Laurents (director, librettist); Herbert Ross (choreographer); Angela Lansbury (star); Lee Remick (star).

Copies of the partiturs are in both the Walker and Rodgers & Hammerstein Organization collections at the Library of Congress. Invoices are in the Walker Collection at the Library of Congress. Base page rate: $8. Invoices indicate that Walker did 89% of the score.

The orchestrations are by Walker, with the following exceptions:

Goland: "Be Like the Bluebird" (song and incidental), "Cora's Chase Part 1," "Cora's Playoff," "I've Got You to Lean On" (incidental), "Lady from Lourdes," "Play Wiz Me Playoff."

Greene: "Anyone Can Whistle," "Fay's Monologue," "Hapgood's Entrance," "Pilgrim March 1," "Pilgrim March 2," "Pumping Music" (before "Miracle").

Other scores:

"Ev'rybody Says Don't" is by Walker, replacing an earlier version by Greene.

"Me and My Town": there are two versions, both by Walker.

"Miracle Song": there are two versions, both by Walker.

Overture is mostly by Walker, with Goland.

Prelude act I is mostly by Walker, with 9 measures by Greene.

"Simple": this extended, 13-minute number is scored in separate sections (8 parts are indicated, but only 7 are included with the materials): part 1, "Interrogation"; part 2, "Hapgood" ("Grass Is Green"); part 3, "A Woman's Place" (featuring güiro [scraper gourd]); part 4, "Can't Judge a Book"; part 5, "Watch Cries" ("rub your stomachs"); part 6, "Hail, Heil" ("which is who?"); part 7, none; part 8, "vaudeville style music." Walker did the entire number except for the 2-page "Interrogation Lead-in" and part 8, by Goland.

> SONDHEIM: Don Walker and Herbie Greene both had great contempt for me, and never let me forget it. I admired Don enormously since *Carousel*, which was probably the best orchestration I ever heard in my life. He was a songwriter manqué, you know. He had written *Courtin' Time*. A very bitter fellow, resented me greatly. Herbie also did, though I'm not sure why. Don would give me a cold smile whenever I made a suggestion, and he'd ignore it. Herbie would do it—but with such resentment, condescension. With Don, I think it was just instinct, he resented working for any young composer. Herbie was insufferable. He gave an interview, years later, saying that everyone was laughing at the score.

David Shire was rehearsal pianist.

> SHIRE: Don was always one of my heroes. You don't get any better than *The Most Happy Fella* and hundreds of other things. But I could see that he didn't understand the uniqueness of Steve's music. When the scores came back, everything was doubled, the textures where

thickened. Don did what he would normally do with other composers. But they didn't write like Stephen Sondheim, and Don didn't understand this.

Instr.: 5 reed, 7 brass (3 tpt, 2 tb/tuba, 2 hrn), 6 strings (0 vln, 0 vla, 5 c, 1 b), piano, accordion, guitar, 2 perc = 23 total.

ANYTHING GOES

Orchestrations credited to Hans **Spialek** and Russell **Bennett**. (Additional orchestrations by Menotti Salta and others.)

Opened November 21, 1934, Alvin, 420 performances. Tryout: November 5, Boston (Colonial).

Music and lyrics by Cole Porter. Musical direction by Earl Busby. Vocal arrangements by Ray Johnson. Other participants: Vinton Freedley (producer); Howard Lindsay (director); Guy Bolton & P. G. Wodehouse, Howard Lindsay, and Russel Crouse (librettists); William Gaxton & Victor Moore (stars); Ethel Merman (star).

A reconstruction of the score by John McGlinn, containing copies of two of the original partiturs, is at the Library of Congress.

Spialek: "The Gypsy in Me," "Opening Act I Scene 1(Bon Voyage)"

The location of the rest of the partiturs is unknown, but they were examined by Tommy Krasker and Robert Kimball for their *Catalog of the American Musical* (1988). Their findings indicate the following:

Spialek: "Be Like the Bluebird," Entr'acte, Finale Act I, Finale Ultimo, Overture, "Public Enemy Number One," "Where Are the Men."

Bennett: "Blow, Gabriel Blow," "I Get a Kick Out of You."

Bennett and **Salta:** "All Through the Night," "Anything Goes."

Orchestrator unknown (de Packh? Salinger?): "Buddie Beware," "There'll Always Be a Lady Fair," "You're the Top."

> SPIALEK: We had a miserable and depressing dress rehearsal in Boston. Ethel Merman hollered for better songs (she had only "I Get a Kick Out of You," "You're the Top," "Blow, Gabriel Blow," and "Anything Goes"). Victor Moore sat alone in a corner and whined in his cracked voice to everyone who cared to listen that never in his career had he had such humiliating material to cope with. William Gaxton implied he would go back on the Paramount-Publix circuit. Russel Crouse and Howard Lindsay, to my inquiry of what this show is all about, answered almost in unison, "Damned if we know!" Yet the show opened the next day without a hitch and to everybody's, but everybody's surprise, as a tremendous and immediate hit.

Instr.: 4 reed (including 1 with celesta), 4 brass (3 tpt, 1 tb), 14? strings (8? vln, 3? vla, 2? c, 1 b), piano, 2 perc = 25? total.

APPLAUSE

Orchestrations credited to Philip J. **Lang**. (Additional orchestrations by Jack Andrews.)
Opened March 30, 1970, Palace, 896 performances. Tryout: Baltimore (Mechanic).

Music by Charles Strouse, lyrics by Lee Adams. Based on the story *All about Eve* by Mary Orr. Musical direction and vocal arrangements by Donald Pippin. Dance arrangements and incidental music by Mel Marvin. Additional arrangements by Marvin Hamlisch (uncredited). Other participants: Ron Field (director, choreographer); Betty Comden & Adolph Green (replacement librettists); Lauren Bacall (star); Len Cariou (featured).

Don Pippin recalls that virtually all of the important material is by Lang, with some utilities and minor incidentals by Andrews. Pippin has the partiturs for several cut numbers, all by Lang: "God Bless," "It Was Always You," "Love Comes First," "She's No Longer a Gypsy" (original version), "Welcome to the Theatre" (original version).

Marvin Hamlisch—as yet in his pre-Hollywood phase, when he was still a Broadway pianist/arranger—had worked with Field on *Golden Rainbow*. He was called in to write the show-stopping "Applause" arrangement, with waiters dancing on the tables to show tunes (including a standoff between *Oklahoma!* and the 1969 erotic revue *Oh! Calcutta!*), which alas was not included on the original cast album.

> CHARLES STROUSE: There was a conflict that was happening within me, that was a little bit discombobulating to *Applause*. *Hair* [the so-called "American Tribal Love-Rock Musical" of 1968] had opened—a fantastic success, as it should have been. I thought it was fantastic. I had written *Applause* right before that, during that, and after that. And the critic of the *Times*, I cannot forget him saying, "from now on, after *Hair*, every show will be rock and roll." Here I am, sitting on this wonderful property, and then we got Bacall, and I thought, well, this was great. But before we opened, I said to Phil, "This is such middle-class music, I'm feeling very self-conscious." And I think I affected everyone with this bug. It affected my writing in what I think now was a destructive way. And I brought Phil into my neurotic thing. I said, these songs sound too much like regular Broadway songs.
>
> I think that, looking back on it, Phil may not have been the right orchestrator. He was an absolutely wonderful man, and a friend, he was like a father to me, but I was like a confused kid trying to get something else. So I don't think I got the best out of Phil, because I maybe wouldn't let him give me the best. When we started *Applause*, it was definitely about the fifties. I think that governed my choice of Phil. It was after we had written it, I said oh my God, it's not *Hair*. And we tried to change it; we even had, in one of the parties, a lot of hippie guys standing around. There was a blatant use of gay men, Ron's way of trying to bring it up to date.
>
> When we opened in Baltimore, it was terrible, the reviews were terrible. I take a lot of the blame for it. My attitude about the show was that it's wonderful, let's change it. I was trying so hard, in a song I loathed called "Hurry Back," to make it seem like it was a "with it" song. Lee isn't that kind of a lyricist, I don't think I'm that kind of composer. Fortunately, Ron Field and the producers and Betty & Adolph were such craftsmen and we improved the show and improved the show and it became a success.

> PIPPIN: I did *Applause* because of Ron Field, whom I worked with in summer stock. I met with Strouse. "I've got to be perfectly honest, maybe you're too old to do this sort of show," he told me. I said, "If I'm too old to conduct it, you're too old to write it."

Walker was called in to help, although it is unknown whether he did any work. He sent an invoice for his trip to Baltimore (dated March 9) with a note:

Hope I was of some help in clearing the air, and that Strouse and Adams have come up with a musical approach that fits the book. I felt from the start that if they solved the problem, Phil Lang would execute it properly; for he is an excellent and competent orchestrator, who does his best to carry out the ideas and direction of the composer and lyricist. Too bad I couldn't have been on the show from the start, for I feel it is right down my alley. But it is Phil's show, and I wish him luck.

THE APPLE TREE

Orchestrations (mostly) by Eddie **Sauter**. Additional scoring by Elliot Lawrence.

Opened October 18, 1966, Shubert, 463 performances. Tryout: unknown.

Music and book by Jerry Bock, lyrics and book by Sheldon Harnick. Based on the stories
The Diary of Adam and Eve by Mark Twain; *The Lady or the Tiger* by Frank R. Stockton; and
Passionella by Jules Feiffer. Musical direction, vocal arrangements, and additional scoring by Elliot Lawrence. Other participants: Stuart Ostrow (producer); Mike Nichols (director); Lee Theodore (choreographer); Herbert Ross (replacement choreographer); Barbara Harris (star); Alan Alda (star).

The partiturs are at Music Theatre International.

The orchestrations are by Sauter, with the following exceptions:

Lawrence: "Forbidden Grandmother," "Make Way (New)," "Movie Star Fanfares," "Movie Star Flip-Flops," final endings for several songs (including "Eve," "Forbidden Love," "Gorgeous," and "I've Got What You Want").

Other scores:

Bows part 1 ("Make Way") is by Lawrence, part 2 ("Gorgeous") is by Sauter.

"Passionella Overture" is marked "bright and wacky"; the introduction to "I Know" is "big and juicy."

> HARNICK: Stu picked Eddie. It was a brilliant choice. Jerry invited me to his first meeting with Eddie. Jerry asked Eddie, "How do you see the opening number?" He said, "I see it as sunlight on marble." Someplace else, he said, "Well, I kind of hear elephants on tiptoe." I remember being so startled, and so pleased.

Instr.: 5 reed (all with saxes), 7 brass (3 tpt, 3 tb, 1 hrn), 8 strings (1 vln, 3 vla, 3 c, 1 b), piano/celesta, harp, guitar (classic/elec/mandolin/banjo), 2 perc = 25 total.

(See page 174.)

ARABIAN NIGHTS

Orchestrations credited to Joe Glover. (Additional orchestrators, if any, unknown.)

Opened June 25, 1954, Jones Beach, New York (Marine).

Music by Carmen Lombardo, lyrics by John Jacob Loeb. Musical direction and vocal arrangements by Pembroke Davenport. Other participants: Guy Lombardo (producer); Yurek Lazowski (choreographer, uncredited; billing read "dances devised by The Ballet Theatre"); Lauritz Melchior (star).

ARE YOU WITH IT?

Orchestrations credited to Joe Glover, Hans **Spialek**, Ted **Royal**, Don **Walker**, and Walter Paul. (Additional orchestrators, if any, unknown.)

Opened November 10, 1945, Century, 264 performances. Tryout: Philadelphia.

Music by Harry Revel, lyrics by Arnold B. Horwitt. Based on the novel *Slightly Perfect* by George Malcolm-Smith. Musical direction by Will Irwin. Vocal arrangements and direction by Clay Warnick. Other participant: Dolores Gray (featured).

ARI

Orchestrations credited to Philip J. **Lang**. (Additional orchestrators, if any, unknown.)

Opened January 15, 1971, Hellinger, 19 performances. Tryout: December, Philadelphia (Shubert); December 22, 1970, Washington, D.C. (National).

Music by Walt Smith, lyrics and book by Leon Uris. Based on the novel *Exodus* by Leon Uris. Musical direction and vocal arrangements by Stanley Lebowsky. Dance arrangements and incidental music by Peter Howard. Other participant: Constance Towers (star).

ARMS AND THE GIRL

Orchestrations credited to Morton Gould and Philip J. **Lang**. (Additional orchestrations by Russell **Bennett** and possibly others.)

Opened February 2, 1950, 46th Street, 134 performances. Tryout: Philadelphia; Boston.

Music by Morton Gould, lyrics and book by Dorothy Fields. Based on the play *The Pursuit of Happiness* by Lawrence Langner and Armina Marshall. Musical direction by Frederick Dvonch. Other participants: Theatre Guild (producer); Rouben Mamoulian (director and co-librettist); Michael Kidd (choreographer); Herbert Fields (co-librettist); Nanette Fabray (star); Pearl Bailey (featured).

Bennett's invoices are preserved in his ledger. Base page rate: $4.95.

Bennett: "I'll Never Learn," "Opening Act II, Opening Scene 14," "Vintage," minor fixes.

With the show in trouble on the road, the producers complained that the arrangements lacked the "Broadway touch" and suggested bringing in Russell Bennett (from their production *Oklahoma!*) to redo the orchestrations. Gould fought this, but allowed Bennett to attend a performance. Irv Kostal reports that Bennett told him that he told the producers, "There's nothing wrong with the orchestrations. But the costumes, the lighting, and the script are absolutely awful. They better try to save the show by looking where the problems really are."

AROUND THE WORLD

Orchestrations credited to Russell **Bennett** and Ted **Royal**. (Additional orchestrators, if any, unknown.)

Opened May 31, 1946, Adelphi, 75 performances. Tryout: April 28, Boston (Boston Opera House); May 7, New Haven (Shubert); May 14, Philadelphia (Shubert).

Music and lyrics by Cole Porter. Based on the novel *Around the World in Eighty Days* by Jules Verne. Musical direction by Harry S. Levant. Vocal arrangements by Mitchell Ayres. Other participant: Orson Welles (producer, director, librettist, star).

Three partiturs are in the Porter Collection at the Library of Congress.

Bennett: "Look What I Found," "Phileas Fogg Dance," "There He Goes, Mr. Phileas Fogg."

AROUND THE WORLD IN EIGHTY DAYS

Orchestrations credited to Philip J. **Lang**. (Additional orchestrators, if any, unknown.)

Opened June 22, 1963, Jones Beach, New York (Marine), 73 performances.

Music by Sammy Fain, lyrics by Harold Adamson. Based on the novel *Around the World in Eighty Days* by Jules Verne. Musical direction by Mitchell Ayres. Other participant: Guy Lombardo (producer).

A prior production of this musical was staged in St. Louis at the Muny on June 11, 1962, although it is unclear whether Lang was involved with that version.

ARTISTS AND MODELS (1943)

Orchestrations credited to Hans **Spialek**, Ted **Royal**, Don **Walker**, Emil Gerstenberger, and Charles L. Cooke. (Additional orchestrators, if any, unknown.)

Opened November 5, 1943, Broadway, 27 performances. Tryout: October 11, Boston.

A revue. Music and lyrics by Dan Shapiro, Milton Pascal, and Phil Charig. Musical direction by Max Meth. Vocal arrangements by Clay Warnick. Other participants: Jane Froman (star); Jackie Gleason (featured).

AS THE GIRLS GO

Orchestrations credited to Ted **Royal**. (Additional orchestrators, if any, unknown.)

Opened November 13, 1948, Winter Garden, 414 performances. Tryout: October 11, Boston (Opera House); November 2, New Haven (Shubert).

Music by Jimmy McHugh, lyrics by Harold Adamson. Musical direction by Max Meth. Vocal arrangements and direction by Hugh Martin. Additional vocal arrangements by Buster Davis. Other participants: Michael Todd (producer); Bobby Clark (star).

Hugh Martin relates that he fought with Mike Todd and was fired during the tryout, with assistant Buster Davis taking over.

AS THOUSANDS CHEER

Orchestrations credited to Adolph Deutsch, Frank Tours, Edward B. Powell, Russell Wooding, and Helmy Kresa. (Additional orchestrators, if any, unknown.)

Opened September 30, 1933, Music Box, 400 performances. Tryout: September 9, Philadelphia (Forrest).

A revue. Music and lyrics by Irving Berlin. Musical direction by Frank Tours. Other participants: Moss Hart (sketches); Marilyn Miller (star); Ethel Waters (star).

AT HOME ABROAD

Orchestrations uncredited. (Orchestrations by Russell **Bennett**, David Raksin, Hans **Spialek**, Don **Walker**, Phil Walsh, Russell Wooding, and possibly others.)

Opened September 19, 1935, Winter Garden, 198 performances. Tryout: unknown.

A revue. Music by Arthur Schwartz, lyrics by Howard Dietz. Musical direction by Al Goodman. Other participants: Vincente Minnelli (director, set designer); Marc Connelly (sketch writer); Beatrice Lillie (star); Ethel Waters (star).

The Walker Collection includes the piano-vocal score for "Get Away from It All," which suggests that Walker did this number.

AT THE GRAND

Orchestrations credited to Albert Sendrey and Arthur Kay. (Additional orchestrations by Al Woodbury and possibly others.)

Tryout: July 7, 1958, Los Angeles (Philharmonic Auditorium). Closed September 13, San Francisco (Curran).

Music and lyrics by Robert Wright & George Forrest. Based on the novel *Grand Hotel* by Vicki Baum. Musical direction by Jay Blackton. Dance and incidental arrangements by Trude Rittman. Other participants: Edwin Lester (producer); Albert Marre (director); Paul Muni (star); Joan Diener (star).

This musical version of Vicki Baum's novel was unearthed thirty years after its early demise, rewritten, and—with half of the score replaced during the tryout by Maury Yeston—taken to Broadway in 1989 under the title *Grand Hotel: The Musical.*

BABES IN ARMS

Orchestrations credited to Hans **Spialek**. (Additional orchestrators unknown.)

Opened April 14, 1937, Shubert, 289 performances. Tryout: March 31, Boston (Shubert).

Music and book by Richard Rodgers, lyrics and book by Lorenz Hart. Musical direction by Gene Salzer. Other participants: George Balanchine (choreographer); Alfred Drake (featured).

BABES IN ARMS (1959 REVIVAL)

Orchestrations by Don **Walker**. (Orchestrations by Walker and Robert **Ginzler**, with Hal Serra.)

Tryout: March 30, 1959, Palm Beach, Florida (Royal Poinciana). Closed April 18, Miami (Coconut Grove).

Musical direction and dance arrangements by Peter Howard. Other participants: Stanley Prager (director); Julie Wilson (featured).

Invoices are in the Walker Collection at the Library of Congress. Base page rate: $5.46.

The orchestrations are by Walker, with the following exceptions:

Ginzler: "Deep North" (ballet), "I Wish I Was in Love Again," "Imagine" (vocal and ballet), "Johnny One Note," "The Lady Is a Tramp," "Way Out West" (dance), "You're Nearer."

Hal Serra: "All at Once."

From Walker to producer Lee Guber, the night after the opening: "The size and type of orchestra, and quality of personnel on tour, are so far removed from the standards I have come to set for myself that until some obvious changes for the better occur, billing will be detrimental to my professional reputation."

BAJOUR

Orchestrations credited to Mort Lindsey. (Additional orchestrators, if any, unknown.)

Opened November 23, 1964, Shubert, 232 performances. Tryout: Boston; October 28, Philadelphia (Shubert).

Music and lyrics by Walter Marks. Based on a series of *New Yorker* stories by Joseph Mitchell. Musical direction and vocal arrangements by Lehman Engel. Dance arrangements by Richard de Benedictis. Other participants: Peter Gennaro (choreographer); Chita Rivera (star).

BAKER STREET

Orchestrations (mostly) by Don **Walker**. (Additional orchestrations by Arnold Goland.)

Opened February 16, 1965, Broadway, 311 performances. Tryout: January, Boston (Shubert); Toronto (O'Keefe).

Music and lyrics by Marian Grudeff and Raymond Jessel. Additional music and lyrics by Jerry Bock and Sheldon Harnick. Based on the *Sherlock Holmes* novels by Sir Arthur Conan Doyle. Musical direction by Harold Hastings. Dance arrangements by John Morris. Other participants: Alexander H. Cohen (producer); Harold Prince (director); Lee Theodore (choreographer); Jerry Bock and Sheldon Harnick (additional music and lyrics, uncredited).

Invoices are in the Walker Collection at the Library of Congress. Base page rate: $8.

The orchestrations are by Walker, with the following exceptions:

Goland: "Diamond Jubilee March," "I'd Do It Again" (changes and reprise), "Leave It to Us, Gov Chase," "Oleo," numerous fixes and incidentals.

Other scores:

Entr'acte (used as Overture on cast album) is by Walker, with 9 pages by Goland.

"Jewelry" is by Walker, incorporating part of an earlier version by Goland.

"Leave It to Us, Gov" is by Walker, with chaser by Goland.

Director Hal Prince inherited a score of fourteen songs from prior director Josh Logan. Prince rejected seven, for which Grudeff and Jessel wrote replacements. (Walker, in a note to Prince after first hearing the songs, complained about the authors' weakness in organizing musical numbers and warned that "their projection of the English period of the show may turn out to be stylistically sterile for orchestration.") During the tryout, Prince insisted on additional songs from Bock & Harnick, with whom he had recently done *She Loves Me* and *Fiddler on the Roof.*

From Walker's journal, during the Boston tryout: "1/6/65: Hal Prince offered me *Flora, the Red Menace* today, played score." "1/8: HP took me to dinner—wants me to do *Flora.*" "1/11: Bock & Harnick here, working on show." "1/12: scored Bock & Harnick's 'I Shall Miss You Holmes' and 'I'm in London Again'."

Walker to general manager Roy Somlyo: "In the final stage of orchestration of a show, it is almost always wise to have some assistance on the least important music (usually the change music) so that you are sure to have everything ready on time and leave a little cushion of time for last minute emergencies. In this case I used Arnold Goland, who is now my regular associate in all fields of orchestration, with the blessings of Hal Hastings."

THANKS AND WISHES   Opening night, from Hastings to Walker: "You've been a brick through this whole bloody mess. Thank you, chum."

THE BAKER'S WIFE

Orchestrations (mostly) by Don **Walker**. (Additional orchestrations by Arnold Goland.)
Tryout: May 11, 1976, Los Angeles (Dorothy Chandler Pavilion); September 15, Boston (Shubert); Washington, D.C. (Opera House). Closed November 13, Washington, D.C.
Music and lyrics by Stephen Schwartz. Based on the film *La Femme de Boulanger* by Marcel Pagnol and Jean Giono. Musical direction by Don Jennings. Dance arrangements by Daniel Troob. Other participants: David Merrick (producer); Joseph Stein (librettist); Topol (star); Paul Sorvino (replacement star); Patti LuPone (featured).

Walker's invoices are at the Library of Congress. Base page rate: $10.89.

Among the numerous changes that occurred on this troubled show was the scrapping of the entire orchestration by Tom Pierson. Walker began work in mid-August and produced new charts in time for the Boston opening. The show had a new star for Washington, but closed there nevertheless. While neither partiturs nor invoices have been located, Walker assigned 15% of the pension payments to Goland.

Instr.: 4 reed, 6 brass (2 tpt, 2 tb [1 with euphonium], 2 hrn), 11 strings (6 vln, 2 vla, 2 c, 1 b), piano, accordion, harp, guitar, perc = 26 total.

BALLAD FOR A FIRING SQUAD

Orchestrations credited to Larry **Wilcox**.
Opened December 11, 1968, de Lys (off-Broadway), 7 performances.

Music by Edward Thomas, lyrics by Martin Charnin. A revised version of the 1967 musical *Mata Hari*. Musical direction by Joyce Brown. Dance arrangements by Joe Rago. Other participant: Martin Charnin (director).

BALLYHOO OF 1932

Orchestrations uncredited. (Orchestrations by Hans **Spialek** and others.)

Opened September 6, 1932, 44th Street, 95 performances. Tryout: August 10, Atlantic City; elsewhere.

A revue. Music by Lewis Gensler, lyrics by E. Y. Harburg. Musical direction by Max Meth. Other participant: Bob Hope (featured).

THE BAND WAGON

Orchestrations (virtually totally) by Russell **Bennett**. (Additional orchestrations by Nathaniel Shilkret.)

Opened June 3, 1931, New Amsterdam, 262 performances. Tryout: unknown.

A revue. Music by Arthur Schwartz, lyrics by Howard Dietz. Musical direction by Al Goodman. Other participants: George S. Kaufman (sketch writer); Fred Astaire (star); Adele Astaire (star).

The partiturs are in the Warner/Chappell Collection at the Library of Congress.

The orchestrations are by Bennett, with the following exception:

Shilkret: "Beggar Scene," "Introduction to Beggar Scene" (written on paper with the imprinted logo of "Shilkret Salon Symphony").

Instr.: 5 reed, 5 brass (3 tpt, 1 tb, 1 hrn), 12? strings (8? vln, 0 vla, 3 c, 1 b), piano, guitar/banjo, perc = 25? total.

BANJO EYES

Orchestrations under the supervision of Domenico Savino. (Additional orchestrations by Charles L. Cooke and others.)

Opened December 26, 1941, Hollywood, 126 performances. Tryout: November 7, New Haven (Shubert); Boston.

Music by Vernon Duke, lyrics by John Latouche. Additional lyrics by Harold Adamson. Based on the play *Three Men on a Horse* by John Cecil Holm and George Abbott. Musical direction by Ray Sinatra. Musical arrangements by Domenico Savino and Charles L. Cooke. Vocal arrangements by Buck (Clay) Warnick. Other participant: Eddie Cantor (star).

BAR MITZVAH BOY

Orchestrations and arrangements credited to Irwin **Kostal**. (Additional orchestrators, if any, unknown.)

Opened October 31, 1978, Her Majesty's (London), 77 performances. Tryout: September 25, Manchester, England (Palace).

Music by Jule Styne, lyrics by Don Black. Based on the teleplay by Jack Rosenthal. Musical direction and vocal arrangements by Alexander Faris. Dance arrangements by Ray Holder. Other participants: Martin Charnin (direction); Peter Gennaro (choreographer).

BARBARY COAST

Orchestrations credited to Philip J. **Lang**. (Additional orchestrations by Peter Myers.) Tryout: February 28, 1978, San Francisco. Closed San Francisco.

Music, lyrics, and book by Jack Penzer. Musical direction by Joseph Stecko. Other participants: Kaye Ballard (star); Eddie Foy, Jr. (star).

BAREFOOT BOY WITH CHEEK

Orchestrations credited to Philip J. **Lang**. (Additional orchestrations by Russell **Bennett** and probably others.)

Opened April 3, 1947, Martin Beck, 108 performances. Tryout: March 3, New Haven (Shubert); Boston.

Music by Sidney Lippman, lyrics by Sylvia Dee. Based on the novel by Max Shulman. Musical direction by Milton Rosenstock. Vocal arrangements by Hugh Martin. Assistant vocal arranger, Buster Davis. Other participants: George Abbott (producer, director); Max Shulman (librettist); Robert E. Griffith (stage manager); Nancy Walker (star).

Bennett's invoice is preserved in his journal. Base page rate: $4.50.

Bennett: "I'll Turn a Little Cog."

BARNUM

Orchestrations credited to Hershy **Kay**. (Orchestrations by Michael Gibson, Larry Fallon, Philip J. **Lang**, and Jim Tyler, with Hershy Kay and Sid **Ramin**.) Opened April 30, 1980, St. James, 854 performances.

Music by Cy Coleman, lyrics by Michael Stewart. Suggested by events in the life of Phineas T. Barnum. Musical direction by Peter Howard. Vocal arrangements by Cy Coleman and Jeremy Stone. Other participants: Joe Layton (director, choreographer); Mark Bramble (librettist); Jim Dale (star); Glenn Close (featured).

The partiturs are at Tams-Witmark.

Kay: "Egress Song," "I Like Your Style" (reprise), "One Brick" (chase), "Women's Emporium Scene."

Fallon: "Black and White," "The Colors of My Life," "I Like Your Style."

Gibson: "Bigger Isn't Better," "The Colors of My Life" (reprise), "One Brick at a Time."

Lang: "Jenny Lind's Entrance," "Join the Circus," "The Prince of Humbug."

Tyler: "Clowns," "Thank God I'm Old," "Whipcrack" (underscoring).

Ramin: "Out There."

Other scores:

"Come Follow the Band" uses part of Kay's chart, finished with "Last Chorus" by Lang.

"Finale" is by Tyler, including a section of Lang's chart for "Join the Circus."

"Love Makes Such Fools of Us All" uses part of Kay's chart, finished with "New 2nd Half" by Gibson.

"There Is a Sucker Born Ev'ry Minute": there are early versions, by Kay and Lang, and a note on the scores that says, "show version is a combination of Hershy Kay and Phil Lang scores, with some additions from Cy Coleman." "Ending," for cast album, is by Tyler.

The orchestra reading was disastrous; unbeknown to anyone, Hershy Kay had suffered a stroke sometime after *Evita* opened (in London, in June 1978). "Everything sounded like 'Turkey in the Straw,'" said librettist Mark Bramble. With previews starting almost immediately—the show opened cold in New York—emergency calls went out to practically every orchestrator in town. Kay retained full and sole billing, but practically all of his work was replaced or altered.

(See page 53.)

BEAT THE BAND

Orchestrations credited to Don **Walker**. (Additional orchestrators, if any, unknown.)

Opened October 14, 1942, 46th Street, 67 performances. Tryout: September 17, New Haven (Shubert); elsewhere.

Music by Johnny Green, lyrics by George Marion, Jr. Musical direction by Archie Bleyer. Replacement conductor, Seymour (Robert) Ginzler. Other participant: George Abbott (producer, director, co-librettist).

Hugh Martin was credited for vocal arrangements in New Haven, but not on Broadway. Martin: "I was thrown out. Johnny went to Abbott and said, 'Either Hugh Martin goes, or I go.' George came to me and said, 'I don't like to do this. I can't lose my composer, but I can lose my vocal arranger.'"

The Walker Collection has two abbreviated "cast list" programs, both dated "week beginning October 14, 1942." One lists Jack Whiting (who was reviewed by the critics) in the role of Damon Dillingham; the other lists the pre-*Oklahoma!* Alfred Drake. Martin says that this must have been an error, as he was a friend of Drake and would have known if he had any involvement with the show.

THE BEAUTY PART

Orchestrations by Don **Walker**.

Opened December 26, 1962, Music Box, 85 performances. Tryout: November 24, New Haven (Shubert); December 4, Philadelphia (Locust Street).

A comedy by S. J. Perelman. Incidental music by Don Walker. Musical direction by Abba Bogin. Other participants: Noel Willman (director); Bert Lahr (star); Charlotte Rae (featured); Alice Ghostley (featured); Larry Hagman (featured).

Invoices are in the Walker Collection at the Library of Congress. Base page rate: $3.86.

THANKS AND WISHES   To Walker: "Dear Don, Thank you for everything and very good luck for tonight. Noël Coward."

BEG, BORROW OR STEAL

Orchestrations credited to Peter Matz and Hal Hidey. (Additional orchestrators, if any, unknown.)

Opened February 10, 1960, Martin Beck, 5 performances.

Music by Leon Pober, lyrics and book by Bud Freeman. Musical direction by Hal Hidey. Other participant: Eddie Bracken (producer, star).

BEGGAR'S HOLIDAY

Orchestrations "under the direction of Billy Strayhorn." (Additional orchestrations by Luther Henderson, Hershy **Kay**, Toots Camarata, Charles L. Cooke, Charles Huffine, and Fred Van Epps.)

Opened December 26, 1946, Broadway, 111 performances. Tryout: Boston.

Music by Duke Ellington, lyrics and book by John Latouche. Based on the play *The Beggar's Opera* by John Gay. Musical direction by Max Meth. Vocal arrangements by Crane Calder. Other participants: Alfred Drake (star); Zero Mostel (featured); Herbert Ross (dancer).

BELLS ARE RINGING

Orchestrations credited to Russell **Bennett**. (Additional orchestrations by Joe Glover and Philip J. **Lang**, with Don **Walker** and Robert Noeltner.)

Opened November 29, 1956, Shubert, 924 performances. Tryout: October 15, New Haven (Shubert); Boston (Shubert); November, Philadelphia (Shubert).

Music by Jule Styne, lyrics and book by Betty Comden & Adolph Green. Musical direction by Milton Rosenstock. Vocal arrangements and direction by Herbert Greene and Buster Davis. Dance arrangements and incidental scoring by John Morris. Other participants: Theatre Guild (producer); Jerome Robbins (director, co-choreographer); Bob Fosse (co-choreographer); Judy Holliday (star); Sydney Chaplin (featured).

Invoices are preserved in Bennett's ledger. Base page rate: $6.21. Invoices indicate: Bennett (58%), Lang (19%), Glover (14%).

Bennett: "Bells Are Ringing" (with a 4-bar tag by Walker), "Better than a Dream" (see below), Entr'acte, "Hello, Hello There!" "I Met a Girl," "I'm Going Back," "Is It a Crime?" "It's a Perfect Relationship" (see below), "It's a Simple Little System," "Just in Time," "Long Before I Knew You," "Oogie," Opening ("Susanswerphone" commercial), Overture, "The Party's Over" (two versions), "Salzburg," "You've Got to Do It" (typewriter scene).

Lang: "The Midas Touch" (see below), "Mu-cha-cha," utility ("Just in Time"), numerous fixes.

Glover: "Party Routine (Drop That Name)," utilities ("I Met a Girl," "Just in Time"), utility ("Just in Time"), numerous fixes.

Walker: "On My Own" ("Independent").

Other scores:

"Better than a Dream," which was written for the film version, was orchestrated by Bennett on November 29, 1957 (exactly one year after the opening), and added to the still-running show.

"It's a Perfect Relationship" is by Bennett, replacing an earlier version by Lang.

"The Midas Touch" is by Lang, although the dance section was rewritten by Noeltner (who also did minor fixes elsewhere in the song).

Bennett, in *The Broadway Sound*, makes a point of stating that he wrote *Bells* entirely by himself: "I take full responsibility for every note." Writing twenty years after the fact, in his eighties, he is clearly referring to the wrong show. According to his journals, which begin in mid-1946, the only show that he orchestrated totally by himself after that date was *The Sound of Music*.

Bennett to Walker, after the opening:

> I feel I owe you a further answer to your note of some time ago about getting into the act with *Bells Are Ringing*. There was considerable horsing around about who should do what, and at one time I made a try to get you on the phone but was unsuccessful for some reason. This is a show where the orchestrations can't possibly be what we set for our modern standards because there are a hundred fixes in each number and what is worse, half of them are "you-do-this" fixes. I don't question the advisability of these minor improvements, but it is a kind of show business I haven't seen for some time.... This had better be confidential, of course.

> BUSTER DAVIS: I was supposed to do a Hollywood job with Hugh Martin. When I became available, they used me instead. The guy who was there [Herb Greene] refused to take his name off the show, although he didn't do a single bar. I did very good vocals on that thing, and I resented terribly the fact that I was listed second.

(See page 182.)

BEN FRANKLIN IN PARIS

Orchestrations credited to Philip J. **Lang**. (Additional orchestrators, if any, unknown.)

Opened October 27, 1964, Lunt-Fontanne, 215 performances. Tryout: August 24, Philadelphia (Shubert); September 16, Boston (Shubert).

Music by Mark Sandrich, Jr., lyrics and book by Sidney Michaels. Additional music and lyrics by Jerry Herman. Suggested by events in the life of Benjamin Franklin. Musical direction and vocal arrangements by Donald Pippin. Dance and incidental music by Roger Adams. Other participants: Michael Kidd (director, choreographer); Jerry Herman (additional music and lyrics, uncredited); Robert Preston (star).

(See page 153.)

BEST FOOT FORWARD

Orchestrations by Don **Walker** and Hans **Spialek**. "Overture by Russell **Bennett**." (Additional orchestrations by Ted **Royal**, Robert Noeltner, Jack Mason, Franklyn Marks, and others.)

Opened October 1, 1941, Ethel Barrymore, 326 performances. Tryout: September 11, New Haven (Shubert); September 14, Philadelphia.

Music and lyrics by Hugh Martin and Ralph Blane. Musical direction by Archie Bleyer. Vocal arrangements by Hugh Martin. Other participants: George Abbott (producer, director); Richard Rodgers (producer, unbilled); Gene Kelly (choreographer).

Some of the partiturs are at Tams-Witmark. Walker's invoices are in the Walker Collection at the Library of Congress. Base page rate: $3.

Walker: "Alive and Kicking," "Don't Sell the Night Short" (song and dance), "Juke Box Ballet part 2," "Shady Lady Bird" (song and dance), "That's How I Love the Blues," "The Three Bs" (and encore), "Three Men on a Date" (song and dance), "Travel Dance," "What Do You Think I Am?"

Spialek: "Ev'ry Time" (and reprise), "My First Promise at My First Prom" (see below).

Bennett: act II Curtain (Opening), "Buckle Down Winsocki," Overture.

Marks: "Just a Little Joint with a Juke Box" (replacing an earlier version by Walker).

Royal: "Don't Sell the Night Short" (utility).

Noeltner: utilities ("Ev'ry Time," "What Do You Think I Am?").

Mason(?): Entr'acte, waltz dance.

Other scores:

Finale Ultimo: part I is by Spialek, part II is by Walker.

"The Guy Who Brought Me": part I is by Mason(?), part II (Patter) is by Walker.

"My First Promise at My First Prom" is by Spialek, with dance section by Mason(?).

Overture: this was likely a string of utilities. Fragments exist, by both Walker and Spialek. At one point, there is an instruction in Walker's hand to "copy from Russell Bennett's score" although the following page, which would identify the song (probably "Buckle Down Winsocki"), is missing.

> MARTIN: Rodgers was the silent co-producer but he handled the musical side. Dick was very surprised when I asked for Don, he thought I'd ask for Russell Bennett or Hans. I remember Dick asking me who I wanted. "Are you sure you want me to choose the orchestrator, Dick? You're the master." He said, "When I write a song, I know how I want it to sound in the pit, and I'm sure you do, too. So I want you to choose."

The orchestrations were apparently split mostly between Walker and Spialek, but relatively little evidence of Spialek's work has survived.

Note to drummer on score of "Alive and Kicking": "Catch acrobat trick."

Instr.: 5 reed (including 5 sax), 6 brass (3 tpt, 3 tb), 6 strings (3 vln, 1 vla, 1 c, 1 b), piano, guitar, perc = 20 total.

(See page 102.)

BETWEEN THE DEVIL

Orchestrations credited to Hans **Spialek** and Conrad Salinger. (Additional orchestrations by Arden Cornwell, Edward B. Powell, Phil Wall, and probably others.)

Opened December 22, 1937, Imperial, 93 performances. Tryout: October 14, New Haven (Shubert); elsewhere.

Music by Arthur Schwartz, lyrics and book by Howard Dietz. Musical direction by Don Vorhees. Other participant: Jack Buchanan (star).

BIG DEAL

Orchestrations credited to Ralph **Burns**. (Additional orchestrators, if any, unknown.)

Opened April 10, 1986, Broadway, 70 performances. Tryout: February 12, Boston (Shubert).

Music and lyrics by various writers. Based on the film *Big Deal on Madonna Street* by Mario Monicelli. Music arranged and conducted by Gordon Lowry Harrell. Other participant: Bob Fosse (director, choreographer, librettist).

BILLION DOLLAR BABY

Orchestrations (totally) by Philip J. **Lang** and Allan Small.

Opened December 21, 1945, Alvin, 219 performances. Tryout: November, Boston.

Music by Morton Gould, lyrics and book by Betty Comden & Adolph Green. Musical direction by Max Goberman. Dance arrangements by Trude Rittman. Other participants: Oliver Smith (co-producer); George Abbott (director); Jerome Robbins (choreographer); Robert E. Griffith (stage manager).

Copies of the partiturs are at Tams-Witmark.

Lang: "Atlantic City" (dance and choral tag), "Bad Timing," "Billion Dollar Baby," "Dreams Come True," "Fight in Dapper's Apartment," "Floats in Reverse," "Funeral," "I've Got a One Track Mind," "Movie Ballet," "Newboy," Overture, "Pals," "Wedding."

Small: "Broadway Blossom," "Charleston" ("Speakeasy Ballet"), "Faithless," "I'm Sure of Your Love," "(I'm Sure of Your) Love Ballet," "Lovely Girl," Marathon Dance, "There I'd Be."

Other scores:

"Time of My Life (Havin' a Time)": song is by Small, "Drum Routine" and utility by Lang.

This unconventional dance musical reunited the entire production team—with the exception of Leonard Bernstein—of *On the Town*, which opened precisely fifty-one weeks before. Lightning didn't strike a second time; the results were innovative and impressive, but the show did not hit the same brilliant chord as its predecessor.

> LANG: It was my first show, and I was all around the theatre. I remember for the first performance I stood in the balcony, and it was really too loud in the balcony. So I went

downstairs and finally got ahold of Mr. Abbott and I said, "You know, Mr. Abbott, I know it isn't my province and I shouldn't say so, but the music is fine in the orchestra," and he said, "Yes, I know, it is delicious." "But," I said, "it is too loud in the balcony." "Phil," Abbott said, "down here they pay $6.60, up there they pay $1.10. Let's pitch it for the people who pay $6.60."

Note to copyist on Small's manuscript of "Speakeasy Ballet": "Sherman, have Phil pick up tag and orchestrate it."

Instr.: 6 reed (4 sax), 8 brass (3 tpt, 3 tb, 2 hrn), ? strings (vln, vla, c, b), 2 perc.

(See page 68.)

BILLY ROSE'S AQUACADE

Orchestrations uncredited. (Orchestrations by Ted **Royal**, Hans **Spialek**, and others.)

Opened May 4, 1939, Flushing, New York (Aquacade, New York World's Fair). Tryout: none.

A revue built around swimming sequences. Music by Dana Suesse, lyrics by Billy Rose and Ted Fetter. Other participants: John Murray Anderson (director); Eleanor Holm (star); Johnny Weismuller (star).

BILLY ROSE'S JUMBO

Orchestrations by Murray Cutter, Joseph Nusbaum, Hans **Spialek**, Adolph Deutsch, and Russell **Bennett**.

Opened November 16, 1935, Hippodrome, 233 performances.

Music by Richard Rodgers, lyrics by Lorenz Hart. Musical direction by Adolph Deutsch. Vocal direction by Charles Henderson. Other participants: Billy Rose (producer); George Abbott (book director); Ben Hecht and Charles MacArthur (librettists); Jimmy Durante (star); Paul Whiteman (star).

The partiturs are in the Billy Rose Collection at the New York Public Library.

Cutter: Circus Train, Circus Waltz, "Diavolo" (see below), "Durante's Wedding Song," "The More I See of Other Girls," "The Most Beautiful Girl in the World" (see below), "Robin, the Musical Clown," "Women" (see below).

Nusbaum: "Memories of Madison Square Garden," "We Won't Go Home."

Spialek: Circus Medley, "My Romance" (see below), Opening.

Deutsch: "Calliope" (Finale act II), "Over and Over Again" (see below).

Other scores:

"The Circus Is on Parade": there are two versions, presumably both used, one by Cutter and one by Nusbaum.

"Diavolo" (song and "agitato & 2nd vocal ensemble") is by Cutter; "Aeroplane," fanfare, and utility are by Nusbaum; "Special" is by Spialek.

"Laugh": first section is by Cutter, second section by Nusbaum.

"March of the Clowns": there are two versions, presumably both used, one by Spialek and one ("revised") by Nusbaum.

"The Most Beautiful Girl in the World": song, "Single Horse Routine," and "Intro to Foster Girls Riding Routine" are by Nusbaum; "Part II" is by Cutter.

"My Romance": song is by Spialek; "Incidental Act I" by Deutsch; finale, utility, and reprise by Cutter. Entr'acte version is a combination of Spialek and Cutter.

"Ostermayer's March": 1st step and tango are by Cutter; 3rd step and 4th step are by Nusbaum.

"Over and Over Again" is by Deutsch; incidental is by Cutter; "Babette's Routine" (wire walker and aerialist) is by Nusbaum.

"Song of the Razorbacks" ("Song of the Roustabouts") is mostly by Nusbaum. There is a second version by Bennett. "Tag" is by Cutter.

"Women": there are two versions by Cutter and an extended introduction by Deutsch.

The score for "Little Girl Blue" is missing, but presumably by Spialek.

Scrawled on the back of the score for "The Most Beautiful Girl in the World": "to be ready by 2 a.m."

Jumbo was a combination of musical comedy, circus, and extravaganza. Thus, a given song might be sung, used for a parade, and accompany a horse act. And then it would be used for the girls on the trapeze. The orchestrations were by committee, with orchestrators often switching off for different sections of the extended numbers. Paul Whiteman brought along his own band arrangers for his sections of the show. (A fair amount of the charts are written on paper that is engraved "Paul Whiteman's JUMBO Orchestra"—one of only two examples we found of score paper printed with the title of a show.) Spialek seems to have been assigned by Chappell to give Rodgers at least one theatre man. His work is readily identifiable, as he used Chappell No. 5 paper. Due to much overlapping and switching of hands, the *Jumbo* identifications are necessarily approximate.

Instr.: 6 reed, 9 brass (4 tpt, 4 tb, tuba), ? strings (vln, vla, c, b), 2 piano (one with organ/celesta), guitar, perc.

BLESS YOU ALL

Orchestrations by Don **Walker**. (Additional orchestrations by Robert **Ginzler**, Irwin **Kostal**, and Philip J. **Lang**, with Allan Small.)

Opened December 14, 1950, Mark Hellinger, 84 performances. Tryout: November 13, New Haven (Shubert); November 21, Philadelphia (Forrest).

A revue. Music and lyrics by Harold Rome. Musical direction and vocal arrangements by Lehman Engel. Ballet music composed and arranged by Mischa Portnoff and Wesley Portnoff, and Don Walker. Other participants: Herman Levin and Oliver Smith (producers); John C. Wilson (director); Pearl Bailey (star).

The partiturs are in the Rome Collection at Yale. Invoices are at the Library of Congress. Base page rate: $5.10.

Walker: "Baby Sitters," "Bless You All" (song and utility), "The Desert Flame" (ballet composed by Walker; page 83 is marked "The End! [for now]"), "I Can Hear It Now" (song, dance, and utility), "Little Things Meant So Much to Me" (with "New Intro" by Ginzler), "Little White House," "Love Letter to Manhattan," "Rose Is a Rose" (song, utility, and "Rose Ballet"), "Take Off the Coat," "You Never Know What Hit You" (and encore).

Ginzler: "Finale Act I," "Finale Ultimo," "Heaven Commercial (A and B)," "Love That Man," "TV Crossover."

Kostal: "Be a Folk Singer," "Do You Know a Better Way to Make a Living?" "Don't Want to Write about the Southland" (with 8-bar "Truman Capote Intro" by Ginzler), "The Paintings," "Victory Blues."

Lang: "Weekend," utilities ("Love Letter to Manhattan," "Summer Dresses," "Take Off the Coat," "Weekend").

Other scores:

Entr'acte: bridgework is by Walker, incorporating utilities by others.

"Summer Dresses" is mostly by Lang, with 20-bar "Intro" by Small and "Insert" by Ginzler.

"Thirty Years Ago" is by Ginzler (7 pages) and Walker (10 pages), with edits throughout by Kostal.

"Take Off the Coat" and "You Never Know What Hit You" were originally used in the Walker-Bennett *That's the Ticket!* (1948). While Walker reorchestrated these numbers for the new show, Bennett's original charts are included with the *Bless You All* partiturs.

THANKS AND WISHES   Opening night, from Rome to Walker: *Thanks for the best orchestrations I've ever had.*

To Walker from critic Robert Coleman: "Don, you did two notable jobs this year: the arrangements for *Call Me Madam* and *Bless You All*. I particularly liked your use of the guitar in the *Bless You All* pit. I also liked Russ Bennett's use of two harps in the *Out of This World* musical ensemble."

Instr.: 5 reed, 7 brass (3 tpt, 3 tb, 1 hrn), 10? strings (4? vln, 2? vla, 3? c, 1 b), piano, guitar, perc = 25? total. (See page 210.)

BLOOMER GIRL

Orchestrations credited to Russell **Bennett**. (Additional orchestrations by Ted **Royal** and
  probably others.)
Opened October 5, 1944, Shubert, 654 performances. Tryout: September 11, Philadel-
  phia (Forrest).
Music by Harold Arlen, lyrics by E. Y. Harburg. Based on an unproduced play by Dan
  James and Lillith James. Musical direction by Leon Leonardi. Rehearsal pianist, Trude
  Rittman. Other participants: John C. Wilson (producer); E. Y. Harburg (director);
  Agnes de Mille (choreographer); Celeste Holm (star).

BLUE EYES

Orchestrations credited to Russell **Bennett**. (Additional orchestrators, if any, unknown.)
Opened April 27, 1928, Piccadilly (London), 276 performances. Tryout: April 9, South-
  sea, England (Kings).
Music by Jerome Kern, lyrics by Graham John. Musical direction by Kennedy Russell.
  Other participants: Guy Bolton and Graham John (librettists).

THE BODY BEAUTIFUL

Orchestrations credited to Ted **Royal**. (Additional orchestrations by John Lesko, Paul Weirick, Charles L. Cooke, and Robert Noeltner.)

Opened January 23, 1958, Broadway, 60 performances. Tryout: December 1957, Philadelphia (Erlanger).

Music by Jerry Bock, lyrics by Sheldon Harnick. Musical direction and vocal arrangements by Milton Greene. Ballet music by Genevieve Pitot. Other participants: Herbert Ross (choreographer); Joseph Stein (co-librettist).

(See page 239.)

BONANZA BOUND

Orchestrations credited to Philip J. **Lang**. (Additional orchestrations by Russell **Bennett** and others.)

Tryout: December 26, 1947, Philadelphia (Shubert). Closed January 3, 1948, Philadelphia.

Music by Saul Chaplin, lyrics and book by Betty Comden & Adolph Green. Musical direction by Lehman Engel. Vocal arrangements by Saul Chaplin. Dance arrangements by Trude Rittman. Other participants: Herman Levin (co-producer); Oliver Smith (co-producer); Jack Cole (choreographer); Adolph Green (featured); Allyn McLerie (featured); Gwen Verdun [*sic*] (dancer).

Bennett's invoice is preserved in his journal. Base page rate: $4.80.

Bennett: "It Was Meant to Be."

THE BOY FRIEND

Orchestrations credited to Ted **Royal** and Charles L. Cooke. (Additional orchestrations by Marion Evans and others.)

Opened September 30, 1954, Royale, 485 performances.

Music, lyrics, and book by Sandy Wilson. Musical direction by Anton Coppola. Conducted by Charles McGrane. Other participants: Feuer & Martin (producers); Julie Andrews (featured).

BOYS AND GIRLS TOGETHER

Orchestrations credited to Hans **Spialek**. (Additional orchestrations by Russell **Bennett**, Don **Walker**, and others.)

Opened October 1, 1940. Broadhurst, 191 performances. Tryout: Boston.

A revue. Music by Sammy Fain, lyrics by Irving Kahal and Jack Yellen. Musical direction by John McManus. Other participant: Ed Wynn (producer, director, star).

Walker's invoice is in the Walker Collection at the Library of Congress. Base page rate: $3.

Walker: "But Can He Dance?" (song and specialty).

THE BOYS FROM SYRACUSE

Orchestrations by Hans **Spialek**. (Additional orchestrations by Maurice de Packh, Hilding Anderson, Walter Paul, Menotti Salta, and others.)

Opened November 23, 1938, Alvin, 235 performances. Tryout: November 3, New Haven (Shubert); November 7, Boston (Shubert).

Music by Richard Rodgers, lyrics by Lorenz Hart. Based on the play *The Comedy of Errors* by William Shakespeare. Musical direction by Harry Levant. Vocal arrangement for "Sing for Your Supper" by Hugh Martin. Other participants: George Abbott (producer, director, librettist); George Balanchine (choreographer); Eddie Albert (star).

Copies of the partiturs are at the offices of the Rodgers & Hammerstein Organization.

Spialek: Entr'acte (except final 3 bars, by unidentified hand #1), "Falling in Love with Love" (except for 4 bars "Added to Intro" by de Packh), "Fanfare," Opening act I ("He Had Twins"), "What Can You Do with a Man" (except for 2-bar modulation into third refrain, by unidentified hand #1), "You Have Cast Your Shadow on the Sea."

Anderson: "Big Brother," "Come with Me."

Paul: "Finale Ultimo."

de Packh: "Masks."

Salta: Ballet, "Finale Act I (Let Antipholus In)."

Other scores:

"Dear Old Syracuse": intro and sections A, B, and C are by Spialek; section D, interlude, and section E are by unidentified hand #2.

"He and She": verse and refrain are by Spialek; encore is by Paul.

"Ladies of the Evening": intro is by Paul; song is by Spialek; "Ladies Dance" is by unidentified hand #1.

"Oh, Diogenes": verse and song are by de Packh; dance is by Paul; "C Chorus" is by de Packh.

Overture: opening, connective sections, and closing are by Spialek; the four song sections are by Paul.

"The Shortest Day of the Year": verse and first refrain are by Spialek; "Chorus B" is by Salta.

"Sing for Your Supper": first and third refrains are by de Packh; second refrain is by Paul; fourth refrain is by Spialek; fifth refrain ("Rhumba" [*sic*]) and "Insert" are by Salta.

"This Can't Be Love": verse and "Refrain A" are by Spialek; "Refrain B" is by Paul; "Reprise Act II (This Must Be Love)" is by de Packh.

Instr.: 4 reed (including 3 sax), 4 brass (2 tpt, 1 tb, 1 hrn), 15? strings (8? vln, 4? vla, 2 c, 1 b), piano, harp, perc = 26? total.

(See page 188.)

THE BOYS FROM SYRACUSE (1963 REVIVAL)

Orchestrations credited to Larry **Wilcox**. (Additional orchestrators, if any, unknown.)

Opened April 15, 1963, Theatre Four (off-Broadway), 502 performances.

Musical and choral direction by Rene Wiegert. Ballet music by Peter Matz. Other participant: Karen Morrow (featured).

THE BOYS FROM SYRACUSE (LONDON)

Orchestrations credited to Ralph **Burns**. (Additional orchestrators, if any, unknown.)
Opened November 7, 1963, Theatre Royal, Drury Lane (London), 100 performances.
Musical direction by Robert Lowe.

Instr.: 7 reed (5 sax), 5 brass (3 tpt, 2 tb), ? strings (vln, 0 vla, c, I b), harp, guitar, perc.

BRAVO GIOVANNI

Orchestrations and arrangements by Robert **Ginzler**. Dance (and other) orchestrations
by Luther Henderson. (Additional orchestrations by Don **Walker**.)
Opened May 19, 1962, Broadhurst, 76 performances. Tryout: Detroit; Philadelphia.
Music by Milton Schafer, lyrics by Ronny Graham. Based on the novel *The Crime of Gio-
vanni Venturi* by Howard Shaw. Musical direction, continuity, and vocal arrangements
by Anton Coppola. Dance music arranged and orchestrated by Luther Henderson.
Other participants: Stanley Prager (director); Carol Haney (choreographer); Cesare
Siepi (star); Michele Lee (featured).

Copies of the partiturs are in a private collection.

The orchestrations are by Ginzler, with the following exceptions:

Henderson: "I'm All I've Got," "Miranda's Entrance," "Night Club Sequence" (introduction, "Signora Pandolfi," and "The Kangaroo"), "Uriti Kitchen" ("Kangaroo" instrumental).

Walker: "Bravo Giovanni" (see below), "Discovery of Tomb," introduction to act I,
"Lobsterscope," "Museum," Pantomime, "Virtue, Arrivederci," "Why Argue?" utilities
("The Argument," "Piazza").

Other scores:

"Ah, Caminare": part 1 (Street Singer), part 2 (utility), part 3 (Block Party), and part
4 (Block Party Continued) are by Henderson; act 2 Finale is by Ginzler.

"Bravo Giovanni": part 1 (song), part 2 (Gavotte), part 3 ("Miranda Angry"), and
part 4 ("Giovanni") are by Walker, with part 3 incorporating a brief section "from RG's
old score."

Temporary Overture: the first part is by Walker, the second by Ginzler.

"Valise Song" ("Jump In") is mostly by Ginzler, with the opening section by Walker.

"We Won't Discuss It" is by Ginzler, with "Tag" by Walker.

RED'S INSTRUCTIONS TO MUSICIANS   On "Beautiful Rome," Ginzler tells the percussionist to use "Bells with mallets softer than the cheeks of a new born baby's ass."

BREAKFAST AT TIFFANY'S

Orchestrations credited to Ralph **Burns**. (Additional orchestrations by Larry **Wilcox** and
possibly others.)
Tryout: (as *Holly Golightly*) October 10, 1966, Philadelphia (Forrest); November 1,
Boston (Shubert). Closed December 14 during previews, New York (Majestic).
Music and lyrics by Bob Merrill. Based on the novella by Truman Capote. Musical direc-
tion by and vocal arrangements by Stanley Lebowsky. Dance arrangements by Marvin

Laird. Other participants: David Merrick (producer); Abe Burrows (original director, original librettist); Michael Kidd (choreographer); Edward Albee (replacement librettist); Mary Tyler Moore (star); Richard Chamberlain (star).

The partiturs are in the Merrick Collection at the Library of Congress (unexamined).

The partiturs were only partially available, but a quick glance revealed contributions by Larry Wilcox (as on other Burns shows of the period).

BRIGADOON

Orchestrations credited to Ted **Royal**. (Additional orchestrations by Robert Noeltner, Philip J. **Lang**, and probably others.)

Opened March 13, 1947, Ziegfeld, 581 performances. Tryout: February 6, New Haven (Shubert); February 10, Boston (Colonial); February 24, Philadelphia (Forrest).

Music by Frederick Loewe, lyrics and book by Alan Jay Lerner. Musical direction by Franz Allers. Vocal arrangements by Frederick Loewe. "Musical assistant to Miss de Mille," Trude Rittman. Other participants: Cheryl Crawford (producer); Robert Lewis (director); Agnes de Mille (choreographer).

Tams-Witmark has a conformed set of partiturs in a copyist's hand. Partial invoices are at the New York Public Library. Base page rate: $4.50.

Lang: "Opening Act One," "My Mother's Wedding Day Dance," utilities ("Almost Like Being in Love," "Come to Me, Bend to Me," "The Heather on the Hill").

Noeltner: "Come to Me, Bend to Me Ballet," "Sword Dance."

Other scores:

Entr'acte incorporates Lang's utilities, as well as an unspecified 13-page section by Noeltner.

(See page 81.)

BRIGHT LIGHTS OF 1944

Orchestrations uncredited. (Orchestrations by Russell **Bennett**, Hans **Spialek**, Ted **Royal**, and others.)

Opened September 16, 1943, Forrest, 4 performances.

A revue. Music by Jerry Livingston, lyrics by Mack David. Musical direction by Max Meth. Other participants: Alexander H. Cohen (producer); Joseph Kipness (associate producer); James Barton (star); Joe Smith & Charles Dale (stars).

BRING BACK BIRDIE

Orchestrations by Ralph **Burns** (supervising orchestrator), Stanley Applebaum, Daniel Troob, Philip J. **Lang**, Jim Tyler, Gary Anderson, Gerald Alters, Scott Kuney, Coleridge-Taylor Perkinson, and Charles Strouse.

Opened March 5, 1981, Martin Beck, 4 performances. Tryout: none.

Music by Charles Strouse, lyrics by Lee Adams. Suggested by characters from the musical *Bye Bye Birdie.* Musical direction and vocal arrangements by Mark Hummel. Dance arrangements by Daniel Troob. Other participants: Michael Stewart (librettist); Joe Layton (director, choreographer); Donald O'Connor (star); Chita Rivera (star).

Most of the partiturs are at Tams-Witmark.

Burns: Finale act I, "Flamenco," "I Like What I Do," "I Love 'Em All," "Middle Age Blues" (and reprise), Overture (see below), "Shape Up," "Twenty Happy Years" (and reprise), "Well, I'm Not!" (and reprise).

Applebaum: "Bring Back Birdie" (see below), "Don't Say I'm F-A-T," "Rosie," "When Will Grown-Ups Grow Up?" "You Can Never Go Back."

Troob: "He's a Man Worth Fightin' For," "Inner Peace," Prelude.

Tyler: "Baby, You Can Count on Me" (see below), "Young."

Lang: "Back in Show Biz Again."

Alters: "Half of a Couple."

Anderson: "Movin' Out."

Perkinson: "There's a Brand New Beat in Heaven."

Other scores:

"Baby, You Can Count on Me" is by Tyler, with a tag by Troob.

"Bring Back Birdie" is by Applebaum, replacing an earlier version by Lang.

Overture and Entr'acte are by Burns, with inserts by Applebaum.

The original cast album lists song-by-song orchestrator credits, which in several cases do not match the handwriting on the scores.

I asked Strouse why *Bring Back Birdie* used ten orchestrators: "That was a problem, the orchestration was in tatters. I was director of music for a big advertising agency, and I met a lot of really, really clever guys who'd worked with synthesizers. I think, in hindsight, one musical consciousness is better than having many of them. Looking back at the experience, I think maybe that was a mistake."

BUTTRIO SQUARE

Orchestrations credited to Don **Walker**. (Additional orchestrators unknown.)

Opened October 14, 1952, Century, 7 performances. Tryout: none.

Music by Arthur Jones and Fred Stamer, lyrics by Gen Genovese.

Based on a play by Hal Cranton. Musical direction and vocal arrangements by Maurice Levine. Dance music composed and arranged by Roger Adams.

One partitur ("The Tarantella" by Walker) is in the Walker Collection at the Library of Congress.

BY JUPITER

Orchestrations credited to Don **Walker**. (Additional orchestrators unknown.)

Opened June 3, 1942, Shubert, 427 performances. Tryout: (as *All's Fair*) May 11, Boston (Shubert).

Music by Richard Rodgers, lyrics by Lorenz Hart, book by Rodgers and Hart. Based on the play *The Warrior's Husband* by Julian F. Thompson. Musical direction by Johnny Green. Replacement conductor, Seymour (Robert) Ginzler. Vocal arrangements by Johnny Green and Buck (Clay) Warnick. Other participants: Joshua Logan (director); Ray Bolger (star).

BY JUPITER (1967 REVIVAL)

Orchestrations credited to Abba Bogin. (Additional orchestrations by Jonathan Tunick.)
Opened January 19, 1967, Theatre Four (off-Broadway), 118 performances.
Music by Richard Rodgers, lyrics by Lorenz Hart. Based on the play *The Warrior's Husband* by Julian F. Thompson. Musical direction by Milton Setzer. Other participants: Fred Ebb (additional material); Bob Dishy (star).

BY THE BEAUTIFUL SEA

Orchestrations by Russell **Bennett**. (Additional orchestrations by Joe Glover.)
Opened April 8, 1954, Majestic, 270 performances. Tryout: February 15, New Haven (Shubert); February 23, Boston; March 16, Philadelphia.
Music by Arthur Schwartz, lyrics and book by Dorothy Fields. Musical direction and vocal arrangements by Jay Blackton. Dance arrangements by Genevieve Pitot (uncredited). Other participants: Robert Fryer (co-producer); Herbert Fields (co-librettist); Shirley Booth (star).

The partiturs are at Music Theatre International. Invoices are preserved in Bennett's ledger. Base page rate: $5.70. Invoices indicate: Bennett (78%), Glover (22%).

Bennett: "Alone Too Long," "Baby Brother" ("Lottie Gibson Specialty"), "Coney Island Boat" (see below), "Dreamland" ("Throw the Anchor Away"), "Hang Up!" "Happy Habit," "Hooray for George the Third" (see below), "I'd Rather Wake Up by Myself," "More Love than Your Love," Overture, "Serpentina Sal" (see below), and numerous incidentals.

Glover: Can-Can, "Happy Habit" (reprise), "Me and Pollyanna" (song and dance), "Mona from Arizona" (see below), "Olio Sequence," and many minor fixes.

Other scores:

"By the Beautiful Sea": the first part is by Bennett. The instrumental continuation, after the end of the vocal, is by Glover.

"Coney Island Boat" is by Bennett, with an added section (labeled "new material") by Glover.

"Good Time Charley" is written in several parts. "New Intro Charley Maestoso" is by Bennett. "Vocal" through the end of the kewpie doll section, is by Bennett. "Good Time Charley Vignettes" are mostly by Bennett, with the final vignette ("The Iceman Cometh") by Glover. "Good Time Chas. Finale" is by Bennett. Reprise is by Glover. The cast album version consists of "Vocal" (preceded by a 2-bar intro) and an abridged version of "Finale."

"Hooray for George the Third" is by Bennett. Glover wrote an earlier version, part of which is used as a utility.

"Mona from Arizona" (Opening act I) is by Glover. "Intro to Mona" is by Bennett.

"Old Enough to Love" is in three parts (all by Bennett). "Old Enough New" is the vocal section. The score then instructs the copyist to "transpose from 'Tuscaloosa,'" "Tuscaloosa" being an earlier version of the song cut from the prior Schwartz/Fields/Bennett/Glover show *A Tree Grows in Brooklyn*. After the "soft shoe (stop-time)" section, the number picks up with "End of Mickey's Dance." The cast recording presents a highly abridged version of the dance.

Overture is by Bennett, incorporating his utilities for "Alone Too Long," "By the Beautiful Sea," and "More Love than Your Love."

"The Sea Song" ("Beautiful Sea"): the first part is by Bennett; the instrumental continuation after the vocal by Glover.

"Serpentina Sal" is mostly by Bennett, with a 24-bar replacement section at the beginning of the song section by Glover (tempo marking: "South American").

This was Bennett's first musical theatre work after a hiatus of two years (during which he worked, most notably, on the TV documentary series *Victory at Sea*). For *Beautiful Sea*, he borrowed scoring sheets from his officemate Don Walker; Walker's name, printed at the bottom of the pages, has been carefully razor-bladed off many, but not all, of the songs.

Instr.: 5 reed, 6 brass (3 tpt, 2 tb, 1 hrn), 15? strings (10?vln, 2?vla, 2 c, 1 b), perc = 27? total.

(See page 195.)

BYE BYE BIRDIE

Orchestrations (mostly) by Robert **Ginzler**. Additional scoring by Elliot Lawrence. (Additional orchestrations by Charles Strouse.)

Opened April 14, 1960, Martin Beck, 607 performances. Tryout: March, Philadelphia (Shubert).

Music by Charles Strouse, lyrics by Lee Adams. Musical direction and additional scoring by Elliott Lawrence. Dance arrangements by John Morris. Other participants: Gower Champion (director, choreographer); Michael Stewart (librettist); Dick Van Dyke (star); Chita Rivera (star).

Copies of the partiturs are at Tams-Witmark.

The orchestrations are by Ginzler, with the following exceptions:

Lawrence: "English Teacher," "Honestly Sincere."

Strouse: "Entr'acte A," "Overture A," "TV Theme Underscoring."

Other scores:

Overture: "Overture A" is by Strouse, although it was used only in New York. (This was synchronized to the fake newsreel footage that opened the show, and is orchestrated in a Chuck Jones cartoon style—and very well, too.) "Entr'acte B," which was used as the Overture in all subsequent productions and is heard as the Overture on the Broadway and London cast albums, is by Ginzler.

Instr.: 5 reed (including 5 sax, 5 clr, 4 fl, 2 picc), 7 brass (3 tpt, 3 tb, 1 hrn), 10 strings (6 vln, 0 vla, 3 c, 1 b), harp, guitar, 2 perc = 26 total.

(See pages 19, 45, 193, 275, 279.)

CABARET

Orchestrations (mostly) by Don **Walker**. (Additional orchestrations by Arthur Beck, with Jim Tyler.)

Opened November 20, 1966, Broadhurst, 1,166 performances. Tryout: October, Boston (Shubert).

Music by John Kander, lyrics by Fred Ebb. Based on the play *I Am a Camera* by John Van Druten, from stories by Christopher Isherwood. Musical direction by Harold Hastings. Dance arrangements by David Baker. Other participants: Harold Prince (producer, director); Ronald Field (choreographer); Lotte Lenya (star); Joel Grey (featured).

A reasonably legible copy of the partiturs (marked and pasted with changes made for the 1987 revival) is at Tams-Witmark. Invoices are in the Walker Collection at the Library of Congress. Base page rate: $10.

The orchestrations are by Walker, with the following exceptions:

Beck: bows, "Married Reprise," Prelude act I, Prelude act II, utilities ("Married," "Pineapple/Couldn't Please Me More").

Tyler: "Kick Line I," "Kick Line II."

Other scores:

"So What?" is by Walker, with revised 8-bar introduction by Beck.

"Telephone Song" is by Walker, with revised 10-bar introduction and "Telephone Tag" by Beck.

"Tomorrow Belongs to Me" is by Walker, with revised 4-bar introduction by Beck.

THANKS AND WISHES Opening night 1966, from Kander to Walker: "It looks to me as if an F seventh must lead naturally to a G seventh; otherwise, how can you explain that line in front of the theatre? Many thanks for making me sound so good."

Opening night 1987, from Kander to Walker (who was ill and unable to participate): "You were certainly very much with us on opening night. Your wonderful work sounds even more impressive after twenty-one years. You will always be an important part of *Cabaret*."

(See page 110.)

CABIN IN THE SKY

Orchestrations credited to Charles L. Cooke, Fudd Livingston, Domenico Savino, and Nathan Lang Van Cleave. (Additional orchestrators, if any, unknown.)

Opened October 25, 1940, Martin Beck, 156 performances. Tryout: none.

Music by Vernon Duke, lyrics by John Latouche. Musical direction by Max Meth. Vocal arrangements by Hugh Martin. Other participants: Vinton Freedley (co-producer); George Balanchine (co-director, choreographer); Ethel Waters (star); Todd Duncan (featured); Katherine Dunham (featured).

CAFE CROWN

Orchestrations credited to Hershy **Kay**. (Additional orchestrations by Bill Stegmeyer, Jack Andrews, and Jay Brower.)

Opened April 17, 1964, Martin Beck, 3 performances. Tryout: unknown.

Music by Albert Hague, lyrics by Marty Brill. Based on the play by Hy Kraft. Musical direction and vocal arrangements by Gershon Kingsley. Dance music by Albert Hague. Other participants: Ronald Field (choreographer); Sam Levene (star).

CALAMITY JANE

Orchestrations credited to Philip J. **Lang.** (Additional orchestrators, if any, unknown.)

Tryout: May 27, 1961, Fort Worth, Texas (Casa Mañana). Closed July, Framingham, Massachusetts.

Music by Sammy Fain, lyrics by Paul Francis Webster. A stage adaptation of the MGM film. Musical direction by Edwin McArthur. Other participant: Edith Adams (star).

CALL ME MADAM

Orchestrations by Don **Walker.** (Additional orchestrations by Joe Glover and probably others.)

Opened October 12, 1950, Imperial, 644 performances. Tryout: September 11, New Haven (Shubert); September 19, Boston (Colonial).

Music and lyrics by Irving Berlin. Musical direction by Jay Blackton. Dance arrangements by Genevieve Pitot and Jesse Meeker. Piano arrangements by Helmy Kresa. Other participants: Leland Hayward (producer); George Abbott (director); Jerome Robbins (choreographer); Ethel Merman (star).

The partiturs for the cut numbers are in the Berlin Collection at the Library of Congress. Walker's invoices are in the Walker Collection at the Library of Congress. Base page rate: $5.10.

Walker: "Best Thing for You" (utility), Finale Act II, "Free" (song and utility), "Our Day of Independence," "They Like Ike" (cut original and "revised and expanded" versions).

Other scores:

New York Overture is apparently by Glover, incorporating utilities by Walker and others.

The location of most of the partiturs is unknown, but they were examined by Tommy Krasker and Robert Kimball for their *Catalog of the American Musical* (1988). Their findings include the following additional attributions:

Walker: "The Best Thing for You," "Can You Use Any Money Today?" "Lichtenburg," "Mrs. Sally Adams," "The Ocarina," "Once upon a Time Today," "They Like Ike," "Washington Square Dance."

Glover: "It's a Lovely Day Today," "Marrying for Love," "Something to Dance About," "You're Just in Love."

They also indicate that "Hostess with the Mostess," among other numbers, was by neither Walker nor Glover (who received program credit for additional orchestrations) but by an unrecognized hand—which is most probably Ginzler, who did the somewhat similar "One Hundred Easy Ways" for Walker in *Wonderful Town.*

The extensive dance arrangement for "Something to Dance About" was most probably arranged by Meeker, whose credit did not appear until after the New Haven opening.

From Walker to general manager Herman Bernstein, during the Boston tryout:

> Although as arranged with Irving I have been holding myself available and have been awaiting a call to Boston, I was rather surprised not to have heard anything. I am still more surprised to hear that others are now working on the orchestration. Please let me know what your desires are so that I can make my plans accordingly. Whatever you set up with your new people, please be sure to call their attention to my billing clause. Also, please tell me what you'd like me to do regarding the show album.

Clearly, someone—either Berlin or Merman—was unhappy enough to force Walker out. This must have been an unpleasant experience for director Abbott and choreographer Robbins, who were already among Don's most loyal customers.

Instr.: 5 reed (including 5 sax), 6 brass (3 tpt, 2 tb, 1 hrn), 13 strings (8 vln [including 1 doubling on mandolin and guitar], 2 vla, 2 c, 1 b), piano, perc = 26 total.

CALL ME MISTER

Orchestrations credited to Ben Ludlow. (Additional orchestrations by Charles Huffine, Julian Work, and probably others.)

Opened April 18, 1946, National, 734 performances. Tryout: March 14, New Haven (Shubert); elsewhere.

A revue. Music and lyrics by Harold Rome. Musical direction and vocal arrangements by Lehman Engel. Other participants: Melvyn Douglas (co-producer); Herman Levin (co-producer).

CALLING ALL STARS

Orchestrations uncredited. (Orchestrations by Hans **Spialek**, Conrad Salinger, and others.)

Opened December 13, 1934, Hollywood, 36 performances.

A revue. Music by Harry Akst, lyrics by Lew Brown. Musical direction by Al Goodman. Other participant: Martha Raye (featured).

CAMELOT

Orchestrations by Russell **Bennett** and Philip J. **Lang**. (Additional orchestrations by Carroll Huxley.)

Opened December 3, 1960, Majestic, 873 performances. Tryout: October, Toronto (O'Keefe); November, Boston (Shubert).

Music by Frederick Loewe, lyrics and book by Alan Jay Lerner. Based on the novel *The Once and Future King* by T. H. White. Musical direction by Franz Allers. Vocal and dance arrangements by Trude Rittman. Other participants: Lerner, Loewe, and Hart (producers); Moss Hart (director); Hanya Holm (choreographer); Richard Burton (star); Julie Andrews (star).

The partiturs are in the American Musical Theatre Collection at the Library of Congress. Invoices are preserved in Bennett's ledger. Base page rate: $6.90.

Invoices indicate: Lang (65%), Bennett (33%).

Bennett: "Before I Gaze at You Again," "C'est Moi," Entr'acte, "Follow Me" (except for 9 bars of instrumental interlude by Huxley), "Guenevere's Welcome" ("Return Procession"), "Invisible Wall," "The Jousts" (except for minor fixes by Lang), "March" ("Parade"), "Pelinore's Entrance," "The Tumblers" (except for 8-bar "new intro" by Lang).

Lang: bows, "Camelot" (and reprise), Corridor Scene, "Curtain Call and Exit," "Enchanted Forest" (replacing an earlier version by Bennett), "Farewell," "Fie on Goodness" (and "Mordred's Fie"), Finale Ultimo, "Guenevere" (replacing Bennett's), "I Loved You Once in Silence" (two versions), "I Wonder What the King Is Doing Tonight?" "If Ever I Would Leave You," "Madrigal," "Overture 12/10" (replacing Bennett's), "The Persuasion" (replacing Bennett's), "The Quests," "The Seven Deadly Virtues," "The Simple Joys of Maidenhood," "Tent Scene," "Then You May Take Me to the Fair," "What Do the Simple Folk Do?"

Huxley: "End of Study Scene."

Other scores:

"Building of Wall/Invisible Wall": the first 95 bars are by Bennett, the final 22 bars are by Lang.

Entr'acte: the first 56 bars, through "Camelot," are by Bennett; the rest, beginning with "How to Handle a Woman," is by Lang.

Finale Act I: the first 172 bars, through "How to Handle a Woman," are by Bennett; the rest, beginning with "I Wonder What the King Is Doing Tonight," is by Lang.

"How to Handle a Woman": the first 56 bars, comprising the introduction and verse, are by Bennett; the refrain is by Lang, replacing Bennett's original version; the instrumental interlude (as heard on the cast album) is by Huxley.

"The Lusty Month of May" is by Lang, with the final 28 bars (including Guenevere's vocal) by Huxley. This replaces an earlier version by Bennett.

It is somewhat surprising to find that Lang did most of the important numbers of this score (including the Overture, "Camelot," "I Wonder What the King," "Simple Joys," "If Ever I Would Leave You," and more)—perhaps Lang's most excellent work. The reason is simple: *Camelot* was extensively rewritten during the tryout, and Bennett was unavailable. It should also be noted that Bennett was apparently unaware that Lang had a ghost working for him; he attributes the Huxley scores in his journal solely to Lang, although the actual partiturs are clearly signed by Huxley.

Instr.: 5 reed (including 2 clr), 8 brass (3 tpt, 2 tb, 3 hrn), ? strings (vln, vla, 2? c, b), harp, guitar/lute, 2 perc.

CAN-CAN

Orchestrations credited to Philip J. **Lang.** (Additional orchestrations by Robert Noeltner and possibly others.)

Opened May 7, 1953, Shubert, 892 performances. Tryout: March 23, Philadelphia (Shubert).

Music and lyrics by Cole Porter. Musical direction by Milton Rosenstock. Dance arrangements by Genevieve Pitot. Other participants: Feuer & Martin (producers); Abe Burrows (director, librettist); Michael Kidd (choreographer); Gwen Verdon (featured).

Porter's preferred orchestrators were unavailable for *Can-Can*; Russell Bennett (from Porter's two prior musicals, *Kiss Me, Kate* and *Out of This World*) was working on *Victory at Sea*, while Don Walker had five other shows within five months. Cy Feuer didn't remember who suggested Lang, but thought he was selected on the basis of his "French" charts for *Make a Wish* (written and directed by *Can-Can*'s Abe Burrows).

While no information other than the billing is available, an educated guess is that the songs are mostly by Lang; the dance and ballet orchestrations—which comprised a significant part of the show—are by Noeltner (who had done ballets for *Brigadoon*, *Paint Your Wagon*, and probably *Out of This World*); and utilities and incidentals are by Jack Mason.

Pembroke Davenport was Porter's conductor on *Kiss Me, Kate* and *Out of This World.* The story goes that, on a two-show day during the Philadelphia tryout of *Can-Can*, Pem was chatting in the pit during the dinner break. He reportedly made a snide remark about the composer's sexuality, unaware that Porter was sitting a few rows back in the darkened house. Milton Rosenstock (of *Make a Wish*) was hired that night.

> ROSENSTOCK: I got a call, saying they wanted me to come down to Philadelphia. I said, I was not going unless Cole says so. Okay, Cole calls me. I said, "What happened?" Cole said, "He is not behaving himself. He is drinking." Cy Feuer calls, "We want you very much." I said, "Okay, are you going to tell Pem?" He said yes. I got out there on Thursday night, they hadn't told him; he turned around, there I was. There was a fight after the show. A terrible fight. Davenport left—taking with him the conductor scores. I stayed up all night with the pianist and the orchestra parts, trying to learn the show. I had never even met the cast, but the next evening I faked my way through the performance.

CANDIDE

Orchestrations credited to Leonard Bernstein and Hershy **Kay**. (Orchestrations mostly by Kay.)

Opened December 1, 1956, Martin Beck, 73 performances. Tryout: October 29, Boston (Colonial); November 19, New Haven (Shubert).

Music by Leonard Bernstein, lyrics by Richard Wilbur. Additional lyrics by John Latouche, Dorothy Parker, and Leonard Bernstein. Based on the novel by Voltaire. Musical direction by Samuel Krachmalnick. Other participants: Tyrone Guthrie (director); Barbara Cook (featured).

About a third of the partiturs (and possibly the entire show) are in the Bernstein Collection at the Library of Congress.

Kay: "Ballad of Eldorado," "Barcarolle," "Candide Begins His Travels," "Candide Continues His Travels," "Candide's Return from Eldorado," "Gambling Scene," "Glitter and Be Gay"

Other scores:

"The Best of All Possible Worlds": There are two scores, both by Kay. The song as used in the show is a cut-down and edited version of what was originally a much longer number. (The existing chart is about 50 pages long, but the final page is numbered 90; numerous passages are missing along the way.) The other chart begins with a hymn to victorious West-phalia and wends its way into passages from the familiar version. This includes a lyric that reads "Emotions that could lead to war or social agitation—and nice post-war inflation."

Overture: This is by Kay. The manuscript is written in the same manner and on the same paper as the other charts, but the bar lines and time signatures have been mechani-cally inked in (unlike on the other scores). Even so, the score has been written by Kay in pencil and is clearly the original. There is also a symphonic version, with the orchestra ex-panded: 5 reed, 4 brass, and 1 percussion have been added. This is in Kay's hand except for the horns (increased from 2 to 4) and some writing for the harp by Bernstein. (Larry Blank guesses that the symphonic version might have been orchestrated first, with Kay subsequently preparing the show version. This would have enabled the copyist to prepare pages preprinted with the bar lines.) There are two bound blueprint copies of this sym-phonic score, one of which was used by Bernstein when he conducted the piece over the years; this one has some minor changes handwritten in by the composer.

It seems that Bernstein closely supervised Kay's orchestrations but did not actually write them—which was precisely the case on Bernstein's subsequent show, *West Side Story*.

Instr.: 6 reed, 6 brass (2 tpt, 2 tb [1 tuba], 2 hrn), 11? strings (6? vln, 2? vla, 2? c, 1? b), harp, perc. = 25? total

(See pages 49, 183, 233.)

CANDIDE (1974 REVIVAL)

Orchestrations credited to Hershy **Kay**.

Opened March 5, 1974, Broadway, 740 performances. Tryout: December 21, 1973, Brooklyn (Academy of Music).

Music by Leonard Bernstein, lyrics by Richard Wilbur. Additional lyrics by Stephen Sondheim and John Latouche. Musical direction by John Mauceri. Other participants: Harold Prince (director); Hugh Wheeler (librettist).

Instr.: 3 reed, 3 brass (2 tpt, 1 tb), 2 strings (1 c, 1 b), 1 piano/elec piano/celesta, 1 piano/vla, perc = 11 total.

(See pages 52, 236.)

THE CAREFREE HEART

Orchestrations credited to Don **Walker**. (Additional orchestrators, if any, unknown.)

Tryout: September 30, 1957, Detroit (Cass). Closed October 26, Cleveland (Hanna).

Music and lyrics by Robert Wright & George Forrest. Based on the play *The Imaginary In-valid* by Molière. Musical direction by Samuel Krachmalnick. Other participants: Lynn Loesser (co-producer); Susan Johnson (star).

CARIB SONG

Orchestrations credited to Ted **Royal**. (Additional orchestrators, if any, unknown.)

Opened September 27, 1945, Adelphi, 36 performances. Tryout: September 1, New Haven (Shubert); Boston.

Music by Baldwin Bergersen, lyrics by William Archibald. Musical direction by Pembroke
Davenport. Other participant: Katherine Dunham (star, choreographer).

CARMELINA

Orchestrations (mostly) by Hershy **Kay**. (Additional orchestrations by Michael Gibson.)
Opened April 8, 1979, St. James, 17 performances. Tryout: March 7, Washington, D.C.
(Opera House).
Music by Burton Lane, lyrics and book by Alan Jay Lerner. Musical direction by Don Jen-
nings. Vocal arrangements by Maurice Levine. Dance arrangements by David Krane.
Other participants: José Ferrer (director); Peter Gennaro (choreographer); Joseph
Stein (co-librettist); Georgia Brown (star); Cesare Siepi (star).

The partiturs are at the Library of Congress.
The orchestrations are by Kay with the following exception:
Gibson: "The Image of Me."
Burton Lane was dissatisfied with Hershy Kay's orchestrations. It is known that Kay
suffered a stroke at some point after *Evita* (which opened in London in June 1978), which
rendered his work on the 1980 *Barnum* unusable. This might similarly have affected his
work on *Carmelina*. In any event, when *Carmelina* was recorded after the closing, a new set
of orchestrations—by Phil Lang—was commissioned at Lane's request.

Instr.: 5 reed, 6 brass (2 tpt, 2 tb, 2 hrn), 10? strings (6? vln, 0 vla, 3 c, 1 b), piano, harp, guitar, perc = 25? total.

CARMEN JONES

Orchestrations (adapted) by Russell **Bennett** (from the originals by Georges Bizet).
Opened December 2, 1943, Broadway, 502 performances. Tryout: October 19, Philadelphia (Erlanger); November 9, Boston (Opera House).
Music by Georges Bizet, lyrics and book by Oscar Hammerstein II. A revised, English-
language adaptation of the opera *Carmen.* Musical direction by Joseph Littau. Choral
direction by Robert Shaw. Other participant: Billy Rose (producer).

The partiturs are at the offices of the Rodgers & Hammerstein Organization.
Hammerstein's adaptation of *Carmen* used Bizet's original orchestrations. Bennett
made the necessary alterations, which for the most part consisted of cutting the third and
fourth French horn parts and revoicing the strings.
This was apparently the first major Broadway musical to use black musicians in the pit.
Billy Rose forced the issue with the Musicians' Union, bringing in five men (including
drummer Cosy Cole, who was featured in the show-stopping "Beat Out Dat Rhythm on
a Drum").

CARNIVAL

Orchestrations credited to Philip J. **Lang**. (Additional orchestrators unknown.)
Opened April 13, 1961, Imperial, 719 performances. Tryout: March 9, Washington, D.C.
(National); Philadelphia (Forrest).

Music and lyrics by Bob Merrill. Based on the film *Lili*, from material by Helen Deutsch. Musical direction and vocal arrangements by Saul Schechtman. Dance arrangements by Peter Howard. Other participants: David Merrick (producer); Gower Champion (director, choreographer).

The partiturs for act II (and the deleted numbers) are in the Merrick Collection at the Library of Congress.

Lang: bows, "Can You Imagine That? (Mira)" (cut version, see below), "Grand Imperial Cirque de Paris" (reprise and ballet), "Her Face," "Hocus Pocus Heaven" (cut), "Humming" (cut section only, see below), "I Hate Him," "It Was Always You" (and reprise), Opening act II (Puppet Sequence): part 1 (Intro), part 2 ("The Rich"), part 3 ("Love Makes the World Go Round"), part 4 ("Beautiful Candy"), "She's My Love," "A Very Nice Man" (cut version).

Unidentified hand: "Magic Underscore," minor incidentals.

When the partiturs were sent to the Library of Congress by Tams, they were accompanied by a register that says "additional orchestrations by Ralph Burns." With act I missing, it is impossible to guess which charts these might be. (The fact that Lang's original charts for "Can You Imagine That?" and "A Very Nice Man" are in the deleted folder means that these songs were reorchestrated, either by Lang or someone else.) In any event, it is highly unlikely that Burns was involved; Peter Howard, who was a good friend of Burns, says he would certainly have known if Ralph were on the show. The Tams-donated scores for Lang's 1959 musical *Take Me Along* include a similar register, in the same hand, that erroneously attributes additional orchestrations. In the case of *Carnival*, the mysterious additional orchestrator might have been Carroll Huxley (who ghosted for Lang on *Take Me Along* and *Camelot*) or Jack Mason.

Instr.: 5 reed, 5 brass (3 tpt [1 hrn], 2 tb), 9? strings (6? vln, 0 vla, 2? c, 1 b/tuba), accordion, harp, guitar, 2 perc = 24? total.

(See page 243.)

CARNIVAL IN FLANDERS

Orchestrations by Don **Walker**. (Additional orchestrations by Robert **Ginzler** and Hans **Spialek**, with Irwin **Kostal**, Jay Blackton, and Jack Mason.)

Opened September 8, 1953, New Century, 6 performances. Tryout: June, Philadelphia; July, Los Angeles.

Music by James Van Heusen, lyrics by Johnny Burke. Based on the film *La Kermesse Heroique* by Jacques Speyer. Musical direction by Harold Hastings. Vocal arrangements by Elie Siegmeister. Dance arrangements by Roger Adams ("Plundering the Town"), John Morris ("Carnival Ballet"), and Elie Siegmeister ("Spanish Dance").

Other participants: Preston Sturges (replacement director, replacement librettist); George Oppenheimer and Herbert Fields (original librettists); Jack Cole (original choreographer); Dolores Gray (star); John Raitt (star).

Invoices are in the Walker Collection at the Library of Congress. Base page rate: $5.70.

Invoices indicate: Walker (43%), Spialek (16%), Ginzler (13%), Mason (11%), Kostal (10%).

Walker: "Admirer," "Castile," "Here's a Rainy Day," "How Far Can a Lady Go?" "Institution," "Military Tactics," "You're Dead."

Ginzler: "Delicate Sex," "For a Moment of Your Love," "Ring the Bell" (see below).

Kostal: "Rustic Opening," Spanish Dance (see below).

Spialek: "Alderman," "Small Things," "The Very Necessary You."

Mason: Overture (see below).

Other scores:

Overture is mostly by Mason (67 pages), with additional material (11 pages) by Walker.

"Ring the Bell" is mostly by Ginzler, with a small section by Blackton; utility is by Mason.

"Spanish Dance" is by Kostal, replacing an earlier version by Spialek.

"Sudden Thrill": there are two versions, one (the earlier?) by Spialek, the other by Kostal; Ginzler invoiced for a new verse and ending, although it is unclear for which version.

CAROUSEL

Orchestrations by Don **Walker**. (Additional orchestrations by Hans **Spialek**, Stephen O. Jones, and Russell **Bennett**, with Joe Glover.)

Opened April 19, 1945, Majestic, 890 performances. Tryout: March 22, New Haven (Shubert); March 27, Boston (Colonial).

Music by Richard Rodgers, lyrics and book by Oscar Hammerstein II. Based on the play *Liliom* by Ferenc Molnár. Musical direction by Joseph Littau. Dance arrangements by Trude Rittman. Other participants: Theatre Guild (producer); Rouben Mamoulian (director); Agnes de Mille (choreographer); John Raitt (star).

The partiturs are in the Rodgers Collection at the Library of Congress.

Walker: Ballet, "Blow High, Blow Low," "Geraniums/Stonecutters," Hornpipe, "If I Loved You/Bench Scene" (see below), "June Is Bustin' Out All Over," "Mister Snow" (see below); Opening act II, "Soliloquy" (see below); "Carousel Waltz" (see below), "What's the Use of Wond'rin'?"

Spialek: "Clambake Specialty" (cut), Death Scene ("If I Loved You") (cut), Opening act I Scene 2, "Storm Scene" (main theme of Waltz) (cut), "What's the Use of Wond'rin'? reprise" (cut), "When the Children Are Asleep."

Jones: "Back to Earth" (cut), "Exit of Heavenly Friend" (partitur missing), "From Judge to Walk" (transition for original cast album), "The Highest Judge of All," "Mister Snow Reprise," "(My Boy) Bill Change" (cut), "My Little Girl Incidental," "This Was a Real Nice Clambake," "You'll Never Walk Alone."

Bennett: "Mister Snow" (see below), "Carousel Waltz" (see below).

Glover: Entr'acte, Finale act I.

Other scores:

Finale is mostly by Jones, with the final 3-bar tag by Walker.

"If I Loved You/Bench Scene" is mostly by Walker. Inserts #1, #2, and #3—underscoring between sections—are by Spialek. The 21-bar tag after the song is by Jones.

"Mister Snow": the extended opening section ("You're a queer one, Julie Jordan") is by Bennett; the song proper ("When I marry Mister Snow") is by Walker (with the final 2 bars by Jones), replacing Bennett's earlier version. Bennett's partitur for the "Mister Snow" section has disappeared, but his orchestration can be heard on the 1945 original cast album.

"Soliloquy" is mostly by Walker, although the location of the partitur is unknown.

"Carousel Waltz": official version, added after the opening, is by Walker. Original version is by Bennett. Bennett's partitur has disappeared, but his orchestration can be heard on the 1945 original cast album.

"What's the Use of Wond'rin' Scene Change" is by Walker, with the first 24 bars by Jones.

DON WALKER: Early in 1945, when I was occupied writing the show that eventually emerged as *Memphis Bound*, I was called into Max Dreyfus' office and told that I would have to take over the orchestration of *Carousel*, which had been in production for about a week. From the beginning, *Carousel* had been Russell's show. Already he had scored the first two numbers: "The Carousel Waltz" and "Mr. Snow." No one would tell me why it was necessary to replace him so suddenly, whether it was illness, family trouble, or conflict of personalities with Rodgers or the show's musical director. All I knew was that while occupied with my own show, I would have to accept responsibility for a production with as much music as an opera to be played by an enormous orchestra, for Broadway, of forty men. Luckily, almost all of my preparatory work for *Memphis* was done, so I tackled *Carousel*. It was a monster. I was able to score the first act myself, but got into trouble with the second act. I called on Hans Spialek for one number and Stephen Jones for another and was able to complete the rest myself in time for the opening in New Haven, scoring the final number in the Hotel Taft while rehearsals were going on. [Writing in 1982, Walker's memory of which numbers were ghosted was hazy.]

Rodgers was delighted with the orchestrations, with the exception of the two numbers Russell had done. He made me promise to rescore "The Carousel Waltz" and "Mr. Snow" in the style I had established with the rest of the score. The show went on to Boston, but I had to go back to New York to take care of *Memphis Bound*. Before that went into rehearsal, I was able to score "Mr. Snow." [Walker scored the second part of the song, "His name is Mister Snow." Bennett's orchestration for the extended opening, "You're a queer one, Julie Jordan," was never replaced and remains in use.] When the show came back to New York, Rodgers needed an Entr'acte. I was deep in my own show and got Joe Glover to make it.

I was too busy with *Memphis Bound* to rescore "The Carousel Waltz" until after the *Memphis* opening. By that time Rodgers not only still wanted me to rescore it, but to score it for a full symphony orchestra, capable of being reduced to play with the forty men in the pit of the show. That was a most difficult assignment, but I did it and from then on my orchestration of the "Waltz" was played not only in the show, but in all concert presentations. [In actuality, Rodgers was asked for a symphonic version of the "Waltz." By having Walker do it in a manner that was reducible to pit orchestra size, Rodgers was able to get his new "Waltz" for the theatre—but have the symphony pay the orchestration cost.] And I still don't know why I was assigned to the show in place of Russell.

Walker also addressed the subject in a 1955 letter to Rodgers, at which time Walker was hoping for involvement in the forthcoming motion picture:

As you will remember, it was not your original intention to have me score *Carousel*, but Russell got tied up in some way, and you asked me to do it. At the time a show of mine—*Memphis Bound*—was approaching production and I was preoccupied, to say the least. Nevertheless, after I read the book and heard the score of *Carousel*, I could not help myself. I gave it my whole heart and I know the result showed it. I feel today that *Carousel* was the best job I have ever done. There was something about the story and your wonderful music that inspired me. . . . It has been my dire misfortune that in the past, with the exception of *Carousel*, I have been involved with your least successful ventures. I have also acquired a reputation as a jazz arranger, but that is all an accident. I know that writing for large groups of strings gives me a chance to use my best technique. I hope *Pipe Dream* is coming along well and I wish you all luck with it. I think Russell is a fine choice for orchestrator.

Instr.: 6 reed (including 2 fl/picc, 2 clr), 9 brass (2 tpt, 3 tb, 1 tuba, 3 hrn), 22 strings (13 vln, 4 vla, 3 c, 2 b), harp, perc = 39 total.

(See pages 104, 125, 203, 304.)

THE CAT AND THE FIDDLE

Orchestrations credited to Russell **Bennett**. (Additional orchestrators, if any, unknown.)
Opened October 15, 1931, Globe, 395 performances. Tryout: September 23, Philadelphia (Garrick); Newark (Shubert).
Music by Jerome Kern, lyrics and book by Otto Harbach. Musical direction by Victor Baravelle. Other participant: Max Gordon (producer).

The partiturs are in the Kern Collection at the Library of Congress (unexamined).

Instr.: 3 reed (including 3 sax), 4 brass (3 tpt, 1 tb), 6 strings (3 vln, 1 vla, 1 c, 1 b/tuba), 3 piano (1 on celesta), 2 perc = 18 total.

CATCH A STAR

Orchestrations credited to Milton Greene. (Additional orchestrators, if any, unknown.)
Opened September 6, 1955, Plymouth, 23 performances. Tryout: unknown.
A revue. Music by Sammy Fain and Paul Charig, lyrics by Paul Webster and Ray Golden. Musical direction by Milton Greene. Ballet music composed by Herb Schutz.
Other participants: Danny Simon and Neil Simon (sketches); Mike Stewart (additional sketch); Jerry Bock (additional music); Larry Holofcener, Lee Adams (additional lyrics).

CAVIAR

Orchestrations uncredited. (Orchestrations by Hans **Spialek**, Edward B. Powell, Don **Walker**, and probably others.)
Opened June 7, 1934, Forrest, 20 performances. Tryout: unknown.
Music by Hayden Church, lyrics by Edward Heyman. Musical direction by Ivan Rudisill. Other participant: Jack Cole (featured).

CELEBRATION

Orchestrations by Jim Tyler. (Additional orchestrators, if any, unknown.)

Opened January 22, 1969, Ambassador, 110 performances.

Music by Harvey Schmidt, lyrics and book by Tom Jones. Musical direction by Rod Dere-finko. Other participants: Cheryl Crawford (co-producer); Tom Jones (director).

> SCHMIDT: The instrumentation evolved at the preliminary workshop. We first got things that actors could play, with a lot of percussion instruments. We eventually added three musicians, getting a lot of orchestral feel by experimenting with different stops on the RMI [electric piano]. When Cheryl Crawford moved the show to Broadway, we felt we needed an orchestra. Jim Tyler was wonderful about taking what we'd done so far, keeping that and adding to it. Jim really did a very good job, bending over backwards to keep the sound of what we'd done.

Instr.: 0 brass, 0 reed, I string (b), 3 keyboards, harp, guitar, 3 perc = 9 total.

CHARLIE AND ALGERNON

Orchestrations credited to Philip J. **Lang**. (Additional orchestrators, if any, unknown.)

Opened September 14, 1980, Helen Hayes, 17 performances. Tryout: August 4, Washington, D.C. (Eisenhower).

Music by Charles Strouse, lyrics and book by David Rogers. Based on the novel *Flowers for Algernon* by Daniel Keyes. Musical direction by Liza Redfield. Additional vocal arrangements by Tom Fay.

CHICAGO

Orchestrations (virtually totally) by Ralph **Burns**.

Opened June 1, 1975, 46th Street, 936 performances. Tryout: May, Philadelphia (Forrest).

Music by John Kander, lyrics and book by Fred Ebb. Based on the play by Maurine Dallas Watkins. Musical direction by Stanley Lebowsky. Dance arrangements by Peter Howard.

Other participants: Robert Fryer (co-producer); Bob Fosse (director, choreographer, co-librettist); Stuart Ostrow ("associate director"); Gwen Verdon (star); Chita Rivera (star); Jerry Orbach (star).

The partiturs are in the composer's possession.

The orchestrations are by Burns with the following exception:

"Cell Block Tango" is mostly by Burns, with a final 10-bar ending (entitled "New Ending") by Michael Gibson.

Burns also did new charts (marked "Chicago 1996") for the Broadway revival, for "A Little Bit of Good" and "My Own Best Friend."

RALPH'S INSTRUCTIONS TO MUSICIANS   "All That Jazz" (to trumpet): "growl plunger solo, give it all hot; quasi Cootie Williams."

"A Little Bit of Good" (to conductor): "Stanley—maybe for this number drums shouldn't play? There wasn't any on the Grace Moore recordings."

"A Little Bit of Good 1996" (to conductor): "Rob Fisher—the harmons on this must be old style—with the bells on quasi–Paul Whiteman orch of 1920s. Also all the tbne solos in solotone should be played seriously but not terribly well, just medium so they don't distract from the vocal, only help it."

"They Both Reached for the Gun" (to trombone, at end of intro): "Growl slide (hold that tiger)"; (to drum, at end after hold): "also—the kitchen sink."

"Roxie" (to trumpets, near end of underscoring before vamp into song): "Stravinsky growl"; (to conductor, at beginning of refrain): "Stan—tpt, tbne, cl and b cl should sound like the old Tommy Dorsey Barrelhouse 5 behind Edith Wright"; (to piano): "add a few Count Basie plinks and plunks." The final 4 bars of this number, which were cut, included a Gershwin quote, with instructions for the clarinet to play "ad lib time quasi 'Rhapsody in Blue.'"

"Razzle Dazzle" (to conductor): "all the way through, quasi-Fellini movie music."

"Class" (to conductor): "piano quasi Shubert. Not theatre, but Franz."

Instr.: 3 reed, 4 brass (2 tpt, 2 tb), 2 strings (1 vln, 0 vla, 0 c, 1 b/tuba), 2 keyboard (1 with accordion), banjo/guitar, perc = 13 total.

(See page 198.)

A CHORUS LINE

Orchestrations credited to Bill Byers, Hershy **Kay**, Jonathan Tunick (replacing Larry **Wilcox**). (Additional orchestrations by Philip J. **Lang**, Harold Wheeler, Ralph **Burns**, and Larry Wilcox.)

Opened October 19, 1975, Shubert, 6,137 performances. Tryout: April 16, Newman at the Public (off-Broadway).

Music by Marvin Hamlisch, lyrics by Edward Kleban. Musical direction and vocal arrangements by Donald Pippin. Other participants: New York Shakespeare Festival/ Joseph Papp (producer); Michael Bennett (director, choreographer).

The Papp Collection at the New York Public Library has a conformed set of partiturs in a copyist's hand. Identifications have been compiled from discussions with Tunick, Pippin, Larry Blank (conductor of the international company), and Larry Abel (supervising copyist).

Tunick: "At the Ballet," "I Hope I Get It" (Opening), "Nothing," "What I Did for Love" (see below).

Kay: "And," "One" (see below), "Sing."

Byers: "I Can Do That."

Lang: "Dance Ten, Looks Three."

Other scores:

"Montage" ("Hello Twelve, Hello Thirteen"/"Mother"/"Gimme the Ball," etc.): much of this multipart number is reportedly by Wilcox, with "about 40 measures" by Byers.

"The Music and the Mirror": song is by Byers; dance (beginning at slow section) is by Wheeler.

"One" is by Kay; "One Reprise/Finale": first section is by Kay, final section (beginning with orchestral buildup and brass blasts) is by Burns.

"What I Did for Love": the original chart, as on the cast recording, is by Tunick. This was replaced in 1977 with a new (and now official) chart—less theatrical but more "commercial"—by Dick Hazard. Yet another version was orchestrated by Tunick for the 2006 revival.

A Chorus Line, being an off-Broadway musical with an unlikely future, was not seen as an especially desirable job. Larry Wilcox, who came in during the tryout of Michael Bennett's prior musical *Seesaw* to reorchestrate the show (without credit), was the original orchestrator. During rehearsals, Hamlisch found Wilcox drunk at the bar of China Song (a Broadway hangout in the Ed Sullivan Theatre building). The sharp-tongued Wilcox apparently insulted Hamlisch and was fired on the spot. Behind schedule, Hamlisch and Pippin called in whoever was available.

Toiling among the anonymous copyists on this production was the octogenarian Hans Spialek, who called his fifty-year-old daughter and said: "You'll never believe this. I'm working on a song for a show, and they call it 'Tits and Ass.'"

Instr.: 4 reed (including 4 sax, 4 clr, 4 fl), 6 brass (3 tpt, 3 tb), 1 string (b/elec b), 2 keyboards (1 with piano/celesta, the other conductor/keyboard), harp, guitar (acoustic/elec/banjo), 2 perc = 17 total.

(See page 96.)

CHRISTINE

Orchestrations credited to Philip J. **Lang**. (Additional orchestrators, if any, unknown.)

Opened April 28, 1960, 46th Street, 12 performances. Tryout: March 21, Philadelphia (Erlanger).

Music by Sammy Fain, lyrics by Paul Francis Webster. Based on the novel *My Indian Family* by Hilda Wernher. Musical direction by Jay Blackton. Vocal and dance arrangements by Trude Rittman. Other participants: Pearl S. Buck (co-librettist); Maureen O'Hara (star).

THE CHRISTMAS SPECTACULAR

Orchestrations credited to Michael Gibson, Danny Troob, Jonathan Tunick, Jim Tyler, Philip J. **Lang**, and others.

Opened November 9, 1990, Radio City Music Hall, 188 performances.

New music by Stanley Lebowsky, new lyrics by Fred Tobias. Musical direction and vocal arrangements by Donald Pippin. Dance arrangements by Marvin Laird.

THE CITY CHAP

Orchestrations uncredited. (Orchestrations by Russell **Bennett** and others.)

Opened October 26, 1925, Liberty, 72 performances. Tryout: September 28, Philadelphia; Brooklyn; Newark.

Music by Jerome Kern, lyrics by Anne Caldwell. Based on *The Fortune Hunter* by Winchell Smith. Musical direction by Victor Baravelle. Other participant: Charles Dillingham (producer).

The partiturs are at the Library of Congress (unexamined).

COCO

Orchestrations credited to Hershy **Kay**. (Additional orchestrations by Russell **Bennett**, Luther Henderson, and possibly others.)

Opened December 18, 1969, Mark Hellinger, 329 performances. Tryout: none.

Music by André Previn, lyrics and book by Alan Jay Lerner. Suggested by events in the life of Gabrielle "Coco" Chanel. Musical direction by Robert Emmett Dolan. Dance arrangements and musical continuity by Harold Wheeler. Other participants: Michael Bennett (choreographer, replacement director [uncredited]); Katharine Hepburn (star).

Bennett's invoices are preserved in his ledger. Henderson's invoices are in his personal papers. Base page rate: $13.

   Bennett: "Always Mademoiselle," "Coco," Film Sequences #1, #2, #6, and #8 (incidentals), "When Your Lover Says Goodbye."

   Henderson: "Fiasco," "Fiasco Fox-Trot," "Personal History" ("Blissfully Unwedded"), "A Woman Is How She Loves" (two versions, song and tag).

   Harold Wheeler confirms that they had a great deal of trouble with "Always Mademoiselle," the nine-minute song threaded through the final scene. Kay tried a couple of charts, as did another orchestrator (whose name Wheeler doesn't remember). Finally, Bennett was called in midway through previews; it is quite likely that the seventy-five-year-old pro—from Lerner's *My Fair Lady*, *Gigi* (film), *Camelot*, and *On a Clear Day*—had turned down the show and recommended Kay in the first place. They were so pleased with Russell's chart that they had him replace two others. Luther Henderson also provided three numbers just before the first preview, leaving one to wonder just how much of the finished show was scored by Kay.

(See page 52.)

COLETTE

Orchestrations (mostly) by Larry **Wilcox**. (Additional orchestrations by Jim Tyler.)

Tryout: February 9, 1982, Seattle, Washington (Fifth Avenue). Closed March 20, Denver, Colorado (Auditorium)

Music by Harvey Schmidt, lyrics and book by Tom Jones. Suggested by the life and writings of Colette. Musical direction and vocal arrangements by Larry Blank. Dance arrangements by David Krane. Other participants: Harry Rigby (co-producer); Dennis Rosa (director); Diana Rigg (star).

According to Larry Blank, the orchestrations are by Wilcox, with the following exceptions:

   Tyler: "Le Vagabond," "Riviera Nights."

COME SUMMER

Orchestrations credited to Carlyle Hall. (Additional orchestrations by Jonathan Tunick and possibly others.)

Opened March 18, 1969, Lunt-Fontanne, 7 performances. Tryout: February, Boston (Colonial).

Music by David Baker, lyrics and book by Will Holt. Based on the novel *Rainbow on the Road* by Esther Forbes. Musical direction by Milton Rosenstock. Vocal arrangements and musical continuity by Trude Rittman. Dance arrangements by David Baker and John Berkman. Other participants: Agnes de Mille (director, choreographer); Ray Bolger (star).

A CONNECTICUT YANKEE (1943 REVIVAL)

Orchestrations credited to Don **Walker**. (Additional orchestrations by Ted **Royal** and others.)

Opened November 17, 1943, Martin Beck, 135 performances. Tryout: October 28, Philadelphia (Forrest).

Music by Richard Rodgers, lyrics by Lorenz Hart. Based on the novel *A Connecticut Yankee in King Arthur's Court* by Mark Twain. Musical direction by George Hirst. Vocal direction by Clay Warnick. Other participants: Richard Rodgers (producer); Herbert Fields (librettist).

Three partiturs are in at the Library of Congress.

Walker: "I Feel at Home with You Utility," "To Keep My Love Alive."

Royal: "You Always Love the Same Girl"

Following the success of *Oklahoma!* and the beginning of his collaboration with Oscar Hammerstein, Rodgers produced this revised version of the 1927 hit in an attempt to get the dissipated Larry Hart back to work. Hart wrote five new songs, but lapsed into an alcohol-fueled case of pneumonia on opening night. He died five days later, at the age of forty-eight.

This was the first of four Rodgers-controlled revivals of Rodgers & Hart musicals. In each case, Rodgers chose to scrap the old orchestrations (*Connecticut Yankee* by Roy Webb, the others by Hans Spialek); the assignments all went to Don Walker, who had done such a fine job the year before on the final Rodgers & Hart musical, *By Jupiter.*

Instr.: 5 reed, 5 brass (3 tpt, 1 tb, 1 hrn), 12? strings (8? vln, 2? vla, 1? c, 1 b), piano, perc = 24? total.

THE CONQUERING HERO

Orchestrations and arrangements credited to Robert **Ginzler** and Sid **Ramin**. (Additional orchestrators, if any, unknown.)

Opened January 16, 1961, ANTA, 8 performances. Tryout: November 19, 1960, New Haven (Shubert); November 29, Washington, D.C. (National).

Music by Moose Charlap, lyrics by Norman Gimbel. Based on the film *Hail, the Conquering Hero* by Preston Sturges. Musical direction and vocal arrangements by Sherman Frank. Dance arrangements by Fred Werner.

Other participants: Bob Fosse (original director, original choreographer); Albert Marre (replacement director, unbilled); Todd Bolender (replacement choreographer, unbilled); Larry Gelbart (librettist).

COOL OFF!

Orchestrations credited to Larry **Wilcox**. (Additional orchestrators, if any, unknown.)
Tryout: March 31, 1964, Philadelphia. Closed April 4, Philadelphia.
Music and lyrics by Howard Blankman. Based on the *Faust* legend. Musical direction by
 John Lesko. Dance arrangements by Genevieve Pitot. Other participants: Jerome
 Weidman (librettist); Stanley Holloway (star); Hermione Baddeley (star).

COPPER AND BRASS

Orchestrations credited to Ralph **Burns**. (Additional orchestrators, if any, unknown.)
Opened October 17, 1957, Martin Beck, 36 performances. Tryout: September 13, New
 Haven (Shubert); Philadelphia.
Music by David Baker, lyrics by David Craig. Musical direction and vocal arrangements
 by Maurice Levine. Dance arrangements by John Morris. Other participants: Bob
 Fosse (uncredited additional choreographer); Nancy Walker (star).

Nancy Walker—wife of lyricist David Craig—played a policewoman ("copper"), with
her leading man a saxophone player ("brass"). The leading man was a member of the popular Williams Brothers singing group. Not Andy, but his older brother Dick.
(See page 34.)

COPPERFIELD

Orchestrations (totally) by Irwin **Kostal**.
Opened April 16, 1981, ANTA, 13 performances. Tryout: March 3, St. Louis (Ameri-
 can).
Music and lyrics by Al Kasha and Joel Hirschhorn. Based on the novel *David Copperfield* by
 Charles Dickens. Musical direction and vocal arrangements by Larry Blank. Dance
 and incidental arrangements by Donald Johnston.

COUNT ME IN

Orchestrations credited to Russell **Bennett**. (Additional orchestrations by Hans **Spialek**,
 Don **Walker**, and probably others.)
Opened October 8, 1942, Ethel Barrymore, 61 performances. Tryout: September 7,
 Boston (Shubert).
A revue. Music and lyrics by Ann Ronell. Musical direction by John McManus. Vocal
 arrangements by Clay Warnick. Other participants: Walter Kerr (co-librettist); Gower
 Champion & Jeanne Tyler (featured).

COURTIN' TIME

Orchestrations credited to Don **Walker**. (Additional orchestrators, if any, unknown.)
Opened June 14, 1951, National, 37 performances. Tryout: April, Boston (Shubert);
 April 30, Philadelphia (Forrest); May 28, Pittsburgh (Nixon).

Music and lyrics by Jack Lawrence and Don Walker. Based on the novel *The Farmer's Wife* by Eden Philpotts. Musical direction by Bill Jonson (replacing Robert Zeller). Vocal arrangements by Don Walker. Other participants: Alexander H. Cohen (associate producer); Alfred Drake (director); George Balanchine (choreographer).

The partiturs are at the Library of Congress (unexamined).

CRAZY FOR YOU

Orchestrations credited to William D. Brohn. Additional orchestration by Sid **Ramin** (and possibly others).

Opened February 19, 1992, Shubert, 1,622 performances. Tryout: December 19, 1991, Washington, D.C. (National).

Music by George Gershwin, lyrics by Ira Gershwin. Suggested by characters and songs from the musical comedy *Girl Crazy*. Musical direction by Paul Gemignani. Dance arrangements and incidental music by Peter Howard. Other participants: Mike Ockrent (director); Susan Stroman (choreographer).

Ramin: "Slap That Bass."

CRISS-CROSS

Orchestrations uncredited. (Orchestrations by Maurice de Packh, Russell **Bennett**, Charles N. Grant, and Hans **Spialek**.)

Opened October 12, 1926, Globe, 210 performances. Tryout: September 22, New Haven (Shubert); Philadelphia (Erlanger).

Music by Jerome Kern, lyrics and book by Otto Harbach and Anne Caldwell. Musical direction by Alfred Newman. Other participants: Charles Dillingham (producer); Fred Stone (star).

The partiturs are in the Kern Collection at the Library of Congress (unexamined).

> SPIALEK: I was sent to New Haven. All I had to do was to develop a 16-bar theme by Mr. Kern into a festive march of about 350 bars, used in the show for a seventeenth-century pageant. This was no little assignment. Mr. Kern was of very small stature and devoid of any outward signs even faintly suggesting his tremendous creative powers. Or that this little man composed so many of the most beautiful songs ever written.
>
> Personally, I thought him dry and a little bit on the nasty side. For instance, in the course of a routine explanation, he suggested the use of an oboe, then asked me, "I hope you know what an oboe is." This festive march was the only arrangement I ever did for Mr. Kern; the arranger in charge of the show, Maurice de Packh, resented my being sent behind his back to do this particular number. He gave Mr. Kern a terrific argument, just about short of body blows. Back in New York, Max Dreyfus presided at his office over a sort of court-martial about the whole affair. I was called as a witness. Jerome Kern asked me just one question: "Tell me, Hans, did I ever insult you?" To which I stupidly answered, "Not yet." Mr. Dreyfus' ensuing remark, "That means, you still have hopes?" provoked laughter, nobody seemed to care any more, and the whole proceedings went out the window. But Kern never forgave me for turning something he took so seriously into a laughing matter, which I always and sincerely regretted.

Spialek tells a good story, but he neglects to mention that he did orchestrate at least one more number for Kern: the all-important "Bill," from *Show Boat*.

CURTAIN GOING UP

Orchestrations by Don **Walker**. (Additional orchestrations by Robert **Ginzler** and Irwin **Kostal**, with Walter Paul.)

Tryout: February 15, 1952, Philadelphia (Forrest). Closed April 1, Philadelphia.

A revue. Music and lyrics by various writers. Musical direction by Milton Rosenstock. Other participants: Mervyn Nelson (producer, director); Max Wilk and George Axelrod (sketch writers); Mel Brooks (additional sketch writer); Larry Storch (star).

Invoices are in the Walker Collection at the Library of Congress. Base page rate: $5. Invoices indicate: Walker (65%), Ginzler (17%), Kostal (13%).

The orchestrations are by Walker, with the following exceptions:

Ginzler: "Dance Hall Routine," Overture, "Rhinestone Presto."

Kostal: "Four Bats," "Lot of Lovin'," "Lot of Lovin' Finale."

Paul: utility ("Four Bats"), fixes.

CYRANO

Orchestrations credited to Philip J. **Lang** (replacing Eddie **Sauter**). (Additional orchestrators, if any, unknown.)

Opened May 13, 1973, Palace, 49 performances. Tryout: January 23, Minneapolis, Minnesota (Guthrie); Boston.

Music by Michael J. Lewis, lyrics by Anthony Burgess. Based on Anthony Burgess's translation of the play *Cyrano de Bergerac* by Edmond Rostand. Musical direction by Thomas Pierson. Incidental music by Clay Fullum. Other participants: Michael Kidd (replacement director); Christopher Plummer (star).

Among the many changes made during the tryout were the replacement of Eddie Sauter's typically iconoclastic charts with more traditional orchestrations by Phil Lang.

DAFFY DILL

Orchestrations uncredited. (Orchestrations by Russell **Bennett** and others.)

Opened August 22, 1922, Apollo, 71 performances. Tryout: August 14, Atlantic City (Apollo).

Music by Herbert Stothart, lyrics by Oscar Hammerstein II. Musical direction by Herbert Stothart. Other participants: Guy Bolton and Oscar Hammerstein II (librettists).

Russell Bennett made his Broadway debut as an orchestrator with this long-forgotten musical comedy.

DAMN YANKEES

Orchestrations by Don **Walker**. (Additional orchestrations by Robert **Ginzler** and Irwin **Kostal**, with Joe Glover.)

Opened May 5, 1955, 46th Street, 1,019 performances. Tryout: April 2, New Haven (Shubert); Boston (Shubert).

Music and lyrics by Richard Adler and Jerry Ross. Based on the novel *The Year the Yankees Lost the Pennant* by Douglass Wallop. Musical direction by Hal Hastings. Dance arrangements by Roger Adams. Other participants: Frederick Brisson, Robert Griffith and Harold Prince (producers); George Abbott (director, co-librettist); Bob Fosse (choreographer); Gwen Verdon (star).

The partiturs are in the Walker Collection at the Library of Congress.

Walker: bows, "The Game," "Goodbye Old Girl" (and reprise), "A Little Brains, a Little Talent," "Shoeless Joe from Hannibal, Mo." (see below), "Six Months Out of Every Year," "Who's Got the Pain?"

Ginzler: "Heart," "Near to You," "Two Lost Souls," "Whatever Lola Wants (Lola Gets)."

Kostal: "Baseball Ballet" (see below), "A Man Doesn't Know" (see below), "Those Were the Good Old Days" (see below).

Glover: Utilities ("Shoeless Joe from Hannibal, Mo." "Whatever Lola Wants (Lola Gets)."

Other scores:

Entr'acte is mostly by Ginzler. "A Man Doesn't Know" and the second part of "Two Lost Souls" are by Walker. (At the end of the score, Ginzler has written "ENUF" in place of "Fine.")

"Heart Reprise" is by Ginzler, although the piano and strings for first 23 bars have been overwritten by Walker.

"A Man Doesn't Know": song and finale are by Kostal. Reprise is by Kostal through the Joe and Meg solo sections; Ginzler does the final 15 bars, beginning with the grand modulation into the duet section.

Overture is written in fragments: "The Game," "A Man Doesn't Know," and "Shoeless Joe" are by Walker. "Near to You" and most of the bridgework is by Ginzler. The abbreviated section heard on the original cast album is by Walker.

"Shoeless Joe from Hannibal, Mo.": song is by Walker; the extended "Baseball Ballet" is by Kostal; "New Joe Finale (Galop)" is by Ginzler.

"Those Were the Good Old Days": there are three versions. The first ("G.O.D.") is by Kostal. The second ("New") combines the vocal with an extended soft-shoe dance section by Ginzler. The final ("B-flat") is by Walker. All three versions are written as a duet for "Ray" and "Gwen"; this was changed after orchestration to a solo for Applegate (Ray Walston).

RED'S INSTRUCTIONS TO MUSICIANS In the dance section of "Whatever Lola Wants," the growling brass (before "boop-boop-ee-doo") is marked "nasty."

At the beginning of the vocal section of "Two Lost Souls," the 5 sax parts are marked "well goosed—a la Billy May."

In the dance section of "Two Lost Souls," Ginzler writes a drum figure for 7 measures, with the instruction "and 52 more!" This continues into a 32-bar solo drum, similar to the Fosse–Roger Adams–Ginzler dance arrangement of "Steam Heat" in *The Pajama Game*.

THANKS AND WISHES   From Rosalind Russell (star of *Wonderful Town*, wife of producer Frederick Brisson) to Walker: "Dear Don, you're batting your usual five hundred again, great luck, Rosalind." From Jerome Robbins to Walker: "Oh, play it daddy! Jerry Robbins."

Instr.: 5 reed, 7 brass (3 tpt [I hrn], 3 tb [I tuba], I hrn), 13 strings (8 vln, 2? vla, 2 c, I b), piano/celesta, guitar/steel guitar/banjo, perc = 28? total.

DANCE ME A SONG

Orchestrations credited to Russell **Bennett**. (Orchestrations by Bennett and Don **Walker**, with Irwin **Kostal**, Robert **Ginzler**, and possibly others.)

Opened January 20, 1950, Royale, 35 performances. Tryout: December 22, 1949, New Haven (Shubert); Boston.

A revue. Music and lyrics by James Shelton (and others.). Musical direction by Tony Cabot. Other participants: Joan McCracken (star); Bob Fosse (dancer).

Bennett's invoices are preserved in his ledger. Other invoices are in the Walker Collection at the Library of Congress. Base page rate: $4.65.

Bennett: "Adam's Rib" (vocal, pantomime, and dance), "Charlie," "Documentary," "Lilac Wine" (2 versions), "Matilda," "Movie Star," "My Little Dog Has Ego" (see below), "We Sing the Love Song."

Walker: "Adam's Rib" (utility), "Dance Me a Song," "Didn't Come to Texas for the Trip," "It's the Weather" (vocal and dance), "Love" (and encore), "Newspaper Ballet," "One Is a Lonely Number," "Strange New Look."

Other scores:

"Dorothy's Name Is Mud" is by Kostal (78 pages) and Ginzler (17 pages).

"My Little Dog Has Ego" is by Bennett, with "Little Dog Intro" by Walker.

"Strange New Look": there are two versions, one each by Bennett and Walker.

> BENNETT: When *The King and I* was running in New York, it was not unusual to hear the question asked: "What would Richard Rodgers have done without you?" They didn't have to wait long for my answer: "He would have engaged another arranger." The answer was all the more appropriate because still in my memory was a recent musical called *Dance Me a Song*, which had a charming dance number called "Matilda" in it. For "Matilda" I had only one waltz refrain given me from which to make a score of 129 pages. In rehearsals it was proclaimed a masterpiece. I will agree only to the point of saying that, compared to anything I did or was required to do for *The King and I*, it was indeed a masterpiece. And yet no one I ever met thought to speak of "Matilda," while quite a number waxed eloquent over the orchestrations of *The King and I*.

(See page 60.)

DANCIN'

Orchestrations credited to Ralph **Burns**. (Additional orchestrators, if any, unknown.)

Opened March 27, 1978, Broadhurst, 1,774 performances. Tryout: February, Boston (Colonial).

A revue. Music and lyrics by various writers. Musical direction, vocal and dance arrangements by Gordon Lowry Harrell. Other participants: Jules Fisher (producer); Bob Fosse (choreographer); Ann Reinking (featured).

DANCING IN THE STREETS

Orchestrations credited to Hans **Spialek** and Ray Sinatra. (Additional orchestrators, if any, unknown.)

Tryout: March 23, 1943, Boston (Shubert). Closed April 10, Boston.

Music by Vernon Duke, lyrics by Howard Dietz. Musical direction by Max Meth. Vocal arrangements by Buck (Clay) Warnick. Other participants: Vinton Freedley (producer); Robert Edmond Jones (set designer); Mary Martin (star).

DARK OF THE MOON

Orchestrations credited to Hershy **Kay**.

Opened March 14, 1945, 46th Street, 318 performances. Tryout: unknown.

A play by Howard Richardson and William Berney. Based on the traditional ballad "Barbara Allen." Incidental music by Walter Hendl. Other participant: Carol Stone (star).

DARLING OF THE DAY

Orchestrations by Ralph **Burns**. (Additional orchestrations by Larry **Wilcox** and Jim Tyler.)

Opened January 27, 1968, George Abbott, 31 performances. Tryout: (as *Darling of the Day*) December 4, 1967, Toronto (O'Keefe); (as *Married Alive!*) December 20, Boston (Shubert).

Music by Jule Styne, lyrics by E. Y. Harburg. Based on the novel *The Great Adventure* by Arnold Bennett. Musical direction and vocal arrangements by Buster Davis. Dance arrangements by Trude Rittman. Other participants: Theatre Guild (co-producer); Lee Theodore (choreographer); Nunnally Johnson (original librettist, billing removed); Vincent Price (star); Patricia Routledge (star).

The partiturs are at the Styne office.

The orchestrations are by Burns, with the following exceptions:

Wilcox: "Crossover" (scene with dialogue), "Lady Triumph Underscore," "Money, Money, Money," "Panache," Prologue.

Tyler: "Bows-Rainbow," "Transition A," "Transition B," "Under the Sunset Tree" (song and utility).

Other scores:

"Act 2 Finale" mostly incorporates Burns's score for "Not on Your Nellie," with the opening and ending by Wilcox.

"Butler in the Abbey" is by Burns, with a new ending by Wilcox.

"Finaletto" ("Money Reprise") is by Wilcox, replacing an earlier "Finale Act I" by Burns.

"A Gentleman's Gentleman": the first part is by Burns; the patter ("Oh, where in this foggy wet dominion . . . ") is by Tyler; the rest is by Burns except for the ending (after "man who serves your cup of tea," by Tyler).

"He's a Genius" is mostly by Burns, with Wilcox providing a new final section (beginning after "knighthood makes a painter distingué") utilizing material from Burns's earlier version.

"I've Got a Rainbow Working for Me": first three sections (solo, choral counter-melody [not on the cast album], and solo/choral counterpart) are by Tyler; "New" final section (solo with chorus) is by Wilcox.

"It's Enough to Make a Lady Fall in Love": song and first part of dance ("Putney Rag," which is not included on the cast album) is by Burns; final section, beginning with the stop-time section ("A single life is a waste of time") is by Wilcox.

"Mad for Art" (opening number) is by Burns, with "New Intro" by Wilcox.

"That Something Extra Special": this is orchestrated under the title "A Little Extra Shilling," with a different lyric, by Burns (except for 3-bar ending by Wilcox).

Burns wrote an Overture that was performed out of town, but there was no overture used in New York. The Overture assembled for the cast album begins with the opening section of Wilcox's Prologue, continuing with portions of "Let's See What Happens" and "I've Got a Rainbow Working for Me" (tempo: "Quasi On Brave Old Army Team") from the Burns Overture. Partiturs for the rest of the recording Overture ("That Something Extra Special" and an ending derived from "What Makes a Marriage Merry") have not been found. The Burns Overture was revised at length before being discarded, with various songs used, including several attempts at inserting "Under the Sunset Tree." On one version, Burns writes, "'Sunset Tree' again!—and don't think this will be the last time!"

An extended and overly long (and inauthentic) alternate version of the Overture was recorded by Jack Everly, which seems to include the entire Burns Overture plus other material that was perhaps written (by Everly?) for the recording.

RALPH'S INSTRUCTIONS TO MUSICIANS   "Let's See What Happens" (to drummer): "All the way through this vocal, play the quietest drums in show business."

"What Makes a Marriage Merry" (to conductor): "Quasi Bach, all the way through. J. S. that is, not Max."

"Under the Sunset Tree" (to harp, at "Spring is a young man's fancy": "with palms, Quasi Harpo Marx."

Instr.: 4 reed, 7 brass (2 tpt, 2 tb, 1 tuba, 2 hrn), 10? strings (6? vln, 0 vla, 3 c, 1 b), piano/harpsichord, harp, perc = 24? total.

THE DAY BEFORE SPRING

Orchestrations credited to Harold Byrns. (Additional orchestrators, if any, unknown.)

Opened November 22, 1945, National, 167 performances. Tryout: October 25, New Haven (Shubert); October 30, Boston (Shubert).

Music by Frederick Loewe, lyrics and book by Alan Jay Lerner. Musical direction by Maurice Abravanel. Vocal arrangements by Frederick Loewe. Other participants: John C. Wilson (producer, director); Anthony Tudor (choreographer).

DEAR SIR

Orchestrations credited to Russell **Bennett**. (Additional orchestrators, if any, unknown.)

Opened September 23, 1924, Times Square, 15 performances. Tryout: September 3, Philadelphia (Forrest).

Music by Jerome Kern, lyrics by Howard Dietz. Musical direction by Gus Salzer.

The partiturs are in the Kern Collection at the Library of Congress (unexamined).

DEAR WORLD

Orchestrations (mostly) by Philip J. **Lang**. (Additional orchestrations by Jack Andrews.)

Opened February 6, 1969, Mark Hellinger, 132 performances. Tryout: Boston (Colonial).

Music and lyrics by Jerry Herman. Based on the play *The Madwoman of Chaillot* by Jean Giraudoux. Musical direction and vocal arrangements by Donald Pippin. Dance and incidental arrangements by Dorothea Freitag (replacing John Morris). Other participants: Alexander H. Cohen (producer); Joe Layton (replacement director and choreographer); Angela Lansbury (star).

The partiturs are in the possession of the composer.

The orchestrations are by Lang, with the following exceptions:

Andrews: "Boat Scene (Riverbank)," "Halls of Justice," "Have a Little Pity on the Rich," "I Like Me," "Rain," "Street Singer," "Tomorrow Morning" (reprise).

Other scores:

Entr'acte: there are two versions, one by Lang and one by Andrews.

Instr.: 5 reed, 6 brass (3 tpt, 2 tb, 1 hrn), 11? strings (8 vln, 0 vla, 2? c, 1 b), organ, accordion, harp, guitar, 2 perc = 28? total.

DESTRY RIDES AGAIN

Orchestrations credited to Philip J. **Lang**. (Additional orchestrations by George Siravo and probably others.)

Opened April 23, 1959, Imperial, 472 performances. Tryout: March 9, Philadelphia (Shubert); April 1, Boston (Shubert).

Music and lyrics by Harold Rome. Based on the story by Max Brand. Musical direction and vocal arrangements by Lehman Engel. Dance arrangements by Genevieve Pitot. Other participants: David Merrick (producer); Michael Kidd (director, choreographer); Andy Griffith (star); Dolores Gray (star).

Two partiturs are in the Merrick Collection at the Library of Congress.

There are two charts for "Fair Warning," one by Lang and the other by Siravo, a top record arranger who worked for Frank Sinatra and other singers (including Dolores Gray). Siravo's chart is marked with the same running-order number (#30B) as Lang's and uses the same instrumentation, so it was clearly used in the show. (The back of Siravo's chart has written on it in big letters: "Dolores Gray. Rush!!!") Both charts are water-damaged, making them difficult to analyze, but the orchestration of "Fair Warning" (as heard on the cast album) sounds considerably different than the rest of the score. Furthermore, Siravo's chart features bongos and fluttertongue flute playing in the refrain, which are more typical of his style and are prominent on the cast recording. It is not unlikely that as in the case of *Jamaica*, two years earlier, Lang stepped aside when the leading lady demanded a "better" orchestration.

Based on Lang's other shows at the time, it is guessed that charts were ghosted by Jack Mason and/or Carroll Huxley, with Bob Noeltner (a Pitot favorite) likely on the dances.

Instr.: 5 reed, 7 brass (3 tpt, 3 tb, 1 hrn), ? strings (vln, 2? vla, c, b), piano, guitar/banjo, perc.

DO I HEAR A WALTZ?

Orchestrations (mostly) by Ralph **Burns**. (Additional orchestrations by Larry **Wilcox**, with Jim Tyler.)

Opened March 18, 1965, 46th Street, 220 performances. Tryout: February 1, New Haven (Shubert); February 16, Boston (Shubert).

Music by Richard Rodgers, lyrics by Stephen Sondheim. Based on the play *The Time of the Cuckoo* by Arthur Laurents. Musical direction by Frederick Dvonch. Dance arrangements by Richard de Benedictis. Other participants: Richard Rodgers (producer); John Dexter (director); Herbert Ross (choreographer); Arthur Laurents (librettist).

The partiturs are at the offices of the Rodgers & Hammerstein Organization.

The orchestrations are by Burns, with the following exceptions:

Wilcox: "Promenade" (see below), "Stay," "Two by Two" (cut).

Tyler: "Philadelphia" (cut), utilities ("Perhaps," "Philadelphia").

Other scores:

"Do I Hear a Waltz?" is by Burns; "Waltz Dance Tag" (within number) and "Waltz Utility" by Wilcox.

"Promenade": the original version was an extended number, in seven parts (and twelve separate charts), all by Wilcox. This included personalized sections for different characters and chorus; the number was built around a major song for Leona, "Two by Two." When replacement choreographer Herb Ross came in, "Promenade" was replaced by "New Promenade." This was a considerably shorter number, including most of the personalized sections but with a new song for Leona, "Here We Go Again." The original

"Promenade" was orchestrated by Wilcox; "New Promenade" was orchestrated by Burns; "(New) Promenade Part 2" included sections by Burns and Wilcox.

"Take the Moment" is by Burns; reprise by Wilcox (including sections from the Burns chart).

> BURNS: I believe Steve was the first person who ever said to Rodgers, "I don't like that melody. Go back and do it again."

Instr.: 4 reed (4 fl, 3 clr), 5 brass (2 tpt, 3 tb), 17 strings (8 vln, 4 vla, 4 c, b), harp/celesta, guitar/mandolin, perc = 29 total.

DO RE MI

Orchestrations by Luther Henderson. (Additional orchestrations by Bill Stegmeyer, Cornel Tanassy, and David Terry.)

Opened December 26, 1960, St. James, 400 performances. Tryout: November 7, Philadelphia; November 29, Boston (Colonial).

Music by Jule Styne, lyrics by Betty Comden & Adolph Green. Based on the novella by Garson Kanin. Musical direction by Lehman Engel. Vocal arrangements and direction by Buster Davis. Dance arrangements by David Baker. Other participants: David Merrick (producer); Garson Kanin (director, librettist); Phil Silvers (star); Nancy Walker (star).

About half of the partiturs are in the American Musical Theatre Collection at the Library of Congress. Henderson's notes are in his personal papers. Base page rate: $6.71.

Henderson: "Ambition," "Juke Box Montage," "Take a Job."

Terry: "Adventure," "The Investigation."

Tanassy: "Divertissement," "Don't Be Afraid of a Teardrop," "Mob Talk," "Pancakes," "Remembering," utilities ("Cry Like the Wind," "Make Someone Happy," "Take a Job").

Stegmeyer: "Venezuela," "Waiting."

Other scores:

"All You Need Is a Quarter": the only partitur found is for the "tape version," by Henderson.

"Double Juke Box": part 4 is by Stegmeyer.

"It's Legitimate": "orchestration scored by Luther Henderson, sketch transcribed by Cornel Tanassy."

Finale act II: part I, beginning with Kay singing "Take a Job," is by Stegmeyer; part II, "Make Someone Happy (Finale)," with Hubie and chorus singing (and which is on the cast album), is by Tanassy.

Missing partiturs:

"All of My Life," "Asking for You," "Cry Like the Wind," "Fireworks," "He's a V.I.P.," "I Know about Love," "The Investigation (Who Is Mr. Big?)," "The Late, Late Show," "Make Someone Happy," "What's New at the Zoo?"

The Tanassy and Terry scores are signed, as are some of Henderson's. Finale act II is written on paper with "arr. by Lindsey" printed on the top and "PAT BOONE" printed on the bottom. This was presumably borrowed from conductor/orchestrator Mort Lindsey.

Do Re Mi was originally offered to Ramin and Ginzler, of Styne and Merrick's *Gypsy*, who were simultaneously committed to *Wildcat.* When work on the film version of *West Side Story* was delayed, Ramin could find time for only one of the two; since *Wildcat* was paying more than *Do Re Mi* (Merrick insisted on bare minimum scale), Ramin and Ginzler opted out. They passed the job on to Kostal, who was just finishing *Fiorello!* He refused minimum, too. With the show already in production, Phil Silvers recommended Henderson (with whom he had worked on television).

The orchestrations were among the most expensive of the time, due to a variety of reasons: an initial delay in having materials ready for orchestration (resulting in heavy overtime costs); the number of extended-length comedy numbers; the many new songs written on the road; and the inordinate number of orchestrated-and-copied numbers which were then transposed or rerouted, resulting in the need for new, overtime charts. (Much of this can be explained by the presence of a director, Garson Kanin, who was unaccustomed to the demands of a musical.) As a result, *Do Re Mi* ran to about 1,500 pages of orchestration, many at overtime rates; a standard musical was more in the 1,000-page range. (*She Loves Me*, a music-intensive show, was only 1,041.)

From Henderson to Merrick: "You mentioned that I was remiss in not 'snitching' to you when the music wasn't coming fast enough. 'Phil Lang,' you said, 'would have called me, and I would have seen to it that you received the music in time.' Obviously, and very visibly to the naked eye, I am not Phil Lang. Snitching is very definitely out of my line."

Instr.: 5 reed, 7 brass (3 tpt, 3 tb, 1 hrn), 10 strings (7 vln, 0 vla, 2 c, 1 b), piano, harp, guitar, 2 perc = 27 total.

DOCTOR JAZZ

Orchestrations by Luther Henderson. (Additional orchestrations by Dick Hyman, Sy Oliver, and possibly others.)

Opened March 19, 1975, Winter Garden, 5 performances. Tryout: none.

Music and lyrics mostly by Buster Davis. Musical direction and vocal arrangements by Buster Davis. Dance arrangements and incidental music composed by Luther Henderson. Other participants: Buster Davis (co-librettist); Donald McKayle (director, choreographer).

(See page 134.)

DONNYBROOK!

Orchestrations and arrangements credited to Robert **Ginzler**. Ballet music orchestrated by Laurence Rosenthal. (Additional orchestrators, if any, unknown.)

Opened May 18, 1961, 46th Street, 68 performances. Tryout: Philadelphia; May 2, Washington, D.C. (National).

Music and lyrics by Johnny Burke. Based on the film *The Quiet Man* by Maurice Walsh. Musical direction and vocal arrangements by Clay Warnick. Ballet music arranged and orchestrated by Laurence Rosenthal. Other participants: Jack Cole (director, choreographer); Eddie Foy (star); Susan Johnson (featured).

DRAT! THE CAT!

Orchestrations credited to Hershy **Kay** and Clare Grundman. (Additional orchestrators, if any, unknown.)

Opened October 10, 1965, Martin Beck, 8 performances. Tryout: Philadelphia (Shubert).

Music by Milton Schafer, lyrics and book by Ira Levin. Musical direction and vocal arrangements by Herbert Grossman. Dance arrangements by Genevieve Pitot. Other participants: Joe Layton (director, choreographer); Ira Levin (librettist); Elliott Gould (star); Lesley Ann Warren (star).

DREAM WITH MUSIC

Orchestrations credited to Russell **Bennett**, Hans **Spialek**, and Ted **Royal**. (Additional orchestrators, if any, unknown.)

Opened May 18, 1944, Majestic, 28 performances. Tryout: April, Boston (Shubert).

Music by Clay Warnick, lyrics by Edward Eager. "Music based on themes from Saint-Saëns, Rimsky-Korsakoff, Schubert, Beethoven, Weber, Grieg, Borodin, Mussorgsky, Wagner, Chopin, Gluck, Schumann, Dvorak, Haydn, and of course Tchaikowsky." Musical direction by Max Meth. Vocal arrangements by Clay Warnick. Other participants: Richard Kollmar (producer, director); Dorothy Kilgallen (co-librettist); Vera Zorina (star).

DU BARRY WAS A LADY

Orchestrations by Hans **Spialek**. (Additional orchestrations by Russell **Bennett**, Ted **Royal**, Walter Paul, and Franklyn Marks.)

Opened December 6, 1939, 46th Street, 408 performances. Tryout: November 9, New Haven (Shubert); November 13, Boston (Shubert); November 27, Philadelphia (Forrest).

Music and Lyrics by Cole Porter. Musical direction by Gene Salzer. Vocal arrangements by Hugh Martin. Other participants: B. G. DeSylva (producer); Herbert Fields and B. G. DeSylva (librettists); Bert Lahr (star); Ethel Merman (star); Betty Grable (featured).

Many of the partiturs are at Tams-Witmark.

Spialek: "But in the Morning, No" (song and encore), "It Was Written in the Stars," "Come On In" (see below), "Entrance of Louie (Where's Louie)," "Do I Love You?" Opening act II ("Danse Tzigane"), "Give Him the Ooh-La-La," "What Have I?" (cut).

Bennett: "Ev'ry Day a Holiday" (and encore); "Mesdames et Messieurs."

Royal: Prologue (Opening act I).

Paul: "Dream Song," "Du Barry's Entrance," utilities ("Do I Love You?" "Ev'ry Day a Holiday," "It Was Written in the Stars").

Other scores:

"Come On In": song is by Spialek; "Burlesque" and "[Betty] Grable/[Charles] Walter Dance Specialty (Danse Victoire)" are by Royal.

Finale act I ("Du Barry Was a Lady"): first section is by Paul, second section by Spialek.

Overture: mostly by Spialek, incorporating Paul's utilities of "Ev'ry Day a Holiday," "It Was Written in the Stars," and "Do I Love You?"

"Well, Did You Evah" is by Spialek, replacing an earlier version by Paul.

"When Love Beckoned (in Fifty-Second Street)" is by Royal, with verse by Spialek.

The following scores are missing: Entr'acte, "Friendship," Gavotte, "It Ain't Etiquette," "Katie Went to Hatie," "L'apres Midi du Beouf." Tommy Krasker and Robert Kimball, in their *Catalog of the American Musical*, attribute "Friendship" and "L'apres Midi du Beouf" to Royal.

Instr.: 5 reed, 5 brass (3 tpt, 1 tb, 1 hrn), 13? strings (8? vln, 2? vla, 2? c, 1 b), piano, harp, perc = 26? total.

THE DUCHESS MISBEHAVES

Orchestrations credited to Don **Walker**. (Additional orchestrators, if any, unknown.)

Opened February 13, 1946, Adelphi, 5 performances. Tryout: January 11, Philadelphia (Shubert).

Music by Dr. Frank Black, lyrics by Gladys Shelley. Musical direction by Charles Sanford. Vocal arrangements by Clay Warnick.

Composer Frank Black was head of the music department at NBC Radio for more than twenty years and offered strong support (and steady work) when Walker was beginning his career in the early 1930s.

EARL CARROLL'S SKETCH BOOK (2ND EDITION)

Orchestrations uncredited. (Orchestrations by Russell **Bennett**, Don **Walker**, Ted **Royal**, David Raksin, and others.)

Opened June 4, 1935, Winter Garden, 207 performances. Tryout: unknown.

A revue. Music and lyrics by Murray Mencher, Charles Newman, and Charles Tobias. Musical direction by Ray Kavanaugh. Other participant: Ken Murray (star).

EARLY TO BED

Orchestrations by Don **Walker**. (Additional orchestrations by Ted **Royal** and Robert Noeltner.)

Opened June 17, 1943, Broadhurst, 380 performances. Tryout: May 24, Boston.

Music by Thomas ("Fats") Waller, lyrics and book by George Marion, Jr. Musical direction by Archie Bleyer. Vocal arrangements by Buck (Clay) Warnick. Special ballet music composed and arranged by Baldwin Bergersen.

A newspaper clipping dated March 11, 1943, announced that Walker would orchestrate *Early to Bed*—at the same time noting that the show's composer, Ferde Grofé, had withdrawn, and the producers were looking for a replacement. The same clipping mentioned that *Away We Go!* (aka *Oklahoma!*) was giving its first performance in New Haven that very night.

Walker's balance sheet through the Boston opening, dated May 27, 1943, provides the following information:

Contract price for all orchestrations and copying up to out-of-town opening: $5,250. Copying expenses: $887.03; arranging expenses: $388.70 (Royal, $313.70; Noeltner, $75); commissions: $525. Net profit on contract: $3,449.27. The copying expense covered seven men, including Ginzler and Noeltner, plus $6.82 for paper. Ginzler is known to have played trombone in the pit for this musical.

EAST WIND

Orchestrations credited to Hans **Spialek**. (Additional orchestrators unknown.)
Opened October 27, 1931, Manhattan, 23 performances. Tryout: October 5, Pittsburgh (Nixon); October 13, Cleveland; October 19, Baltimore.
Music by Sigmund Romberg, lyrics and book by Oscar Hammerstein II. Musical direction by Oscar Bradley. Other participant: Oscar Hammerstein II (director).

THE EDUCATION OF H*Y*M*A*N K*A*P*L*A*N

Orchestrations credited to Larry **Wilcox**. (Additional orchestrators, if any, unknown.)
Opened April 4, 1968, Alvin, 29 performances. Tryout: March 4, Philadelphia (Erlanger).
Music and lyrics by Oscar Brand and Paul Nassau. Based on the novel by Leo Rosten. Musical direction and vocal arrangements by Julian Stein. Dance arrangements by Lee Holdridge. Other participants: George Abbott (director); Tom Bosley (star); Donna McKechnie (featured).

As if this show didn't have enough problems, word spread through the Alvin during intermission of the opening night performance that Dr. Martin Luther King, Jr., had been assassinated. Mayor John Lindsay, who was in the house, rushed out in fear of riots in Harlem, while much (though not all) of the audience remained for the rest of the dispiriting evening.

AN EVENING WITH CAROL BURNETT

Orchestrations credited to Irwin **Kostal**. (Additional orchestrators, if any, unknown.)
Opened July 1962, Detroit (Fisher). Closed August 1962.
Music and lyrics by various writers. Musical direction by Irwin Kostal. Other participants: Ernest Flatt (choreographer); Mike Nichols (sketches); Mitzi and Ken Welch (sketches); Carol Burnett (star).

This eight-week tour was a follow-up to the 1962 television special *Julie and Carol at Carnegie Hall.* When Julie Andrews became unavailable, the revue went out with Carol Burnett plus chorus (and Kostal conducting), and was reportedly quite uproarious.
(See page 247.)

EVER GREEN

Orchestrations credited to Russell **Bennett**. (Additional orchestrators, if any, unknown.)

Opened December 3, 1930, Adelphi (London), 254 performances. Tryout: October 13, Glasgow, Scotland (King's).

Music by Richard Rodgers, lyrics by Lorenz Hart. Musical direction by Richard Crean. Other participants: Charles B. Cochran (producer); Jessie Matthews (star).

EVERYBODY'S WELCOME

Orchestrations uncredited. (Orchestrations by Hans **Spialek**, Edward B. Powell, Hilding Anderson, Joe Jordon, F. Henri Klickmann, and possibly others.)

Opened October 13, 1931, Shubert, 127 performances. Tryout: September 14, Newark; elsewhere.

Music by Sammy Fain, lyrics by Irving Kahal. Additional songs by Herman Hupfeld and others. Based on the play *Up Pops the Devil* by Frances Goodrich and Albert Hackett. Musical direction by Tom Jones.

Many of the partiturs are in the Shubert Archives.

Spialek: "As Time Goes By," "Even as You and I" (song, incidental), Overture, "You've Got a Lease on My Heart."

Powell: "All Wrapped Up in You," "Nature Played a Dirty Trick on You," "Tango," "Valse Medley" (including "You and You").

Anderson: "He Looked at Her and She Looked at Him," "Ta-Ta Old Bean."

Jordon: "Lover's Luck," "One-in-a-Million."

Klickmann: "Greenwich Village."

Spialek's partitur for the Overture reads, "Music composed by Everybody and H. Spialek."

Instr.: 3 reed (3 sax), 5 brass (3 tpt, 2 tb), ? strings (? vln, 0 vla, 2 c, 1 b), piano, perc.

(See page 21.)

EVITA

Orchestrations credited to Hershy **Kay** and Andrew Lloyd Webber.

Opened September 25, 1979, Broadway, 1,567 performances. Tryout: May 8, Los Angeles (Dorothy Chandler Pavilion); San Francisco.

Music by Andrew Lloyd Webber, lyrics by Tim Rice. Suggested by events in the life of Eva Peron. Musical direction by René Wiegert. Other participants: Harold Prince (director); Patti LuPone (star); Mandy Patinkin (star).

All orchestrations are credited (on the original cast album) to Kay and Webber except for "Don't Cry for Me Argentina," "Oh, What a Circus," "On the Balcony of the Casa Rosada," "Requiem for Evita," and "Waltz for Eva and Che," which are attributed solely to the composer. Credits of this manner are often more official than actual.

(See page 53.)

FACE THE MUSIC

Orchestrations credited to Russell **Bennett**, Frank Tours, and Maurice de Packh. (Additional orchestrators unknown.)

Opened February 17, 1932, New Amsterdam, 165 performances. Tryout: February 3, Philadelphia (Shubert).

Music and lyrics by Irving Berlin. Musical direction by Frank Tours. Other participants: Sam H. Harris (producer); George S. Kaufman (director); Moss Hart (librettist); Mary Boland (star).

The original orchestrations were reconstructed for performance at Encores! in 2007, working from the pit parts (as the partiturs could not be located). However, I have been able to make some educated guesses as to who did what. Frank Tours was a veteran conductor who arrived on Broadway in 1903 and was best known for a series of Jolson shows; he had worked with Berlin as early as 1916, with *Step This Way*. As an orchestrator, he seems to have had limited experience, occasionally contributing a few charts to shows he was conducting. With Bennett aboard, it is unlikely that Tours would have orchestrated any major numbers. Rather, he would have contributed incidentals or scene changes. De Packh had also been around before Bennett came to Broadway; when Frank Saddler died, de Packh was one of the orchestrators Dreyfus tried out before moving Bennett into the number one spot. By 1932, he was often assisting Bennett or Spialek by writing utilities and "finishing" longer numbers that were started by the head man. Thus, I would suppose that the shorter songs and the beginning sections of the longer ones are by Bennett; the rest of these split songs are by de Packh (or other assistants). Minor incidentals and perhaps a chorus number would be by Tours. It is also quite likely that other orchestrators—Spialek, specifically—contributed a song or two.

FADE OUT, FADE IN

Orchestrations by Ralph **Burns** and Ray Ellis. Ballet orchestration by Robert Prince. (Additional orchestrations by Harry Zimmerman, Richard de Benedictis, Larry **Wilcox**, and Jim Tyler.)

Opened May 26, 1964, Mark Hellinger, 199 performances (plus 72 additional performances after its reopening on February 15, 1965). Tryout: April 18, New Haven (Shubert); April 29, Boston (Colonial).

Music by Jule Styne, lyrics and book by Betty Comden & Adolph Green. Musical direction by Colin Romoff. Vocal arrangements by Buster Davis. Dance arrangements by Richard de Benedictis. Other participants: Jule Styne (co-producer); George Abbott (director); Carol Burnett (star).

Most of the partiturs are in the Warner/Chappell Collection at the Library of Congress.

Ellis: "At the Post" (cut, two versions), "Byron Prong" (cut), "Close Harmony" (two versions), "Fear" (song, "Byron's Fear," and utility), "Forbidden Fruit" (cut), "I Can't Go Back" (cut), "I'm with You" (see below), "Lila Tremaine," "L.Z.'s Playoff," "L.Z.'s Scherzo," "L.Z.'s Vienna," "My Fortune Is My Face" (three versions), "The Nineteen Thirties," Opening, "The Usher from the Mezzanine," "You Mustn't Feel Discouraged."

Burns: "It's Good to Be Back Home" (see below), Overture (see below).

Zimmerman: "Fade Out, Fade In" (see below), "Go Home Train" (see below).

de Benedictis: "Carol's Paganini Bit," "Lila Bungalow to Gate."

Prince: "Dangerous Age Nightmare" (ballet).

Wilcox: "My Heart Is Like a Violin," "What Is this Thing I've Got?" (cut).

Tyler: "Take the Time to Fall in Love" (cut).

Other scores:

"Dangerous Age" (song): unidentified hand.

"Fade Out, Fade In" ("Duet–Dance 5/11/64") is mostly by Harry Zimmerman, with the final section (beginning 4 bars from the end of the dance break, and including the vocal tag) by Wilcox. There are three earlier scores: a solo version for Hope (Burnett), by Tyler; a revised version (4/23) by Tyler, with dance by Wilcox; and another (5/2) by Ellis, by which point the song had become a duet.

"Go Home Train" (5/11) is by Zimmerman, replacing two earlier versions (4/27 and 5/1) by Ellis.

"I'm with You": there are no less than eight(?) scores, all by Ellis. The longest incorporates a dance by de Benedictis. Ellis also did the utility and act II reprise.

"It's Good to Be Back Home" is by Burns. There are three earlier versions, incorporating large sections of movie star impressions by Burnett (which were cut). Utility is by Ellis.

Overture is in three sections. Part I (Fanfare, "Violin/I'm with You," "Usher from the Mezzanine," "Fade Out") is by Burns. The clarinet solo in the title song is marked "play like Benny Goodman." Part II ("Call Me Savage," "I'm with You") is by Jim Tyler. Coda (starting with the fast section after "I'm with You," leading into the aggravated waltz and continuing through the end) is by Burns.

Missing: "Call Me Savage."

Early lyric for "The Usher from the Mezzanine": "The usher turned her flashlight in / To study singing and Gunga Din."

Burns's commitment to Styne's already-in-production *Funny Girl*—which extended its tryout—resulted in the hiring of a co-orchestrator, Ray Ellis (who earlier that season had orchestrated Styne's incidental music for the David Merrick/Tony Richardson production of Brecht's *Arturo Ui*). As *Fade Out* underwent its own troubles, Burns seems to have been generally unavailable, resulting in numerous ghosts, including Harry Zimmerman (of that April's *High Spirits*, with which Styne was also associated). Zimmerman went on to become Burnett's television orchestrator.

Instr.: 5 reed, 8 brass (3 tpt, 3 tb, 2 hrn), 9? strings (6 vln, 0 vla, 2? c, 1 b), piano, harp, 2 perc = 26? total.

A FAMILY AFFAIR

Orchestrations (mostly) by Robert **Ginzler**. (Additional orchestrations by Don **Walker**, with Sid **Ramin** and others.)

Opened January 27, 1962, Billy Rose, 65 performances. Tryout: December 26, 1961, Philadelphia (Erlanger).

Music by John Kander, lyrics and book by James Goldman and William Goldman. (Official billing: "by James Goldman, John Kander and William Goldman.") Musical and vocal direction by Stanley Lebowsky. Dance arrangements by Gerald Alters. Other participant: Harold Prince (replacement director).

The partiturs are at Music Theatre International.

Ginzler: "Anything for You" (see below), "Beautiful" ("Alfie," "Tillie," and utility), "Every Girl Wants to Get Married," "Kahlua Bay," "Harmony" (song and utility), "My Son the Lawyer," "Now Morris," "Revenge," "Right Girls" (see below), "Summer Is Over," "There's a Room in My House" (song and utility), "Wedding" ("Family Affair"/ "Room in My House"), "What I Say Goes."

Walker: Various incidentals and transitions.

Ramin: "Milwaukee" (cut).

Unidentified hand #1 (Gerald Alters?): "Bachelor Blues."

Other scores:

Act I Finale ("Harmony") is by Ginzler, with final 5 bars (for curtain) by Walker.

"Anything for You" is by Ginzler, with 20-bar extension (not on the recording) by Walker. Entr'acte ("Harmony Utility") is by Ginzler, with 4-bar "Intro to Entr'acte" by Walker.

"Football New" is by unidentified hand #1 (Alters?). This leads into Ginzler's "Football V" (starting with "Friends of Alfie Nathan").

"I'm Worse than Anybody": part I is by Ginzler, part II (starting with "Misery" trio, 120 bars) by Walker. The Walker chart replaced an earlier trio routine. Sample of original lyric: "I could resign from Hadassah."

Overture: there are two versions, one by Ginzler and one by Walker (which starts with "Every Girl Wants to Be Married"). At bar 44 of Ginzler's score, he writes "cut to bar #15 of new overture"; Walker's score starts with bar 15, so the final Overture apparently combined the two versions. The opening on the cast recording, featuring a choral rendition of the title song, is abridged from Ginzler's original Overture.

"Oh, What a Wonderful Party" is mostly by Ginzler, with part of the dance—"Bachelor Party Re-write," a wild jazz section—by unidentified hand #1 (Alters?).

"Right Girls" is by Ginzler, with the final 2-bar fanfare by Walker.

A Family Affair was initially directed by Word Baker (best known for the 1960 off-Broadway hit *The Fantasticks*). After a poor reception in Philadelphia, Hal Prince came in to salvage the show; by all reports, he did an impressive job, laying the groundwork for his career as a director.

Ginzler came to the show through his relationship with Kander (who was dance arranger on two shows he orchestrated, *Gypsy* and *Irma La Douce*). When Prince started making changes, Ginzler—already busy on *All American*—called in his friend and former boss Don Walker to take over. Prince's alterations called for numerous musical bridges from scene to scene, which were done by Walker. In interviews during the research for this book, neither Kander nor Prince recalled Walker's involvement.

"Milwaukee" starts as a solo for the Shelley Berman character, followed by three-part harmony. This is followed by an instrumental section for four saxes and brass, with the tempo marked "Cool!" (from Ramin, who orchestrated "Cool" in *West Side Story*).

RED'S INSTRUCTIONS TO MUSICIANS   "Oh, What a Wonderful Party": trumpet solo is marked "early Dizzy"; trombone solo says "rip into it like raw meat"; (to brass at end): "remove mouthpieces from collar buttons."

Overture (to copyist Mathilde Pincus): "shift the whole mess up to naturals, dear."

"Revenge," at final bar: "Fine—Thank Gawd!!!"

"Wedding" (to violins): "one half pint higher"; (to timpanist): "change Ab to G while you are saving the show with the C."

Instr.: 4 reed, 5 brass (3 tpt, I tb, I hrn), 9 strings (4 vln, 0 vla, 4 c, I b), piano/harp, guitar/banjo, perc = 21 total.

FANNY

Orchestrations (mostly) by Philip J. **Lang**. (Additional orchestrations by Jack Mason, with Joe Glover.)

Opened November 4, 1954, Majestic, 888 performances. Tryout: October 12, Boston (Shubert); October 28, Philadelphia (Shubert).

Music and lyrics by Harold Rome. Based on the trilogy by Marcel Pagnol. Musical direction by Lehman Engel. Vocal arrangements by Lehman Engel. Musical continuity by Trude Rittman. Other participants: David Merrick (producer); Joshua Logan (producer, director); Ezio Pinza (star).

The partiturs are in the Merrick Collection at the Library of Congress.

The orchestrations are by Lang, with the following exceptions:

Mason: "Street" ("Restless Heart Underscore #2"), "The Thought of You," "#16 underscore," "#25 underscore," "#27 underscore."

Glover: "#7A" ("Fanny" incidental).

Other scores:

"Be Kind to Your Parents" is by Lang, replacing an earlier version by Mason; the brief verse (with bells) is from Mason's chart.

"Fanny" (duet and reprise) is by Lang; intro to verse of reprise is by Mason.

"Garage Scene" is by Lang and Mason.

"I Have to Tell You": there are several sections and multiple versions, the earliest by Lang; "Version 2" includes Mason's 16-bar "Introduction to verse of 'I Have to Tell You.'"

"Oysters, Cockles and Mussels": part 1 is by Lang; part 2, beginning with the four-part choral underscoring, is by Mason.

"To My Wife" is by Lang, with an 18-bar introduction by Mason.

"Welcome Home": there are several versions, more than one of which might have been used in the course of the performance. "Final #14 (Cesar)" is by Lang, with a 12-bar introduction by Mason; "Marius Welcome Home #24" is by Mason; "Introduction to Welcome Home" is by Mason; "Reprise and Street Scene," with a duet for Marius and Brun, is by Mason.

The partiturs include numerous numbers that needed to be reorchestrated, as well as much cut material. (Many of the incidentals and dances in the published vocal score are severely truncated.) It appears that many of the songs were submitted to Lang for orchestration before the connecting musical material and introductions had been written, necessitating numerous changes.

> LANG: I went to Ezio Pinza and asked him what he wanted. He said, "They tell me you're a good orchestrator. You orchestrate, I sing."

Instr.: 5 reed, 6 brass (2 tpt, 2 tb, 2 hrn), 13 strings (8 vln [1 mandolin], 2 vla, 2 c, 1 b), concertina, harp, guitar, perc = 28 total.

(See page 70.)

FIDDLER ON THE ROOF

Orchestrations by Don **Walker**. (Additional orchestrations by Arnold Goland, with Jim Tyler.)

Opened September 22, 1964, Imperial, 3,242 performances. Tryout: Detroit (Fisher); August 26, Washington, D.C. (National).

Music by Jerry Bock, lyrics by Sheldon Harnick. Based on the *Tevye* stories by Sholom Aleichem. Musical direction and vocal arrangements by Milton Greene. Dance arrangements by Betty Walberg. Other participants: Harold Prince (producer); Jerome Robbins (director, choreographer); Joseph Stein (librettist); Zero Mostel (star).

The location of most of the partiturs is unknown.

Four partiturs by Walker ("Chava Sequence" (original ballet version), "If I Were a Rich Man," "To Life," "Wedding Dance") are in a private collection. Invoices are in the Walker Collection at the Library of Congress. Base page rate: $6.52.

The orchestrations are by Walker, with the following exceptions:

Goland: "Anatevka Underscoring," "Opening Act II," utility ("To Life"), miscellaneous fixes.

Tyler: "To Life" (dance).

THANKS AND WISHES   From Walker to general manager Carl Fisher: "How does a lowly arranger get house seats to this fabulous hit?"

Instr.: 5 reed (including a bassoon/heckelphone chair), 7 brass (3 tpt, 2 tb [including 1 euphonium], 2 hrn), 9 strings (6 vln, 1 vla, 1 c, 1 b), accordion, 2 guitar/mandolin, perc = 25 total.

(See pages 65, 201, 246.)

FIFTY MILLION FRENCHMEN

Orchestrations uncredited. (Orchestrations by Hans **Spialek**, F. Henri Klickmann, Russell **Bennett**, Maurice de Packh, and Charles Miller.)

Opened November 27, 1929, Lyric, 254 performances. Tryout: November 14, Boston (Colonial).

Music and lyrics by Cole Porter. Musical direction by Gene Salzer. Other participants: Herbert Fields (librettist); William Gaxton (star).

The location of the partiturs is unknown, but they were examined by Tommy Krasker while he was preparing a performing edition of the show in 1988 (which resulted in a 1991 cast album). His findings indicate the following:

Spialek: "Do You Want to See Paris?" Entr'acte, "I Worship You," "It Isn't Done," "Let's Step Out," "Paree, What Did You Do to Me?" "Somebody's Going to Throw a Big Party," "You Do Something to Me," "You've Got That Thing."

Klickmann: "At Longchamps Today," "I'm in Love," Overture, "Please Don't Make Me Be Good," "Why Shouldn't I Have You?"

Bennett: "Find Me a Primitive Man."

de Packh: "I'm Unlucky at Gambling."

Miller: "Where Would You Get Your Coat?"

FINE AND DANDY

Orchestrations uncredited. (Orchestrations by Hans **Spialek** and others.)

Opened September 23, 1930, Erlanger, 255 performances. Tryout: unknown.

Music by Kay Swift, lyrics by Paul James. Musical direction by Gene Salzer. Other participant: Joe Cook (star).

One of the partiturs is at the Library of Congress.

Spialek: "Nobody Breaks My Heart."

FINIAN'S RAINBOW

Orchestrations by Russell **Bennett** and Don **Walker**. (Additional orchestrators, if any, unknown.)

Opened January 10, 1947, 46th Street, 725 performances. Tryout: December 10, 1946, Philadelphia.

Music by Burton Lane, lyrics and book by E. Y. Harburg. Musical direction by Milton Rosenstock. Choral arrangements by Lyn Murray. Additional vocal arrangements by Milton Rosenstock. Dance arrangements by Trude Rittman. Other participants: Michael Kidd (choreographer); Fred Saidy (co-librettist); David Wayne (featured).

Bennett's invoices are preserved in his ledger. Base page rate: $4.05.

> WALKER: I was called into Max Dreyfus's office and told that I would have to go down to Philadelphia and work on *Finian's Rainbow*. "But," I argued, "it's Russell's show!" "Never mind, he's off it now and it's up to you." So I caught a train to the City of Brotherly Love and found that there wasn't much love flying around *Finian's Rainbow*. There had been many disagreements about the way Russell had handled a number of the scores and he had not been cooperative. Anyhow, I rescored five or six numbers, and everyone was happy.

Pending discovery of the partiturs, it is impossible to identify these "five or six numbers," other than "The Begat" and "Necessity." (Harburg to Walker: "Thanks for the additional shine you gave the *Rainbow*. Thanks for saving 'Necessity' and 'Begat.' Stick around—we need you.") The Library of Congress has Walker's copies of the rehearsal versions of "How Are Things in Glocca Morra?" "Old Devil Moon," and "If This Isn't Love"; given that the keys are handwritten on the pages in pencil, one theorizes that Walker reorchestrated these numbers (replacing earlier versions by Bennett). It is possible to definitely identify the official Overture as by Bennett, as he wrote it in New York three weeks after his departure from the show.

> ROSENSTOCK: They ran out of money when we were in Philadelphia. There were terrible fights. They threw out two numbers, and I went to them and said, "You are out of your f***ing mind." Yip Harburg said, "Who are you to talk to me like that, you no good s***." I said, "All right, I think you are wrong." Yip said, "Okay, fix it." I said, "Are you telling me to fix it?" He said, "Yes." Lyn Murray did the numbers originally. They had four boys singing "Necessity," and then they had the four boys doing "The Begat," back to back. But Lyn had a whole big vocal thing in "The Begat," and when they finished, it was too heavy. There was too much harmony in there, it didn't get right to it. Bretaigne Windust, the director, said, "It's a living room number; it's very good in the living room but it doesn't work onstage." So I took "Necessity" and worked it out with the chorus girls, evenings after the performance. Finally, I took in the new versions of the two numbers. Everybody refused to listen to them. "Look," I said, "we have been working every night; you said to fix it. The least you could do is listen to it." So Harburg said, "Okay, smartass, let's hear those songs."

FIORELLO!

Orchestrations (virtually totally) by Irwin **Kostal**. (Additional orchestrations by Don **Walker**.)

Opened November 23, 1959, Broadhurst, 795 performances. Tryout: October 19, New Haven (Shubert); October 27, Philadelphia (Erlanger); Boston (Shubert).

Music by Jerry Bock, lyrics by Sheldon Harnick. Suggested by events in the life of Fiorello H. La Guardia. Musical direction by Hal Hastings. Dance arrangements by Jack Elliott. Other participants: Robert Griffith and Harold Prince (producers); George Abbott (director, co-librettist); Peter Gennaro (choreographer); Tom Bosley (featured).

Most of the partiturs are in the Bock Collection at the New York Public Library.

The orchestrations are by Kostal, with the following exception:

Walker: utility ("Till Tomorrow," 32 bars).

The following charts are presumably by Kostal but have not been located: "Gentleman Jimmy," "Little Tin Box," and "Where Do I Go from Here?" (cut).

Walker's brief chart for the "Till Tomorrow" utility was prerecorded, for use on a phonograph with the pit eventually joining in while Fiorello dances with Marie; this then led into the song version, orchestrated by Kostal.

In the "Gentleman Jimmy" section of the Overture ("Overture #3 [Help!]"), Kostal instructs the three saxes (two soprano and one alto) to "hoke it up" and stand for the solo.

Charts exist for extended versions of "Home Again," featuring Ben (Howard Da Silva), which was mostly deleted; a "Gentleman Jimmy" reprise, which pits politicians singing "business is fundamentally sound" against Prohibition apple sellers (an idea which seems to have been recycled into Prince's *Flora, the Red Menace*); and a complete "Marie Version" of "On the Side of the Angels," with verse and refrain. There are also complete charts for the deleted numbers "'Til the Bootlegger Comes" (Dora) and "Impatient" (Thea).

Instr.: 5 reed (including 3 sax, 5 clr, 4 fl, 2 picc), 5 brass (3 tpt, 2 tb), 12 strings (7 vln, 2 vla, 2 c, b/tuba), piano/celesta/accordion, guitar/banjo/mandolin (plus reed II chair also doubles on mandolin), perc = 25 total. (See pages 92, 231, 269.)

THE FIREBRAND OF FLORENCE

Orchestrations by Kurt **Weill**. (Additional orchestrations by Ted **Royal**.)

Opened March 22, 1945, Alvin, 43 performances. Tryout: (as *Much Ado about Love*) February 23, Boston (Colonial).

Music by Kurt Weill, lyrics and book by Ira Gershwin. Based on the play *The Firebrand* by Edwin Justus Mayer. Musical direction by Maurice Abravanel. Other participants: Max Gordon (producer); Edwin Justus Mayer (co-librettist); Lotte Lenya (featured).

The partiturs are in the Weill Collection at Yale.

The orchestrations are by Weill, with the following exceptions:

Royal: "Come to Paris," "Duchess's Letter," Entr'acte (originally the Overture), "Gigue" (final scene, with an 8-bar intro by Weill), Prelude.

Other scores:

"Just in Case" ("We're soldiers of the Duchy"): song section is by Royal, extended opening instrumental by Weill.

"A Rhyme for Angela": first section (94 bars) is by Weill, "Angela Last" (79 bars) is by Royal.

"Sing Me Not a Ballad": first section is by Weill, second section (for Duchess and Quartet) is by Royal.

"Finaletto Act I, Scene 3 (Quintet)": listed elsewhere as being by Royal, this is actually by Weill.

Instr.: 5 reed, 6 brass (3 tpt, 1 tb, 2 hrn), 17 strings (12 vln, 2 vla, 2 c, 1 b), harp, guitar, perc = 31 total.

FIRST IMPRESSIONS

Orchestrations credited to Don **Walker**. (Additional orchestrations by Robert **Ginzler** and possibly others.)

Opened March 19, 1959, Alvin, 84 performances. Tryout: February 2, New Haven (Shubert); February 10, Philadelphia (Forrest); Boston (Shubert).

Music and lyrics by Robert Goldman, Glenn Paxton, and George Weiss. Based on the novel *Pride and Prejudice* by Jane Austen. Musical direction by Frederick Dvonch. Vocal arrangements and direction by Buster Davis. Dance arrangements by John Morris.

Other participants: Jule Styne Organization (producer: "Jule Styne's services courtesy of Producers Music Publishing Co., Inc."); Abe Burrows (director, librettist).

Although no partiturs or invoices have been found, one can guess that "I Feel Sorry for the Girl" and "I'm Me" are among Ginzler's contributions.

A FLAG IS BORN

Orchestrations credited to Isaac van Grove. (Additional orchestrations by Hershy **Kay**.)

Opened September 5, 1946, Alvin, 120 performances. Tryout: unknown.

A play by Ben Hecht. Incidental music by Kurt Weill. Other participants: Luther Adler (director); American League for a Free Palestine (producer); Paul Muni (star); Marlon Brando (featured).

The partiturs are at the Jobotinsky Institute in Tel Aviv, Israel.
    Kay: Overture (Prelude).

FLAHOOLEY

Orchestrations credited to Ted **Royal**. (Additional orchestrations by Robert Noeltner and others.)

Opened May 14, 1951, Broadhurst, 40 performances. Tryout: April 9, New Haven (Shubert); Philadelphia.

Music by Sammy Fain, lyrics by E. Y. Harburg. Musical direction and vocal arrangements by Maurice Levine. Dance arrangements by Freda Miller. Other participants: Cheryl Crawford (producer); E. Y. Harburg (director and co-librettist); Barbara Cook (featured).

Marion Evans, a student of Royal, didn't start ghosting until the next Royal musical, *Paint Your Wagon.* He recalls that Noeltner was definitely on *Flahooley,* as was (most probably) Charles L. Cooke. Following the show's ignominious failure, a revised version was presented in Los Angeles by Edwin Lester under the title *Jollyanna.*

FLORA, THE RED MENACE

Orchestrations (mostly) by Don **Walker**. (Additional orchestrations by Arthur Beck and Arnold Goland.)

Opened May 11, 1965, Alvin, 87 performances. Tryout: April 3, New Haven (Shubert); April 14, Boston (Colonial).

Music by John Kander, lyrics by Fred Ebb. Based on the novel *Love Is Just Around the Corner* by Lester Atwell. Musical direction by Harold Hastings. Dance arrangements by David Baker (and John Berkman). Other participants: Harold Prince (producer); George Abbott (director, co-librettist); Lee Theodore (choreographer); Liza Minnelli (star).

Invoices are in the Walker Collection at the Library of Congress. Base page rate: $8.
    The orchestrations are by Walker, with the following exceptions:
    Goland: bows, fixes on seven songs.
    Beck: "Blood on 23rd Street Ballet," other fixes.
    Other scores:
    "Among the People" (cut) is by Walker, with dance by Goland.
    Entr'acte is by Walker (42 pages) and Goland (7 pages).

THANKS AND WISHES From Hastings to Walker: "We have done so many this year. I think I forgot this last time to say again what a marvelous job you have done and how much I enjoy the process. Thanks always, Hal."

Instr.: 5 reed (including 7 sax, 5 clr, 3 fl), 7 brass (3 tpt, 3 tb, 1 hrn), 10 strings (6 vln, 2 vla, c, b), piano/celesta, guitar/banjo, perc = 25 total.

FLOWER DRUM SONG

Orchestrations by Russell **Bennett**. (Additional orchestrations by Joe Glover and Luther Henderson.)

Opened December 1, 1958, St. James, 600 performances. Tryout: October 27, Boston (Shubert).

Music by Richard Rodgers, lyrics and book by Oscar Hammerstein II. Based on the novel by C. Y. Lee. Musical direction by Salvatore Dell'Isola. Dance arrangements by Luther Henderson. Other participants: Richard Rodgers and Oscar Hammerstein II (producers); Joseph Fields (co-librettist); Gene Kelly (director); Carol Haney (choreographer).

The partiturs are in the Rodgers Collection at the Library of Congress, with copies at the offices of the Rodgers & Hammerstein Organization. Invoices are preserved in Bennett's ledger. Base page rate: $6.17. Invoices indicate: Bennett (71%), Glover (27%).

The orchestrations are by Bennett, with the following exceptions:

Glover: "Chop Suey" (song and encore), "Chop Suey Jazz Bit," "Gliding Through My Memoree," "The Other Generation" (see below), utilities ("Like a God," "Love Look Away," "One Hundred Million Miracles," "She Is Beautiful," "Sunday").

Other scores:

Finale Ultimo is by Bennett, with the final 8 bars from Glover's earlier version.

"Grant Avenue": there are four versions. The first is by Bennett; the second (which includes an extended dance) is by Henderson; the third—marked "New New Grant Avenue"—is by Glover. The final version begins with Bennett (through bar 162) and continues with Glover, incorporating part of Henderson's version. The reprise "Grant Avenue," incorporated in the "Gliding Through My Memoree" number, is by Glover.

"My Best Love" (cut) is by Bennett; reprise and utility are by Glover.

"The Other Generation" (song, reprise, and utility) is by Glover; "Other Generation Dance" is by Bennett.

"Processional": there are two versions, one by Bennett and one by Glover.

On several of the scores (including "She Is Beautiful," "I Am Going to Like It Here," and "Love, Look Away"), Bennett uses Chinese symbols to write the character names.

Instr.: 6 reed (including 3 sax), 8 brass (3 tpt, 2 tb, 1 tuba, 2 hrn), 13 strings (8 vln, 2 vla, 2 c, 1 b), harp, guitar/mandolin/banjo, perc = 30 total.

FLYING COLORS

Orchestrations uncredited. (Orchestrations by Hans **Spialek**, Edward B. Powell, Arthur Schutt, Russell **Bennett**, and others.)

Opened September 15, 1932, Imperial, 181 performances. Tryout: Philadelphia (Forrest).

A revue. Music by Arthur Schwartz, lyrics and sketches by Howard Dietz. Musical direction by Al Goodman. Vocal arrangements by André Kostelanetz and Robert Emmett Dolan. Other participants: Max Gordon (producer); George S. Kaufman (additional sketches); Clifton Webb (star).

The partiturs are in the Schwartz and Warner/Chappell collections at the Library of Congress.

Spialek: "Alone Together," "Christmas Carol," "My Heart Is Part of You," Opening.

Powell: "Day after Day," "Riding Habit," "Sleepy Shore," "Triplets," "Two-Faced Woman."

Schutt: "Break the Rhythm," "A Shine on Your Shoes."

Bennett: "Mother Told Me So."

Other scores:

"The Butler Carries On" is by Powell, with an additional shorter score (utility?) by Spialek.

"A Rainy Day" is by Spialek, with dance by Schutt.

FOLLOW THE GIRLS

Orchestrations credited to Joe Glover, Charles L. Cooke, Nathan Lang Van Cleave, Walter Paul, Bob Haggart, Julian Work, Geo. Leeman, Ernie Watson, Cornell Tannasy, and Henry Cowen.

Opened April 8, 1944, Century, 882 performances. Tryout: March 2, New Haven (Shubert); Boston.

Music and lyrics by Dan Shapiro, Milton Pascal, and Phil Charig. Musical direction by Will Irwin. Vocal arrangements by Bobby Tucker. Other participants: Gertrude Niesen (star); Jackie Gleason (featured).

FOOLS RUSH IN

Orchestrations uncredited. (Orchestrations by Conrad Salinger, Hans **Spialek**, Russell **Bennett**, and others.)

Opened December 25, 1934, Playhouse, 14 performances. Tryout: unknown.

A revue. Music by Will Irwin, lyrics by Norman Zeno. Musical direction by Max Meth. Other participants: Leonard Sillman (producer, director, featured); Imogene Coca (featured).

FORBIDDEN MELODY

Orchestrations credited to Don **Walker**. (Additional orchestrators, if any, unknown.)

Opened November 2, 1936, New Amsterdam, 32 performances. Tryout: October 9, Philadelphia (Erlanger); Boston (Shubert).

Music by Sigmund Romberg, lyrics and book by Otto Harbach. Musical direction by Robert Emmett Dolan. Other participant: Carl Brisson (star).

One partitur ("You Are All I Wanted," by Walker) is in the Walker Collection at the Library of Congress.

42ND STREET

Orchestrations credited to Philip J. **Lang**. (Additional orchestrators, if any, unknown.)

Opened August 25, 1980, Winter Garden, 3,486 performances. Tryout: June 21, Washington, D.C. (Opera House).

Music by Harry Warren, lyrics by Al Dubin. Based on the novel by Bradford Ropes. Musical direction and vocal arrangements by John Lesko. Dance arrangements by Donald Johnston. Other participants: David Merrick (producer); Gower Champion (director, choreographer); Michael Stewart and Mark Bramble (librettists); Jerry Orbach (star); Tammy Grimes (star).

FOSSE

Orchestrations credited to Ralph **Burns** and Douglas Besterman. (Additional orchestrators, if any, unknown.)

Opened January 14, 1999, Broadhurst, 1,093 performances. Tryout: July 16, 1998, Toronto (Ford); September 10, Boston (Colonial); October 21, Los Angeles (Ahmanson).

A revue. Music and lyrics by various writers. Musical direction by Patrick S. Brady. Musical arrangements and musical supervision by Gordon Lowry Harrell. Other participants: Richard Maltby (director); Ann Reinking (co-director, co-choreographer); Gwen Verdon ("artistic advisor").

1491

Orchestrations credited to Irwin **Kostal**. (Additional orchestrators, if any, unknown.)

Tryout: September 2, 1969, Los Angeles. Closed December 13, San Francisco (Curran).

Music and lyrics by Meredith Willson. Suggested by events in the life of Christopher Columbus. Musical direction, vocal and dance arrangements by Julian Stein. Other participants: Edwin Lester (producer); John Cullum (star); Chita Rivera (star).

FOXY

Orchestrations credited to Eddie **Sauter** (replaced by Hershy **Kay**). Dance (and other) orchestrations by Hal Schaefer.

Opened February 16, 1964, Ziegfeld, 72 performances. Tryout: January 13, Detroit (Fisher).

Music by Robert Emmett Dolan, lyrics by Johnny Mercer. Based on the play *Volpone* by Ben Jonson. Musical direction and vocal arrangements by Donald Pippin. Dance arrangements and orchestrations by Hal Schaefer. Other participants: David Merrick (producer); Robert Whitehead (preliminary producer); Billy Rose (post-opening producer); Ring Lardner, Jr. (co-librettist); Robert Lewis (director); Jack Cole (choreographer); Bert Lahr (star).

The partiturs are in the Billy Rose Collection at the New York Public Library.

Kay: "The Balcony," "Celia's First Essay," Finale act I, "I'm Way Ahead of the Game," "It's Easy when You Know How," "Larceny and Love," "Money Isn't Everything," "My Night to Howl" (song and dance), "Opening Act I Scene 6," Overture, "Respectability," "Run, Run, Run Cinderella," "Talk to Me, Baby" (see below), "Worth My Weight."

Sauter: "Bon Vivant," "Buzzard Cabin #3," "In Loving Memory" (funeral version of

"Money Isn't Everything"), "Intro to Cinderella," "Many Ways to Skin a Cat" (see below), "S.S. Ebeneezer MacAfee the Third."

Schaefer: "Buzzard's Cabin" (#1 and #2); "Celia's Dilemma" ballet (including the song, "A Case of Rape"), Entr'acte, "Gold Routine," "Intro to Bridal Suite," Opening act II, "Rollin' in Gold" (song and utility), "S.S. Ebeneezer MacAfee the Third" (utility), "Trial (new)."

Other scores:

"Many Ways to Skin a Cat": song and reprise #2 are by Sauter; reprise #1 and utility are by Schaefer.

"New Finale Ultimo" is by Kay, replacing an earlier version by Sauter.

"Prelude–New" is by Kay, replacing an earlier version by Sauter.

"Talk to Me, Baby" is by Kay, with 4-bar intro by Schaefer; reprise by Schaefer.

Instr.: 6 reed, 5 brass (3 tpt, 2 tb, 1 hrn), ? strings (? vln, 0 vla, ? c, 1 b), piano, guitar/banjo, perc.

(See page 85.)

FROM A TO Z

Orchestrations credited to Jay Brower and Jonathan Tunick. (Additional orchestrators, if any, unknown.)

Opened April 20, 1960, Plymouth, 21 performances. Tryout: March 26, New Haven (Shubert); elsewhere.

A revue. Music and lyrics by various writers (including Mary Rodgers, Jerry Herman, and Fred Ebb). Musical direction and vocal arrangements by Milton Greene. Dance arrangements by Jack Holmes. Other participants: Woody Allen (sketch writer); Hermione Gingold (star).

When Hermione Gingold was asked by Texas millionaires Carroll and Harris Masterson to do a revue, she recommended as director her friend Christopher Hewett (Zoltan Karpathy in the original *My Fair Lady*, Roger De Bris in the original motion picture *The Producers*). Hewett had been directing at Tamiment, the adult summer camp, so he assembled *From A to Z* with a cast and staff from Tamiment. Jonathan Tunick, a student at Juilliard, had spent one summer at the camp. He turned twenty-two on opening night, making him what was presumably the youngest credited orchestrator in Broadway history. It would take eight years before his next Broadway credit, as one of three orchestrators on *Here's Where I Belong*.

FUNNY FACE

Orchestrations uncredited. (Orchestrations by Hans **Spialek**, George Gershwin, and others.)

Opened November 22, 1927, Alvin, 244 performances. Tryout: (as *Smarty*): October 11, Philadelphia (Shubert); (as *Funny Face*) October 31, Washington, D.C. (Poli's); November 7, Atlantic City (Nixon's Apollo); November 14, Wilmington, Delaware (Playhouse).

Music by George Gershwin, lyrics by Ira Gershwin. Musical direction by Alfred Newman. Other participants: Fred Astaire and Adele Astaire (stars).

Two of the partiturs are in the Gershwin Collection at the Library of Congress.

FUNNY GIRL

Orchestrations by Ralph **Burns**. Dance (and other) orchestrations by Luther Henderson. (Additional orchestrations by Larry **Wilcox** and Jim Tyler.)

Opened March 26, 1964, Winter Garden, 1,348 performances. Tryout: January 13, Boston (Shubert); February 4, Philadelphia (Forrest); Philadelphia (Erlanger).

Music by Jule Styne, lyrics by Bob Merrill. Suggested by events in the life of Fanny Brice. Musical direction by Milton Rosenstock. Vocal arrangements by Buster Davis. Assistant vocal arranger, Marvin Hamlisch. Dance arrangements and orchestrations by Luther Henderson. Other participants: Ray Stark (producer); David Merrick (original producer); Garson Kanin (original director); Jerome Robbins (replacement director, billed as "production supervisor"); Carol Haney (choreographer); Barbra Streisand (star); Sydney Chaplin (star).

About two-thirds of the partiturs are in the American Musical Theatre Collection at the Library of Congress. Partiturs of the deleted songs are at Tams-Witmark.

Burns: "Don't Rain on My Parade," "Find Yourself a Man" (similar but not identical to what is heard on the cast album), "I Want to Be Seen with You," "I'd Be Good for Her" (cut), "I'm the Greatest Star" (see below), "Nicky Arnstein #2," "Henry Street," "The Music That Makes Me Dance" (similar but not identical to what is heard on the cast album), "New Overture," "People" (similar but not identical to what is heard on the cast album), "Sadie, Sadie" (tempo: "quasi Molly Picon 1920"), "Nicky's Parade," "Something about Me" (cut), "A Temporary Arrangement" (cut).

Wilcox: "People Reprise" (cut), "Who Are You Now?" (except for 5-bar "New Ending" by Burns).

Henderson: "One Step–Two Step/Downtown Rag," Opening Scene 7 (replacing an earlier version by Wilcox).

Tyler: "Train Music for Montage" (cut).

Other scores:

"Cornet Man": the existing material, all of which was cut, includes "New Ending" by Wilcox (written on Don Walker's personalized paper, with Walker's name razor-bladed out) and a section of vocal production number ("Let me tell you, it's hot" and "Shinbone Lizzie"), prior to Fanny's entrance, by Henderson. An early version of Fanny's vocal ("The lady ain't seen light") exists, by Wilcox; some of this seems to have been reused in the final version, which is missing.

"His Love Makes Me Beautiful": "Part 2" is by Wilcox, "Part 3 (Follies)" is by Burns; "Part 1" (the song proper) is missing.

"I'm the Greatest Star": the first section, through "Mr. Ziegfeld here I am!" is by Burns; "Greatest Star New 2/18/64" is by Burns and two other hands (almost certainly copyists incorporating sections from earlier versions by Burns). Tempo marking: "Cute Corny, Not Funny."

"New Entr'acte": the first 26 bars, through the beginning of "People," are by Wilcox; the rest is by Burns, including a large section reused from the Overture.

"Rat-a-Tat-Tat": "Part 3, Germans" (cut) is by Henderson; the Broadway chart is missing.

"What a Helluva Day/Helluva Group Block Party" (cut): one version is by Tyler, the other version has part I by Burns, part II by Wilcox.

"You Are Woman" ("old version") is by Wilcox. The Broadway chart is missing.

Also missing: "If a Girl Isn't Pretty" and "Who Taught Her Everything?"

There is a major cut in the final Overture ("New Overture") from the end of "People" to the xylophone solo leading into "Don't Rain on My Parade," at bar 100 of the vocal score, with 41 bars of "I've Got to Be Seen with You" deleted.

RALPH'S INSTRUCTIONS TO MUSICIANS   Overture (to horn at "Nicky Arnstein Chant," prior to "People" [bar 73]): "Sing It—Espressione!"; (to trumpet at end of bridge of "Don't Rain on My Parade" [bar 134]): "if in the mood play an octave up."

Instr.: 5 reed (all sax), 7 brass (3 tpt, 3 tb, I hrn), 10 strings (6 vln, 0 vla, 3 c, b), piano/celesta, guitar, perc = 25 total.

(See pages 172, 271.)

A FUNNY THING HAPPENED ON THE WAY TO THE FORUM

Orchestrations (totally) by Irwin **Kostal** and Sid **Ramin**.

Opened May 8, 1962, Alvin, 964 performances. Tryout: March 31, New Haven (Shubert); April 11, Washington, D.C. (National).

Music and lyrics by Stephen Sondheim. Musical direction by Harold Hastings. Dance arrangements by Hal Schaefer. Additional dance arrangements by Betty Walberg. Other participants: Harold Prince (producer); George Abbott (director); Jack Cole (choreographer); Jerome Robbins (additional direction and choreography, uncredited); Burt Shevelove and Larry Gelbart (librettists); Zero Mostel (star).

The partiturs are at Music Theatre International. Copies, including cut material, are in the Ramin Collection at the Butler Library, Columbia University.

Kostal: Chase (cut); "Everybody Ought to Have a Maid" (see below), "Funeral Sequence," "Love, I Hear" (two versions; see below), "Once upon a Time" (cut), "Pretty Little Picture," "Set the Scene (Opening Act I Fanfare)," "That'll Show Him" (see below).

Ramin: "Bring Me My Bride," "Echo Song" (cut), Finale Ultimo, "Free," "Hornpipe," "Love Is Going Around" (see below), "Lovely" (see below), "That Dirty Old Man."

Other scores:

"Comedy Tonight": the beginning through bar 127 in the vocal score (crescendo after "open up the curtain") is by Ramin; slapstick section (128–163, "Erronious in search of his children") is by Kostal. Thereafter, score switches back and forth, with Ramin doing most of the vocal portions and Kostal doing the comedic sections ("Punch and Judy," "Shrinking Tall Man [Charles Chaplin]," "Disguises"). The total bar count is 415, which might have set a new record for an opening number. ("Carousel Waltz" is 461, but that served as the show's Overture as well as its opening pantomime.) The version heard on the original cast album is severely cut.

Entr'acte is mostly by Kostal, except for bars 9–27 ("House of Marcus Lycus").

"Everybody Ought to Have a Maid" is almost all by Kostal. Ramin contributed the changes, namely the 1-bar intro, the first ending ("skittering down the hallway" until end), and the encore rideout (repeating the words "the house" four times).

"House of Marcus Lycus" ("New") is by Ramin, except for the first 26 bars.

"I'm Calm" is mostly by Kostal, except for the ending (77–88).

"Impossible" is mostly by Kostal, except for the 4-bar interlude between the first and second refrain, and the final ending (85–94).

"Love Is Going Around" (4/4/62) (cut) is by Ramin except for the "New Intro" (4/15/62).

"Lovely" is mostly by Ramin. The Pseudolus-Hysterium duet is the original chart, with all except for the final 9 bars (beginning "world will never seem the same") by Ramin. During the tryout of the show, it was decided to replace Hero and Philia's first act duet with a reprise—or should we say *pre*-prise?—of "Lovely." This version begins with an intro (based on "Love, I Hear") by Kostal. The song, beginning with the vamp, is a straight transposition (up a half-tone) from Ramin's Pseudolus-Hysterium chart with Kostal's ending.

Overture ("New 4/15/62") is mostly by Ramin, except for "Free" and the transition from "Lovely" back to "Free," by Kostal. The closing version of "Free" is by Ramin. There are two earlier overtures. "Old" is by Ramin; this starts with D trumpets for the first 16 bars, before moving to B♭ trumpets. "Overture #2 (4/3/62)" is by Kostal. This features the first two trumpets in D and the third in B♭. Both of these overtures are martial in tone, featuring the show's two brass fanfares (heard elsewhere in "Opening Act I" and the beginning of "Bring Me My Bride").

"That'll Show Him (Noo)" (4/23/62) is by Kostal, except for the final 4-bar ending by Ramin. This replaced an earlier version (4/4/62; without verse) by Ramin.

> RAMIN: We decided not to use violins. Irv said, "You know, we gotta do something that is different." I hadn't used violas on *West Side* or *Gypsy*, so I said let's use three violas and not violins. I think they were missed, I really do, because people got used to hearing that sound of violins.

Kostal credits Sondheim with the idea of omitting violins: "At first, the violists found it difficult to be playing such important parts, but when they got the idea, it was a very pleasing effect. . . . Sid and I were both quite amused when Goddard Lieberson, recording expert, complimented Sid and I after he had seen the show, telling us the violins had never sounded better. We didn't have the nerve to tell him there weren't any."

The trumpets were problematic too, initially.

> RAMIN: Steve wanted to use trumpets in D, instead of the standard B♭ trumpet. They sound higher, they're more difficult to play, nobody plays them. We said we didn't think it was a good idea, but he was the composer. So Irv and I tried to use trumpets in D. We said to Steve, "We'll write it in the overture; we guarantee that they will need to be transposed." They tried to play it in D up in New Haven; it didn't work.

Kostal also comments on his two charts for the hero Hero's opening number, "Love, I Hear":

> Steve gave me a sketch that had some strange things in it. There were clusters in the low register that could only be played by a trombone, a bassoon, the cellos, the piano, and the string bass. These clusters had nothing whatsoever to do with this great song, and against my will and because of my rather strained relationship at this time with Steve, I did use these ideas in the orchestration. As luck would have it, Leonard Bernstein happened to be in the audience at the very first performance of this arrangement, out of town. Lenny came storming backstage after the closing curtain and tackled Steve, criticizing the arrangement, and knowing that these clusters must have been Steve's ideas, said, "Who do you think you are? Me?" Lenny then turned to me, and let me have it. "How could you not have known better? Do it over, and do it right." With a more harmonic orchestration, this song was a highlight of the show.

When the show was prepared for touring and stock & amateur purposes, the instrumentation was altered—even more drastically than usual—with the addition of six violins (necessitating a reduction of other colors).

Instr.: 7 reed, 7 brass (3 tpt, 1 tb, 3 hrn), 7 strings (0 vln, 3 vla, 3 c, 1 b), piano, harp, guitar, perc = 25 total. (See pages 211, 246, 268, 290.)

THE GANG'S ALL HERE

Orchestrations uncredited. (Orchestrations by Hans **Spialek** and others.)

Opened February 18, 1931, Imperial, 23 performances. Tryout: January 26, Philadelphia (Shubert); February 9, Newark (Shubert).

Music by Lewis E. Gensler, lyrics by Owen Murphy and Robert A. Simon. Musical direction by Gene Salzer. Other participants: Russel Crouse (librettist); Oscar Hammerstein II (additional librettist).

GANTRY

Orchestrations credited to Jim Tyler. (Additional orchestrators, if any, unknown.)

Opened February 14, 1970, George Abbott, 1 performance.

Music by Stanley Lebowsky, lyrics by Fred Tobias. Based on the novel *Elmer Gantry* by Sinclair Lewis. Musical direction by Arthur Rubinstein. Vocal arrangements by Stanley Lebowsky. Dance arrangements by Dorothea Freitag. Other participants: Onna White (director, choreographer); Robert Shaw (star); Rita Moreno (star).

GARRICK GAIETIES (1926 EDITION)

Orchestrations uncredited. (Orchestrations by Hans **Spialek** and others.)

Opened May 10, 1926, Garrick, 174 performances. Tryout: none.

A revue. Music by Richard Rodgers, lyrics by Lorenz Hart. Musical direction by Roy Webb. Other participant: Theatre Guild (producer).

(See page 93.)

GAY DIVORCE

Orchestrations credited to Hans **Spialek**. (Additional orchestrations by Russell **Bennett**, F. Henri Klickmann, and others.)

Opened November 29, 1932, Ethel Barrymore, 248 performances. Tryout: November 7, Boston (Wilbur); November 21, New Haven (Shubert).

Music and lyrics by Cole Porter. Based on an unproduced play by J. Hartley Manners. Musical direction by Gene Salzer. Other participants: Howard Lindsay (director); Dwight Taylor (son of Laurette Taylor, stepson of J. Hartley Manners) (original librettist); Fred Astaire (star).

Some partiturs are at the Shubert Archives, Spialek's orchestration of "Night and Day" is at Yale, and copies of others are at the Library of Congress.

    Spialek: Entr'acte, "How's Your Romance?" "I Still Love the Red, White and Blue," "I've Got You on My Mind," "Mimi's Entrance," "Opening Final Scene," "What Will Become of Our England?" (song, "Dance," and "England Dance",) "Why Marry Them?"

    Bennett: "After You, Who?" "Breakfast Incidental," "Night and Day" (see below), "You're in Love."

    Klickmann: "Change Music," "Egbert and Tonetti," "Lipstick Incidental," "Tonetti's Entrance."

    Unidentified hand: "Mimi Incidental," "Opening Act II," "Tango Incidental."

    Other scores:

    "After You, Who?" Reprise is by Klickmann and Bennett.

    "Girls Specialty (I've Got You on My Mind)" – first 34 bars are by Klickman, final 34 by Spialek.

    "Night and Day" is by Bennett, replacing a chart by Spialek.

    Overture is by Spialek and Bennett.

    "Salt Air" is by Bennett with the opening 17 bars by an unidentified hand, replacing a chart by Spialek.

Instr.: 3 reed (3 sax), 4 brass (3 tpt, 1 tb), 10? strings (6? vln, 0 vla, 3? c, 1 b), piano, guitar/banjo, perc = 20? total.

(See page 91.)

THE GAY LIFE

Orchestrations (mostly) by Don **Walker**. (Additional orchestrations by Herbert Greene and others.)

Opened November 18, 1961, Shubert, 113 performances. Tryout: October 2, Detroit (Fisher); October 24, Toronto (O'Keefe).

Music by Arthur Schwartz, lyrics by Howard Dietz. Based on the play *Anatol* by Arthur Schnitzler. Musical direction and vocal arrangements by Herbert Greene. Dance arrangements by Robert Starer. Other participants: Kermit Bloomgarden (producer); Herbert Ross (choreographer); Barbara Cook (star).

The partiturs are in a private collection. Invoices are in the Walker Collection at the Library of Congress. Base page rate: $5.95. Invoices indicate a breakdown as follows: Walker (89%), Greene (11%).

The orchestrations are by Walker, with the following exceptions:

Greene: "The Magician" (all-string instrumental of "Why Go Anywhere at All").

Other scores:

"Bloom Is off the Rose" is by Walker, except for final 11-bar "new tag" ("your show of shows") by Greene.

"Come A-Wandering with Me" is mostly by Greene, with some brief sections and overwrites in an unidentified hand (possibly a copyist).

Finale act I: "Rumor Change" ("Frau" instrumental) is by Greene; the rest, "Congratulations" (instrumental), Anatol's "Frau," and Liesl's "Magic Moment," is by Walker.

"Wild Hungarian Czardas" (tempo: "Sempre Furioso") is mostly by Greene, with the first 16 bars in an unidentified hand (copyist?) and the second 16 by Walker. At the end of the chart, instead of the traditional "Fine," Greene has written "Help!!!!"

At the top of Greene's chart for "Come A-Wandering with Me," Walker instructs the copyist to take it up a half-tone and writes, "NOTE: Original violin cadenza impossible when transposed to key of A♭. Use this." He then writes in a new cadenza.

The Walker Collection includes correspondence dated March 10, 1952, in which Walker—in his composing days—attempted to option the musicalization rights to *Anatol* for himself.

Instr.: 4 reed, 7 brass (3 tpt, 1 tb/tuba, 3 hrn), 13? strings (12? vln, 0 vla, 0 c, 1 b), accordion/celesta, cimbalom, perc = 27? total.

(See page 109.)

GENTLEMEN PREFER BLONDES

Orchestrations credited to Don **Walker**. (Additional orchestrators, if any, unknown.)

Opened December 8, 1949, Ziegfeld, 740 performances. Tryout: November 21, Philadelphia (Forrest).

Music by Jule Styne, lyrics by Leo Robin. Based on the novel by Anita Loos. Musical direction by Milton Rosenstock. Vocal arrangements and direction by Hugh Martin. "Assistant to Messrs. Martin and Styne: Bus Davis." Dance arrangements by Trude Rittman. Other participants: Herman Levin and Oliver Smith (producers); John C. Wilson (director); Agnes de Mille (choreographer); Joseph Fields and Anita Loos (librettists); Carol Channing (star).

Walker's journal is at the Library of Congress. Base page rate: $5.10.

Walker, in his notes, breaks down the songs into four groups: vocals, group vocals, dance, and orchestral.

> STAGE MANAGER BIFF LIFF: I was with Agnes most of the time, and so I was very familiar with what she did on that show. Jack Wilson, the director, didn't know a lot about the musical aspect of it. He didn't get into that at all. It was mostly Hugh Martin working with the actors, and Agnes staging the musical numbers.
>
> HUGH MARTIN: Jule and I did it together—we set keys, I did vocal arrangements when they

were called for. Jule was a very good musician, a very creative person. [But] Jule set all of Carol's keys too high. She got laryngitis; I came in and got her back where it belonged. That meant reorchestrating everything.

THANKS AND WISHES   Styne to Walker, Philadelphia: "It is really the biggest thrill of my life hearing your wonderful orchestrations of my music. Thanks for everything."

Styne to Walker, New York: "I make myself a promise. No one shall ever touch a note of my music but Don Walker on Broadway. It's been a thrill to work with such a nice guy and great talent. Please always make yourself available to me."

Instr.: 5 reed (including 5 sax, 4 clr), 6 brass (3 tpt, 2 tb, 1 hrn), 12 strings (8 vln, 2 vla, c, b/tuba), piano/celesta, guitar/banjo, perc = 26 total.

(See pages 190, 195, 229, 230.)

GENTLEMEN UNAFRAID

Orchestrations credited to Russell **Bennett**. (Additional orchestrators, if any, unknown.)
Tryout: June 3, 1938, St. Louis (Muny), 6 performances.
Music by Jerome Kern, lyrics and book by Oscar Hammerstein II and Otto Harbach. Based on a story by Edward Boykin. Musical direction by George Hirst. Associate musical director, Jacob Schwartzdorf [Jay S. Blackton].

GEORGE M!

Orchestrations credited to Philip J. **Lang**. (Additional orchestrations by Eddie **Sauter** and others.)
Opened April 10, 1968, Palace, 433 performances. Tryout: February, Detroit (Fisher).
Music and lyrics by George M. Cohan, lyric and musical revisions by Mary Cohan.
Suggested by events in the life of George M. Cohan. Musical direction and vocal arrangements by Jay Blackton. Musical supervision by Laurence Rosenthal. Other participants: Joe Layton (director, choreographer); Michael Stewart (co-librettist); Joel Grey (star).

Eleven partiturs are at Tams-Witmark. Copies of four are in the Sauter Collection at Yale University.

Lang: "Down by the Erie Canal," "Harrigan," "I've Never Been Over There," "The Man Who Owns Broadway," Montage, "Nellie Kelly, I Love You," "Over There," Overture, "Yankee Doodle Finale."

Sauter: Finale act I, "Give My Regards to Broadway," "The Voice in My Heart," "Yankee Doodle Boy."

GEORGE WHITE'S SCANDALS OF 1935

Orchestrations uncredited. (Orchestrations by Russell **Bennett**, Conrad Salinger, and others.)
Opened December 25, 1935, New Amsterdam, 110 performances. Tryout: December 9, Washington, D.C. (National); elsewhere.

A revue. Music by Ray Henderson, lyrics by Jack Yellen. Musical direction by Tom Jones. Other participants: George White (producer, director, sketch writer); Rudy Vallee (star); Bert Lahr (star).

GEORGE WHITE'S SCANDALS OF 1939

Orchestrations uncredited. (Orchestrations by Hans **Spialek**, Don Walker, Lew Harris, Ted **Royal**, and others.)

Opened August 28, 1939, Alvin, 120 performances. Tryout: unknown.

A revue. Music by Sammy Fain, lyrics by Jack Yellen. Musical direction by Charles Drury. Other participants: George White (producer, director, sketch writer); Ella Logan (star); The Three Stooges (featured); Ann Miller (featured).

GEORGY

Orchestrations credited to Eddie **Sauter**. (Additional orchestrators, if any, unknown.)

Opened February 26, 1969, Winter Garden, 4 performances. Tryout: January 10, New Haven (Shubert); Boston.

Music by George Fischoff, lyrics by Carole Bayer. Based on the screenplay by Peter Nichols, from a novel by Margaret Forster. Musical direction and vocal arrangements by Elliot Lawrence. Dance arrangements by Marvin Laird. Other participant: Peter Hunt (director).

GIGI

Orchestrations (totally) by Irwin **Kostal**.

Opened November 13, 1973, Uris, 103 performances. Tryout: May 15, San Francisco (Curran); Detroit (Fisher); elsewhere.

Music by Frederick Loewe, lyrics and book by Alan Jay Lerner. Based on a screenplay by Alan Jay Lerner, from a novel by Colette. Musical direction by Ross Reimueller. Dance arrangements by Trude Rittman. Other participants: Saint Subber (producer); Edwin Lester (producer); Joseph Hardy (director); Onna White (choreographer); Alfred Drake (star).

Copies of the partiturs are at Tams-Witmark.

> KOSTAL: Most of the time I found myself with Fritz Loewe in his hotel room. It was not necessary for Fritz and Alan to sit at a piano and work together, they did it on the phone. While most of the songs were written for the movie, new songs were going in and out on a fairly regular basis. This is how they worked: the phone would ring and Fritz would write down lyrics dictated to him by Alan. Sometimes, Fritz would ask, "Does it go, da da da da da, or da da da da," or syllables of this sort. Many times, the lyric would be quite long. Then Fritz would go to the piano and set this lyric to music. When he thought he had it, he would call Alan and play the melody on the piano while Alan listened. Sometimes, Alan would say fine, and at others they would have quite a heated discussion, never angry, but working towards a final decision. Never did I see them work together in the same room. . . .

According to Fritz, Alan had already been divorced six times, and each divorce had cost Alan a million dollars, making a total of six million dollars. Fritz, on the other hand, admitted to being quite immoral. Each year, he hired a young French girl who stayed with him until he properly educated her, and then he sent her on her way to lead a better life. In six years, Alan had been very moral, always marrying the women he fell in love with, and as Fritz put it, "Alan is broke, I have six million dollars."

During a cast party, Kostal entertained at the keyboard. Alfred Drake came over and asked where he learned to play piano like that.

> KOSTAL: I answered, when I was twelve years old, my very first professional job was playing in the reception room of a house of prostitution, called in those uneducated days "a hoor house." I didn't know what was going on, the girls would pat me on the head as they walked by, and I didn't even learn to spell it until four years later.
>
> Alfred didn't quite believe me, and I assured him of the truth of the matter, and I explained that many pianists had started their careers in this fashion. He sort of pooh-poohed me, so I called Fritz Loewe over and asked him, "Fritz, what was your first job as a pianist?" Fritz said, "I was just a little boy, it was a whore house in Vienna." We laughed, but Fritz added his own bit of humor. "I didn't get paid," he said, "but I took it out in trade!"

GIRL CRAZY

Orchestrations credited to Russell **Bennett**. (Additional orchestrations by William Daly, George Gershwin, and possibly others.)

Opened October 14, 1930, Alvin, 272 performances. Tryout: September 29, Philadelphia (Shubert).

Music by George Gershwin, lyrics by Ira Gershwin. Musical direction by Earle Busby.

Other participants: Alex Aarons and Vinton Freedley (producers); Ginger Rogers (lead); Ethel Merman (featured).

The partiturs are in the Gershwin Collection at the Library of Congress (unexamined).

Bennett points out that the pit band included the Red Nichols Band: Nichols on first trumpet, Glenn Miller on trombone, Gene Krupa on drums, and Benny Goodman on first clarinet/sax. This same group had played the Gershwins' January 1930 musical, *Strike Up the Band*, with Jimmy Dorsey instead of Goodman. The *Girl Crazy* pianist was Roger Edens.

THE GIRL FRIEND

Orchestrations uncredited. (Orchestrations by Maurice de Packh and others.)

Opened March 17, 1926, Vanderbilt, 301 performances. Tryout: March 8, Atlantic City (Apollo).

Music by Richard Rodgers, lyrics by Lorenz Hart. Musical direction by Ernest Cutting. Other participants: Lew Fields (producer); Herbert Fields (librettist).

THE GIRL FROM NANTUCKET

Orchestrations and vocal arrangements credited to Jacques Belasco. (Additional orchestrations by Ted **Royal** and probably others.)

Opened November 8, 1945, Adelphi, 12 performances. Tryout: October, Philadelphia (Forrest); Boston.

Music by Jacques Belasco, lyrics by Kay Twomey. Additional songs by Hughie Prince and Dick Rogers. Musical direction by Harry Levant.

THE GIRL IN PINK TIGHTS

Orchestrations by Don **Walker**. (Additional orchestrations by Robert **Ginzler**, Robert Farnon, Walter Paul, Hans **Spialek**, and Jack Mason.)

Opened March 5, 1954, Mark Hellinger, 115 performances. Tryout: January 25, New Haven (Shubert); Philadelphia.

Music by Sigmund Romberg, "developed" by Don Walker, lyrics by Leo Robin. Musical direction by Sylvan Levin. Vocal arrangements by Don Walker. Ballet music arranged by Trude Rittman. Other participant: Agnes de Mille (choreographer).

The partiturs and invoices are in the Walker Collection at the Library of Congress. Base page rate: $5.87. Invoices indicate: Walker (68%), Ginzler (10%).

Walker: "Bacchanal," "The Bats," "Finale Act I," "Love Is the Funniest Thing," "My Heart Won't Say Goodbye" ("solo version"), "Pas de Deux," "We're All in the Same Boat," "When I Am Free to Love."

Ginzler: "The Flag," "Fun," "Opening Act II," "Lost in Loveliness" (and reprise).

Farnon: Cake Walk, "You've Got to Be a Little Crazy."

Spialek: "The Siren Ballet" ("by Trude Rittman, by H. Sp.").

Mason: utilities ("In Paris and in Love," "Lost in Loveliness," "My Heart Won't Say Goodbye," "Up in the Elevated Railway," "We're All in the Same Boat," "When I Am Free to Love").

Paul: "Cardinal's Guard," Etude, "I Promised Their Mothers."

Other scores:

"In Paris and in Love" ("Let's Pretend") is by Walker, replacing earlier chart by Farnon.

Overture is a composite in several hands.

"Up in the Elevated Railway": verse and first two refrains are by Ginzler; choral interlude and the rest ("Elevated Finale") are by Farnon.

THANKS AND WISHES   Walker to featured actress Brenda Lewis: "You are undoubtedly the best looking one-woman quintette to whom I have ever set!"

Instr.: 4 reed (including 4 clr), 6 brass (2 tpt, 1 tb, 3 hrn), ? strings (vln, 0 vla, c, b), piano, accordion, harp, perc.

(See page 310.)

THE GIRL WHO CAME TO SUPPER

Orchestrations by Russell **Bennett**. (Additional orchestrations by Jack Andrews, Philip J. **Lang**, William Stegmeyer, and Hans **Spialek**, with Jay Blackton.)

Opened December 8, 1963, Broadway, 112 performances. Tryout: September, Boston (Colonial); Toronto (O'Keefe); November, Philadelphia (Shubert).

Music and lyrics by Noël Coward. Based on the play *The Sleeping Prince* by Terence Rattigan. Musical direction and vocal arrangements by Jay Blackton. Dance arrangements by Genevieve Pitot. Other participants: Herman Levin (producer); Joe Layton (director, choreographer); José Ferrer (star).

Invoices are preserved in Bennett's ledger. Base page rate: $10. Invoices indicate: Bennett (72%), Andrews (10%).

The orchestrations are by Bennett, with the following exceptions:

Andrews: "The Coconut Girl," "Curt, Clear and Concise Revised Boston" (replacing version by Spialek), "Here and Now," "Here and Now Reprise" (including "This Time It's True Love"), "Saturday Night."

Lang: "Foreign Princes."

Stegmeyer: "Lonely" (song and encore, with fixes by Andrews), "Opening Scene 7."

Spialek: "London after Tango."

Other scores:

"Curt, Clear and Concise Revised Boston" (presumably the final version) is by Andrews, replacing original chart by Spialek.

"London": part 1 and part 2 are by Bennett; part 3 ("Charlie") is by Lang; part 4 ("Saturday Night") is by Spialek; part 5 ("Finale") is by Lang; fixes are by Blackton; "London Utility (New)" is by Andrews.

"New Middle Age" is by Bennett with fixes by Blackton, replacing a version by Stegmeyer.

THE GIRLS AGAINST THE BOYS

Orchestrations credited to Sid **Ramin** and Robert **Ginzler**. (Additional orchestrators, if any, unknown.)

Opened November 2, 1959, Alvin, 16 performances. Tryout: unknown.

A revue. Music by Richard Lewine. Additional music by Albert Hague, lyrics and sketches by Arnold B. Horwitt. Musical direction by Irving Actman. Vocal arrangements by Charles Strouse (uncredited). Dance arrangements by John Morris. Other participants: Bert Lahr (star); Nancy Walker (star); Dick Van Dyke (featured).

GLAD TO SEE YOU

Orchestrators uncredited.

Tryout: November 13, 1944, Philadelphia (Shubert). Closed January 6, 1945, Boston.

Music by Jule Styne, lyrics by Sammy Cahn. Musical direction by Max Meth. Vocal arrangements by Buck (Clay) Warnick. Other participants: Busby Berkeley (director, choreographer); Alexander H. Cohen (production assistant).

The Walker Collection includes a rehearsal copy of "I'm Laying Away a Buck," indicating that Walker orchestrated the song.

THE GOLDEN APPLE

Orchestrations (totally) by Jerome Moross and Hershy **Kay.**

Opened April 20, 1954, Phoenix (off-Broadway), 46 performances (plus an additional 127 at the Alvin).

Music by Jerome Moross, lyrics by John Latouche. Based on *The Odyssey* by Homer. Musical direction by Hugh Ross.

The partiturs are in the Moross Collection at the Butler Library at Columbia University (partially examined).

Moross: "Lazy Afternoon."

Instr.: 5 reed (including 2 sax), 5 brass (2 tpt, 1 tb, 2 hrn), ? strings (vln, 2? vla, 2? c, 1 b), piano/celesta, harp, perc.

(See page 49.)

GOLDEN BOY

Orchestrations credited to Ralph **Burns.** Additional scoring by Elliot Lawrence. (Additional orchestrations by Larry **Wilcox,** Jim Tyler, and possibly others.)

Opened October 20, 1964, Majestic, 568 performances. Tryout: June 25, Philadelphia (Shubert); July 29, Boston (Shubert); August 25, Detroit (Fisher).

Music by Charles Strouse, lyrics by Lee Adams. Based on the play by Clifford Odets. Musical direction and additional scoring by Elliot Lawrence. Dance arrangements and ballet music by Dorothea Freitag. Other participants: Peter Coe (original director); Arthur Penn (replacement director); Donald McKayle (choreographer); Clifford Odets (original librettist); William Gibson (co-librettist, following Odets's death); Sammy Davis (star).

This show, which underwent a long and troubled tryout tour, was reportedly heavily ghosted by Larry Wilcox. It is known that "Night Song," Sammy Davis's opening number, was orchestrated by Jim Tyler.

> ELLIOT LAWRENCE: Almost every show in the old days, you take it out of town, you work on it, it comes back, it's better. *Golden Boy* is the only show I've done, when we opened in Philadelphia I thought it was really unbelievable, one of the best shows. It gradually got worse. All of Sammy Davis's friends from the clubs said, you're not doing enough this, you're not doing enough that.

(See pages 37, 199.)

GOLDEN RAINBOW

Orchestrations credited to Pat Williams and Jack Andrews. Additional scoring by Elliot Lawrence. (Additional orchestrators, if any, unknown.)

Opened February 4, 1968, Shubert, 383 performances. Tryout: December 1967, Philadelphia (Forrest); elsewhere.

Music and lyrics by Walter Marks. Based on the play *A Hole in the Head* by Arnold Schulman. Musical direction, additional scoring, and vocal arrangements by Elliot Lawrence. Dance arrangements by Marvin Hamlisch and Luther Henderson. Other participants: Ron Field (original choreographer, replaced); Steve Lawrence (star); Eydie Gorme (star).

GOLDILOCKS

Orchestrations by Leroy Anderson and Philip J. **Lang**. (Additional orchestrations by Russell **Bennett**, Robert Noeltner, Laurence Rosenthal, and Jack Mason.)

Opened October 11, 1958, Lunt-Fontanne, 161 performances. Tryout: September 9, Philadelphia (Erlanger); Boston (Shubert).

Music by Leroy Anderson, lyrics by Joan Ford, Walter Kerr, and Jean Kerr. Musical direction by Lehman Engel. Dance arrangements by Laurence Rosenthal. Other participants: Robert Whitehead (producer); Walter Kerr (director); Agnes de Mille (choreographer); Walter Kerr and Jean Kerr (librettists); Elaine Stritch (star).

The partiturs are in the Anderson Collection at Yale University. Bennett's invoices are preserved in his ledger. Base page rate: $6.

Lang: "Fat Cat," "I Can't Be in Love," "I Never Know When to Say When," "Indian Scene," "Lady in Waiting," "Lady in Waiting Dance" (488 bars, with an 8-bar fix by Rosenthal), "Little Girls" (cut), "My Last Spring" (cut), Opening act II, "Opera" (cut), "Overture" (see below).

Anderson: "Come to Me" (cut), "Save a Kiss," "Shall I Take My Heart?"

Noeltner: "The Beast in You," "Cavalry Scene," "General Utility" ("Lazy Moon"), "No One Will Ever Love You" (with final 2 bars by Lang), "Town Hall Maxixe" (with extended coda by Lang), "Trailer (Two Years in the Making)."

Bennett: "Bad Companions," "Guess Who?" (cut), "Lazy Moon."

Mason: utilities ("Guess Who?" "Save a Kiss").

Other scores:

"Give the Little Girl a Hand": song is by Lang; "Finale Tag" by Anderson; "Ending for Recording" by Mason.

"Heart of Stone" is by Lang; "Egypt Dance" is by Anderson.

"Hello" (cut) is by Lang, replacing an earlier version by Noeltner.

"If I Can't Take It with Me" (cut): there are two versions, one marked "#6A" by Lang and one (a reprise?) marked "#18A" by Noeltner.

"Overture New" is by Lang, replacing "Overture I" (by Lang, incorporating utilities by Anderson and Mason).

"Pirate Dance" (253 bars) is mostly by Noeltner, with a 63-bar inserted section by Lang.

"The Pussy Foot": song is by Lang; "Dance" (248 bars) is by Lang, with several extended patches by Rosenthal and a final section by Anderson; "Reprise–New" is by Anderson.

"Tag-Along Kid" (cut) alternates between Lang and Noeltner, with a utility by Noeltner.

"There Never Was a Woman" is by Anderson (replacing a version by Lang); "Woman Dance" by Noeltner; "Woman Tag" by Lang.

"Who's Been Sitting in My Chair?" is by Anderson (labeled for "Maggie"), replacing an earlier version by Bennett (labeled for "Elaine" [Stritch], who played the role); "Chair Dance" is by Mason; "Chair Reprise/Pirate Scene" by Lang. Many years later, Anderson annotated his score of this song with the note: "orchestrated by Russell Bennett and patched up. Later, new orchestration by Leroy Anderson in New York." The cast album uses Anderson's chart.

The Anderson Collection includes a second, full orchestration entirely by the composer, for a slightly smaller orchestra (including reduced string parts).

Instr.: 5 reed, 7 brass (3 tpt, 2 tb, 2 hrn), ? strings (6? vln, vla, c, b), piano, harp, perc.

GONE WITH THE WIND

Orchestrations credited to Keith Amos. (Additional orchestrations by William David
  Brohn and probably others.)
Tryout: August 28, 1973, Los Angeles (Dorothy Chandler Pavilion). Closed November
  24, San Francisco (Curran).
Music and lyrics by Harold Rome. Based on the novel *Gone with the Wind* by Margaret
  Mitchell. Musical direction by Jay Blackton. Vocal and dance arrangements by Trude
  Rittman. Other participants: Joe Layton (director, choreographer); Horton Foote (librettist); Lesley Ann Warren (star); Pernell Roberts (star).

One partitur is in the Rome Collection at Yale.
  Brohn: "A Time for Love."

GOOD NEWS (1974 REVIVAL)

Orchestrations credited to Philip J. **Lang**. (Additional orchestrators, if any, unknown.)
Opened December 23, 1974, St. James, 16 performances. Tryout: December 7, 1973,
  Philadelphia; December 17, Boston (Colonial); January 30, 1974, Washington, D.C.
  (Opera House); elsewhere.
Music by Ray Henderson, lyrics by B. G. DeSylva and Lew Brown. Musical direction by
  Lisa Redfield. Musical supervision, arrangements, and vocal arrangements by Hugh
  Martin and Timothy Gray. Dance and incidental arrangements by Luther Henderson.
  Other participants: Harry Rigby (co-producer); Abe Burrows (director); Donald Saddler (choreographer); Alice Faye (star); Gene Nelson (star); Stubby Kaye (star).

THE GRAND TOUR

Orchestrations (totally) by Philip J. **Lang**.

Opened January 11, 1979, Palace, 61 performances. Tryout: San Francisco (Curran).

Music and lyrics by Jerry Herman. Based on the play *Jacobowsky and the Colonel* by Franz
   Werfel. Musical direction by Wally Harper. Vocal arrangements by Donald Pippin.
   Dance arrangements by Peter Howard. Other participants: Donald Saddler (choreog-
   rapher); Michael Stewart and Mark Bramble (librettists); Joel Grey (star).

The partiturs are in the possession of the composer.

Instr.: 4 reed, 5 brass (2 tpt, 2 tb, 1 hrn), 11 strings (6 vln, 2 vla, 2 c, 1 b), piano, harp, mandolin/banjo, 2
perc = 25 total.

THE GRASS HARP

Orchestrations credited to J. (Billy) VerPlanck. (Additional orchestrations by Jonathan
   Tunick and Russell **Bennett**.)

Opened November 2, 1971, Martin Beck, 7 performances. Tryout: Ann Arbor, Michigan
   (Power Center, University of Michigan).

Music by Claibe Richardson, lyrics and book by Kenward Elmslie. Based on the novella
   by Truman Capote. Musical direction by Theodore Saidenberg. Dance arrangements
   and incidental music by John Berkman. Other participant: Barbara Cook (star).

Bennett's invoice is preserved in his journal.
   Bennett: Finale ("Reach Out").
   Tunick orchestrated the show's preliminary production in 1966, at Trinity Rep in
Providence, Rhode Island. When he was unavailable for the Michigan tryout, the show
was reorchestrated by VerPlanck. When the show reached Broadway, Tunick stepped back
in to provide about half the orchestrations. He also suggested inviting Bennett, for whom
he ghosted on the 1966 revival of *Show Boat*, to write the finale. (Both Tunick and Bennett
received program credit for additional orchestrations.)

(See page 30.)

GREAT DAY!

Orchestrations uncredited. (Orchestrations by Paul Lannin, Stephen O. Jones, Frank
   Skinner, W.H. Challis, and others.)

Opened October 17, 1929, Cosmopolitan, 36 performances. Tryout: June 4, Philadelphia (Garrick); July, Jamaica, New York (Werba's); Boston (Colonial); elsewhere.

Music by Vincent Youmans, lyrics by William (Billy) Rose and Edward Eliscu. Musical
   direction by Paul Lannin. Other participants: Vincent Youmans (producer).

Several partiturs are in the Youmans Collection at the Library of Congress.
   Lannin: "Happy Because I'm in Love," "I Ask You Does It Pay to Be a Lady."
   Skinner: "Great Day," "Without a Song."
   Challis: "More Than You Know."

Unidentified hand: "Open up Your Heart."

Instr.: 6 reed, 6 brass (3 tpt, 1 tb, 2 hrn), 14? strings (8? vln, 2? vla, 2? c, 2 b [1 tuba]), piano/celesta, harp, 1 perc = 29? total.

GREAT LADY

Orchestrations credited to Hans **Spialek**. (Additional orchestrators unknown.)

Opened December 1, 1938, Majestic, 20 performances. Tryout: November 15, 1938, New Haven (Shubert); elsewhere.

Music by Frederick Loewe, lyrics by Earle Crooker. Suggested by events in the life of Eliza Jumel. Musical direction by John Fredhoven. Other participants: Jerome Robbins (dancer); Nora Kaye (dancer).

GREAT TO BE ALIVE!

Orchestrations by Russell **Bennett** and Don **Walker**. (Additional orchestrators, if any, unknown.)

Opened March 23, 1950, Winter Garden, 52 performances. Tryout: (as *What a Day!*): February 23, New Haven (Shubert); February 28, Philadelphia (Forrest).

Music by Abraham Ellstein, lyrics by Walter Bullock. Musical direction by Max Meth. Dance arrangements by Genevieve Pitot. Vocal arrangements by Crane Calder. Other participants: Vinton Freedley (producer); Vivienne Segal (star).

Bennett's invoice is preserved in his journal. Walker's invoices (made out under the original title of the show, *What a Day!*) are at the Library of Congress. Base page rate: $5.25.

Bennett: "Blue Day," "Dreams Ago," "Final Curtain (Headin' for a Weddin')," "It's a Long Time," "Opening Act II," "This Is Love," "What a Day."

Walker: "Act II Ballet," "Believe Me," "Headin' for a Weddin'" (song, dance, and tag), "There's Nothing Like It" (song, encore, and intro), "Re-Decorate" (song, dance, and tag), "There's a Man Every Time" (song and encore), Wedding Sequence, "When the Sheets Come Back from the Laundry," "Who Done It?" (reprise), "You Appeal to Me" (and encore).

GREENWICH VILLAGE FOLLIES (3RD EDITION)

Orchestrations uncredited. (Orchestrations by Russell **Bennett** and others.)

Opened September 12, 1922, Shubert, 209 performances. Tryout: unknown.

A revue. Music by Louis Hirsch, Bert Kalmar, and others; lyrics by Irving Caesar, John Murray Anderson, Harry Ruby and others. Musical direction by Alfred Newman.

GREENWILLOW

Orchestrations (virtually totally) by Don **Walker**.

Opened March 8, 1960, Alvin, 97 performances. Tryout: January 30, Philadelphia (Shubert).

Music and lyrics by Frank Loesser. Based on the novel by B. J. Chute. Musical direction
by Abba Bogin. Vocal arrangements by Don Walker (uncredited). Dance arrangements
by Billy Goldenberg (replacing Charles Strouse). Other participants: Frank Produc-
tions/Frank Loesser (associate producer); Frank Loesser (co-librettist); Joe Layton
(choreographer); Anthony Perkins (star).

Copies of the partiturs are at the Loesser office. Walker's invoices are at the Library of
Congress. Base page rate: $5.83.

Orchestrations are by Walker, with the following exceptions:

Finale act 1 is by Walker, except for the 5-bar ending by Bogin (heard on the cast
album at the end of "Greenwillow Christmas").

"Walking Away Whistling" is by Walker, with a 5-bar ending by Bogin.

During rehearsals, *Greenwillow* lost its dance arranger, Charles "Buddy" Strouse; he departed, understandably, when the long-in-gestation *Bye Bye Birdie* finally went into production.

DON'S INSTRUCTIONS TO MUSICIANS   Note to percussionist, for the sound of "the neighbor's choppin' axe" in "The Music of Home": "Hit wooden side of pit with metal stick."

Instr.: 6 reed, 7 brass (2 tpt, 2 tb, 3 hrn), 13? strings (8? vln, 2? vla, 2 c, 1 b), harp, 2 perc = 29? total.

(See page 224.)

GRIND

Orchestrations by Billy Byers. (Additional orchestrations by Jim Tyler with Harold
Wheeler.)

Opened April 16, 1985, Mark Hellinger, 71 performances. Tryout: March, Baltimore.

Music by Larry Grossman, lyrics by Ellen Fitzhugh. Musical direction by Paul Ge-
mignani. Dance arrangements by Tom Fay. Dance arrangement for "A New Man" by
Gordon Harrell. Other participants: Harold Prince (co-producer, director); Fay
Kanin (librettist); Ben Vereen (star); Leilani Jones (star); Timothy Nolen (star);
Stubby Kaye (star).

The partiturs are in the City Center Encores! collection.

The orchestrations are by Byers with the following exceptions:

Tyler: "From the Ankles Down," "The Grind" (see below), "I Get Myself Out," "My
Daddy," "A New Man," "Yes, Ma'am."

Other scores:

"The Grind" is mostly by Tyler, with several pages from an earlier version by Byers.

"The Line" is by Byers except for the middle section ("That's What I Should Have
Said"), which is by Tyler.

Overture: there are at least two versions. The earlier surviving version is by Wheeler.
The final version opens and closes with sections by Byers (originally used in the Entr'acte), surrounding Wheeler's orchestration of "All Things to One Man." The Overture
used on the recording contains edits and new bridgework by Tyler.

"Why, Mama, Why?" is by Byers, with inserts and fixes by Tyler.

During the tryout, Byers left the show and was replaced by Tyler.

GUYS AND DOLLS

Orchestrations by George Bassman and Ted **Royal**. (Additional orchestrators, if any, unknown.)

Opened November 24, 1950, 46th Street, 1,200 performances. Tryout: October 14, Philadelphia (Shubert and Erlanger).

Music and lyrics by Frank Loesser. Based on stories by Damon Runyon. Musical direction by Irving Actman. Vocal arrangements and direction by Herbert Greene. Dance arrangements by Billy Kyle (uncredited). Other participants: Feuer & Martin (producers); George S. Kaufman (director); Michael Kidd (choreographer); Abe Burrows (librettist); Peter Gennaro, Onna White (dancers).

The Loesser office has a conformed set of partiturs in a copyist's hand, with corrections by Royal. It also has Loesser's copy of a bound, handwritten piano-conductor score, on which most of the songs are labeled with the name of the orchestrator.

Bassman, a respected Hollywood orchestrator, was fired during the Philadelphia tryout when Feuer discovered that he was demanding kickbacks from the musicians. Royal, the supervising orchestrator on the prior Loesser/Feuer & Martin musical, *Where's Charley?* came in to finish the show.

According to identifications in the bound score, most of the show is by Bassman. The exceptions are "If I Were a Bell," "The Oldest Established," and "Take Back Your Mink" (by Royal); and "Adelaide's Lament Duet Reprise," Entr'acte, "I'll Know," and "My Time of Day" (unattributed.) Identification notes aside, it is known that Royal made changes and revisions to Bassman's charts.

The conformed score was apparently prepared to match the published piano-vocal score, which reflects the stock & amateur version of the show. Checking the scores against the songs included on the 1950 original cast album, one finds that most are reasonably similar, although there are a fair number of instrumental solos and countermelodies on the recording that are not reflected in the score. While the conformed score is in a copyist's hand, there are considerable corrections and reed assignments written in by Royal, even on songs that he did not originally orchestrate. This leads one to suspect that he revised the Bassman charts, cleaning things up in the weeks after the opening (by which point the cast album had already been recorded).

The version of "I'll Know" heard on the 1950 album is totally different from the partitur (and the published vocal score). It is guessed that Bassman's chart was replaced shortly after the post-opening recording with a new one by Royal. The other major change is in "Adelaide's Lament." The vocal score has a modulation at the bottom of page 44 after "a person can develop a cough," which is not heard on the recording (where the song remains in key). The conformed score includes an orchestration by Walker for the rest of the song, beginning with "and furthermore, just from stalling . . . the wedding trip." As the founding president of MTI, Walker was presumably involved in the preparation of the stock & amateur release.

The bound score also bears the legend "rehearsal score prepared by Billy Kyle" on the two major dances, "Crapshooter's Ballet" and "Opening Street Scene" ("Runyonland

Music"). Both Kyle and Bassman appear to have been brought on the project by musical director Irving Actman (who had been composer to lyricist Loesser when the pair first hit Broadway in 1936 and then headed to Hollywood). Actman, Kyle, and Bassman all worked together on the negligible 1950 revue *Alive and Kicking*.

THANKS AND WISHES   From Robert Coleman, musically perceptive critic of the *Daily Mirror*, to Walker:

> I can only regret that I couldn't persuade Ernie Martin to engage you to arrange Frank Loes-ser's score for *Guys and Dolls*, but believe me—I tried. I was called to Philadelphia before the New York opening, to make suggestions—and that was a major one of them. I had the feel-ing that Loesser had at least four pop song hits in this score, but that two of them [perhaps "I'll Know" and "I've Never Been in Love Before"] would take a long time to make the grade on any hit parade because of mediocre arrangements. Ernie told me that he realized I was right, but that he couldn't do anything about it at that late date.

Instr.: 5 reed, 5 brass (3 tpt, 1 tb, 1 hrn), ? strings (? vln, 0 vla, ? c, b), piano, perc.
(See page 186.)

GYPSY

Orchestrations credited to Sid **Ramin** with Robert **Ginzler**. (Orchestrations totally by Ramin *and* Ginzler.)
Opened May 21, 1959, Broadway, 702 performances. Tryout: April 13, Philadelphia.
Music by Jule Styne, lyrics by Stephen Sondheim. Based on the memoir by Gypsy Rose Lee. Musical direction by Milton Rosenstock. Dance arrangements by John Kander. Additional dance music by Betty Walberg. Other participants: David Merrick and Le-land Hayward (producers); Jerome Robbins (director, choreographer); Arthur Lau-rents (librettist); Ethel Merman (star).

Copies of the partiturs are in the Ramin Collection at the Butler Library, Columbia Uni-versity.

The song analysis below, which in places descends to a bar-by-bar description, takes into account the unusual amount of shared scores and the importance of this musical to the overall sound of Broadway music. It is included with apologies to those readers who might find it incomprehensible or overly detailed.

"All I Need Is the Girl": song is by Ginzler. The partitur for the dance is missing, but probably by Ginzler.

"Baby June and Her Newsboys": the opening is by Ginzler except for a 6-bar fix (at "barrel of charm"). The rest of the sequence—including "Let Me Entertain You," "Recitation and Military Routine," and "Military Part II"—is by Ginzler except for Ramin's piccolo solo at bar 67 of the vocal score ("Stars and Stripes Forever").

"Curtain Music" and "Exit Music" are by Ginzler.

Entr'acte is mostly by Ginzler. There is also an older version, which begins with the same fanfare as the Overture.

"Everything's Coming Up Roses": the introduction ("I had a dream") is by Ramin;

the refrain (beginning with "swell") is mostly by Ginzler, with important interior solos by Ramin. These include the brass at 58 and the strings at 60 ("set it spinning"). The section beginning at "Curtain up" (68) is mostly by Ramin, with strings by Ginzler. Red takes over at "Lucky star" (84), including the horn solo at "We can do it" (102). The final section, beginning at 131 ("Everything's coming up roses and daffodils"), has celesta, violin, and cello by Ramin, with the rest by Ginzler.

"Farm Sequence": "Broadway" is mostly by Ginzler, with overwrites by Ramin. "Cow Recitation" is by Ginzler. "Farmboys' Opening" ("Extra! Extra!") is missing, but probably by Ginzler. "Extra Utility" is by Ginzler.

"Gypsy Strip Routine (Let Me Entertain You)" is mostly by Ginzler, with brass edits by Ramin.

"If Momma Was Married" is mostly by Ginzler, with assorted solos—like the strings after "Godspeed and God bless") and the horn at 84 ("Oh, momma get married today")—by Ramin.

"Little Lamb Show Version (May 7)" is by Ginzler. Two earlier versions—used as an interlude in "Goldstone," coming between the double-time section and "there are good stones"—are both by Ramin.

"May We Entertain You": the song section is mostly by Ginzler; the underscoring for Rose/Jocko is by Ramin.

"Mr. Goldstone": first 33 bars (through "have a lichee") are by Ramin. The next large section, through the più mosso ("have a goldstone"), is mostly by Ginzler, with Ramin filling in key passages (usually violins). The rest of the number is mostly by Ramin.

Overture: the beginning of the opening fanfare (bars 1–7) is by Ginzler. (The strings and piano, played under the brass holds—which were cut but restored for the 2004 revival—are by Ramin.) The reeds/strings/brass pyramid section (8–15) is by Ginzler. The descending brass (16–19) is by Ramin. "Roses" is mostly by Ginzler; the trumpet runs in the bridge and the strings are by Ramin. Ramin takes over at the transition to "You'll Never Get Away from Me"; most of this song is by Ramin, except for the trumpet fills at the end of the A (122–123) and B (130–131) sections. There is a major cut at bar 146, deleting "Caroline" ("vaudeville style" with sax solo and wah-wah trumpets, by Ramin) and "Together" (trombone melody, with triplets from reeds, by Ramin with reed runs by Ginzler) . The majestic section (leading to "Small World") is by Ginzler, with the strings and the violin trill by Ramin. "Small World" is by Ginzler, with that distinctive 2-note pizzicato in the strings at 160 by Ramin. In the bridge, Ramin writes the strings and celesta. The 2-bar transition into the strip, with brass triplets, is by Ginzler. Ramin takes over with the triplets at 172 and continues through the entire "burlesque strip style" section. Ginzler resumes at "Goldstone," including all those high flourishes from the reeds. The final section, beginning at 226 ("I–love–") is by Ramin.

"Rose's Turn" (called "Mama's Turn" on the partitur) is mostly by Ginzler. The "Mama's talkin' loud" section, from 48 to 62, is by Ramin. Ramin also wrote the trombone line at 103 ("wasn't for me, Herbie") and the violins and cello at 107.

"Seattle to Los Angeles" ("Some People Reprise"): the section in which Rose "drafts" the boys for the act is by Ramin.

"Small World" is by Ginzler (the cast album uses an altered version). The earlier extended version includes "Mama's Talkin Soft" and a quartet section for Louise, Clare (June), Rose, and Herbie; this is almost all by Ginzler, with Ramin doing most of the bridgework. "Small World (Act II Reprise)" is by Ginzler; utility is by Ramin.

"Some People" is mostly by Ginzler. The first 10 bars, through "sitting still," were rewritten by Ramin. String runs in the bridge are by Ginzler. The cello, trumpet, and violin solos—indicated in the vocal score starting at bar 88 (echoing "I had a dream, just as real as can be")—are by Ramin. Ginzler resumes by himself at "get yourself some new orchestrations." The 4-bar transition after "88 cents" is by Ramin. "Goodbye to blueberry pie" (139) is Ginzler, with the flute runs (marked as strings in the score) by Ramin. Ramin takes over at 163 ("That's living for some people") through the end.

"Together" is mostly by Ginzler. Ramin provides solos throughout, like the brass fills in the bridge, the tremolo thumb line beginning at 71 ("whatever the boat I row"), and the brass accompanying the title phrase at the end of the refrain.

"Toreadorables": the first 18 bars are by Ginzler; the next section (beginning with "barrel of charm" and ending with Louise's split) is by Ramin. The "Toreador" section is by Ginzler. The partiturs include an extended "Spanish" number for the girls, to the melody of "Broadway" (from the "Farmboy Sequence"), by Ginzler.

"You Gotta Get a Gimmick": The clarinet solo at the beginning and most of the brass are by Ramin; most of the reeds are by Ginzler. The accompaniment to the bugle strip is by Ramin, as is the brass figure at 68 (after "Gypsy, girl, you've got it made"). The violin solo for the ballet strip (78) is by Ramin. The end of the song, from 94 ("dressy Tessie Tura"), is by Ginzler. The lyric "all them other ladies because" was changed from "all them other mothers-in-laws."

"You'll Never Get Away from Me" is mostly by Ginzler, including all those runs from the reeds. The original version, by the way, began with Rose singing part of "Together" as a verse.

Sid described himself as "the idea man" of the team of Ramin and Ginzler. They had spent almost a decade working together on *The Milton Berle Show*. Ramin often mapped out the charts and wrote in major solos. He also occasionally dictated parts to Ginzler, who was a considerably faster writer. Thus, while Ginzler's hand is far more present on the *Gypsy* partiturs, there seems to have been an equal collaboration on the show.

Among the unused charts are several fully orchestrated sections of "stripper" underscoring, which have been given whimsical names ("The Bloozy Cool," "The Exotic"). One of them has an especially unwieldy title, "June Is a Jew, So Change It to Clare." This referred to a late-developing crisis, when *Gypsy*'s real-life sister, June Havoc, refused to allow her name to be used in the musical. Thus, June was changed to Clare. (Yes, for a while it was "Baby Clare and Her Newsboys.") No sooner had this occurred than Havoc—perhaps realizing that she had more to gain than lose by being memorialized in *Gypsy*—agreed to a settlement. What is of import in all this, though, is the music itself. I have always wondered just where that now-famous strip music—heard in the Overture (accompanying the wild trumpet solo) and as the opening vamp of "Rose's Turn"—came from; unlike everything else in the Overture (and, for that matter, in "Rose's Turn"), it is not developed from one of the songs. The answer can be found in the deleted 43-bar "June Is a Jew, So Change It to Clare."

SID AND RED'S INSTRUCTIONS TO MUSICIANS   On the Overture: those three horn notes—in the fourth and third bars from the end—are marked "Whoop Whoop Whoop."

On "You Gotta Get a Gimmick": "You can (bump!)" is marked "Viol behind the bridge, Jack Benny style." Ramin's accompaniment to the bugle strip (at bar 37) is marked "Quasi Pomp and Circ." Ginzler's trumpet flutters at 56, after "They'll never make her rich," are marked "3rd valve false finger."

On the exit music: the trombone in the final measure is marked "Solo (finally)!"

Instr.: 5 reed (including 6 sax, 5 clr),, 7 brass (3 tpt, 3 tb, 1 hrn), 11 strings (6 vln, 0 vla, 4 c, 1 b), piano, harp, , perc = 26 total.

(See pages 45, 75, 186, 207, 211, 228, 232, 258.)

HALF A SIXPENCE

Orchestrations credited to Jim Tyler. Dance orchestrations by Robert Prince. (Additional orchestrators, if any, unknown.)

Opened April 25, 1965, Broadhurst, 512 performances. Tryout: March 15, Boston (Colonial); March 30, Toronto (O'Keefe).

Music and lyrics by David Heneker. Based on the novel *Kipps* by H. G. Wells. Musical direction by Stanley Lebowsky. Vocal arrangements by Buster Davis. Dance arrangements, ballet music, and dance orchestrations by Robert Prince.

Other participants: Gene Saks (replacement director); Onna White (choreographer); Tommy Steele (star).

HALLELUJAH, BABY!

Orchestrations by Peter Matz. Dance (and other) orchestrations by Luther Henderson. (Additional orchestrations by Ralph Wilkinson and Jim Tyler.)

Opened April 26, 1967, Martin Beck, 293 performances. Tryout: March 20, Boston (Colonial).

Music by Jule Styne, lyrics by Betty Comden & Adolph Green. Musical direction and vocal arrangements by Buster Davis. Dance arrangements and orchestrations by Luther Henderson. Other participants: Burt Shevelove (director); Arthur Laurents (librettist); Leslie Uggams (star).

The partiturs are at the Styne office. Henderson's invoices are in his personal papers. Base page rate: $8.39.

The orchestrations are by Matz, with the following exceptions:

Henderson: "Cakewalk," "Clem's Drill," exit music, "Feet Do Your Stuff" (and "Feet Fox Trot"), "Freedom Parade" (a small portion of which introduces the final track on the original cast album), "Hallelujah, Baby!" (song and dance), "Under the Ropes," "Voodoo Ritual," "Witches" (introduction to "Double, Double"), "When the Weather's Better" (see below), "You Ain't Gonna Shake Your Feathers."

Wilkinson: "Mama in the '40s," "A Wolf from Grandma," "Wrong Time, Wrong Place."

Other scores:

"Another Day" is by Matz, reprise by Wilkinson.

"My Own Morning" and two reprises are by Matz, underscore by Wilkinson.

"When the Weather's Better" (cut) and "Weather Opening" are by Henderson; "Weather Underscore" and "Weather Finale" by Matz; utility is by Tyler.

"You're Welcome" (cut) is by Matz; "Welcome Underscore" and reprise by Wilkinson.

Instr.: 5 reed (5 sax), 7 brass (3 tpt, 3 tb, 1 hrn), 10 strings (6 vln, 0 vla, 3 c, 1 b), piano, guitar, 2 perc = 26 total.

HANS CHRISTIAN ANDERSEN

Orchestrations credited to Don **Walker**. (Additional orchestrators, if any, unknown.)

Opened February 5, 1976, Dallas, Texas (Music Hall). Closed Dallas(?).

Music and lyrics by Frank Loesser. Suggested by events in the life of Hans Christian Andersen. Other participant: Tom Hughes (producer).

The partiturs (unexamined) and invoices are in the Walker Collection at the Library of Congress. Base page rate: $14.72.

This was the second authorized stage musicalization of the Samuel Goldwyn film. Harold Fielding produced an earlier one, *Hans Andersen*, at the London Palladium, starring Tommy Steele, which opened on December 17, 1974, with orchestrations by a team headed by Alyn Ainsworth.

THE HAPPIEST GIRL IN THE WORLD

Orchestrations (totally) by Russell **Bennett** and Hershy **Kay**.

Opened April 3, 1961, Martin Beck, 96 performances. Tryout: February 18, New Haven (Shubert); Philadelphia (Shubert).

Music by Jacques Offenbach, lyrics and "story" by E. Y. Harburg. Based on the play *Lysistrata* by Aristophanes. Musical direction and vocal arrangements by Robert De Cormier. Musical research by Jay Gorney. Dance arrangements by Gerald Alters.

Other participant: Cyril Ritchard (director, star).

The partiturs are at Tams-Witmark. Bennett's invoices are preserved in his ledger. Base page rate: $6.52.

Kay: "Adrift on a Star" (see below), "Cheers for the Hero," "Diana's Decree," "Eureka," Finale act II, "Five Minutes of Spring" (see below), "The Glory That Is Greece," "The Greek Marines," "The Happiest Girl in the World" (see below), "Hup–2–3," "The Magic Fa-Lute" (ballet), "Never Bedevil the Devil," "The Oath," "The Olympics," "The Olympics Revisited," "Persian Women" (instrumental), "Sez She, to Me" (song and reprise), "The Transformation."

Bennett: "Honesty" (parts I and II), "How Soon, Oh Moon," "Never Trust a Virgin," Overture (New York and Temporary), "Shall We Say Farewell," "Shepherd's Serenade," "Vive La Virtue" (see below), "Whatever That May Be."

Other scores:

"Adrift on a Star" is by Kay, replacing an earlier chart by Bennett.

"Five Minutes of Spring" is by Kay, replacing an earlier chart by Bennett; "Diana's Reprise" by Kay.

"The Happiest Girl in the World" is by Kay, replacing an earlier chart by Bennett; reprise by Bennett.

"Opening Galop": part I is by Kay; part II is by Bennett.

"Vive La Virtue" is by Bennett except for the 17-bar second verse ("Vice is not averse to virtue") by Kay.

The score was originally split evenly, but a significant amount of Bennett's material was replaced during the tryout by Kay. Bennett worked on the show in New York only. Kay, the supervising orchestrator, took the show on the road and did the rest of the job (except for the "New York Overture," which Bennett wrote on March 29). The replacement of three major Bennett charts might well be attributable to changes in the routines, rather than dissatisfaction with the material.

HAPPY AS LARRY

Orchestrations credited to Rudolph Goehr and Charles L. Cooke. (Additional orchestrators, if any, unknown.)

Opened January 6, 1950, Coronet, 3 performances. Tryout: unknown.

Music by Mischa and Wesley Portnoff, lyrics and book by Donagh MacDonagh. Musical direction by Franz Allers. Vocal arrangements by Herbert Greene. Other participants: Leonard Sillman (producer), Burgess Meredith (director, star).

HAPPY BIRTHDAY

Orchestrations and incidental music composed by Russell **Bennett**.

Opened October 31, 1946, Broadhurst, 564 performances. Tryout: October, Boston (Boston).

A play by Anita Loos, with one song by Richard Rodgers and Oscar Hammerstein II. Other participants: Richard Rodgers and Oscar Hammerstein II (producers); Joshua Logan (director); Helen Hayes (star).

Bennett's invoices are preserved in his ledger. Base page rate: $3.

This play with music included one original song, "I Haven't Got a Worry in the World" by Rodgers and Hammerstein. Three standards were used, "Honeysuckle Rose," "My Melancholy Baby," and "The Only Girl." The play also included fourteen pieces of incidental music, some of which were twice as long as the songs and which were composed by Bennett.

HAPPY HUNTING

Orchestrations credited to Ted **Royal**. Additional orchestrations by Joe Glover, Don **Walker**, and Seymour "Red" **Ginzler** (and possibly others).

Opened December 6, 1956, Majestic, 412 performances. Tryout: October 22, Philadelphia (Shubert); Boston.

Music by Harold Karr, lyrics by Matt Dubey. Musical direction by Jay Blackton. Dance music devised by Roger Adams.

Other participants: Jo Mielziner (producer); Abe Burrows (director); Ethel Merman (star).

The orchestrations were clearly problematic, as Glover, Walker, and Ginzler all received title-page credit for additional orchestrations. An opening night greeting from the songwriters to Walker (*Glad you were in at the finish to do the opening.* —*Matt and Harold*) suggests that Walker's contributions included Merman's rousing opening number, "Gee, But It's Good to Be Here," which was added during the tryout. "If'n" sounds like it is probably by Ginzler.

HAPPY NEW YEAR

Orchestrations credited to Luther Henderson. (Additional orchestrations by Daniel Troob.)

Opened April 27, 1980, Morosco, 17 performances.

Music and lyrics by Cole Porter. Based on the play *Holiday* by Philip Barry. Musical direction and vocal arrangements by Buster Davis. Dance arrangements by Charles Coleman. Other participants: Burt Shevelove (director, librettist); Donald Saddler (choreographer).

THE HAPPY TIME

Orchestrations (mostly) by Don **Walker**. (Additional orchestrations by Jim Tyler.)

Opened January 18, 1968, Broadway, 286 performances. Tryout: Los Angeles (Dorothy Chandler Pavilion).

Music by John Kander, lyrics by Fred Ebb. Based on the play by Samuel Taylor, from stories by Robert Fontaine. Musical direction and vocal arrangements by Oscar Kosarin. Dance arrangements and incidental music by Marvin Laird. Other participants: David Merrick (producer); Gower Champion (director, choreographer); Robert Goulet (star); David Wayne (star).

Invoices are in the Walker Collection at the Library of Congress. Base page rate: $12.50. Invoices indicate: Walker (96%).

The orchestrations are by Walker, with the following exceptions.

Tyler: "Catch My Garter," minor fixes.

KANDER: Gower was almost totally in charge of it, and it was very hard to interfere with whatever he was doing. He fired Don without telling me. 'Cause Don was very quiet. He didn't speak much. He'd come in with his tape recorder, watch the number, talk to me, and he'd go off and write an orchestration. I think Gower felt, basically, "if he's not asking me more questions, he can't be very good." So one day he called me to tell me that he fired Don without asking me. I was devastated. He brought in Phil Lang, who I didn't know; Gower had worked with him before. I got off the phone with Gower, and I didn't know what to do. And Don said—he really spoke very soft, not many words, I think he lay in wait for Gower—something to the effect of "it's okay that you're firing me. But that will cost you x-thousand dollars." I don't remember the figure, but Don had it all worked out. He was right, it would cost a fortune. And suddenly Gower loved all the work that Don did. So Don stayed and did a wonderful job.

I guess that the figure, in 1968, would have been in the $30,000 range—for reorchestration of the score at overtime road rates, as well as importing a bevy of expert copyists at round-the-clock double-time. *The Happy Time* was already seriously over budget—it wound up as the first Broadway show to lose a million dollars—and Merrick was holding Gower responsible.

Tunick remembers Mathilde Pincus's version of the story: "Don came into the rehearsal, saw a number, and packed up his papers. He started to leave. Gower said, 'Don't you want to see it again?' Don said, 'I've seen it all a million times.' And Gower was livid."

By my estimates, *The Happy Time* was Walker's eighty-second musical (of ninety-three) as principal orchestrator.

THANKS AND WISHES   Opening night, from Kander to Walker: "Without you, I'm nothing. Love always, John."

HAZEL FLAGG

Orchestrations by Don **Walker**. (Additional orchestrations by Jack Mason, Joe Glover, and Robert **Ginzler**, with Irwin **Kostal**, Walter Paul, Philip J. **Lang**, Jay Blackton, and Sid **Ramin**.)

Opened February 11, 1953, Mark Hellinger, 190 performances. Tryout: January 12, Philadelphia (Shubert).

Music by Jule Styne, lyrics by Bob Hilliard. Based on the film *Nothing Sacred* by Ben Hecht, from a story by James Street. Musical direction by Pembroke Davenport. Vocal arrangements and direction by Hugh Martin. Assistant to Hugh Martin, Buster Davis. Ballet arrangements by Oscar Kosarin.

Other participants: Jule Styne (producer); Ben Hecht (librettist); Helen Gallagher (star).

Invoices are in the Walker Collection at the Library of Congress. Base page rate: $5.70.

Invoices indicate: Walker (45%), Ginzler (15%), Mason (13%).

Walker: "Egelhoffer's Coming" (cut), "Every Street's a Boulevard in Old New York," "How Do You Speak to an Angel?" "I Feel Like I'm Gonna Live Forever" (see below), "Make the People Cry" (cut), "Money Burns a Hole in My Pocket," "My Wild Imagination" (cut), "Paris Gown Ballet (How Do You Speak to an Angel?)," "People Forget" (cut), "Radium Gal (Hello, Hazel)," "The Rutland Bounce," "Salome," "The World Is Beautiful Today."

Ginzler: "Every Street's a Boulevard in Old New York" (encore), Finale act 1, Finale act 2, "Laura de Maupassant," "A Little More Heart" (see below).

Mason: "Autograph Chant," "Funeral Parade," "Just Think How Many People Never Fall in Love" (cut).

Kostal: "Carried Away (Big Parade Ballet)."

Paul: "Who Is the Bravest?"

Other scores:

Entr'acte is a compilation of utilities, with bridgework by Glover.

"Everybody Loves to Take a Bow" is by Walker (the vocal) and Ginzler (beginning with the choral interlude).

"I Feel Like I'm Gonna Live Forever" is by Walker, with fixes by Lang.

"I'm Glad I'm Leaving" appears to be orchestrated in three parts, Hazel's section (by Glover), the chorus section (by Blackton), and the dance section (by Paul).

"A Little More Heart" is by Ginzler and Ramin (the latter making his Broadway debut), with the dance by Ginzler.

Overture is a compilation of utilities, with bridgework by Glover.

"You're Gonna Dance with Me, Willie": part 1 (Hazel's vocal) is by Walker; part 2 (choral and dance sections) is by Ginzler.

Orchestration and copying costs through the New York opening were $19,099.01. This is a remarkably high figure for the time, reflecting the numerous discarded numbers and costly overtime replacements. Hopes were apparently high all around; the piano-vocal scores used in rehearsal were written on paper with the show title printed on the bottom, the only case of show-personalized paper I ran across other than Paul Whiteman's scores for *Jumbo*.

THANKS AND WISHES   From star Helen Gallagher to Walker: "Merde alors!"

(See page 108.)

HEADS UP!

Orchestrations uncredited. (Orchestrations by Russell **Bennett** and others.)

Opened November 11, 1929, Alvin, 144 performances. Tryout: (as *Me for You*) September 15, Detroit (Shubert); (as *Heads Up!*) October 25, Philadelphia (Shubert).

Music by Richard Rodgers, lyrics by Lorenz Hart. Musical direction by Alfred Newman.
    Other participants: Alex Aarons and Vinton Freedley (producers).

HEAVEN ON EARTH

Orchestrations (mostly) by Russell **Bennett** and Don **Walker**. (Additional orchestrations by George Bassman.)

Opened September 16, 1948, Century, 12 performances. Tryout: Philadelphia.

Music by Jay Gorney, lyrics by Barry Trivers. Musical direction by Clay Warnick. Vocal arrangements and direction by Hugh Martin. Additional vocal arrangements by Bus [Buster] Davis. Dance arrangements by Alan Morand.

Most of the partiturs are in the Gorney Collection at the New York Public Library. Bennett's invoices are preserved in his ledger. Walker's invoices are in the Walker Collection at the Library of Congress. Base page rate: $4.95.

Bennett: "Back of Hack," "The Brawl," "Drunk Specialty," Finale act 2, "The Future of America," "Glad I'm Married," "Heaven on Earth" (plus "Duo Dance" and "New

Dance"), "Home Is Where the Heart Is," "The Letter," "No Room for Love," "Oh, Friday (Come-All-Ya)," "Peter Lind Hayes Specialty (Tour of the City)," "Tradesman's Chorus," "Wedding Gifts (Dorothy Jarnac Specialty)," "What's the Matter with Our City?"

Walker: "Applejack" (song, choral version, dance, reprise), "Bow in My Hair (song, quintet, dance, and tag), "Coffee" (song, choral version, part III, part IV, part V), "Don't Forget to Dream" (song and utility), "The Lady Police," "Wedding in the Park."

Bassman: "Just Push a Button" (with "Push Exit" by Bennett), "Opening."

Other scores:

"Punchy's Dance" is mostly by Bennett, with 4 pages by Walker.

"So Near and Yet So Far" is by Bennett; "Specialty" by Walker.

"Temporary Overture" has bridgework by Bennett, incorporating utilities by Bennett and Walker.

Instr.: 5 reed (including 5 sax), 6 brass (3 tpt, 2 tb, 1 hrn), ? strings (, 0 vla, c, 1 b), piano, perc.

(See page 209.)

HELLO, DADDY!

Orchestrations uncredited. (Orchestrations by Hans Spialek, Stephen O. Jones, Maurice de Packh, Fudd Livingston, Arthur Johnstone, and possibly others.)

Opened December 26, 1928, Mansfield, 196 performances. Tryout: unknown.

Music by Jimmy McHugh, lyrics by Dorothy Fields. Based on the play *The High Cost of Loving* by Frank Mandel. Musical direction by Max Steiner. Other participants: Lew Fields (producer, star); Herbert Fields (librettist).

HELLO, DOLLY!

Orchestrations by Philip J. **Lang**. (Additional orchestrations by Jack Andrews.)

Opened January 16, 1964, St. James, 2,844 performances. Tryout: November 18, 1963, Detroit (Fisher); December 17, Washington, D.C. (National).

Music and lyrics by Jerry Herman. Based on the play *The Matchmaker* by Thornton Wilder. Musical direction and vocal arrangements by Shepard Coleman. Dance arrangements and incidental music by Peter Howard. Other participants: David Merrick (producer); Gower Champion (director, choreographer); Michael Stewart (librettist); Carol Channing (star).

The partiturs of cut material and the revised orchestrations for replacement stars are in the possession of the composer. The charts for the original Broadway version, however, cannot presently be located.

Lang: "Butterfly Scramble," "Exasperating Woman," "G'bye Song," "I Had a Penny," utility ("Sunday Clothes").

Andrews: "It Takes a Woman" (original version, an altogether different song than what is used in the final show), "No! A Million Times, No!"

Unidentified hand: "New Opening 12/8/63" ("I Put My Hand In" vamp, incorporated into final version).

Other scores:

"Opening Act II": there are two versions by Lang, one segueing into "Exasperating Women" and the other (dated 12/16/1963) based on the "Call on Dolly" theme.

Overture: there are at least four overtures. The original, routined by Peter Howard and written by Lang, was written for the tryout but unused. The Overture heard on the Pearl Bailey cast album is by Glenn Osser. Lang wrote another Overture for the Houston Grand Opera production, which played Broadway in 1978. The current Overture, routined by Don Pippin and orchestrated by Larry Blank, was written for the 1995 Broadway revival (although the cast album, recorded prior to the New York run, uses the 1978 Overture).

"Ribbons Down My Back": the existing partitur is for an early version that was cut. It begins with an extended 78-bar instrumental. The song is by Andrews except for the first 39 bars of the intro, by Lang. Lang has also written in new trumpet parts for the refrain.

While the scores used for the original Broadway production are missing, the composer has an assortment of later scores, all by Lang, most of which are based on the original orchestrations. These fall into three categories:

Transpositions and new arrangements for the Mary Martin company (labeled "Mary Martin"): "Before the Parade" (first 124 bars), "Before the Parade Insert" ("for optional insertion in Mary Martin transposition"), "Dancing" (first 116 bars), "Finale Act II," "Hello, Dolly!" (first 127 bars), "I Put My Hand In" (complete number), "Motherhood" (complete), "New March to Harmonia," "Put on Your Sunday Clothes" (40 bars only), "So Long Dearie" (with the vocal marked "Mary 8 basso").

Revised scores labeled "Red. Inst.," whatever that might mean: "I Put My Hand In," "It Takes a Woman," "It Takes a Woman (reprise)," "Yonkers March."

Added songs for Ethel Merman: "Love, Look in My Window," "World, Take Me Back."

In his *Playbill* bio for the 1969 musical *Jimmy*, Jack Andrews identified the show among his orchestration credits.

The four scores illegibly labeled "Red. Inst." have a slightly different orchestration (violins A and B instead of A, B, C, D; no harp; and the addition of a viola line). Written on one of the wrappers is "Schubert [*sic*] Theatre, State and Monroe"—which suggests that these might have been written for the Chicago company.

> PETER HOWARD: I'd hate to defame Shepard Coleman, but he had not done many shows and he wangled his way into the job. Carol Channing hated him, and he really messed up her performance many times. He only lasted a few months, and I replaced him. After he was fired, he won the Tony. There was something in Dorothy Kilgallen's column about the conductor being fired but winning the Tony anyway. So they stopped giving out the award for conductor.

Instr.: 4 reed, 5 brass (3 tpt, 2 tb), 11? strings (8? vln, 0 vla, 2 c, 1 b), piano/celesta, harp, guitar/banjo, 2 perc = 25? total.

(See pages 174, 198, 203, 306.)

HELLZAPOPPIN (1967 VERSION)

Orchestrations credited to Don **Walker**. (Additional orchestrators, if any, unknown.)

Tryout: July 1, 1967, Montreal (Garden of Stars, Expo '67). Closed September 16, Montreal.

A revue. Music by Marian Grudeff, lyrics by Raymond Jessel. Suggested by the 1938 revue devised by Ole Olsen and Chic Johnson. Musical direction and dance arrangements by John Berkman. Other participants: Alexander H. Cohen (producer); Jerry Adler (director); Soupy Sales (star).

Invoices are in the Walker Collection at the Library of Congress. Base page rate: $12.50.

HELLZAPOPPIN (1976 VERSION)

Orchestrations credited to Ralph **Burns**. (Additional orchestrators, if any, unknown.)

Tryout: November 22, 1976, Baltimore (Mechanic); December 7, Washington, D.C. (National). Closed January 22, 1977, Boston (Shubert).

A revue. Music mostly by Jule Styne and Hank Beebe, lyrics mostly by Carolyn Leigh and Bill Heyer. Additional song by Cy Coleman and Dorothy Fields. Suggested by the 1938 revue devised by Ole Olsen and Chic Johnson. Musical direction by John Lesko. Dance arrangements by Gordon Lowry Harrell. Other participants: Alexander H. Cohen (co-producer); Abe Burrows (original director, sketch writer); Jerry Adler (replacement director); Donald Saddler (choreographer); Tommy Tune (additional choreographer, uncredited); Joseph Stein (sketch writer); Jerry Lewis (star); Lynn Redgrave (star).

HENRY, SWEET HENRY

Orchestrations credited to Eddie **Sauter**. (Additional orchestrators, if any, unknown.)

Opened October 23, 1967, Palace, 80 performances. Tryout: Detroit (Fisher); Philadelphia.

Music and lyrics by Bob Merrill. Based on the novel *The World of Henry Orient* by Nora Ephron. Musical direction and vocal arrangements by Shepard Coleman. Dance arrangements by William Goldenberg and Marvin Hamlisch. Other participants: Michael Bennett (choreographer); Nunnally Johnson (librettist); Don Ameche (star).

Herb Harris was the contractor:

> I worked for the producer, Norman Twain. He let me choose the orchestrator, I brought in Eddie Sauter. Early on, we needed someone to play auditions. I called a friend who recommended a pianist from NYU. Marvin Hamlisch played auditions, soon became rehearsal pianist, went on the road with us, and when Billy Goldenberg had to leave Detroit to do a film, Marvin moved in as dance arranger. I had breakfast with Eddie, he was furious. "Who's this guy? Now he's making changes in the dance music I already orchestrated."

HER FIRST ROMAN

Orchestrations by Don **Walker**. (Additional orchestrations by Jim Tyler.)

Opened October 20, 1968, Lunt-Fontanne, 17 performances. Tryout: Boston (Colonial).

Music, lyrics, and book by Ervin Drake. Additional music and lyrics by Jerry Bock and Sheldon Harnick (uncredited). Based on *Caesar and Cleopatra* by George Bernard Shaw. Musical direction, dance arrangements, and incidental music by Peter Howard. Vocal arrangements by Don Walker. Other participants: Richard Kiley (star); Leslie Uggams (star).

Invoices are in the Walker Collection at the Library of Congress. Base page rate: $10. The orchestrations are by Walker (who also had a separate contract in the amount of $2,000 for vocal arrangments) , with the following exceptions:

Tyler: "Bacchanale," "Caesar Is Wrong," "Evil Companions," Opening act II, "Ptolemy," "What Are We Doing in Egypt?" "When My Back Is to the Wall," various fixes.

Other score:

"Her First Roman": song is by Walker; dance and tag by Tyler.

Instr.: 6 reed, 9 brass (3 tpt, 3 tb, 3 hrn), 6 strings (0 vln, 0 vla, 5 c, 1 b), Rocksichord (keyboard), harp, 2 perc = 25 total.

(See page 111.)

HERE'S LOVE

Orchestrations (mostly) by Don **Walker**. Additional scoring by Elliot Lawrence.

Opened October 3, 1963, Shubert, 334 performances. Tryout: July 30, Detroit (Fisher); August 27, Washington, D.C. (National).

Music, lyrics, and book by Meredith Willson. Based on the film *Miracle on 34th Street* by George Seaton, from a story by Valentine Davies. Musical direction, vocal arrangements, and additional scoring by Elliot Lawrence. Dance arrangements by Peter Howard. Other participants: Stuart Ostrow (producer, replacement director); Michael Kidd (choreographer).

Invoices are in the Walker Collection at the Library of Congress. Base page rate: $6.71. Invoices indicate the following breakdown: Walker (90%), Lawrence (10%).

The orchestrations are by Walker, with the following exceptions:

Lawrence: Overture, "The Plastic Alligator," "That Man Over There," minor fixes.

The opening, as heard on the cast recording, begins with an abbreviated Overture (by Lawrence); a short "Prelude" (Walker); "Big Clown Balloons" (Walker); "Parade" (Walker); "Adeste Fidelis Finale" (Lawrence).

From Walker to Stuart Ostrow, en route from Detroit to Washington:

> I am not very happy about the orchestrations. They are a stylistic hodgepodge, opportunistic and often lacking in musical integrity. Part of the problem arises because we are evoking no definite musical period, which often gives a score an overall style. There is nothing we can do about this situation, it is built into any show that is supposed to be today. . . . Everything that Elliot has scored—although I am first to agree that it works—is so far away from my approach as to be in another musical. . . . the show rises to such a musical peak so early with the "Adeste" [the climax of the opening number] that all dynamic levels are distorted from then on. . . . when Fred grabs Doris and kisses her the music should be the biggest climax of all—but unfortunately the diet has been too rich and the musical effect is not startling. We have a brassy, blatant score [due in part to "goosing it up" to fill the cavernous Fisher] that I shudder to expose to the NY critics. . . . I doubt very much that we can repair the damage that's been done here. The changes have been too universal. Sometimes I think you'd have been better off with Phil Lang. There sure weren't any "weak spots" in *Li'l Abner.*

This last, presumably, refers to a recurring complaint from choreographer Michael Kidd. Stuart Ostrow produced the show and, during the tryout, took over as director. Before going out on his own as a producer, Ostrow had worked with Frank Loesser on *The Most Happy Fella*, *The Music Man*, and *Greenwillow* (all orchestrated by Walker):

> I spoke with Don. He was nay-saying when everybody was celebrating the good out-of-town reviews. It got me nervous—why is Don talking to me about this? I asked Meredith about the orchestrations: "No, I love them," he said. So we didn't do anything. Maybe we should have. . . . I guess Don was feeling sorry for himself; it may have been related with the erosion of his relationship with Loesser; I wasn't part of it, but he naturally associated me with Frank. With the "Parade," I think Don hated the idea that Peter had sketched it out with Kidd, hated that he wasn't in on the creative process as he was on *Happy Fella*.

> PETER HOWARD: *Here's Love* could have been and should have been a much better show. We had a lot of problems. When people are not together on their thinking, that's when you have problems. It wasn't the best score in the world, either. The "Parade" number, of course, was great. That's where I took all of the themes and used them on all the instruments of the orchestra. Those themes on "Big Clown Balloons" are all countermelodies. Piccolo, trombone, the xylophone—we used two of the kids on a big xylophone, tap dancing. What I did with Michael Kidd, it was all homework. I'd get ideas, bring them into the studio, and we'd try things out.

(See page 199.)

HERE'S WHERE I BELONG

Orchestrations credited to Glenn Osser, Norman Leyden, and Jonathan Tunick. Opened March 3, 1968, Billy Rose, 1 performance. Tryout: Philadelphia.

Music by Robert Waldman, lyrics by Alfred Uhry. Based on the novel *East of Eden* by John Steinbeck. Musical direction and vocal arrangements by Theodore Saidenberg. Dance arrangements by Arnold Goland (replacing Genevieve Pitot). Other participants: Mitch Miller (producer); Terrence McNally (original librettist, credit withdrawn).

HI YA, GENTLEMEN!

Orchestrations credited to Russell **Bennett**, Hans **Spialek**, and Don **Walker**. (Additional orchestrators, if any, unknown.)

Tryout: November 29, 1940, Hartford, Connecticut (Bushnell); December 1940, Boston (Colonial). Closed December, Boston.

Music by Johnny Green, lyrics by Harold Adamson. Musical direction by Johnny Green. Vocal arrangements by Hugh Martin, Gene de Paul, and Pete King. Other participants: Joshua Logan (director); Alex A. Aarons (co-producer).

> HUGH MARTIN: Don's orchestrations were so exciting. That's why I brought him to Dick Rodgers for *Best Foot Forward*. There was a song, "I'll take the high note, you'll take the low note," with a vocal arrangement like "Sing for Your Supper." It was later used in the Red Skelton/Esther Williams movie *Bathing Beauty*.

Telegram from composer Green to Walker: "In reading score vocal verse and chorus blues, have found couple instances definite reharmonization to extent of being recomposition object to this strenuously and suggest if you have done this elsewhere you correct same now and save us unpleasantness."

Further unpleasantness was saved. A year later, Green wrote to Walker from Hollywood, discussing progress on his next Broadway musical, *The Umpire's Daughter*, with a book by George Abbott (either unproduced, or retitled *Beat the Band*): "I want it to be Walker, from overture to exit."

HIGH BUTTON SHOES

Orchestrations credited to Philip J. **Lang**. (Additional orchestrators, if any, unknown.)
Opened October 9, 1947, Century, 727 performances. Tryout: unknown.
Music by Jule Styne, lyrics by Sammy Cahn. Based on the novel *The Sisters Liked Them Handsome* by Stephen Longstreet. Musical direction by Milton Rosenstock. Vocal arrangements by Bob [*sic*] Martin. Other participants: George Abbott (director); Jerome Robbins (choreographer); Phil Silvers (star); Nanette Fabray (featured).

The vocal arrangements were credited to "Bob Martin," but Hugh Martin confirms that he did "Papa, Won't You Dance with Me" and "There's Nothing Like a Model 'T'" (which, indeed, incorporates a bit of Martin's "The Trolley Song").

The dance arrangement for Jerome Robbins's "Bathing Beauty Ballet" has in some places been unofficially credited to Genevieve Pitot, although this is almost certainly erroneous. (Pitot's entry in *The Biographical Encyclopedia and Who's Who of the American Theatre*, which is otherwise comprehensive, does not mention *High Button Shoes*—which is a credit she would surely not have overlooked.) The *Playbill* includes the following credit: "Ballet music by Mr. Styne. Assistant to Mr. Styne, Jess Meeker."

It is similarly unclear who orchestrated the ballet; it seems unlikely that Lang would have had the time or the inclination. Two educated guesses: Allan Small, Lang's coorchestrator on *Billion Dollar Baby*, the 1945 Robbins-Abbott musical; or Bob Noeltner, who was especially comfortable with ballet and served with Lang as a fellow ghost on *Brigadoon.* This orchestration, whoever did it, remains available for rental. When the ballet was recorded by Lehman Engel for RCA in 1958, it was reorchestrated by RCA staffer Sid Ramin; this chart was also used, with revisions, in the 1989 revue *Jerome Robbins' Broadway.* The Pitot attribution seems to have first appeared in the liner notes for Engel's album. (See page 196.)

HIGH KICKERS OF 1942

Orchestrations uncredited. (Additional orchestrations by Hans **Spialek**, Don **Walker**, Ted **Royal**, and others.)
Opened October 31, 1941, Broadhurst, 171 performances. Tryout: October 13, Philadelphia (Forrest).
Music and lyrics by Bert Kalmar and Harry Ruby. "Based on an idea by Phil Silvers." Musical direction by Val Ernie. Vocal arrangements by Buck (Clay) Warnick. Other participants: Bert Kalmar, Harry Ruby, and George Jessel (librettists); George Jessel (star); Sophie Tucker (star).

Walker's invoices are at the Library of Congress. Base page rate: $3.

Walker: "Cigarettes" (and "Betty Bruce Specialty"), "Panic in Panama."

HIGH SPIRITS

Orchestrations credited to Harry Zimmerman. (Overture by Luther Henderson. Additional orchestrators, if any, unknown.)

Opened April 7, 1964, Alvin, 375 performances. Tryout: February 1, New Haven (Shubert); February, Boston (Colonial); March, Philadelphia (Shubert).

Music, lyrics, and book by Hugh Martin and Timothy Gray. Based on the play *Blithe Spirit* by Noël Coward. Musical direction by Fred Werner. Vocal arrangements and direction by Hugh Martin and Timothy Gray. Dance music by William Goldenberg. Other participants: On-Stage Productions/Jule Styne (co-producers); Noël Coward (original director); Gower Champion (replacement director, uncredited); Beatrice Lillie (star); Tammy Grimes (star).

Henderson: Overture.

> HUGH MARTIN: Don Walker walked out at the last minute [apparently because the dates conflicted with *Anyone Can Whistle*], and everybody was busy. We ended up with Harry Zimmerman. The orchestrations weren't very exciting, just ordinary.... We had a very tame Overture, which sort of put people to sleep. Noël came to me and said, "Can't you goose up the Overture a bit?" We got Luther Henderson, who did the new Overture. It is terrific. I wish he had done the whole show.

Harry Zimmerman was a TV orchestrator who had replaced Kostal on *The Garry Moore Show* in 1962.

> KOSTAL: When I was introduced to Harry, I immediately recognized him. Thirty-six years earlier, he was playing the organ at the Illington Theatre in Chicago. We high school kids used to bombard him with spit balls as he played popular tunes while the bouncing ball followed the lyrics on the silver screen. He'd turn around and stare at us, and we'd belt him a few more times. Harry remembered it well.

According to Fred Werner, Henderson was suggested by Tammy Grimes.

HIGHER AND HIGHER

Orchestrations by Hans **Spialek**. (Additional orchestrations by Walter Paul, Don **Walker**, Ted **Royal**, and R. P. DuPage.)

Opened April 4, 1940, Shubert, 108 performances. Tryout: March 7, New Haven (Shubert); March 12, Boston (Shubert).

Music by Richard Rodgers, lyrics by Lorenz Hart. Musical direction by Al Goodman. Other participant: Joshua Logan (director, co-librettist).

The partiturs are at the offices of the Rodgers & Hammerstein Organization.

Spialek: "Blue Monday," "Ev'ry Sunday Afternoon," "From Another World" (see below), "It Never Entered My Mind," "Nothing but You" (see below).

Walker: "A Barking Baby Never Bites" (see below), "Morning's at Seven" (see below).

Paul: utilities ("A Barking Baby Never Bites," "Ev'ry Sunday Afternoon," "From Another World," "Nothing but You").

Other scores:

"A Barking Baby Never Bites" is by Walker, with verse by Spialek; dance (cut) by Royal.

"Disgustingly Rich": first two sections (27 pages) are by Spialek; the remaining six sections (51 pages, including "Swing Interlude," vocal chorus, and "Wind-Up") are by Royal.

Entr'acte consists of 2 pages by Spialek with inserts by Paul of "From Another World" and "Nothing but You."

Finale act I is by Royal (with the first 3 pages by Spialek).

Finale act II consists of 8 bars of bridgework by Spialek with inserts of "Ev'ry Sunday Afternoon" (Spialek) and "From Another World" (Paul).

"From Another World": song, "Development," and "Insert after Development" are by Spialek; "Choral Refrain" is by Royal (replacing "Singing Specialty" by Spialek).

"I'm Afraid": the first and third sections are by Spialek; the second and final by Royal.

"It's Pretty in the City" (cut) is by Spialek, replacing a version by DuPage.

"Life! Liberty!" (cut) is by Paul, DuPage, and Walker.

"A Lovely Day for a Murder": the first and third sections are by Spialek; the second and final by Royal; this replaces an earlier version by DuPage.

"Morning's at Seven" is by Walker (with an 18-bar insert by Spialek); utility by Spialek.

"Nothing but You" is by Spialek; "Choral Encore" is by Paul.

"Opening Act I": this extended number is mostly by Spialek, with 4 pages by Royal and 10 by Paul.

Overture has bridgework by Spialek, with inserts of "Ev'ry Sunday Afternoon" (Spialek), "Morning's at Seven" (Walker), and Paul's versions of "From Another World," "Nothing but You," and "A Barking Baby Never Bites."

TED'S INSTRUCTIONS TO MUSICIANS   On the 95th and final page of "A Lovely Day for a Murder": "Thank God."

To the trombonist, regarding a horn cue in "Opening Act I": "Better play this (especially in Boston)."

Instr.: 5 reed (4 sax), 4 brass (2 tpt, 1 tb, 1 hrn), 16? strings (8? vln, 4? vla, 3? c, 1 b), piano, harp, perc = 28? total.

HIT THE DECK!

Orchestrations uncredited. (Orchestrations by Paul Lannin, Stephen O. Jones and others.)

Opened April 25, 1927, Belasco, 352 performances. Tryout: March 28, Philadelphia (Chestnut Street).

Music by Vincent Youmans, lyrics by Clifford Grey and Leo Robin. Musical direction by Paul Lannin. Other participants: Vincent Youmans and Lew Fields (producers).

Two partiturs are in the Youmans Collection at the Library of Congress.

Jones: "An Armful of You," "Hallelujah."

Instr.: 5 reed, 5 brass (2 tpt, 1 tb, 2 hrn), 15? strings (8? vln, 4? vla, 2? c, 1? b), piano, 1 perc ("batterie") = 27? total.

HIT THE TRAIL

Orchestrations by Don **Walker**. (Additional orchestrations by Hans **Spialek** and Robert **Ginzler**, with Joe Glover.)

Opened December 2, 1954, Mark Hellinger, 4 performances. Tryout: (as *On with the Show*) November 4, New Haven (Shubert); Boston.

Music by Frederico Valerio, lyrics by Elizabeth Miele. Musical direction and vocal arrangements by Arthur Norris. Other participants: Elizabeth Miele (producer); Irra Petina (star).

Invoices are in the Walker Collection at the Library of Congress. Base page rate: $5.87.
  Invoices indicate: Walker (58%), Spialek (20%), Ginzler (16%).
  The orchestrations are by Walker, with the following exceptions:
  Spialek: "Gypsy's Curse," "A New Look," "No! No! No!" "Somehow Stranded," "Waltzing on a Cloud," "Wherever I May Go," utility ("Set Me Free").
  Ginzler: "Dynamic Spaces," "On with the Show," "Tell Me How It Was Destiny," "What's My Fatal Charm."
  Other scores:
  Entr'acte and Overture are compilations of utilities, with bridgework by Joe Glover.
  The Walker Collection contains a letter dated August 3, 1954, from Walker to producer-lyricist Elizabeth Miele: "Because of other commitments, I find I am unable to be personally responsible for the orchestration. There are several excellent orchestrators available who have worked in the past under my supervision and if you would be interested in engaging any one of them I will promise to keep an eye on what they are doing; help them if possible; and have the arranging and copying done in my office."
  Miele accepted this arrangement; as an inducement, she agreed to give Walker a royalty (½%), apparently the first received by a Broadway orchestrator.

HITCHY-KOO OF 1920 (4TH EDITION)

Orchestrations uncredited. (Orchestrations by Frank Saddler, Russell **Bennett**, and others.)

Opened October 19, 1920, New Amsterdam, 71 performances. Tryout: September 6, Boston (Colonial).

A revue. Music by Jerome Kern, lyrics by Anne Caldwell. Musical direction by Cassius Freeborn. Other participant: Raymond Hitchcock (producer, star).

HOLD IT!

Orchestrations credited to Hans **Spialek** and Ted **Royal**. (Additional orchestrators, if any, unknown.)

Opened May 5, 1948, National, 46 performances. Tryout: March 25, New Haven (Shubert); elsewhere.

Music by Gerald Marks, lyrics by Sam Lerner. Musical direction and vocal arrangements by Clay Warnick. Ballet arrangements by Irma Jurist. Other participant: Michael Kidd (choreographer).

HOLD ON TO YOUR HATS

Orchestrations credited to Hans **Spialek** and Don **Walker**. (Additional orchestrators, if any, unknown.)

Opened September 11, 1940, Shubert, 158 performances. Tryout: Detroit; Boston.

Music by Burton Lane, lyrics by E. Y. Harburg. Musical direction by Al Goodman. Vocal arrangements by Joseph Lilley. Other participants: Al Jolson (star); Martha Raye (featured).

HOLD YOUR HORSES

Orchestrations credited to Russell **Bennett**. (Additional orchestrators, if any, unknown.)

Opened September 25, 1933, Winter Garden, 88 performances. Tryout: unknown.

Music by Russell Bennett, lyrics by Owen Murphy and Robert A. Simon. Musical direction by Gene Salzer. Other participants: Russel Crouse (co-librettist); Joe Cook (star).

HOLLYWOOD PINAFORE; OR, THE LAD WHO LOVED A SALARY

Orchestrations credited to Hans **Spialek**. (Additional orchestrations by Stephen O. Jones and probably others.)

Opened May 31, 1945, Alvin, 53 performances. Tryout: May, Philadelphia (Shubert).

Music by Arthur Sullivan, lyrics adapted from the work of W. S. Gilbert. A revised version of the operetta *H.M.S. Pinafore*. Musical direction by George Hirst. Other participants: Max Gordon (producer); George S. Kaufman (director, librettist "with apologies to the lyrics of W. S. Gilbert"); William Gaxton (star); Victor Moore (star); Shirley Booth (featured).

HOME AGAIN, HOME AGAIN

Orchestrations credited to Jim Tyler. (Additional orchestrators, if any, unknown.)

Tryout: March 12, 1979, Stratford, Connecticut (American Shakespeare Festival). Closed April 14, Toronto (Royal Alexandra).

Music by Cy Coleman, lyrics by Barbara Fried. Musical direction by Stanley Lebowsky. Vocal arrangements by Stanley Lebowsky and Cy Coleman. Dance arrangements by Cy Coleman. Dance music coordinator, Dorothea Freitag. Other participants: Gene Saks (director); Onna White (choreographer); Russell Baker (librettist); Dick Shawn (star).

HOORAY FOR WHAT!

Orchestrations by Don **Walker**. (Additional orchestrations by Walter Paul, Conrad Salinger, Joe Glover, Paul Sterrett, and possibly others.)

Opened December 1, 1937, Winter Garden, 200 performances. Tryout: October 30, Boston (Colonial); November 16, Philadelphia.

Music by Harold Arlen, lyrics by E. Y. Harburg. Musical direction by Robert Emmett Dolan. Vocal arrangements by Kay Thompson and Hugh Martin. Other participants: Howard Lindsay (director, co-librettist); Russel Crouse (co-librettist); Ed Wynn (star); Vivian Vance (featured); Hugh Martin (featured); Ralph Blane (featured).

Some of the partiturs are located at the Shubert Archive.

Walker: "God's Country," "I've Gone Romantic on You" (song, dance, tag), "Viva Geneva."

Paul: Overture.

Salinger: Entr'acte.

Other scores:

"In the Shade of the New Apple Tree": partitur is missing, except for "Stone's Apple Tree Specialty" (for replacement actress Dorothy Stone) by Walker.

Hooray for What! gives us a fine example of the utility overture, in this case built around the hoped-for song hit "Down with Love." The partitur, by Walter Paul, contains only bridges and modulations; most of the Overture was drawn from existing utilities. Part 1 is 16 bars, leading to "Down with Love." Part 2 (4 bars) leads to "On with the Waltz." Then, part 3 (8 bars) leads to "I've Gone Romantic on You"; part 4 (4 bars) continues to "page 10, Down with Love, 33rd measure"; part 5 (12 bars) is the final coda, following "Down with Love."

DON'S INSTRUCTIONS TO MUSICIANS   On the partitur for "God's Country," Walker instructs the clarinet fills to be played "slightly flat." He also instructs the percussionist to use a factory whistle.

Instr.: 5 reed (4 sax), 4 brass (3 tpt, 1 tb), 13? strings (9? vln, 0 vla, 3 c, 1 b), piano, harp, perc = 25? total.

HOT-CHA!

Orchestrations credited to Russell **Bennett**. (Additional orchestrators unknown.)

Opened March 8, 1932, Ziegfeld, 119 performances. Tryout: February 15, Washington, D.C. (National); elsewhere.

Music by Ray Henderson, lyrics by Lew Brown. Musical direction by Al Goodman.

Other participants: Florenz Ziegfeld, Jr. (producer); Bert Lahr (star); Lupe Velez (star).

THE HOT MIKADO

Orchestrations credited to Charles L. Cooke. (Additional orchestrators unknown.)

Opened March 23, 1939, Broadhurst, 85 performances. Tryout: unknown.

Music by Arthur Sullivan, lyrics adapted from the work of W. S. Gilbert. "Modern rhythm adaptations by Charles L. Cooke." A revised version of the operetta *The Mikado*. Musical direction by William Parson. Other participants: Mike Todd (producer); Bill Robinson (star).

HOT SEPTEMBER

Orchestrations credited to Philip J. **Lang**. Dance orchestrations by Robert Prince. (Additional orchestrators, if any, unknown.)

Tryout: September 14, 1965, Boston (Shubert). Closed October 9, Boston.

Music by Kenneth Jacobson, lyrics by Rhoda Roberts. Based on the play *Picnic* by William Inge. Musical direction and vocal arrangements by Milton Rosenstock. Dance music and orchestrations by Robert Prince. Other participants: David Merrick and Leland Hayward (producers); Joshua Logan (director); Paul Oborn (librettist).

HOT SPOT

Orchestrations credited to Luther Henderson and Ralph **Burns**.

Opened April 19, 1963, Majestic, 43 performances. Tryout: February 5, Washington, D.C. (National); February 28, Philadelphia (Shubert).

Music by Mary Rodgers, lyrics by Martin Charnin. Musical direction by Milton Rosenstock. Vocal arrangements and dance arrangements by Trude Rittman and John Morris. Other participants: Robert Fryer (producer); Morton Da Costa (original director); Herbert Ross (replacement director, uncredited); Onna White (original choreographer); Judy Holliday (star).

Some of the piano-conductor scores identify the orchestrators, as follows: Henderson: "Gabie," "A Matter of Time," "Anderson and Henderson" (act I version). Burns: "Bossa Nova," "A Little Trouble," "Anderson and Henderson" (act II version), "Yakacabana."

Red Ginzler, who was scheduled to orchestrate *Hot Spot*, died a week before the beginning of rehearsals. Mary Rodgers recalls that Jonathan Tunick (slated to assist Ginzler) lobbied for the job, but the producers wanted someone with more experience. The first-position billing of Henderson (of Richard Rodgers's *Flower Drum Song*) implies that Burns (of Rodgers's *No Strings*) wasn't fully available, but agreed to back up Luther.

HOUSE OF FLOWERS

Orchestrations credited to Ted **Royal**. (Additional orchestrations by Marion Evans, Charles L. Cooke, Don Redmond, and others.)

Opened December 30, 1954, Alvin, 165 performances. Tryout: November 24, Philadelphia (Erlanger).

Music by Harold Arlen, lyrics by Harold Arlen and Truman Capote. Based on the novella by Truman Capote. Musical direction by Jerry Arlen. Vocal and dance arrangements by Peter Matz. Other participants: Saint Subber (producer); Peter Brook (director); George Balanchine (choreographer); Herbert Ross (replacement choreographer); Truman Capote (librettist); Pearl Bailey (star); Diahann Carroll (featured).

The location of the partiturs is unknown except for two utilities ("I Never Has Seen Snow" and "A Sleepin' Bee," both by Royal) in the City Center Encores! collection.

According to Marion Evans, fifty years after the fact, he did the song versions of "I Never Has Seen Snow" and "A Sleepin' Bee"; Charles Cooke did "Carnival" ("Mardi Gras"); and Don Redmond did "One Man Ain't Quite Enough" and "What Is a Friend For?" "Two Ladies in de Shade of de Banana Tree" was mostly by Evans and Cooke, with Royal possibly providing some parts as well.

MARION EVANS: A classic example of the producer and the director losing total control. Opening night at the Erlanger, Josephine Premice stopped the show, she broke it up. Next morning, Pearlie goes to Harold, says it's me or her. By the time it got to Broadway, everybody left. The director, the choreographer, it was a night with Pearl Bailey on Broadway.

I remember, what a hassle. I'd never written anything for steel drums, that was really an interesting thing. Pearl wanted to do her own versions of things; she brought in a guy named Don Redmond, who was a very good musician, he wrote most of the stuff that Pearl sings. I did for the most part all of Diahann Carroll's things, "Sleepin' Bee," "I Never Has Seen Snow." And then we had "Two Ladies in de Shade of de Banana Tree." I did that with Charlie Cooke.

Instr.: 5 reed, 6 brass (3 tpt, 1 tb, 2 hrn), 13? strings (8? vln, 2? vla, 2 c, 1 b), piano/celesta, perc = 26? total.

HOW DO YOU DO? I LOVE YOU

Orchestrations credited to Jonathan Tunick.

Tryout: October 31, 1967, Westbury, New York (Music Fair). Closed November 12, Westbury.

Music by David Shire, lyrics by Richard Maltby, Jr. Musical direction and vocal arrangements by Arthur Rubinstein. Other participants: Michael Stewart (librettist); Phyllis Newman (star).

(See page 518.)

HOW NOW, DOW JONES

Orchestrations credited to Philip J. **Lang**. (Additional orchestrators unknown.)

Opened December 7, 1967, Lunt-Fontanne, 220 performances. Tryout: September 30, New Haven (Shubert); October 10, Philadelphia (Shubert); October 31, Boston (Colonial).

Music by Elmer Bernstein, lyrics by Carolyn Leigh. Musical direction, vocal and dance arrangements by Peter Howard. Other participants: David Merrick (producer); Arthur Penn (original director); George Abbott (replacement director); Gillian Lynne (original choreographer); Michael Bennett (replacement choreographer, uncredited); Max Shulman (librettist).

Lang was most probably assisted by Jack Andrews (and possibly Jim Tyler).

HOW TO SUCCEED IN BUSINESS WITHOUT REALLY TRYING

Orchestrations (mostly) by Robert **Ginzler**. Additional scoring by Elliot Lawrence.

Opened October 14, 1961, 46th Street, 1,417 performances. Tryout: September 4, Philadelphia (Shubert).

Music and lyrics by Frank Loesser. Based on the satirical self-help book by Shepard Mead. Musical direction and additional scoring by Elliot Lawrence. Dance arrangements by Donald Smith (uncredited). Other participants: Feuer & Martin (producers); Frank Productions/Frank Loesser (associate producer); Abe Burrows (director, replacement librettist); Bob Fosse (replacement choreographer); Robert Morse (star).

The partiturs are at Music Theatre International.

The orchestrations are by Ginzler, with the following exceptions:

Lawrence: "Get Me Finch," "Knitorama," "New TV Announcement," other minor incidentals.

Other scores:

"Coffee Break" is by Ginzler, with extensive overwriting by Lawrence (tempo marking: "Ominous Cha-Cha").

"Company Way": there are at least three versions (beginning as a solo for Twimble), plus a reprise (for Frump) and a Finale version, all by Ginzler.

"I Worry about You" (cut), Rosemary's opening number, is by Ginzler.

"Pirate Dance" ("The Yo-Ho-Ho") is mostly by Ginzler, through the beginning of section "P" on page 146 of vocal score; the rest ("New Pirate Ending") is by Lawrence.

"Rosemary–New" is by Ginzler, replacing an earlier version (by Ginzler, with extensive overwrites by Lawrence).

"A Secretary Is Not a Toy": "Secretary Version III," the final version, is by Ginzler, replacing his earlier charts; "Secretary Orchestra Tag" is by Lawrence.

RED'S INSTRUCTIONS TO MUSICIANS   The score of "Grand Old Ivy" instructs the three trombones to "cheat one at a time thru unison to rest the chops, two playing at a time—but not on LP."

Instr.: 5 reed (including 5 sax, 5 clr, 5 kazoo), 7 brass (3 tpt, 3 tb, 1 hrn), 11 strings (6 vln [1 doubled on piano for the Grieg excerpts in "Rosemary"], 0 vla, 4 c, 1 b), harp, guitar, 2 perc = 27 total.

(See pages 220, 223, 241, 273.)

I CAN GET IT FOR YOU WHOLESALE

Orchestrations by Sid **Ramin**. (Additional orchestrations by Arthur Beck.)

Opened March 22, 1962, Shubert, 300 performances. Tryout: February, Philadelphia (Shubert); February 27, Boston (Colonial).

Music and lyrics by Harold Rome. Based on the novel by Jerome Weidman. Musical direction and vocal arrangements by Lehman Engel. Dance arrangements by Peter Howard. Other participants: David Merrick (producer); Arthur Laurents (director); Herbert Ross (choreographer); Jerome Weidman (librettist); Elliott Gould (star); Barbra Streisand (featured).

Copies of the partiturs are in the Ramin Collection at the Butler Library, Columbia University.

Ramin: "Ballad of Garment Trade," "Eat a Little Something," "A Funny Thing Happened," "Have I Told You Lately?" "I'm Not a Well Man," Prologue, "The Sound of Money" (see below), "The Way Things Are," "What Are They Doing to Us Now?" (see below), "What's in It for Me," "When Gemini Meets Capricorn," "Who Knows."

Beck: Entr'acte, "The Family Way" (song and utility), "Fashion Show," "A Gift Today," "Miss Marmelstein," "Too Soon," utilities ("A Funny Thing Happened," "When Gemini Meets Capricorn").

Other scores:

"The Sound of Money": song is by Ramin, dance (beginning with "Listen . . . ") is by Beck; underscoring (act II) is by Beck.

"What Are They Doing to Us Now?": song is by Ramin, dance (from bar 137, bongo solo) is by Beck.

I DO! I DO!

Orchestrations credited to Philip J. **Lang**. (Additional orchestrators, if any, unknown.)

Opened December 5, 1966, 46th Street, 560 performances. Tryout: Boston (Colonial); October 18, Washington, D.C. (National); Cincinnati.

Music by Harvey Schmidt, lyrics and book by Tom Jones. Based on the play *The Fourposter* by Jan de Hartog. Musical direction by John Lesko. Other participants: David Merrick (producer); Gower Champion (director, choreographer); Mary Martin (star); Robert Preston (star).

I HAD A BALL

Orchestrations credited to Philip J. **Lang**. (Additional orchestrators unknown.)

Opened December 15, 1964, Martin Beck, 199 performances. Tryout: Detroit (Fisher); November, Philadelphia (Forrest).

Music and lyrics by Jack Lawrence and Stan Freeman. Musical direction and vocal arrangements by Pembroke Davenport. Associate musical director, René Wiegert. Dance arrangements by Luther Henderson. Other participants: Lloyd Richards (original director); Onna White (choreographer); Buddy Hackett (star); Richard Kiley (featured); Karen Morrow (featured).

Red Press, who played the reed I chair, said that the sax solos were too swinging for Phil, and thinks they must have been written by Luther Henderson. Henderson almost certainly orchestrated the dance music, and it is believed that Jack Andrews also worked on the show.

I MARRIED AN ANGEL

Orchestrations credited to Hans **Spialek**. (Additional orchestrators unknown.)

Opened May 11, 1938, Shubert, 338 performances. Tryout: April 14, New Haven (Shubert); April 19, Boston (Shubert).

Music and book by Richard Rodgers, lyrics and book by Lorenz Hart. Based on a play by John Vaszary. Musical direction by Gene Salzer. Other participants: Joshua Logan (director); George Balanchine (choreographer).

I REMEMBER MAMA

Orchestrations credited to Philip J. **Lang**. (Additional orchestrators, if any, unknown.)

Opened May 31, 1979, Majestic, 108 performances. Tryout: March 9, Philadelphia (Shubert).

Music by Richard Rodgers, lyrics by Martin Charnin. Additional lyrics by Raymond Jessel. Based on the play by John Van Druten, from *Mama's Bank Account* and other stories by Kathryn Forbes. Musical direction and vocal arrangements by Jay Blackton.

Other participants: Alexander H. Cohen (producer); Martin Charnin (original director); Cy Feuer (replacement director); Thomas Meehan (librettist); Liv Ullmann (star).

The partiturs are in the Rodgers Collection at the Library of Congress (unexamined).

ICE-TRAVAGANZA

Orchestrations credited to Ralph **Burns**. (Additional orchestrators, if any, unknown.)

Opened May 5, 1964, Flushing, New York (New York City Pavilion, World's Fair).

A revue. Music by John Morris, lyrics by Gerald Freedman and John Morris. Musical direction by John Morris. Other participant: Dick Button (co-producer, director, choreographer).

I'D RATHER BE RIGHT

Orchestrations by Hans **Spialek**. (Additional orchestrations by Don **Walker**, Conrad Salinger, Maurice de Packh, Ted **Royal**, Walter Paul, and others.)

Opened November 2, 1937, Alvin, 290 performances. Tryout: October 11, Boston (Colonial); October 24, Baltimore (Ford's).

Music by Richard Rodgers, lyrics by Lorenz Hart. Musical direction by Harry Levant. Other participants: George S. Kaufman (director); George S. Kaufman and Moss Hart (librettists); George M. Cohan (star).

The partiturs are at the offices of the Rodgers & Hammerstein Organization.

Spialek: "Agitato" (instrumental), "Ev'rybody Loves You," "Have You Met Miss Jones?," "I'd Rather Be Right" (see below), "Kaleidoscope," "Labor Is the Thing," "Spring in Vienna (The World Is an Oyster)," "Take and Take and Take."

Walker: "A Baby Bond for Baby."

Salinger: "We're Going to Balance the Budget."

de Packh: "A Homogenous Cabinet" (see below), "I'd Rather Be Right" (see below).

Royal: "Off the Record."

Paul: "Curtain Music," utilities ("Ev'rybody Loves You," "Have You Met Miss Jones?").

Other scores:

"Beauty Sequence": part 1 (instrumental) is by Spialek; part 2 ("Take and Take and Take") is by Paul; part 3 is by Salinger; "Continued" is by Salinger.

"A Homogenous Cabinet" is mostly by de Packh, with two brief sections ("Farley" and "Miss Perkins") by Spialek.

"I'd Rather Be Right": there are two distinctly different songs with this title. The first (which was subsequently used in another show, with the new title "Now That I Know You") was by de Packh, with three additional scores: "Routine" by unknown hand #1; "Section G" and an additional version (utility?) by Paul.

"Not So Innocent Fun (A Little Bit of Constitutional Fun)": part 1 is by Spialek; part 2 is by unknown hand #1; part 3 is by Paul.

Overture: all that can be located is some bridgework by Spialek and inserts for "Have You Met Miss Jones?" "I'd Rather Be Right" (second version; by Paul), and "We're Going to Balance the Budget" (by Salinger).

"Sweet Sixty-Five": first refrain and "extra" are by Spialek; dance is by Walker.

"(Georgie) Tapp Routines": first ("Saga") and second are by Spialek; "New Tapp Routine" is by unknown hand #1.

SPIALEK: I am sure that no theatregoer ever suspects or, for that matter, gives an iota that an arranger's heart can be broken. Rodgers's score for *I'd Rather be Right*, especially coming on the heels of *On Your Toes* and *Babes in Arms*, was a disappointing if serviceable one. But Rodgers wrote for the show a magnificent number, a Chinese ballet [performed in the course of the plot by a wandering WPA ballet group]. Not only the music, but Irene Sharaff's radiant costumes and Charles Weidman's brilliant dance direction made the ballet an outstanding production number.

I worked on this ballet score harder than on all the rest of the show, to give it all the expected originality, flavor, and splendor. Everything went fine during the orchestra and company rehearsals, everybody congratulated everybody, and everybody concerned was proud, having contributed to this number. Then came the dress rehearsal. When the Chinese ballet was over, George Kaufman, in his quiet, tall, and commanding manner, got up from his seat and said, "Out!"—then, after an almost-unison gasp from the concerned parties—"it slows the show up." The decision stood, and though heartsick I had to admit that Mr. Kaufman was right.

HANS'S INSTRUCTIONS TO MUSICIANS   On the score for "Agitato," in Spialek's hand: "Woodwinds, Brass, Drums, Harp and Piano were arranged directly on the parts by Mr. Spialek personally. Signed: Dick Rodgers, President of the Hartford Nailbiting Co."

Instr.: 5 reed (4 sax, 1 oboe/Eng hrn), 4 brass (2 tpt, 1 tb, 1 hrn), ? strings (vln, vla, c, 1 b), piano, harp, perc.

IF THE SHOE FITS

Orchestrations by Russell **Bennett**. (Additional orchestrations by Ted **Royal**, Hans **Spialek**, Walter Paul, and Joe Glover.)
Opened December 5, 1946, Century, 20 performances. Tryout: November, Boston.
Music by David Raksin, lyrics by June Carroll. Based on *Cinderella*. Musical direction by

Will Irwin. Vocal direction by Joe Moon. Other participants: Leonard Sillman (producer); Joe Besser (featured).

Bennett's invoices are preserved in his ledger. Base page rate: $3.75. Tentative attributions per invoice.

Bennett: "Cindy Gets Shoes," "End of Shoe Ballet," Overture, "Vignettes," "Waltz Parody," "Wave of My Wand."

Instr.: 6 reed (all sax), 6 brass (3 tpt, 2 tb, 1 hrn), ? strings (vln, vla, c, 1 b), piano, harp, perc.

THE ILLUSTRATORS' SHOW

Orchestrations uncredited. (Orchestrations by Hans **Spialek** and others.)

Opened January 22, 1936, 48th Street, 5 performances.

A revue. Music mostly by Irving Actman, additional music by Frederick Loewe and others, lyrics mostly by Frank Loesser. Musical direction by Gene Salzer. Other participant: Society of Illustrators (producer).

ILLYA DARLING

Orchestrations by Ralph **Burns**. (Additional orchestrations by Larry **Wilcox**.)

Opened April 11, 1967, Mark Hellinger, 320 performances. Tryout: Washington, D.C. (National); Toronto (O'Keefe); Boston.

Music by Manos Hadjidakis, lyrics by Joe Darion. Based on the film *Never on Sunday* by Jules Dassin. Musical direction by Karen Gustafson (replacing Lehman Engel). Dance arrangements by Roger Adams. Other participants: Kermit Bloomgarden (producer); Jules Dassin (director, librettist); Onna White (choreographer); Melina Mercouri (star).

Copies of most of the partiturs are at Tams-Witmark.

Burns: "Golden Land," "Medea Tango," "Never on Sunday" (see below), Overture ("Bouzouki Nights").

Wilcox: "Dear Mr. Schubert" (see below), "I'll Never Lay Down Anymore," "Yorgo's Dance."

Burns and Wilcox: "Heaven Help a Sailor on a Night Like This," "I Think She Needs Me," "Piraeus, My Love," "Po, Po, Po," "Taverna Dance."

Other scores:

"Dear Mr. Schubert" is by Wilcox, although the melody line and lyric are in Burns's hand; apparently, Burns started to lay out the score but handed it over to Wilcox for orchestration.

"Illya Darling": part I (song) and part III (finale) are mostly by Burns; part II (dance) is mostly by Wilcox.

"Never on Sunday" is mostly by Burns.

In most of the joint scores, Burns wrote the string, Chordovox/keyboard, and percussion parts; Wilcox wrote the reeds and brass.

The location of the following partiturs is unknown: "After Love" and "Love, Love, Love."

RALPH'S INSTRUCTIONS TO MUSICIANS   On page 20 of score for Overture, to copyist Mathilde Pincus: "At this point shipyard noises and Illya's laugh etc. should come in if not before, as without them the audience will have left the theatre!!"

Instr.: 3 reed, 6 brass (2 tpt, 2 tb, 2 hrn), ? strings, keyboard/Chordovox, 2 mandolins, 2 bouzoukis, 2 perc. (See page 37.)

I'M SOLOMON

Orchestrations credited to Hershy **Kay**. (Additional orchestrations by Jonathan Tunick and others.)

Opened April 23, 1968, Mark Hellinger, 7 performances. Tryout: (as *In Someone Else's Sandals*) March 8, New Haven (Shubert); elsewhere.

Music by Ernest Gold, lyrics and book by Anne Croswell. Based on the play *King Solomon and the Cobbler* by Sammy Gronemann. Musical direction and vocal arrangements by Gershon Kingsley. Dance arrangements by Dorothea Freitag. Other participants: Michael Benthall (director); Donald McKayle (choreographer); Dick Shawn (star); Karen Morrow (featured).

> JONATHAN TUNICK: I got a call to go to the Hellinger. When I got there, just about every arranger in New York was lined up at the stage door, like a committee meeting. Luther Henderson, Jack Andrews, Larry Wilcox, Phil Lang were all there. We all did numbers. I did several, including a big expansive ballad for Karen Morrow. I didn't want to offend Hershy, so I said, "Is it okay with you?" Hershy was carrying a big pile of music. He said, "I don't give a shit," and he threw the music in the air. All I remember about the show is one lyric. It went: "We'll sit while the tea brews / Like two happy Hebrews."

IN GAY NEW ORLEANS

Orchestrations credited to Russell **Bennett**. (Additional orchestrators unknown.)

Tryout: December 25, 1946, Boston (Colonial). Closed December 31, Boston.

Music by Carl Fredrickson, lyrics by Forbes Randolph. Musical direction by Ray Kavanaugh.

Bennett's invoices are preserved in his ledger. Base page rate: $4.75. Tentative attributions per invoice.

Bennett: "The Heavens Declare," "Lonely Straggler," "New Orleans Saga," "Opening Act I," "Song of the Nile," "Wind from the Bayou," various incidentals.

The scenery, by Watson Barratt, was reused later that season in *Louisiana Lady*—which featured a score that was altogether different (but orchestrated by Bennett).

INSIDE U.S.A.

Orchestrations credited to Russell **Bennett**. (Additional orchestrations by Don **Walker** and probably others.)

Opened April 30, 1948, New Century, 399 performances. Tryout: Philadelphia.

A revue. Music by Arthur Schwartz, lyrics by Howard Dietz. Musical direction by Jay

Blackton. "Incidental music for dances" by Genevieve Pitot. Other participants: Arthur Schwartz (producer); Helen Tamiris (choreographer); Moss Hart (sketch contributor); Beatrice Lillie (star); Jack Haley (star).

One partitur ("Rhode Island Is Famous for You" by Walker) is in the Walker Collection at the Library of Congress. Bennett's invoices are preserved in his ledger. Walker's invoices are in the Walker Collection at the Library of Congress. Base page rate: $4.65.

Bennett: "Bea's Oklahoma," "Come O Come (to Pittsburgh)," "County Fair," Finale act I, "First Prize at the Fair," "Haunted Heart" (song and ballet), "If We Had a Little More Time," "Inside U.S.A." (and encore), "Mardi Gras," "Massachusetts Mermaid," "The Movie," "My Gal Is Mine," New York Overture, Temporary Overture, "Tiger Lily," numerous incidentals.

Walker: "Atlanta," Finale Ultimo, "Leave My Pulse Alone," "Protect Me," "Rhode Island Is Famous for You."

Other scores:

"Blue Grass": Bennett billed for "Estelle Loring vocal" (40 pages); Walker billed for another version (54 pages).

IRENE (1973 REVIVAL)

Orchestrations (mostly) by Ralph **Burns.** (Additional orchestrations by Jim Tyler and Larry **Wilcox.**)

Opened March 13, 1973, Minskoff, 594 performances. Tryout: November 28, 1972, Toronto (O'Keefe); Philadelphia (Shubert); February 1, 1973, Washington, D.C. (National).

Music by Harry Tierney, lyrics by Joseph A. McCarthy. Additional music and lyrics by Charles Gaynor and Otis Clements. Based on the play *Irene O'Dare* by James Montgomery. Musical direction by Jack Lee. Vocal and dance arrangements by Wally Harper. Other participants: John Gielgud (original director, credit removed); Gower Champion (replacement director); Peter Gennaro (choreographer); Hugh Wheeler (original librettist); Joseph Stein (replacement librettist); Debbie Reynolds (star).

The partiturs are at Tams-Witmark.

The orchestrations are by Burns, with the following exceptions:

Tyler: "Style Show" (instrumental).

Other scores:

"I'm Always Chasing Rainbows," "Mother, Angel, Darling," and "You Made Me Love You" are by Burns, with minor fixes by Wilcox.

RALPH'S INSTRUCTIONS TO MUSICIANS   On the third version of the Overture, note to copyist: "New, Improved, with extra added applause line."

Instr.: 5 reed, 7 brass (4 tpt, 3 tb), 7 strings (4 vln, 0 vla, 2 c, 1 b), piano, harp, guitar, 3 perc = 25 total.

IRMA LA DOUCE

Orchestrations by André Popp. Additional (new) orchestrations by Robert **Ginzler.**

Opened September 29, 1960, Plymouth, 524 performances. Tryout: September 8, Washington, D.C. (National).

Music by Marguerite Monnot, original lyrics and book by Alexandre Breffort, English lyrics and book by Julian More, David Heneker, and Monty Norman. Musical direction by Stanley Lebowsky. Vocal arrangements by Bert Waller and Stanley Lebowsky. Dance music by John Kander. Other participants: David Merrick (producer); Peter Brook (director); Onna White (choreographer); Donald Pippin (pianist).

Copies of the partiturs are at Tams Witmark.

Ginzler: "Dis-Donc Dance," "Freedom of the Seas Ballet," Overture.

Other scores:

"But" starts with the British chart, with Ginzler writing the final 40 bars.

"From a Prison Cell" starts with the British chart, with Ginzler's score beginning at the modulation where the chorus joins Nestor.

"Irma La Douce" starts with the British chart, with Ginzler's chart (and Lebowsky's vocal arrangement) beginning where the chorus joins Irma, for the final 20 measures.

Overture act II: part 1 is from the original British chart; part 2 is by Ginzler.

"There Is Only One Paris for That" is mostly by Ginzler, except for an 18-measure instrumental section retained from the British chart.

The copyists worked from scores for the British production, with inserts and additional scores by Red Ginzler. The British material is all in one hand (apparently that of a copyist).

Instr.: 2 reed (fl, clr), 2 brass (2 tb), 1 string (b), piano, accordion, guitar/mandolin, perc = 9 total.

(See page 195.)

IT'S A BIRD . . . IT'S A PLANE . . . IT'S SUPERMAN

Orchestrations (mostly) by Eddie **Sauter**. (Additional orchestrations by Don **Walker** and Jim Tyler.)

Opened March 29, 1966, Alvin, 129 performances. Tryout: February 15, Philadelphia (Shubert).

Music by Charles Strouse, lyrics by Lee Adams. Based on the comic book *Superman.* Musical direction by Hal Hastings. Dance arrangements by Betty Walberg. Other participant: Harold Prince (producer, director).

The partiturs are in the Sauter Collection at Yale University, with copies at Tams-Witmark.

The orchestrations are by Sauter with the following exceptions:

Walker: "It's Superman (Lois Version)," "We Need Him Playoff."

Tyler: Finale Ultimo.

Overtures (all by Sauter): "3/17/66" is the final version (and used on the cast album); "3/7/66" is used as Entr'acte; "2/14/66" is used as exit music.

The doubles on the reed I chair alone are flute, piccolo, alto flute, clarinet, E♭ clarinet, alto sax, and kazoo.

> STROUSE: It was my idea to use Eddie Sauter; *Superman,* after all, was not the usual "This Nearly Was Mine." It was my idea not to use violins. Eddie just had a wonderful, swing jazz band background. I thought it was a really smart choice on my part. Probably these

come as close to an arranger doing his own arrangements on any of my shows. There's a slight edge—even though I wrote certain things in the piano parts, there were certain choices Eddie made coloristically and stylistically that were his. I thought it was a terrific-sounding show.

EDDIE'S INSTRUCTIONS TO MUSICIANS   Opening section of Overture (to bass): "Pull strings straight out and let them slap back."

Instr.: 6 reed, 9 brass (3 tpt, 3 tb [1 tuba], 3 hrn), 6 strings (0 vln, 3 vla, 2 c, 1 b), organ/celesta, harp, 2 perc = 25 total.

IT'S SPRING: THE GLORY OF EASTER

Orchestrations credited to Philip J. **Lang**, Michael Gibson, Elman Anderson, and Gary Anderson.

Opened March 14, 1980, Radio City Music Hall, 56 performances.

New songs by Donald Pippin and Sammy Cahn. Musical direction by Donald Pippin. Conductor, Elman Anderson. Other participant: Radio City Music Hall Productions (producer).

JACKPOT

Orchestrations credited to Hans **Spialek**, Russell **Bennett**, and Vernon Duke. (Additional orchestrations by Ted **Royal** and possibly others.)

Opened January 13, 1944, Alvin, 67 performances. Tryout: December 2, 1943, New Haven (Shubert); Boston; January 3, 1944, Washington, D.C. (National).

Music by Vernon Duke, lyrics by Howard Dietz. Musical direction by Max Meth. Vocal arrangements by Clay Warnick. Other participants: Vinton Freedley (producer); Sidney Sheldon (co-librettist); Nanette Fabray (lead); Jacqueline Susann (featured).

JAMAICA

Orchestrations by Philip J. **Lang**. (Additional orchestrations by Lennie Hayton, with Peter Matz.)

Opened October 31, 1957, Imperial, 555 performances. Tryout: September 16, Philadelphia (Shubert); October 8, Boston (Shubert).

Music by Harold Arlen, lyrics and book by E. Y. Harburg. Musical direction, vocal arrangements, and continuity by Lehman Engel (replacing Jay Blackton). Dance music and additional vocal arrangements by Peter Matz. Other participants: David Merrick (producer); Robert Lewis (director); Jack Cole (choreographer); Fred Saidy (co-librettist); Lena Horne (star); Ricardo Montalban (star).

The partiturs are at Tams-Witmark.

The orchestrations are by Lang, with the following exceptions:

Hayton: "Ain't It de Truth" (see below), "Coconut Sweet" (see below), "Napoleon," "Pretty to Walk With," "Push de Button," "Take It Slow, Joe."

Matz: "Café Scene," "Napoleon" chaser; "New 'Truth' Tag."

Other scores:

"Ain't It de Truth" (song and reprise) is by Hayton, replacing Lang's version. In the reprise, Horne's section is by Hayton. The later section—with three girls taking over the vocal, and the subsequent dance—is retained from Lang's original version.

"Coconut Sweet": there are three scores. The first, by Neal Hefti, is heard on the cast album. (This track was recorded for release as a single during the rehearsal period, long before the cast album was recorded.) The second version is by Lang. It was replaced by the final version by Hayton, which draws on Hefti's chart. The two reprises are by Hayton.

"Pity de Sunset" is by Lang through the end of Koli's (Montalban's) section. Starting at Horne's section ("Fancy that now"), Lang's score was replaced with a new one by Hayton.

Virtually all of Lang's orchestrations for star Lena Horne were replaced during the tryout with new (and first-rate) charts by her husband, Hollywood arranger Lenny Hayton.

Musical director Jay Blackton, who had turned down the unlikely-sounding *West Side Story* for *Jamaica*, found himself on the wrong side of Horne and was fired in Philadelphia. Missing out on two long-run hits, he wound up with *Oh Captain!* (Blackton's signed vocal arrangement for "Savannah's Wedding Day" did remain in the show.) Lehman Engel was rushed down to take over:

> After three performances, I said, "Lena, I know what's the matter with the orchestrations. You have five saxophones playing all the time, and you can't possibly sing over five saxophones." And I said, "Why not have five clarinets play those parts?" "I like saxophones," she said, and that was the end of that. She was miked, and we had a man in the back, a mixer, but you can't control the volume of five saxophones. It's not a matter of volume. It's a matter of timbre. Saxophones wipe out voices.

Instr.: 5 reed (including 5 sax), 6 brass (3 tpt, 3 tb), 11? strings (6? vln, 2? vla, 2? c, 1 b), guitar, 2 perc = 25? total.

JEEVES

Orchestrations credited to Don **Walker** and Andrew Lloyd Webber. (Additional orchestrations by Keith Amos and David Cullen.)

Opened April 22, 1975, Her Majesty's (London). Tryout: Bristol, England.

Music by Andrew Lloyd Webber, lyrics and book by Alan Ayckbourn. Based on the series of novels by P. G. Wodehouse. Musical direction and vocal arrangements by Anthony Bowles. Other participant: Robert Stigwood (producer).

During the tryout, orchestrations were credited to Andrew Lloyd Webber, Keith Amos, and David Cullen. With the show facing massive (and apparently unsolvable) problems, Walker was flown in from the States to rescore the show. At the first London preview, the orchestrations were credited to Walker, Lloyd Webber, Amos, and Cullen; by the opening, Amos's and Cullen's credits had been removed. *Jeeves* quickly shuttered. Lloyd Webber and Ayckbourn, later in their enormously successful careers, attempted to rejuvenate their Wodehouse-based musical. *By Jeeves* finally reached Broadway, briefly, in 2001.

From Walker's journal: "4/22: party at Stigwood's"; "4/23: read reviews—Ugh!"

JENNIE

Orchestrations credited to Philip J. **Lang** and Robert Russell **Bennett**. (Additional orchestrators, if any, unknown.)

Opened October 17, 1963, Majestic, 82 performances. Tryout: Boston (Colonial); Detroit (Fisher).

Music by Arthur Schwartz, lyrics by Howard Dietz. Suggested by events in the life of Laurette Taylor. Musical direction by John Lesko. Vocal and dance arrangements by Trude Rittman. Other participants: Cheryl Crawford (producer); Mary Martin (star).

Bennett's invoices are preserved in his ledger. Base page rate: $10.

Bennett: "Before I Kiss the World Goodbye," "Dinner Is Served," "Harem (to fire)," "I Still Look at You That Way," "I Think I'm Going to Like It," "Melodrama I," "Waitin' for the Evenin' Train," "Where You Are."

> LANG: Mary Martin is a lovely person to work with. She's very particular and very fussy, and you don't get away with anything. There are times when you can tell her that she's wrong—as long as you keep talking.
>
> RED PRESS: *Jennie* was terrible. And they had a waterfall on the stage, until they figured out it used to leak into the pit. I remember the first performance in New York, we played through the exit music, and as we finished we heard someone yell down, "Better luck next time, Mary."

JEROME ROBBINS' BROADWAY

Orchestrations credited to Sid **Ramin** and William David Brohn. (Additional orchestrators, if any, unknown.)

Opened February 26, 1989, Imperial, 633 performances.

A revue. Music and lyrics by various writers. Musical direction by Paul Gemignani. Musical continuity by Scott Frankel. Other participant: Jerome Robbins (director, choreographer).

JIMMY

Orchestrations credited to Jack Andrews. (Additional orchestrations by Jonathan Tunick and possibly others.)

Opened October 23, 1969, Winter Garden, 84 performances. Tryout: September, Philadelphia (Forrest).

Music and lyrics by Bill Jacob and Patti Jacob. Based on *Beau James* by Gene Fowler, suggested by events in the life of James J. Walker. Musical direction and vocal arrangements by Milton Rosenstock. Dance arrangements by John Berkman. Other participants: Jack L. Warner (producer); Joseph Anthony (director); Peter Gennaro (choreographer); Frank Gorshin (star).

Tunick recalls that Rosenstock called him to help out. He did numerous charts, among them "I Only Wanna Laugh," "That Old Familiar Ring," and "What's Out There for Me?"

> KEYBOARD PLAYER JOHN FRANCESCHINA: The Overture begins in a messy perpetual motion for everyone except the brass, who are stuck with a deadly nonmelody. We all used to laugh at the attempt to cover up the lack of musical interest with more lack of musical interest.

JOHN HENRY

Orchestrations credited to Hans **Spialek** and Charles L. Cooke. (Additional orchestrators, if any, unknown.)

Opened January 10, 1940, 44th Street, 7 performances. Tryout: Boston.

A play by Roark Bradford. Music by Jacques Wolfe, lyrics by Roark Bradford. Based on the legend of John Henry. Musical direction by Don Voorhees. Vocal arrangements and musical supervision by Leonard De Paur. Other participant: Paul Robeson (star).

JOHN MURRAY ANDERSON'S ALMANAC

Orchestrations credited to Ted **Royal**. (Additional orchestrations by Marion Evans and others.)

Opened December 10, 1953, 229 performances. Tryout: November, Boston (Shubert).

A revue. Music and lyrics by Richard Adler and Jerry Ross (and others.). Musical direction and vocal arrangements by Buster Davis. Dance arrangements by Gerald Alters. Other participants: John Murray Anderson ("devised and staged by"); Cyril Ritchard (sketch director); Donald Saddler (choreographer); Hermione Gingold (star); Harry Belafonte (star).

(See page 134.)

JOHNNY JOHNSON

Orchestrations (totally) by Kurt Weill.

Opened November 19, 1936, 44th Street, 68 performances. Tryout: none.

Music by Kurt Weill, lyrics and book by Paul Green. Musical direction by Lehman Engel. Other participants: Group Theatre (producer); Cheryl Crawford (producer); Lee Strasberg (director); Elia Kazan (featured); Robert Lewis (featured); Lee J. Cobb (featured); John Garfield (featured).

The partiturs are in the Weill Collection at Yale.

Instr.: 2 reed, 3 brass (2 tpt, 1 tb), 3 strings (2 vln, 1 c), Hammond organ/piano, guitar/banjo, perc = 11 total.

JOKERS

Orchestrations credited to Larry **Wilcox**. (Additional orchestrators, if any, unknown.)

Tryout: October 14, 1986, Chester, Connecticut (Norma Terris). Closed Chester.

Music, lyrics, and book by Hugo Peretti, Luigi Creatore, and George David Weiss. Based on the play *The Gin Game* by D. L. Coburn. Musical direction and vocal arrangements by Paul Trueblood. Dance arrangements by Michael Skloff. Other participant: Martin Charnin (director).

JOLLYANNA

New orchestrations credited to Hershy **Kay**. (Original orchestrations by Ted **Royal** and others.)

Opened August 11, 1952, San Francisco (Curran). Closed San Francisco, September 6.

Music by Sammy Fain, additional music by Burton Lane, lyrics by E. Y. Harburg. A revised version of the musical *Flahooley*. Musical direction by Louis Adrian. Other participants: Edwin Lester (producer); E. Y. Harburg (co-librettist); Bobby Clark (star); Mitzi Gaynor (star).

This attempt to fix the 1951 musical *Flahooley* came up naught. Harburg continued to work on the musical the following year with a brief Los Angeles production, with additional songs this time by William Friml (son of Rudolf). Harburg continued to intermittently work on the project for the next quarter-century, to no avail.

A JOYFUL NOISE

Orchestrations credited to William Stegmeyer. (Additional orchestrators, if any, unknown.)

Opened December 15, 1966, Mark Hellinger, 12 performances. Tryout: Boston.

Music and lyrics by Oscar Brand and Paul Nassau. Based on the novel *The Insolent Breed* by Borden Deal. Musical direction by René Wiegert. Vocal arrangements by William Stegmeyer. Dance arrangements by Lee Holdridge. Other participants: Michael Bennett (choreographer); John Raitt (star); Karen Morrow (featured); Tommy Tune (dancer).

JUBILEE

Orchestrations credited to Russell **Bennett**. (Additional orchestrators, if any, unknown.)

Opened October 12, 1935, Imperial, 169 performances. Tryout: September 21, Boston (Shubert).

Music and lyrics by Cole Porter. Musical direction by Frank Tours. Other participants: Sam H. Harris and Max Gordon (producers); Monty Woolley (director); Moss Hart (librettist); Mary Boland (star); Montgomery Clift (featured).

JUNO

Orchestrations by Russell **Bennett**, Marc Blitzstein, and Hershy **Kay**. (Orchestrations mostly by Bennett and Kay, with Blitzstein and Philip J. **Lang**.)

Opened March 9, 1959, Winter Garden, 16 performances. Tryout: January 17, Washington, D.C. (National); February 4, Boston (Shubert).

Music and lyrics by Marc Blitzstein. Based on the play *Juno and the Paycock* by Sean O'Casey. Musical direction by Robert Emmett Dolan. "Additional ballet music" by Trude Rittman. Other participants: Oliver Smith (co-producer); José Ferrer (replacement director); Agnes de Mille (choreographer); Joseph Stein (librettist); Shirley Booth (star); Melvyn Douglas (star).

Nine partiturs (some fragmentary) are in the possession of the Blitzstein estate. Invoices are preserved in Bennett's ledger. Base page rate: $6. Invoices indicate: Kay (58%), Bennett (35%).

Kay: "Daarlin' Man," "Dublin Night Ballet," "Farewell, Me Butty," "From This Out," "Hymn," "Johnny's Dance," "Old Sayin's" (song and reprise), "On a Day Like This," Prologue ("We're Alive"), "Where?," "You Poor Thing."

Bennett: Entr'acte (with 4 pages by Kay), Finale act II, "For Love," "I Wish It So," "Ireland's Eye" (dance), "It's Not Irish" (as heard from onstage phonograph), "The Liffey Waltz" (plus two reprises), "Music in the House," "One Kind Word," Overture, "Song of the Ma," "We Can Be Proud."

Lang: "His Own Peculiar Charm," "Ireland's Eye" (song), "My True Heart" (see below).

Blitzstein: "Bird upon the Tree," "Kids."

Other scores:

"My True Heart" is by Lang, with a replacement bridge by Bennett.

"What Is the Stars?": Kay wrote the original chart, but most of it was replaced with a "New Refrain" by Bennett.

The invoices make clear that Bennett did most of his work during rehearsals in New York, with a few charts contributed by Lang and Blitzstein. Kay did not begin until after the Washington opening, at which point an enormous amount of work was necessary (at overtime rates). Bennett did some relatively minor additional work during the first week in Washington, after which he seems to have entirely left it to Kay.

Instr.: 6 reed, 5 brass (2 tpt, 2 tb, 1 hrn), 16? strings (9? vln, 4? vla, 2 c, 1 b), piano, accordion, guitar/mandolin, perc. = 31? total.

KEAN

Orchestrations credited to Philip J. **Lang**. (Additional orchestrators, if any, unknown.)

Opened November 2, 1961, Broadway, 92 performances. Tryout: September, Boston (Shubert); October, Philadelphia (Shubert).

Music and lyrics by Robert Wright & George Forrest. Based on a play by Jean-Paul Sartre, from a play by Alexandre Dumas. Musical direction and vocal arrangements by Pembroke Davenport. Dance arrangements by Elie Siegmeister. Other participants: Jack Cole (director, choreographer); Peter Stone (librettist); Alfred Drake (star).

An unreleased recording of the Entr'acte—taped, perhaps, at orchestra rehearsal or as warm-up at the recording session—reveals it to be exceptional. It is so different in tone from the rest of the score that one guesses it was routined and orchestrated by Elie Siegmeister.

KEEP OFF THE GRASS

Orchestrations credited to Hans **Spialek** and Don **Walker**. (Additional orchestrators, if any, unknown.)

Opened May 23, 1940, Broadhurst, 44 performances. Tryout: April 29, Boston (Shubert).

A revue. Music by Jimmy McHugh, lyrics by Al Dubin and Howard Dietz. Ballet ("Raffles") by Vernon Duke. Musical direction by John McManus. Vocal arrangements by Anthony R. Morelli. Additional vocal arrangements by Arthur Wilson. Other participants: George Balanchine (choreographer); Ray Bolger (star); Jimmy Durante (star); Jack [Jackie] Gleason (featured).

KELLY

Orchestrations credited to Hershy **Kay**. (Additional orchestrators, if any, unknown.)

Opened February 6, 1965, Broadhurst, 1 performance. Tryout: December 28, 1964, Philadelphia (Shubert); January 20, 1965, Boston (Shubert).

Music by Moose Charlap, lyrics and book by Eddie Lawrence. Musical direction by Samuel Matlovsky. Dance arrangements by Betty Walberg. Other participants: David Susskind (co-producer); Joseph E. Levine (co-producer); Herbert Ross (director, choreographer); Mel Brooks (replacement co-librettist, uncredited).

KICKS & CO.

Orchestrations credited to Alonzo Levister. (Additional orchestrators, if any, unknown.)

Tryout: October 11, 1961, Chicago (Arie Crown). Closed October 14, Chicago.

Music and lyrics by Oscar Brown, Jr. Musical direction and vocal arrangements by Jack Lee. Arrangements and additional music by Alonzo Levister. Dance arrangements and additional arrangements by Dorothea Freitag. Other participants: Robert Nemiroff (co-producer, co-librettist); Lorraine Hansberry (director); Donald McKayle (choreographer); Burgess Meredith (star).

THE KING AND I

Orchestrations by Russell **Bennett**. (Additional orchestrations by Don **Walker** and Hans **Spialek**, with Walter Paul.)

Opened March 29, 1951, St. James, 1,246 performances. Tryout: February 26, New Haven (Shubert); March 5, Boston (Shubert).

Music by Richard Rodgers, lyrics and book by Oscar Hammerstein II. Based on the novel

Anna and the King of Siam by Margaret Landon. Musical direction by Frederick Dvonch. Dance arrangements by Trude Rittman. Other participants: Richard Rodgers and Oscar Hammerstein II (producers); Jerome Robbins (choreographer); Gertrude Lawrence (star); Yul Brynner (featured).

The partiturs are in the Rodgers Collection at the Library of Congress, with copies at the offices of the Rodgers & Hammerstein Organization. Invoices are preserved in Bennett's ledger. Base page rate: $5.70.

The orchestrations are by Bennett, with the following exceptions:

Walker: "Boy's Soliloquy" (reprise of "A Puzzlement"), "Shall We Dance" (see below), "Vignettes and Dance."

Spialek: "Dance of Anna and Sir Edward (Varsovienne)," "Fireworks," Postlude of Ballet, "So Big a World" (incidental, page 71 of vocal score), "Song of the King" ("A woman is a female who is human . . . ").

Paul: utility ("Hello, Young Lovers").

Other scores:

Entr'acte is by Bennett, except for "Hello, Young Lovers Utility" by Walter Paul. (In Bennett's hand: "Copy W. P. score 'Young Lovers,' no intro, no ending").

"Processional": the beginning is by Bennett until the prince's entrance (section 5 on page 181 of vocal score); the rest is by Spialek.

"Shall We Dance": the first part, until the beginning of the dance lesson (section D on page 171 of vocal score) is by Walker; the rest of the scene ("New Refrain") alternates between Bennett and Walker.

"Uncle Tom's Cabin Ballet" ("The Small House of Uncle Thomas") is by Bennett, who names the composer on the first page as "Trude Rodgers."

Most of Bennett's early scores list the working title of the show, *Anna and the King of Siam*. The final version of the Overture lists the show as *Le Roi et Moi*.

The show was orchestrated for seven reeds and nine brass, just about the largest such sections I have come across in my research (other than the stringless *No Strings*, with eight reeds and seven brass in a twenty-one-piece pit).

Instr.: 7 reed, 9 brass (3 tpt, 2 tb, I tuba, 3 hrn), 10 strings (5 vln, 2 vla, 2 c, I b), harp, 2 perc = 29 total. (See pages 206, 256.)

KISMET

Orchestrations and choral arrangements by Arthur Kay. (Additional orchestrators, if any, unknown.)

Opened December 3, 1953, 583 performances. Tryout: August 17, Los Angeles (Philharmonic Auditorium); San Francisco; Boston; November, Philadelphia (Shubert).

Music from Alexandre Borodin. Musical adaptation and lyrics by Robert Wright & George Forrest. Based on the play by Edward Knoblock. Musical direction by Louis Adrian. Other participants: Edwin Lester (producer); Albert Marre (director); Jack Cole (choreographer); Alfred Drake (star); Joan Diener (featured); Richard Kiley (featured).

KISS ME, KATE

Orchestrations by Russell **Bennett**. (Additional orchestrations by Don **Walker**, with Walter Paul and Hans **Spialek**.)

Opened December 30, 1948, New Century, 1,077 performances. Tryout: December 2, Philadelphia (Shubert).

Music and lyrics by Cole Porter. A musical incorporating scenes adapted from the play *The Taming of the Shrew* by William Shakespeare. Musical direction by Pembroke Davenport. "Incidental ballet arrangements" by Genevieve Pitot. Other participants: Saint Subber (co-producer); John C. Wilson (director); Hanya Holm (choreographer); Alfred Drake (star).

Somewhat altered copies of the partiturs are in the American Musical Theatre Collection at the Library of Congress. This score is labeled "Road Version" and was prepared by Robert Noeltner, with edits and minor changes in his hand. However, most of the pages of the original partiturs are included. Bennett's invoices are preserved in his ledger. Walker's ledger is in the Walker Collection at the Library of Congress. Base page rate: $5.10.

Bennett: "Always True to You in My Fashion," "Brush Up Your Shakespeare," "Harlequin Ballerina," Hornpipe, "I Am Ashamed That Women Are So Simple," "I Hate Men," "I've Come to Wive It Wealthily," "Last Curtain" ("Brush Up Your Shakespeare" reprise), "Padua Street Scene" ("We Open in Venice"), "Pavane," "So in Love" (Kate's version, act 1), "Too Darn Hot" (vocal and dance), "Why Can't You Behave?" "Wunderbar."

Walker: "Another Op'nin," "Bianca" (see below), "First Act Finale," "I Sing of Love," Rose Dance (see below), "Shrew Finale Part II" ("So Kiss Me, Kate"), "So in Love" (Fred's version, act 2), Tarantella (Finale dance), "Tom, Dick and Harry" (song and encore), "Where Is the Life That Late I Led?"

Paul: utilities ("So in Love," "Were Thine That Special Face").

Spialek: "Wunderbar" (incidental, #18A).

Other scores:

"Bianca" (song) is by Walker; introduction ("Package for Miss Lois Lane"), added later during the tryout, is by Bennett; "Bianca Dance" is by Bennett.

Overture is by Bennett; the Entr'acte—which was used as the Overture on the original cast album—is by Bennett except for "Were Thine That Special Face," by Paul (Bennett's handwritten score says "Copy W. P. util.").

"Rose Dance" is mostly by Walker, with a new 15-page section added by Bennett.

"Were Thine That Special Face" is by Bennett, with new string and guitar parts for the dance section by Paul.

For the "Road Version," the first 120 bars of Walker's chart for "Another Op'nin" was severely truncated by Noeltner; however, he appears, in some cases, to be copying sections from Walker's original chart.

> WALKER: It was Russell's show, but for some reason he couldn't get any numbers released for orchestration until ten days before the orchestra reading. Everybody had to pitch in. I orchestrated at least five or six numbers. Once again, Russell gave me my percentage of the royalties from the show album.

From Bennett to Walker: "In view of my agreement with Columbia Records whereby I am to receive certain royalties earned on the sale of the album with the original cast and using our orchestral arrangements, I agree to turn over to you one-third of all sums received."

Instr.: 5 reed (including 5 sax), 5 brass (3 tpt, 1 tb, 1 hrn), ? strings (vln, vla, c, b), piano/celesta, harp, guitar/mandolin, perc.

KNICKERBOCKER HOLIDAY

Orchestrations (mostly) by Kurt Weill. (Additional orchestrations by Irving Schlein.)
Opened October 19, 1938, Ethel Barrymore, 168 performances. Tryout: September 28, Hartford, Connecticut (Bushnell); Boston; October 10, Washington, D.C. (National).
Music by Kurt Weill, lyrics and book by Maxwell Anderson. Based on the *Knickerbocker History of New York* stories by Washington Irving. Musical direction by Maurice d'Abravanel [Abravanel]. Other participants: Joshua Logan (director); Walter Huston (star).

The partiturs are in the Weill Collection at Yale.

The orchestrations are by Weill, with an added viola part by Schlein. This is, in many cases, written on a blank line at the bottom of the page, although often adapted from and written in on the cello or second-violin line.

Instr.: 4 reed (including 3 sax, 3 clr, 2 bcl), 4 brass (2 tpt, 2 tb), ? strings (vln, 1 vla, ? c, 1 b), piano/organ, guitar/banjo, perc.

KWAMINA

Orchestrations credited to Sid **Ramin** and Irwin **Kostal**. (Additional orchestrators, if any, unknown.)
Opened October 23, 1961, 54th Street, 32 performances. Tryout: Toronto (O'Keefe); September, Boston (Colonial).
Music and lyrics by Richard Adler. Musical and choral direction by Colin Romoff. Assistant conductor, John Berkman. Dance arrangements by John Morris. Other participants: Robert Lewis (director); Agnes de Mille (choreographer); Sally Ann Howes (star).

> KOSTAL: Sid and I, being entranced by the possibilities of using ethnic music, did a lot of research on African music. The orchestra pit of *Kwamina* looked like the jungle itself. We had branches of trees, which when shaken by our percussionists, sounded like Aeolian whispering palms. We used elephant gongs that sounded many pitches, and a Chinese piano that really came from Africa.
>
> RAMIN: I was doing *Candid Camera*, Irv was doing *The Garry Moore Show*, so we decided that we would cover for each other. *Kwamina* was trying out in Toronto. One week, I would go up to Toronto; the next week, Irv would go up. The concert master in Toronto was a very good violinist; he later wrote a book about the violin. [This was apparently Theodor H. Podnos, author of *Intonation for Strings, Winds, and Singers*.] So I was up in Canada, and I listened to one of the songs and I heard this beautiful violin obbligato, and I thought, "Gee, Irv, you wrote this beautiful obbligato when I wasn't there." When I told

him, he said, "I heard that obbligato. I thought you did it." The violinist had written his own obbligato! It was so beautiful, we were both congratulating each other.

LA BELLE

Orchestrations credited to Philip J. **Lang**. (Additional orchestrators, if any, unknown.)
Tryout: August 13, 1962, Philadelphia (Shubert). Closed August 25, Philadelphia.
Music by William Roy, based on themes by Offenbach, lyrics by Marshall Barer.
Based on the story of Helen of Troy. Musical direction and vocal arrangements by Pembroke Davenport. Dance arrangements by Genevieve Pitot. Other participants: Albert Marre (director); Brendan Gill (librettist); Menasha Skulnik (star); Joan Diener (star); George Segal (featured).

LA BELLE HELENE

Orchestrations uncredited. (Orchestrations by Don **Walker**, Hans **Spialek**, and others.)
Tryout: July 7, 1941, Westport, Connecticut (Country Playhouse). Closed Westport.
Music by Jacques Offenbach. Based on the story of Helen of Troy. Arranged by Herbert Kingsley. Other participants: Lawrence Langner and Armina Marshall (producers); Anne Brown (star).

Base page rate: $2.

Don Walker put in a bill for this production for 114 pages (with song titles unspecified).

Offenbach's opéra bouffe *La Belle Helene* was first performed in Paris in 1864. Director Max Reinhardt directed a celebrated English-language version in the West End in 1932, under the title *Helen!* with a libretto by A. P. Herbert and musical adaptation by Erich Wolfgang Korngold. Herbert's libretto served as the basis for the Westport *La Belle Helene*, from the Langners (of the Theatre Guild). This was an all-black version, starring Anne Brown (of *Porgy and Bess*) as Helen of Troy. Following the quick closing, the Reinhardt-Korngold version was presented on Broadway in 1944, with a nonblack cast, under the title *Helen Goes to Troy*. Walker's charts were most certainly not used in that production. Yet another version of the Offenbach piece, with no connection to the aforementioned, was produced in 1962 under the title *La Belle* (see the listing above). This one closed out of town, too.

LA CAGE AUX FOLLES

Orchestrations (mostly) by Jim Tyler. (Additional orchestrations by Harold Wheeler and Joe Gianono.)
Opened August 21, 1983, Palace, 1,761 performances. Tryout: Boston (Shubert).
Music and lyrics by Jerry Herman. Based on the play by Jean Poiret. Musical direction and vocal arrangements by Donald Pippin. Dance arrangements by Gordon Harrell. Other participants: Alan Carr (co-producer); Arthur Laurents (director); Harvey Fierstein (librettist).

The orchestrations are by Tyler, with the following exceptions:

Wheeler: "Masculinity."

Gianono: "Dindon March" (incidental), "Don Clementini" (incidental).

> PIPPIN: Jerry had no doubt it would be Phil Lang. Phil's health was failing; we talked to him, he thought it was too much for him to take on. He thought he was going to recover. Searching around one day, somebody put on the record of *Oh, Brother!*—bad show, but wonderful orchestrations. I went to Jerry and asked him to listen to it in terms of an orchestrator. So Tyler got the job.

> HERMAN: I said to Jim, who was a wonderful guy and without ego—I said, "This is a terrible thing to say to an orchestrator, but I want this show to sound like Phil Lang." He said, "Of course, I wouldn't do it any other way."

> PIPPIN: Later, we get to the big song, "The Best of Times." Jerry and I looked at each other— "Wouldn't it be marvelous if Phil would do this one number?" We ran it by Jim. "Oh, I would be honored if Phil would do this number—it *is* a Phil Lang number." Phil agreed that he would do it. I wrote out a meticulous sketch, went over it with him in great detail. Phil brought it back. It was pitiful—he was so ill, he couldn't write any more. No figures, wrong notes. So we gave it to Jim; he wrote it overnight. Jim was like a chameleon.

LA STRADA

Orchestrations (mostly) by Eddie **Sauter**. (Additional orchestrations by Elliot Lawrence.)

Opened December 14, 1969, Lunt-Fontanne, 1 performance. Tryout: October 27, Detroit (Fisher).

Music and lyrics by Lionel Bart. Additional music by Elliot Lawrence. Additional lyrics by Martin Charnin. Based on the film by Federico Fellini. Musical direction by Hal Hastings. Dance arrangements by Peter Howard. Other participants: Alan Schneider (director); Alvin Ailey (choreographer); Bernadette Peters (star).

The partiturs are in the Sauter Collection at Yale.

The orchestrations are by Sauter, with the following exceptions:

Lawrence: "I Don't Like You a Lot," "With a Man" (song and incidental).

LADY BE GOOD

Orchestrations uncredited. (Orchestrations by Paul Lannin, Russell **Bennett**, William Daly, Charles Grant, Stephen O. Jones, and Max Steiner.)

Opened December 1, 1924, Liberty, 330 performances. Tryout: November 17, Philadelphia (Forrest).

Music by George Gershwin, lyrics by Ira Gershwin. Musical direction by Paul Lannin. Other participants: Guy Bolton (librettist); Fred & Adele Astaire (stars).

Some of the partiturs are in the Gershwin Collection at the Library of Congress.

Lannin: "Scene 2, Act I," "Scene 3, Act I," "We're Here Because."

Bennett: "Linger in the Lobby (Opening Act II)."
Daly: "Opening Act I."
Steiner: "Finale Act I."

THE LADY COMES ACROSS

Orchestrations under the supervision of Domenico Savino. (Additional orchestrations by Charles L. Cooke and others.)

Opened January 9, 1942, 44th Street, 3 performances. Tryout: December 11, 1941, New Haven (Shubert); elsewhere.

Music by Vernon Duke, lyrics by John Latouche. Musical arrangements by Domenico Savino and Charles L. Cooke. Vocal arrangements by Hugh Martin. Other participants: George Balanchine (choreographer); Gower Champion (featured dancer); the Martins (including Hugh Martin and Ralph Blane; featured singers).

LADY FINGERS

Orchestrations uncredited. (Orchestrations by Roy Webb, Hans **Spialek**, and others.)

Opened January 31, 1929, Vanderbilt, 132 performances. Tryout: unknown.

Music by Joseph Meyer, lyrics by Edward Eliscu. Additional songs by Richard Rodgers and Lorenz Hart. Based on the play *Easy Come, Easy Go* by Owen Davis. Musical direction by Roy Webb.

LADY IN THE DARK

Orchestrations (mostly) by Kurt Weill. (Additional orchestrations by Ted **Royal**.)

Opened January 23, 1941, Alvin, 467 performances. Tryout: December 30, 1940, Boston (Colonial).

Music by Kurt Weill, lyrics by Ira Gershwin. Musical direction by Maurice Abravanel. Other participants: Moss Hart (director, librettist); Gertrude Lawrence (star); Danny Kaye (featured).

The partiturs are in the Weill Collection at Yale.

The orchestrations are by Weill, with the following exception:

Royal: "Bats about You" (cut).

Other score:

"One Life to Live" is mostly by Weill, with 38 bars of dance orchestration by Royal.

It has been written elsewhere, in error, that Royal also orchestrated the cut song "You Are Unforgettable" (which was never, in fact, orchestrated).

Instr.: 4 reed (including 3 sax), 4 brass (3 tpt, 1 tb), 9 strings (6 vln, 0 vla, 2 c, 1 b), piano, Hammond organ, perc = 20 total.

THE LAUGH PARADE

Orchestrations credited to Russell **Bennett**, Hans **Speilac** [*sic*], and Henry Sallinger [*sic*]. (Additional orchestrators, if any, unknown.)

Opened November 2, 1931, Imperial, 231 performances. Tryout: unknown.

A revue. Music by Harry Warren, lyrics by Mort Dixon and Joe Young. Musical direction by John McManus. Other participant: Ed Wynn (producer, co-librettist, director, "conceived by," star).

Spialek's credit is clearly a misspelling. "Henry Sallinger" is Conrad Salinger, whose first Broadway credit using his correct name came the night after *The Laugh Parade* opened, with *Here Comes the Bride.*

LEAVE IT TO ME!

Orchestrations credited to Donald J. **Walker** [*sic*]. (Additional orchestrations by W. C. Lindenmann and probably others.)

Opened November 9, 1938, Imperial, 307 performances. Tryout: October 13, New Haven (Shubert); October 17, Boston (Shubert).

Music and lyrics by Cole Porter. Based on the play *Clear All Wires* by Bella Spewack and Samuel Spewack. Musical direction by Robert Emmett Dolan. Vocal arrangements by Don Walker (uncredited). Other participants: Vinton Freedley (producer); Bella Spewack and Samuel Spewack (librettists); William Gaxton and Victor Moore (stars); Sophie Tucker (star); Mary Martin (featured).

The partiturs for three numbers are at Tams-Witmark.

    Walker: Overture, "Taking the Steppes to Russia."

    Lindenmann: "Far Away."

    Tams also has vocal arrangements, in Walker's hand, for "From Now On" (for double quartet); "Get Out of Town" (for male octet); and "I Want to Go Home," which specifies "quartet, one solo baritone (very weak)."

    "Taking the Steppes to Russia" lists the show's two earlier titles, *First in the Hearts* and *Clear All Wires.*

    The partitur for "My Heart Belongs to Daddy" is missing, but Walker has described how he orchestrated it.

Instr.: 4 reed, 6 brass (3 tpt, 2 tb, 1 hrn), ? strings (vln, vla, c, b), piano, harp, guitar, perc.

(See page 184.)

LEND AN EAR

Orchestrations credited to Clare Grundman. (Additional orchestrators, if any, unknown.)

Opened December 16, 1948, National, 460 performances. Tryout: June, Los Angeles (Las Palmas), Boston (Wilbur).

Music, lyrics, and sketches by Charles Gaynor. Musical direction by George Bauer. Vocal arrangements by Dorothea Freitag. Other participants: Gower Champion ("staging," choreographer); Carol Channing (featured).

LET 'EM EAT CAKE

Orchestrations credited to Edward B. Powell. (Additional orchestrators, if any, unknown.)

Opened October 21, 1933, Imperial, 89 performances. Tryout: October 2, Boston (Shubert).

Music by George Gershwin, lyrics by Ira Gershwin. Musical direction by William Daly. Other participant: George S. Kaufman (director, co-librettist).

LET FREEDOM SING

Orchestrations credited to Morton Gould and Philip J. **Lang**. (Additional orchestrators, if any, unknown.)

Opened October 5, 1942, Longacre, 8 performances.

A revue. Music and lyrics by various writers (including Harold J. Rome). Musical direction by Lou Cooper. Other participants: Youth Theatre (producer); Mitzi Green (featured); Betty Garrett (featured).

LET IT RIDE!

Orchestrations credited to Raymond Jaimes. (Additional orchestrations by Jack Andrews, Jacques Belasco, Dave Grusin, Luther Henderson, and Walter Eiger.)

Opened October 12, 1961, Eugene O'Neill, 68 performances. Tryout: September 7, Philadelphia (Erlanger).

Music and lyrics by Jay Livingston and Ray Evans. Based on the play *Three Men on a Horse* by John Cecil Holm and George Abbott. Musical direction by Jay Blackton. Vocal direction by Jerry Packer. Dance arrangements by Billy Goldenberg. Other participants: Onna White (choreographer); George Gobel (star); Sam Levene (star).

> RED PRESS: By the time I worked with Blackton on *Let It Ride!* everyone disliked him. All through the run, he would sit at the podium and take notes of every wrong note, and send them back to whoever played them. Once, someone stole some pages from his "a note from Jay Blackton" pad. During a performance, they sent a note to the first trumpet that said, "You two trumpets, move over and change places with the trombones." The trumpeter looked over to Blackton questioningly; Blackton seemed to nod (although he was conducting at the time). So, in the middle of the performance, the trumpets stood up and started to move their music.

LET'S FACE IT!

Orchestrations by Hans **Spialek** and Don **Walker**. (Additional orchestrations by Ted **Royal**, Walter Paul, and probably others.)

Opened October 29, 1941, Imperial, 547 performances. Tryout: October 6, Boston (Colonial).

Music and lyrics by Cole Porter. Based on the play *The Cradle Snatchers* by Norma Mitchell and Russell Medford. Musical direction by Max Meth. Vocal arrangements by Lyn Murray, Carley Mills, and Miss Edna Fox. Other participants: Vinton Freedley (producer); Herbert & Dorothy Fields (librettists); Danny Kaye (star).

Walker's ledger is at the Library of Congress. Base page rate: $3.

Walker: "Ace in the Hole" (song and dance), "Farming" (song, dance, and tag), "Jerry, My Soldier Boy" (song and dance), "Let's Face It," Overture, "Rub Your Lamp" (song, dance, and tag), "Unfinished Business" (song and dance).

From the program: "vocal arrangements for 'Ace in the Hole,' 'A Lady Needs a Rest' and 'Ev'rything I Love' by Lyn Murray and Carley Mills. Vocal arrangements for The Royal Guards by Miss Edna Fox."

The Royal Guards' numbers were "Let's Face It" and "A Little Rumba Numba." Tommy Gleason and His Royal Guards were, according to the show's promotional material, "a six-voiced combination made up of collegiate vocalists from Notre Dame, Texas U., Michigan, Stanford, Northwestern and Oregon. They are former gridiron stars, athletes and band instrumentalists."

Instr.: 5 reed (including 5 sax), 6 brass (3 tpt, 3 tb), 9 strings (6 vln, 0 vla, 2 c, 1 b), piano, harp, perc = 23 total.

LET'S MAKE AN OPERA

Orchestrations uncredited. (Orchestrations by Benjamin Britten.)

Opened December 13, 1950, John Golden, 5 performances. Tryout: November 22, New Haven (Shubert); elsewhere.

Music by Benjamin Britten, lyrics by Eric Crozier. Musical direction by Norman Del Mar. Other participants: Marc Blitzstein (director); Jo Sullivan (featured).

THE LIAR

Orchestrations credited to Lehman Engel and Ben Ludlow, Jr. (Additional orchestrators, if any, unknown.)

Opened May 18, 1950, Broadhurst, 12 performances. Tryout: April 24, Philadelphia.

Music by John Mundy, lyrics and book by Edward Eager. Based on the play *La Locandiera* by Carlo Goldoni. Musical direction by Lehman Engel. Other participants: Alfred Drake (director, co-librettist); William Eythe (star); Walter Matthau ensemble).

LIFE BEGINS AT 8:40

Orchestrations uncredited. (Orchestrations by Hans **Spialek**, Russell **Bennett**, Don **Walker**, Walter Paul, Ted **Royal**, and others.)

Opened August 27, 1934, Winter Garden, 237 performances. Tryout: August 6, Boston (Shubert).

A revue. Music by Harold Arlen, lyrics by Ira Gershwin and E. Y. Harburg. Musical direction by Al Goodman (replacing Max Meth). Other participants: Messrs. Shubert (producers); Bert Lahr (star); Ray Bolger (star).

The partiturs are at the Shubert Archive.

Spialek: "C'est La Vie" (see below), "The Elks and the Masons" (see below), "I Couldn't Hold My Man," "I Knew Him When," "LaGuardia," "Let's Take a Walk Around the Block," "Long Ago, Far Away and Once upon a Time (Album Song)," "Opening Act I," "Quartet Erotica (Rabelais)," "Roxy Rose," "Things," "What Can You Say in a Love Song?" (see below).

Walker: "Window Dresser" (see below).

Royal: "Finale 1st Act."

Bennett: "I'm Not Myself" (see below), "Spring Fever."

Other scores:

"C'est La Vie": song and "Acrobat" are by Spialek; utility is by Walker(?); "Waltz after C'est La Vie" is by Bennett.

"The Elks and the Masons" is by Spialek, except for the first 28 bars (probably a revision) by unidentified hand #1.

"Fun to Be Fooled" is by Spialek; 11-page dance introduction is by unidentified hand #2.

"I'm Not Myself": song is by Bennett; dance is by Walker.

"Shoein' the Mare": song, "Weidman's Dance," and "Ensemble Chorus" are by Spialek; "Shoein' Dance" and "Utility Chorus" are by Walker; "Specialty" is by Paul.

"What Can You Say in a Love Song?" is by Spialek, with utility by Walker.

"Will You Love Me Monday Morning? (Weekend Excursion)": "Verse Dance," "Forty Chorus," and "Light Dance: Jackie Starr's Specialty" are by Bennett; "Ray Bolger Specialty," "Bolger Encore" (piano and strings), and utility(?) are by Walker.

"You're a Builder-Upper": first refrain is by Spialek; dance, "Specialty," and "Vocal Second" are by Walker.

Instr.: 4 reed (3 sax), 4 brass (3 tpt, 1 tb), 12? strings (8? vln, 2? vla, 1? c, 1 b), 2 piano [1 celesta], perc = 23? total.

LIFE OF THE PARTY

Orchestrations credited to Hans **Spialek**, Russell **Bennett**, and Ted **Royal**. (Additional orchestrators, if any, unknown.)

Tryout: October 8, 1942, Detroit (Wilson). Closed November, Detroit.

Music by Frederick Loewe, lyrics by Earle Crooker. Based on the play *The Patsy* by Barry Connors. Musical direction by Ray Kavanaugh. Vocal arrangements by Ted Scott. Other participants: Alan Jay Lerner (librettist); Dorothy Stone (star); Margaret Dumont (featured).

LI'L ABNER

Orchestrations credited to Philip J. **Lang**. (Additional orchestrators, if any, unknown.)

Opened November 15, 1956, St. James, 693 performances. Tryout: September 17, Washington, D.C. (National); Boston; Philadelphia.

Music by Gene de Paul, lyrics by Johnny Mercer. Based on the comic strip by Al Capp. Musical direction, vocal arrangements, and continuity by Lehman Engel. Ballet music arranged by Genevieve Pitot. Other participant: Michael Kidd (co-producer, director, choreographer).

(See page 243.)

THE LITTLE DOG LAUGHED

Orchestrations credited to Hans **Spialek**. (Additional orchestrators, if any, unknown.)
Tryout: August 13, 1940, Atlantic City (Garden Pier). Closed August 24, Boston.
Music and lyrics by Harold Rome. Musical direction and vocal arrangements by Lehman
   Engel. Other participant: Eddie Dowling (producer, director).

> SPIALEK: The show was so revoltingly bad that, instead of attending the preparations for the
> opening night, I spent my time in the adjacent arena watching much funnier rehearsals
> for the scheduled wrestling matches. Although the first showing met with a very lenient
> audience, the show was still bad, and all the concerted efforts of the talented Paul
> Draper, Lehman Engel, Philip Loeb, Harold Rome, etc., failed to transform this child-
> ishly symbolic monstrosity into a modicum of entertainment.

LITTLE JESSE JAMES (1953 REVIVAL)

Orchestrations (new) by Don **Walker**. (Additional orchestrations by Robert **Ginzler**.)
Tryout: November 30, 1953, Cincinnati (Taft). Closed December 19, Baltimore (Ford's).
Music by Harry Archer, lyrics by Harlan Thompson. New lyrics by Gladys Shelley.
Musical direction by Harry Archer.

Invoices are in the Walker Collection at the Library of Congress. Base page rate: $4.65.
Invoices indicate: Walker (83%), Ginzler (17%).
   The orchestrations are by Walker, with the following exceptions:
   Ginzler: Entr'acte, "How Did You Ever Happen to Me," "Women Never Fool This
Man."

LITTLE JOHNNY JONES (1982 REVIVAL)

Additional orchestrations (new) by Eddie **Sauter** and Mack Schlefer.
Opened March 21, 1982, Alvin, 1 performance. Tryout: July 1, 1980, East Haddam, Connecticut (Goodspeed Opera House). Pre-Broadway: February 1982, Boston (Metropolitan Center).
Music, lyrics, and book by George M. Cohan. Musical direction by Lynn Crigler. Vocal
   arrangements and additional dance arrangements by Robert (Rob) Fisher. Dance
   arrangements by Russell Warner. Other participants: Gerald Gutierrez (director); Alfred Uhry (book adaptation); Donny Osmond (star).

LITTLE ME

Orchestrations credited to Ralph **Burns**. (Additional orchestrators, if any, unknown.)
Opened November 17, 1962, Lunt-Fontanne, 257 performances. Tryout: October 8,
   Philadelphia (Erlanger).
Music by Cy Coleman, lyrics by Carolyn Leigh. Based on the fictional memoir by Patrick
   Dennis. Musical direction by Charles Sanford. Vocal arrangements by Clay Warnick.
   Dance arrangements by Fred Werner. Other participants: Feuer & Martin (producers);

Cy Feuer and Bob Fosse (directors); Bob Fosse (choreographer); Neil Simon (librettist); Sid Caesar (star).

It is known that Larry Wilcox worked on this show as a copyist and perhaps as an orchestrator.

(See page 35.)

THE LITTLE PRINCE AND THE AVIATOR

Orchestrations by Don **Walker**. (Additional orchestrations by Danny Troob, Harold Serra, Jim Tyler, and Craig Shuler.)

Tryout: December 26, 1981, New York (Alvin). Closed in previews, January 17, 1982.

Music by John Barry, lyrics by Don Black. Based on the story *Le Petit Prince* by Antoine de Saint-Exupéry. Musical direction and vocal arrangements by David Friedman. Dance arrangements by Grant Sturiale. Other participants: Hugh Wheeler (librettist); Michael York (star).

The partiturs and invoices are in the Walker Collection at the Library of Congress. Base page rate: $13.12.

Instr.: 4 reed (4 sax, 4 clr, 3 fl), 4 brass (2 tpt, 1 tb, 1 hrn), 7 strings (4 vln, 1 vla, 1 c, 1 b), keyboard, harp, 2 perc = 19 total.

(See page 230.)

THE LITTLEST REVUE

Orchestrations credited to John Strauss. (Additional orchestrations by Joe Glover and Tommy Goodman.)

Opened May 22, 1956, Phoenix (off-Broadway), 32 performances.

A revue. Music by Vernon Duke, lyrics by Ogden Nash. Additional songs by Sheldon Harnick, Sammy Cahn, John Latouche, Charles Strouse, and Lee Adams. Musical direction by Will Irwin. Other participants: Phoenix Theatre (producer); Tammy Grimes (featured); Charlotte Rae (featured); Joel Grey (featured).

LIVIN' THE LIFE

Orchestrations credited to Hershy **Kay** and Joe Glover. (Additional orchestrations by Ralph **Burns**.)

Opened April 27, 1957, Phoenix (off-Broadway), 25 performances.

Music by Jack Urbont, lyrics by Bruce Geller. Based on the novel *Tom Sawyer* by Mark Twain. Musical direction by Anton Coppola. Vocal arrangements by Jack Urbont. Dance arrangements by Genevieve Pitot.

LOLITA, MY LOVE

Orchestrations credited to Eddie **Sauter**. (Additional orchestrations by Larry **Wilcox** and possibly others.)

Tryout: February 16, 1971, Philadelphia (Shubert). Closed March 27, Boston (Shubert).

Music by John Barry, lyrics and book by Alan Jay Lerner. Based on the novel *Lolita* by Vladimir Nabokov. Musical direction and vocal arrangements by Herbert Grossman. Dance arrangements by John Morris. Other participants: John Neville (star); Dorothy Loudon (featured).

It has been reported that Sauter did most of the show, with the Overture orchestrated by Larry Wilcox.

LOLLIPOP

Orchestrations uncredited. (Orchestrations by Stephen Jones, Russell **Bennett**, Maurice de Packh and others.)

Opened January 21, 1924, Knickerbocker, 152 performances. Tryout: (as *The Left Over*) September 20, 1923, New Haven (Shubert); elsewhere.

Music by Vincent Youmans, lyrics by Zelda Sears and Walter DeLeon. Musical direction by Russell Tarbox.

Several partiturs are at the Library of Congress.

Jones: "Deep in My Heart," "It Must Be Love."

Bennett: Take a Little One-Step (signed "VY/Rus").

de Packh: "Honey Bun" (originally used as "Fairbanks Twins Dance" in *Two Little Girls in Blue*).

LOOK MA, I'M DANCIN'!

Orchestrations credited to Don **Walker**. (Additional orchestrations by Russell **Bennett**, Robert **Ginzler**, and probably others.)

Opened January 29, 1948, Adelphi, 188 performances. Tryout: December 25, 1947, Boston (Shubert); Philadelphia (Forrest).

Music and lyrics by Hugh Martin. Musical direction by Pembroke Davenport. Vocal arrangements by Hugh Martin. Assistant vocal arranger, Buster Davis. Ballet arrangements by Trude Rittman. Other participants: George Abbott (producer, co-director); Jerome Robbins (co-director, choreographer, conception); Robert E. Griffith (stage manager); Nancy Walker (star).

Bennett's invoice is preserved in his journal. Base page rate: $5.30.

Bennett: "Mlle. Scandale Ballet" (also known as "Mademoiselle Marie," composed by Rittman).

While no partiturs or invoices for this show have been located, Red Ginzler's daughters specifically recall him going out of town with the pre-Broadway tryout.

Robbins's "Mlle. Scandale Ballet" featured Nancy Walker as "Mademoiselle Marie, a young bride" and—as "Her Beloved"—Herbert Ross.

THANKS AND WISHES From Martin to Walker: "How does it feel to be the best?"

From Robbins to Walker: "All I can say is from now on when Robbins appears as choreographer, Walker appears as orchestrator. Thanks, love and luck, Jerry."

Instr.: 5 reed, 4 brass (3 tpt, 1 tb), 8 strings (5 vln, 1 vla, 1 c, 1 b), piano, harp, guitar, 2 perc = 22 total.

LOOK TO THE LILIES

Orchestrations (mostly) by Larry **Wilcox**. (Additional orchestrations by Peter Matz.)

Opened March 29, 1970, Lunt-Fontanne, 25 performances. Tryout: unknown.

Music by Jule Styne, lyrics by Sammy Cahn. Based on the novel *Lilies of the Field* by William Barrett. Musical direction by Milton Rosenstock. Vocal arrangements and direction by Buster Davis. Dance arrangements by John Morris. Other participants: Joshua Logan (director); Shirley Booth (star).

The partiturs are at the Styne office.

The orchestrations are by Wilcox, with the following exception:

Matz: "Give It a Shot Dance New."

LORELEI

Orchestrations by Philip J. **Lang** and Don **Walker**. (Additional orchestrations by Russell **Bennett**, Ray Ellis, and possibly others.)

Opened January 27, 1974, Palace, 320 performances. Tryout: February 26, 1973, Oklahoma City, Oklahoma (Civic Center); May 15, 1973, Washington, D.C. (National); November 1973, Philadelphia (Forrest); elsewhere.

Music by Jule Styne, lyrics by Leo Robin. Additional lyrics by Betty Comden & Adolph Green. A revised version of the musical *Gentlemen Prefer Blondes*. Musical direction by Milton Rosenstock. Vocal arrangements by Hugh Martin and Buster Davis. Dance arrangements by Jay Thompson. Other participants: Joe Layton (original director, choreographer); Robert Moore (replacement director); Carol Channing (star).

Bennett's invoice is preserved in his journal.

Bennett: "A Girl Like I" (cut).

Lorelei was an unsuccessful update of the 1949 hit *Gentlemen Prefer Blondes*, conceived to allow Carol Channing (at fifty-three) to recreate the role that made her famous (at twenty-eight). A new book, with flashbacks, was written, while composer Styne was joined by long-time collaborators Comden and Green for the requisite new songs.

Instr.: 5 reed (including 5 sax), 7 brass (3 tpt, 2 tb, 2 hrn), 11 strings (6 vln, 2 vla, 2 c, 1 b), piano, guitar, 2 perc = 27 total.

LOST IN THE STARS

Musical arrangements and orchestrations (mostly) by Kurt Weill. (Additional orchestrations by Irving Schlein.)

Opened October 30, 1949, Music Box, 273 performances. Tryout: none.

Music by Kurt Weill, lyrics and book by Maxwell Anderson. Based on the novel *Cry, the Beloved Country* by Alan Paton. Musical direction by Maurice Levine. Other participants: Rouben Mamoulian (director); Todd Duncan (star).

Copies of the partiturs are in the Weill Collection at Yale.

The orchestrations are by Weill, with the following exception:

Schlein: "Who'll Buy?"

Instr.: 3 reed (3 sax, 3 clr), 1 brass (tpt), 5 strings (0 vln, 2 vla, 2 c, 1 b), piano/accordion/organ, harp, perc = 12 total.

LOUISIANA LADY

Orchestrations credited to Hans **Spialek** and Russell **Bennett**. (Additional orchestrators, if any, unknown.)

Opened June 2, 1947, Century, 4 performances. Tryout: May 8, New Haven (Shubert); elsewhere.

Music and lyrics by Monte Carlo and Alma Sanders. Based on the play *Creoles* by Samuel Shipman and Kenneth Perkins. Musical direction and vocal arrangements by Hilding Anderson.

Bennett's invoices are preserved in his ledger. Base page rate: $5.

Bennett: "Can Can," "The Cuckoo-Cheena" (vocal and dance), Finale act I (reprise), "Lou Wills Dance," opening dance, "When You Are Close to Me" (two versions).

LOUISIANA PURCHASE

Orchestrations by Russell **Bennett**. (Additional orchestrations by Nathan Lang Van Cleave and Ted **Royal**.)

Opened May 28, 1940, Imperial, 444 performances. Tryout: May 2, New Haven (Shubert); May 6, Washington, D.C. (National); May 13, Philadelphia (Forrest).

Music and lyrics by Irving Berlin. Musical direction by Robert Emmett Dolan. Vocal arrangements by Hugh Martin. Other participants: B. G. DeSylva (producer); George Balanchine (choreographer). William Gaxton and Victor Moore (stars).

The partiturs are in the Berlin Collection at the Library of Congress.

Orchestrations are by Bennett (with Royal), with the following exceptions:

Van Cleave: "Cakewalk," "I'd Love to Be Shot from a Cannon with You" (replacing an earlier version by Bennett).

Other scores:

"Louisiana Purchase": song and reprise are by Bennett; "April Specialty" and "Nicodemus Specialty" by Van Cleave. "The Lord Done Fix Up My Soul": opening (through bar 17) is by Bennett; bars 18–55 are by Van Cleave; ending (beginning with "Bless the Lord") is by Bennett.

"Outside of That I Love You" is by Van Cleave; "Nick Long Specialty" by Bennett.

"Sex Marches On": first part is by Bennett; interlude through ending is by Van Cleave.

"You're Lonely and I'm Lonely": song is by Bennett; "Nicodemus Specialty" by Van Cleave.

Louisiana Purchase was conceived as a "hot" show, musically, with numerous swing numbers. It has always been a bit of a mystery how Bennett—Broadway's finest "legit" orchestrator—was able to write these charts (especially the saxophones). Along with the original partiturs, the Berlin Collection has a set of charts for some (though not all) of the songs, which contain only the five reed parts, by Ted Royal. These are enumerated, measure for measure, to match the full partiturs. The individual lines are relatively identical to the full scores; here and there, the notation is different, one of the indicated instruments has been changed, or the actual notes are different. Royal was apparently hired to write the reed parts. (He had been added to the staff at Chappell in 1939, specifically to give the house someone who could provide the swing band sound.) From an examination of the materials, it appears that Bennett and Van Cleave initially left the reed lines blank. Royal, working from their scores, wrote—on separate pages—suggested reed parts. (It would have been impossible to write these five lines alone, without knowledge of what the rest of the orchestra was playing.) Bennett and Van Cleave then took Royal's scores, copied them onto the full scores, and freely made whatever changes they desired to integrate the reeds with the rest of the orchestra. The results, as can be heard on the cast album of the 1996 City Center Encores! restoration of the score, are indeed "hot"—especially for a Bennett musical.

Instr.: 5 reed (including 5 sax, 4 clr), 5 brass (3 tpt, 2 tb), 14? strings (9? vln, 2? vla, 2? c, 1 b), piano, guitar, perc = 27? total.

LOVE LIFE

Musical arrangements and orchestrations by Kurt Weill. Ballet (and other) orchestrations by Irving Schlein.

Opened October 7, 1948, 46th Street, 252 performances. Tryout: September 9, New Haven (Shubert); September 13, Boston (Shubert).

Music by Kurt Weill, lyrics and book by Alan Jay Lerner. Musical direction by Joseph Littau. "Punch and Judy" ballet arranged and orchestrated by Irving Schlein. Other participants: Cheryl Crawford (producer); Elia Kazan (director); Michael Kidd (choreographer); Nanette Fabray (star).

The partiturs are in the Weill Collection at Yale.

The orchestrations are by Weill, with the following exception:

Schlein: "Punch and Judy's Divorce Ballet."

Other scores:

"Green-Up Time" is by Weill; "Green-Up Polka" by Schlein.

"Mother's Getting Nervous" is by Weill; "Foxtrot Variations" by Schlein.

"Progress" is by Weill; "Progress Soft Shoe" by Schlein.

"Women's Club Blues" is by Weill, with "Boogie-Woogie" section by Schlein.

Instr.: 5 reed (all sax/clr), 4 brass (3 tpt, 1 tb), 12 strings (9 vln, 0 vla, 2 c, 1 b), piano/accordion, guitar/mandolin/banjo, perc = 24 total.

LOVE MATCH

Orchestrations credited to Hershy **Kay**. (Additional orchestrators, if any, unknown.)

Tryout: November 3, 1968, Phoenix, Arizona (Palace West). Closed January 4, 1969, Los Angeles (Ahmanson).

Music by David Shire, lyrics by Richard Maltby, Jr. Suggested by events in the life of Queen Victoria. Musical direction by Theodore Saidenberg. Vocal and dance arrangements by David Shire. Other participant: Patricia Routledge (star).

LOVELY LADIES, KIND GENTLEMEN

Orchestrations credited to Philip J. **Lang** (replaced by Irwin **Kostal**). (Additional orchestrators, if any, unknown.)

Opened December 28, 1970, Majestic, 16 performances. Tryout: August 19, Philadelphia (Shubert); Los Angeles; San Francisco.

Music and lyrics by Stan Freeman and Franklin Underwood. Based on the play *The Teahouse of the August Moon* by John Patrick. Musical direction and vocal arrangements by Theodore Saidenberg. Dance arrangements by Albert Mello. Other participants: Herman Levin (producer); John Patrick (librettist).

Times critic Clive Barnes memorialized this musical with the opening line of his review, "I come to bury *Lovely Ladies, Kind Gentlemen*, not to praise it." The show began in Philadelphia with a quasi-Japanese orchestration. When the tryout continued at the Civic Light Opera, local producer Ed Lester insisted on something more in the Broadway/Rodgers & Hammerstein vein and called in his frequent orchestrator Kostal. While Lang retained credit, Kostal's charts were used for Broadway; apparently, only one Lang chart remained, "Call Me Back."

> KOSTAL: Phil Lang, at Stan Freeman's suggestion, had made the original orchestrations exploiting the oriental aspects of the story, using Japanese ethnic musical instruments of all sorts. Ed Lester had his own idea and proceeded to make the most elaborate changes in the script, reversing scenes and reworking the entire show. In just a few weeks of rehearsal, he minimized the emphasis on the Japanese background and built up the importance of the American soldiers. Without a Marlon Brando [who played the principal role of Sakini in the film version], Ed rightfully decided to go a different route. He did not care for the original arrangements and hired me. I very quickly reorchestrated the entire score in just sixteen days, highlighting the contrasting cultures, using some odd Japanese instruments, accompanied by a lot of American jazz, and sometimes superimposing one style on top of the other.

LUCKY

Orchestrations uncredited. (Orchestrations by Russell **Bennett**, Hans **Spialek**, Stephen O. Jones, and others.)

Opened March 22, 1927, New Amsterdam, 71 performances. Tryout: March 8, Philadelphia (Garrick).

Music by Jerome Kern, lyrics by Otto Harbach, additional songs by Bert Kalmar and Harry Ruby. Musical direction by Gus Salzer. Other participants: Charles Dillingham (producer); Ruby Keeler (featured); Paul Whiteman (featured).

The partiturs are in the Kern Collection at the Library of Congress (unexamined).

LUTE SONG

Orchestrations credited to Raymond Scott. (Additional orchestrators, if any, unknown.)
Opened February 6, 1946, Plymouth, 142 performances. Tryout: December 13, 1945, New Haven (Shubert); elsewhere.
Music by Raymond Scott, lyrics by Bernard Hanighen. Based on the play *Pi-Pa-Ki* by Kao-Tong-Kia and Mao-Tseo. Musical direction by Eugene Kusmiak. Other participants: Mary Martin (star); Yul Brynner (featured).

LUTE SONG (1959 REVIVAL)

Orchestrations by Irwin **Kostal** (uncredited). (Additional orchestrators, if any, unknown.)
Opened March 12, 1959, City Center, 14 performances.
Musical direction by Sylvan Levin. Other participants: Dolly Haas (star); André Gregory ([member of] ensemble).

According to Kostal, composer Scott asked him to prepare new orchestrations for this revival by the City Center Light Opera Company.

MACK & MABEL

Orchestrations credited to Philip J. **Lang**. (Additional orchestrators, if any, unknown.)
Opened October 6, 1974, Majestic, 66 performances. Tryout: June 17, San Diego; June 25, Los Angeles (Dorothy Chandler Pavilion); St. Louis; September 3, Washington, D.C. (Opera House).
Music and lyrics by Jerry Herman. Suggested by events in the lives of Mack Sennett and Mabel Normand. Musical direction and vocal arrangements by Donald Pippin. Dance arrangements by John Morris. Other participants: David Merrick (producer); Gower Champion (director, choreographer); Michael Stewart (librettist); Robert Preston (star); Bernadette Peters (star).

> PIPPIN: This was Phil at his most Phil Lang–ish style, with Johnny Morris writing fabulous arrangements. Musically speaking, it was an easy thing for Phil. He knew exactly what he was doing, that's his meat; you didn't have to tell him anything.

(See page 166.)

MAGGIE

Orchestrations credited to Don **Walker**. (Additional orchestrations by Walter Paul, Joe Glover, Philip J. **Lang**, Russell **Bennett**, Robert **Ginzler**, and Jack Mason.)
Opened February 18, 1953, National, 5 performances. Tryout: January 19, Philadelphia (Forrest); February 9, New Haven (Shubert).
Music and lyrics by William Roy. Based on the play *What Every Woman Knows* by James M. Barrie. Musical direction by Maurice Levine. Dance arrangements by Dean Fuller.

Invoices are in the Walker Collection at the Library of Congress. Base page rate: $5.35.
Invoices indicate: Walker (31%), Paul (22%), Glover (10%).

The orchestrations are by Walker and Paul, with the following exceptions:

Glover: "Dream," "Triangle," "You Become Me."

Lang: "Any Afternoon," "Dream Sequence," "Train."

Bennett: "Bug Dance," "Montage."

Other scores:

Overture and Entr'acte are compilations of utilities, with bridgework by Mason and Ginzler.

MAGGIE FLYNN

Orchestrations credited to Philip J. **Lang**. (Additional orchestrators, if any, unknown.)

Opened October 23, 1968, ANTA, 82 performances. Tryout: September, Detroit (Fisher).

Music, lyrics, and book by Hugo Peretti, Luigi Creatore, and George David Weiss. Musical direction and vocal arrangements by John Lesko. Dance arrangements by Trude Rittman. Other participants: Morton Da Costa (director, "book in association with"); Shirley Jones (star); Jack Cassidy (star).

It is likely that Jack Andrews worked on this show.

THE MAGNOLIA LADY

Orchestrations uncredited. (Orchestrations by Russell **Bennett** and others.)

Opened November 25, 1924, Shubert, 49 performances. Tryout: November 9, Washington, D.C.

Music by Harold A. Levey, lyrics and book by Anne Caldwell. Based on the play *Come Out of the Kitchen* by Alice Duer Miller and A. E. Thomas. Musical direction by Harold A. Levey.

MAKE A WISH

Orchestrations credited to Philip J. **Lang** and Allan Small. (Additional orchestrations by George Bassman and possibly others.)

Opened April 18, 1951, Winter Garden, 102 performances. Tryout: March 12, Philadelphia (Shubert).

Music and lyrics by Hugh Martin. (Additional lyrics by Timothy Gray.) Based on the play *The Good Fairy* by Ferenc Molnár. Musical direction by Milton Rosenstock. Vocal arrangements by Hugh Martin. Vocal direction by Buster Davis. Dance arrangements by Richard Pribor. Other participants: Jule Styne (co-producer); Alexander H. Cohen (co-producer); Preston Sturges (librettist); John C. Wilson (director); Abe Burrows (replacement librettist, director); Gower Champion (choreographer); Nanette Fabray (star).

A December 1950 clipping announced that Walker would orchestrate—and Balanchine choreograph—this show, which was then called *Suits Me Fine.* The show was delayed, though, and proceeded without Walker or Balanchine.

HUGH MARTIN: I was disappointed in the orchestration; I really expected more. I wish they'd been a little more exciting. They were all acceptable, but not outstanding. We couldn't get people that I love; they were not available, so we had to go to other people who were available.

The only chart whose orchestrator Martin specifically recalls is "Suits Me Fine," by George Bassman.

MAKE MINE MANHATTAN

Orchestrations credited to Ted **Royal**. (Additional orchestrations by Russell **Bennett** and others.)

Opened January 15, 1948, Broadhurst, 429 performances. Tryout: December 17, 1947, New Haven (Shubert); elsewhere.

A revue. Music by Richard Lewine, lyrics and sketches by Arnold B. Horwitt. Musical direction by Charles Sanford. Vocal arrangements by Lois Moseley. Dance arrangements by Mel Pahl. Other participants: Max Liebman (director); Sid Caesar (featured).

Bennett's invoices are preserved in his ledger. Base page rate: $4.50. Tentative attributions per invoice.

Bennett: "The Good Old Days," "Never Again."

From Max Dreyfus to Walker: "On my return to the office Doc [Albert Sirmay] told me about your call concerning your release for the Lewine-Horwitt show. You will recall that I agreed in principle to release you for this show provided Chappell would have first choice to publish the score. I have not changed my mind about that at all and it still goes." As it happened, the dates conflicted with *Look Ma, I'm Dancin'!* so Walker was unavailable. Royal became the supervising orchestrator on the show, which was indeed published by Chappell.

MAMBA'S DAUGHTERS

Orchestration by Hans **Spialek**.

Opened January 3, 1939, Empire, 162 performances. Tryout: unknown.

A play by Dorothy and DuBose Heyward, with a song by Jerome Kern and DuBose Heyward. Vocal arrangement by Reginald Beane. Other participants: Ethel Waters (star); José Ferrer (featured).

MAME

Orchestrations (mostly) by Philip J. **Lang**. (Additional orchestrations by Jack Andrews.)

Opened May 24, 1966, Winter Garden, 1,508 performances. Tryout: Boston; April 4, Philadelphia (Shubert).

Music and lyrics by Jerry Herman. Based on the play *Auntie Mame* by Jerome Lawrence and Robert E. Lee, from the novel by Patrick Dennis. Musical direction and vocal arrangements by Donald Pippin. Dance arrangements by Roger Adams. Other participants:

Robert Fryer (co-producer); Gene Saks (director); Onna White (choreographer); Jerome Lawrence and Robert E. Lee (librettists); Angela Lansbury (star).

The partiturs are in the possession of the composer.

The orchestrations are by Lang, with the following exceptions:

"Bosom Buddies" is by Lang (with 12 bars in part 2 by Andrews).

"It's Today" is by Lang; "Reprise (Party)" is by Andrews. There are two utilities, one by Lang and one by Andrews.

"We Need a Little Christmas" is by Lang; "Tag" is mostly by Lang, with the final ending by Andrews.

> JERRY HERMAN: I personally think that *Mame* is Phil's crowning glory. The orchestration of "It's Today" is the absolute model of a Broadway song. It blew me away when first I heard it, made hair stand up on my arms.

Pippin remembers that, when Jerry heard the woodwinds figurations in this number at the orchestra reading, "his eyes just opened wide."

Instr.: 5 reed, 6 brass (3 tpt, 3 tb), 11 strings (6 vln, 2 vla, 2 c, 1 b/tuba), piano/celesta, harp, guitar/banjo, perc = 26 total.

(See pages 169, 200, 210, 265.)

MAN OF LA MANCHA

Orchestrations credited to Music Makers Inc. (Carlyle Hall). (Additional orchestrators, if any, unknown.)

Opened November 22, 1965, ANTA Washington Square, 2,328 performances. Tryout: June 24, East Haddam, Connecticut (Goodspeed Opera House).

Music by Mitch Leigh, lyrics by Joe Darion. Based on the novel *Don Quixote* by Miguel de Cervantes. Musical direction by Neil Warner. Other participants: Albert Marre (director); Richard Kiley (star); Joan Diener (star).

MANHATTAN SHOWBOAT

Orchestrations credited to Philip J. **Lang**, Michael Gibson, and others.

Opened June 30, 1980, Radio City Music Hall, 191 performances. Tryout: none.

A revue. Music by Donald Pippin, lyrics by Sammy Cahn. Musical direction by Donald Pippin. Musical routining by Stanley Lebowsky. Other participant: Radio City Music Hall Productions (producer).

MARDI GRAS

Orchestrations credited to Philip J. **Lang**. (Additional orchestrators, if any, unknown.)

Opened June 26, 1965, Jones Beach, New York (Marine), 68 performances.

Music by Carmen Lombardo, lyrics by John Jacob Loeb. Other participant: Guy Lombardo (producer).

MARINKA

Orchestrations credited to Hans **Spialek**. (Additional orchestrators unknown.)

Opened July 18, 1945, Winter Garden, 165 performances. Tryout: (as *Marinka*) May 31, New Haven (Shubert); (as *Song of Vienna*) June 11, Washington, D.C. (National); elsewhere.

Music by Emmerich Kalman, lyrics by George Marion, Jr. Based on the Mayerling incident of 1889. Musical direction by Ray Kavanaugh. Other participants: Joan Roberts (star); Ethel Levey (featured).

MARJORIE

Orchestrations uncredited. (Orchestrations by Stephen O. Jones, Hans **Spialek**, and, possibly, others.)

Opened August 11, 1924, Shubert, 144 performances. Tryout: (as *Margerie Daw*) Atlantic City.

Music by Sigmund Romberg, Herbert Stothart, Philip Culkin, and Stephen O. Jones, lyrics and book by Fred Thompson and Clifford Grey. Based on the play *Margery Daw* by George D. Parker. Musical direction by John L. McManus.

This is the show which introduced Hans Spialek to the Broadway theatre. One can't help but noticing that they kept changing the spelling of the heroine's name; did it help any? (See page 91.)

MARY JANE MCKANE

Orchestrations uncredited. (Orchestrations by Russell **Bennett** and others.)

Opened December 25, 1923, Imperial, 151 performances. Tryout: October 25, Wilkes-Barre, Pennsylvania (Irving); October 31, Baltimore (Auditorium); November 5, Boston (Shubert).

Music by Vincent Youmans and Herbert Stothart, lyrics and book by William Cary Duncan and Oscar Hammerstein II. Musical direction by Herbert Stothart.

MASS

Orchestrations by Hershy **Kay**, Jonathan Tunick, and Leonard Bernstein. (Additional orchestrations by Sid **Ramin**.)

Opened September 8, 1971, Washington, D.C. (Kennedy Center Opera House), 12 performances.

Music by Leonard Bernstein. Text from the liturgy of the Roman Mass. Additional texts by Stephen Schwartz and Leonard Bernstein. Musical direction by Maurice Peress. Other participants: Roger L. Stevens (producer); Gordon Davidson (director); Alvin Ailey (choreographer).

The partiturs are at the Library of Congress (unexamined).

The orchestrations are by Kay, Tunick, and Bernstein, with the following exception: **Ramin:** "Prefatory Prayers (Kyrie Eleison)."

MATA HARI

Orchestrations by Russell **Bennett**. (Additional orchestrations by Hans **Spialek**, Jay Brower, Philip J. **Lang**, Edward Thomas, and Colin Romoff.)

Tryout: November 18, 1967, Washington, D.C. (National). Closed December 9, Washington, D.C.

Music by Edward Thomas, lyrics by Martin Charnin. Suggested by events in the life of Mata Hari. Musical direction and vocal arrangements by Colin Romoff. Dance arrangements by Roger Adams. Other participants: David Merrick (producer); Vincente Minnelli (director); Jack Cole (choreographer).

Invoices are preserved in Bennett's ledger. Base page rate: $6.90.

Bennett: "Arabic," "The Choice Is Yours" (see below), "Curiousity," "Everyone Has Something to Hide," Finale act I, "Hello, Yank," "How Young You Were Tonight," "I Don't See Him Much Any More," "I'm Saving Myself for a Soldier," "Is This Fact?" "Maman," "No More than a Moment," Prelude, "Salon Waltz," "Sextet" (and reprise), "Soliloquy," "This Is Not a Very Nice War," "You Have No Idea."

Spialek: "Chalet," "I'm Saving Myself for a Soldier" (reprise), "Temporary Overture," various utilities.

Brower: Finale ("Marseillaise"), "Taxicab," various incidentals.

Thomas (the composer): "In Madrid," "There Will Be Love."

Lang: "Malaysian."

Romoff: "Backstage."

Other scores:

"Blue Ballet" and "White Ballet" are by Brower; "Red Ballet" is by Brower and Bennett.

"The Choice Is Yours" is by Bennett; "Bolero version" is by Romoff and Bennett.

This turned out to be the final credited show for the seventy-three-year-old Bennett, although he continued to contribute charts to other musicals (through the 1975 revue *Rodgers & Hart*). It was also apparently the final orchestration assignment of Spialek, who was two months older than Bennett. (Hans later supervised the reconstruction of *On Your Toes* in 1983, and also worked as a copyist on such shows as *A Chorus Line*.) It was a fitting assignment for Spialek; like Mata Hari, he spent time in a Russian prison camp; unlike Mata Hari, he managed to narrowly escape the firing squad. After the quick folding in Washington, *Mata Hari* was rewritten and mounted off-Broadway as *Ballad for a Firing Squad*.

MAY WINE

Orchestrations credited to Don **Walker** and Russell **Bennett**. (Orchestrations by Walker, additional orchestrations by Bennett and possibly others.)

Opened December 5, 1935, St. James, 213 performances. Tryout: November 22, Wilmington, Delaware (Playhouse); November 25, Baltimore (Ford's).

Music by Sigmund Romberg, lyrics by Oscar Hammerstein II. Based on the novel *The Happy Alienist* by Wallace Smith, from a story by Eric von Stroheim. Musical direction by Robert Emmett Dolan. Other participant: Jack Cole (featured).

> WALKER: Because of my close association with Romberg, being in charge of his orchestrations for his radio program, he insisted that I score *May Wine*. It was my first show! There was a lot of music in it. In the final week of rehearsal, with problems I had to handle on the radio program, Rommie asked me if I would mind if we had Russell Bennett orchestrate one fairly long number. I reluctantly agreed.

ME AND JULIET

Orchestrations (mostly) by Don **Walker**. (Additional orchestrations by Hans **Spialek**, Robert **Ginzler**, and Jack Mason.)

Opened May 28, 1953, Majestic, 358 performances. Tryout: April 20, Cleveland (Hanna); May 6, Boston (Shubert).

Music by Richard Rodgers, lyrics and book by Oscar Hammerstein II. Musical direction by Salvatore Dell'Isola. Vocal arrangements by Don Walker. Dance arrangements by Roger Adams. Other participants: Richard Rodgers and Oscar Hammerstein II (producers); George Abbott (director).

The partiturs are at the offices of the Rodgers & Hammerstein Organization. Invoices are in the Walker Collection at the Library of Congress. Base page rate: $6.04. Invoices indicate: Walker (85%), Spialek (8%). Walker also turned in bills for several vocal arrangements, including "Marriage Type Love" and "Keep It Gay."

The orchestrations are by Walker, with the following exceptions:

Spialek: "Act Two Sequence" (a 100-page chart, not included in the published vocal score).

Ginzler: "Act Two Sequence Part D," "Alley Scene," "Audition."

Mason: utilities ("Keep It Gay," "Marriage Type Love," "No Other Love").

Pianist/vocalist Barbara Carroll performed her two numbers ("A Very Special Day" and "That's the Way It Happens") onstage with two musicians. Walker's final invoice explains that these numbers were "not orchestrated under the terms of my contract with Mr. Rodgers, and are therefore omitted from this bill."

From the *New York Times* review of the original cast album: "Even the better moments are handicapped by the repetitiously patterned arrangements of Don Walker and the heavy hand of conductor Salvatore Dell'Isola."

THANKS AND WISHES   From Walker to Abbott: "Hope a real easy one comes along someday."

From Abbott to Walker: "We deserve each other, and a rest." ("We Deserve Each Other" was a lighthearted insult duet in the second act.)

From Walker to star Joan McCracken (Fosse), who had a notoriously weak voice: "A flat, B flat, what's the difference? Best, Don Walker."

Instr.: 5 reed, 8 brass (4 tpt, 3 tb, 1 hrn), 9? strings (6? vln, 1 vla, 1 c, 1 b), piano, harp, perc = 25? total.

MEET ME IN ST. LOUIS (1960 VERSION)

Orchestrations credited to Philip J. **Lang**. (Additional orchestrators, if any, unknown.)
Tryout: June 9, 1960, St. Louis (Muny). Closed St. Louis.
Music and lyrics by Hugh Martin and Ralph Blane. A stage version of the film, from *The Kensington Stories* by Sally Benson. Other participant: Sally Benson (librettist).

MEET ME IN ST. LOUIS (1989 VERSION)

Orchestrations by Michael Gibson. (Additional orchestrations by Frederick Willard, Jim Tyler, Art Harris, and possibly others.)
Opened November 2, 1989, Gershwin, 253 performances.
Musical direction by Bruce Pomahac. Vocal arrangements by Hugh Martin and Bruce Pomahac. Dance arrangements by James Raitt. Other participants: Hugh Wheeler (librettist); George Hearn (star).

> HUGH MARTIN: I was disappointed by the orchestrations. Michael Gibson was very nice, I liked him; but he farmed out a lot. I made a point of finding out who did the songs I especially liked, and all of them had been farmed out.

According to Bruce Pomahac, most of the orchestrations were done by Gibson, with others by Jim Tyler and some incidentals by Art Harris. The chart Martin most liked, "You Are for Loving," was by Tyler.

MEET THE PEOPLE 1955

Orchestrations credited to Joe Glover. (Additional orchestrators, if any, unknown.)
Opened April 13, 1955, Café Theatre, Paramount Hotel (off-Broadway), 13 performances.
A new edition of the 1940 revue. Music by Jay Gorney, lyrics by Henry Myers and Edward Eliscu. Musical direction by Herb Schutz. Other participants: Lionel Stander and Jay Gorney (producers).

MEMPHIS BOUND

Orchestrations credited to Don **Walker**. "Additional orchestrations for Mr. Robinson" by Ted **Royal**. (Additional orchestrators unknown.)
Opened May 24, 1945, Broadway, 36 performances. Tryout: May 3, Boston (Colonial).
Music and lyrics by Don Walker and Clay Warnick. A revised version of the operetta *H.M.S. Pinafore* by W. S. Gilbert and Arthur Sullivan. Musical direction by Charles Sanford. Vocal arrangements by Clay Warnick. Other participants: Vinton Freedley (production supervisor); "with gratitude to W. S. Gilbert and Sir Arthur Sullivan"; Bill Robinson (star).

Society bandleader Meyer Davis, the original producer of *Memphis Bound*, approached George S. Kaufman to direct Walker and Warnick's adaptation of *H.M.S. Pinafore*. Kaufman turned the project down, but quickly decided to write his own adaptation of the Gilbert & Sullivan operetta; set in Hollywood, it became *Hollywood Pinafore*. Kaufman's partner, Max Gordon, produced it, "in association with Meyer Davis." Walker and Warnick cried foul, but to little avail. The two musicals were produced simultaneously, this one with Bill Robinson and the other with the team of William Gaxton & Victor Moore. Both reupholstered *Pinafores* were quick failures.

MERLIN

Orchestrations credited to Larry **Wilcox**. (Additional orchestrators, if any, unknown.)

Opened February 13, 1983, Mark Hellinger, 199 performances. Tryout: none.

Music by Elmer Bernstein, lyrics by Don Black. Musical direction and vocal arrangements by David Spear. Dance arrangements by Mark Hummel. Other participants: Ivan Reitman (director); Doug Henning (magic illusions, star); Chita Rivera (star); Christian Slater (featured); Nathan Lane (featured).

MEXICAN HAYRIDE

Orchestrations credited to Russell **Bennett** and Ted **Royal**. (Additional orchestrators unknown.)

Opened January 28, 1944, Winter Garden, 481 performances. Tryout: December 29, 1943, Boston (Shubert).

Music and lyrics by Cole Porter. Musical direction by Harry Levant. Vocal arrangements by William Parson. Other participants: Michael Todd (producer); Herbert & Dorothy Fields (librettists); Bobby Clark (star).

The song "Carlotta," sung by Corinna Mura, reportedly underwent seven different orchestrations before opening night—despite which it never did amount to much.

MICHAEL TODD'S PEEP SHOW

Orchestrations credited to Ken Hopkins and Irwin **Kostal**. (Additional orchestrators, if any, unknown.)

Opened June 28, 1950, Winter Garden, 278 performances.

A revue. Music by various composers, including Bhumibol Chakraband (aka the King of Siam [Thailand]), Sammy Fain, Jule Styne, and Harold Rome, lyrics by Herb Magidson, Bob Hilliard, and Harold Rome. Musical direction and vocal arrangements by Clay Warnick. Musical arrangements by Mel Pahl. "Music for all dances and production numbers arranged by Mel Pahl." Other participants: Michael Todd (producer); Bobby Clark (sketches, direction).

According to Kostal, orchestrator Kenyon Hopkins—who didn't have much of a feel for burlesque—was terminated early on, leaving Kostal to do most of the show.

MILK AND HONEY

Orchestrations credited to Hershy **Kay** and Eddie **Sauter**. (Additional orchestrators, if any, unknown.)

Opened October 10, 1961, Martin Beck, 543 performances. Tryout: August 28, New Haven (Shubert); September 5, Boston (Colonial).

Music and lyrics by Jerry Herman. Musical direction by Max Goberman. Vocal arrangements by Robert De Cormier. Dance arrangements by Genevieve Pitot. Other participants: Albert Marre (director); Donald Saddler (choreographer); Robert Weede (star); Mimi Benzell (star); Molly Picon (star).

The location of the partiturs is unknown except for "The Wedding" (including "Let's Not Waste a Moment/There's No Reason in the World" reprise), by Kay, which is in the possession of Don Pippin.

> JERRY HERMAN: I wanted as close to a classical sound as I could find, even though I was writing show music. Because of Weede and Benzell, who were opera stars, and some of the melodic lines, it was more operetta than musical comedy. I always admired Hershy; it turned out to be the right sound. I thought it gave the show a special sound, that none of my other shows had, almost semi-classical.

After forty-five years, Herman recalls that Kay did most of the show, with Sauter providing (he thinks) "As Simple as That," "Chin Up Ladies," and "I Will Follow You." It also seems likely that Sauter provided the comedic orchestration for "Hymn to Hymie." Herman also gives full praise to the contributions of arrangers Genevieve Pitot and Bob De Cormier.

(See page 51.)

MINNIE'S BOYS

Orchestrations credited to Ralph **Burns**. (Additional orchestrators, if any, unknown.)

Opened March 26, 1970, Imperial, 80 performances. Tryout: none.

Music by Larry Grossman, lyrics by Hal Hackady. Suggested by events in the lives of the Marx Bros. Musical direction and vocal arrangements by John Berkman. Dance arrangements and incidental music by Marvin Hamlisch and Peter Howard. Other participants: Groucho Marx (production consultant); Shelley Winters (star).

Burns provided some especially nice harp writing (especially in the songs "Mama a Rainbow" and "Empty")—fitting, in that one of the real-life characters was America's most famous harpist.

MISS LIBERTY

Orchestrations by Don **Walker**. (Additional orchestrations by Robert **Ginzler**, Russell **Bennett**, and Joe Glover.)

Opened July 15, 1949, Imperial, 308 performances. Tryout: June 13, Philadelphia (Forrest).
Music and lyrics by Irving Berlin. Musical direction and vocal arrangements by Jay S.
   Blackton. Piano arrangements by Helmy Kresa. Dance arrangements by Genevieve
   Pitot. "The Train" ballet composed and arranged by Trude Rittman. Other partici-
   pants: Irving Berlin, Robert E. Sherwood, and Moss Hart (producers); Moss Hart
   (director); Jerome Robbins (choreographer); Robert E. Sherwood (librettist).

The partiturs are in the Berlin Collection at the Library of Congress. Base page rate: $5.10.
   The orchestrations are by Walker, with the following exceptions:
   Ginzler: "Fight Music," "Finale Ultimo," "Homework Reprise," "March Crossover,"
utility ("Policeman's Ball").
   Bennett: "Paris Wakes Up," "The Train" Ballet.
   Glover: "New Finale Act II."
   Other scores:
   "Give Me Your Tired, Your Poor" is by Walker (except for the reeds and brass in the
4-bar intro, by Glover).
   "Let's Take an Old-Fashioned Walk": there are three versions. The first is an early one
by Ginzler; the second one, also by Ginzler, appears to have been used during the tryout.
The third, by Walker, appears to incorporate some of Ginzler's second version. "Old-
Fashioned Walk Scene Change" is by Ginzler.
   "Little Fish in a Big Pond" (song and dance) is by Walker. At the modulation from the
dance back into the song, there are 2 bars by Bennett, literally pasted onto the partitur.
   "Miss Liberty" is by Walker, with several substantial sections of revisions by Ginzler.
   "Mr. Monotony": song and ballet are by Walker.

THANKS AND WISHES   From Robbins to Walker: "This is just a reprise of the *Look, Ma* telegram
with three extra choruses thanks a million again thanks a million again and again. Sincerely, Jerry."
   From Berlin to Walker: "Many thanks for that very nice wire. As I wired you for the opening, I think you did a swell job and I hope in spite of the bad reviews we will eventually over-
come them and come through as a hit."

Instr.: 5 reed (including 5 sax, 5 clr, 3 fl), 6 brass (3 tpt, 2 tb, 1 hrn), 13 strings (8 vln, 2 vla, 2 c, b), piano/ce-
lesta, harp, perc = 27 total.

MISS MOFFAT

Orchestrations credited to Robert M. Freedman. (Additional orchestrators, if any, un-
   known.)
Tryout: October 10, 1974, Philadelphia (Shubert). Closed October 17, Philadelphia.
Music by Albert Hague, lyrics by Emlyn Williams. Based on the play *The Corn Is Green* by
   Emlyn Williams. Musical direction by Jay Blackton. Other participants: Joshua Logan
   (director, co-librettist); Emlyn Williams (co-librettist); Bette Davis (star).

MR. PRESIDENT

Orchestrations by Philip J. **Lang.** (Additional orchestrations by Jack Elliott.)
Opened October 20, 1962, St. James, 265 performances. Tryout: August 27, Boston
   (Colonial); September 25, Washington, D.C. (National).

Music and lyrics by Irving Berlin. Musical direction and underscoring by Jay Blackton.
Dance arrangements by Jack Elliott. Other participants: Leland Hayward (producer);
Joshua Logan (director); Peter Gennaro (choreographer); Howard Lindsay and Rus-
sell Crouse (librettists); Nanette Fabray (star).

The partiturs are in the Berlin Collection at the Library of Congress.

The orchestrations are by Lang, with the following exceptions:

Elliott: "Opening Twist" (leading to Lang's "Let's Go Back to the Waltz"), "President
Change and Dance #8" ("Not the Kennedys" incidental), "The Trip" (extended scene
leading to Lang's "They Love Me").

Other scores:

"Empty Pockets Filled with Love" is by Lang, with a 5-bar interlude ("I don't want
silver, I don't want gold") by Elliott.

"In Our Hide-Away": there are two versions by Lang, one of which includes a 28-bar
dance interlude by Elliott.

"Let's Go Back to the Waltz": song is by Lang; extended dance is by Elliott; "Vocal
Ending for Recording" is by Lang.

"The Only Dance I Know (Song for Belly Dancer)": there are three versions; in each,
song is by Lang and dance by Elliott.

"Washington Twist": there are three versions; in each, song is by Lang and dance by
Elliott.

"You Need a Hobby": song is by Lang; extended dance—with sections entitled
"Corny," "Samba," "Tango," "Cha-cha-cha," "Polka," "Charleston"—is by Elliott.

There are three versions of at least four numbers, and two each of several more. Such
constant changing indicates a show in severe trouble; one suspects that they kept trying
to make the orchestrations sound more exciting because the seventy-four-year-old composer was incapable of providing more exciting songs.

Instr.: 6 reed, 7 brass (3 tpt, 2 tb, 2 hrn), ? strings (vln, vla, c, b), piano/celesta, harp, guitar, perc.

MR. WONDERFUL

Orchestrations credited to Ted **Royal** and Morton L. Stevens. (Additional orchestrations
by Marion Evans, Don Costa, Sy Oliver, and others.)

Opened March 22, 1956, Broadway, 383 performances. Tryout: February 21, Philadelphia (Shubert).

Music and lyrics by Jerry Bock, Larry Holofcener, and George Weiss. Musical direction
by Morton L. Stevens. Vocal arrangements by Hugh Martin (uncredited). Musical and
vocal supervision by Oscar Kosarin. Other participants: Jule Styne (producer, "production conceived by"); Joseph Stein (co-librettist); Sammy Davis, Jr. (star); Chita
Rivera (featured).

Morty Stevens was Sammy Davis's musical director. According to Jerry Bock, Stevens orchestrated most of Davis's numbers; the "theatrical" numbers were done by Royal (by
Royal and his ghosts, that is, of whom Bock was unaware).

Marion Evans gave a further explanation: the nightclub section, which used interpolated songs by other composers, was lifted from Sammy's recent date at the Copa. When

Davis started working as a single act, shortly before *Mr. Wonderful*, he hired Stevens as his musical director. Stevens asked Evans—a fellow student at Juilliard—and Don Costa to do the Copa charts, which wound up in the pit of *Mr. Wonderful*.

Evans also worked on the "show" section of the score, along with Royal's other assistants. His only specific recollection was "Too Close for Comfort": part 1 is by Sy Oliver; part 2—the stop-time, soft shoe encore—is by Evans. Hugh Martin's contract, at the Styne Office, provides $1,750 for three vocal arrangements ("1617 Broadway," "Charlie Welch," and perhaps the quartet "I've Been Too Busy").

MISTRESS OF THE INN

Orchestrations credited to Don **Walker**. (Additional orchestrators, if any, unknown.)

Tryout: August 1957, New Hope, Pennsylvania (Bucks County Playhouse).

Music by Don Walker, lyrics and book by Ira Wallach. Based on the play by Carlo Goldoni. Musical direction by Bruce Prince-Joseph. Other participants: Jack Cassidy (featured); Beatrice Arthur (featured); Gene Saks (featured).

MOLLY

Orchestrations credited to Eddie **Sauter**. (Additional orchestrators, if any, unknown.)

Opened November 1, 1973, Alvin, 68 performances. Tryout: September, Boston (Shubert).

Music by Jerry Livingston, lyrics by Mack David and Leonard Adelson. Based on the radio and television series *The Goldbergs* by Gertrude Berg. Musical direction and vocal arrangements by Jerry Goldberg. Dance arrangements by Arnold Gross. Other participants: Alan Arkin (replacement director); Grover Dale (replacement choreographer); Kaye Ballard (star).

A MONTH OF SUNDAYS

Orchestrations credited to Ted **Royal**. (Additional orchestrators, if any, unknown.)

Tryout: December 25, 1951, Boston (Shubert). Closed January 26, 1952, Philadelphia (Forrest).

Music by Albert Selden, lyrics, book, and direction by B. G. (Burt) Shevelove. Based on the play *Excursion* by Victor Wolfson. Musical direction and vocal arrangements by Lehman Engel. Dance arrangements by David Baker (and John Morris). Other participants: Nancy Walker (star); Richard Kiley (featured).

THE MOST HAPPY FELLA

Orchestrations (mostly) by Don **Walker**. (Additional orchestrations by Robert **Ginzler**, with Mark Bucci.)

Opened May 3, 1956, Imperial, 676 performances. Tryout: March 13, Boston (Shubert); April 10, Philadelphia (Shubert).

Music, lyrics, and book by Frank Loesser. Based on the play *They Knew What They Wanted* by Sidney Howard. Musical direction and choral direction by Herbert Greene. Musical assistants, Tommy Goodman and Abba Bogin. Other participants: Kermit Bloomgarden and Lynn Loesser (producers); Robert Weede (star); Jo Sullivan (star); Susan Johnson (featured).

The partiturs are at the Loesser office. Invoices are in the Walker Collection at the Library of Congress. Base page rate: $6.21.

The orchestrations are by Walker, with the following exceptions:

Ginzler: "Fresno Beauties," interior sections of "Abbondanza" and minor incidentals.

Bucci: minor incidentals.

> WALKER: One of the landmarks of what I've done in this business. I play it, the 3-record complete recording, once a year, just to remind myself of what I did. We went into preliminary rehearsals with two pianos, in December. Frank made a special deal with Equity so he could record it, he said because it was a first-time director. They did it with pianos in December, so I had that track and I started to orchestrate after Christmas. The show went into full rehearsals in February. There were changes, but at least I had the basis to make the changes. Where Frank made his mistake was that when he went from just pure musical numbers to recitative or dialogue, he didn't realize how long that would take. When we opened in Boston, it ran until 12:20. To go into rehearsal with a show like that, and not have timed it, was crazy. But he wanted to hear every note he'd written, so how are you going to cut it? The way to cut that show would have been to rewrite, consolidate. Instead, Frank just took out numbers and substituted dialogue which took about a third of the time, and that's what's wrong with it. I mean, that was a great opera, really. There were two marvelous songs for the character of the sister—he invented the character, it wasn't in the original play. Well, he took out most of the sister's role, cut her down. She had an aria, "You look at me with the eyes of a stranger," which was one of the most marvelous things Frank ever wrote. And he took it out.

Virtually all of the show is by Walker, with very minor assists (one song plus connective bridgework) by Ginzler and Bucci.

Loesser had two assistants, pianist Tommy Goodman (who transcribed most of the music) and Abba Bogin (who was brought in to work mostly on the choral parts and went on to conduct the touring company).

> BOGIN: Basically, Frank was a guy who knew what he wanted, but he very often was not able technically to put it down the way he wanted it. When you played it back, he would listen and say "That's not what I wrote, that's not what I wanted." At orchestra readings, Frank would say: "I don't want this, I don't want that." Don would take it back and fix it. And Frank would say, "That's it!" He pretty much supervised everything. There were lots of little bridges and things that I wrote, or Don Walker or Tommy Goodman wrote. Eight-bar transitions, things like that. Eventually, it would get okayed by Frank.

DON'S INSTRUCTIONS TO MUSICIANS   In "Sposalizio," marked on the trumpet solo at "the lanterns growing": "Loesser Italiano Style—try valiantly not to kill singers."

THANKS AND WISHES   The Walker Collection includes an opening night note from Susan Johnson, who played the long-suffering waitress Cleo (and in one memorable moment laments the stingy tips she receives): an index card saying, "And one Canadian dime for good luck—plus many thanx!" Taped to the card: one Canadian dime.

Instr.: 4 reed (including 4 clr, 3 fl), 7 brass (2 tpt, 2 tb, 3 hrn), 22 strings (12 vln, 4 vla, 4 c, 2 b), harp, guitar, 2 perc (1 with accordion/celesta) = 37 total.

(See page 107.)

A MOTHER'S KISSES

Orchestrations credited to Jack Andrews (replaced by Larry **Wilcox**). (Additional orchestrators, if any, unknown.)

Tryout: September 23, 1968, New Haven (Shubert). Closed October 19, Baltimore (Mechanic).

Music and lyrics by Richard Adler. Based on the novel by Bruce Jay Friedman. Musical direction and vocal arrangements by Colin Romoff. Dance arrangements by Roger Adams. Other participants: Gene Saks (director); Onna White (choreographer); Bruce Jay Friedman (librettist); Beatrice Arthur (star).

> RED PRESS: I was playing the tryout in New Haven. The arranger went to his hotel room, filled the bathtub, and slit his wrists. The water overflowed out into the hall, the hotel manager found him and got him to the hospital in time.

Press didn't remember whether it was one of the orchestrators or one of the other arrangers. Ken Billington, who was there as the assistant to lighting designer Tharon Musser, confirms that it was Roger Adams.

MURDER AT THE VANITIES

Orchestrations uncredited. (Orchestrations by Edward B. Powell, Hans **Spialek**, and others.)

Opened September 8, 1933, New Amsterdam, 207 performances. Tryout: unknown.

Music and lyrics by various writers. Musical direction by Ray Kavanaugh. Other participants: Earl Carroll (producer, director, co-librettist); Bela Lugosi (star).

MUSIC IN MY HEART

Orchestrations credited to Hans **Spialek**. (Additional orchestrators unknown.)

Opened October 2, 1947, Adelphi, 124 performances. Tryout: (as *Song Without Words*) August 20, 1945, Los Angeles (Philharmonic Auditorium).

"With melodies by Tchaikovsky," adapted by Franz Steininger, lyrics by Forman Brown. Musical direction by Franz Steininger. Vocal arrangements by Clay Warnick.

An earlier version of this show (without Spialek's participation) was given a tryout in 1945, under the title *Song Without Words*. A third version, *The Lady from Paris*—presumably using Spialek's charts—opened September 26, 1950, in Philadelphia (Erlanger) and shuttered there after two weeks.

MUSIC IN THE AIR

Orchestrations (totally) by Russell **Bennett**.

Opened November 8, 1932, Alvin, 342 performances. Tryout: October 17, Philadelphia (Garrick).

Music by Jerome Kern, lyrics and book by Oscar Hammerstein II. Musical direction by Victor Baravelle. Other participants: Jerome Kern and Oscar Hammerstein II (co-directors).

The partiturs are in the Kern Collection at the Library of Congress.

Instr.: 5 reed (including 2 clr, 2 fl/picc), 4 brass (2 tpt, 1 tb, 1 hrn), 15? strings (7? vln, 4? vla, 3? c, 1 b), 2 piano (1 organ, 1 cel), harp, perc = 28? total.

MUSIC IN THE AIR (1951 REVIVAL)

Orchestrations credited to Russell **Bennett**. (Additional orchestrators, if any, unknown.)

Opened October 8, 1951, Ziegfeld, 56 performances. Tryout: September 25, Olney, Maryland (Olney).

Musical direction by Maurice Levine. Other participant: Oscar Hammerstein II (director).

Bennett's invoices are preserved in his ledger. Base page rate: $4.35.

Bennett: "After Frieda's Bedroom," "All the Things You Are" (cut), Overture (full score, plus an 8-page section for two solo pianos).

Bennett presented invoices for only three numbers plus underscoring, totaling 128 pages (which indicates that this revival used the stock & amateur rental materials). He also received a $100 fee for "laying out transpositions, editing and revising."

MUSIC IS

Orchestrations (mostly) by Hershy **Kay**. (Additional orchestrations by Jim Tyler.)

Opened December 20, 1976, St. James, 8 performances. Tryout: October 13, Seattle, Washington (Seattle Rep); November 10, Washington, D.C. (Eisenhower).

Music by Richard Adler, lyrics by Will Holt. Based on the play *Twelfth Night* by William Shakespeare. Musical direction by Paul Gemignani. Vocal and dance arrangements by William Cox. Other participants: Richard Adler (co-producer); George Abbott (director, librettist); Patricia Birch (choreographer).

The partiturs are at the Library of Congress.

The orchestrations are by Kay, except as noted:

Tyler: "I Am It," "Should I Speak of Loving You," "Time Goes By."

Richard Adler recalls that he fired Hershy Kay, whom he considered the most unpleasant person with whom he worked in his career. The scores, though, indicate that Kay finished most of the show.

THE MUSIC MAN

Orchestrations by Don **Walker**. (Additional orchestrations by Sidney Fine, Irwin **Kostal**, Seymour "Red" **Ginzler**, Walter Eiger, and Laurence Rosenthal.)

Opened December 19, 1957, Majestic, 1,375 performances. Tryout: November 18, Philadelphia (Shubert).

Music, lyrics, and book by Meredith Willson. Based on the memoir *And There I Stood with My Piccolo* by Meredith Willson. Musical direction and vocal arrangements by Herbert Greene. Dance arrangements by Laurence Rosenthal. Other participants: Kermit Bloomgarden (producer); Frank Loesser/Frank Productions (associate producer); Herbert Greene (associate producer); Morton Da Costa (director); Onna White (choreographer); Robert Preston (star); Barbara Cook (featured).

The partiturs are at Music Theatre International. Invoices are in the Walker Collection at the Library of Congress. Base page rate: $5.70.

Invoices indicate: Walker (38%), Fine (33%), Kostal (12%), Ginzler (10%).

Walker: "Rock Island" (see below), "Train Opening," "Ya Got Trouble" (see below).

Fine: bows ("Seventy-Six Trombones"), "Chase," "Double Reprise," Entr'acte, "Gary, Indiana," "Goodnight My Someone" (see below), "If You Don't Mind My Saying So (Piano Lesson)," "Iowa Stubborn," "Pick a Little, Talk a Little" (song and reprise).

Kostal: "Lida Rose (Will I Ever Tell You)," "The Sadder but Wiser Girl," "Shipoopi" (including dance: part I "Energetic Couple," part II "Eccentric Couple," and part III "One-Step").

Ginzler: exit music, Finale act I, Finale act II, "The Wells Fargo Wagon."

Eiger: "Till There Was You" (song, reprise, and incidental).

Rosenthal: "Marian the Librarian Dance."

Other scores:

"Cross-Over (Footbridge)": first 18 bars are by Fine; 35-bar "Footbridge Waltz" ("It's You") is by Walker; the rest alternates between Walker and Ginzler.

"Goodnight My Someone" is mostly by Fine, with much of the bassoon, English horn, and bass clarinet rewritten by Ginzler.

"Ice Cream Sociable" is mostly by Kostal, with the final section by Ginzler.

"Marian the Librarian": first part is by Fine; the rest (beginning with "now in the moonlight") is by Kostal.

"My White Knight": first 32 bars (through "than he is in him-") are by Fine. Remainder is mostly by Walker, except for ending (starting with the final word "die") by Fine.

"Overture III" is mostly by Walker (who also did Overtures I and II). Twelve bars of the "Wells Fargo" section have violins, piano, and some reeds filled in by Fine. The abbreviated Overture on the cast album is entirely by Walker, segueing into "Train Opening."

"Rock Island (Train Talk)" is by Walker. The orchestration was cut in Philadelphia, where it was determined that the song was more effective a cappella.

"Seventy-Six Trombones" (song) is mostly shared by Walker (on violin, brass, and bass sax parts) and Ginzler (on percussion, piano, and most of the reeds). In the "Dixieland" section, the trombones and clarinets are Walker, the rest Ginzler. The 16-bar chorus section ("Seventy-six trombones hit the counterpoint") is by Fine. There is also a 10-page dance by Rosenthal. The verse ("May I have your attention please") is a separate score, entitled "Trouble Reprise," by Walker.

"Train Opening" is by Walker and Ginzler.

The partitur for "Ya Got Trouble" contains two choral interludes: a 12-bar section just before "and all week long your River City youth'll be fritterin' away," and an 8-bar section before "now I know all you folks are the right kind-a' parents." These were presumably included to give the singer breathing room, but Bob Preston didn't need it.

The use of so many orchestrators can be explained by Walker's (and Ginzler's) conflicting obligations. Walker became conductor for the television show *Your Hit Parade* on July 15, 1957, with Ginzler under contract as his orchestrator. Walker and *Your Hit Parade* were not a good combination, and his contract was mutually terminated on December 5, as *Music Man* was ending its pre-Broadway tryout.

From Walker to general manager Max Allentuck, five months after the opening:

Sidney [Fine] is not happy with his billing. I assure you that this is the first I have known of it, since he seemed quite satisfied when we opened. However, since the show is a great hit it is only natural that he would like to be as prominently accredited as possible. Under union regulations he is actually entitled to different credit than he is receiving, and if he demands the program you are required by the union to give it to him. Therefore, I am officially notifying you that I have been instructed by Local 802 to bill the orchestrations as follows. In New York the following credits must be given, in as prominent a place as possible: ADDITIONAL ORCHESTRATIONS by Sidney Fine, and Irwin Kostal, Seymour Ginzler, Walter Eiger. In the California production the following credit must be given, as close to mine as physically possible: ADDITIONAL ORCHESTRATIONS by Sidney Fine. And, in as good a position as possible, wherever you can find the space, ASSOCIATE ARRANGERS: Irwin Kostal, Seymour Ginzler, Walter Eiger.

DON'S INSTRUCTIONS TO MUSICIANS   Walker has written detailed blocking on the partitur for the Overture. Samples: "Conductor blows police whistle and stands up"; "the whole right side of the orchestra stands up"; "violins stand up" (at "Till There Was You").

On "Seventy-Six Trombones," at end of song portion: "Segue to Herb (Conway Creatore Sousa Pryor Handy Liberatti) Greene's Follies."

Instr.: 5 reed, 6 brass (3 tpt, 3 tb/1 tuba), 13? strings (8? vln, 0 vla, 4 c, 1 b), piano, perc = 26? total. (See pages 107, 264.)

MUSIC! MUSIC!

Orchestrations credited to Elliot Lawrence. Additional orchestrations by Al Cohn, William Elton, and possibly others.

Opened April 11, 1974, City Center, 37 performances.

A revue. Music and lyrics by various writers. Musical supervision by Lehman Engel. Musical direction and vocal arrangements by John Lesko. Dance arrangements by Wally Harper. Other participants: Alan Jay Lerner ("Footnotes"); Martin Charnin (director); Tony Stevens (choreographer); Larry Kert (featured); Donna McKechnie (featured); Gene Nelson (featured); Karen Morrow (featured).

A MUSICAL JUBILEE

Orchestrations credited to Philip J. Lang, Hershy Kay, and Elman Anderson. (Additional orchestrators, if any, unknown.)
Opened November 13, 1975, St. James, 92 performances.
A revue. Music and lyrics by various writers. Musical supervision by Lehman Engel. Musical direction by John Lesko. Dance arrangements and incidental music by Trude Rittman. Other participants: Theatre Guild (producer); Morton Da Costa (director); John Raitt (star); Cyril Ritchard (star); Tammy Grimes (star); Lillian Gish (star).

MY DARLIN' AIDA

Orchestrations credited to Hans **Spialek**. (Additional orchestrators, if any, unknown.)
Opened October 27, 1952, Winter Garden, 89 performances.
Music by Giuseppe Verdi, lyrics, book, and direction by Charles Friedman. A revised version of the opera *Aida*. Music adapted by Hans Spialek. Musical direction by Franz Allers. Vocal direction by Robert Shaw. Dance arrangements by Trude Rittman.

Charles Friedman, who had directed *Carmen Jones*—Oscar Hammerstein's reworking of Bizet's *Carmen*, set in the South during World War II—attempted to do the same with Verdi. *My Darlin' Aida* was notable as one of the most opulent productions of its day, but this Civil War adaptation did not follow *Carmen Jones* to success.

MY DEAR PUBLIC

Orchestrations credited to Hans **Spialek**, Don **Walker**, and Ted **Royal**. (Additional orchestrators, if any, unknown.)
Tryout: March 5, 1942, New Haven (Shubert). Closed March 28, Philadelphia.
Music and lyrics by Irving Caesar, Sam Lerner, and Gerald Marks. Musical direction by Gene Salzar. Other participants: Irving Caesar (producer, co-librettist); Joe Smith & Charles Dale (stars); Mitzi Green (star).

Two special acts of note were included in the cast. The singing group the Martins, including Hugh Martin and Ralph Blane, were featured. Also present was the nightclub act the Revuers, a quintet that included Betty Comden, Adolph Green, and Judith Tuvim (soon to become Judy Holliday). The Revuers wrote the three numbers they performed, including "The Baroness Bazooka."

MY DEAR PUBLIC (1943 REVISION)

Orchestrations credited to Hans **Spialek** and Ted **Royal**. (Additional orchestrators, if any, unknown.)

Opened September 9, 1943, 46th Street, 45 performances. Tryout: August 15.

Music and lyrics by Irving Caesar, Sam Lerner, and Gerald Marks. Musical direction by
Harry Levant. Vocal arrangements by Buck (Clay) Warnick. Other participants: Irving
Caesar (producer, co-librettist); Willie Howard (star); Nanette Fabray (featured).

> SPIALEK: The deadliest stage offering of all times. *My Dear Public* appeared in two equally bad
> versions, with two different, equally talented casts but unfortunately with the same book.

MY FAIR LADY

Orchestrations by Russell Bennett and Philip J. **Lang**. (Additional orchestrations by Jack
Mason.)

Opened March 15, 1956, Mark Hellinger, 2,717 performances. Tryout: February 4, New
Haven (Shubert); February 15, Philadelphia (Erlanger).

Music by Frederick Loewe, lyrics and book by Alan Jay Lerner. Based on the play *Pyg-
malion* by George Bernard Shaw. Musical direction by Franz Allers. Assistant conductor, Peter Howard. Choral arrangements by Gino Smart. Dance arrangements by
Trude Rittman. Other participants: Herman Levin (producer); Moss Hart (director);
Rex Harrison (star); Julie Andrews (star).

The partiturs are in the American Musical Theatre Collection at the Library of Congress.
Invoices are preserved in Bennett's ledger. Base page rate: $5.70. Invoices indicate: Bennett
(59%), Lang (37%).

The orchestrations are by Bennett, with the following exceptions:

Lang: bows, "Eliza's Entrance," "Get Me to the Church on Time" (song, 81 pages;
chorale, 11 pages; ballet, 51 pages; utility, 18 pages), "Hymn to Him (Why Can't a
Woman Be More Like a Man)," "On the Street Where You Live" (see below), "Opening
Scene (Covent Garden)," "Promenade," utilities ("I Could Have Danced," "On the Street
Where You Live," "Why Can't the English?").

Mason: "A Little Bit of Luck" (except for the added 20-bar extension ["He hasn't got
a thruppence in his pocket"] by Lang), "A Little Bit of Luck" (reprise), "Say a Prayer for
Me Tonight" (cut), utility ("Wouldn't It Be Loverly?").

Other scores:

"On the Street Where You Live" is mostly by Lang. The original, extended verse (by
Lang) was cut and replaced by a different and considerably shorter verse by Bennett. There
is also an earlier, cut version of this song (verse and refrain) by Lang.

"Why Can't the English?" is by Bennett until measure 96 ("set a good example"), with
the rest of the number by Lang.

"Without You" is by Bennett, replacing an earlier version by Lang.

Bennett was the orchestrator of record until after the Broadway opening. From Bennett's *The Broadway Sound*: "One morning some extra-sensory something called to me and
said, 'Hey! Philip J. Lang has done quite a bit of this and he would probably like you to
give him credit on the program. . . .' The idea struck me very clearly, wherever it came
from. And, wherever it came from, I'm so glad it did." This was highly uncommon for
Bennett; of all his shows for which I've found scores, all but one was ghosted (in some

cases, more so than *My Fair Lady*). The only other time I've found when he altered the credits was when he was replaced by Walker on *Finian's Rainbow*.

The Broadway Sound also includes an editor's note which states, "Lang takes credit for *My Fair Lady*'s 'With a Little Bit of Luck,' 'The Ascot Gavotte,' 'On the Street Where You Live,' 'The Embassy Waltz,' 'Get Me to the Church on Time,' and 'Without You.'" This list, as we can see, is inaccurate; only two of the numbers are in fact by Lang. However, it must be considered that Lang provided this list thirty-odd years later.

After *My Fair Lady* opened, Lang prepared both a reduced stock & amateur orchestration and a "bandstration" (a no-strings orchestration, popular with groups without string players). Thus, Lang's confusion is perhaps understandable; he did orchestrate "Ascot Gavotte" and the others, only not for Broadway.

Samuel "Biff" Liff, production stage manager:

> Rex, who spoke his songs, worked with a pianist. Every day we did the thing, he'd have piano rehearsals and so forth, and he would do the numbers. When we started to put it together, the piano would be there. He was at the orchestra rehearsal. He heard it, and he was a little frightened by it but not overboard.
>
> We got to the dress rehearsal in New Haven, it was the day we opened in the afternoon. A miserable, wintry day. We got to "Accustomed to Her Face." He was out there doing it, and it was a shambles. He could not do it. The orchestra was playing, but he couldn't follow it. It was just too difficult, so he said, "I'm not going on. I'm not going to go on tonight." The problem was, he didn't hear the melody from the piano any more. There was no piano in the orchestra; you only heard the orchestration underneath it. He said, "I'm not doing it."
>
> We sent the company off in the middle of the afternoon; they went to see a movie or something. What I said was, "Give him a chair, let him hear the orchestration. Sit him down right in front of the conductor, let him hear it, so he knows where he comes in." And, finally, he got it. And he went ahead with the opening that night. Now, let us skip over a few months, into the run of the show. One night, we had a very bad accident backstage, where one of the sets fell right in the middle of his number and made an extraordinary explosion. Nobody got hurt. But Rex was out there, and it stopped the show cold because of this large noise. And Rex, he had to stop in the middle of the song. So he turned to Franz Allers, and he said: "Take it from the oboe." I'll never forget it. "Take it from the oboe," he said. I thought, "Jesus, we've come a long way from that orchestra rehearsal."

Instr.: 4 reed, 7 brass (3 tpt, 2 tb, 2 hrn), 16? strings (10?vln, 2 vla, 2 c, 2 b [1 with tuba]), harp, perc = 29? total.

(See pages 18, 122, 261.)

MY ROMANCE

Orchestrations credited to Don **Walker**. (Additional orchestrators, if any, unknown.)

Opened October 19, 1948, Shubert, 95 performances. Tryout: October 6, Boston (Shubert).

Music by Sigmund Romberg, lyrics and book by Rowland Leigh. Based on the play *Romance* by Edward Sheldon. Musical direction by Roland Fiore. Other participants: Messrs. Shubert (producers); Rowland Leigh (director).

An earlier version of this show, with the same lyricist, librettist, director, and leading lady (Anne Jeffreys), but neither composer Romberg nor orchestrator Walker, opened in New Haven on February 12, 1948, and closed in Chicago on May 9.

Instr.: 5 reed (including 1 sax), 6 brass (2 tpt, 1 tb, 3 hrn), 13 strings (8 vln, 2 vla, 2 c, 1 b), harp, perc/celesta = 26 total.

(See page 18.)

MYSTERY MOON

Orchestrations uncredited. (Orchestrations by Hans **Spialek**, Hilding Anderson, Maurice de Packh, Joe Weiss, and possibly others.)

Opened June 23, 1930, Royale, 1 performance. Tryout: unknown.

Music and lyrics by Monte Carlo and Alma Sanders. Book by Fred Herendeen.

Musical direction by Ernie Valle.

NELLIE BLY

Orchestrations credited to Ted **Royal** and Elliott Jacoby. (Additional orchestrators, if any, unknown.)

Opened January 21, 1946, Adelphi, 16 performances. Tryout: December 1945, Philadelphia; Boston.

Music by James Van Heusen, lyrics by Johnny Burke. Suggested by events in the life of Nellie Bly. Musical direction by Charles Drury. Vocal direction by Simon Rady. Dance arrangements by Buster Davis. Other participants: Eddie Cantor (co-producer); William Gaxton & Victor Moore (stars).

NEW FACES

Orchestrations uncredited. (Orchestrations by Hans **Spialek** and others.)

Opened March 15, 1934, Fulton, 149 performances.

A revue. Music and lyrics by various writers (including June [Sillman] Carroll, Nancy Hamilton, and James Shelton). Musical direction by Gus Salzer. Other participants: Charles Dillingham (producer); Leonard Sillman (director, featured); Henry Fonda (featured); Imogene Coca (featured).

NEW FACES OF 1936

Orchestrations uncredited. (Orchestrations by Hans **Spialek**, David Raksin, and others.)

Opened May 19, 1936, Vanderbilt, 192 performances.

A revue. Music and lyrics by various writers (including June Carroll, Nancy Hamilton, and Irvin Graham). Musical direction by Ray Kavanaugh. Other participants: Leonard Sillman (producer, co-director); Van Johnson (featured); Imogene Coca (featured); Ralph Blane (featured).

NEW FACES OF 1952

Orchestrations credited to Ted **Royal**. (Additional orchestrations by Marion Evans, Robert Noeltner, Charles L. Cooke, and possibly others.)

Opened May 16, 1952, Royale, 365 performances. Tryout: Philadelphia.

A revue. Music and lyrics by various writers (including June Carroll, Arthur Siegel, Ronny Graham, and Sheldon Harnick). Musical direction and "special orchestration" by Anton Coppola. Dance arrangements by Trude Rittman. Other participants: Leonard Sillman (producer); Melvin [Mel] Brooks (sketch writer); Ronny Graham (sketch writer, featured); Paul Lynde (sketch writer, featured); Eartha Kitt (featured).

Marion Evans remembers that this show was scored by committee in New York. The day before the tryout opened, Royal's father died and he had to leave the show. Evans and Noeltner remained and finished the job. The show was scored for about a dozen players (as the Royale was a "penalty house"), including three reeds, three brass, and a string quartet.

Speaking fifty years after the fact, Evans recollected that he did "Guess Who I Saw Today" (possibly with fixes by Royal) and "I'm in Love with Miss Logan." Royal did "Boston Beguine" (with fixes by Evans) and "Lizzie Borden." Cooke did "Penny Candy." "Love Is a Simple Thing" was done in several variations, with a couple by Noeltner and one by Evans. Evans also recalls that he did a couple of the several versions of "He Takes Me Off His Income Tax," which were scattered through the revue as a running joke.

NEW FACES OF '56

Orchestrations credited to Ted **Royal**, Albert Sendrey, Joe Glover. (Additional orchestrators, if any, unknown.)

Opened June 14, 1956, Barrymore, 220 performances. Tryout: unknown.

A revue. Music and lyrics by various writers (including June Carroll, Arthur Siegel, Matt Dubey, Harold Karr, and Paul Nassau). Musical direction by Jay Blackton. Other participants: Leonard Sillman (producer); Paul Lynde (director, sketch writer); Neil Simon (sketch writer); Maggie Smith (featured).

NEW FACES OF 1962

Orchestrations credited to Ted **Royal**, Jay Brower, Mark Bucci, Sy Oliver, and David Terry. (Additional orchestrators, if any, unknown.)

Opened February 1, 1962, Alvin, 28 performances. Tryout: December 28, 1961, New Haven (Shubert); elsewhere.

A revue. Music and lyrics by various writers (including June Carroll, Arthur Siegel, and Ronny Graham). Musical direction by Abba Bogin. Dance arrangements by Jack Holmes. Other participant: Leonard Sillman (director, "conceived by").

NEW FACES OF 1968

Orchestrations credited to Lanny Meyers. (Additional orchestrators, if any, unknown.)

Opened May 2, 1968, Booth, 56 performances.

A revue. Music and lyrics by various writers (including June Carroll, Arthur Siegel, Ronny Graham, David Shire, and Richard Maltby, Jr.). Musical direction, Ted Simons. Other participants: Leonard Sillman (producer, stager, "conceived by"); Madeline Kahn (featured); Robert Klein (featured).

NEW GIRL IN TOWN

Orchestrations credited to Russell **Bennett** and Philip J. **Lang**. (Additional orchestrators, if any, unknown.)

Opened May 14, 1957, 46th Street, 431 performances. Tryout: April 8, New Haven (Shubert); April, Boston (Shubert).

Music and lyrics by Bob Merrill. Based on the play *Anna Christie* by Eugene O'Neill. Musical direction by Hal Hastings. Dance music devised by Roger Adams. Other participants: Robert Griffith and Harold Prince (producers); George Abbott (director, librettist); Bob Fosse (choreographer); Gwen Verdon (star).

Bennett's invoices are preserved in his ledger. Base page rate: $5.70.

Bennett: "Ain't No Flies on Me"; four dance variations for "Finale Act I" ("Cakewalk," "Jelly Roll," "Promenade," and "Soft Shoe"); "Roll Yer Socks Up."

THE NEW MOON

Orchestrations uncredited. (Orchestrations by Emil Gerstenberger, Al Goodman, Hans **Spialek**, and possibly others.)

Opened September 19, 1928, Imperial, 509 performances. Tryout: December 26, 1927, Philadelphia (Chestnut Street Opera House); (revisions) August 27, 1928, Cleveland (Hanna); September 10, Pittsburgh (Shubert Alvin).

Music by Sigmund Romberg, lyrics by Oscar Hammerstein II. Musical direction by Al Goodman. Other participant: Oscar Hammerstein II (co-librettist).

Some of the partiturs are in the Warner/Chappell Collection at the Library of Congress.

A NEW YORK SUMMER

Orchestrations credited to Philip J. **Lang**, Larry **Wilcox**, Quincy Jones, Peter Matz, Michael Gibson, and others.

Opened June 1, 1979, Radio City Music Hall, 203 performances. Tryout: none.

A revue. Music and lyrics by Tom Bahler and Mark Viega. Musical direction by Donald Pippin. Other participant: Radio City Music Hall Productions (producer).

THE NEW YORKERS

Orchestrations uncredited. (Orchestrations by Hans **Spialek** and others.)

Opened December 8, 1930, Broadway, 168 performances. Tryout: November 12, Philadelphia (Chestnut Street Opera House); November 24, Newark (Shubert).

Music and lyrics by Cole Porter. Musical direction by Al Goodman. Other participants: Herbert Fields (librettist); Jimmy Durante (featured).

NICE GOIN'

Orchestrations credited to Don **Walker**. (Additional orchestrators, if any, unknown.)

Tryout: October 21, 1939, New Haven (Shubert). Closed November 4, Boston (Shubert).

Music and lyrics by Ralph Rainger and Leo Robin. Based on the play *Sailor, Beware!* by Kenyon Nicholson. Musical direction by Don Walker. Other participants: Laurence Schwab (producer, librettist); Mary Martin (star); Jack Cole and His Dancers (featured).

A NIGHT OUT

Orchestrations uncredited. (Orchestrations by Stephen O. Jones, Paul Lannin, Hans **Spialek**, and others.)

Tryout: September 7, 1925, Philadelphia (Garrick). Closed September 19, Philadelphia.

Music by Vincent Youmans, lyrics by Clifford Grey and Irving Caesar. Based on the British musical of the same title by Willie Redstone, George Grossmith, and Arthur Miller. Musical direction by Charles Previn.

Several partiturs are at the Library of Congress.

Jones: "Kissing" (same orchestration as "It Must Be Love" from *Lollipop*).
Unidentified hand: "I Want a Yes Man."

NINA ROSA

Orchestrations uncredited. (Orchestrations by Hans **Spialek** and others.)

Opened September 20, 1930, Majestic, 137 performances. Tryout: unknown.

Music by Sigmund Romberg, lyrics by Irving Caesar. Musical direction by Max Meth. Other participant: Otto Harbach (librettist).

NINE

Orchestrations credited to Jonathan Tunick. (Additional orchestrations by Larry **Wilcox**.)

Opened May 9, 1982, 46th Street, 739 performances. Tryout: none.

Music and lyrics by Maury Yeston. Musical direction by Wally Harper. Choral composition and musical continuity by Maury Yeston. Other participant: Tommy Tune (director).

NO, NO, NANETTE

Orchestrations uncredited. (Orchestrations by Stephen O. Jones, Russell **Bennett**, Emil Gerstenberger and others.)

Opened September 16, 1925, Globe, 321 performances. Tryout: April 23, 1924, Detroit
(Garrick); April 30, Cincinnati (Shubert); May 7, Chicago (Harris); Boston; elsewhere.

Music by Vincent Youmans, lyrics by Irving Caesar and Otto Harbach. Based on the play
My Lady Friends by Emil Nyitray and Frank Mandel. Musical direction by Nicholas
Kempner.

Several partiturs are at the Library of Congress.

Jones: "I Want to Be Happy," "I've Confessed to the Breeze," "Where Has My Hubby
Gone Blues" (chart incomplete).

Bennett: "Santa Claus" (signed "VY/RB") "Take a Little One-Step" (originally used
in *Lollipop*, signed "VY/Rus").

Gerstenberger: "No, No Nanette."

Instr.: 4 reed, 4 brass (2 tpt, 1 tb, 1 hrn), 18? strings (8? vln, 6? vla, 3? c, 1 b), harp, perc = 28? total.
(See page 181.)

NO, NO, NANETTE (1971 REVIVAL)

Orchestrations by Ralph **Burns.** (Additional orchestrations by Luther Henderson, with
Hershy **Kay.**)

Opened January 19, 1971, 46th Street, 861 performances. Tryout: October 1970, Boston
(Shubert); November, Toronto (O'Keefe); December, Philadelphia (Forrest); Baltimore (Mechanic).

Music by Vincent Youmans, lyrics by Irving Caesar and Otto Harbach. Based on the play
My Lady Friends by Emil Nyitray and Frank Mandel. Musical direction and vocal arrangements by Buster Davis. Dance arrangements and incidental music by Luther Henderson. Other participants: Cyma Rubin (producer); Harry Rigby (producer, billing
removed); Busby Berkeley (production supervisor); Burt Shevelove (director, book adaptation); Donald Saddler (choreographer); Ruby Keeler (star); Helen Gallagher (star).

The partiturs are at Tams-Witmark. Henderson's invoices are in his personal papers.

The orchestrations are by Burns, with the following exceptions:

Henderson: "The Call of the Sea" (song and dance), "Dress Parade (Waiting for
You)," "Only a Moment Ago" (cut), "Peach on the Beach" (song and dance).

Other scores:

"Don't Turn Your Back on a Bluebird": Burns's version was cut during the tryout. The
song was reinstated after the opening for star replacement Martha Raye, with a new orchestration by Henderson.

"Fight over Me" (cut): vocal is by Burns; dance part 1 is by Henderson, parts 2 and 3
are by Kay.

"I Want to Be Happy": vocal is by Burns; "dance chaser" is by Henderson. The score
for the dance section (the biggest show-stopper of the production) is missing, but was invoiced by Henderson and is surely his. "Martha Raye Happy," a new vocal version for replacement Raye, is by Henderson.

"Take a Little One Step": vocal is by Burns; dance and tag are by Henderson.

"Tea for Two": song is by Burns; dance tag is by Henderson. The score for the dance is missing, but was invoiced by Henderson and is surely his.

"Telephone Girlie": song is by Burns; dance is by Henderson.

"'Where Has My Hubby Gone' Blues": song is by Burns; "Patter" (with male chorus) and finish by Henderson.

"You Can Dance with Any Girl": song is by Burns; tags 1, 2, and 3 (dance variations) are by Henderson.

On the chart for "I Want to Be Happy," Burns assigns the vocals not to the characters Jimmy and Nanette but to "Hiram" (Sherman) and "Carole" (Demas)—both of whom were fired during the tryout.

The assignment: to make the ancient, 1925 *Nanette* sound like a twenties musical to the jaded ears of post-*Hair* theatregoers at the start of the swingin' seventies. Burns and his partner Luther Henderson did so by increasing the brass (from 4 to 7) and, most importantly, adding the two-piano sound of Phil Ohman and Victor Arden, who were prominently featured in a string of seven Gershwin and Rodgers & Hart musicals during that decade (beginning with *Lady Be Good* in 1924). The results made for delectably refreshing entertainment, while poor old lady *Nanette*'s original strings-and-harp combine would presumably have sounded unbearably quaint.

RALPH'S INSTRUCTIONS TO MUSICIANS: On the score for "Tea for Two" (to copyist Lillete Hindin concerning a mistake in the instrumentation): "Viols 1 and 2 are not important. Don't call me up in the middle of the night and tell me Lennie Hayton has started on different doubles. (Transfer notes to other reeds on your own). Love + kisses, Roger Edens. P.P.S.—Besides, I've been singing this song all night in my sleep and it's too repetitious. Vincent will probably write a new one in Boston to take its place!" (For those to whom these references are too obscure, Burns was jokingly referring to musical giants from M-G-M in the 1940s, arranger Lennie Hayton [husband to Lena Horne] and arranger-producer Roger Edens. And no, Vincent Youmans [who died in 1946] did not write a new song in Boston to replace "Tea for Two.")

Instr.: 5 reed, 6 brass (3 tpt, 2 tb, 1 hrn), 11 strings (6 vln, 2 vla, 2 c, 1 b), 2 piano, guitar, perc = 26 total.

NO STRINGS

Orchestrations by Ralph **Burns**. (Additional orchestrations by Peter Matz.)

Opened March 15, 1962, 54th Street, 580 performances. Tryout: January 15, Detroit (Fisher); February 6, Toronto (O'Keefe); February 19, Cleveland (Hanna); February 27, New Haven (Shubert).

Music and lyrics by Richard Rodgers. Musical direction and dance arrangements by Peter Matz. Other participants: Richard Rodgers (producer); Joe Layton (director, choreographer); Diahann Carroll (star); Richard Kiley (star).

The partiturs for the cut numbers only are at the offices of the Rodgers & Hammerstein Organization.

The deleted scores include two by Matz, "Sweetest Sounds Dance" and "Sweetest Sounds Reprise." This suggests that he did more of the orchestration, which might logically include the "Casino Ballet" and the "Eager Beaver" dance. R&H does have a reduced road orchestration for ten pieces (half of the twenty-one used on Broadway). This is mostly by Wilcox—who didn't start working with Burns until *Little Me*, which opened eight months after *No Strings*—with some charts by Matz.

> JOE LAYTON: Richard Rodgers started out by saying that he wanted to do a show without strings. That was a good title, and so on and so forth, and then I said, "Well, why not put the music on the stage as well?" And he bought that, because he always has invention in his head. He loves that. I sat down with David Hays, the designer, and came up with the concept. And Rodgers loved it. He said, "Oh, that's terrific!" But he never asked us to go into detail or wanted us to. I just said what we were going to do, and he agreed.

Instr.: 8 reed (8 sax, 8 clr, 7 fl, 4 bcl), 7 brass (4 tpt, 3 tb), "no strings," I b, piano (played by conductor), harp, guitar, 2 perc = 21 total.

(See pages 34, 230.)

NOWHERE TO GO BUT UP

Orchestrations and arrangements by Robert **Ginzler**. (Additional orchestrations by Don **Walker**, with Sid **Ramin**.)

Opened November 10, 1962, Winter Garden, 9 performances. Tryout: Philadelphia (Shubert).

Music by Sol Berkowitz, lyrics and book by James Lipton. Musical direction and vocal arrangements by Herbert Greene. Other participants: Kermit Bloomgarden (co-producer); Sidney Lumet (director); Ron Field (choreographer); Michael Bennett (assistant choreographer); Tom Bosley (star); Dorothy Loudon (featured).

Copies of the partiturs are in a private collection.

The orchestrations are by Ginzler, with the following exceptions:

Walker: Finale act I; Overture 2 (orchestrated four days before the Broadway opening). Other scores:

"A Couple of Clowns": part 1 is by Ginzler; part 2 by Ramin.

"Gimme" is by Ginzler; playoff by Walker.

"Montage": this is a long (458-bar) number scored in thirteen sections, with more than half by Walker.

"Out of Sight" is by Ginzler (except for extended intro—"Into Out of Sight"—by Walker).

Prologue is by Ginzler, with "Coda" by Walker.

The Overture for this show, about Prohibition era G-men, starts with "4 pistol shots."

Sid Ramin's chart for the second half of "A Couple of Clowns" is headed as follows: "Clowns !?!X 6:30 AM. No sleep 24 hours! Maybe a few mistakes." The music is marked "very broad and dirty."

Instr.: 5 reed (including 3 soprano sax), 6 brass (3 tpt, 2 tb, I hrn), 11 strings (7 vln, 0 vla, 3 c, I b), piano/celesta, harp, perc.

NYMPH ERRANT

Orchestrations credited to Russell **Bennett**. (Additional orchestrators, if any, unknown.)

Opened October 6, 1933, Adelphi (London), 154 performances. Tryout: September 11, Manchester, England (Opera House).

Music and lyrics by Cole Porter. Based on the novel by James Laver. Musical direction by Hyman Greenbaum. Other participants: Charles B. Cochran (producer); Agnes de Mille (choreographer); Gertrude Lawrence (star); Elisabeth Welch (featured).

OF THEE I SING

Orchestrations credited to Russell **Bennett**, William Daly, and George Gershwin. (Additional orchestrators, if any, unknown.)

Opened December 26, 1931, Imperial, 441 performances. Tryout: December 8, Boston (Majestic).

Music by George Gershwin, lyrics by Ira Gershwin. Musical direction by Charles Previn. Other participants: Sam H. Harris (producer); George S. Kaufman (director); George S. Kaufman and Morrie Ryskind (librettists); William Gaxton & Victor Moore (stars).

One partitur only, "Opening Act II" (by Gershwin and Daly), is in the Gershwin Collection at the Library of Congress.

OF THEE I SING (1952 REVIVAL)

Orchestrations by Don **Walker**. Assistant orchestrator, Seymour (Red) **Ginzler**. (Additional orchestrations by Guido Tutrinoli and Irwin **Kostal**.)

Opened May 5, 1952, Ziegfeld, 72 performances. Tryout: April 7, New Haven (Shubert); April 14, Philadelphia (Shubert).

Musical direction by Maurice Levine. Dance arrangements by David Baker. Additional dance arrangements by John Morris. Other participant: George S. Kaufman (director, co-librettist).

The partiturs and invoices are in the Walker Collection at the Library of Congress. Invoices indicate: Walker (58%), Tutrinoli (18%), Ginzler (17%).

Kostal did an Overture based on the original by Bennett, which was replaced during the tryout by a medley Overture by Walker. The Walker Collection includes a note headed, in Walker's writing, "Themes for Overture (with big ending for applause)."

OH, BROTHER!

Orchestrations credited to Jim Tyler. (Additional orchestrators, if any, unknown.)

Opened November 19, 1981, ANTA, 3 performances. Tryout: Washington, D.C. (Eisenhower).

Music by Michael Valenti, lyrics and book by Donald Driver. Based on the play *The Comedy of Errors* by William Shakespeare. Musical direction, vocal and dance arrangements by Marvin Laird. Other participant: Donald Driver (director, choreographer).

(See page 453.)

OH CAPTAIN!

Orchestrations credited to Robert **Ginzler**, Joe Glover, Ray Jaimes, Philip J. **Lang**, Walter Eiger, Sy Oliver, Cornel Tanassy, and Oscar Kosarin.

Opened February 4, 1958, Alvin, 192 performances. Tryout: Philadelphia (Shubert).

Music and lyrics by Jay Livingston and Ray Evans. Based on the film *The Captain's Paradise* by Alec Coppel. Musical direction, vocal and ballet arrangements by Jay Blackton. Assistant to Jay Blackton, Peter Howard. Other participants: José Ferrer (director, co-librettist); Tony Randall (star).

It seems likely that "Surprise," "Life Does a Man a Favor (Paris)"/"Hey, Madame!" and "Femininity" are by Ginzler and that "A Very Proper Town" is by Lang.

OH, PLEASE!

Orchestrations uncredited. (Orchestrations by Hans **Spialek** and others.)

Opened December 17, 1926, Fulton, 75 performances. Tryout: November 19, Philadelphia (Forrest); Hartford; December 2, New Haven (Shubert); Atlantic City.

Music by Vincent Youmans, lyrics by Anne Caldwell. Based on a play by Maurice Hennequin and Pierre Veber. Musical direction by Gus Salzer. Other participants: Charles Dillingham (producer); Beatrice Lillie (star).

OKLAHOMA!

Orchestrations (mostly) by Russell **Bennett**. (Additional orchestrations by Menotti Salta.)

Opened March 31, 1943, St. James, 2,212 performances. Tryout: (as *Away We Go!*) March 11, New Haven (Shubert); March 15, Boston (Colonial).

Music by Richard Rodgers, lyrics and book by Oscar Hammerstein II. Based on the play *Green Grow the Lilacs* by Lynn Rigg. Musical direction by Jacob Schwartzdorf [Jay S. Blackton]. Dance arrangements by Morgan Lewis (uncredited). Other participants: Theatre Guild (producer); Rouben Mamoulian (director); Agnes de Mille (choreographer); Alfred Drake (featured).

The partiturs are in the Rodgers Collection at the Library of Congress.

Bennett's early scores use the source material as working title, *Green Grow the Lilacs* or simply *Lilacs*. The orchestrations are by Bennett, with the following exceptions:

Salta: "Interlude to Ballet," "Laurey's Entrance (Beautiful Mornin')."

Other scores:

"It's a Scandal, It's an Outrage" (entitled with the original name, "Scandal for the Jaybirds") is by Bennett; "Exit" (after song section), beginning on page 83 of vocal score, is by Salta.

"Many a New Day": song is by Bennett; dance (entitled "Many a New York Dance"), beginning with "exit of singers" on the last line of page 69, is by Salta.

"Oklahoma" is by Bennett, except for 4-bar scale-like intro leading into "II Special Chorus" on top of page 188, by Salta.

"People Will Say We're in Love" is by Bennett; "end of scene" underscoring, beginning with Jud's entrance on page 88 and continuing with Laurey and Eller, is by Salta.

BENNETT'S INSTRUCTIONS TO MUSICIANS:　On "Many a New Day": "If the copyist copies this first note G-natural, I will beat the stuffing out of him. Yours truly, RRB."

Instr.: 4 reed, 5 brass (2 tpt, 1 tb, 2 hrn), 16 strings (10 vln, 3 vla, 2 c, 1 b), harp, guitar, perc = 28 total. (See pages 185, 190, 197, 204.)

OLIVER!

Orchestrations by Eric Rogers.

Opened January 6, 1963, 774 performances. Tryout: August 1962, Los Angeles; San Francisco; Detroit (Fisher); Toronto.

Music, lyrics, and book by Lionel Bart. Based on the novel *Oliver Twist* by Charles Dickens. Musical direction by Donald Pippin. Other participants: David Merrick (producer); Peter Coe (director); Sean Kenny (designer).

Copies of the partiturs are in the Merrick Collection at the Library of Congress.

Don Pippin, assistant conductor of *Irma La Douce* (and conductor of the Las Vegas company), saw *Oliver!* in London and lobbied for the job.

> PIPPIN: Merrick asked why he should give the show to me. "Because I love the show, and nobody can do it better than I can," I said. "Okay," said Merrick, "it's yours. You better be as good as you think you are."
>
> Merrick was determined that it be rewritten for twenty-five pieces instead of thirteen. I went to England to see Eric Rogers, and asked him if we could expand stereophonically, but retain the intimacy. He rewrote it so that we kept the thirteen-piece orchestra for the intimacy, then as the songs ended we'd start sneaking in the additional instruments. Merrick said, "I love it! Didn't I tell you?"

ON A CLEAR DAY YOU CAN SEE FOREVER

Orchestrations by Russell **Bennett**. (Additional orchestrations by Robert Noeltner, with Trude Rittman.)

Opened October 17, 1965, Mark Hellinger, 280 performances. Tryout: September 7, Boston (Colonial).

Music by Burton Lane, lyrics and book by Alan Jay Lerner. Musical direction by Theodore Saidenberg. Vocal arrangements and musical continuity by Trude Rittman. Dance arrangements by Betty Walberg.

Other participants: Alan Jay Lerner (co-producer); Robert Lewis (director); Herbert Ross (choreographer); Barbara Harris (star); Louis Jourdan (tryout star); John Cullum (star replacement).

Copies of the partiturs are in the American Musical Theatre Collection at the Library of Congress. Invoices are preserved in Bennett's ledger. Base page rate: $10. Invoices indicate: Bennett (79%), Noeltner (19%).

The orchestrations are by Bennett, with the following exceptions:

Noeltner: "Come Back to Me" (reprise), "Domestic Champagne Waltz," "Melinda Incidental," "Royal Academy," "When I'm Being Born Again" (song and playoff), utilities ("Melinda," "On a Clear Day," "What Did I Have?"), numerous fixes.

Rittman: "Dolly's Seduction," "Intro to Marriage Contract (Father of the Bride)."
Other Score

"On the S.S. Bernard Cohn" is by Bennett, with several sections in the later portion of the dance by Noeltner. As the dance routine continued to change during the Boston tryout, Noeltner also provided an additional 36-page score of "new dance music."

Lerner, in his later years, was notorious for his inability to complete his lyrics. (Richard Rodgers walked off this project—then known as *I Picked a Daisy*—in frustration.) In one score, Bennett writes, "New lyric due." Also of note is an early lyric in Bennett's score for "Come Back to Me": "Mademoiselle, where in hell can you be? / Wear a robe, wear a rag / Come in frills, come in drag / In a Rolls or Sedan."

Instr.: 6 reed, 7 brass (3 tpt, 2 tb, 2 hrn), 15 strings (8 vln, 3 vla, 3 c, 1 b), piano/harpsichord, harp, perc = 31 total.

ON THE TOWN

Orchestrations by Hershy **Kay**, Don **Walker**, Elliott Jacoby, and Ted **Royal**.
Opened December 28, 1944, Adelphi, 462 performances. Tryout: December 13, Boston (Colonial).
Music by Leonard Bernstein, lyrics by Betty Comden & Adolph Green, additional lyrics by Leonard Bernstein. Suggested by the ballet *Fancy Free* by Leonard Bernstein. Musical direction by Max Goberman. Other participants: Oliver Smith (co-producer); George Abbott (director); Jerome Robbins (choreographer, original idea); Betty Comden & Adolph Green (librettists, featured players); Nancy Walker (featured); Herbert Greene (singer).

The Library of Congress and Tams both have conformed copies of the orchestration, on which the copyist has written the name of an orchestrator on the first page of each number. Walker's invoices are at the Library of Congress.

Kay: Opening (including "I Feel Like I'm Not Out of Bed Yet" and "Miss Turnstiles Variations"), "Lonely Town" (including "High School Girls" and "Lonely Town Pas de Deux"), "Carnegie Hall Pavane" (including "Do-Do-Re-Do"), "Times Square," Finale act I, "I Wish I Was Dead" (Spanish variation), "Ya Got Me" (encore only), "Subway Ride and Imaginary Coney Island," "Great Lover Displays Himself Pas de Deux," "Some Other Time," "Real Coney Island," Finale.

Walker: "I Can Cook Too," "Carried Away," "So Long Baby" (marked "Moderato Pomposo" for the first 6 measures, after which it turns "Fast and Corny"), "Taxi Scene"/"Come Up to My Place."

Jacoby: "I Wish I Was Dead" (and two of its several sections, "Conga Cabana" and "Slam Bang Blues Dixieland"), "Ya Got Me."

Royal: "Lucky to Be Me."
Other scores:

"Intermission Song" (cut), "It's Gotta Be Bad to Be Good" (cut), "Pickup Song" (cut), and "Say When"/"I'm Afraid It's Love" (cut) were all invoiced by Walker.

"Pitkin's Song (I Understand)": the copyist's score lists this as being by Kay, but probably in error as Walker (who was assigned most of the comedy material) invoiced both "Pitkin's Song" and "Pitkin's Coda."

Apparently wanting his ballets to sound more symphonic than the typical Broadway score, Bernstein selected Kay as the main orchestrator (Kay's first Broadway assignment). Walker, who was already George Abbott's favorite orchestrator, was assigned the comedy numbers; he ultimately wrote 209 pages, roughly 25% of the show.

Instr.: 5 reed (including 3 sax), 8 brass (3 tpt, 3 tb, 2 hrn), 15? strings (9? vln, 3 vla, 2 c, b), piano, perc = 30? total.

(See pages 48, 103.)

ON THE TWENTIETH CENTURY

Orchestrations credited to Hershy **Kay**. (Additional orchestrations by Jim Tyler.)

Opened February 19, 1978, St. James, 449 performances. Tryout: January 7, Boston (Colonial).

Music by Cy Coleman, lyrics and book by Betty Comden & Adolph Green. Based on the play *Twentieth Century* by Ben Hecht and Charles MacArthur. Musical direction by Paul Gemignani. Other participants: Robert Fryer (co-producer); Harold Prince (director); Madeline Kahn (star); John Cullum (star); Kevin Kline (featured).

"Babette" is known to be by Jim Tyler; otherwise, it is believed that Kay did most of the score.

(See page 52.)

ON YOUR TOES

Orchestrations credited to Hans **Spialek**. (Additional orchestrations by David Raksin, with Ted **Royal**.)

Opened April 11, 1936, Imperial, 315 performances. Tryout: March 21, Boston (Shubert).

Music by Richard Rodgers, lyrics by Lorenz Hart. Musical direction by Gene Salzer.

Other participants: Rodgers & Hart and George Abbott (librettists); George Abbott (replacement director, uncredited); George Balanchine (choreographer); Ray Bolger (star).

The partiturs are at the offices of the Rodgers & Hammerstein Organization.

Spialek: "Glad to Be Unhappy," "The Heart Is Quicker than the Eye" (see below), "Olympic Games," "Slaughter on Tenth Avenue" (see below), "There's a Small Hotel," "The Three B's," "Too Good for the Average Man."

Raksin: "It's Got to Be Love" (see below), "On Your Toes" (see below), "Ragtime" (see below).

Royal: "Two-a-Day for Keith."

Other scores:

"The Heart Is Quicker Than the Eye": song is by Spialek; utility (?) by Raksin. "It's Got to Be Love": song is by Raksin, although there are notations referring to "new score" (by Raksin or Spialek?); "1st Encore" and "2nd Encore" are by Raksin. There are also two scores marked "Reprise," one by Spialek and one by Raksin.

"On Your Toes": song (instrumental, refrain, verse, refrain) is by Raksin. There are two dances; the version by Spialek probably replaced the one by Raksin.

Overture: bridgework is by Spialek, referring to inserts (utilities?) by unidentified orchestrators.

"Princess Zenobia Ballet": part 1 and part 2 are incomplete (but probably by Spialek); part 3 (beginning at "Slave Dance," bar 343 on page 87 of vocal score, through end) is by Raksin.

"Quiet Night": part 1 (song) is by Spialek; part 2 (instrumental) and part 3 ("Unquiet Chorus") are by Raksin.

"Ragtime"—by Raksin—is a set of dance variations to an unidentifiable tune. The sections are "Ragtime" ("with a B. F. Keith Circuit Swing"), "Charleston," "Black Buttock," and "Modrin" ("Modern").

"Slaughter on Tenth Avenue" is missing, but surely by Spialek.

At the orchestra rehearsal, Rodgers vehemently objected to a harmony in one of Raksin's charts. "What have you done to my music!" Rodgers yelled. Raksin retorted, "What music?"—which hastened his departure from the orchestrators' room at Chappell. (Raksin, who became a noted Hollywood composer, told Michael Feinstein many years later that the note had been illegible on the copy of the piano-vocal arrangement. Working in the middle of the night, he simply guessed what the composer intended.)

RAKSIN'S INSTRUCTIONS TO MUSICIANS: On "It's Gotta Be Love" reprise, to violins: "See if you can melt M. Rodgers' hard heart, mes amis."

Instr.: 5 reed, 5 brass (3 tpt, 1 tb, 1 hrn), 11 strings (6 vln, 2 vla, 2c, 1 b), 2 piano (1 celesta), perc = 25 total. (See page 93.)

ON YOUR TOES (1954 REVIVAL)

Orchestrations by Don **Walker**. (Additional orchestrations by Robert **Ginzler** with Irwin **Kostal**.)

Opened October 11, 1954, 46th Street, 64 performances. Tryout: September 25, New Haven (Shubert).

Musical direction by Salvatore Dell'Isola. Vocal arrangement for "You Took Advantage of Me" by Portia Nelson. Other participants: George Abbott (producer, director); George Balanchine (choreographer); Robert Griffith (stage manager); Elaine Stritch (featured).

The partiturs are at the offices of the Rodgers & Hammerstein Organization.

Invoices are in the Walker Collection at the Library of Congress. Base page rate: $5.87. Invoices indicate: Walker (71%), Ginzler (27%).

The orchestrations are by Walker, with the following exceptions:

Ginzler: "It's Got to Be Love," "Opening Act II," "Quiet Night," "You Took Advantage of Me."

Kostal: Finale.

Other scores:

"On Your Toes": song is by Walker; dance by Ginzler.

Overture is by Walker and Ginzler (roughly one-half each).

"Three B's" is mostly by Walker, with Kostal billing for the 12-page "Extension."

From Rodgers to his secretary: "I am happy that the contract with Don has been set because this will put my mind at ease as to the quality of the job."

Walker, preparing for an interview with the *New York Times*, checked with Rodgers as to precisely what he should say. From Walker to Rodgers:

> I feel that a general cleaning up and elimination of that which is not your own in the score should be done. . . . I am dedicated to carrying out your wishes in your absence to the best of my ability and discretion, in preserving your excellent score as intact as possible while enhancing it with the orchestral richness that has developed in the years since the original production. I would like to know any definite wishes or violent convictions you have so that I may not unknowingly cause you distress.

From Rodgers (on location shooting for *Oklahoma!*) to Walker: "Thanks for your assurances that you will do everything to the best of your ability to preserve my score. I need hardly tell you that you don't have to reassure me. You have never done anything else for my work since I've known you."

The resulting explanation, which appeared in the *New York Times* in August: "The show will be reorchestrated by Don Walker, who plans to make the treatment simpler than the original. Although the layman might not be aware of it, the orchestrations two decades ago were quite a bit more flowery than those that we accept today."

THANKS AND WISHES   Opening night, from Walker to Elaine Stritch: "Zip the Hostest with the Mostest Is Too Good for the Average Man."

Instr.: 6 reed, 7 brass (3 tpt, 3 tb, 1 hrn), ? strings (vln, vla, c, 1 b), piano, perc.

ONCE UPON A MATTRESS

Orchestrations credited to Hershy **Kay**, Arthur Beck, and Carroll Huxley. (Additional orchestrators, if any, unknown.)

Opened May 11, 1959, Phoenix (off-Broadway), 216 performances (followed by an additional 244 performances, initially at the Alvin).

Music by Mary Rodgers, lyrics by Marshall Barer. Based on *The Princess and the Pea*. Musical direction by Hal Hastings. Dance arrangements by Roger Adams. Other participants: George Abbott (director); Joe Layton (choreographer); Carol Burnett (star).

> MARY RODGERS: The orchestrators were kind of assigned. I didn't know much about it, anyway. Originally we had Hershy Kay. He stopped in the middle. "I can't go any further," he said. "I have to go orchestrate something for George Balanchine." "You didn't tell us about that," we said. "You didn't ask." Hershy did just about half of the show. The biggest problem is that when I heard things that sounded wrong, I could say, "There, that sounds wrong," but I couldn't fix it. I didn't know how to repair it. There were all kinds of things that were not right.

(See page 50.)

ONE DAM THING AFTER ANOTHER

Orchestrations uncredited. (Orchestrations by Russell **Bennett** and others.)
Opened May 19, 1927, London (Pavilion), 237 performances. Tryout: unknown.
A revue. Music by Richard Rodgers, lyrics by Lorenz Hart. Musical direction by J. B.
Hastings. Other participant: C. B. Cochran (producer).

ONE FOR THE MONEY

Orchestrations credited to Hans **Spialek**. (Additional orchestrators unknown.)
Opened February 3, 1939, Booth, 132 performances. Tryout: unknown.
Music by Morgan Lewis, lyrics and sketches by Nancy Hamilton. Musical direction by
Ray Kavanaugh. Vocal arrangements by Hugh Martin. Other participants: Alfred
Drake (featured); Gene Kelly (featured).

> SPIALEK: While rehearsing *One for the Money* I had an encounter with Gene Kelly, best described as an unpleasant one. Trying one of Kelly's numbers with the orchestra, he stopped repeatedly, dissatisfied by either tempo or sound. I cut his rehearsal time short with something like, "It's always the little hams causing trouble, never the big ones." Later, watching him at the first runthrough of *Pal Joey* in New York, I was not only astonished but thrilled by his performance. I rushed backstage and told him so. He said, "Well, thanks. That's something, coming from you!"

110 IN THE SHADE

Orchestrations credited to Hershy **Kay**. Assistant orchestrator, Bill Stegmeyer. (Additional orchestrators, if any, unknown.)
Opened October 24, 1963, Broadhurst, 330 performances. Tryout: September 9, Boston
(Shubert); October, Philadelphia (Shubert).
Music by Harvey Schmidt, lyrics by Tom Jones. Based on the play *The Rainmaker* by
N. Richard Nash. Musical direction by Donald Pippin. Vocal arrangements by Robert
De Cormier. Dance arrangements by Billy Goldenberg. Other participants: David
Merrick (producer); Agnes de Mille (choreographer); N. Richard Nash (librettist).

The partiturs for two numbers, "Gonna Be Another Hot Day" and "Rain Song" (both
by Kay), are in a private collection.
    Neither Schmidt nor Pippin remembers Stegmeyer's involvement, but he was clearly
credited in the *Playbill.*

Instr.: 6 reed, 6 brass (3 tpt, 1 tb, 2 hrn), 7 strings (0 vln, 4 vla, 2 c, 1 b), harp, guitar, 2 perc = 23 total.
(See page 51.)

ONE NIGHT STAND

Orchestrations (totally) by Philip J. **Lang**.
Tryout: October 20, 1980, New York (Nederlander). Closed during previews, October 25.

Music by Jule Styne, lyrics and book by Herb Gardner. Musical direction by Eric Stern. Dance arrangements by Marvin Laird. Other participants: John Dexter (director); Peter Gennaro (choreographer); Jack Weston (star).

The partiturs are at the Styne office.

Instr.: 4 reed, 5 brass (3 tpt, 1 tb, 1 hrn), 8 strings (5 vln, 1 vla, 1 c, 1 b/elec b), guitar/ukulele, 2 perc/1 "mallets" = 20 total.

ONE TOUCH OF VENUS

Orchestrations and arrangements (virtually totally) by Kurt Weill. (Additional orchestrations by Russell **Bennett**.)

Opened October 7, 1943, Imperial, 567 performances. Tryout: September 17, Boston (Shubert).

Music by Kurt Weill, lyrics by Ogden Nash. Based on the story *The Tinted Venus* by F. Anstey. Musical direction by Maurice Abravanel. Other participants: Cheryl Crawford (producer); Elia Kazan (director); Agnes de Mille (choreographer); S. J. Perelman and Ogden Nash (librettists); Mary Martin (star).

The partiturs are in the Weill Collection at Yale.

The orchestrations are by Weill, with the following exceptions:

"Artists Ball" is by Weill, with a revised opening (15 bars) and closing (22 bars) by Bennett.

Overture (used as Entr'acte?): the first half, including the introduction and opening section, is by Bennett, the rest by Weill.

The last-minute fixes are by Bennett, however unlikely it may seem. The common denominator: choreographer Agnes de Mille of *Oklahoma!*

Instr.: 4 reed (all sax/clr), 4 brass (3 tpt, 1 tb), 18? strings (12? vln, 3 vla, 2 c, 1 b), piano/accordion, perc = 28? total.

OUT OF THIS WORLD

Orchestrations credited to Russell **Bennett**. (Additional orchestrations by Joe Glover and probably others.)

Opened December 21, 1950, New Century, 157 performances. Tryout: November 4, Philadelphia (Shubert); November 28, Boston (Shubert).

Music and lyrics by Cole Porter. Based on the Amphitryon legend. Musical direction by Pembroke Davenport. Dance arrangements by Genevieve Pitot. Incidental music arranged by Trude Rittman. Other participants: Saint Subber and Lemuel Ayers (producers); Agnes de Mille (director); George Abbott (unbilled replacement director); Hanya Holm (choreographer).

Bennett's invoices are preserved in his ledger. Base page rate: $5.70. Tentative attributions per invoice.

Bennett: "Ballet I," Entr'acte, "Hark to the Song of the Night," "Hush" (cut), "I Am Loved" (and reprise), "I Got Beauty," "I Sleep Easier Now," "Longest Night," "Maiden

Fair," "Mountain Dance," "Nobody's Chasing Me," "Opening Act II," Overture, "Peasant Dance," Prologue, "They Couldn't Compare to You," "Use Your Imagination," "What Do You Think about Men?" "Where, Oh, Where," "You Don't Remind Me."

Unknown (not invoiced by Bennett): "The Dawn," "Entrance of Night," "Hail, Hail, Hail," "No Lover for Me."

Other scores:

"Cherry Pies Ought to Be You": song by unknown; Juno-Niki reprise by Bennett.

"Climb Up the Mountain": song by unknown; dance by unknown and Bennett.

"From This Moment On": song by unknown; dance by Bennett.

"I Jupiter, I Rex": song by unknown, with intro by Bennett.

Bennett notes in his ledger that he was forced to increase his agreed-upon page rate due to a new union page rate: "$5.40 was changed to $5.70 on account of Mr. 802 J.G."—which is to say, Joe Glover. While Glover often did auxiliary numbers for Bennett, Russell farmed out more important numbers (such as "Cherry Pies Ought to Be You" and "No Lover") to Don Walker on other shows of this period. It was also usual for Bennett to assign secondary numbers and dance-heavy pieces, like "The Dawn" and "Entrance of Night," to Bob Noeltner, who did ballet orchestrations on Porter's *Seven Lively Arts* and de Mille's *Brigadoon.*

Trude Rittman (*Carousel, Brigadoon*) worked on incidental arrangements but not the dances, as de Mille was not choreographing the show. Genevieve Pitot (*Kiss Me, Kate, Call Me Madam*) did the dance arrangements for choreographer Hanya Holm.

Instr.: 5 reed, 6 brass (2 tpt, 2 tb, 2 hrn), 15? strings (8? vln, 3? vla, 3? c, 1 b), 2 harp, 2 guitar, perc = 31? total. (See page 221.)

PAINT YOUR WAGON

Orchestrations by Ted **Royal**. (Additional orchestrations by Russell **Bennett**, Rudolph Goehr, Hans **Spialek**, Robert Noeltner, and Marion Evans.)

Opened November 12, 1951, Shubert, 289 performances. Tryout: September 17, Philadelphia (Shubert); October 9, Boston (Shubert).

Music by Frederick Loewe, lyrics and book by Alan Jay Lerner. Musical direction by Franz Allers. Dance arrangements by Trude Rittman. Other participants: Cheryl Crawford (producer); Agnes de Mille (choreographer).

Copies of the partiturs (with post-Broadway changes and edits) are at the offices of the Rodgers & Hammerstein Organization. Bennett's invoices are preserved in his ledger. Partial invoices from Evans and Noeltner are in the Royal Collection at the New York Public Library. Base page rate: $5.55.

Royal: "All for Him," "Another Autumn," "Cariño Mio," "Fandango's Farewell," "How Can I Wait?" "I Still See Elisa," "I Talk to the Trees," "I'm on My Way" (song and reprise), "In Between," "Movin'," "Rumson Town," "Trio," "What's Goin' On?" "Whoop-ti-ay."

Bennett: Ballet (part I and part IV), "Opening Act II (Hand Me Down That Can o' Beans)."

Goehr: "Fandango Entrance and Dance," "Fandango Exit," "Lonely Men Ballet."

Noeltner: "Intro to Coach Ballet."

Evans: "Wanderin' Star" (see below), numerous fixes.

Other scores:

"Can-Can": the first section, through #13 on page 169 of vocal score, is by Royal; the next section, through #24, is by Spialek; the rest ("Ballet: Section 4"), beginning with "Allegro Vivace" on page 174, is by Bennett.

Entr'acte is mostly by Royal, with the final section ("There's a Coach Comin' In") by Evans.

Overture: Spialek wrote three sections: the opening 8-bar fanfare, the end of the "Maria" section (leading into "Elisa"), and the final 4 bars. Evans contributed bridge-work. The song sections are mostly by Royal. (The "I Talk to the Trees" section, by Royal, is marked "Trees–Overture, 17th Version").

"Rope Dance": part I (#27) is by Bennett (who identifies the author as "Lerner Loewe Rittman"); part II (#27A) is by Spialek (who credits "Trude's Frederick Loewe"); part III (27B) is by Royal.

"There's a Coach Comin' In" is by Royal and Evans.

"They Call the Wind Maria" is missing, but probably by Royal.

"Wanderin' Star": song is by Evans; reprise (with chorus) is by Royal. These are truncated and joined on the cast album, although they were performed separately in the show. This is the only full score credited to Royal that has been located. As can be seen, he needed a considerable amount of help. Unlike in his other shows of the fifties, which were seemingly assembled by committee, Royal did an enormous amount of work—and very good work—on *Paint Your Wagon*, including almost all of the songs. However, the show was musically overlong; the five ballets, alone, encompassed 320 pages. (Comparatively, a moderate-length musical can come in under 800 pages.) In this case, Royal enlisted others for the ballets: Bennett, Spialek, and the German-born Rudolph Goehr, who did two major de Mille ballets by himself.

Instr.: 5 reed (including 5 clr, 3 fl), 9 brass (3 tpt, 2 tb, I tuba, 3 hrn), 14 strings (8 vln, 2 vla/I mandolin, 2 c, 2 b), piano, guitar/banjo, perc = 31 total.

(See page 206.)

THE PAJAMA GAME

Orchestrations by Don **Walker**. (Additional orchestrations by Robert **Ginzler**, Irwin **Kostal**, and Joe Glover, with Walter Paul.)

Opened May 13, 1954, St. James, 1,063 performances. Tryout: April 12, New Haven (Shubert); Boston.

Music and lyrics by Richard Adler and Jerry Ross. Based on the novel *7½ Cents* by Richard Bissell. Musical direction by Hal Hastings. Dance arrangements by Roger Adams. Other participants: Frederick Brisson, Robert Griffith and Harold Prince (producers); George Abbott (director, co-librettist); Jerome Robbins (co-director); Bob Fosse (choreographer); John Raitt (star).

The partiturs are in the Walker Collection at the Library of Congress.

Walker: Closing act II, "Her Is" (song and dance), "I'm Not at All in Love,"

"Leibchen," Montage, "Once a Year Day" (song and ballet), Opening act I, "Racing with the Clock," "Sewing Machines," "Slowdown," "There Once Was a Man (I Love You More)," "Think of the Time I Save."

Ginzler: "I'll Never Be Jealous Again," "A New Town Is a Blue Town," Opening act II, "Seven-and-a-Half Cents," "S-S-S-Steam Heat" [*sic*].

Kostal: Finale act I ("Hey There"), "Hernando's Hideaway" (see below), "Hey There."

Glover: "I'm Not at All in Love Scene Change," "Small Talk."

Other scores:

Entr'acte: "I'll Never Be Jealous Again" is by Walker; "Small Talk" and "Once a Year Day" by Glover; "Hey There" by Paul; "I'm Not at All in Love" through end by Walker.

"Hernando's Hideaway" is by Kostal, except for the interior scene change and brief dance patches by Walker; version on the cast album is totally by Kostal.

"Hey There Reprise" (act II) is by Walker and Glover.

"I'm Not at All in Love" incidental and scene change are by Paul, utility by Ginzler.

"Jealousy Ballet" alternates among Walker, Kostal, and unidentified hand.

"Watch Your Heart" (added to the 1973 Broadway revival) was orchestrated by Jim Tyler.

Walker's name has been cut off the bottom of the partiturs for "Small Talk" and the "Small Talk" section of the Entr'acte. Following the opening, Glover (who ghosted on several Walker shows from 1952 to 1954) began an extended fight with Walker about money.

THANKS AND WISHES   From Walker to Fosse: "I really enjoyed orchestrating those crazy numbers, man. Let's do it again."

From Walker to co-producer Frederick Brisson and his wife, Rosalind Russell: "Hope to orchestrate every musical either one of you is ever connected with. Somehow there seem to be less headaches."

From Walker to Hal Hastings: "Well we fooled them again, kid. But someday somebody will find out that we do it with slide rules."

From Walker to Abbott: "Not sure that your remark 'but you always have to end up with Don Walker' is a compliment or a complaint. All I know is that if I end up with George Abbott, I consider myself lucky."

From Abbott to Walker: "Judging by all the rave reviews you got, I take it the orchestra wasn't at such a bad height after all."

From Abbott to Walker and Mathilde Pincus, upon receiving a bound copy of the score: "You could have knocked me over with a pair of pajamas. I love my book. I can't play but it will look just elegant on the grand piano."

From the producers to Walker: "Never before in the pajama game has material been so finely orchestrated. Thanks for a special job, Freddie, Bobby and Hal."

Instr.: 5 reed, 6 brass (3 tpt, 3 tb), 11? strings (6? vln, 2? vla, 2? c, 1 b), piano/accordion, guitar (acoustic, elec), perc = 25? total.

(See pages 10, 244.)

PAL JOEY

Orchestrations credited to Hans **Spialek.** (Additional orchestrations by Ted **Royal** and others.)

Opened December 25, 1940, Ethel Barrymore, 374 performances. Tryout: December 16, Philadelphia (Forrest).

Music by Richard Rodgers, lyrics by Lorenz Hart. Based on the stories by John O'Hara. Musical direction by Harry Levant. Vocal arrangement for "Plant You Now, Dig You Later" by Hugh Martin. Other participants: George Abbott (producer, director); John O'Hara (librettist); Gene Kelly (star).

> SPIALEK: After an evening performance in Philadelphia, at the Penny Club (an after-curfew drink dispensary), I shared a table with Mr. O'Hara and Larry Hart. Naturally, the topic of our discussions was *Pal Joey*. During a standstill in our conversation, Hart fondled his glass, looked in his abstract, head-tilted-to-the-left manner at the drink and mused: "I love *Pal Joey*. Frankly, I love it more than any of my previous shows. . . . I wonder how many, if any, are yet to come." There came only one more show for Larry Hart before his tragic and untimely end in 1943.

Instr.: 5 reed (including 5 sax, 4 clr, 3 bcl), 5 brass (3 tpt, 1 tb, 1 hrn), ? strings (vln, vla, c, 1 b), piano, perc. (See page 94.)

PAL JOEY (1952 REVIVAL)

"Special orchestrations" by Don **Walker**. (Additional orchestrations by Irwin **Kostal** and Robert **Ginzler**.)

Opened January 2, 1952, Broadhurst, 542 performances. Tryout: December 25, 1951, New Haven (Shubert).

Musical direction by Max Meth. Vocal arrangements by Don Walker. Dance and ballet arrangements by Oscar Kosarin. Other participants: Jule Styne (producer); Vivienne Segal (star); Harold Lang (star); Helen Gallagher (featured).

Invoices are in the Walker Collection at the Library of Congress. The Walker Collection includes Walker's response to a letter from one Fredrica Winters, who praised the revival but complained that the exciting orchestration for "Zip" heard on the 1952 studio cast recording (starring Vivienne Segal and Harold Lang) was not used in the show:

> The points you raised were so interesting that I went out and bought a Columbia album of *Pal Joey*. This is practically treason since my new orchestrations are being released by Capitol Records. The Columbia recording of "Zip" startled me, since I know the original arrangement was made by Hans Spialek, a very gifted legitimate arranger, who, however, is strictly from Vienna, if you know what I mean. In fact I have seen the score of his original arrangement and there isn't a whisper of what happens in what appears to be your favorite recording.
>
> This mystery intrigued me enough to want to unravel it. I have talked to the musicians who were on the Columbia date, and this is the story: When they started to record "Zip," they found that the arrangement was hopelessly square, and in desperation just told the boys to go ahead and fake anything they could think of. The musicians on the date were just about the finest and highest paid men in the business, and they came through beautifully.
>
> So your favorite record is truly a "jam session." What they played was never written down, and even the men themselves could never duplicate it exactly. It is a fine example of free improvisation. Let me add that I think that even if the arrangement could be duplicated in the theatre, it would not be right under those conditions. Pit musicians are not of the caliber of

recording men, and what you feel is satire on the record would, in the theatre, become heavily obvious comment. You must admit that subtlety pays off in the present production. Miss Stritch stops the show with a number that has nothing to do with the plot. What more do you want? All this and Harry James, too?

Instr.: 5 reed (including 5 sax, 5 clr), 5 brass (3 tpt, 2 tb), 9 strings (6 vln, 0 vla, 1 c, 2 b), piano, guitar, perc = 22 total.

PANAMA HATTIE

Orchestrations credited to Don **Walker**. (Additional orchestrations by Russell Bennett, Hans **Spialek**, Ted **Royal**, and possibly others.)

Opened October 30, 1940, 46th Street, 501 performances. Tryout: October 3, New Haven (Shubert); October 8, Boston (Shubert).

Music and lyrics by Cole Porter. Musical direction by Gene Salzer. Vocal arrangements by Lyn Murray. Other participants: B. G. DeSylva (producer); Herbert Fields and B. G. DeSylva (librettists); Ethel Merman (star).

PARADE

Orchestrations uncredited. (Orchestrations by Conrad Salinger, Russell **Bennett**, David Raksin, Jerome Moross, and probably others.)

Opened May 20, 1935, Guild, 40 performances.

Music by Jerome Moross, lyrics by Paul Peters. Musical direction by Max Meth. Other participant: Theatre Guild (producer).

PARADISE ISLAND

Orchestrations credited to Joe Glover. (Additional orchestrators, if any, unknown.)

Opened June 22, 1961, Marine (Jones Beach, New York), 75 performances.

Music by Carmen Lombardo, lyrics by John Jacob Loeb. Musical direction and vocal arrangements by Pembroke Davenport. Dance arrangements by Milt Sherman. Other participants: Guy Lombardo (producer); William Gaxton (star).

PARDON MY ENGLISH

Orchestrations credited to William Daly and Russell Bennett. (Additional orchestrations by Adolph Deutsch.)

Opened January 20, 1933, Majestic, 46 performances. Tryout: December 2, 1932, Philadelphia (Garrick); December 26, Brooklyn (Majestic); January 2, 1933, Newark (Broad Street); January 9, Boston (Colonial).

Music by George Gershwin, lyrics by Ira Gershwin. Musical direction by Earl Busby. Other participants: Alex A. Aarons & Vinton Freedley (producers); Herbert Fields (librettist).

The partiturs are at the Library of Congress (unexamined).

Daly: "The Dresden Northwest Mounted," "Fatherland (Mother of the Band)," "Finaletto Act I," "Freud and Jung and Adler" (two versions), Overture, "Pardon My English," "Together at Last."

Bennett: "Dancing in the Streets," "Finale Act II," "Finaletto," "In Three-Quarter Time," "Isn't It a Pity," "The Luckiest Man in the World," "Nurses," "So What?"

Deutsch: "Golo Theme," "I've Got to Be There," "Michael Theme," "My Cousin in Milwaukee."

Missing: "The Lorelei" (probably by Deutsch).

Instr.: 4 reed (including 3 sax, 3 clr), 5 brass (2 tpt, 1 tb, 2 hrn), 15? strings (10? vln, 2? vla, 2? c, 1? b), piano, perc = 26? total.

PARIS

Orchestrations uncredited. (Orchestrations by Hans **Spialek** and others.)

Opened October 8, 1928, Music Box, 195 performances. Tryout: February 6, Atlantic City (Nixon's Apollo); February 13, Philadelphia (Adelphi); May 7, Boston (Wilbur); September 30, Washington, D.C. (Poli's).

Music and lyrics by Cole Porter (and others). Other participants: Irene Bordoni (star).

PARIS '90

Orchestrations (totally) by Russell **Bennett**.

Opened March 4, 1952, Booth, 87 performances. Tryout: January 24, New Haven (Shubert); elsewhere.

A one-woman revue. Music and lyrics by Kay Swift. Musical direction by Nathaniel Shilkret. Other participant: Cornelia Otis Skinner (author, star).

Bennett's invoices are preserved in his ledger. Base page rate: $3.15.

PARK AVENUE

Orchestrations credited to Don **Walker**. (Additional orchestrators, if any, unknown.)

Opened November 4, 1946, Shubert, 72 performances. Tryout: September 23, Boston (Colonial); October 7, Philadelphia (Shubert); October 19, New Haven (Shubert).

Music by Arthur Schwartz, lyrics by Ira Gershwin. Musical direction by Charles Sanford. Vocal and dance arrangements by Clay Warnick. Other participants: George S. Kaufman (director, co-librettist); Nunnally Johnson (co-librettist); Arnold Saint Subber (production supervisor).

Base page rate: $3.70.

Instr.: 5 reed (with 5 sax), 4 brass (3 tpt, 1 tb), 13 strings (8 vln, 2 vla, 2 c, 1 b), piano, harp, guitar, perc = 26 total.

PEG (1967 VERSION)

Orchestrations credited to Philip J. **Lang**. (Additional orchestrations by Russell **Bennett** and probably others.)

Tryout: August 1, 1967, Westbury [New York] Music Fair. Closed in Valley Forge, Pennsylvania.

Music and lyrics by Johnny Brandon. Based on the play *Peg o' My Heart* by J. Hartley Manners. Musical direction and vocal arrangements by Theodore Saidenberg. Dance arrangements and orchestrations by Leslie Harnley. Other participants: Christopher Hewett (director); Katherine Dunham (choreographer); Eartha Kitt (star).

Bennett's invoices are preserved in his ledger.

Bennett: Entr'acte, Finale act I, "Look at Me," "The Right Kind of People."

PEG (1983 REVUE)

Orchestrations by Philip J. **Lang**, Johnny Mandel, Billy May, Don Sebesky, Larry **Wilcox**, Torrie Zito, and others.

Opened December 14, 1983, Lunt-Fontanne, 5 performances.

"A musical autobiography" of Peggy Lee. Music and lyrics by various writers. New lyrics and book by Peggy Lee. Musical direction by Larry Fallon. Vocal arrangements by Ray Charles. Other participants: Cy Coleman (creative consultant); Peggy Lee (star).

PEG (1984 VERSION)

Orchestrations credited to Larry **Wilcox**. (Additional orchestrators, if any, unknown.)

Opened April 12, 1984, Phoenix (London), 146 performances. Tryout: Guilford, England.

Music by David Heneker, lyrics by David Heneker and John Taylor. Based on the play *Peg o' My Heart* by J. Hartley Manners. Musical direction by Kevin Amos.

PERFECTLY FRANK

Orchestrations credited to Billy Byers. (Additional orchestrations by Luther Henderson and probably others.)

Opened November 30, 1980, Helen Hayes, 16 performances. Tryout: September 10, Los Angeles (Westwood).

A revue. Music and lyrics by Frank Loesser. Musical direction by Yolanda Segovia. Music consultant, Larry Grossman. Dance arrangements, Ronald Melrose. Other participant: Jo Sullivan (featured).

Henderson's invoices are in his personal papers. Base page rate: $13. Tentative attributions per invoice.

Henderson: "Manhattan Sequence (Finale Act I)," "Prologue (Revised)," "Spring Will Be a Little Late This Year."

The Los Angeles tryout used a different set of orchestrations, by Irv Kostal.

Instr.: 4 reed (including 4 sax, 4 clr, 4 fl), 5 brass (3 tpt, 2 tb), 1 strings (1 b), piano/celesta, perc = 12 total.

PETER PAN (1950 VERSION)

Orchestrations credited to Hershy **Kay**. (Additional orchestrators, if any, unknown.)

Opened April 24, 1950, Imperial, 321 performances. Tryout: unknown.

Music and lyrics by Leonard Bernstein. A revised version of the play by J. M. Barrie, with new songs. Conducted by Ben Steinberg. Music coordination and arrangements by Trude Rittman. Other participants: Jean Arthur (star); Boris Karloff (star).

Leonard Bernstein wrote six songs for this version of *Peter Pan*, his second Broadway effort.

Instr.: 6 reed, 1 brass (hrn), ? strings, Novachord (keyboard), 2 perc.

PETER PAN (1954 VERSION)

Orchestrations credited to Albert Sendrey. (Additional orchestrations by Don **Walker**, Robert **Ginzler**, and probably others.)

Opened October 20, 1954, Winter Garden, 152 performances. Tryout: July 19, San Francisco (Curran); Los Angeles (Philharmonic Auditorium).

Music by Mark "Moose" Charlap, additional music by Jule Styne, lyrics by Carolyn Leigh, additional lyrics by Betty Comden & Adolph Green. Based on the play by J. M. Barrie. Musical direction by Louis Adrian. Incidental music by Elmer Bernstein and Trude Rittman. Dance arrangements by Trude Rittman (and the uncredited Roger Adams and John Morris). Other participants: Edwin Lester (co-producer); Jerome Robbins (director, choreographer); Mary Martin (star).

Two charts are in a private collection. Walker's orchestration invoice is at the Library of Congress. Base page rate: $5.52.

"Indian Dance" is by Walker.

"Ugg-a-Wug" is by Walker and Ginzler, with Red providing the "I'll just send for Tiger Lily" section.

The Walker Collection contains an extraordinary letter from Roger Adams:

> Here I am back in L.A. having gone through probably the worst experience I have ever been through. I cannot begin to tell you the story of the mess of *Peter Pan* but all I can say is that I am resting for three days with the help of phenobarbitall, nembutal, aspirin, heating pads and a full-size doctor's bill. I have suffered through bad moments—but to be charged with the combined neuroses of M. Martin, J. Robbins, E. Lester and L. Adrian is something to write home about! During this period I had a back seat driver to guide me—by name, T. Rittman. All in all, I have parted company with said group in good form, with everyone just as nice as they could be. However, this constant effort to retain the "smiling through" attitude has landed me close to the mental ward of the local clinic. Needless to say, the indecision of Mary "How horrible can you get" Martin was too much and I decided to depart from this holocaust of madness and chose to go with Bob Fosse on *My Sister Eileen* at Columbia. [This was a film version of the same source material that had been used for the musical *Wonderful Town*. Adams had been Fosse's arranger on *The Pajama Game* and would work on his next three musicals.] Jerry has been very sweet and gracious to me and at all times conscious of the pressing situation. I would have liked to have been able to see him through but I feel that under the circumstances, I have done more than my duty to the show and now I should not turn down an opportunity that might benefit my bank account. He understands completely and we have parted the best of friends.

THANKS AND WISHES   From Robbins to Walker: "All my deepest appreciation and gratitude for the help you gave when I needed it most, Jerry."

PETER PAN (1979 REVIVAL)

Orchestrations (new) credited to Ralph **Burns**. (Additional orchestrators, if any, unknown.)

Opened September 6, 1979, Lunt-Fontanne, 554 performances. Tryout: Dallas; Atlanta; July 18, Washington, D.C. (Opera House). Musical and vocal direction by Jack Lee. Dance arrangements by Wally Harper. Additional dance arrangements by David Krane. Other participants: Ron Field (replacement director, uncredited); Sandy Duncan (star).

PHIL THE FLUTER

Orchestrations credited to Irwin **Kostal**. (Additional orchestrators, if any, unknown.)

Opened November 13, 1969, Palace (London), 125 performances. Tryout: (as *The Golden Years*) Dublin (Gaiety).

Music and lyrics by David Heneker and Percy French. Suggested by events in the life of Percy French. Musical direction by Ray Cook. Other participants: Harold Fielding (producer); Gillian Lynne (choreographer); Evelyn Laye (star).

Kostal's Overture—which combines the styles of Irish composer Percy French (1854–1920), traditional musical comedy composer Heneker (of *Half a Sixpence*), and pop music of the sixties—is a highly impressive example of both arranging and orchestrating. Seek it out if you can.

PHOENIX '55

Orchestrations credited to Ralph **Burns** and Clare Grundman. (Additional orchestrators, if any, unknown.)

Opened April 23, 1955, Phoenix (off-Broadway), 97 performances.

A revue. Music by David Baker, lyrics by David Craig. Musical direction by Buster Davis. Ballet arrangements by John Morris. Other participant: Nancy Walker (star).

(See page 34.)

THE PINK JUNGLE

Orchestrations credited to Albert Sendrey. (Additional orchestrators, if any, unknown.)

Tryout: October 14, 1959, San Francisco (Alcazar); Detroit (Fisher). Closed December 12, Boston (Shubert).

Music and lyrics by Vernon Duke. Musical direction by Sherman Frank. Vocal arrangements by Jack Lattimer. Other participants: Ginger Rogers (star); Agnes Moorehead (featured).

PIPE DREAM

Orchestrations by Russell **Bennett**. (Additional orchestrations by Joe Glover, Philip J. **Lang**, Jack Mason, Robert Noeltner, Don **Walker**, and Hans **Spialek**.)

Opened November 30, 1955, Shubert, 246 performances. Tryout: October 22, New Haven (Shubert); November 1, Boston (Shubert).

Music by Richard Rodgers, lyrics and book by Oscar Hammerstein II. Based on the novel *Sweet Thursday* by John Steinbeck. Musical direction by Salvatore Dell'Isola. Dance arrangements by John Morris. Other participants: Richard Rodgers and Oscar Hammerstein II (producers); Harold Clurman (director).

The partiturs are in the Rodgers Collection at the Library of Congress, with copies at the offices of the Rodgers & Hammerstein Organization. Invoices are preserved in Bennett's ledger. Base page rate: $6.21. Invoices indicate: Bennett (60%), Glover (16%), Lang (10%).

The orchestrations are by Bennett, with the following exceptions:

Glover: "All Kinds of People" (reprise), "The Man I Used to Be" (see below). "The Party That We're Gonna Have Tomorrow Night" (song, dance, utility), "Sweet Thursday" (reprise), "Temporary Overture," many fixes and incidentals.

Lang: "Masquerade Brawl" (page 152 of vocal score), "Party Dance" (a 102-page score, which is highly abbreviated in the vocal score).

Mason: utilities ("All at Once You Love Her," "Everybody's Got a Home," "Sweet Thursday").

Noeltner: "Bum's Opera Reprise" and utility.

Spialek: "I Am a Witch (Gang of Witches)."

Other scores:

"All Kinds of People" is by Bennett, with a 16-bar insert (not in the published vocal score) by Glover.

"All at Once You Love Her" is by Bennett; reprise ("Helen's Version") is by Glover, with a verse by Bennett.

"A Lopsided Bus" is by Bennett, with a large insert (at bars 175–310, on page 53 of the vocal score) by Noeltner; "Reprise Ending" is by Noeltner.

"The Man I Used to Be" is by Glover, except for an 8-bar instrumental (at 123–131, on page 87 of the vocal score) by Bennett, from a cut chart called "Doc's Essence Dance."

"The Next Time It Happens" is by Bennett, replacing an earlier version by Spialek.

"Suzy Is a Good Thing": there are two versions, one by Bennett and one by Walker.

"Will You Marry Me?" is by Lang; for the version used on the cast album, Bennett rewrote Doc's section of the song.

Instr.: 5 reed, 8 brass (3 tpt, 2 tb, 1 tuba, 2 hrn), 13 strings (8 vln, 2 vla, 2 c, 1 b), piano, harp, perc = 29 total.

PIPPIN

Orchestrations credited to Ralph **Burns**. (Additional orchestrations by Jonathan Tunick and, possibly, others.)

Opened October 23, 1972, Imperial, 1,944 performances. Tryout: September 20, Washington, D.C. (Opera House).

Music and lyrics by Stephen Schwartz. Musical direction by Stanley Lebowsky. Dance arrangements by John Berkman. Other participants: Stuart Ostrow (producer); Bob Fosse (director, choreographer).

TUNICK: Ralph gave me a jazz dance to do, and told me the instrumentation. I said, "Ralph, with a score like this, why did you choose only two trombones and one trumpet?" He said, "They told me it was a medieval operetta."

Instr.: 2 reed, 4 brass (I tpt, 2 tb, I hrn), 4 strings (I vln, I vla, I c, I b), 2 piano (I organ, I harpsichord), harp, guitar/banjo/elec guitar, 2 perc = 16 total.

PLAIN AND FANCY

Orchestrations credited to Philip J. **Lang**. (Additional orchestrators, if any, unknown.)

Opened January 27, 1955, Mark Hellinger, 461 performances. Tryout: December 11, 1954, New Haven (Shubert); elsewhere.

Music by Albert Hague, lyrics by Arnold B. Horwitt. Musical direction by Franz Allers. Assistant to Franz Allers, Peter Howard. Vocal arrangements and direction by Crane Calder. Other participants: Morton Da Costa (director); Joseph Stein (co-librettist); Barbara Cook (featured).

It is likely that the orchestrations were ghosted by Jack Mason and, possibly, Bob Noeltner on the extensive dance sections.

PLEASURE DOME

Orchestrations credited to Ralph **Burns**. (Additional orchestrators, if any, unknown.)

Closed in rehearsal, prior to the first preview scheduled for December 1, 1955, in Washington, D.C. (Shubert).

A revue. Music and lyrics mostly by Dean Fuller and Marshall Barer. Musical direction and vocal arrangements by Buster Davis. Other participants: Ira Wallach (sketch writer); Kaye Ballard (star).

This revue, which would have been Ralph Burns's first Broadway job, ran out of money during rehearsals and was forced to disband.

BUSTER DAVIS: *Pleasure Dome* was frightening. Everybody practically bought their way into the show. We had three really good performers who didn't, but the rest of the people were unbelievable. George Abbott came in to see a rehearsal. And he liked it. It was good material, Abbott said, "but this is the strangest show I have ever seen. The leads are marvelous, but the supporting people are just shocking, they are so bad." As for the producer—it was the first time that I had ever seen the naked use of money and sex to cast a show. Of course, it couldn't work. You cannot put someone's lover or husband on the stage just because he put in $5,000 or $12,000—not if they don't have any talent. Most of the material showed up in *New Faces of 1956*.

(See page 34.)

PLEASURES AND PALACES

Orchestrations (totally) by Philip J. **Lang**.

Tryout: March 11, 1965, Detroit (Fisher). Closed April 10, Detroit.

Music and lyrics by Frank Loesser. Based on the play *Once There Was a Russian* by Sam Spewack. Musical direction by Fred Werner. Other participants: Allen Whitehead (producer); Frank Productions/Frank Loesser (associate producer); Bob Fosse (director, choreographer); Frank Loesser (co-librettist); Phyllis Newman (star).

> WHITEHEAD: It was beyond Phil—I don't think he was qualified to do that type of show. He was just a layman, wasn't an inventive kind of person. I think it was just desperation—we were ready to go, suddenly things fell into place. It seems like he was the only person available.

Phyllis Newman remembered her husband, lyricist/librettist Adolph Green, visiting Detroit: "Adolph, of course, wouldn't say anything negative. But he did ask, "Don't they think it might be inadvisable to write a musical based on a play that closed after only one performance?"

Instr.: 5 reed (5 clr, 3 fl), 7 brass (2 tpt, 2 tb/1 with baritone and carillon, 3 hrn), 14 strings (8 vln, 0 vla, 4 c, 2 b/1 with tuba), harp, guitar/mandolin, 2 perc = 29 total.

(See page 243.)

POLONAISE

Orchestrations credited to Don **Walker**. (Additional orchestrators, if any, unknown.)

Opened October 6, 1945, Alvin, 113 performances. Tryout: September 24, Washington, D.C. (National); elsewhere.

Music by Frederic Chopin. Adaptations and original numbers by Bronislaw Kaper. Lyrics by John Latouche. Musical direction by Max Goberman. Vocal direction by Irving Landau. Other participants: Jan Kiepura (star); Martha Eggerth (star).

PORGY AND BESS

Orchestrations (virtually totally) by George Gershwin (with Russell **Bennett**, Hans **Spialek** and William Daly?).

Opened October 10, 1935, Alvin, 124 performances. Tryout: September 30, Boston (Colonial).

An opera. Music by George Gershwin, lyrics by DuBose Heyward and Ira Gershwin. Based on the novel *Porgy* by Heyward and the play by DuBose and Dorothy Heyward. Musical direction by Alexander Smallens. Assistant conductor, Alexander Steinert. Choral direction by Eva Jessye. Other participants: Theatre Guild (producer); Rouben Mamoulian (director); DuBose Heyward (librettist).

The partiturs are at the Library of Congress.

Gershwin's original partiturs, bound and carefully preserved at the Library of Congress, are a monumental piece of art: 548 pages in a beautiful, stylish and expressive hand that recall nothing so much as a medieval manuscript. (These 548 pages are not comparable to the standard page count, which is calculated at the union rate of 4 bars per page, as many pages contain twice that amount or more.) Gershwin writes not only every musical note but also every word of the libretto, as well as stage and musical directions, in an emotional and impassioned hand that is breathtaking. (The composer had immersed himself into painting at the time, which seems to enhance the visual appeal of the manuscript.) He has signed the scores with a finish date of September 2, 1935, four weeks before the first performance. Which leads to an obvious question: what happened next? There are no known cases of a Broadway musical that was not changed and altered during the rehearsal and tryout periods. Routines are revamped; material is cut or added; keys are altered to accommodate performers; adjustments in the orchestration, itself, are *always* necessary during and after the orchestra readings. Changes are necessary for missed notes, for places where the singers might need more or less support, for passages that don't sound precisely as the composer or orchestrator expected.

Porgy and Bess was a monumentally complex piece, featuring performers who for the most part were unaccustomed to performing on the musical theatre stage, a director with operatic but not musical theatre experience, and what one might consider a novice orchestrator. Gershwin by this point had scored some of his later symphonic pieces and perhaps two or three numbers in each of a half-dozen or so musicals. He had little experience at orchestrating passages that were intended to be sung, and nothing on the scale of *Porgy and Bess*. It seems impossible to expect the September 2 scores to have been played intact on September 30 in Boston and October 10 in New York. In fact, time and performance constraints necessitated severe cuts in the 1935 production of *Porgy*.

The partiturs are pristine, with no cuts indicated (although there are erasures, crossouts, and pages on which Gershwin either laid out lines for instruments that he did not ultimately use or crammed in an instrument he did not anticipate needing). These tryout cuts and changes were presumably made on a copy of the partiturs; nothing has survived, though, other than the original copy of the score—which is in such fine condition that one suspects that George carefully stored it away in New York for safekeeping and worked solely from copies.

Tryouts are hectic times, with alterations happening around the clock. In those days, the composer and director would consult on changes late at night following the performance, consulting with the orchestrator at 1 a.m. or so; he would then work through the new pages and would pass them over to the copyists at 6 a.m. so new parts could be prepared and assembled in time for that evening's performance. Which necessitated the professional workhorse-type of theatre orchestrator like Bennett, Spialek, Walker, or Royal, who was conditioned to work fast and without sleep. (Gershwin did a masterful job on the *Porgy* orchestration, but he spent more than nine months on it; Bennett appears to have done *Show Boat*, which is close to comparable in size if you include all the deleted material, in a month or so.) Severe cuts such as occurred on *Porgy* are not a mere question of removing pages; changes and alterations need to be made to get from one point to another. All of which is why, as we have discussed on earlier pages, it is impractical for a theatre composer to orchestrate his own musical. Given the activity going on at the Colonial in Boston in the last days of September and the first week of October, it seems beyond the realm of possibility for George to have orchestrated the corrections, changes, and fixes by himself.

Pending the discovery of amended orchestral scores, no definitive information on who did the additional work on *Porgy* is likely to surface. Two anecdotal accounts, however, indicate that changes indeed came from other hands. When Larry Blank discovered the semi-retired Spialek anonymously copying parts in 1975 (as related elsewhere), their conversation was far-ranging. Blank recalls Spialek specifically mentioning that he and Russell went to Boston on *Porgy* to "finish everything up for George"; he did not claim major contributions, but described the job as "cleaning up stuff." Spialek possessed a perfect memory, even in his later years, and was not the sort to take credit where it was unwarranted; that being the case, one would have to accept this statement as being factual. (It also seems likely that Gershwin consulted with his friend Bennett during the long months he spent orchestrating the score; under the circumstances, Bennett most certainly would have offered constructive advice without feeling the need to tell anyone about it.) Morris Stonzek, the long-active musical contractor who played first cello on the show, claimed in his 1978 interview with Lehman Engel that Gershwin's close friend Bill Daly—conductor and orchestrator of many of Gershwin musicals—did significant work on *Porgy*. Daly's input is likely, given the close nature of his professional relationship with Gershwin and the fact that he was very much present (though not officially working on the show). Given the entirety of Stonzek's interview, though, I am not as sanguine about his overall accuracy.

It should be added that while the full partiturs at the Library of Congress are completely in Gershwin's hand, there is technically another hand present. Gershwin used clean, 30-stave paper without any instrument names printed on it. (Chappell orchestrators usually worked on paper with instrument names preprinted along the left-hand column, available with various instrumental lineups.) Gershwin wrote the needed instruments on each of the 548 pages, in ink (fountain pen?), in his artistic, mellifluous hand. On about half-a-dozen pages, though, in Act One Scene II (the funeral scene incorporating "My Man's Gone Now"), Gershwin has labeled the reeds (at the top) and the strings (on the bottom) but the lines in the middle of the score page are written in, in ink, in a markedly different hand. (This is almost surely that of Walter Paul, a friend of Bennett's who did charts for many Chappell shows of the period.) Paul didn't write any of the orchestration, mind you; he only labeled the instruments that Gershwin for some reason omitted. There are also some minor pencil additions to actual orchestration; these are presumably (though not certainly) in Gershwin's hand. The other mystery of the score is the banjo, which is sparingly used—I count 61 bars—for "I Got Plenty of Nuttin'" and its brief reprise. There was surely not a separate banjo chair; was this played by one of the viola players, or perhaps a violinist; or perhaps an on-stage member of the cast?

In any event, it is safe to say that the orchestration of *Porgy and Bess* was for all intents and purposes done by Gershwin himself, with minor help from Bennett and Spialek. Gershwin never again attempted anything on this scale—he died within two years of the opening of his opera—but one thing is for certain: this is a monumental score and a monumental orchestration, and it is pretty much all George.

Instr.: 9 reed (including 4 clr [3 sax], 2 fl, 2 oboe/Eng hrn. I bssn), 9 brass (3 tpt, 2 tb, I tuba, 3 hrn), 21? strings (12? vln, 4? vla [including I banjo?], 3 c, 2 b), piano, 2 perc = 42? total.

PORTOFINO

Orchestrations credited to Philip J. **Lang**. (Additional orchestrators, if any, unknown.) Opened February 21, 1958, Adelphi, 3 performances. Tryout: Philadelphia.

Music by Louis Bellson and Will Irwin, lyrics by Richard Ney. Additional lyrics by Sheldon Harnick. Musical direction by Will Irwin. Vocal arrangements by Joe Moon. Other participants: Helen Gallagher (star); Georges Guetary (star).

POUSSE CAFÉ

Orchestrations credited to Larry **Wilcox**. (Additional orchestrators, if any, unknown.)

Opened March 18, 1966, 46th Street, 3 performances. Tryout: January 25, Toronto (O'Keefe); Detroit (Fisher).

Music by Duke Ellington, lyrics by Marshall Barer and Fred Tobias. Based on the film *The Blue Angel*, from the play *Professor Unrath* by Heinrich Mann. Musical direction by Sherman Frank. Other participants: José Quintero (replacement director); Jerome Weidman (replacement librettist); Lilo (star).

> COPYIST EMILE CHARLAP: We opened the tryout in Toronto. We got a band there that was so great, the fourth trumpet could have played first. So our first trumpet player, all he did was play ad libs, sweet parts. It was a Duke Ellington score, it was so great, the best band we ever had. We went to Detroit after that, the band was so bad, the lead trumpet player couldn't even play the first part.

A live tape—presumably from Toronto—demonstrates that the orchestrations are vibrant, with the Overture featuring a phenomenal trumpet part (with a high G), on the level of *Gypsy* and *Funny Girl.*

PRESENT ARMS!

Orchestrations uncredited. (Orchestrations by Hans **Spialek** and others.)

Opened April 26, 1928, Mansfield, 155 performances. Tryout: April 9, Wilmington, DE (Shubert); April 18, Atlantic City (Apollo).

Music by Richard Rodgers, lyrics by Lorenz Hart. Musical direction by Roy Webb. Other participants: Lew Fields (producer); Busby Berkeley (choreographer, featured); Ray Bolger (featured).

One partitur is in the Rodgers Collection at the Library of Congress.

Spialek: "Atlantic Blues."

PRETTYBELLE

Orchestrations credited to Elliot Lawrence and Jack Cortner. (Additional orchestrators, if any, unknown.)

Tryout: February 1, 1971, Boston (Shubert). Closed March 6, Boston.

Music by Jule Styne, lyrics and book by Bob Merrill. Based on the novel by Jean Arnold. Musical direction and incidental music by Peter Howard. Other participants: Alexander H. Cohen (producer); Gower Champion (director, choreographer); Angela Lansbury (star).

The partiturs are at the Styne office (partially examined).

Luther Henderson's papers include receipts for a trip to Boston to see *Prettybelle* on February 2, although it is unknown whether he did any work. The Overture on the studio cast album—recorded twenty years after the show opened and closed—was orchestrated by Phil Lang.

PROMENADE

Orchestrations credited to Eddie **Sauter**. (Additional orchestrators, if any, unknown.)

Opened June 4, 1969, Promenade (off-Broadway), 259 performances.

Music by Al Carmines, lyrics by Maria Irene Fornes. Musical direction and vocal arrangements by Al Carmines. Conductor, Susan Romann. Other participant: Madeline Kahn (featured).

PROMISES, PROMISES

Orchestrations (virtually totally) by Jonathan Tunick.

Opened December 1, 1968, Shubert, 1,281 performances. Tryout: Boston (Colonial); October 29, Washington, D.C. (National).

Music by Burt Bacharach, lyrics by Hal David. Based on the film *The Apartment* by Billy Wilder and I. A. L. Diamond. Musical direction by Harold Wheeler (replacing Arthur Rubinstein). Dance arrangements by Harold Wheeler. Other participants: David Merrick (producer); Michael Bennett (choreographer); Jerry Orbach (star); Donna McKechnie (dancer).

Copies of the partiturs are at Tams-Witmark.

The orchestrations are by Tunick, with the exception of a 24-bar introduction to "Christmas Party" by Harold Wheeler.

> STEPHEN SONDHEIM: A good friend, Mike Stewart, had written a script called *How Do You Do? I Love You*. He asked me to do the score. I turned it down, but I said, "I have a couple of promising and talented young composers. I'm mentoring them slightly, I would recommend them." Mike said, "Great." So Maltby and Shire wrote the score. It was done in one of the tents, Westbury, with Phyllis Newman, who was also a friend. I went to see it. I was completely knocked out that they had such a huge orchestra. At intermission, I went and looked in the pit. Twelve people! I thought, "This guy's great!"
>
> Burt Bacharach, who I knew slightly, came to New York to do *Promises, Promises*. He called me and said, "You're one of the few people I know in the theatre—who should orchestrate the show?" I said, "This guy named Jonathan Tunick strikes me as terrific." I heard the stuff for *Promises*. Between that and *How Do You Do?* I figured I'd ask Jonathan to do my orchestrations for *Company*.

Harold Wheeler was a first-time Broadway dance arranger. When the original conductor was fired during the Boston tryout, Merrick offered the job to Wheeler despite his lack of conducting experience. Similarly, Tunick—who had spent eight years in search of his own break—offered Wheeler a minor incidental, letting him break in as a Broadway orchestrator. (See page 222.)

PURLIE

Orchestrations and choral arrangements credited to Gary Sherman and Luther Henderson. (Additional orchestrators, if any, unknown.)

Opened March 15, 1970, Broadway, 688 performances. Tryout: none.

Music by Gary Geld, lyrics by Peter Udell. Based on the play *Purlie Victorious* by Ossie Davis. Musical direction by Joyce Brown. Dance arrangements by Luther Henderson. Additional arrangements by Ray Wright. Other participants: Ossie Davis (colibrettist); Cleavon Little (star); Melba Moore (star).

Some of Henderson's invoices are in his personal papers. Base page rate: $10. Tentative attributions per invoice.

Henderson: "Big Fish," "Cotchipee's Dream" ballet (125 pages), "Easy-Going Man" (cut), "He Can Do It."

It is believed that Henderson also orchestrated "Walk Him Up the Stairs," although no corroboration can be found.

QUEEN HIGH

Orchestrations uncredited. (Orchestrations by Russell **Bennett** and others.)

Opened September 5, 1926, Ambassador, 367 performances. Tryout: April 1, New Haven (Shubert); elsewhere.

Music by Lewis Gensler, lyrics by B. G. DeSylva. Based on the play *A Pair of Sixes* by Edward Peple. Musical direction by Ivan Rudisill. Other participant: Laurence Schwab (producer, co-librettist).

RAINBOW

Orchestrations uncredited. (Orchestrations by Arthur Lange, Russell **Bennett**, Max Steiner and others.)

Opened November 21, 1928, Gallo (Studio 54), 29 performances. Tryout: October 29, Philadelphia (Chestnut Street); November 12, Baltimore (Maryland).

Music by Vincent Youmans, lyrics and book by Oscar Hammerstein II. Musical direction by Max Steiner. Other participants: Busby Berkeley (choreographer); Laurence Stallings (colibrettist); Libby Holman (star).

Several partiturs are in the Youmans Collection at the Library of Congress.

Lange: "Hay, Straw," "I Want a Man," "The One Girl"
Steiner: "The Bride Was Dressed in White," "Who Am I?"
Bennett: "My Mother Told Me Not to Trust a Soldier"
Unidentified hand: "I Like You As You Are."

RED, HOT AND BLUE!

Orchestrations credited to Russell **Bennett**. (Additional orchestrations by Hans **Spialek**, Don **Walker**, and probably others.)

Opened October 29, 1936, Alvin, 183 performances. Tryout: October 7, Boston (Colonial); October 19, New Haven (Shubert).

Music and lyrics by Cole Porter. Musical direction by Frank Tours. Other participants: Vinton Freedley (producer); Howard Lindsay and Russel Crouse (librettists); Ethel Merman (star); Jimmy Durante (star); Bob Hope (star).

Walker: "Down in the Depths (on the 90th Floor)."

Sitting in Boston with the tryout of Romberg's *Forbidden Melody*, Walker received an emergency call. *Red, Hot and Blue!* was finishing its engagement that weekend, around the corner at the Colonial. Everybody had been displeased with Ethel Merman's opening number; Cole Porter had just finished a new one. The song needed to go in that night; there was an orchestra rehearsal called just before that evening's performance; and the orchestrators (Bennett and Spialek) were back in New York. Walker got to work. Merman, who missed the pre-show rehearsal, performed "Down in the Depths (on the 90th Floor)" cold that evening—and stopped the show. "Who did the arrangement?" she asked. "He did," they said, pointing to Walker. "It's okay," said the Merm.

THE RED SHOES

Orchestrations credited to Sid **Ramin** and William D. Brohn. (Additional orchestrators, if any, unknown.)

Opened December 16, 1993, Gershwin, 5 performances.

Music by Jule Styne, lyrics by Marsha Norman and Paul Stryker (aka Bob Merrill). A stage adaptation of the film by Emeric Pressburger and Michael Powell. Musical direction and vocal arrangements by Donald Pippin. Ballet and dance music arrangements by Gordon Harrell. Other participants: Stanley Donen (replacement director); Lar Lubovitch (choreographer); Marsha Norman (librettist).

The partiturs are at the Styne office (unexamined).

REDHEAD

Orchestrations credited to Philip J. **Lang** and Russell **Bennett**. (Additional orchestrators, if any, unknown.)

Opened February 5, 1959, 46th Street, 452 performances. Tryout: December 20, 1958, New Haven (Shubert); Washington, D.C. (National); January 1959, Philadelphia (Shubert);

Music by Albert Hague, lyrics by Dorothy Fields. Musical direction and vocal arrangements by Jay Blackton. Dance arrangements by Roger Adams. Other participants: Robert Fryer (producer); Bob Fosse (director, choreographer); Herbert & Dorothy Fields (co-librettists); Gwen Verdon (star); Richard Kiley (featured).

Bennett's invoices are preserved in his ledger. Base page rate: $6.

Bennett: "Behave Yourself" (song and vignettes), "Chase," "Don't Mention It," Finale ("Chase"/"Merely Marvelous" reprise), "The Girl Is Not Enough Woman," "My Girl Is Just Enough Woman," "Opening," "Simpson Sisters," "Two Faces in the Dark."

Bennett did the original versions of these numbers, although during the tryout some of them might have been replaced. The version of "The Pick-Pocket Tango" on the original cast album is not the version used in the show; it was written by and is credited to Sid Ramin. RCA assigned staff orchestrator Ramin to score the "Tango" specifically for the recording. While the partiturs for the theatre version are missing, the piano-conductor score (at MTI) has a reduction of this different and weaker version (which is by Lang or a ghost). This can be heard, with a somewhat reduced orchestra, on *La Pelirroja*, the 1960 Mexican cast album of *Redhead*. (The soloist in the "Two Faces in the Dark" number is a nineteen-year-old tenor named Placido Domingo.)

REGINA

Orchestrations credited to Marc Blitzstein. (Additional orchestrators, if any, unknown.)
Opened October 31, 1949, 46th Street, 56 performances. Tryout: October 6, New Haven (Shubert); elsewhere.
Music, lyrics, and book by Marc Blitzstein. Based on the play *The Little Foxes* by Lillian Hellman. Musical direction by Maurice Abravanel. Other participants: Cheryl Crawford (producer); Robert Lewis (director).

REUBEN REUBEN

Orchestrations credited to Marc Blitzstein, "assisted by Hershy **Kay** and Bill Stegmeyer."
Tryout: October 10, 1955, Boston (Shubert). Closed October 22, Boston.
Music, lyrics, and book by Marc Blitzstein. Musical direction by Samuel Krachmalnick. Choral direction by Abba Bogin. Other participants: Cheryl Crawford (producer); Robert Lewis (director); Eddie Albert (star).

> BOGIN: Hershy did most of everything. Marc didn't want people to think he didn't know what he was doing. After the show, we had meetings eight nights a week.

(See page 49.)

REVENGE WITH MUSIC

Orchestrations credited to Russell **Bennett**. (Additional orchestrators, if any, unknown.)
Opened November 28, 1934, New Amsterdam, 158 performances. Tryout: unknown.
Music by Arthur Schwartz, lyrics and book by Howard Dietz. Based on the novel *The Three-Cornered Hat* by Pedro de Alarcón. Musical direction by Victor Baravelle. Other participants: Charles Winninger (star); Libby Holman (star).

REX

Orchestrations (totally) by Irwin **Kostal**.
Opened April 25, 1976, Lunt-Fontanne, 49 performances. Tryout: February 23, Wilmington, Delaware (Playhouse); March 4, Washington, D.C. (Opera House); March 23, Boston (Shubert).

Music by Richard Rodgers, lyrics by Sheldon Harnick. Suggested by events in the life of Henry VIII. Musical direction by Jay Blackton. Dance arrangements by David Baker. Other participants: Richard Adler (producer); Edwin Sherin (director); Harold Prince (replacement director, uncredited); Nicol Williamson (star).

The partiturs are at the offices of the Rodgers & Hammerstein Organization.

> IRV KOSTAL: The director, Edwin Sherin, asked me to orchestrate the show in the style of music played in the time of Henry VIII. He presented me with a tape of a small baroque group playing songs composed by the king. When I discussed this with Dick Rodgers, he said, "I didn't go to Siam to write the songs for *The King and I*." He had no interest in being authentic. Sherin was insistent and unbending. He demanded I use "krum horns" because he had found, in his own research, these were the kinds of horns used in the sixteenth century. In my own research, I learned these krum horns were made of wood; there are only two still in existence, in a museum in Copenhagen. When I informed Ed of this tidbit of information, he really blew his stack, and we proceeded in extreme difficulty.
>
> Then, Barbara Andres, as Queen Catherine, stopped the show with "As Once I Loved You." Sherin couldn't stand it. He called a meeting, and opened up with, "It's against my religion to allow a song to interfere with the progression of the story line by causing the audience to unnecessarily applaud." And Dick answered in his difficult to control voice: "And it's against my religion to take out a song that stops the show!" Jay Blackton advised me on how to orchestrate this number. He even sang some of the fills he wanted me to use, claiming he knew exactly what Richard Rodgers would expect. At the first orchestra rehearsal, when Dick heard this treatment, he asked me to remove the ridiculous fills I had written. Never mentioning who had suggested these fills, I dutifully and pleasurably removed all these unnecessary orchestral embellishments, much to Jay's displeasure. He never forgave me. And that's how things went with *Rex*.

Don Walker had begun the job, going so far as to set the instrumentation. While he had a long and cordial relationship with producer Richard Adler (co-author of *The Pajama Game*), his contract had to be approved by composer Rodgers. Walker to Adler:

> As soon as negotiations began, my manager found that Rodgers and [attorney Edward] Colton were trying to push me back to 1955. Even then, trying to help you because of your obvious royalty problems, I made the first reductions in my demands since 1956. But that wasn't enough. Rodgers-Colton wanted to put me back with Russell Bennett circa 1955. Luckily, I don't need *Rex*. I am now in the position where I only wish to do shows that I can enjoy, with people who need my contributions and are willing to pay for them. It would not be fair to all those producers and writers who have accepted my contract to suddenly emasculate it for Dick Rodgers. I hope you have a hit.

Kostal, who had orchestrated and conducted the film version of *The Sound of Music*, came in to do *Rex*. The reverse happened on *Fiddler on the Roof*, with Walker stepping in when Kostal withdrew to do *Mary Poppins*.

Instr.: 4 reed (including recorder), 6 brass (3 tpt, 1 tb, 2 hrn), 9 strings (4 vln, 2 vla, 2 c, b), harpsichord/celesta, harp, guitar, 2 perc = 24 total.

RHAPSODY

Orchestrations credited to Russell **Bennett**. (Additional orchestrators, if any, unknown.)
Opened November 22, 1944, Century, 13 performances. Tryout: unknown.
Music by Fritz Kreisler, musical adaptation by Russell Bennett, lyrics by John Latouche, additional lyrics by Russell Bennett and Blevins Davis. Musical direction by Fritz Mahler.

RIGHT THIS WAY

Orchestrations uncredited. (Orchestrations by Hans **Spialek**, Maurice de Packh, Claude Austin, and probably others.)
Opened January 4, 1938, 46th Street, 15 performances. Tryout: unknown.
Music by Bradford Greene and Sammy Fain, lyrics by Marianne Brown Waters and Irving Kahal. Musical direction by Max Meth.

THE ROAR OF THE GREASEPAINT—THE SMELL OF THE CROWD

Orchestrations by Philip J. **Lang**. (Additional orchestrations by Russell **Bennett** and possibly others.)
Opened: May 16, 1965, Shubert, 231 performances. Tryout: Wilmington, Delaware (Playhouse); February 8, Washington, D.C. (National); Philadelphia (Forrest); March 15, New Haven (Shubert); March 22, Boston (Shubert); Cleveland; Toronto (O'Keefe).
Music, lyrics, and book by Leslie Bricusse and Anthony Newley. Musical direction by Herbert Grossman. Vocal and dance arrangements by Peter Howard. Other participants: David Merrick (producer); Anthony Newley (director, star); Gillian Lynne (choreographer).

The partiturs are at Tams-Witmark.

The orchestrations are by Lang, with the following exceptions:

Bennett: Overture (written on National Broadcasting Company paper).

Stored along with Lang's partiturs of "Love Song," "Put It in the Book," "Things to Remember" (reprise), and "Who Can I Turn To?" are the charts from the original UK production (each labeled "English Arrangement"), making one question whether these were adapted by Lang, or perhaps replaced his charts. The pit book of partiturs, which conductor Herb Grossman used at the podium, includes the English arrangement (presumably by Ian Fraser) of "Who Can I Turn To?" This version seems to have been used in performance.

ROBERTA

Orchestrations (totally) by Russell **Bennett**.

Opened November 18, 1933, New Amsterdam, 295 performances. Tryout: (as *Gowns by Roberta*) October 21, Philadelphia (Forrest).

Music by Jerome Kern, lyrics and book by Otto Harbach. Based on the novel *Gowns by Roberta* by Alice Duer Miller. Musical direction by Victor Baravelle. Other participants: Max Gordon (producer); Jerome Kern (original director); Hassard Short (replacement director, unbilled); Bob Hope (featured).

The partiturs are in the Kern Collection at the Library of Congress.

> BENNETT: I can report another one of those mistakes I made that never stop yapping at my heels. There was a song called "I'll Be Hard to Handle." The singer was Lyda Roberti, one of the most original personalities on the stage at that time. I took a good look at her, sized up her style, and missed it by nine nautical miles. I gave her an arrangement that might have been effective with a number of red-hot mamas of the day, but poor Roberti stood in the middle of the stage trying to figure out what hit her. What I had missed was the very keynote of her act. She was a tender character trying to be tough and only succeeding in being adorable. Sweet she was, but not hot. It took only a few minutes to take all the sassiness out of the orchestra, but a good music arranger is supposed to see those things coming.

Instr.: 4 reed, 3 brass (2 tpt, 1 tb), 15? strings (8? vln, 3? vla, 3? c, 1 b), 2 piano (1 celesta), perc = 25? total.

RODGERS & HART

Orchestrations by Luther Henderson. (Additional orchestrations by William D. Brohn, Jim Tyler, and Russell **Bennett**.)

Opened May 13, 1975, Helen Hayes (aka Fulton), 111 performances.

A revue. Music by Richard Rodgers, lyrics by Lorenz Hart. Musical direction by Buster Davis. Dance arrangements by Luther Henderson. Other participants: Burt Shevelove (director); Donald Saddler (choreographer).

Invoices are preserved in Henderson's papers. Bennett's invoices are preserved in his ledger. Base page rate: $8.

This revue featured about 100 songs, sectioned in medleys (which makes a number-by-number listing impractical). Henderson and Brohn each did over a third of the charts; Tyler wrote about 250 pages; and Bennett contributed his final Broadway work, with 18 pages of the act I Finale and 16 pages of the Entr'acte.

RONDELAY

Orchestrations credited to Philip J. **Lang**. (Additional orchestrators, if any, unknown.)

Opened November 5, 1969, Hudson West (off-Broadway), 11 performances.

Music and lyrics by Jerry Douglas. Based on the play *La Ronde* by Arthur Schnitzler. Musical direction and vocal arrangements by Karen Gustafson. Other participant: Jacques d'Amboise (choreographer).

ROSALIE

Orchestrations uncredited. (Orchestrations by Emil Gerstenberger, Hans **Spialek**, Max
   Steiner, Maurice de Packh, William Daly, Hilding Anderson, and possibly others.)
Opened January 10, 1928, New Amsterdam, 335 performances. Tryout: December 5,
   1927, Boston (Colonial).
Music by George Gershwin and Sigmund Romberg, lyrics by P. G. Wodehouse and Ira
   Gershwin. Musical direction by Oscar Bradley. Other participants: Florenz Ziegfeld
   (producer); Marilyn Miller (star).

The partiturs are at the Library of Congress (unexamined).
   Gerstenberger: "Entrance of Hussars," "Opening Scene 1, Act 1," "Rosalie Waltz,"
"Say So," "Trio," "West Point March," "West Point Song."
   Spialek: "Flunkeys," Overture, "Show Me the Town."
   de Packh: "An Ace, a King and a Jack," Ballet, "New York Serenade."
   Daly: "Setting Up Exercise."
   Anderson: "Finale Act 1."
   Steiner: "Opening Act 2."
   Other scores:
   Ballet: the existing partiturs include two ballet scores. One is denoted as "by" Rom-
berg (that is, adapted from songs by Romberg), scored by de Packh. The other is "by"
Romberg and Gershwin, scored by Gerstenberger.

ROSE-MARIE

Orchestrations credited to Russell **Bennett**. (Additional orchestrations by Maurice de
   Packh and, presumably, others.)
Opened September 2, 1924, Imperial, 557 performances. Tryout: August 18, Atlantic
   City (Apollo); Long Branch, New Jersey (Auditorium).
Music by Rudolf Friml and Herbert Stothart, lyrics and book by Otto Harbach and
   Oscar Hammerstein II. Musical direction by Herbert Stothart.

(See page 27.)

THE ROTHSCHILDS

Orchestrations credited to Don **Walker**. (Additional orchestrators, if any, unknown.)
Opened October 19, 1970, Lunt-Fontanne, 505 performances. Tryout: August 11, Detroit (Fisher); September 17, Philadelphia (Forrest).
Music by Jerry Bock, lyrics by Sheldon Harnick. Based on the biography by Frederic Morton. Musical direction and vocal arrangements by Milton Greene. Dance arrangements by
   Clay Fullum. Other participants: Hillard Elkins (co-producer); Derek Goldby (original
   director); Michael Kidd (choreographer, replacement director); Hal Linden (star).

Walker's ledger is at the Library of Congress. Base page rate: $11.44.
   Walker's personal notations, recording charts, and number of pages for billing purposes indicate that he did all of the score himself.
THANKS AND WISHES   From Harnick to Walker: "Considering that *The Rothschilds* is actually an
impossible show to bring off, I think we did pretty well! Again let me tell you how constantly im-

pressed I remain with your endless ingenuity and your feeling for what each musical moment is trying to accomplish. What a constant pleasure to hear your work."

Instr.: 5 reed, 7 brass (2 tpt, 1 tb, 1 euphonium, 3 hrn), 12 strings (7 vln, 2 vla, 2 c, b), Allen organ, harp, 2 perc = 28 total.

ROYAL FLUSH

Orchestrations credited to Larry **Wilcox**. (Additional orchestrators, if any, unknown.)

Tryout: December 30, 1964, New Haven (Shubert); January 5, 1965, Toronto (Royal Alexandra). Closed January 23, Philadelphia (Shubert).

Music and lyrics by Jay Thompson. Based on the play *The Green Bird* by Carlo Gozzi. Musical direction by Skip Redwine. Dance arrangements by Hal Schaefer. Other participants: Jack Cole (original director, choreographer); Kaye Ballard (star).

RUMPLE

Orchestrations credited to Ted **Royal**. (Additional orchestrators unknown.)

Opened November 6, 1957, Alvin, 45 performances. Tryout: October 5, Boston; October 28, Philadelphia (Shubert).

Music by Ernest G. Schweikert, lyrics by Frank Reardon. Musical direction by Frederick Dvonch. Dance arrangements by Robert Atwood.

The Walker Collection includes an unsigned contract dated February 13, 1957, in which Walker agrees to "work with the writers" in exchange for 1% from the author's share of the gross, along with $350 a week as musical director. Whether this agreement was ever signed is unknown, but by the time the show went into production Walker was the musical director of the weekly TV series *Your Hit Parade* and—simultaneously—orchestrator of *The Music Man.*

SADIE THOMPSON

Orchestrations credited to Charles L. Cooke, Walter Eiger, John Klein, Joseph [Joe] Glover, Irving Landau, Julian Work, and Vernon Duke.

Opened November 16, 1944, Alvin, 60 performances. Tryout: Philadelphia (Forrest).

Music by Vernon Duke, lyrics by Howard Dietz. Based on the play *Rain* by W. Somerset Maugham and John Colton. Musical direction by Charles Sanford. Vocal arrangements by Vernon Duke. Vocal direction by Millard Gibson. Dance arrangements by Trude Rittman. Other participants: Rouben Mamoulian (director, co-librettist); Howard Dietz (co-librettist); June Havoc (star).

This ambitious musical was doomed from the moment Ethel Merman walked out during rehearsals.

SAIL AWAY

Orchestrations by Irwin **Kostal**. (Additional orchestrators, if any, unknown.)

Opened October 3, 1961, Broadhurst, 167 performances. Tryout: August 9, Boston (Colonial); September 7, Philadelphia (Forrest).

Music, lyrics, and book by Noël Coward. Musical direction and dance arrangements by Peter Matz. Vocal arrangements by Fred Werner. Other participants: Noël Coward (director); Joe Layton (choreographer); Elaine Stritch (star).

According to people who saw the scores when they last surfaced in 1999, most of the orchestrations are by Kostal. There are, apparently, minor contributions—possibly including "Don't Run Away from Love"—from conductor/dance arranger Matz.

> KOSTAL: After the first orchestra rehearsal, Noël Coward stood up on a chair, and paid me one of my highest compliments. He singled me out and said, "The orchestrations make me feel like a real composer."

ST. LOUIS WOMAN

Orchestrations credited to Ted **Royal**, Allan Small, Menotti Salta, and Walter Paul. (Additional orchestrators, if any, unknown.)

Opened March 30, 1946, Martin Beck, 113 performances. Tryout: February 14, New Haven (Shubert); February 19, Boston; March, Philadelphia.

Music by Harold Arlen, lyrics by Johnny Mercer. Based on the novel *God Sends Sunday* by Arna Bontemps. Musical direction and vocal arrangements by Leon Leonardi. Other participants: Rouben Mamoulian (director); Pearl Bailey (featured).

ST. LOUIS WOMAN (1998 REVIVAL)

Orchestrations by Ralph **Burns** and Luther Henderson.

Opened April 30, 1998, City Center, 4 performances.

Music by Harold Arlen, lyrics by Johnny Mercer. Musical direction by Rob Fisher. Dance arrangements and orchestrations by Luther Henderson. Other participants: City Center Encores! (producer); Jack O'Brien (director); George Faison (choreographer); Vanessa L. Williams (star).

The partiturs are in the City Center Encores! Collection (unexamined).

SALLY (1948 REVIVAL)

Orchestrations by Russell **Bennett**. (Additional orchestrations by Philip J. **Lang**, Allan Small, and possibly others.)

Opened May 6, 1948, Martin Beck, 36 performances. Tryout: unknown.

Music by Jerome Kern, lyrics by P. G. Wodehouse and Clifford Grey. Musical direction by Pembroke Davenport. Conducted by David Mordecai. Other participants: Bambi Linn (star); Willie Howard (star).

The partiturs are in the Kern Collection at the Library of Congress (unexamined). Bennett's invoices are preserved in his ledger. Base page rate: $4.80. Tentative attributions per invoice.

Bennett: Entr'acte, Finale Ultimo, "The Follies," "Once in a While" (dance), Opening act I, Opening act II, Overture, "Sally's Dance," "Siren's Song," "Tulip Time," "Wild Rose" (part I).

Small: "Little Church Around the Corner."

SANDHOG

Orchestrations credited to Hershy **Kay**. (Additional orchestrators, if any, unknown.)

Opened November 29, 1954, Phoenix (off-Broadway), 48 performances.

Music by Earl Robinson, lyrics by Waldo Salt. Musical direction by Ben Steinberg. Other participants: Howard Da Silva (director); Bernard Gersten (stage manager).

SARATOGA

Orchestrations credited to Philip J. **Lang**. (Additional orchestrators, if any, unknown.)

Opened December 7, 1959, Winter Garden, 80 performances. Tryout: October 26, Philadelphia (Shubert).

Music by Harold Arlen, lyrics by Johnny Mercer. Based on the novel *Saratoga Trunk* by Edna Ferber. Musical direction by Jerry Arlen. Vocal arrangements by Herbert Greene. "Music for dances" by Genevieve Pitot. Other participants: Robert Fryer (producer); Morton Da Costa (director, librettist).

A friend of producer Bobby Fryer recounted a story that Fryer delighted in telling (at least, he delighted in telling it thirty years later). With everything going wrong during the disastrous tryout, Ferber encountered Fryer standing down by the orchestra pit one evening. "Why don't you go into the pit and play the harp tonight?" said Edna. "You've already f***ed up everything else."

SAY, DARLING

Orchestrations credited to Sid **Ramin**. (Orchestrations totally by Ramin and Robert **Ginzler**.)

Opened April 3, 1958, ANTA, 332 performances. Tryout: February 22, New Haven (Shubert); Boston (Shubert).

Music by Jule Styne, lyrics by Betty Comden & Adolph Green. Based on the novel by Richard Bissell. "At the pianos, Colin Romoff and Peter Howard." Dance arrangements by Peter Howard. Other participants: Jule Styne (producer); Abe Burrows (director, co-librettist).

The partiturs are at Tams-Witmark.

Ramin: "The Husking Bee," "Let the Lower Lights Be Burning."

Other scores:

"Chief of Love" and "Say, Darling" are mostly by Ramin, with sections by Ginzler.

"The Carnival Song" and "It's Doom" are mostly by Ginzler, with sections by Ramin.

"Dance Only with Me," "Say, Darling (Finale)," "The Second Time You Meet," and

"Something's Always Happening on the River" are equally split between Ramin and Ginzler.

Overture: the opening is by Ramin; "Something's Always Happening on the River" is by Ginzler; on "Dance Only with Me" and "Try to Love Me," violin A, first trumpet, and French horn solo are by Ramin; the rest is by Ginzler.

"Try to Love Me" is mostly by Ginzler, with string parts by Ramin. Reprise (Johnny Desmond version) is mostly by Ginzler, with Ramin providing the three trombone parts and the "showy" string sections.

Say, Darling was a play with songs about the making of a musical comedy (a thinly disguised *Pajama Game*). The show featured a two-piano accompaniment with a small combo. When RCA proposed a cast album, it commissioned a full orchestration from in-house arranger Sid Ramin. (Ramin shared the job with Ginzler, but RCA deemed that Ramin receive sole credit.) The orchestration was subsequently used for at least one of the not very many post-Broadway productions and remains available for stock & amateur purposes.

Most of the scores are by Ramin and Ginzler combined. In the shared scores, Ramin usually wrote the first trumpet and violin A lines, with Ginzler filling in the rest of the brass and string sections as well as the reeds.

(See page 75.)

SAY WHEN

Orchestrations uncredited. (Orchestrations by Conrad Salinger, Russell **Bennett**, and others.)

Opened November 8, 1934, Imperial, 76 performances. Tryout: unknown.

A revue. Music by Ray Henderson, lyrics by Ted Koehler. Musical direction by Max Meth. Other participants: Harry Richman (star); Bob Hope (star).

SEESAW

Orchestrations credited to Larry Fallon (replaced by Larry **Wilcox**). (Additional orchestrations by Jonathan Tunick and possibly others.)

Opened March 18, 1973, Uris, 296 performances. Tryout: January 16, Detroit (Fisher).

Music by Cy Coleman, lyrics by Dorothy Fields. Based on the play *Two for the Seesaw* by William Gibson. Musical direction and vocal arrangements by Donald Pippin. Dance arrangements supervised by Cy Coleman. Dance arrangements by Elman Anderson, Cy Coleman, Marvin Hamlisch, and David Spangler. Other participants: Joseph Kipness (producer); Edwin Sherin (original director); Grover Dale (original choreographer); Michael Bennett (replacement director, replacement choreographer, replacement librettist); Tommy Tune (associate choreographer); Michael Stewart (original librettist); Lainie Kazan (original star); Michele Lee (replacement star).

PIPPIN: The show had the wrong director, the wrong cast. I went in on two days' notice because John Morris backed out; I got a desperate call from Joe Kipness. Cy had a terminal case of musicality. He had so much facility, but he would start playing and he would say—"We could use a C 7th. Or, we could add the 13th." He could spend hours on one bar of music. Every idea he would come up with, he'd tell you to write. In rehearsal, the show was really off-kilter. Fallon had done commercials or something, but we had an orchestrator who had never done a Broadway show, a copyist who had never done a Broadway show, a composer who couldn't make up his mind. We finally opened in Detroit. The orchestrations were just awful. There wasn't one bar that sounded good; they were just ridiculous. The copying was bad, the musicians were complaining. At the reading, Cy stopped us every three beats, trying to change everything.

When Michael Bennett came in, the first thing he said was, "The orchestrations are terrible." Bennett tried to see who he could get. Tunick, who had done *Promises*, *Company*, and *Follies* with Bennett, was in Boston for the tryout of *A Little Night Music*. He made a quick trip to Detroit, but Sondheim was still writing so Tunick was unavailable. It is to be assumed that Bennett called Ralph Burns, and that Ralph—as in many other cases—recommended Larry Wilcox.

> PIPPIN: Larry Wilcox was a genius, but I knew he had a drinking problem. He came in and rewrote just about the entire show; I'll bet there weren't a hundred bars left over that had been written by Fallon. Larry would walk into the rehearsals clearly under the influence of alcohol, I don't know how he managed to do the writing. He never brought up the idea of getting credit; maybe he simply never asked. Cy has made some of the most ridiculous decisions about who he worked with. He always had different people on every show; he never seemed to understand when he had a good group that he should stay with people who work well with him.

Heavy rewriting continued through the New York previews. Tunick came in to help during this period; among his contributions were "Welcome to Holiday Inn."

SET TO MUSIC

Orchestrations credited to Hans **Spialek**. (Additional orchestrators unknown.)

Opened January 18, 1939, Music Box, 129 performances. Tryout: January 9, Washington, D.C. (National); elsewhere.

A revue. Music, lyrics, and sketches by Noël Coward. Musical direction by John McManus. Other participants: Noël Coward (director); Beatrice Lillie (star).

SEVEN BRIDES FOR SEVEN BROTHERS

Orchestrations credited to Irwin **Kostal**. (Additional orchestrations by Gus Levene.)

Opened July 8, 1982, Alvin, 5 performances. Tryout: December 21, 1981, San Diego (Fox); elsewhere.

Music by Gene de Paul, lyrics by Johnny Mercer. New songs by Al Kasha and Larry Hirschhorn. A stage adaptation of the film, based on *The Sobbin' Women* by Stephen Vincent Benet. Musical direction by Richard Parrinello. Dance arrangements by Robert Webb. Other participants: Lawrence Kasha (director, co-librettist, co-producer); Debby Boone (star); David-James Carroll (star).

According to Kostal, various utilities and playoffs were orchestrated by Gus Levene.

SEVEN LIVELY ARTS

Orchestrations by Hans **Spialek**, Russell **Bennett**, and Ted **Royal**. (Additional orchestrations by Don **Walker**, Robert Noeltner, and Hawley Ades.)

Opened December 7, 1944, Ziegfeld, 183 performances. Tryout: November 24, Philadelphia (Forrest).

A revue. Music and lyrics by Cole Porter, ballet by Igor Stravinsky. Musical direction by Maurice Abravanel. Choral direction by Robert Shaw. Other participants: Billy Rose (producer); Moss Hart (sketches); Salvador Dali ("surrealistic conceptions of the seven lively arts," which were exhibited in the lounge); Beatrice Lillie (star); Bert Lahr (star).

Many of the partiturs—but none of Bennett's charts—are in the Billy Rose Collection at the New York Public Library for the Performing Arts.

Royal: "Drink, Drink, Drink," Opening ("Big Town"), "When I Was a Cuckoo."

Spialek: "Is It the Girl or Is It the Gown?" Opening act I, Overture.

Walker: "Hence, It Don't Make Sense" (song and specialty), "Pas de Deux."

Noeltner: "The Band Started Swinging a Song," "Tom Jones," "Waltz Song."

Other scores:

"Ev'ry Time We Say Goodbye" is by Spialek, with the orchestration for the Fred Waring choral section by Ades.

"Frangee Pahnee": there are two versions. One is by Royal; the other is by Walker, with Waring insert by Ades.

"Only a Boy and Girl": duet is by Spialek; "Schottische" (for Waring) is by Ades;

specialty refrains ("Jere McMahon," "Nan Wynn," "Dolores Gray," "Lillie & Lahr") are by Walker; "Waltz" is by Ades.

"Opera Finale": part 1 is by Spialek; part 2 (march) and part 3 ("Toreador Specialty") are by Walker. The final 2 pages are by Royal.

"Wow-oh-Wolf": sections A and C are by Walker; section B by Royal.

The New York Public Library also has a fragment of "It Can't Happen Here," in Bennett's hand.

When Billy Rose bought the Ziegfeld Theatre, he determined to fill it with the most ambitious revue ever. Hence, Lillie and Lahr, Porter and Stravinsky, Benny Goodman in the pit and even Salvador Dali. An oft-repeated tale has producer Billy Rose sending a telegram to Stravinsky: *Congratulations stop your music is sensational stop suggest we get Robert Russell Bennett to reorchestrate stop.* Stravinsky's answer: *Satisfied with sensational stop.*

Instr.: 7 reed, 9 brass (3 tpt, 3 tb, 1 tuba, 2 hrn), 21 strings (12 vln, 4 vla, 3 c, 2 b), piano, 2 perc = 40 total.

(See page 229.)

SEVENTEEN

Orchestrations credited to Ted **Royal**. (Additional orchestrators unknown.)

Opened June 21, 1951, Broadhurst, 180 performances. Tryout: unknown.

Music by Walter Kent, lyrics by Kim Gannon. Based on the novel by Booth Tarkington. Musical direction by Vincent Travers. Vocal arrangements by Crane Calder. Dance arrangements by Jesse Meeker. Other participant: Milton Berle (co-producer).

It is probable that Robert Noeltner, Charles L. Cooke, and others contributed orchestrations.

1776

Orchestrations (totally) by Eddie **Sauter**.

Opened March 16, 1969, 46th Street, 1,217 performances. Tryout: February 8, New Haven (Shubert); February 18, Washington, D.C. (National).

Music and lyrics by Sherman Edwards. Musical and dance arrangements by Peter Howard. Orchestra personnel manager, Elliot Lawrence. Vocal arrangements by Elise Bretton. Other participants: Stuart Ostrow (producer); Peter Stone (librettist); Onna White (choreographer).

Copies of the partiturs are in the Sauter Collection at Yale.

In addition to the partiturs for the full twenty-two-musician orchestration, Sauter prepared a reduced, thirteen-person orchestration (also in the Sauter Collection).

> OSTROW: We had a problem with the ending. We had the members of the cast signing the Declaration, a tableau. I thought, what do we do about that goddam Liberty Bell? I said to Eddie, "Is there any way to foreshadow what is going to happen to this country?" "Dissonance," he said. So I said, "Go listen to 'Wozzeck.'" He said, "What's that?" He got a copy, went crazy when he heard it. And he came in with the ending, one chord played over and over and over again, with dissonance. It foreshadowed what was going to happen, that the future would not be all patriotic and full of hope.

Stephen Sondheim (rating orchestrators): "Eddie Sauter? Knowing he was responsible for the last thirty seconds of *1776*, I would give him a gold star."

Instr.: 4 reed, 6 brass (1 tpt, 2 tb, 3 hrn), 9 strings (4 vln, 3 vla, 1 c, 1 b), harpsichord, harp, perc = 22 total.

SEVENTH HEAVEN

Orchestrations credited to David Terry. (Additional orchestrations by Irwin **Kostal** and possibly others.)

Opened May 26, 1955, ANTA, 44 performances. Tryout: April 16, New Haven; Philadelphia; Boston.

Music by Victor Young, lyrics by Stella Unger. Based on the play by Austin Strong.

Musical direction by Max Meth. Vocal direction by Crane Calder. Dance arrangements by Trude Rittman. Other participants: Peter Gennaro (choreographer); Jerome Robbins (uncredited doctoring); Chita Rivera (featured).

David Terry—a recording arranger—had trouble writing for theatre, so Young called in his old Chicago friend Kostal (who said that he ultimately redid most of the orchestrations). The clever musical comedy numbers—"Camille, Colette, Fifi," "Happy Little Crook," "Love Sneaks Up on You"—sound especially like Kostal.

70, GIRLS, 70

Orchestrations (totally) by Don **Walker**.

Opened April 15, 1971, Broadhurst, 35 performances. Tryout: March 7, Philadelphia (Forrest).

Music by John Kander, lyrics by Fred Ebb. Based on the play *Breath of Spring* by Peter Coke. Musical direction and vocal arrangements by Oscar Kosarin. Dance arrangements by Dorothea Freitag. Other participants: Onna White (choreographer); Mildred Natwick (star); Dorothea Freitag (featured).

The partiturs are in the collection of the composer. Walker's invoices are at the Library of Congress. Base page rate: $10.

The charts reveal a deceptively spare instrumentation: only thirteen pieces, including three trombones. Much of the fill was supplied by the RMI (or Rocksichord, an electronic keyboard with primitive synthesizer capabilities). One of the characters (Lorraine, played by dance arranger Dorothea Freitag) held court onstage at a piano on a small turntable. Most of the show is scored for piano, organ, guitar, and drums; accents come from the reeds and—in the loud parts—the brass.

"Hit It, Lorraine"—which was performed by the cast serenading the pianist while she played up a storm—is filled with stage directions ("pianist jumps up," "arms stretched overhead," "pianist snaps fingers of left hand"—then "L.H. makes arc back to keys"). At the Dixieland wail, three brass and two reeds are instructed to suddenly appear out of the portals; the third trombone and the bassoon stay in the pit to play while the others go up to the stage.

"Go Visit Your Grandmother" is written as a duet between Eddie (the show's bell-bottomed youngster) and Sadie (an octogenarian). The dance section still contains stage directions for original co-star Davey Burns ("wait until Harry picks up pants"). Burns died in Philadelphia, collapsing in the wings of the Forrest after performing this number.

THANKS AND WISHES   From Kander to Walker: ". . . and just think, it was all so easy."

Instr.: 3 reed, 4 brass (I tpt, 3 tb), I strings (b), piano (onstage), RMI (elec piano), guitar, 2 perc = 13 total. (See page 111.)

SHANGRI-LA

Orchestrations credited to Philip J. **Lang**. (Additional orchestrations by Russell **Bennett** and probably others.)

Opened June 13, 1956, Winter Garden, 21 performances. Tryout: April 21, New Haven (Shubert); Boston (Shubert).

Music by Harry Warren, lyrics by Jerome Lawrence and Robert E. Lee. Based on the novel *Lost Horizon* by James Hilton. Musical direction, vocal arrangements, and musical continuity by Lehman Engel. Ballet music composed and arranged by Genevieve Pitot. Additional dance arrangements by John Morris. Other participants: Robert Fryer (producer); Albert Marre (director).

Bennett's invoices are preserved in his ledger. Base page rate: $6.04.

Bennett: "The Beetle Race," "Somewhere."

SHE LOVES ME

Orchestrations (mostly) by Don **Walker**. (Additional orchestrations by Jack Elliott.)

Opened April 23, 1963, Eugene O'Neill, 302 performances. Tryout: March 18, New Haven (Shubert); March 26, Philadelphia (Forrest).

Music by Jerry Bock, lyrics by Sheldon Harnick. Based on the play *Parfumerie* by Miklos Laszlo. Musical direction by Harold Hastings. Incidental music arranged by Jack Elliott. Other participants: Harold Prince (producer, director); Carol Haney (choreographer); Barbara Cook (star).

Copies of the partiturs are in a private collection. Walker's invoices are at the Library of Congress. Base page rate: $6.52. Invoices indicate: Walker (97%).

The orchestrations are by Walker, with the following exceptions:

Elliott: "Romantic Atmosphere," "Shop Opening."

Partiturs for the two additional songs added to the 1964 London production, "Heads I Win" and "Three Letters"—both orchestrated by Alyn Ainsworth—are in the Jerry Bock Collection at the New York Public Library.

> HARNICK: Some of the best orchestrations I ever heard, just silken. Don understood character. He didn't have the melodic gifts he needed to be a composer, but he certainly understood character.

THANKS AND WISHES   From the songwriters: "Dear Don Walker—you've taken us to our lieder. With gratitude and love, Sheldon and Jerry."

From Hugh Martin to Walker: "When I do my thesis entitled 'Sex in Music,' I am going to use as my reference works Salome's dance by Strauss, 'Escales' by Ibert, and your orchestration of 'Ilona.'"

Instr.: 4 reed, 5 brass (1 tpt, 1 tb, 3 hrn), 9 strings (4 vln, 2 vla, 2 c, 1 b), accordion/celesta, harp, perc = 21 total.

(See page 110.)

SHEBA

Orchestrations credited to Ralph **Burns.** (Additional orchestrators, if any, unknown.)

Tryout: July 24, 1974, Chicago (First Chicago Center). Closed July 28, Chicago.

Music by Clint Ballard, Jr., lyrics and book by Lee Goldsmith. Based on the play *Come Back, Little Sheba* by William Inge. Musical direction and vocal arrangements by Glen Clugston. Other participant: Kaye Ballard (star).

SHENANDOAH

Orchestrations credited to Don **Walker.** (Additional orchestrators, if any, unknown.)

Opened January 7, 1975, Alvin, 1,050 performances. Tryout: November 22, 1974, Boston (Colonial).

Music by Gary Geld, lyrics by Peter Udell. Based on the film by James Lee Barrett. Musical direction by Lynn Crigler. Dance arrangements by Russell Warner. Other participant: John Cullum (star).

Walker's ledger is at the Library of Congress. Base page rate: $10.

Walker's personal notations, recording charts, and number of pages for billing purposes indicate that he did all of the score himself.

SHERRY!

Orchestrations credited to Philip J. **Lang** (replacing Larry **Wilcox**). (Additional orchestrations by Jack Andrews and Clare Grundman.)

Opened March 28, 1967, Alvin, 65 performances. Tryout: Boston (Colonial); February 8, Philadelphia (Shubert).

Music by Laurence Rosenthal, lyrics and book by James Lipton. Based on the play *The Man Who Came to Dinner* by George S. Kaufman and Moss Hart. Musical direction and vocal arrangements by Jay Blackton. Dance arrangements by John Morris. Other participants: Morton Da Costa (original director); Joe Layton (replacement director); George Sanders (original star); Clive Revill (replacement star); Dolores Gray (star).

Lang: "Christmas Eve," "How Can You Kiss Those Good Times Goodbye?" "Putty in Your Hands" (reprise), "With This Ring."

Andrews: "Harriet Sedley."

Grundman: "Listen Cosette," "The Proposal Duet."

Wilcox: "I Always Stay at the Ritz."

During the tryout, Wilcox was replaced by Phil Lang; Andrews and Grundman were probably involved as ghosts before Lang joined the show. (Wilcox was credited out of town; no orchestrator was billed on opening night in New York; Lang's name was added to the credits following the Broadway opening.) Orchestrations were only one of the problems; the show also lost its director, choreographer, and star.

The 2004 studio cast album is an amalgamation of charts, including some written specifically for the recording and thus not reflecting the show as it sounded in the theatre. The attributions above are as listed on the cast album and not verified.

SHINBONE ALLEY

Orchestrations credited to George Kleinsinger. (Additional orchestrations by Irwin **Kostal** and Ralph **Burns**.)

Opened April 13, 1957, Broadway, 49 performances.

Music by George Kleinsinger, lyrics by Joe Darion. A stage adaptation of the concept album *archy and mehitabel*, based on the book by Don Marquis. Musical and choral direction by Maurice Levine. Additional musical routines by John Morris. Other participants: Joe Darion and Mel Brooks (librettists); Eartha Kitt (star); Eddie Bracken (star).

Irv Kostal, who received credit for "additional orchestrations," claimed that he did most of the show; modernist jazz composer Kleinsinger, who had no theatre experience, proved unable to write for a pit band. Ralph Burns says he wrote a couple of charts for Eartha Kitt and listed *Shinbone Alley* in his program bio later that year for *Copper and Brass*, his first full Broadway musical.

SHOOTIN' STAR

Orchestrations credited to Hershy **Kay**. (Additional orchestrators, if any, unknown.)
Tryout: April 4, 1946, New Haven (Shubert). Closed April 27, Boston (Shubert).
Music by Sol Kaplan, lyrics by Bob Russell. Musical direction by Pembroke Davenport.
    Other participants: Max Liebman (co-producer); David Brooks (star); Doretta Morrow (star).

This show was subtitled "The Musical Story of Billy the Kid." It premiered at the Shubert in New Haven just one week after that other musical about another shootin' star, Annie Oakley.

    Kay made his ballet debut five years later, on April 11, 1951, with *The Thief Who Loved a Ghost* (derived from music by Carl Maria von Weber). Joining him was a young choreographer also making his Ballet Theatre debut, Herbert Ross—from the chorus of *Shootin' Star.*

SHOW BOAT

Orchestrations (mostly) by Russell **Bennett**. (Additional orchestration by Hans **Spialek.**)
Opened December 27, 1927, Ziegfeld, 572 performances. Tryout: November 15, Washington, D.C. (National); November 21, Pittsburgh (Nixon); November 28, Cleveland, Ohio; December 5, Philadelphia (Erlanger).
Music by Jerome Kern, lyrics and book by Oscar Hammerstein II. Based on the novel by Edna Ferber. Musical direction by Victor Baravelle. Choral direction by Will Vodery.
    Other participants: Florenz Ziegfeld (producer); Oscar Hammerstein II (replacement director, uncredited); Charles Winninger (star); Helen Morgan (star).
The partiturs are at the Library of Congress.
    The orchestrations are by Bennett, with the following exception(s):
    Spialek: "Bill"
    Missing: "Goodbye, My Lady Love," "Ol' Man River" (probably by Bennett)
    Bennett scored the show for separate banjo and guitar chairs, rather than the usual method of combining the two. What's more, he had the guitar player double on tuba (which is one of the stranger combinations we've found).
    While earlier versions of "Bill" were used in two prior musicals, *Oh Lady! Lady!!* (1918) and *Zip, Goes a Million* (1919), Spialek's chart was written in 1927 for *Show Boat.* (The earlier shows were produced while Spialek was still in Siberia, literally so.)
Instr.: 5 reed, 5 brass (2 tpt, 1 tb, 2 hrn), 18? strings (10? vln, 4? vla, 3 c, 1 b), piano, guitar/tuba, banjo, perc = 32? total.

SHOW BOAT (1946 REVIVAL)

Orchestrations (virtually totally) by Russell **Bennett**. (Additional orchestrator unknown.)
Opened January 5, 1946, Ziegfeld, 418 performances.

Musical direction by Edwin McArthur. Choral direction by Pembroke Davenport. Other
participants: Kern and Hammerstein (producers); Oscar Hammerstein II (director).

The partiturs are at the offices of the Rodgers & Hammerstein Organization.

The orchestrations are by Bennett, with the following exceptions:

"Why Do I Love You?" is mostly by Bennett, with the 30-bar choral refrain by an unknown hand.

"Why Do I Love You? (Waltz and Polka)" is mostly by Bennett, with two 12-bar sections by the same unknown hand.

Instr.: 5 reed, 5 brass (2 tpt, 2 tb, ? tuba, 1 hrn), ? strings (vln, vla, c, b), piano, guitar/banjo, perc.

SHOW BOAT (1966 REVIVAL)

Orchestrations by Russell **Bennett**. (Additional orchestrations by Ruth Anderson, with
Jonathan Tunick.)

Opened July 19, 1966, New York State, 64 performances.

Musical direction by Franz Allers. Associate conductor, William Brohn. Dance arrangements by Richard de Benedictis. Other participants: Music Theater of Lincoln Cen-
ter/Richard Rodgers (producer); Lawrence Kasha (director); Ronald Field (choreographer); David Wayne (star); Barbara Cook (star); Constance Towers (star).

The partiturs are at the offices of the Rodgers & Hammerstein Organization. Invoices are
preserved in Bennett's ledger. Base page rate: $7.05.

The orchestrations are by Bennett, with the following exceptions:

Anderson: "Can't Help Lovin' Dat Man Reprise," Finale act I, "Life upon the Wicked
Stage," "St. Agatha's Convent, "You Are Love Reprise."

Tunick: "Goodbye, My Lady Love."

Other scores:

"Why Do I Love You?" duet is by Bennett; patter and final choral refrain are by Anderson.

SHOW GIRL

Orchestrations by Maurice B. de Packh and William Daly (and probably others).

Opened July 2, 1929, Ziegfeld, 111 performances. Tryout: June 24, Boston (Colonial).

Music by George Gershwin, lyrics by Ira Gershwin and Gus Kahn. Additional music by
Vincent Youmans. Musical direction by William Daly. Other participants: Florenz
Ziegfeld (producer); Ruby Keeler Jolson (star); Jimmy Durante (featured).

"Tonight's the Night" is in the Gershwin Collection at the Library of Congress, "Mississippi Dry" is in the Youmans Collection at the Library of Congress.

de Packh: "Tonight's the Night."

Unidentified hand: "Mississippi Dry"

THE SHOW IS ON

Orchestrations credited to Gordon Jenkins. (Additional orchestrations by Russell **Bennett**, Hans **Spialek**, and others.)

Opened December 25, 1936, Winter Garden, 237 performances. Tryout: November, Boston; December 7, Washington, D.C. (National); Philadelphia (Forrest).

A revue. Music by Vernon Duke, George Gershwin, Richard Rodgers, Harold Arlen, and others; lyrics by Ted Fetter, Ira Gershwin, Lorenz Hart, E. Y. Harburg, and others. Sketches by Moss Hart and others. Musical direction by Gordon Jenkins. Other participants: Messrs. Shubert (producers); Vincente Minnelli (co-director, designer); Beatrice Lillie (star); Bert Lahr (star).

SHOW ME WHERE THE GOOD TIMES ARE

Orchestrations credited to Philip J. **Lang**. (Additional orchestrators, if any, unknown.)

Opened March 5, 1970, Edison (off-Broadway), 29 performances.

Music by Kenneth Jacobson, lyrics by Rhoda Roberts. Based on the play *The Imaginary Invalid* by Molière. Musical direction and vocal arrangements by Karen Gustafson. Other participant: Morton Da Costa (director).

SHUFFLE ALONG (1952 REVIVAL)

Orchestrations credited to Charles L. Cooke. (Additional orchestrations by Ted **Royal**, Marion Evans and others.)

Opened May 8, 1952, Broadway, 4 performances. Tryout: April 23, New Haven (Shubert); elsewhere.

A revue. Music by Eubie Blake, lyrics by Noble Sissle. Vocal arrangements by Claude Garreau. Other participants: Eubie Blake (featured); Noble Sissle (featured).

SILK STOCKINGS

Orchestrations by Don **Walker**. (Additional orchestrations by Robert **Ginzler**, with Irwin **Kostal** and Hans **Spialek**.)

Opened February 24, 1955, Imperial, 477 performances. Tryout: November 26, 1954, Philadelphia (Shubert); January 4, 1955, Boston (Shubert); February 1, Detroit (Shubert).

Music and lyrics by Cole Porter. Based on the film *Ninotchka*, from a story by Melchior Lengyel. Musical direction and vocal arrangements by Herbert Greene. Dance arrangements by Tommy Goodman. Other participants: Feuer & Martin (producers); George S. Kaufman (co-librettist, original director); Cy Feuer (replacement director); Abe Burrows (replacement librettist).

Copies of the partiturs are in the American Musical Theatre Collection at the Library of Congress. Invoices are in the Walker Collection at the Library of Congress. Base page rate: $6.21. Invoices indicate: Walker (64%), Ginzler (30%).

Walker: "As on Through the Seasons We Sail," "It's a Chemical Reaction, That's All," "Paris Loves Lovers," "Silk Stockings," "Stereophonic Sound" (song and reprise), "Too Bad," "Without Love."

Ginzler: exit music, "Hail, Bibinski," "Josephine" (except for new opening fanfare, by Walker), "Satin and Silk," utility ("Too Bad").

Kostal: "Siberia" (except for the first 8 bars of dance section, which were replaced during the tryout by Ginzler).

Spialek: "Ode to a Tractor."

Other scores:

"All of You" is by Walker and Ginzler.

Entr'acte is by Walker, Ginzler, and Kostal.

Overture: Opening (gypsy violins) and "Hail, Bibinski" are by Walker; "All of You" is by Ginzler; "Too Bad" is by Walker; "Silk Stockings" is by Kostal; "Stereophonic Sound" is by Walker.

"The Red Blues": first refrain is by Walker; second and fourth refrain are by Ginzler; third refrain is by Ginzler, with patches by Walker.

With the show in trouble during an extended tryout and the ailing Porter back in New York, Walker was called upon to fill in for the composer, as described in a letter from Walker to general manager Monty Schaff: "As practically everyone connected with *Silk Stockings* knows, I had quite a bit to do with the tune of 'Red Blues.' In case this situation worries you, you may file this statement. I hereby, in consideration of this payment of $500, relinquish any claim upon the aforesaid production and or Cole Porter for any composing I may have done in connection with 'Red Blues.'"

This was apparently the first successful musical for which Walker received what would become his standard royalty, ½% of the gross.

Instr.: 5 reed (including 5 sax), 7 brass (3 tpt, 3 tb, 1 hrn), 13 strings (8 vln, 2 vla, 2 c, b), piano/celesta, harp, perc = 28 total.

(See page 310.)

SIMPLY HEAVENLY

Orchestrations credited to David Martin. (Additional orchestrators, if any, unknown [Ted **Royal**?].)

Opened August 20, 1957, Playhouse, 62 performances. Tryout: May 21, off-Broadway (85th Street Playhouse).

Music by David Martin, lyrics and book by Langston Hughes. Based on the novel *Simple Takes a Wife* by Langston Hughes. Musical direction by Sticks Evans. Vocal arrangements by Bill Heyer. Other participant: Claudia McNeil (star).

SING OUT THE NEWS

Orchestrations uncredited. (Orchestrations by Hans **Spialek** and others.)

Opened September 24, 1938, Music Box, 105 performances. Tryout: unknown.

A revue. Music and lyrics by Harold Rome. Musical direction by Max Meth. Ballet music by Will Irwin. Other participants: Max Gordon (producer); George S. Kaufman and Moss Hart (associate producers).

SINGIN' IN THE RAIN

Orchestrations (virtually totally) by Larry **Wilcox**. (Additional orchestration by Michael Gibson.)

Opened July 2, 1985, Gershwin, 367 performances.

Music by Nacio Herb Brown, lyrics by Arthur Freed. A stage adaptation of the MGM film. Musical direction by Robert Billig. Musical supervision and vocal arrangements by Stanley Lebowsky. Dance arrangements and incidental music by Michael Dansicker. Other participant: Twyla Tharp (director, choreographer).

The partiturs are in a private collection.

The orchestrations are by Wilcox, with the following exceptions:

Gibson: "Before Fiddle" (intro to "Fit As a Fiddle," vaudeville section).

Stan Lebowsky told a story about a production meeting. Twyla said she wanted the show to sound like an authentic musical from the twenties: two trumpets, two clarinets, two flutes, a tuba. Wilcox, who was more than a little tipsy, said that this was a famous MGM musical from the fifties, and the audience will be expecting that sound. He suggested that they use three trumpets, three trombones, five reeds, and strings. "But that's a standard Broadway-type orchestra," Twyla complained. "That way," Larry said, "I won't have to redo it when Joe Layton takes over." And Stan whisked him out of the room.

Instr.: 4 reed (including 4 sax), 5 brass (3 tpt, 2 tb), 7 strings (4 vln, 1 vla, 1 c, 1 b/tuba), piano/celesta, harp, guitar/banjo, 2 perc = 21 total.

SINGIN' THE BLUES

Orchestrations uncredited. (Orchestrations by Russell **Bennett** and others.)

Opened September 16, 1931, Liberty, 46 performances. Tryout: unknown.

Music by Jimmy McHugh, lyrics by Dorothy Fields. Musical direction by Eubie Blake. Other participants: Alex A. Aarons and Vinton Freedley (producers).

SITTING PRETTY

Orchestrations uncredited. (Orchestrations by Russell **Bennett**, Max Steiner, Hilding Anderson, and possibly others.)

Opened April 8, 1924, Fulton, 95 performances. Tryout: March 23, Detroit (Shubert); Buffalo.

Music by Jerome Kern, lyrics by P. G. Wodehouse. Musical direction by Max Steiner. Other participants: P. G. Wodehouse and Guy Bolton (librettists).

The partiturs are in the Kern Collection at the Library of Congress (unexamined).

1600 PENNSYLVANIA AVENUE

Orchestrations credited to Sid **Ramin** and Hershy **Kay**. (Additional orchestrators, if any, unknown.)

Opened May 4, 1976, Mark Hellinger, 7 performances. Tryout: Philadelphia (Forrest); March 17, Washington, D.C. (National).

Music by Leonard Bernstein, lyrics and book by Alan Jay Lerner. Musical direction by Roland Gagnon. Other participants: Saint Subber (original producer); Ken Howard (star); Patricia Routledge (star).

The partiturs are in the Bernstein Collection at the Library of Congress (unexamined).

Herb Harris worked with Bernstein throughout the latter's career; he started as drummer on *On the Town* and played Bernstein's opera *Trouble in Tahiti*, *Wonderful Town*, and with the New York Philharmonic. He also served as contractor for *Candide*, *Mass*, and *1600 Pennsylvania Avenue*.

> HARRIS: Lenny's toughest role was writing music. He really suffered with it. Playing piano was easy for him, conducting was easy; but writing was hard.

SKYSCRAPER

Orchestrations credited to Fred Werner. (Additional orchestrations by Larry **Wilcox** and possibly others.)

Opened November 13, 1965, Lunt-Fontanne, 241 performances. Tryout: September 13, Detroit (Fisher).

Music by James Van Heusen, lyrics by Sammy Cahn. Based on the play *Dream Girl* by Elmer Rice. Musical direction by John Lesko. Dance arrangements by Marvin Laird. Other participants: Feuer & Martin (producers); Cy Feuer (director); Michael Kidd (choreographer); Peter Stone (librettist); Julie Harris (star).

Larry Wilcox stepped in to do additional orchestrations, including the "Delicatessen" number and dance. Wilcox told Larry Blank that when Feuer heard the chart, he came over and told Wilcox that he had the job on the next Feuer & Martin/Van Heusen & Cahn musical, *Walking Happy*.

SLEEPY HOLLOW

Orchestrations credited to Hans **Spialek**, Ted **Royal**, and George Lessner. (Additional orchestrators, if any, unknown.)

Opened June 3, 1948, St. James, 12 performances. Tryout: April 29, New Haven (Shubert); elsewhere.

Music by George Lessner, lyrics and book by Russell Maloney and Miriam Battista. Based on the story *The Legend of Sleepy Hollow* by Washington Irving. Musical direction by Irving Actman. Assistant conductor, Hal Hastings. Vocal arrangements by Elie Siegmeister. Other participant: Marc Connelly (co-director).

This musical, based on the legend of Ichabod Crane, had the distinction of following *Oklahoma!* into the St. James. *Sleepy Hollow* lasted precisely 2,200 performances less.

SMALL WONDER

Orchestrations credited to Ted **Royal**. (Additional orchestrators unknown.)

Opened September 15, 1948, Coronet, 134 performances. Tryout: August 26, New Haven (Shubert); Boston (Majestic).

A revue. Music by Baldwin Bergersen and Albert Selden, lyrics by Phyllis McGinley and Billings Brown [Burt Shevelove]. Musical direction by William Parson. Vocal arrangements by Herbert Greene. "Musical development for the dance" by Richard Priborsky [Pribor]. Other participants: Burt Shevelove (director); Gower Champion (choreographer); Tom Ewell (featured); Mary McCarty (featured).

Co-lyricist "Billings Brown" was actually the show's first-time director, Burt Shevelove. There was also a first-time choreographer onboard, with the unlikely name Gower Champion.

SMILE

Orchestrations by Sid **Ramin**, Bill Byers, Dick Hazard, and Torrie Zito. (Additional orchestrators, if any, unknown.)
Opened November 24, 1986, Lunt-Fontanne, 48 performances. Tryout: Baltimore.
Music by Marvin Hamlisch, lyrics and book by Howard Ashman. Based on the film by Jerry Belson. Musical direction by Paul Gemignani. Vocal arrangements by Buster Davis. Other participants: Howard Ashman (director); Carolyn Leigh (original lyricist).

SMILES

Orchestrations uncredited. (Orchestrations by Stephen O. Jones, Edward P. Powell, Maurice de Packh, King Ross, Paul Lannin, and others.)
Opened November 18, 1930, Ziegfeld, 63 performances. Tryout: October 29, Boston (Colonial).
Music by Vincent Youmans, lyrics by Harold Adamson, additional lyrics by Clifford Grey and Ring Lardner. Musical direction by Frank Tours. Other participants: Florenz Ziegfeld (producer); Marilyn Miller (star); Fred & Adele Astaire (stars).

Several partiturs are in the Youmans Collection at the Library of Congress.
Jones: "More Than Ever."
Powell: "Blue Bowery" (also used as "My Lover" in *Take a Chance.*)
de Packh: "Be Good to Me."
King Ross: "I'm Glad I Waited."
Unidentified hand: "Carry on, Keep Smiling," "If I Were You, Love."

SNOW WHITE AND THE SEVEN DWARFS

Orchestrations credited to Philip J. **Lang**. (Additional orchestrators, if any, unknown.)
Opened October 18, 1979, Radio City Music Hall, 33 performances (plus 70 additional performances upon its return engagement in January 1980).
Music by Frank Churchill, lyrics by Larry Morey. New music by Jay Blackton, new lyrics by Joe Cook. A stage adaptation of the film. Musical direction by Donald Pippin. Conductor, Don Smith. Other participant: Radio City Music Hall Productions (producer).

SO LONG, 174TH STREET

Orchestrations credited to Luther Henderson. (Additional orchestrators, if any, unknown.)

Opened April 27, 1976, Harkness, 16 performances. Tryout: Philadelphia (Shubert).

Music and lyrics by Stan Daniels. Based on the play *Enter Laughing* by Joseph Stein, from the novel by Carl Reiner. Musical direction by John Lesko. Dance arrangements by Wally Harper. Other participants: Frederick Brisson (producer); Burt Shevelove (director); Joseph Stein (librettist); Robert Morse (star).

SOMETHING FOR THE BOYS

Orchestrations by Hans **Spialek** and Don **Walker**. (Additional orchestrations by Russell **Bennett**, Ted **Royal**, Walter Paul, and possibly others.)

Opened January 7, 1943, Alvin, 422 performances. Tryout: December 18, 1942, Boston (Shubert).

Music and lyrics by Cole Porter. Musical direction and vocal arrangements by William Parson. Other participants: Michael Todd (producer); Herbert & Dorothy Fields (librettists); Jack Cole (co-choreographer); Ethel Merman (star).

The location of the partiturs is unknown, but they were examined by Tommy Krasker and Robert Kimball for their *Catalog of the American Musical* (1988). Their findings include the following:

Spialek: "By the Mississinewah," "He's a Right Guy," Overture (with Paul), "See That You're Born in Texas" (with Paul), "So Long, San Antonio," "When We're Home on the Range."

Walker: "Hey, Good-Lookin'" (with Paul), "The Leader of a Big-Time Band," "Something for the Boys," "Square Dance," "There's a Happy Land in the Sky," "When My Baby Goes to Town."

Bennett: "Could It Be You?" "Prologue."

Royal: "Assembly Line," "Betty Bruce Specialty (Born in Texas)."

Instr.: 5 reed (including 5 sax), 5 brass (3 tpt, 2 tb), 12? strings (9? vln, 0 vla, 2? c, 1 b), piano, perc = 24? total.

SOMETHING MORE!

Orchestrations by Ralph **Burns**. (Additional orchestrations by Larry **Wilcox** and Robert Prince.)

Opened November 10, 1964, Eugene O'Neill, 15 performances. Tryout: September 28, Philadelphia (Shubert); elsewhere.

Music by Sammy Fain, lyrics by Marilyn and Alan Bergman. Based on the novel *Portofino P.T.A.* by Gerald Green. Musical direction by Oscar Kosarin. Vocal arrangements and direction by Buster Davis. Dance arrangements by Robert Prince. (Preliminary ads credited the orchestrations jointly to Burns and Prince.) Other participants: Jule Styne (producer, director); Barbara Cook (star).

The partiturs are in the Warner/Chappell Collection at the Library of Congress.

Burns: "Act I Travel Montage," "Better All the Time," "Bravo, Bravo, Novelisto," "Buster's Ultra-New 9/27 Lush Grazie and Final Scene Act II," "Children Make Friends," "The Church of My Choice," "I've Got Nothing to Do," "Jule's Beach Opening," "Life Is Too Short," "Mineola March," "New Opening," "No Questions Asked," "No Time at All," "Ode to a Pencil," "Something More" (song and reprise), "The Straw That Broke the Camel's Back," "That Faraway Look," "Throw the Net Around Jule" (underscore), "To the Beach," "Wanna Trade," "Why Did You Want Something More" (new), "Who Fills the Bill?" "You Gotta Taste All the Fruit" ("small combo jazz" arrangement).

Wilcox: Finaletto act I, "I Feel Like New Year's Eve," "Master of the Greatest Art of All," utilities ("Grazie Mille per Niente," "Something More," "You Gotta Taste All the Fruit").

Prince: "Beach Dance" (composed by Prince), "Portofino Square."

Other scores:

"Come Sta": "Opening (Beach)" is by Prince; "Vocal B" by Burns.

"Don't Make a Move": parts 1 (song) and 3 (finale) are by Burns; part 2 (dance) by Prince.

"Grazie Mille per Niente": song ("Ronny [Graham]") is by Wilcox; "Party Dance" by Prince; vocal tag by Wilcox.

"Jaded, Degraded Am I" is by Burns, with extension by Wilcox.

Overture is by Burns, except for "Life Is Too Short" and the ending, by Wilcox.

Missing: "The Prettiest Girl at the Party."

It has long been rumored that, during the disastrous tryout, several songs were composed by Jule Styne (who also produced the show and directed it until he brought in the uncredited Joe Layton to replace himself). The materials donated to the Library of Congress by Chappell, the publisher, specifically identify Styne as composer of several songs, including "I Feel Like New Year's Eve" and "The Prettiest Girl at the Party."

Instr.: 3 reed (including 3 sax), 5 brass (2 tpt, 2 tb, 1 hrn), 9? strings (6? vln, 1? vla, 1 c, 1 b), piano/accordion, guitar, perc = 20? total.

SONG OF NORWAY

Orchestrations credited to Arthur Kay. (Additional orchestrations by Don **Walker**, Al Woodbury, Henry Vars, and, presumably, others.)

Opened August 21, 1944, Imperial, 860 performances. Tryout: June 12, Los Angeles; San Francisco.

Music by Edvard Grieg, musical adaptation and lyrics by Robert Wright & George Forrest. Based on a play by Homer Curran. Musical direction and vocal arrangements by Arthur Kay. Other participants: Edwin Lester (producer); George Balanchine (choreographer).

Five partiturs are at Tams-Witmark. Walker's invoices are at the Library of Congress. Walker attributions per invoice.

Kay: "Now (Rome Reprise)," "Scene from *Peer Gynt.*"
Walker: "Freddy and His Fiddle," "Strange Music."
Woodbury: "The Ball" #34.
Vars: "Music under Dialogue."

The two Arthur Kay scores at Tams are joined by several pieces of incidental music orchestrated by Al Woodbury and Henry Vars. There is also an Overture by Philip J. Lang, which appears to have been scored for a later production (quite likely the 1958 outdoor production at Jones Beach). "Freddy and His Fiddle" and "Strange Music"—both of which are missing—are attributed to Walker based on his invoices; they most probably replaced earlier versions used during the West Coast tryout. Don also put in an invoice, marked "piano only," for a 74-page score for "I Love You."

SONG OF THE FLAME

Orchestrations uncredited. (Orchestrations by Russell **Bennett** and others.)

Opened December 30, 1925, 44th Street, 219 performances. Tryout: December 10, Wilmington, Delaware (Playhouse); December 14, Baltimore (Academy of Music); December 21, Philadelphia (Shubert).

Music by George Gershwin and Herbert Stothart, lyrics and book by Otto Harbach and Oscar Hammerstein II. Musical direction by Herbert Stothart.

SONS O' FUN

Orchestrations "under the supervision of Domenico Savino." (Additional orchestrations by Charles L. Cooke and, presumably, others.)

Opened December 1, 1941, Winter Garden, 742 performances. Tryout: November 1, , Washington, D.C. (National); elsewhere.

A revue. Music by Sammy Fain, lyrics by Jack Yellen. Musical arrangements by Domenico Savino and Charles L. Cooke. Musical direction by John McManus. Vocal arrangements by Pembroke Davenport. Dance music composed by Will Irwin. Other participants: Ole Olsen and Chic Johnson (co-producers, sketch writers, stars).

SOPHIE

Orchestrations and arrangements credited to Sid **Ramin** and Arthur Beck. (Additional orchestrators unknown.)

Opened April 15, 1963, Winter Garden, 8 performances. Tryout: Columbus, Ohio; Detroit (Fisher); Philadelphia.

Music and lyrics by Steve Allen. Suggested by events in the life of Sophie Tucker.

Musical direction and vocal arrangements by Liza Redfield. Dance arrangements by Genevieve Pitot. Other participants: Donald Saddler (choreographer); Libi Staiger (star); Art Lund (star).

(See page 77.)

THE SOUND OF MUSIC

Orchestrations (totally) by Russell **Bennett**.

Opened November 16, 1959, Lunt-Fontanne, 1,443 performances. Tryout: October 3, New Haven (Shubert); October 13, Boston (Shubert).

Music by Richard Rodgers, lyrics by Oscar Hammerstein II. Based on the biography *The Trapp Family Singers* by Maria Augusta Trapp. Musical direction by Frederick Dvonch. Assistant conductor, Peter Howard. Choral arrangements by Trude Rittman. Other participants: Richard Rodgers and Oscar Hammerstein II (co-producers); Joe Layton (choreographer); Howard Lindsay and Russel Crouse (librettists); Mary Martin (star).

The partiturs are in the Rodgers Collection at the Library of Congress, with copies at the offices of the Rodgers & Hammerstein Organization. Invoices are preserved in Bennett's ledger. Base page rate: $5.70.

This is the only post-1990 score that has been located that was written solely by Bennett. He also worked on the reorchestration for the 1962 bus & truck tour of *The Sound of Music*, one of the few post-Broadway tours for which I found him submitting invoices. (He was usually too busy with new shows to revisit old ones.) Bennett did about 10% of the new charts for the tour, with the rest by Ruth Anderson. For the 1967 City Center Light Opera revival (April 26, 1967), Bennett did new charts for "How Can Love Survive?" and "The Sound of Music" ("in F"), as well as orchestrating the interpolated "Something Good" (which was written by Rodgers, music and lyrics, for the motion picture version).

Instr.: 6 reed, 9 brass (3 tpt, 2 tb, 1 tuba, 3 hrn), 13 strings (8 vln [1 with guitar/mandolin], 2 vla, 2 c, 1 b), harp, perc = 30 total.

(See pages 29, 103, 260.)

SOUTH PACIFIC

Orchestrations (mostly) by Russell **Bennett**. (Additional orchestrations by Don **Walker**.)

Opened April 7, 1949, Majestic, 1,925 performances. Tryout: March 7, New Haven (Shubert); March 15, Boston (Shubert).

Music by Richard Rodgers, lyrics by Oscar Hammerstein II. Based on stories from *Tales of the South Pacific* by James Michener. Musical direction by Salvatore Dell'Isola. Musical continuity and incidental arrangements by Trude Rittman. Other participants: Richard Rodgers and Oscar Hammerstein II (producers); Joshua Logan (director, associate producer); Oscar Hammerstein and Joshua Logan (librettists); Mary Martin (star); Ezio Pinza (star).

The partiturs are in the Rodgers Collection at the Library of Congress, with copies at the offices of the Rodgers & Hammerstein Organization. Bennett's invoices are preserved in his ledger. Base page rate: $5.10.

The orchestrations are by Bennett, with the following exceptions:

Walker: "Carefully Taught."

Missing: "A Wonderful Guy."

There is a later reconstruction of "A Wonderful Guy" in a copyist's hand (apparently, Mathilde Pincus) with a slightly different instrumentation, omitting the tuba. Included in this score is one page by Bennett, apparently from the original. While there has been some suggestion that this chart is by Walker, I am virtually certain that it is by Bennett. The encore, which does exist, is by Bennett.

On April 12, 1950, a year after the opening, Bennett put in a bill labeled "Carefully Taught (*South Pacific* [Road])." This chart was presumably used for the tour—or not; it could also be the continuation of the scene ("I was cheated before, and I'm cheated again") that was added as an insert into some copies of the published vocal score (#39A, pages 146a–c). At any rate, Walker's chart remains the official version.

Instr.: 5 reed, 9 brass (3 tpt, 2 tb, 1 tuba, 3 hrn), 14 strings (8 vln, 3 vla, 2 c, 1 b), harp, perc = 30 total.

SPRING IN BRAZIL

Orchestrations and choral arrangements by Arthur Kay. (Additional orchestrations by Don **Walker** and probably others.)

Tryout: October 1, 1945, Boston (Shubert); November 27, Washington, D.C. (National); elsewhere. Closed January 12, 1946, Chicago (Great Northern).

Music and lyrics by Robert Wright & George Forrest. Musical direction by Anthony R. Morelli. Other participant: Milton Berle (star).

Orchestrator Arthur Kay was a classically oriented musician, best known at the time for the still-running Wright and Forrest hit *Song of Norway*—an unlikely choice for a broad musical comedy vehicle for Milton Berle. The Library of Congress has a signed contract between Walker and the producers dated November 1, 1945, which indicates that he was brought in during the tryout to rewrite the orchestrations (without credit).

Instr.: 5 reed (all sax), 5 brass (3 tpt, 2 tb), ? strings (vln, 0 vla, c, 1 b), piano, perc.

STARS IN YOUR EYES

Orchestrations credited to Don **Walker** and Hans **Spialek**. (Additional orchestrations by Al Goodman and probably others.)

Opened February 9, 1939, Majestic, 127 performances. Tryout: January 13, New Haven (Shubert); January 17, Boston (Shubert).

Music by Arthur Schwartz, lyrics by Dorothy Fields. Musical direction by Al Goodman. Other participants: Joshua Logan (director); Ethel Merman (star); Jimmy Durante (star); Jerome Robbins (dancer); Nora Kaye (dancer); Maria Karniloff [Karnilova] (dancer).

One partitur (the encore to "This Is It," by Walker) is in the Walker Collection at the Library of Congress. The collection also has piano-vocal scores for "All the Time," "Just a Little Bit More," and "This Is It," indicating that these were likely orchestrated by Walker as well.

THE STEPPING STONES

Orchestrations uncredited. (Orchestrations by Russell **Bennett**, Hilding Anderson, and others.)

Opened November 6, 1923, Globe, 281 performances. Tryout: October 16, New Haven (Shubert); Hartford, Connecticut; Providence, Rhode Island.

Music by Jerome Kern, lyrics by Anne Caldwell. Musical direction by Victor Baravelle. Other participants: Charles Dillingham (producer); Anne Caldwell (co-librettist); Fred Stone (star).

The partiturs are in the Kern Collection at the Library of Congress (unexamined).

STOP THE WORLD—I WANT TO GET OFF

Orchestrations credited to Ian Fraser with David Lindup, Burt Rhodes, and Gordon Langford.

Opened October 3, 1962, Shubert, 555 performances. Tryout: September, Philadelphia (Shubert).

Music, lyrics, and book by Leslie Bricusse and Anthony Newley. Musical direction by Milton Rosenstock. Musical supervision by Ian Fraser. Other participants: David Merrick (producer); Anthony Newley (director, star).

Copies of the partiturs are at Tams-Witmark.

The Broadway copyists worked from a conformed score for the British production. The British material is all in one hand (apparently that of a copyist). The original chart for "Once in a Lifetime" was replaced by a new one for the Broadway production. It is likely that this is by Ian Fraser.

THE STRAW HAT REVUE

Orchestrations uncredited.

Opened September 29, 1939, Ambassador, 75 performances. Tryout: unknown.

A revue. Music and lyrics by Sylvia Fine. Additional songs by James Shelton. Musical direction by Edward A. Hunt. Other participants: Max Liebman (director, sketches); Danny Kaye (featured); Alfred Drake (featured); Jerome Robbins (dancer).

STREET SCENE

Musical arrangements and orchestrations by Kurt Weill. (Additional orchestrations by Ted **Royal**.)

Opened January 9, 1947, Adelphi, 148 performances. Tryout: December 16, 1946, Philadelphia (Shubert).

Music by Kurt Weill, lyrics by Langston Hughes. Additional lyrics by Elmer Rice.

Based on the play by Elmer Rice. Musical direction by Maurice Abravanel.

The partiturs are in the Weill Collection at Yale.

The orchestrations are by Weill, with the following exceptions:

Royal: "Moon-Faced, Starry Eyed," "Wrapped in a Ribbon."

The trumpet solo in Royal's "Moon-Faced" dance is labeled "gut-bucket blues"—which is not what one would expect to find in Weill's *Street Scene!*

Instr.: 6 reed, 6 brass (2 tpt, 2 tb, 2 hrn), ? strings (vln, vla, c, b), piano/celesta, harp, 2 perc.

STREETS OF PARIS

Orchestrations credited to Hans **Spialek**. (Additional orchestrators unknown.)

Opened June 19, 1939, Broadhurst, 274 performances. Tryout: unknown.

A revue. Music by Jimmy McHugh, lyrics by Al Dubin. Additional song by Harold Rome. Musical direction by John McManus. Vocal arrangements by Hugh Martin.

Other participants: Bobby Clark (star); Bud Abbott and Lou Costello (stars); Carmen Miranda (star); Gower Champion (featured); the Martins (including Hugh Martin and Ralph Blane, featured).

STRIKE UP THE BAND

Orchestrations uncredited. (Orchestrations by William Daly and others.)

Tryout: August 29, 1927, Long Branch, New Jersey (Reade's Broadway); September 25, 1927, Philadelphia (Shubert). Closed Philadelphia.

Music by George Gershwin, lyrics by Ira Gershwin. Book by George S. Kaufman. Musical direction by William Daly.

One partitur is in the Gershwin Collection at the Library of Congress.

Daly: "The Man I Love."

STRIP FOR ACTION

Orchestrations credited to Ralph **Burns**. (Additional orchestrators, if any, unknown.)

Tryout: March 17, 1956, New Haven (Shubert). Closed April 14, Pittsburgh (Nixon).

Music by Jimmy McHugh, lyrics by Harold Adamson. Based on the play by Howard Lindsay and Russel Crouse. Musical direction by Buster Davis. Dance music devised by Roger Adams. Other participant: John C. Wilson (director).

This musical, based on a play of the same name about life in burlesque, was Ralph Burns's first Broadway assignment (unless one counts *Pleasure Dome*, which closed during rehearsals).

SUBWAYS ARE FOR SLEEPING

Orchestrations credited to Philip J. **Lang**. (Additional orchestrators, if any, unknown.)

Opened December 27, 1961, St. James, 205 performances. Tryout: November 6, Philadelphia (Shubert); November 28, Boston (Colonial).

Music by Jule Styne, lyrics and book by Betty Comden & Adolph Green. Based on stories by Edmund G. Love. Musical direction by Milton Rosenstock. Dance arrangements by Peter Howard. Other participants: David Merrick (producer); Michael Kidd (director, choreographer).

One partitur ("When You Help a Friend Out," by Lang) is in the Merrick Collection at the Library of Congress.

> PETER HOWARD: I liked *Subways*. I was one of the few people who did, but there was such *tsuris* [aggravation] from the very beginning. Everybody was at each other's throat. Jule Styne wasn't the easiest person, and Comden & Green were trying to soothe everything, and we had Carol Lawrence who was not the easiest person either, to put it nicely. Jule could be very difficult. I remember, we were having a big fight; Carol Lawrence, Betty, Adolph, Kidd, and Jule were all trying to outshout each other. Finally, Jule hollered over them all, "Well, I agree with you fully! In part."

Instr.: 5 reed, 6 brass (3 tpt, 2 tb, 1 hrn), ? strings (vln, vla, c, 1 b), piano, harp, perc.
(See page 210.)

SUGAR

Orchestrations (totally) by Philip J. **Lang**.

Opened April 9, 1972, Majestic, 505 performances. Tryout: January 17, Washington, D.C. (Opera House); February 6, Toronto (O'Keefe); February 22, Philadelphia (Forrest); March 7, Boston (Shubert).

Music by Jule Styne, lyrics by Bob Merrill. Based on the film *Some Like It Hot* by Billy Wilder and I. A. L. Diamond. Musical direction and vocal arrangements by Elliot Lawrence. Dance arrangements by John Berkman. Other participants: David Merrick (producer); Gower Champion (director, choreographer); Peter Stone (librettist); Robert Morse (star).

The partiturs are at the Styne office.

The final Overture is entitled "Overture (Jule)," which suggests that it was routined by Styne himself.

Instr.: 4 reed, 8 brass (4 tpt, 3 tb, 1 hrn), 7? strings (4? vln, 0 vla, 2 c, 1 b), piano, harp, guitar, 2 perc = 24? total.

SUGAR BABIES

Orchestrations credited to Dick Hyman. (Additional orchestrations by Dick Leib, Stan Freeman, Joe Lipman, and Sy Johnson.)

Opened October 8, 1979, Mark Hellinger, 1,208 performances. Tryout: May 8, 1978, San Francisco (Curran); August 1979, Philadelphia (Shubert); elsewhere.

A revue. Music by Jimmy McHugh, lyrics by Dorothy Fields and Al Dubin. Musical direction by Glen Roven. Vocal arrangements by Arthur Malvin. Additional vocal arrangements by Hugh Martin and Ralph Blane. Dance arrangements by Arnold Gross. Other participants: Harry Rigby (co-producer); Mickey Rooney (star); Ann Miller (star).

The cast album Overture was orchestrated by Phil Lang.

SUNNY

Orchestrations credited to Russell **Bennett**. (Additional orchestrators, if any, unknown.)

Opened September 22, 1925, New Amsterdam, 517 performances. Tryout: September 9, Philadelphia (Forrest).

Music by Jerome Kern, lyrics and book by Otto Harbach and Oscar Hammerstein II. Musical direction by Gus Salzer. Other participants: Charles Dillingham (producer); Marilyn Miller (star).

The partiturs are in the Kern Collection at the Library of Congress (unexamined).

SUNNY RIVER

Orchestrations credited to Don **Walker**. (Additional orchestrators, if any, unknown.)

Opened December 4, 1941, St. James, 36 performances. Tryout: November 27, New Haven (Shubert).

Music by Sigmund Romberg, lyrics and book by Oscar Hammerstein II. Musical direction by Jacob Schwartzdorf [Jay S. Blackton]. Other participants: Max Gordon (producer); Oscar Hammerstein II (director).

Base page rate: $3.

SWEET ADELINE

Orchestrations credited to Russell **Bennett**. (Additional orchestrations by Max Steiner and others.)

Opened September 3, 1929, Hammerstein's, 234 performances. Tryout: August 19, Atlantic City (Apollo); August 26, Newark (Shubert).

Music by Jerome Kern, lyrics and book by Oscar Hammerstein II. Musical direction by Gus Salzer. Other participants: Arthur Hammerstein (producer); Reginald Hammerstein (director); Helen Morgan (star).

SWEET BYE AND BYE

Orchestrations credited to Ted **Royal**. (Additional orchestrations by Walter Eiger, Charles L. Cooke, John Kline, Allan Small, and Hershy **Kay**.)

Tryout: October 10, 1946, New Haven (Shubert). Closed November 5, Philadelphia (Erlanger).

Music by Vernon Duke, lyrics by Ogden Nash. Musical direction by Charles Blackman. Vocal arrangements by Vernon Duke and George Bauer. Dance arrangements by Buster Davis. Other participants: Fred Kelly (choreographer); S. J. Perelman and Al Hirschfeld (librettists); Dolores Gray (star).

SWEET CHARITY

Orchestrations credited to Ralph **Burns**. (Additional orchestrations by Larry **Wilcox** and probably others.)

Opened January 29, 1966, Palace, 608 performances. Tryout: Detroit (Fisher); December 6, 1965, Philadelphia (Shubert).

Music by Cy Coleman, lyrics by Dorothy Fields. Based on the film *Nights of Cabiria* by Federico Fellini, Tullio Pinelli, and Ennio Flaiano. Musical direction and dance arrangements by Fred Werner. Assistant conductor, Oscar Kosarin. Other participants: Robert Fryer (producer); Bob Fosse (director, choreographer); Neil Simon (librettist); Gwen Verdon (star).

According to reliable sources, Burns had a good deal of assistance on this show (from Wilcox and, presumably, Jim Tyler). "I Love to Cry at Weddings" is known to be by Wilcox. (See page 39.)

SWEETHEARTS (1947 REVIVAL)

Orchestrations and arrangements credited to Russell **Bennett**. (Additional orchestrators unknown.)

Opened January 21, 1947, Shubert, 288 performances. Tryout: unknown.

Music by Victor Herbert, lyrics by Robert B. Smith. Musical direction by Edwin McArthur. Vocal direction by Pembroke Davenport. Other participant: Bobby Clark (star).

Bennett's invoices are preserved in his ledger. Base page rate: $3.75.

Bennett: "Angeline," "Land of Romance," "Once in a While," "Opening Act I," "Opening Act II," "Overture."

SWING

Orchestrations credited to Eddie **Sauter**. (Additional orchestrators, if any, unknown.)

Tryout: February 25, 1980, Wilmington, Delaware (Playhouse). Closed March 30, Washington, D.C. (Opera House).

Music by Robert Waldman, lyrics by Alfred Uhry. Musical direction and dance arrangements by Peter Howard. Vocal arrangements by Elise Bretton. Other participant: Stuart Ostrow (producer, director).

TAKE A CHANCE

Orchestrations uncredited. (Orchestrations by Stephen O. Jones, Edward B. Powell, Russell **Bennett**, Hans **Spialek**, William Daly, and probably others.)

Opened November 26, 1932, Apollo, 243 performances. Tryout: (as *Humpty Dumpty*) September 12, Pittsburgh (Nixon); (as *Take a Chance*) November 7, Philadelphia (Garrick).

Music by Richard A. Whiting and Herb Brown Nacio (aka Nacio Herb Brown). Additional music by Vincent Youmans, lyrics by B. G. DeSylva. Musical direction by Max Meth (replacing Lou Silvers). Vocal arrangements (Merman) by Roger Edens. Other participants: B. G. DeSylva (co-producer, co-librettist); Ethel Merman (star).

This show was revamped, rewritten, and retitled during the tryout, with composer Vincent Youmans coming in to add new songs.

TAKE ME ALONG

Orchestrations (mostly) by Philip J. **Lang**. (Additional orchestrations by Laurence **Rosenthal** and Carroll Huxley.)

Opened October 22, 1959, Shubert, 448 performances. Tryout: September 9, New Haven (Shubert); September 21, Boston (Shubert); Philadelphia.

Music and lyrics by Bob Merrill. Based on the play *Ah, Wilderness!* by Eugene O'Neill. Musical direction and vocal arrangements by Lehman Engel. Ballet and incidental music by Laurence Rosenthal. Other participants: David Merrick (producer); Joseph Stein (co-librettist); Peter Glenville (director); Onna White (choreographer); Jackie Gleason (star); Robert Morse (featured).

Copies of the partiturs are in the American Musical Theatre Collection at the Library of Congress.

The orchestrations are by Lang, with the following exceptions:

Rosenthal: "Beardsley Ballet."

Huxley: Overture.

Other scores:

Entr'acte is by Rosenthal, except for the final section, "Take Me Along," which is by Lang.

BOB MERRILL: Gleason wanted an 11 o'clock song like Merman had in *Gypsy*. Merrick, Peter Glenville, and Charlie Baker (Jackie's agent from William Morris) agreed it was wrong for the show, so we decided that I would keep saying I was working on it. Gleason caught on and was furious; it ended up with us having to be pulled apart backstage because he was swinging at me. One day, Jackie called at the hotel and said, "Listen, Phil Lang is going to orchestrate a number, and these boys—Lyn Duddy and Jerry Bressler—have written a number, and your name is on the show. It's for your own benefit to listen to this number, and if you can give them some help I think you should because your name is going to be on it." So that made sense to me. And I went over and I heard a number that I am not going to criticize. And Jackie said, "What do you think?" And before I could answer, he said, "I agree." And he stood onstage and said, "Listen, you guys, go back to New York." And that was the end of it. I did write him one number—I appreciated him being honest with me, and I did write him a number and I think we put it in for three nights. He liked it, but I didn't; it was just wrong for him to do a number there.

The Overture was orchestrated by (and signed by) Carroll Huxley, a friend of Engel's from the army. A frequent orchestrator for André Kostelanetz, Huxley's only official Broadway credit was as co-orchestrator of *Once upon a Mattress*. He also ghosted for Lang on *Camelot* and quite possibly on other shows of the era for which the partiturs have not been located (including *Destry Rides Again* and *Subways Are for Sleeping*).

Instr.: 5 reed (including 4 clr), 5 brass (2 tpt, 1 tb, 2 hrn), ? strings (vln, 0 vla, c, b), harp, perc.

TENDERLOIN

Orchestrations (totally) by Irwin **Kostal**.

Opened October 17, 1960, 46th Street, 216 performances. Tryout: September 10, New Haven (Shubert); September 20, Boston (Shubert).

Music by Jerry Bock, lyrics by Sheldon Harnick. Based on the novel by Samuel Hopkins Adams. Musical direction by Hal Hastings. Dance arrangements by Jack Elliott. Other participants: Robert E. Griffith and Harold Prince (producers); George Abbott (director, co-librettist); Joe Layton (choreographer); Maurice Evans (star).

The partiturs are in the Bock Collection at the New York Public Library.

The final Overture is Overture #3. This includes "Artificial Flowers" from Overture #2 and "The Picture of Happiness" from the original Entr'acte. The bravura trumpet solo, at bar 234, is from Overture #1. The second part of the solo, a variation on "Army of the Just," is marked "band in the park style." The music of the opening galop, following the religioso introduction, is from "The Orgy."

Entr'acte #2 begins with the first 66 bars of Entr'acte #1 (through "Artificial Flowers") and the 16-bar "Tommy, Tommy" section of Overture #1.

Instr.: 4 reed, 6 brass (2 tpt, 2 tb, 2 hrn), 13? strings (6? vln, 4? vla, 2 c, 1 b), piano/organ/celesta, harp, guitar/banjo/mandolin, perc = 27? total.

(See pages 63, 233.)

TEXAS, LI'L DARLIN'

Orchestrations credited to Russell **Bennett**. (Additional orchestrators unknown.)

Opened November 25, 1949, Mark Hellinger, 293 performances. Tryout: August 29, Westport, Connecticut (Playhouse); October 25, New Haven (Shubert); elsewhere.

Music by Robert Emmett Dolan, lyrics by Johnny Mercer. Musical direction by Will Irwin.

Bennett's invoices are preserved in his ledger. Base page rate: $4.80.

Bennett: "Affable, Balding Me," "Big Movie Show in the Sky," Entr'acte, "Hootin' Owl Trail," "Horseshoes Are Lucky," "It's Great to Be Alive," "A Month of Sundays," "Opening Dance," Overture, "Politics," "Ride 'Em, Cowboy," "Square Dance," "Take a Crank Letter," "Texas, Li'l Darlin'," "Whichaway'd They Go," "Yodel Blues (They Talk a Different Language)" (song and reprise).

Among the songs not invoiced by Bennett are "Down in the Valley," "Love Me, Love My Dog," and "Whoopin' and A-Hollerin'." The Finale version of "It's Great to Be Alive," too, sounds like it is by someone other than Bennett.

A tryout casualty was the twenty-four-year-old leading lady, Elaine Stritch, who left the show after Westport.

THAT'S THE TICKET!

Orchestrations credited to Don **Walker** and Russell **Bennett**. (Additional orchestrators, if any, unknown.)

Tryout: September 24, 1948, Philadelphia (Shubert). Closed October 2, Philadelphia.

Music and lyrics by Harold Rome. Musical direction and vocal arrangements by Lehman Engel. Incidental music by Bus [Buster] Davis. Other participant: Jerome Robbins (director).

Two of the partiturs ("Take Off the Coat" and "You Never Know," both by Bennett) were subsequently used in *Bless You All* and are located with the scores for the latter production in the Rome Collection at Yale. Walker's invoices are at the Library of Congress. Bennett's invoices are preserved in his ledger. Base page rate: $4.95.

Walker: "The Ballad of Marcia LaRue," "Clank! Clank!" "The Fair Sex," "Gin Rummy Rhapsody," "I Shouldn't Love You," "Newsreel," "The Money Song."

Bennett: "Cry Baby," "Determined Woman," "Dost Thou," "Entr'acte," "The Five Knights," "Looking for a Candidate," "Opening," "Overture," "Read All about It," "Take Off the Coat," "You Never Know."

This election-year political satire—originally entitled *Alfred the Average*—has the distinction of being the first Broadway musical directed by Jerome Robbins. One week in Philadelphia, and out.

Instr.: 5 reed, 6 brass (3 tpt, 2 tb, 1 hrn), 10 strings (6 vln, 2 vla, c, b), piano, harp, perc = 24 total.

THEY'RE PLAYING OUR SONG

Orchestrations by Ralph **Burns**, Dick Hazard, and Gene Page.

Opened February 11, 1979, Imperial, 1,082 performances. Tryout: December 1, 1978, Los Angeles (Ahmanson).

Music by Marvin Hamlisch, lyrics by Carole Bayer Sager. Musical direction by Larry Blank. Other participants: Neil Simon (librettist); Robert Klein (star); Lucie Arnaz (star).

Attributions per conductor's score (verified by Larry Blank).

Burns: bows, exit music, "Fallin'," "Fill in the Words," Overture, "Right," "They're Playing My Song," "Workin' It Out."

Hazard: "Act I Curtain," "I Still Believe in Love," "If He Really Knew Me," "Just for Tonight."

Page: "When You're in My Arms."

Other score:

Entr'acte is mostly by Burns, with Hazard contributing the "If He Really Knew Me" section.

13 DAUGHTERS

Orchestrations credited to Joe Glover. (Additional orchestrations by Russell **Bennett** and possibly others.)

Opened March 2, 1961, 54th Street, 28 performances. Tryout: unknown.

Music, lyrics, and book by Eaton Magoon, Jr. Musical direction and vocal arrangements by Pembroke Davenport. Dance arrangements by Bob Atwood. Other participant: Don Ameche (star).

Bennett's invoice is preserved in his journal.

> **Bennett:** Opening ("13 Daughters").

Cy Coleman has stated that he wrote "You Fascinate Me So" as a proposed interpolation into this show. This is clearly erroneous, as the Coleman-Leigh standard was introduced in the 1958 Jules Monk nightclub revue *Demi-Dozen*. One suspects that the song *was* written for a spot in a musical, but Coleman remembered the wrong show title.

THIS IS THE ARMY

Orchestrations uncredited. (Orchestrations by Walter Paul, Nathan Lang Van Cleave, Don **Walker**, Hans **Spialek**, Ralph Wilkinson, Philip J. **Lang**, Allan Small, Bob Warren, Ben Ludlow, Bill Jones, Ralph Kessler, Abe Osser, Al Goering, Tony Gale, and others.)

Opened July 4, 1942, Broadway, 113 performances.

A revue. Music and lyrics by Irving Berlin. Musical direction by Corporal Milton Rosenstock. Dance arrangements by Private Melvin Pahl. Other participants: "Uncle Sam, in cooperation with Irving Berlin" (producer); Irving Berlin (featured).

The partiturs are in the Berlin Collection at the Library of Congress.

> **Paul:** "American Eagles," "I'm Getting Tired So I Can Sleep Reprise," opening chorus.
> **Van Cleave:** Ballet, "This Is the Army, Mr. Jones" (see below).
> **Wilkinson:** "I Left My Heart at the Stage Door Canteen" (see below), "I'm Getting Tired So I Can Sleep" (see below).
> **Warren:** "The Army's Made a Man Out of Me" (see below), "My Sergeant and I Are Buddies."
> **Ludlow:** "That's What the Well-Dressed Man in Harlem Will Wear" (see below).
> **Small:** "Siboney."
> **Lang:** "Oh, To Be Home Again."
> **Spialek:** "Overture #2."
> **Walker:** "Mandy Finale."
> **Jones:** "The Kick in the Pants" (added during tour), "Off to France" (added during tour), "Oh, How I Long to Be Home Again" (added during tour), "There Are No Wings on a Foxhole" (added during tour).
> **Kessler:** "Heaven Watch Out for the Philippines Finale" (added during tour).
> Other scores:

"The Army's Made a Man Out of Me": there are two versions, one (#15, probably the show version) by Warren and the other unidentified.

"I Left My Heart at the Stage Door Canteen": song is by Wilkinson; "It's a Lovely Day Tomorrow" and "A Pretty Girl Is Like a Melody" excerpts are by Kessler.

"I'm Getting Tired So I Can Sleep": there are two versions, one (#8) by Wilkinson and the other unidentified.

"Oh, How I Hate to Get Up in the Morning": there are three versions, one (in G major) by Lang; one (in A major) by Goering; and one (in A-flat) by an unidentified hand.

"That Russian Winter": song is by "Kogan" (full name unknown); dance is by Osser.

"That's What the Well-Dressed Man in Harlem Will Wear": there are two versions, one (with an extended routine) by Ludlow and the other unidentified.

"This Is the Army, Mr. Jones": there are three versions, one (#6, probably the show version) by Van Cleave and two unidentified.

"This Time" is by Tony Gale; "First Ending" is by Jones.

It was long stated that this legendary armed forces show was fully staffed by servicemen. But examination of the partiturs shows that the orchestrations were sent out to the usual suspects, with willing participation from members of the Chappell stable (including Walker, Spialek, Paul, and Van Cleave). There are multiple versions of many charts, presumably to accommodate different-sized orchestras during the extensive worldwide tour of military installations.

THOROUGHLY MODERN MILLIE

Orchestrations by Doug Besterman and Ralph **Burns**. (Additional orchestrations by Larry Blank.)

Opened April 18, 2002, Marquis, 903 performances. Tryout: October 10, 2000, La Jolla, California (Playhouse).

New music by Jeanine Tesori, new lyrics by Dick Scanlan. A stage adaptation of the film and story by Richard Morris. Musical direction by Michael Rafter. Vocal arrangements by Jeanine Tesori. Dance arrangements by David Chase. Other participant: Sutton Foster (star).

Ralph Burns died on November 21, 2001. His final theatre work, *Thoroughly Modern Millie*, had been produced in October 2000 in a developmental production at the La Jolla Playhouse in California. Doug Besterman, who had worked with Burns on *Fosse*, took over *Millie* and orchestrated it for Broadway—retaining many of Ralph's figures, preserving his final credit, and winning Burns a posthumous Tony.

A THOUSAND CLOWNS

Orchestrations and incidental music composed by Don **Walker**.

Opened April 5, 1962, Eugene O'Neill, 428 performances. Tryout: March 15, Boston (Wilbur).

A comedy by Herb Gardner. Other participants: Fred Coe (co-producer, director); Jason
Robards (star); Sandy Dennis (featured); William Daniels (featured); Gene Saks (featured).

THE THREE MUSKETEERS

Orchestrations uncredited. (Orchestrations by Hans **Spialek** and others.)

Opened March 13, 1928, Lyric, 319 performances. Tryout: February 21, Washington,
D.C. (National); elsewhere.

Music by Rudolf Friml, lyrics by P. G. Wodehouse and Clifford Grey. Based on the novel
by Alexandre Dumas. Musical direction by Gus Salzer. Other participant: Florenz
Ziegfeld, Jr. (producer).

THE THREE MUSKETEERS (1984 REVIVAL)

Orchestrations credited to Larry Wilcox. (Additional orchestrations by Bill Byers, Harold
Wheeler, and Danny Troob.)

Opened November 4, 1984, Broadway, 9 performances. Tryout: Stamford, Connecticut.

Music by Rudolf Friml, lyrics by P. G. Wodehouse and Clifford Grey. Based on the novel
by Alexandre Dumas. Music adapted, arranged, and supervised by Kirk Nurock. Conducted by Gordon Lowry Harrell. Dance arrangements by Wally Harper and Mark
Hummel. Other participant: Tom O'Horgan (director).

THREE SISTERS

Orchestrations credited to Russell **Bennett**. (Additional orchestrators, if any, unknown.)

Opened April 9, 1934, Theatre Royal, Drury Lane (London), 45 performances. Tryout:
none.

Music by Jerome Kern, lyrics and book by Oscar Hammerstein II. Musical direction by
Charles Prentice. Other participants: Jerome Kern and Oscar Hammerstein II (directors).

Bennett's partitur for "Dorrie Barges"—which incorporates the song that became "I
Won't Dance" when it was reused in the 1935 film version of *Roberta*—is located with the
partiturs for *Roberta* in the Kern Collection at the Library of Congress.

Instr.: 8 reed, 4 brass (2 tpt, 2 tb), ? strings (vln, vla, c, b), piano, harp, guitar, perc.

THREE TO MAKE READY

Orchestrations credited to Russell **Bennett**, Charles L. Cooke, Elliott Jacoby, Ted **Royal**,
Hans **Spialek**, and Walter Paul.

Opened March 7, 1946, Adelphi, 327 performances. Tryout: February, Boston.

A revue. Music by Morgan Lewis, lyrics and sketches by Nancy Hamilton. Musical direction by Ray Kavanaugh. Continuity by Melvin Pahl. Vocal arrangements by Joe Moon.
Other participants: Ray Bolger (star); Gordon MacRae (featured); Arthur Godfrey
(featured).

THREE WALTZES

Orchestrations uncredited. (Orchestrations by Conrad Salinger, Hilding Anderson, Don **Walker**, and others.)

Opened December 25, 1937, Majestic, 122 performances. Tryout: unknown.

Music by Johann Strauss, Sr., Johann Strauss, Jr., and Oscar Straus, lyrics by Clare Kummer. Based on the play by Paul Knepler and Armin Robinson. Musical direction by Harold Levey. Other participant: Kitty Carlisle (star).

THREE WISHES FOR JAMIE

Orchestrations credited to Russell **Bennett**. (Additional orchestrations by Philip J. **Lang** and possibly others.)

Opened March 21, 1952, Mark Hellinger, 92 performances. Tryout: February 4, New Haven (Shubert); Philadelphia; Boston.

Music and lyrics by Ralph Blane. Based on the novel by Charles O'Neal. Musical direction by Joseph Littau. Vocal arrangements by William Ellfeldt. Dance arrangements by Roger Adams. Other participants: Abe Burrows (director, co-librettist); John Raitt (star).

Bennett's invoices are preserved in his ledger. Base page rate: $4.95.

Bennett: "April Face" (song and reprise), "The Chase," Entr'acte, "The Girl That I Court in My Mind," "Goin' on a Hayride" (song and reprise), "I'll Sing You a Song," "I'm Gonna Be Rich," "It Must Be Spring," "It's a Wishing World," "Love Has Nothing to Do with Looks," "Magic Tree," "Maybe," "My Heart's Darlin'," Prelude, "The Search," "Trottin' to the Fair," "We're for Love," "What Do I Know?"

Among the songs not invoiced by Bennett are "The Army Mule Song," "Kevin's Prayer," "My Home's a Highway," "The Wake," and "Wedding March.," The likeliest ghosts for the songs Bennett didn't do are Phil Lang (who at one point listed the show among his credits) and possibly Joe Glover.

Bennett did most of this show during one of his California sojourns, as it was first mounted in Los Angeles in June 1951 as part of Edwin Lester's Civic Light Opera season.

THE THREEPENNY OPERA

Orchestrations (totally) by Kurt Weill.

Opened April 13, 1933, Empire, 12 performances.

Music by Kurt Weill, lyrics by Bertolt Brecht. English adaptation of lyrics and book by Gifford Cochran and Jerrold Krimsky. Based on the play *The Beggar's Opera* by John Gay. Musical direction by Macklin Marrow.

The original partiturs (from the 1928 Berlin premiere) are at the Sibley Music Library in Rochester, New York.

THE THREEPENNY OPERA (1954 VERSION)

Orchestrations (totally) by Kurt Weill.

Opened March 10, 1954, de Lys (off-Broadway), 2,706 performances.

English adaptation of lyrics and book by Marc Blitzstein. Musical direction by Samuel Matlowsky. Other participant: Lotte Lenya (featured).

Instr.: 2 reed (clr/sax), 3 brass (2 tpt, 1 tb), 0 strings, piano/celesta/harmonium, guitar/banjo, perc = 8 total.

THROUGH THE YEARS

Orchestrations uncredited. (Orchestrations by Domenico Savino, Stephen O. Jones, Deems Taylor, Howard Jackson, and probably others.)

Opened January 28, 1932, Manhattan, 20 performances. Tryout (as *Smilin' Through*): December 28, 1931, Philadelphia (Garrick); January, Washington, D.C.

Music by Vincent Youmans, lyrics by Edward Heyman. Musical direction by William Daly. Other participants: Vincent Youmans (producer).

Several partiturs are in the Youmans Collection at the Library of Congress.
    Savino: "It's Every Girl's Ambition," "Kathleen Mine," "You're Everywhere."
    Jackson: "Drums in My Heart," "Kinda Like You."
    Jones: "More Than Ever."
    Other scores:
    "Ghost Music": there are two scores, one by Deems Taylor and one by Savino.

THUMBS UP!

Orchestrations uncredited. (Orchestrations by Hans **Spialek**, Conrad Salinger, David Raksin, and others.)

Opened December 27, 1934, St. James, 156 performances. Tryout: Philadelphia.

A revue. Music and lyrics by various writers, including James F. Hanley and Vernon Duke. Musical direction by Gene Salzer. Other participants: Bobby Clark & Paul McCullough (stars); Jack Cole (featured).

TICKETS, PLEASE!

Orchestrations credited to Ted **Royal**. (Additional orchestrators, if any, unknown.)

Opened April 27, 1950, Coronet, 245 performances. Tryout: April 6, New Haven (Shubert); Boston.

A revue. Music by Lyn Duddy (and others); lyrics by Joan Edwards (and others). Musical direction by Phil Ingalls. Incidental music by Phil Ingalls and Hal Hastings. Other participants: George Abbott (unbilled replacement director); H. Smith Prince (assistant stage manager); Paul & Grace Hartman (stars); Larry Kert (member of chorus).

This forgotten revue is memorable for the presence of assistant stage manager "H. Smith Prince," who within four years would turn producer with *The Pajama Game*. Also present: Prince's longtime musical director, Hal Hastings.

TIMBUKTU!

"Additional" orchestrations credited to William David Brohn, from the original orchestrations credited to Arthur Kay. (Additional orchestrators, if any, unknown.)

Opened March 1, 1978, Mark Hellinger, 221 performances. Tryout: December 1977, Philadelphia; January 5, 1978, Washington, D.C. (Opera House).

Music from Alexandre Borodin. Musical adaptation and lyrics by Robert Wright & George Forrest. Based on the musical *Kismet*. Musical direction, arrangements, and incidental music by Charles H. Coleman. Other participants: Geoffrey Holder (director, choreographer); Eartha Kitt (star); Melba Moore (featured).

A TIME FOR SINGING

Orchestrations by Don **Walker**. (Additional orchestrations by Ted Raph, with Harvey Wuest and Mark Bucci.)

Opened May 21, 1966, Broadway, 41 performances. Tryout: April 14, Boston (Colonial).

Music by John Morris, lyrics and book by John Morris and Gerald Freedman. Based on the novel *How Green Was My Valley* by Richard Llewellyn. Musical direction by Jay Blackton. Other participants: Alexander H. Cohen (producer); Gerald Freedman (director); Donald McKayle (choreographer); Gower Champion (replacement choreographer, uncredited).

Walker's invoices are at the Library of Congress. Base page rate: $10. Invoices indicate: Walker (73%), Raph (25%).

Walker: "Angharad's Love," final scene, "Old Long John," "That's What Young Ladies Do," "The Wedding."

Walker and **Raph:** "And the Mountains Sing Back," Entr'acte, "Far from Home," "Here We Stand," "I'm Always Wrong," "Miner's March," "Saturday," "Someone Must Try," "There Is Beautiful You Are," "A Time for Singing," "Wedding Dance," "What a Party," "When He Looks at Me," "When the Baby Comes," "Why Would Anyone Want to Get Married?"

Other scores:

"How Green Was My Valley" and "Window Scene (Let Me Love You)" are mostly by Walker, with minor contributions by Raph.

"I Wonder If" is by Walker and Bucci; reprise by Walker.

"Tell Her I Love Her" is mostly by Walker and Wuest, with minor contributions by Raph.

"Three Ships" is mostly by Raph (28 pages), with Walker (14 pages).

TIME REMEMBERED

Orchestrations credited to Vernon Duke.

Opened November 12, 1957, Morosco, 247 performances. Tryout: September 30, New Haven (Shubert); elsewhere.

A play by Jean Anouilh, with incidental music and lyrics by Vernon Duke. Other participants: Albert Marre (director); Helen Hayes (star); Richard Burton (star).

TO BROADWAY WITH LOVE

Orchestrations credited to Philip J. **Lang**. (Additional orchestrations by Russell **Bennett** and probably others.)

Opened April 29, 1964, Flushing, New York (Texas Pavilion Music Hall, World's Fair). Tryout: none.

A revue. New songs by Jerry Bock and Sheldon Harnick. Musical direction by Franz Allers. Other participants: Morton Da Costa (director, "conceived by"); Donald Saddler (choreographer).

Bennett's invoice is preserved in his journal. Base page rate: $6.90.

Bock and Harnick wrote five songs for this World's Fair revue. Bennett's account book indicates that he scored 62 pages, without specific titles, "for Phil Lang."

TOO MANY GIRLS

Orchestrations credited to Hans **Spialek**. (Additional orchestrations by Franklyn Marks, Hilding Anderson, Walter Paul, Don **Walker**, Ted **Royal**, R. P. DuPage, and others.)

Opened October 18, 1939, Imperial, 249 performances. Tryout: October 2, Boston (Shubert).

Music by Richard Rodgers, lyrics by Lorenz Hart. Musical direction by Harry Levant. Vocal arrangements by Hugh Martin. Other participant: George Abbott (producer, director).

The partiturs are at the offices of the Rodgers & Hammerstein Organization.

Spialek: "Give It Back to the Indians" (see below), "Heroes in the Fall" (Opening act I), "Hunted Stag" (cut), "I Didn't Know What Time It Was" (see below), "I Like to Recognize the Tune" (see below), "Look Out," "Love Never Went to College" (see below), "My Prince (What a Prince)," "Sweethearts of the Team," "You're Nearer" (written for the motion picture version).

Anderson: "Pottawatomie."

Other scores:

" 'Cause We Got Cake": there are several scores. Song is by Spialek; dance is by Royal; "Cake (Interlude)" is by Spialek. The number continues with a section by DuPage. "Encore (Hugh's Arrangement)" is by Marks.

"Give It Back to the Indians": song and dance are by Spialek; encore by unknown hand #1.

"I Didn't Know What Time It Was" is by Spialek, with incidental by Royal.

"I Like to Recognize the Tune" is mostly by Spialek, with 4 pages by DuPage. Encore is by Spialek.

"Love Never Went to College": song is by Spialek, tag by Anderson, continuation by unknown hand #1.

Overture: opening, interior bridgework, and end are by Spialek. Interludes are "Too Many Girls" (Royal), "I Didn't Know What Time It Was" (Paul), "Love Never Went to College" (missing, probably Spialek), and "Spic and Spanish" (Paul).

"She Could Shake the Maracas": part 1 is by Spialek; part 2 by Walker; dance (cut) is by Spialek.

"Spic and Spanish": song is by Spialek; dance routine by Royal; encore and reprise by unknown hand #1; "Specialty for Solo Dance" (cut) by Marks.

"Too Many Girls": song is by Paul; "Hugh's Vocal Arrangement" by Marks; dance by Anderson; tag by Marks.

Instr.: 5 reed, 5 brass (3 tpt, 1 tb, 1 hrn), 11? strings (8? vln, 0 vla, 2? c, 1 b), piano, perc = 23? total..

TOP BANANA

Orchestrations credited to Don **Walker**. (Additional orchestrations by Bill Finegan, Robert **Ginzler**, Luther Henderson, and others.)

Opened November 1, 1951, Winter Garden, 350 performances. Tryout: September 17, Boston (Shubert); October 9, Philadelphia (Shubert).

Music and lyrics by Johnny Mercer. Musical direction by Harold Hastings. Vocal arrangements and direction by Hugh Martin. Assistant to Hugh Martin, Buster Davis. Dance arrangements by Lee Pockriss. Other participant: Phil Silvers (star).

Finegan: "I Fought Every Step of the Way," "Sans Souci."

Big band arranger Bill Finegan, formerly staff orchestrator for the Glenn Miller Orchestra, was given specific program credit (as "Finnigan") for "I Fought Every Step of the Way" and "Sans Souci." In 1952, just after *Top Banana*, he joined with Eddie Sauter to form the fabled Sauter-Finegan band.

On his rehearsal copy of "You're O.K. for TV," which contained a number of impressions by Phil Silvers, Walker has labeled the relevant sections with the names Chevalier, Durante, and Wynn as a guide to orchestration style.

TOPLITZKY OF NOTRE DAME

Orchestrations credited to Menotti Salta, Allan Small, and Lewis Raymond. (Additional orchestrators, if any, unknown.)

Opened December 26, 1946, Century, 60 performances. Tryout: unknown.

Music by Sammy Fain, lyrics and book by George Marion, Jr. Musical direction and vocal arrangements by Leon Leonardi.

TOUCH AND GO

Orchestrations by Don **Walker**. (Additional orchestrations by Russell **Bennett**.)

Opened October 13, 1949, Broadhurst, 176 performances. Tryout: September 21, New Haven (Shubert); September 26, Philadelphia (Forrest).

A revue. Music by Jay Gorney, lyrics and sketches by Jean and Walter Kerr. Musical direction and vocal arrangements by Antonio Morelli. Ballet music by Genevieve Pitot. Other participants: George Abbott (producer); Walter Kerr (director).

Most of the partiturs are in the Gorney Collection at the New York Public Library.

Walker's invoices are at the Library of Congress. Bennett's invoices are preserved in his ledger. Base page rate: $5.10. Invoices indicate: Walker (78%), Bennett (22%).

Walker: "Be a Mess," "Bendix," "Broadway Love Song," "Cinderella Skit," "Easy Does It," "Highbrow," "I Love Them Bums," "It'll Be Alright in 100 Years" (song and utility), "Miss Platt Seeks Mate," "Mr. Brown, Miss Dupree," "Private Detective," Opening, Overture, "This Is the Church" (see below), "Under the Sleeping Volcano," "Wish Me Luck."

Bennett: "Comic Books," "Hamlet," utilities ("Glorious, Atkinson, Times," "Mr. Brown," "Touch and Go").

Other scores:

"This Had Better Be Love" is by Bennett, with an 8-bar patch near the end of part I by Walker; utility is by Walker.

"This Is the Church (American Primitive)": song (87 bars) is by Walker; ballet (with chorus, 178 bars) is by Bennett.

This was the only show, out of all for which partiturs were located, in which the reed section included dedicated legit players. That is, there were six conventional reed chairs— two clarinets, four sax, all of whom doubled. In addition, there were chairs labeled "legit flute" and "legit oboe." These extra musicians necessitated relatively small brass and string sections.

Instr.: 8 reed (including 4 sax), 4 brass (2 tpt, 1 tb, 1 hrn), 7? strings (4? vln, 1 vla, 1 c, 1 b), piano, Novachord (keyboard), guitar, perc = 23? total.

TOVARICH

Orchestrations credited to Philip J. **Lang**. (Additional orchestrators, if any, unknown.)

Opened March 18, 1963, Broadway, 264 performances. Tryout: January, Philadelphia (Erlanger); February 12, Boston (Colonial).

Music by Lee Pockriss, lyrics by Anne Croswell. Based on Robert E. Sherwood's adaptation of the play by Jacques Deval. Musical direction and vocal arrangements by Stanley Lebowsky. Dance arrangements by Lee Pockriss. Additional dance music by Dorothea Freitag. Other participants: Herbert Ross (choreographer); Vivien Leigh (star); Jean Pierre Aumont (star).

A TREE GROWS IN BROOKLYN

Orchestrations by Joe Glover and Russell **Bennett**. (Additional orchestrations by Ted **Royal** and possibly others.)

Opened April 19, 1951, Alvin, 267 performances. Tryout: March 19, New Haven (Shubert); Philadelphia.

Music by Arthur Schwartz, lyrics by Dorothy Fields. Based on the novel by Betty Smith. Musical direction by Max Goberman. Musical supervision by Jay Blackton. Dance arrangements by Oscar Kosarin. Other participants: George Abbott (producer, director, co-librettist); Robert Fryer (associate producer); Herbert Ross (choreographer); Shirley Booth (star).

Most of the partiturs are in the possession of the composer's estate. Bennett's invoices are preserved in his ledger. Base page rate: $4.80.

The orchestrations are by Glover, with the following exceptions:

Bennett: "The Bride," "Lament" part 1 and part 2 ("Where Is My Prince"), Opening part I ("Payday") and part II ("Mine till Monday").

Royal: "Halloween" (ballet).

Unidentified hand: "New Broom" incidental.

Other scores:

"I'll Buy You a Star": the first refrain is by Bennett; the second (choral) refrain by Glover; the partitur for the verse is missing, but probably by Bennett.

"He Had Refinement" is by Glover, replacing an earlier version by Bennett.

"Make the Man Love Me" is by Glover, replacing an earlier version by Bennett.

"If You Haven't Got a Sweetheart," "Don't Be Afraid," and the "Halloween" ballet are missing. The first two are probably by Glover. The ballet, reports dance arranger Oscar Kosarin, was orchestrated by Royal. "Halloween" was replaced for the brief tour with a second, modernistic ballet, "The Raffle" (ballet music arranged by Dean Fuller). The partiturs for this are also missing, but almost surely are not by Glover.

Paul Schwartz, son of the composer (and a composer in his own right), remembered that his father didn't much like the orchestrations. A look at the invoices and the calendar explains what happened. Bennett usually worked just over three weeks on a show, returning as necessary to handle changes during the tryout. He worked on *The King and I* from February 10 through March 8, returning from New Haven to start on his next assignment. But he only spent one week on *Brooklyn*, hastily departing March 15 for Boston—where *The King and I* was undergoing major rewrites. (He actually did one *Brooklyn* chart in Boston, on the same day as "I Have Dreamed.") Glover was already lined up to assist Bennett on *Brooklyn*. He had also replaced Walker earlier that season on *Call Me Madam*, which was conducted by *Brooklyn* musical supervisor Jay Blackton. Under the circumstances, it was apparently decided to let Glover take over the contract. Glover was understandably rushed, which resulted in some rather sketchy charts. As a matter of personality, it seems like he was determined not to farm out anything as a way of proving that he was capable of doing a whole show (at a time when Bennett and Walker regularly used multiple ghosts).

Bennett received sole billing on the tryout advertising and first printing of the sheet music. Elsewhere, Glover and Bennett are billed equally, with Glover usually in first position.

Instr.: 5 reed, 6 brass (2 tpt, 2 tb, 2 hrn), 13? strings (8? vln, 2 vla, 2 c, b), piano, perc = 26? total.

TRIXIE TRUE TEEN DETECTIVE

Orchestrations by Eddie **Sauter**. (Additional orchestrators, if any, unknown.)

Opened December 7, 1980, de Lys (off-Broadway), 94 performances.

Music and lyrics by Kelly Hamilton, musical direction and vocal arrangements by Robert (Rob) Fisher. Dance arrangements by Jimmy Roberts.

TWO BY TWO

Orchestrations (totally) by Eddie **Sauter**.

Opened November 10, 1970, Imperial, 343 performances. Tryout: September 14, New Haven (Shubert); September 29, Boston (Shubert).

Music by Richard Rodgers, lyrics by Martin Charnin. Based on the play *The Flowering Peach* by Clifford Odets. Musical direction by Jay Blackton. Vocal and dance arrangements by Trude Rittman. Other participants: Richard Rodgers (producer); Joe Layton (director); Peter Stone (librettist); Danny Kaye (star).

The partiturs are at the offices of the Rodgers & Hammerstein Organization.

There is also a second set of orchestrations for a smaller orchestra—3 reed, 3 brass, 2 percussion, organ, and 7(?) strings—by Larry Wilcox.

Instr.: 5 reed, 6 brass (2 tpt, 2 tb, 2 hrn), 11 strings (7 vln, 1 vla, 2 c, 1 b), organ/celesta, harp, 2 perc = 26 total.

TWO FOR THE SHOW

Orchestrations credited to Hans **Spialek** and Don **Walker**. (Additional orchestrators, if any, unknown.)

Opened February 8, 1940, Booth, 124 performances. Tryout: January 23, Boston.

A revue. Music by Morgan Lewis, lyrics by Nancy Hamilton. Musical direction by Ray Kavanaugh. Vocal arrangements by Harold Cooke. Other participants: Joshua Logan (director); Alfred Drake (featured).

TWO ON THE AISLE

Orchestrations credited to Philip J. **Lang**. (Additional orchestrators, if any, unknown.)

Opened July 19, 1951, Mark Hellinger, 276 performances. Tryout: June 11, New Haven (Shubert); June 20, Philadelphia (Forrest).

A revue. Music by Jule Styne, lyrics and sketches by Betty Comden & Adolph Green. Musical direction and vocal arrangements by Herbert Greene. Dance arrangements by Genevieve Pitot. Other participants: Abe Burrows (director); Bert Lahr (star); Dolores Gray (star).

TWO'S COMPANY

Orchestrations by Don **Walker**. (Additional orchestrations by Clare Grundman and Philip J. **Lang**.)

Opened December 15, 1952, Alvin, 90 performances. Tryout: October 19, Detroit (Shubert); Pittsburgh; November 17, Boston (Shubert).

A revue. Music by Vernon Duke, lyrics by Ogden Nash, additional lyrics by Sammy Cahn. Musical direction and vocal arrangements by Milton Rosenstock. Dance arrangements by Genevieve Pitot and David Baker. Other participants: Michael Ellis (co-producer; Jerome Robbins (choreographer); Jules Dassin (sketch director); Charles Sherman (sketch writer); Bette Davis (star).

Invoices are in the Walker Collection at the Library of Congress. Base page rate: $5.52.

Walker: "Esther," "Finale," "Haunted Hot Spot" (except for revised section of dance, by Grundman), "A Man's Home," "Out of a Clear Blue Sky."

Grundman: "Baby Couldn't Dance," "Glug-Glug," "I Think You're Pretty, Too," "It Just Occurred to Me" (song, intro, and dance), "Just Turn Me Loose on Broadway," "Magician Sketch," Overture, utilities ("Good Little Girls," "Out of a Clear Blue Sky," "Roundabout," "The Theatre Is a Lady").

Lang: "Ball Song," "Good Little Girls" (song and encores), "Herbert," "Just Like a Man," "Purple Rose" (song and utility), "Roll Along, Sadie" (with new ending by Grundman), "Roundabout," "Zumbali (Purple Rose Opening)."

Other scores:

"The Theatre Is a Lady" is by Walker and Grundman.

> MICHAEL ELLIS: We started because we had a lot of unused revue material by Charles Sherman. "Let's do a revue," we said—"but with a star who's not associated with musicals." First, we went to Judith Anderson. She was interested, but couldn't make herself available. We had rented office space from Ralph Alswang, the set designer. One day, he was talking on the phone to Gary Merrill, who had just married Bette Davis. Jimmy Russo, my co-producer, yelled out as a joke for Ralph to ask if Bette Davis would do it. And she did.

The show marked a brief reunion for Walker. When he first came to New York early in the Depression, in October 1930, he slept on the window seat in the apartment (at 72nd Street and Riverside Drive) of Phil Cohen, a fellow sax player from Princeton. Cohen was head of the music department at the Paramount Astoria Studios; his two rent-paying roommates were a team of neophyte songwriters working at Paramount, Vernon Duke and Yip Harburg.

At one point during the extended tryout, *Two's Company* bore the legend "entire production supervised by Jerome Robbins." As the extent of the disaster became apparent, Robbins voluntarily rescinded the credit.

Instr.: 5 reed (including 5 sax), 5 brass (3 tpt, 2 tb), 9 strings (6 vln, 1 vla, 1 c, 1 b), piano, guitar, perc = 22 total.

THE UNSINKABLE MOLLY BROWN

Orchestrations (mostly) by Don **Walker**. (Additional orchestrations by Sol Berkowitz[?].)

Opened November 3, 1960, Winter Garden, 532 performances. Tryout: September 26, Philadelphia (Shubert).

Music and lyrics by Meredith Willson. Suggested by events in the life of Molly Tobin Brown. Musical direction and vocal arrangements by Herbert Greene. Dance arrangements by Sol Berkowitz. Other participants: Theatre Guild (co-producer); Dore Schary (co-producer, director); Peter Gennaro (choreographer); Tammy Grimes (star).

The partiturs are at Music Theatre International. Walker's invoices are at the Library of Congress.

The orchestrations are by Walker, with the following exceptions:

Unidentified hand (Sol Berkowitz?): "Belly Up" dance (two versions), several minor incidentals.

Other scores:

"Blue Danube I" is by Walker; "Blue Danube II" is by Walker, except for first 6 bars by unidentified hand.

Instr.: 5 reed, 7 brass (3 tpt, 1 tb, 3 hrn), 12? strings (8? vln, 0 vla, 4 c, 1 b), piano, perc = 26? total.

UP IN CENTRAL PARK

Orchestrations credited to Don **Walker**. (Additional orchestrators, if any, unknown.)

Opened January 27, 1945, Century, 504 performances. Tryout: December 28, 1944, Philadelphia (Forrest).

Music by Sigmund Romberg, lyrics by Dorothy Fields. Musical direction by Max Meth. Other participants: Michael Todd (producer); Herbert & Dorothy Fields (co-librettists).

Three charts ("The Big Back Yard Encore," "Close as Pages in a Book," and "When You Walk in the Room Recording Version," all by Walker) are in the Walker Collection at the Library of Congress.

Instr.: 6 reed, 6 brass (2 tpt, 2 tb, 2 hrn), ? strings (vln, vla, c, b), piano/celesta, harp, perc.

THE UTTER GLORY OF MORRISEY HALL

Orchestrations credited to Jay Blackton and Russell Warner. (Additional orchestrators, if any, unknown.)

Opened May 13, 1979, Mark Hellinger, 1 performance. Tryout: November 3, 1978, Princeton, New Jersey (McCarter).

Music and lyrics by Clark Gesner. Musical direction by John Lesko. Dance arrangements by Allen Cohen. Other participant: Celeste Holm (star).

THE VAMP

Orchestrations credited to James Mundy (replacing Don **Walker**). (Additional orchestrations by Frank Ventre, Jay Brower, and probably others.)

Opened November 10, 1955, Winter Garden, 60 performances. Tryout: (as *Delilah*) September, Detroit; October 11, New Haven (Shubert); October 18, Washington, D.C. (National).

Music by James Mundy, lyrics by John Latouche. Musical direction and vocal arrangements by Milton Rosenstock. Incidental music by Jack Pfeiffer. Other participants:

Alexander Carson (co-producer); John Latouche (co-librettist); Carol Channing [Carson] (star).

Walker's invoices are at the Library of Congress. Base page rate: $6.04.

Walker was the initial orchestrator on the show, with additional orchestrations by composer Jimmy Mundy. Walker voluntarily terminated his contract—with an open offer to help out—on September 28, in order to allow Mundy to take over. By then, Walker (and ghosts) had done 52% percent of the score (with 42% by Mundy), although Mundy surely had written more by the time the show reached New York.

Instr.: 5 reed (including 5 sax), 5 brass (3 tpt, 2 tb), 10 strings (6 vln, 0 vla, 3 c, b), piano, harp, guitar, perc = 24 total.

VENUS IN SILK

Orchestrations credited to Robert Stolz, Hans **Spialek**, and George Hirst. (Additional orchestrators, if any, unknown.)

Tryout: October 1, 1935, Pittsburgh; October 7, Washington, D.C. (National). Closed October 12, Washington, D.C.

Music by Robert Stolz, lyrics by Lester O'Keefe. Musical direction and vocal arrangements by George Hirst.

VERY WARM FOR MAY

Orchestrations credited to Russell **Bennett**. (Additional orchestrations by Gus Levene, Nathan Lang Van Cleave, Menotti Salta, Hans **Spialek** and others.)

Opened November 17, 1939, Alvin, 59 performances. Tryout: October 20, Wilmington, Delaware (Playhouse); October 23, Washington, D.C. (National); October 30, Philadelphia (Forrest); November 6, Boston (Shubert).

Music by Jerome Kern, lyrics and book by Oscar Hammerstein II. Musical direction by Robert Emmett Dolan. Dance arrangements by Will Irwin. Other participants: Vincente Minnelli (director, designer); Oscar Hammerstein II (book director).

The partiturs are in the Kern Collection at the Library of Congress.

The orchestrations are by Bennett, with the following exceptions:

Van Cleave: "High Up in Harlem"

Salta: "Muskat" (Opening Act 2 Part 2)

Spialek: "Soft Shoe Dance"

Unidentified hands: "Flight of the Bumble Bee," "Sally Dances"

Other scores:

"All the Things You Are": verse and first two refrains are by Bennett. There is an additional chart by Levene, apparently used as a continuation of the number

"Finale Ultimo": twelve parts of this number are by Bennett, the other two by Levene

"Heaven in My Arms": song is by Bennett, dance ("Music in My Heart Dance Night Club") is by Van Cleave.

Instr.: 5 reed, 5 brass (3 tpt, 2 tb),? strings (vln, vla, 2? c, 1 b), 2 piano, guitar, 2 perc..

VINTAGE '60

Orchestrations credited to Allyn Fergusen. (Additional orchestrations by Sid **Ramin**, Robert **Ginzler**, Peter Matz, Johnny Mandel, John Lesko, and Gershon Kingsley.)

Opened September 17, 1960, Brooks Atkinson, 8 performances. Tryout: unknown.

A revue. Music and lyrics by various writers, including Sheldon Harnick. Musical direction by Gershon Kingsley. Other participants: David Merrick (producer); Michele Lee (featured).

VIRGINIA

Orchestrations credited to Hans **Spialek**, Phil Wall, and Will Vodery. (Additional orchestrations by Arden Cornwell and Maurice Baron.)

Opened September 2, 1937, Center, 60 performances.

Music by Arthur Schwartz, lyrics by Albert Stillman. Musical direction by John McManus. Vocal arrangements by Lee Montgomery and Ken Christie.

> SPIALEK: Partly as a gag, partly on a bet that nobody would recognize it, for the first act Finale, I used—no, "lifted," note for note—a few very poignant pages from Richard Wagner's *Götterdämmerung*—and got away with it. Only a very old horn player in the orchestra almost spoiled my fun and bet, by shaking his finger at me, squawking, "That's from *Valkyre!*"

WALK A LITTLE FASTER

Orchestrations uncredited. (Orchestrations by Russell **Bennett**, Conrad Salinger, and others.)

Opened December 7, 1932, St. James, 121 performances. Tryout: Boston (Majestic).

A revue. Music by Vernon Duke, lyrics by E. Y. Harburg. Musical direction by Nicholas Kempner. Other participants: Monty Woolley (director); Beatrice Lillie (star); Bobby Clark & Paul McCullough (stars).

WALK WITH MUSIC

Orchestrations credited to Hans **Spialek**, Don **Walker**, Arden Cornwell, Fred Van Epps, and Joe Dubin.

Opened June 4, 1940, Ethel Barrymore, 55 performances. Tryout: (as *Three after Three*) November 24, 1939, New Haven (Shubert); January 8, 1940, Washington, D.C. (National); Chicago; elsewhere. Closed March 16, 1940, Detroit.

Music by Hoagy Carmichael, lyrics by Johnny Mercer. Based on the play *Three Blind Mice* by Stephen Powys. Musical direction by Joseph Littau (replacing Buck [Clay] Warnick). Vocal arrangements by Hugh Martin. Other participants: Mitzi Green (star); Kitty Carlisle (star, replacing Simone Simon); Stepin Fetchit (featured); the Martins (including Hugh Martin and Ralph Blane, featured).

WALKING HAPPY

Orchestrations credited to Larry **Wilcox**. (Additional orchestrators, if any, unknown.)

Opened November 26, 1966, Lunt-Fontanne, 161 performances. Tryout: October, Philadelphia (Shubert); Detroit (Fisher).

Music by James Van Heusen, lyrics by Sammy Cahn. Based on the play *Hobson's Choice* by Harold Brighouse. Musical direction and vocal arrangements by Herbert Grossman. Dance arrangements by Ed Scott. Other participants: Feuer & Martin (producers); Cy Feuer (director); Peter Stone (co-librettist).

WE TAKE THE TOWN

Orchestrations credited to Russell **Bennett** and Hershy **Kay**. (Additional orchestrators, if any, unknown.)

Tryout: February 19, 1962, New Haven (Shubert). Closed March 31, Philadelphia (Shubert).

Music by Harold Karr, lyrics by Matt Dubey. Suggested by events in the life of Pancho Villa. Musical direction and vocal direction by Colin Romoff. Assistant musical director, John Berkman. Dance arrangements by Mordecai Sheinkman. Other participants: Stuart Ostrow (producer); Alex Segal (director); Donald Saddler (choreographer); Robert Preston (star); John Cullum (featured).

Bennett's invoices are preserved in his ledger.

Bennett: "Beautiful People," How Does the Wine Taste?" (song and utility), "I Don't Know How to Talk," "I've Got a Girl" ("first refrain" and utility), "Jesus" (utility), "Ode to a Friend," "Pancho the Bull," "Pancho's Thoughts," "Revolution" (parts "A3" and "A4–5"), "Talk to a Lady."

WEST SIDE STORY

Orchestrations by Leonard Bernstein with Sid **Ramin** and Irwin **Kostal**. (Orchestrations totally by Sid Ramin and Irwin Kostal.)

Opened September 26, 1957, Winter Garden, 732 performances. Tryout: August 19, Washington, D.C. (National); Philadelphia.

Music by Leonard Bernstein, lyrics by Stephen Sondheim. Musical direction by Max Goberman. Coordinator of dance music, Betty Walberg. Other participants: Robert Griffith and Harold Prince (producers); Jerome Robbins (director, choreographer, "based on a conception by"); Peter Gennaro (co-choreographer); Arthur Laurents (librettist).

The partiturs (Bernstein's copies) are in the Bernstein Collection at the Library of Congress, with another set (Ramin's copies) in the Ramin Collection at the Butler Library, Columbia University.

The song analysis, which in places descends to a bar-by-bar description, takes into account the unusual amount of shared scores and the importance of this musical to the overall sound of Broadway music. It is included with apologies to those readers who might find it incomprehensible or overly detailed.

Kostal: "A Boy Like That," "I Have a Love," "Maria," "One (One Hand, One Heart)," "Quintet," "Tonight (New Balcony Scene)."

Ramin: "I Feel Pretty."

Other scores:

"America" is written in alternating sections. The beginning ("Puerto Rico") is by Kostal; the first two refrains ("I like to be in America") are by Ramin; the "Whistle Dance," through the end of that refrain, is by Kostal. Thereafter, the vocal sections ("I'll Bring a TV to San Juan" and others) are by Ramin; the dance sections (including the final dance) are by Kostal.

"Ballet Sequence" (including "Somewhere"): opening section (underscoring, "I'll take you away," the section with Tony and Maria running, and the slow "Transition to Scherzo," pages 148–152 of vocal score) is by Ramin. "Scherzo" ("fast and light section" in altering tempo, with finger snaps) is by Kostal. "Somewhere" is in both hands: Ramin did much of the chart, while Kostal wrote in some of the reeds and horns. A significant amount was deleted: violin, cello, bass plus the piano part (a rolling accompaniment, as heard on the final track of the original cast album). "Procession and Nightmare" is mostly by Kostal.

"Cool": song is by Ramin; fugue (page 91 through end of 95) is by Kostal; closing dance and vocal are by Ramin, with final flute solo added by Kostal.

"Dance at the Gym": "Blues," "Promenade," "Cha-Cha," and "Meeting Scene" are by Kostal. "Mambo," part 1, through the key change on page 44, is by Ramin; part 2, written on three staves in the vocal score, pages 44–47, is by Kostal; part 3, beginning "Tony and Maria see each other," is by Ramin. "Jump" is missing, but probably by Ramin.

"Finale" is by Kostal. This is a longer chart than in the printed vocal score, corresponding to what is heard on the original cast album.

"Gee, Officer Krupke": opening and skits 1 and 2 are by Ramin; "Skit 3" (social worker) through end is by Kostal.

"Jet Song" is by Kostal, except for the 11-bar bridge sections (see below) and the music under dialogue—prior to the vocal and after "In, out, let's get crackin'"—which are by Ramin.

"Something's Coming": the first section is by Ramin; the second (beginning with "Around the corner," through the end) is mostly by Kostal.

"Prologue": the beginning, through the end of the drum section ("Jets exit" on page 5 of vocal score), is by Ramin; the next section, through the long hold (Sharks' entrance, page 9), is by Kostal; "A shark trips a jet" through end of "Frack on the track" (page 11, third line) is by Ramin; canon, marked "marc." on mid-page 11 through page 12, third line, is by Kostal. The next 10 bars are by Ramin, then Kostal continues until just after "Bernardo pierces A-rab's ear." "The Brawl" (starting at the key change on the fourth line of page 13) is by Ramin; Kostal takes over at the police whistle; Ramin picks up at the time change "under dialogue" through the end.

"The Rumble": part 1, until Tony takes the knife from the dying Riff, is mostly by

Ramin (with Kostal pasting in brief sections to accommodate changes in the ballet routine); part 2 is by Kostal.

"Taunting Scene": part 1 is by Ramin; part 2, beginning at the key and time change near the bottom of page 197, is by Kostal.

"Temporary Overture": this was not written until the 1960 return engagement; Bernstein wanted to conduct at the opening night, so they literally threw together an Overture for him. It is assembled mostly from copies of existing sections from the "Quintet" (Kostal), "Somewhere" (Ramin), and "Mambo" (Kostal), with the lyrics crossed out. "New Ending" is by Ramin.

"Tonight" is by Kostal, with all of Maria's lyrics assigned to "Mary"; the "Balcony Scene" introduction (pages 60–61, until "See only me") is by Ramin.

While I haven't done an actual page count, it seems that Kostal wrote considerably more than Ramin. This is understandable in that Sid was—admittedly—much slower than Irv. (Not slower to figure out the orchestration, but slower to write it down.) In some cases, Sid apparently sang lines, which Irv wrote down and developed. As discussed at length elsewhere, Bernstein supervised but did not actually write any of the orchestration (although he received a larger and more prominent credit than Ramin and Kostal).

"Jet Song," with bridges by Ramin, looked mighty suspicious. By reading beneath some pasted-in sections, I was able to determine that the song was originally orchestrated by Kostal (except for the dialogue sections, which used Ramin's material from the Prologue). At some point during the tryout, the original 8-bar bridge was replaced by the 11-bar "You're never alone" section. (On the scores, this is a 12-bar section; there had originally been an extra bar's worth of beats after "disconnected.") When the new bridge was written, Kostal was apparently unavailable, so Ramin pasted in the required measures.

"One Hand, One Heart" was scored as "One," containing the original melody and lyric (using whole notes, with the lyric "One–hand–one–heart" instead of "make of our hands, one hand"). At Sondheim's urging, Bernstein gave him some quarter-notes, but no changes were made to the orchestration. Also worth noting on the partiturs is this early lyric for the second line of "Maria": "the most beautiful, wonderful, marvelous magic word." And this, on the "I Feel Pretty" chart, in Bernstein's hand: "*Ich fuhle mich hubsch*" ("I feel pretty" in German).

The Bernstein Web site indicates four percussion players, and the published full score indicates up to five drum lines playing at once. However, Ramin confirms that the show on Broadway was done by a trap drummer and one very busy percussionist. (Herb Harris, who subbed on the show and became Bernstein's contractor, verifies that there were only two players.) When the show was revived at the New York State Theatre in 1968, a third player was added. The extra lines on the score were seemingly added thereafter by Bernstein.

IRV'S INSTRUCTIONS TO MUSICIANS   On "Cool" (to flute player, 2 bars before page 95): "Grab ze piccolo!"—giving him five beats to make the switch from flute.

Instr.: 5 reed (including 4 sax, 4 clr), 7 brass (3 tpt, 2 tb, 2 hrn), 12 strings (7 vln, 0 vla, 4 c, b), piano/celesta, guitar, 2 perc = 28 total.

(See pages 62, 74, 192, 203, 239, 245.)

WHAT MAKES SAMMY RUN?

Orchestrations (mostly) by Don **Walker**. (Additional orchestrations by Arnold Goland, Willis Schaefer, and Marion Evans.)

Opened February 27, 1964, 54th Street, 540 performances. Tryout: December 26, 1963, Philadelphia (Erlanger); elsewhere.

Music and lyrics by Ervin Drake. Based on the novel by Budd Schulberg. Musical direction and vocal arrangements by Lehman Engel. Dance arrangements by Arnold Goland. Other participants: Abe Burrows (director); Steve Lawrence (star).

Invoices are in the Walker Collection at the Library of Congress. Base page rate: $6.71.
The orchestrations are by Walker, with the following exceptions:

Schaefer: "I Feel Humble New," fixes.

Evans: "My Hometown."

Goland: "Monsoon," "Sheba," incidentals.

Other scores:

"New York Overture" is by Walker (46 pages) and Shaffer (18 pages).

When the chart for "My Hometown" was not to the star's liking, Steve Lawrence called in his record arranger, Marion Evans, to orchestrate it.

From Walker to producer Joe Cates: "Not included in the total [$12,326.70] is any work done by Marion Evans, which did not go through my books. I'd like to point out that such procedure is highly irregular, but I am willing to let sleeping dogs lie, as long as everybody else does."

WHAT'S UP?

Orchestrations credited to Nathan Lang Van Cleave. (Additional orchestrators, if any, unknown.)

Opened November 11, 1943, National, 63 performances. Tryout: October 22, Wilmington, Delaware (Playhouse); October 25, Philadelphia (Walnut Street).

Music by Frederick Loewe, lyrics by Alan Jay Lerner. Musical direction by Will Irwin. Vocal arrangements by Bobby Tucker. Other participants: George Balanchine (director, choreographer); Alan Jay Lerner (co-librettist).

WHERE'S CHARLEY?

Orchestrations credited to Ted **Royal**, Hans **Spialek**, and Philip J. **Lang**. (Additional orchestrators, if any, unknown.)

Opened October 11, 1948, St. James, 792 performances. Tryout: September 13, Philadelphia (Forrest).

Music and lyrics by Frank Loesser. Based on the play *Charley's Aunt* by Brandon Thomas. Musical direction by Max Goberman. Vocal arrangements and direction by Gerry Dolin. Other participants: Feuer & Martin (producers); George Abbott (director, librettist); George Balanchine (choreographer); Robert Griffith (stage manager); Ray Bolger (star).

Spialek and Lang's co-orchestration billing was added during the tryout. *Where's Charley?* (and Bolger) played a return engagement at the Broadway (opened January 29, 1951, 56 performances). At this time, the orchestrations were credited to Royal and Spialek, without Lang; vocal direction and arrangements were credited to Herbert Greene, who in the interim had done Loesser's *Guys and Dolls.*

Larry Moore, who prepared a reconstruction of the orchestrations for presentation at the Kennedy Center's Words and Music series in 1998, offers the following informed guesses. Royal, just off *Brigadoon,* presumably did most of the show. Spialek, who had done several Rodgers-Balanchine ballets (including "Slaughter on Tenth Avenue"), probably did the "Pernambuco" ballet and the extended dance for "At the Red Rose Cotillion." Moore guesses that Spialek did "Lovelier Than Ever" as well, citing the solo violin part, which is similar to earlier Spialek scores. "The New Ashmolean Marching Society and Students' Conservatory Band," which featured (and kidded) marching bands, is almost surely the work of Phil Lang; he was an acknowledged expert on concert band scoring, even writing a textbook on the subject. (This orchestration turned out to be highly humorous; at one point, the orchestrator has the musicians playing in opposing tempos and keys.) Lang told an anecdote in his 1978 interview with Lehman Engel which implies that he did "Once in Love with Amy."

THE WHITE HORSE INN

Orchestrations credited to Hans **Spialek**. (Additional orchestrators, if any, unknown.)
Opened October 1, 1936, Center, 223 performances. Tryout: unknown.
Music by Ralph Benatzky, lyrics by Irving Caesar. Musical direction by Victor Baravelle. Other participants: William Gaxton (star); Kitty Carlisle (star); Alfred Drake (singer).

WHOOP-UP

Orchestrations credited to Philip J. **Lang**. (Additional orchestrators, if any, unknown.)
Opened December 22, 1958, Shubert, 56 performances. Tryout: November 10, Philadelphia (Shubert); elsewhere.
Music by Moose Charlap, lyrics by Norman Gimbel. Based on the novel *Stay Away, Joe* by Dan Cushman. Musical and vocal direction by Stanley Lebowsky. Dance arrangements by Peter Matz. Other participants: Feuer & Martin (producers); Cy Feuer (director); Onna White (choreographer).

It is probable that Lang had assistance on this show; the likeliest candidates are Jack Mason and Carroll Huxley. The dance sections, with blaring brass, were almost surely orchestrated by dance arranger Matz.

WILD AND WONDERFUL

Orchestrations credited to Luther Henderson. (Additional orchestrators, if any, unknown.)

Opened December 7, 1971, Lyceum, 1 performance. Tryout: none.

Music and lyrics by Bob Goodman. Musical direction, dance and vocal arrangements by Thom Janusz.

WILDCAT

Orchestrations and arrangements (totally) by Robert **Ginzler** and Sid **Ramin**.

Opened December 16, 1960, Alvin, 171 performances. Tryout: Philadelphia (Erlanger).

Music by Cy Coleman, lyrics by Carolyn Leigh. Musical direction, vocal and dance arrangements by John Morris. Other participants: Michael Kidd (co-producer, director, choreographer); Lucille Ball (star).

Copies of most of the partiturs are in the American Musical Theatre Collection at the Library of Congress.

Ginzler: "Corduroy Road," "Dancing on My Tippy-Tippy Toes," "Hey, Look Me Over!" "You're a Liar."

Ramin: "El Sombrero," "Oil," "One Day We Dance," "Tall Hope," "You've Come Home" (reprise and utility).

Other scores:

"Give a Little Whistle" is by Ginzler and Ramin; in many places, Ginzler writes the reeds and brass while Ramin writes the strings, guitar, and piccolo. The choral refrain is mostly by Ramin.

Overture: the first section (through "You've Come Home") is by Ginzler; the second section (beginning with "What Takes My Fancy") is by Ramin. (This section differs somewhat from the version of the Overture on the cast recording and in the vocal score.) The final march section ("Hey, Look Me Over!") is not included in the partiturs, but is probably by Ginzler.

"What Takes My Fancy" is by Ginzler and Ramin. The chart calls for tack piano and "country-style" violins.

Missing: "That's What I Want for Jamie," "Wildcat," and the song version of "You've Come Home." The string writing in the latter suggests that it is by Ramin.

Instr.: 5 reed, 7 brass (3 tpt, 3 tb, 1 hrn), 9 strings (6? vln, 0 vla, 2 c, 1 b), piano, guitar, 2 perc = 25? total.

WILDFLOWER

Orchestrations uncredited. (Orchestrations by Herbert Stothart, Russell **Bennett**, Stephen O. Jones, Charles Miller and others.)

Opened February 7, 1923, Casino, 477 performances. Tryout: January 26, Wilkes-Barre, Pennsylvania (Grand); January 29, Baltimore (Auditorium).

Music by Vincent Youmans and Herbert Stothart, lyrics and book by Otto Harbach and Oscar Hammerstein II. Musical direction by Herbert Stothart.

Several partiturs are at the Library of Congress.

Jones: "Bambalina."

Other scores:

"Wildflower": there are two scores, one by Jones and one by Miller.

Bennett, in *The Broadway Sound*, praised Stephen Jones for his expert orchestration of the song hit, "Bambalina."

WINDY CITY

Orchestrations credited to Don **Walker**. (Additional orchestrators, if any, unknown.)

Tryout: April 18, 1946, New Haven (Shubert); Boston; May 16, Chicago (Great Northern). Closed June 6, Chicago.

Music by Walter Jurman, lyrics by Paul Francis Webster. Musical direction by Charles Sanford. Musical supervision by Don Walker and Clay Warnick. Vocal arrangements by Clay Warnick. Dance arrangements by Dorothea Freitag. Other participant: Katherine Dunham (choreographer).

The Walker Collection includes a contract for Walker and Warnick as musical supervisors, with a weekly royalty of $150.

Instr.: 5 reed, 4 brass (2 tpt, 1 tb, 1 hrn), 7 strings (4 vln, 1 vla, 1 c, 1 b), Novachord (keyboard), guitar, harp, perc = 20 total.

WISH YOU WERE HERE

Orchestrations credited to Don **Walker**. (Additional orchestrations by Robert **Ginzler** and others.)

Opened June 25, 1952, Imperial, 598 performances. Tryout: none.

Music and lyrics by Harold Rome. Based on the play *Having Wonderful Time* by Arthur Kober. Musical direction by Jay Blackton. Musical continuity by Trude Rittman. Other participants: Leland Hayward (producer); Joshua Logan (co-producer, director, co-librettist); Robert Griffith (stage manager).

It is assumed that this show was heavily ghosted, which was Walker's practice at the time. Ginzler listed the show among his credits; other prime candidates include Glover, Walter Paul, and possibly Kostal. "Flattery" and "Shopping Around," especially, sound like Ginzler, while "Don José from Far Rockaway" is probably Ginzler or Kostal. "Where Did the Night Go?" "Summer Afternoon," and the title song are probably by Walker.

THANKS AND WISHES   From Jack Mason to Walker: "I can honestly and simply say that it's the finest job of theatre orchestrating I've ever heard. If that's an example of what is going to come out of W. 22nd St. [the newly formed Chelsea Music], I'm looking forward to being a part of the organization."

THE WIZARD OF OZ

Orchestrations credited to Larry **Wilcox**. (Additional orchestrators, if any, unknown.)

Opened December 17, 1987, Barbicon (London).

Music by Harold Arlen, lyrics by E. Y. Harburg. Based on the novel by L. Frank Baum and the 1939 MGM motion picture. Background music by Herbert Stothart. Dance and vocal arrangements by Peter Howard. Other participant: Royal Shakespeare Company (producer).

WONDERFUL TOWN

Orchestrations by Don **Walker**. Assistants to Don Walker: Seymour (Red) **Ginzler** and Sidney **Ramin**. (Additional orchestrations by Joe Glover, Irwin **Kostal**, Walter Paul, Jack Mason, Julian Work, and Mark Bucci.)

Opened February 25, 1953, Winter Garden, 559 performances. Tryout: January 19, New Haven (Shubert); Boston (Shubert).

Music by Leonard Bernstein, lyrics by Betty Comden & Adolph Green. Based on the play *My Sister Eileen* by Joseph Fields and Jerome Chodorov, from stories by Ruth McKenney. Musical direction and vocal arrangements by Lehman Engel. Other participants: Robert Fryer (producer); George Abbott (director); Donald Saddler (choreographer); Jerome Robbins (unbilled additional choreographer); Robert E. Griffith (stage manager); Harold Prince (assistant stage manager); Rosalind Russell (star).

Copies of most of the partiturs are at Tams-Witmark and in the Bernstein Collection at the Library of Congress. Invoices are in the Walker Collection at the Library of Congress. Invoices indicate: Ginzler (44%), Walker (14%), Glover (13%).

Walker: "Conquering the City Ballet" (with four small sections by Bucci), "One Hundred Easy Ways Scene Change," "Ohio" (see below), "A Quiet Girl" (see below), "The Story of My Life" (cut).

Ginzler: "Ballet at the Village Vortex (Let It Come Down)" (vocal [cut] and dance), "Christopher Street (see below), "Conga," "Conversation Piece," "It's Love," "One Hundred Easy Ways."

Glover: "What a Waste" (see below), "Wrong Note Rag."

Kostal: "Pass That Football" (song and dance).

Ramin: "Swing" (see below), numerous fixes.

Paul: "Lollapalooza" song and reprise (cut), "Ohio Reprise," utilities ("Ohio," "Swing," "What a Waste").

Bucci: "Story Vignettes."

Other scores:

"Christopher Street" is mostly by Ginzler. Tempo marking at top: "Molto Duchino." Walker provided the first instrumental section; on the later instrumental section, Walker inserted a few brass lines. All told, about 90% of the (extended) number is by Ginzler.

"Courtroom Ballet" (three movements, cut) is mostly by Work, with sections by Bucci.

"Finale Act Two" is by Ginzler, except for first 8 bars by Glover.

"A Little Bit in Love" is in two parts, the first by Walker and the second (after dialogue between Eileen and Baker) by Glover.

"My Darlin' Eileen": song is by Walker; dance (jig) is by Work.

"Ohio" is by Walker, except for the middle section ("now listen, Eileen, Ohio was stifling" through "thank heaven we're free"), by Glover "in the style of Shep Fields."

Overture is mostly by Mason; Walker does 8 bars (the transition from "My Darlin'

Eileen" into "It's Love"); and Glover provides the final section beginning with the trumpets leading into "Wrong Note Rag."

"A Quiet Girl" is mostly by Walker, with new intro and verse by Ginzler.

"Swing": the location of the partiturs is unknown, but it is all or mostly by Ramin; invoices indicate that Walker might have done the scat "extension."

"What a Waste" is by Glover, but in Boston, reed parts were pasted over and replaced by Ginzler.

The total orchestration cost of $7,365 was spread among eight men. This drastic ghosting stems from the fact that *Wonderful Town* was Walker's third Broadway musical within fourteen days.

"Let It Come Down" was a major production number that opened the last scene. During the tryout, the lyric was cut, and it was performed as "Ballet at the Village Vortex." Ramin: "I tried to do it, but it was too difficult for me; I struggled with it so much. Red finally did it because I couldn't figure the damned thing out." The arrangement is intricate and extremely reed-heavy. Ginzler wrote on his invoice: "twenty-seven pages of blood."

THANKS AND WISHES From Ramin to Walker: "The thrill of working with you will always be remembered. Program credit meant so very much to me and I want you to know I'll always think of your kindness. Gratefully, The Jewish Don Walker (Sid)."

Instr.: 5 reed (5 sax, 5 clr), 7 brass (4 tpt, 3 tb), ? strings (vln, vla, c, l b), piano/celesta, 2 perc.

(See pages 74, 106, 196.)

XMAS IN LAS VEGAS

Orchestrations and incidental music composed by Don **Walker**.

Opened November 4, 1965, Ethel Barrymore, 4 performances. Tryout: unknown.

A play by Jack Richardson. Title song by Don Walker and Arnold Goland. Other participants: Fred Coe (co-producer, director); Tom Ewell (star).

The partitur for "Opening Act I" is in the Walker Collection at the Library of Congress.

THE YEARLING

Orchestrations credited to Larry **Wilcox**. (Additional orchestrators, if any, unknown.)

Opened December 10, 1965, Alvin, 3 performances. Tryout: October 30, New Haven (Shubert); November 9, Philadelphia (Shubert).

Music by Michael Leonard, lyrics by Herbert Martin. Based on the novel by Marjorie Kinnan Rawlings. Musical direction and vocal arrangements by Julian Stein. Dance arrangements by David Baker. Other participants: Lloyd Richards (original director); David Wayne (star).

Hershy Kay was originally announced as orchestrator, but he left the project after a couple of early meetings with the composer. (The pair did not get along, which was not an uncommon occurrence with Kay.) Larry Wilcox received sole billing and markings on the piano-conductor scores suggest that he orchestrated the entire show.

YOU NEVER KNOW

Orchestrations by Hans **Spialek**. (Additional orchestrations by Maurice de Packh, Don
   Walker, Claude Austin, Menotti Salta, Max Hoffman, and Elliott Jacoby.)
Opened September 21, 1938, Winter Garden, 78 performances. Tryout: March 3, New
   Haven (Shubert); March 7, Boston (Shubert); March 21, Washington, D.C. (National); and nine other venues.
Music by Cole Porter and Robert Katscher, lyrics by Cole Porter. Additional lyrics by
   Rowland Leigh and Edwin Gilbert. Based on the play *By Candlelight* by Siegfried Geyer.
   Musical direction by John McManus. Other participant: Clifton Webb (star).

Many of the partiturs are at the Shubert Archives.
   Spialek: "Don't Let It Get You Down" (see below), Entr'acte, "I'm Yours," "Maria"
(see below), Opening act I, Overture Prologue, "What Is That Tune?" (see below), "You
Never Know."
   Walker: "From Alpha to Omega."
   Other scores:
   "Candlelight": "Waltz" is by de Packh; "Incidental" is by an unidentified hand.
   "Don't Let It Get You Down": song is by Spialek; "Preiser Dance" is by de Packh;
"Hartman Specialty" is by Salta; additional score (utility?) is by Austin.
   "For No Rhyme or Reason": "Debonairs" intro (31 pages) is by Austin; "Hartman"
(main song) is by Spialek.
   "Maria": song and "2nd section, to dance" are by Spialek; "New Part" is by de Packh.
   "What Is That Tune?" is by Spialek; "That Tune (Rhumba)" is by Salta.

Instr.: 5 reed (3 sax), 4 brass (3 tpt, 1 tb), 13? strings (8? vln, 0 vla, 4? c, 1 b), piano, harp, perc = 25? total.

ZENDA

Orchestrations and arrangements credited to Irwin **Kostal**. (Additional orchestrators, if
   any, unknown.)
Tryout: August 5, 1963, San Francisco (Curran). Closed November 16, Pasadena, California (Civic Auditorium).
Music by Vernon Duke, lyrics by Lenny Adelson, Sid Kuller, and Martin Charnin.
Based on the novel *The Prisoner of Zenda* by Anthony Hope. Musical direction by Pembroke
   Davenport. Dance arrangements by Harper McKay. Other participants: Edwin Lester
   (producer); Jack Cole (choreographer); Alfred Drake (star); Chita Rivera (star).

The partiturs are in the Duke Collection at the Library of Congress.

ZIEGFELD FOLLIES OF 1924

Orchestrations uncredited. (Orchestrations by Russell **Bennett**, Stephen O. Jones, Raymond Hubbell, Fred Barry, Harold Sandford, and probably others.)
Opened June 24, 1924, New Amsterdam, 295 performances. Tryout: unknown.
A revue. Music and lyrics by various writers, including Victor Herbert, Dave Stamper, and

Raymond Hubbell. Musical direction by Victor Baravelle. Other participant: Florenz Ziegfeld, Jr. (producer).

ZIEGFELD FOLLIES OF 1925

Orchestrations uncredited. (Orchestrations by Russell **Bennett**, Stephen O. Jones, Fred Barry, Harold Sandford, and probably others.)

Opened July 6, 1925, New Amsterdam, 88 performances. Tryout: March 22, Washington, D.C. (National); elsewhere.

A revue. Music and lyrics by various writers, including Raymond Hubbell, Dave Stamper, and Sigmund Romberg. Musical direction by Victor Baravelle. Other participant: Florenz Ziegfeld, Jr. (producer).

ZIEGFELD FOLLIES OF 1934

Orchestrations uncredited. (Orchestrations by Edward B. Powell, Hans **Spialek**, Don **Walker**, Paul Sterrett, and others.)

Opened January 4, 1934, Winter Garden, 182 performances. Tryout: Boston; Philadelphia; December 4, 1933, Washington, D.C. (National).

A revue. Music by Vernon Duke and others, lyrics by E. Y. Harburg and others. Musical direction by John McManus. Other participants: Mrs. Florenz Ziegfeld [Billie Burke] (producer); Lee Shubert (producer, uncredited); Fanny Brice (star).

Some of the partiturs are at the Shubert Archive.

    Powell: "Green Eyes," "I Like the Likes of You," "Suddenly" (song, "Finale Act I," Entr'acte version), "This Is Not a Song" (song, tag, reprise), "What Is There to Say?"

    Spialek: Ballet, "Big Bad Wolf Oratorio," "Moon about Town," "Sarah, the Sunshine Girl," "Soul Saving Sadie."

    Other scores:

    "Fifth Avenue": this was an extended, nine-part, 709-bar number—the longest found in the course of my research. (Whether all—or any—of it was used is another question.) "Part G" has 29 bars (of 80) by Sterrett. The final section, "Ebsen's Fifth Avenue (Specialty for Buddy and Vilma Ebsen)" is by Powell (60 bars). The rest—an astounding 620 bars—is by Walker, his first major Broadway chart on what was apparently his second show.

Powell's Instructions to Musicians

    On "Suddenly," to the pianist: "quasi-harpsichord—lay sheet of paper on the strings."

Instr.: 6 reed (3 sax), 5 brass (3 tpt, 2 tb), 14? strings (10? vln [1 guitar?], 0 vla, 3? c, 1 b), 2 piano, perc = 28? total.

ZIEGFELD FOLLIES OF 1936

Orchestrations uncredited. (Orchestrations by Hans **Spialek**, Conrad Salinger, Russell **Bennett**, Don **Walker**, and others.)

Opened January 30, 1936, Winter Garden, 115 performances. Tryout: December 30, 1935, Boston (Opera House); January 14, 1936, Philadelphia (Forrest).

A revue. Music by Vernon Duke, lyrics by Ira Gershwin. Musical direction by John Mc-
Manus. Other participants: Mrs. Florenz Ziegfeld [Billie Burke] (producer); Lee Shubert (producer, uncredited); George Balanchine (choreographer); Vincente Minnelli
(designer); Fanny Brice (star); Bob Hope (star).

Walker: "I Can't Get Started."

> SPIALEK: It seldom fails, but during the preparatory stage of any musical, every leading
> singer invariably complains either about the quality of their songs, or not having enough
> songs in the show. The complainants in this case were Josephine Baker and Gertrude
> Niesen. In the course of a morning rehearsal, Vernon Duke and Ira Gershwin were re-
> quested to write a sentimental song for Miss Baker and a rhythm tune for Miss Niesen.
> Vernon Duke, a strange combination of being in equal quantities gifted, arrogant, ver-
> satile, conceited, prolific, stuffed-shirtedly snobbish; and Ira Gershwin, one of the very
> few original, genuine lyric writers, wrote the two requested numbers in a single day.
>
> The lead sheets of the new songs were handed to the respective prima donnas dur-
> ing the evening. Of course, both singers were anxious to hear, rehearse, and have the
> songs in the show as soon as possible. A rehearsal was set right after the evening per-
> formance. The orchestra combination for the *Follies* included two pianos. The two
> singers, the two pianists, and everybody concerned with the proceedings met after the
> show by the orchestra pit. And there the rumpus started. Of course, neither Miss Baker
> nor Miss Niesen agreed as to who was going to be the first one to rehearse. The singers
> practiced and were coached simultaneously, causing one of the most angry, vile, and id-
> iotic cacophonies I've ever listened to. The songs went in the following night, only to be
> immediately thereafter thrown out of the show.

ZIEGFELD FOLLIES OF 1943

Orchestrations by Don **Walker**. (Additional orchestrations by Robert Noeltner, Ted
Royal, Ben Ludlow, Clay Warnick, Robert **Ginzler**, and others.)

Opened April 1, 1943, Winter Garden, 553 performances. Tryout: January, Boston.

A revue. Music by Ray Henderson, lyrics by Jack Yellen. Musical direction by John Mc-
Manus. Other participant: Milton Berle (star).

Invoices are in the Walker Collection at the Library of Congress.

A financial recap at the Library of Congress shows that Walker received a $3,500 fee
for orchestrating the show, out of which he paid slices to seven other orchestrators.
Walker's net profit on the job: $2,603.45.

ZIEGFELD FOLLIES OF 1956

Orchestrations credited to George Bassman and Albert Sendrey. (Additional orchestrators unknown.)

Tryout: April 16, 1956, Boston (Shubert). Closed May 12, Philadelphia (Shubert).

A revue. Music and lyrics by various writers, including Jerry Bock and Larry Holofcener,
Albert Hague and Arnold B. Horwitt, and Cy Coleman. Musical direction by Anton

Coppola. Vocal arrangements by Hugh Martin. Dance arrangements by Hal Schaefer. Other participants: Jack Cole (choreographer); Tallulah Bankhead (star).

ZIEGFELD FOLLIES OF 1957

Orchestrations credited to Russell **Bennett**, Bill Stegmeyer, Joe Glover, and Robert Noelt-ner. (Additional orchestrations by Philip J. **Lang** and probably others.)

Opened March 1, 1957, Winter Garden, 123 performances. Tryout: February 4, New Haven (Shubert); February 11, Washington, D.C. (National); elsewhere.

A revue. Music and lyrics by various writers. Musical direction by Max Meth. Vocal arrangements by Earl Rogers. Dance arrangements by René Wiegert. Other partici-pant: Beatrice Lillie (star).

Bennett's invoices are preserved in his ledger. Base page rate: $5.70.

Bennett: "Buy Yourself a Balloon," "Intoxication," "Make Me" (song and utility), "Music for Madame" (vocal, routine, and dance).

Other score:

Opening is by Bennett and Lang.

ZORBÀ

Orchestrations (mostly) by Don **Walker**. (Additional orchestrations by Jim Tyler.)

Opened November 17, 1968, Imperial, 305 performances. Tryout: October 7, New Haven (Shubert); Boston (Shubert).

Music by John Kander, lyrics by Fred Ebb. Based on the novel *Zorba the Greek* by Nikos Kazantzakis. Musical direction by Harold Hastings. Dance arrangements by Doro-thea Freitag. Other participants: Harold Prince (producer, director); Ronald Field (choreographer); Joseph Stein (librettist); Herschel Bernardi (star); Maria Karnilova (star).

The partiturs and invoices are in the Walker Collection at the Library of Congress. Base page rate: $10.

The orchestrations are by Walker, with the following exception:

Tyler: Entr'acte.

Walker's files include a copy of the book *How to Play the Bouzouki* by Takis Marakis.

The scoring cost for the Broadway production was $10,223. For the national com-pany, Walker received an additional $2,381 for rescoring all of the reeds, brass, and strings. When the show went out on a cut-down bus & truck tour, Walker received an ad-ditional $4,000 "for adding additional parts plus completely orchestrating material played by ethnic instruments on stage."

THANKS AND WISHES   From Kander to Walker, with opening night gift: "In memory of all our trips together—to French Canada, Berlin, New York in the '30s and Crete."

(See page 110.)

SECTION III.
ADDITIONAL SHOWS BY
OTHER ORCHESTRATORS

The following shows fall outside our area of discussion. Even so, many of them are of interest, orchestration-wise and otherwise wise, and are thus included for reference.

AIN'T BROADWAY GRAND

Orchestrations credited to Chris Bankey.
Opened April 18, 1993, Lunt-Fontanne, 25 performances.
Music by Mitch Leigh, lyrics by Lee Adams. Musical direction by Nicholas Archer. Musical supervision and vocal arrangements by Neil Warner. Dance arrangements by Scot Woolley.

AND THE WORLD GOES 'ROUND

Orchestrations credited to David Krane.
Opened March 5, 1991, Westside (off-Broadway), 408 performances.
Music by John Kander, lyrics by Fred Ebb. Musical direction, vocal and dance arrangements by David Loud.

ANNA KARENINA

Orchestrations credited to Peter Matz.
Opened August 26, 1992, Circle in the Square, 46 performances.
Music by Daniel Levine, lyrics by Peter Kellogg. Musical direction and dance arrangements by Nicholas Archer.

ANNIE GET YOUR GUN (1999 REVIVAL)

New orchestrations credited to Bruce Coughlin.
Opened March 4, 1999, Marquis, 1,046 performances.
Musical direction and dance arrangements by Marvin Laird. Supervising musical director, vocal and incidental arrangements by John McDaniel.

ANNIE WARBUCKS

Orchestrations credited to Keith Levenson.
Opened August 9, 1993, Variety Arts (off-Broadway), 200 performances.
Music by Charles Strouse, lyrics by Martin Charnin. Musical direction by Keith Levenson.

ASSASSINS

Orchestrations credited to Michael Starobin.
Opened January 27, 1991, Playwrights Horizons (off-Broadway), 72 performances.
Music and lyrics by Stephen Sondheim. Musical direction by Paul Gemignani.

BABY

Orchestrations credited to Jonathan Tunick.
Opened December 4, 1983, Ethel Barrymore, 241 performances.
Music by David Shire, lyrics by Richard Maltby, Jr. Musical direction by Peter Howard.

BALLROOM

Orchestrations credited to Jonathan Tunick.
Opened December 14, 1978, Majestic, 116 performances.
Music by Billy Goldenberg, lyrics by Alan Bergman and Marilyn Bergman. Musical direction by Don Jennings.

THE BEAST IN ME

Orchestrations credited to Billy Byers.
Opened May 16, 1963, Plymouth, 4 performances.
Music by Don Elliott, lyrics by James Costigan. Musical direction by Don Elliott. Conducted by Lehman Engel. Dance arrangements by Judd Woldin.

BEAUTY AND THE BEAST

Orchestrations credited to Danny Troob. (Additional orchestrations by Michael Starobin.)
Opened April 18, 1994, Palace, 5,464 performances.
Music by Alan Menken, lyrics by Howard Ashman and Tim Rice. Musical direction and incidental arrangements by Michael Kosarin. Musical supervision and vocal arrangements by David Friedman.

THE BEST LITTLE WHOREHOUSE GOES PUBLIC

Orchestrations credited to Peter Matz.
Opened May 10, 1994, Lunt-Fontanne, 16 performances.
Music and lyrics by Carol Hall. Musical direction by Karl Jurman. Musical supervision, vocal and dance arrangements by Wally Harper.

BIG

Orchestrations credited to Doug Besterman. (Additional orchestrations by Billy Byers.)
Opened April 28, 1996, Shubert, 192 performances.

Music by David Shire, lyrics by Richard Maltby, Jr. Musical direction by Paul Gemignani. Dance arrangements by David Krane.

BIG RIVER

Orchestrations credited to Steve Margoshes and Danny Troob.

Opened April 25, 1985, Eugene O'Neill, 1,005 performances.

Music and lyrics by Roger Miller. Musical direction and vocal arrangements by Linda Twine. Dance and incidental music by John Richard Lewis.

BLACK AND BLUE

Orchestrations credited to Sy Johnson. (Additional orchestrations by Luther Henderson.)

Opened January 26, 1989, Minskoff, 829 performances.

Music and lyrics by various writers. Musical supervision by Sy Johnson. Conducted by Leonard Oxley.

BLOOD RED ROSES

Orchestrations credited to Julian Stein and Abba Bogin.

Opened March 22, 1970, Golden, 1 performance.

Music by Michael Valenti, lyrics by John Lewin. Musical direction by Milton Setzer.

A BROADWAY MUSICAL

Orchestrations credited to Robert M. Freedman.

Opened December 21, 1978, Lunt-Fontanne, 1 performance.

Music by Charles Strouse, lyrics by Lee Adams. Musical supervision and vocal arrangements by Donald Pippin. Conductor, Kevin Farrell. Dance arrangements by Donald Johnston.

CABARET (1987 REVIVAL)

Additional orchestrations by Michael Gibson.

Opened October 22, 1987, Minskoff, 261 performances.

Musical direction by Donald Chan. Additional dance arrangements by Ronald Melrose.

CABARET (1998 REVIVAL)

New orchestrations credited to Michael Gibson.

Opened March 19, 1998, Kit Kat Klub (Henry Miller's), 2,377 performances.

Musical direction by Patrick Vaccariello. New dance arrangements by David Krane.

CAROUSEL (1994 REVIVAL)

Orchestrations credited to William David Brohn.
Opened March 24, 1994, Vivian Beaumont, 322 performances.
Musical direction by Eric Stern.

CARRIE

Orchestrations credited to Anders Eljas, Harold Wheeler, and Michael Starobin.
Opened May 12, 1988, Virginia, 5 performances.
Music by Michael Gore, lyrics by Dean Pitchford. Musical direction by Paul Schwartz.
    Musical supervision by Harold Wheeler.

CHAPLIN

Orchestrations credited to Billy Byers, Chris Boardman, and Angela Morley.
Tryout: August 13, 1984, Los Angeles (Dorothy Chandler Pavilion). Closed September
    24.
Music and lyrics by Anthony Newley and Stanley Ralph Ross. Musical direction and
    arrangements by Ian Fraser.

A CHRISTMAS CAROL

Orchestrations credited to Michael Starobin. (Additional orchestrations by Doug Bester-
    man.)
Opened December 1, 1994, Paramount (Madison Square Garden), 71 performances.
Music by Alan Menken, lyrics by Lynn Ahrens. Musical direction by Paul Gemignani.
    Dance arrangements by Glen Kelly.

CHU CHEM

Orchestrations credited to Music Makers, Inc. (Carlyle Hall?).
Tryout: November 15, 1966, Philadelphia (New Locust Street). Closed November 19.
Music by Mitch Leigh, lyrics by Jim Haines and Jack Wohl. Musical direction by How-
    ard Cable. Vocal and dance arrangements by Neil Warner.

CHU CHEM (1989 REVIVAL)

Orchestrations credited to Michael Gibson.
Opened April 7, 1989, Ritz, 45 performances.
Music by Mitch Leigh, lyrics by Jim Haines and Jack Wohl. Musical direction by Don
    Jones.

CITY OF ANGELS

Orchestrations credited to Billy Byers.

Opened December 11, 1989, Virginia, 878 performances.

Music by Cy Coleman, lyrics by David Zippel. Musical direction by Gordon Lowry Harrell. Vocal arrangements by Cy Coleman and Yaron Gershovsky.

THE CIVIL WAR

Orchestrations credited to Kim Scharnberg.

Opened April 22, 1999, St. James, 61 performances.

Music by Frank Wildhorn, lyrics by Jack Murphy. Musical direction by Jeff Lams. Musical supervision by Jason Howland.

COMPANY

Orchestrations credited to Jonathan Tunick.

Opened April 26, 1970, Alvin, 706 performances.

Music and lyrics by Stephen Sondheim. Musical direction by Hal Hastings. Dance arrangement by Wally Harper.

THE CONSUL

Orchestrations by Gian Carlo Menotti.

Opened March 15, 1950, Barrymore, 269 performances.

An opera by Gian Carlo Menotti. Musical direction by Lehman Engel. Musical coordination by Thomas Schippers.

CRY FOR US ALL

Orchestrations credited to Carlyle Hall.

Opened April 8, 1970, Broadhurst, 18 performances.

Music by Mitch Leigh, lyrics by William Alfred and Phyllis Robinson. Musical direction by Herbert Grossman. Music supervision by Sam Pottle.

CYRANO: THE MUSICAL

Orchestrations credited to Don Sebesky and Tony Cox.

Opened November 21, 1993, Neil Simon, 137 performances.

Music by Ad Van Dijk, lyrics by Koen Van Dijk, additional lyrics by Sheldon Harnick. Musical direction by Constantine Kitsopoulos.

DAMN YANKEES (1994 REVIVAL)

Orchestrations credited to Doug Besterman.

Opened March 3, 1994, Marquis, 510 performances.

Musical direction uncredited (James Raitt). Musical supervision and vocal arrangements by James Raitt. Conductor, assistant musical director, David Chase. Dance arrangements by Tom Fay. Additional dance arrangements by David Krane.

DANCE A LITTLE CLOSER

Orchestrations credited to Jonathan Tunick.

Opened May 11, 1983, Minskoff, 1 performance.

Music by Charles Strouse, lyrics by Alan Jay Lerner. Musical direction by Peter Howard. Dance arrangements by Glen Kelly.

A DOLL'S LIFE

Orchestrations credited to Billy Byers.

Opened September 23, 1982, Mark Hellinger, 5 performances.

Music by Larry Grossman, lyrics by Betty Comden & Adolph Green. Musical direction by Paul Gemignani.

DREAM

Orchestrations credited to Dick Lieb.

Opened April 3, 1997, Royale, 109 performances.

Music by various writers, lyrics by Johnny Mercer. Musical direction and vocal arrangements by Bryan Louiselle. Dance arrangements by Jeanine Tesori.

DREAMGIRLS

Orchestrations credited to Harold Wheeler (replacing Michael Gibson).

Opened December 20, 1981, Imperial, 1,521 performances.

Music by Henry Krieger, lyrics by Tom Eyen. Musical direction by Yolanda Segovia. Vocal arrangements by Cleavant Derricks.

FALSETTOS

Orchestrations credited to Michael Starobin.

Opened April 29, 1992, John Golden, 487 performances.

Music and lyrics by William Finn. Musical direction by Scott Frankel.

THE FIG LEAVES ARE FALLING

Orchestrations credited to Manny Albam.

Opened January 2, 1969, Broadhurst, 4 performances.

Music by Albert Hague, lyrics by Allan Sherman. Musical direction by Abba Bogin. Dance arrangements by Jack Lee.

THE FIRST

Orchestrations credited to Luther Henderson.

Opened November 17, 1981, Martin Beck, 37 performances.

Music by Bob Brush, lyrics by Martin Charnin. Musical direction by Mark Hummel. Vocal arrangements by Joyce Brown. Dance arrangements by Luther Henderson.

5-6-7-8 . . . DANCE!

Orchestrations credited to Billy Byers.

Opened June 15, 1983, Radio City Music Hall, 149 performances.

New music and lyrics by Wally Harper and David Zippel. Musical direction by Thomas Helm. Musical supervisor, Wally Harper. Dance arrangements by Mark Hummel and Donald York.

FOLLIES

Orchestrations credited to Jonathan Tunick.

Opened April 4, 1971, Winter Garden, 522 performances.

Music and lyrics by Stephen Sondheim. Musical direction by Hal Hastings. Dance arrangements by John Berkman.

FOOTLOOSE

Orchestrations credited to Danny Troob.

Opened October 22, 1998, Richard Rodgers, 708 performances.

Music by Tom Snow and others, lyrics by Dean Pitchford and others. Musical direction and vocal arrangements by Doug Katsaros. Dance arrangements by Joe Baker.

A FUNNY THING HAPPENED ON THE WAY TO THE FORUM (1996 REVIVAL)

Orchestrations credited to Jonathan Tunick.

Opened April 18, 1996, St. James, 715 performances.

Musical direction by Edward Strauss. Dance arrangements by David Chase.

THE GERSHWINS' FASCINATING RHYTHM

Orchestrations credited to Larry Hochman.

Opened April 25, 1999, Longacre, 17 performances.

Music by George Gershwin, lyrics by Ira Gershwin. Musical direction by Cynthia Kort-
man. Musical and vocal arrangements by Marvin Laird.

THE GOODBYE GIRL

Orchestrations credited to Billy Byers and Torrie Zito.

Opened March 4, 1993, Marquis, 188 performances.

Music by Marvin Hamlisch, lyrics by David Zippel. Musical direction by Jack Everly.
Dance arrangements by Mark Hummel.

GOODTIME CHARLEY

Orchestrations credited to Jonathan Tunick.

Opened March 3, 1975, Palace, 104 performances.

Music by Larry Grossman, lyrics by Hal Hackady. Musical direction and vocal arrangements by Arthur B. Rubinstein. Dance arrangements by Danny Troob.

GRAND HOTEL: THE MUSICAL

Orchestrations credited to Peter Matz.

Opened November 12, 1989, Martin Beck, 1,018 performances.

Music and lyrics by Robert Wright & George Forrest. Additional music and lyrics by
Maury Yeston. Musical and vocal direction by Jack Lee. Musical supervision and additional music by Wally Harper.

A GRAND NIGHT FOR SINGING

Orchestrations credited to Michael Gibson and Jonathan Tunick.

Opened November 17, 1993, Criterion Stage Right, 52 performances.

Music by Richard Rodgers, lyrics by Oscar Hammerstein II. Musical direction by Fred
Wells.

GREASE

Orchestrations credited to Michael Leonard.

Opened February 14, 1972, Eden, 3,388 performances.

Music and lyrics by Jim Jacobs and Warren Casey. Musical direction, dance and vocal
arrangements by Louis St. Louis.

GROVER'S CORNERS

Orchestrations credited to David Siegel.

Tryout: July 22, 1987, Chicago (Marriott's Lincolnshire). Closed November 11.

Music by Harvey Schmidt, lyrics by Tom Jones. Musical direction and vocal arrangements by Kevin Stites.

GUYS AND DOLLS (1976 REVIVAL)

New orchestrations credited to Danny Holgate and Horace Ott.

Opened July 21, 1976, Broadway, 239 performances.

Music and lyrics by Frank Loesser. Musical direction and vocal arrangements by Howard Roberts.

GUYS AND DOLLS (1992 REVIVAL)

New orchestrations credited to Michael Starobin. Additional orchestrations by Michael Gibson.

Opened April 14, 1992, Martin Beck, 1,143 performances.

Music and lyrics by Frank Loesser. Musical direction by Edward Strauss. Dance arrangements by Mark Hummel.

HAIR

Orchestrations uncredited (Galt MacDermot).

Opened April 29, 1968, Biltmore, 1,750 performances.

Music by Galt MacDermot, lyrics by James Rado and Gerome Ragni. Musical direction by Galt MacDermot.

HIGH SOCIETY

Orchestrations credited to William David Brohn.

Opened April 27, 1998, St. James, 144 performances.

Music and lyrics by Cole Porter. Musical direction by Paul Gemignani. Dance arrangements by Glen Kelly.

HOME SWEET HOMER

Orchestrations credited to Buryl Red.

Opened January 4, 1976, Palace, 1 performance.

Music by Mitch Leigh, lyrics by Charles Burr and Forman Brown. Musical direction by Ross Reimueller.

HONKY TONK NIGHTS

Orchestrations credited to Jim Tyler.

Opened August 7, 1986, Biltmore, 4 performances.

Music by Michael Valenti, lyrics by Ralph Allen and David Campbell. Musical direction and vocal arrangements by George Broderick. Dance arrangements by David Krane.

HOW TO SUCCEED IN BUSINESS WITHOUT REALLY TRYING (1995 REVIVAL)

New orchestrations credited to Danny Troob and David Siegel.

Opened March 23, 1995, Richard Rodgers, 548 performances.

Musical direction and vocal arrangements by Ted Sperling.

I LOVE MY WIFE

Orchestrations uncredited.

Opened April 17, 1977, Ethel Barrymore, 857 performances.

Music and arrangements by Cy Coleman, lyrics by Michael Stewart. Musical direction by John Miller.

INTO THE WOODS

Orchestrations credited to Jonathan Tunick.

Opened November 5, 1987, Martin Beck, 764 performances.

Music and lyrics by Stephen Sondheim. Musical direction by Paul Gemignani.

IS THERE LIFE AFTER HIGH SCHOOL?

Orchestrations credited to Bruce Coughlin.

Opened May 7, 1982, Ethel Barrymore, 12 performances.

Music and lyrics by Craig Carnelia. Musical direction by Bruce Coughlin.

JEKYLL & HYDE

Orchestrations credited to Kim Scharnberg.

Opened April 28, 1997, Plymouth, 1,543 performances.

Music by Frank Wildhorn, lyrics by Leslie Bricusse. Musical direction by Jason Howland. Vocal arrangements by Jason Howland and Ron Melrose.

JELLY'S LAST JAM

Orchestrations credited to Luther Henderson.

Opened April 26, 1992, Virginia, 569 performances.

Music by Jelly Roll Morton, lyrics by Susan Birkenhead. Additional music by Luther Henderson. Musical direction by Linda Twine.

JERRY'S GIRLS

Orchestrations credited to Christopher Bankey, Joseph Gianono, and Jim Tyler.
Opened December 18, 1985, St. James, 139 performances.
Music and lyrics by Jerry Herman. Musical direction by Janet Glazener. Musical supervision by Donald Pippin. Dance arrangements by Mark Hummel.

THE KING AND I (1996 REVIVAL)

New orchestrations credited to Bruce Coughlin.
Opened April 11, 1996, Neil Simon, 807 performances.
Musical direction by Michael Rafter. Musical supervision by Eric Stern.

KING DAVID

Orchestrations credited to Doug Besterman.
Opened May 18, 1997, New Amsterdam, 6 performances.
Music by Alan Menken, lyrics by Tim Rice. Musical direction and vocal arrangements by Michael Kosarin.

KING OF HEARTS

Orchestrations credited to William David Brohn. (Additional orchestrations by Michael Gibson and Jim Tyler.)
Opened October 22, 1978, Minskoff, 48 performances.
Music by Peter Link, lyrics by Jacob Brackman. Musical direction by Karen Gustafson. Dance arrangements by Dorothea Freitag.

KISS ME, KATE (1999 REVIVAL)

Orchestrations credited to Don Sebesky.
Opened November 18, 1999, Martin Beck, 881 performances.
Musical direction by Paul Gemignani. Dance arrangements by David Chase.

THE KISS OF THE SPIDER WOMAN

Orchestrations credited to Michael Gibson.
Opened May 3, 1993, Broadhurst, 906 performances.
Music by John Kander, lyrics by Fred Ebb. Musical direction by Jeffrey Huard. Dance arrangements by David Krane.

LA GROSSE VALISE

Orchestrations credited to Gerard Calvi.
Opened December 14, 1965, 54th Street, 7 performances.
Music by Gerard Calvi, lyrics by Harold Rome. Musical direction by Lehman Engel.

LATE NITE COMIC

Orchestrations credited to Larry Hochman.
Opened October 15, 1987, Ritz, 4 performances.
Music and lyrics by Brian Gari. Musical direction by Gregory J. Dlugos. Dance arrangements by James Raitt.

LEADER OF THE PACK

Orchestrations uncredited. (Additional orchestrations by Harold Wheeler.)
Opened April 8, 1985, Ambassador, 120 performances.
Music and lyrics by Ellie Greenwich and others. Musical direction by Jimmy Vivino. Vocal arrangements by Marc Shaiman. Dance arrangements by Timothy Graphenreed. Opening dance sequence composed and orchestrated by Harold Wheeler.

LEGS DIAMOND

Orchestrations credited to Michael Starobin.
Opened December 26, 1988, Mark Hellinger, 64 performances.
Music and lyrics by Peter Allen. Musical direction and vocal arrangements by Eric Stern. Dance arrangements by Mark Hummel.

THE LIFE

Orchestrations credited to Don Sebesky and Harold Wheeler.
Opened April 26, 1997, Ethel Barrymore, 466 performances.
Music by Cy Coleman, lyrics by Ira Gasman. Musical direction by Gordon Lowry Harrell. Vocal and dance arrangements by Cy Coleman and Doug Katsaros.

THE LION KING

Orchestrations credited to Robert Elhai, David Metzger, and Bruce Fowler.
Opened November 13, 1997, New Amsterdam. (Still playing January 1, 2009.)
Music by Elton John and others, lyrics by Tim Rice and others. Musical direction by Joseph Church. Vocal arrangements by Lebo M.

LITTLE ME (1982 REVIVAL)

Orchestrations credited to Harold Wheeler.
Opened January 21, 1982, Eugene O'Neill, 36 performances.
Music by Cy Coleman, lyrics by Carolyn Leigh. Musical direction by Donald York. Vocal
and dance arrangements by Cy Coleman.

LITTLE ME (1998 REVIVAL)

Orchestrations credited to Harold Wheeler.
Opened November 12, 1998, Criterion, 99 performances.
Music by Cy Coleman, lyrics by Carolyn Leigh. Musical direction by David Chase. Dance
arrangements by David Krane.

A LITTLE NIGHT MUSIC

Orchestrations credited to Jonathan Tunick.
Opened February 25, 1973, Shubert, 601 performances.
Music and lyrics by Stephen Sondheim. Musical direction by Hal Hastings.

MAIL

Orchestrations credited to Michael Gibson.
Opened April 14, 1988, Music Box, 36 performances.
Music by Michael Rupert, lyrics by Jerry Colker. Musical direction and dance arrange-
ments by Tom Fay. Musical supervision by Paul Gemignani.

MARIE CHRISTINE

Orchestrations credited to Jonathan Tunick.
Opened December 2, 1999, Vivian Beaumont, 44 performances.
Music and lyrics by Michael John LaChiusa. Musical direction by David Evans.

MARILYN: AN AMERICAN FABLE

Orchestrations credited to William David Brohn.
Opened November 20, 1983, Minskoff, 16 performances.
Music and lyrics by various writers. Musical direction, vocal and orchestral arrangements
by Steve Margoshes. Dance arrangements and additional orchestrations by Donald
Johnston.

MERRILY WE ROLL ALONG

Orchestrations credited to Jonathan Tunick.
Opened November 16, 1981, Alvin, 16 performances.
Music and lyrics by Stephen Sondheim. Musical direction by Paul Gemignani.

MISS SAIGON

Orchestrations credited to William David Brohn (replacing John Cameron).
Opened April 11, 1991, Broadway, 4,092 performances.
Music by Claude-Michel Schönberg, lyrics by Alain Boublil and Richard Maltby, Jr. Musical direction by Edward G. Robinson.

MY FAVORITE YEAR

Orchestrations credited to Michael Starobin. (Additional orchestrations by Danny Troob and Michael Gibson.)
Opened December 10, 1992, Vivian Beaumont, 37 performances.
Music by Stephen Flaherty, lyrics by Lynn Ahrens. Musical direction by Ted Sperling. Dance arrangements by Wally Harper.

MY ONE AND ONLY

Orchestrations credited to Michael Gibson.
Opened May 1, 1983, St. James, 767 performances.
Music by George Gershwin, lyrics by Ira Gershwin. Musical direction and vocal arrangements by Jack Lee. Musical concept by Wally Harper. Dance arrangements by Wally Harper and Peter Larson.

THE MYSTERY OF EDWIN DROOD

Orchestrations credited to Rupert Holmes.
Opened December 2, 1985, Imperial, 608 performances.
Music and lyrics by Rupert Holmes. Musical direction by Michael Starobin.

NASH AT NINE

Orchestrations credited to John Morris.
Opened May 17, 1973, Helen Hayes (aka Fulton), 21 performances.
Music by Milton Rosenstock, lyrics by Ogden Nash. Musical direction by Karen Gustafson.

NEFERTITI

Orchestrations credited to Robert M. Freedman.
Tryout: September 20, 1977, Chicago (Blackstone). Closed October 22.
Music by David Spangler, lyrics by Christopher Gore. Musical direction by John DeMain.
   Conductor, Robert Billig. Dance arrangements by Wally Harper.

NICK & NORA

Orchestrations credited to Jonathan Tunick.
Opened December 8, 1991, Minskoff, 9 performances.
Music by Charles Strouse, lyrics by Richard Maltby, Jr. Musical direction and vocal arrange-
   ments by Jack Lee. Dance and incidental arrangements by Gordon Lowry Harrell.

OH, KAY! (1978 REVIVAL)

Orchestrations credited to Billy Byers. (Additional orchestrations by Michael Gibson.)
Tryout: July 20, 1978, Toronto (Royal Alexandra). Closed September 23, Washington,
   D.C. (Opera House).
Music by George Gershwin, lyrics by Ira Gershwin. Musical direction and dance arrange-
   ments by Wally Harper. Vocal arrangements by William Elliott.

OH, KAY! (1990 REVIVAL)

Orchestrations credited to Arnold Goland.
Opened November 1, 1990, Richard Rodgers, 77 performances.
Musical direction, vocal and additional dance arrangements by Tom Fay. Dance arrange-
   ments by Donald Johnston.

ON THE TOWN (1998 REVIVAL)

Orchestrations credited to Bruce Coughlin.
Opened November 22, 1998, Gershwin, 65 performances.
Musical direction by Kevin Stites.

ONCE ON THIS ISLAND

Orchestrations credited to Michael Starobin.
Opened October 18, 1990, Booth, 469 performances.
Music and vocal and dance arrangements by Stephen Flaherty, lyrics by Lynn Ahrens.
   Musical direction by Steve Marzullo.

ONCE UPON A MATTRESS (1996 REVIVAL)

Orchestrations credited to Bruce Coughlin.
Opened December 19, 1996, Broadhurst, 187 performances.
Musical direction and vocal arrangements by Eric Stern. Dance arrangements by Tom Fay.

ONWARD VICTORIA

Orchestrations credited to Michael Gibson. (Additional orchestrations by Jim Tyler.)
Opened December 14, 1980, Martin Beck, 1 performance.
Music by Keith Herrmann, lyrics by Charlotte Anker and Irene Rosenberg. Musical di-
    rection by Larry Blank. Vocal arrangements by Keith Herrmann and Larry Blank.
    Dance arrangements by Donald Johnston.

OVER HERE!

Orchestrations credited to Michael Gibson and Jim Tyler.
Opened March 6, 1974, Shubert, 341 performances.
Music and lyrics by Richard M. Sherman and Robert B. Sherman. Musical direction by
    Joseph Klein. Vocal arrangements and special dance music by Louis St. Louis.

PACIFIC OVERTURES

Orchestrations credited to Jonathan Tunick.
Opened January 11, 1976, Winter Garden, 193 performances.
Music and lyrics by Stephen Sondheim. Musical direction by Paul Gemignani.

PARADE

Orchestrations credited to Don Sebesky.
Opened December 17, 1998, Vivian Beaumont, 84 performances.
Music and lyrics by Jason Robert Brown. Musical direction by Eric Stern.

PASSION

Orchestrations credited to Jonathan Tunick.
Opened May 9, 1994, Plymouth, 280 performances.
Music and lyrics by Stephen Sondheim. Musical direction by Paul Gemignani.

PICKWICK

Orchestrations credited to Eric Rogers.
Opened October 4, 1965, 46th Street, 56 performances.

Music by Cyril Ornadel, lyrics by Leslie Bricusse. Musical direction and vocal arrangements by Ian Fraser.

PLAY ON!

Orchestrations credited to Luther Henderson.
Opened March 20, 1997, Brooks Atkinson, 61 performances.
Music by Duke Ellington, lyrics by various writers. Musical direction by J. Leonard Oxley. Musical supervision by Luther Henderson.

PRINCE OF CENTRAL PARK

Orchestrations credited to Don Sebesky. (Additional orchestrations by Larry Hochman.)
Opened November 9, 1989, Belasco, 4 performances.
Music by Don Sebesky, lyrics by Gloria Nissenson. Musical direction and vocal arrangements by Joel Silberman. Dance arrangements by Henry Aronson.

THE PRINCE OF GRAND STREET

Orchestrations credited to Michael Gibson.
Tryout: March 7, 1978, Philadelphia (Forrest). Closed April 15, Boston (Shubert).
Music and lyrics by Bob Merrill. Musical direction and vocal arrangements by Colin Romoff. Dance arrangements by David Baker.

PUTTING IT TOGETHER

Orchestrations uncredited.
Opened March 2, 1993, Manhattan Theatre Club Stage 1, 96 performances.
Music and lyrics mostly by Stephen Sondheim. Musical direction by Scott Frankel. Arrangements by Chris Walker.

PUTTING IT TOGETHER (1999 VERSION)

Orchestrations credited to Jonathan Tunick.
Opened November 21, 1999, Ethel Barrymore, 101 performances.
Musical direction by Paul Raiman.

RAGS

Orchestrations credited to Michael Starobin.
Opened August 21, 1986, Mark Hellinger, 4 performances.
Music by Charles Strouse, lyrics by Stephen Schwartz. Musical direction and additional arrangements by Eric Stern.

RAGTIME

Orchestrations credited to William David Brohn.

Opened January 18, 1998, Ford Center, 861 performances.

Music by Stephen Flaherty, lyrics by Lynn Ahrens. Musical direction by David Loud. Musical supervisor, Jeffrey Huard. Dance arrangements by David Krane.

RAISIN

Orchestrations credited to Al Cohn and Robert M. Freedman.

Opened October 18, 1973, 46th Street, 847 performances.

Music by Judd Woldin, lyrics by Robert Brittan. Musical direction by Howard A. Roberts. Vocal arrangements by Joyce Brown and Howard A. Roberts. Dance arrangements by Judd Woldin. Incidental arrangements by Dorothea Freitag.

THE RINK

Orchestrations credited to Michael Gibson.

Opened February 9, 1984, Martin Beck, 204 performances.

Music by John Kander, lyrics by Fred Ebb. Musical direction by Paul Gemignani. Dance arrangements by Tom Fay.

THE ROBBER BRIDEGROOM

Orchestrations credited to Robert Waldman.

Opened October 9, 1976, Ethel Barrymore, 145 performances.

Music by Robert Waldman, lyrics by Alfred Uhry. Musical direction uncredited.

ROMANCE, ROMANCE

Orchestrations credited to Michael Starobin.

Opened May 1, 1988, Helen Hayes, 297 performances.

Music by Keith Herrmann, lyrics by Barry Harman. Musical direction by Kathy Sommer. Vocal and dance arrangements by Keith Herrmann and Kathy Sommer.

ROZA

Orchestrations credited to Michael Gibson.

Opened October 1, 1987, Royale, 12 performances.

Music by Gilbert Becaud, lyrics by Julian More. Musical direction, vocal and dance arrangements by Louis St. Louis.

SARAVÀ

Orchestrations credited to Danny Troob.

Opened February 23, 1979, Mark Hellinger, 140 performances.

Music by Mitch Leigh, lyrics by N. Richard Nash. Musical direction and vocal arrangements by David Friedman.

THE SCARLET PIMPERNEL

Orchestrations credited to Kim Scharnberg.

Opened November 9, 1997, Minskoff, 640 performances.

Music by Frank Wildhorn, lyrics by Nan Knighton. Musical direction by Ron Melrose. Musical supervision by Jason Howland.

THE SECRET GARDEN

Orchestrations credited to William David Brohn.

Opened April 25, 1991, St. James, 706 performances.

Music by Lucy Simon, lyrics by Marsha Norman. Musical direction and vocal arrangements by Michael Kosarin. Dance arrangements by Jeanine Levenson [Tesori].

THE SELLING OF THE PRESIDENT

Orchestrations credited to Jonathan Tunick.

Opened March 22, 1972, Shubert, 5 performances.

Music by Bob James, lyrics by Jack O'Brien. Musical direction by Harold Hastings.

SHE LOVES ME (1993 REVIVAL)

Orchestrations credited to Don Walker and Frank Matosich, Jr. (Additional orchestration by David Krane.)

Opened June 10, 1993, Criterion, 354 performances.

Music by Jerry Bock, lyrics by Sheldon Harnick. Musical direction by David Loud. "A Romantic Atmosphere" orchestrated by David Krane.

SHOGUN: THE MUSICAL

Orchestrations credited to David Cullen and Steve Margoshes.

Opened November 29, 1990, Marquis, 72 performances.

Music by Paul Chihara, lyrics by John Driver. Musical direction by Edward G. Robinson.

SHOW BOAT (1994 REVIVAL)

New orchestrations credited to William David Brohn.
Opened October 2, 1994, Gershwin, 946 performances.
Musical direction by Jeffrey Huard. Dance arrangements by David Krane.

SMITH

Orchestrations credited to Jonathan Tunick.
Opened May 19, 1973, Eden (off-Broadway), 18 performances.
Music and lyrics by Matt Dubey and Dean Fuller. Musical direction by Richard Parrinello. Vocal arrangements by Dean Fuller. Dance arrangements by John Berkman.

SMOKEY JOE'S CAFE

Orchestrations credited to Steve Margoshes.
Opened March 2, 1995, Virginia, 2,036 performances.
Music and lyrics by Jerry Leiber and Mike Stoller and others. Musical direction by Louis St. Louis.

SOMETHING'S AFOOT

Orchestrations credited to Peter M. Larson.
Opened May 27, 1976, Lyceum, 61 performances.
Music and lyrics by James McDonald, David Vos, and Robert Gerlach. Musical direction by Buster Davis.

SOPHISTICATED LADIES

Orchestrations credited to Al Cohn.
Opened March 1, 1981, Lunt-Fontanne, 767 performances.
Music by Duke Ellington and others. Musical direction by Mercer Ellington. Musical and dance arrangements by Lloyd Mayers. Vocal arrangements by Malcolm Dodds and Lloyd Mayers.

THE SOUND OF MUSIC (1998 REVIVAL)

New orchestrations credited to Bruce Coughlin.
Opened March 12, 1998, Martin Beck, 533 performances.
Musical direction by Michael Rafter. Dance arrangements by Jeanine Tesori.

SPOTLIGHT

Orchestrations credited to Will Schaefer.

Tryout: January 11, 1978, Washington, D.C. (National). Closed January 14, Washington, D.C.

Music by Jerry Bresler, lyrics by Lyn Duddy. Musical direction and vocal arrangements by Jack Lee. Dance arrangements by Wally Harper.

STATE FAIR

Orchestrations credited to Bruce Pomahac.

Opened March 27, 1996, Music Box, 111 performances.

Music by Richard Rodgers, lyrics by Oscar Hammerstein II. Musical direction and vocal arrangements by Kay Cameron. Dance arrangements by Scot Woolley.

STEEL PIER

Orchestrations credited to Michael Gibson.

Opened April 24, 1997, Richard Rodgers, 76 performances.

Music by John Kander, lyrics by Fred Ebb. Musical direction and vocal arrangements by David Loud. Dance arrangements by Glen Kelly.

THE STUDENT GYPSY; OR, THE PRINCE OF LIEDERKRANZ

Orchestrations credited to Arnold Goland.

Opened September 30, 1961, 54th Street, 16 performances.

Music and lyrics by Rick Besoyan. Musical direction by Shepard Coleman.

SUNDAY IN THE PARK WITH GEORGE

Orchestrations credited to Michael Starobin.

Opened May 2, 1984, Booth, 604 performances.

Music and lyrics by Stephen Sondheim. Musical direction by Paul Gemignani.

SWEENEY TODD

Orchestrations credited to Jonathan Tunick.

Opened March 1, 1979, Uris, 558 performances.

Music and lyrics by Stephen Sondheim. Musical direction by Paul Gemignani.

SWING

Orchestrations credited to Harold Wheeler.

Opened December 9, 1999, St. James, 461 performances.

Music and lyrics by various writers. Musical direction by Jonathan Smith. Musical supervision by Michael Rafter.

THE TAP DANCE KID

Orchestrations credited to Harold Wheeler.

Opened December 21, 1983, Broadhurst, 669 performances.

Music by Henry Krieger, lyrics by Robert Lorick. Musical direction by Don Jones. Vocal arrangements by Harold Wheeler. Dance arrangements by Peter Howard.

TEDDY AND ALICE

Orchestrations credited to Jim Tyler. (Additional orchestrations by Michael Gibson, Chris Bankey, and Larry Blank.)

Opened November 12, 1987, Minskoff, 77 performances.

Music by John Philip Sousa, lyrics by Hal Hackady. Musical direction by Larry Blank. Musical supervision and vocal arrangements by Donald Pippin. Dance arrangements by Gordon Lowry Harrell.

TITANIC

Orchestrations credited to Jonathan Tunick.

Opened April 23, 1997, Lunt-Fontanne, 804 performances.

Music and lyrics by Maury Yeston. Musical direction by Kevin Stites.

TRIUMPH OF LOVE

Orchestrations credited to Bruce Coughlin.

Opened October 23, 1997, 84 performances.

Music by Jeffrey Stock, lyrics by Susan Birkenhead. Musical direction by Patrick Brady. Musical supervision and arrangements by Michael Kosarin.

TWO GENTLEMEN OF VERONA

Orchestrations credited to Harold Wheeler.

Opened December 1, 1971, St. James, 614 performances.

Music by Galt MacDermot, lyrics by John Guare. Musical direction by Harold Wheeler.

VICTOR/VICTORIA

Orchestrations credited to Billy Byers.

Opened October 25, 1995, Marquis, 734 performances.

Music by Henry Mancini, lyrics by Leslie Bricusse. Additional music by Frank Wildhorn. Musical direction and vocal arrangements by Ian Fraser. Dance and incidental music by David Krane.

WELCOME TO THE CLUB

Orchestrations credited to Doug Katsaros.

Opened April 13, 1989, Music Box, 12 performances.

Music by Cy Coleman, lyrics by Cy Coleman and A. E. Hotchner. Musical direction by David Pogue. Vocal arrangements by Cy Coleman and David Pogue.

THE WHO'S TOMMY

Orchestrations credited to Steve Margoshes.

Opened April 22, 1993, St. James, 899 performances.

Music and lyrics by Pete Townshend and others. Musical direction by Joseph Church. Assistant conductor, Jeanine Levenson [Tesori].

THE WILL ROGERS FOLLIES

Orchestrations credited to Billy Byers.

Opened May 1, 1991, Palace, 983 performances.

Music by Cy Coleman, lyrics by Betty Comden & Adolph Green. Musical direction by Eric Stern.

WIND IN THE WILLOWS

Orchestrations credited to William David Brohn.

Opened December 21, 1985, Nederlander, 4 performances.

Music by William Perry, lyrics by Roger McGough and William Perry. Musical direction and vocal arrangements by Robert Rogers. Musical supervision by Jonathan Tunick. Dance and incidental music by David Krane.

WOMAN OF THE YEAR

Orchestrations credited to Michael Gibson.

Opened March 29, 1981, Palace, 770 performances.

Music by John Kander, lyrics by Fred Ebb. Musical direction and vocal arrangements by Donald Pippin. Dance arrangements by Ronald Melrose.

WORKING

Orchestrations credited to Kirk Nurock.

Opened May 14, 1978, 46th Street, 25 performances.

Music and lyrics by Stephen Schwartz, Craig Carnelia, James Taylor, and others. Musical direction and vocal arrangements by Stephen Reinhardt. Dance and incidental music by Michele Brourman.

YOU'RE A GOOD MAN, CHARLIE BROWN (1999 REVIVAL)

New orchestrations credited to Michael Gibson.

Opened February 4, 1999, Ambassador, 150 performances.

Music and lyrics by Clark Gesner. New songs and arrangements by Andrew Lippa. Musical direction by Kimberly Grigsby.

THE ZULU AND THE ZAYDA

Orchestrations credited to Meyer Kupferman.

Opened November 10, 1965, Cort, 179 performances.

A play with songs by Harold Rome. Musical direction by Michael Spivakowsky.

Overture from *The King and I* by Richard Rodgers and Oscar Hammerstein II. Orchestration by Robert Russell Bennett. The opening two chords—marked "long"—are played by the orchestra in unison; the next two "presto" measures feature reeds, strings, harp, and cymbal. An uncharacteristically playful Bennett writes the title in French, "Le Roi et Moi." Copyright © 1951 by Richard Rodgers and Oscar Hammerstein II. Copyright renewed. Williamson Music, owner of publication and allied rights throughout the world. International copyright secured. All rights reserved. Used by permission. From the Richard Rodgers Collection in the Music Division of the Library of Congress.

CODA

SECTION I. CHRONOLOGY

Arranging the show listings in alphabetical order is the most logical way to do so, as it enables the reader to handily locate a given production. Part of the story of Broadway orchestrators, though, has to do with not only what they did but when they did it—and what else they were doing at the same time. This chronological list of the shows contained in our main listing section (but not the shows in the supplemental "additional shows" section) will provide an idea of when the shows were produced in relation to each other.

The date of the official Broadway opening is used, naturally enough. In the case of shows that did not open on Broadway, however, we use not the opening but the closing date. The orchestrator, generally speaking, works up until the day of the Broadway opening; thus, the date closest to the intended opening best serves our purpose of showing simultaneous activity.

The final column indicates the orchestrators of the shows—or, rather, those shows that were orchestrated by our twelve major orchestrators or others included in our "Valued Members of the Music Department" section (Luther Henderson, Joe Glover, Bob Noeltner, Jim Tyler, and more). The main orchestrators are listed first; those who made relatively minor contributions, either credited or ghosted, are listed in parentheses. (This is not an exact call, especially on earlier shows where billing was inexact or nonexistent.) This column will serve to give a picture of just how active these orchestrators were; different people, at different times, seem to have been working on almost every show that came along. Also listed in this column are some orchestrators who are not among those on our list but whom it seems reasonable to include (including Jonathan Tunick and such composer/ orchestrators as Kurt Weill and Marc Blitzstein). For the relatively few shows on which none of our orchestrators were involved, this column has been left empty.

1920

	October 19	Hitchy-Koo of 1920	(Bennett)

1922

	August 22	Daffy Dill	(Bennett)
	September 12	Greenwich Village Follies (3rd)	(Bennett)

1923

	February 7	Wildflower	(Bennett)
	November 6	The Stepping Stones	(Bennett)
	December 25	Mary Jane McKane	(Bennett)

1924

	January 21	Lollipop	(Bennett)
	April 8	Sitting Pretty	(Bennett)
	June 24	Ziegfeld Follies of 1924	(Bennett)
	August 11	Marjorie	(Spialek)
	September 2	Rose-Marie	Bennett
	September 23	Dear Sir	Bennett
	November 25	The Magnolia Lady	(Bennett)
	December 1	Lady Be Good	(Bennett)

1925

	July 6	Ziegfeld Follies of 1925	(Bennett)
	September 16	No, No, Nanette	(Bennett)
	September 19	A Night Out	(Spialek)
	September 22	Sunny	Bennett
	October 26	The City Chap	(Bennett)
	December 30	Song of the Flame	(Bennett)

1926

	March 17	The Girl Friend	
	May 10	Garrick Gaieties	(Spialek)
	July 26	Americana	(Spialek)
	September 5	Queen High	(Bennett)
	October 12	Criss-Cross	(Bennett, Spialek)
	December 17	Oh, Please!	(Spialek)

1927

	March 22	Lucky	(Bennett, Spialek)
	April 25	Hit the Deck!	
	May 19	One Dam Thing after Another	(Bennett)
	August 17	À La Carte	(Spialek)

	October	Strike Up the Band	
	November 22	Funny Face	(Spialek)
	December 27	Show Boat	Bennett (Spialek)
1928			
	January 10	Rosalie	(Spialek)
	March 13	The Three Musketeers	(Spialek)
	April 26	Present Arms!	(Spialek)
	April 27	Blue Eyes	Bennett
	September 19	The New Moon	(Spialek)
	October 8	Paris	(Spialek)
	October 30	Americana	(Spialek)
	November 21	Rainbow	(Bennett)
	December 26	Hello, Daddy!	(Spialek)
1929			
	January 31	Lady Fingers	(Spialek)
	July 2	Show Girl	
	September 3	Sweet Adeline	Bennett
	October 17	Great Day!	
	November 11	Heads Up!	(Bennett)
	November 27	Fifty Million Frenchmen	(Spialek, Bennett)
1930			
	June 23	Mystery Moon	(Spialek)
	September 20	Nina Rosa	(Spialek)
	September 23	Fine and Dandy	(Spialek)
	October 14	Girl Crazy	Bennett
	November 18	Smiles	
	December 3	Ever Green	Bennett
	December 8	The New Yorkers	(Spialek)
1931			
	February 10	America's Sweetheart	Bennett
	February 18	The Gang's All Here	(Spialek)
	June 3	The Band Wagon	Bennett
	September 16	Singin' the Blues	(Bennett)
	October 13	Everybody's Welcome	(Spialek)
	October 15	The Cat and the Fiddle	Bennett
	October 27	East Wind	Spialek
	November 2	The Laugh Parade	Bennett, Spialek
	December 26	Of Thee I Sing	Bennett
1932			
	January 28	Through the Years	
	February 17	Face the Music	Bennett
	March 8	Hot-Cha!	Bennett
	September 6	Ballyhoo of 1932	(Spialek)
	September 15	Flying Colors	(Spialek, Bennett)

October 5	Americana	
November 8	Music in the Air	Bennett
November 26	Take a Chance	(Bennett)
November 29	Gay Divorce	Spialek (Bennett)
December 7	Walk a Little Faster	(Bennett)

1933

January 20	Pardon My English	Bennett
April 13	The Threepenny Opera	Weill
September 8	Murder at the Vanities	(Spialek)
September 25	Hold Your Horses	Bennett
September 30	As Thousands Cheer	
October 6	Nymph Errant	Bennett
October 21	Let 'Em Eat Cake	
November 18	Roberta	Bennett

1934

January 4	Ziegfeld Follies of 1934	(Spialek, Walker)
January 30	All the King's Horses	(Bennett, Spialek)
March 15	New Faces	(Spialek)
April 9	Three Sisters	Bennett
June 7	Caviar	(Spialek, Walker)
August 27	Life Begins at 8:40	(Spialek, Bennett, Walker, Paul, Royal)
November 8	Say When	(Bennett)
November 21	Anything Goes	Spialek, Bennett (Salta)
November 28	Revenge with Music	Bennett
December 13	Calling All Stars	(Spialek)
December 25	Fools Rush In	(Spialek, Bennett)
December 27	Thumbs Up!	(Spialek)

1935

May 20	Parade	(Bennett)
June 4	Earl Carroll's Sketch Book (2nd)	(Bennett, Walker)
September 19	At Home Abroad	(Bennett, Spialek, Walker)
October 10	Porgy and Bess	Gershwin (Bennett, Spialek)
October 12	Jubilee	Bennett
October 12	Venus in Silk	(Spialek)
November 16	Billy Rose's Jumbo	(Spialek, Bennett)
December 5	May Wine	Walker (Bennett)
December 25	George White's Scandals of 1935	(Bennett)

1936

January 22	The Illustrators' Show	(Spialek)
January 30	Ziegfeld Follies of 1936	(Spialek, Bennett, Walker)

	April 11	On Your Toes	Spialek (Royal)
	May 19	New Faces of 1936	(Spialek)
	October 1	The White Horse Inn	Spialek
	October 29	Red, Hot and Blue!	Bennett (Spialek, Walker)
	November 2	Forbidden Melody	Walker
	November 19	Johnny Johnson	Weill
	December 25	The Show Is On	(Bennett, Spialek)
1937			
	April 14	Babes in Arms	Spialek
	September 2	Virginia	Spialek
	November 2	I'd Rather Be Right	Spialek (Walker, Royal, Paul)
	December 1	Hooray for What!	Walker (Paul, Glover)
	December 22	Between the Devil	Spialek
	December 25	Three Waltzes	(Walker)
1938			
	January 4	Right This Way	(Spialek)
	May 11	I Married an Angel	Spialek
	June 3	Gentlemen Unafraid	Bennett
	September 21	You Never Know	Spialek (Walker, Salta)
	September 24	Sing Out the News	(Spialek)
	October 19	Knickerbocker Holiday	Weill
	November 9	Leave It to Me!	Walker
	November 23	The Boys from Syracuse	Spialek (Paul, Salta)
	December 1	Great Lady	Spialek
1939			
	January 3	Mamba's Daughters	Spialek
	January 18	Set to Music	Spialek
	February 3	One for the Money	Spialek
	February 9	Stars in Your Eyes	Walker, Spialek
	March 23	The Hot Mikado	
	May 4	Billy Rose's Aquacade	(Royal, Spialek)
	June 19	Streets of Paris	Spialek
	August 28	George White's Scandals of 1939	(Spialek, Walker, Royal)
	September 29	The Straw Hat Revue	
	October 18	Too Many Girls	Spialek (Paul, Walker, Royal)
	November 4	Nice Goin'	Walker
	November 17	Very Warm for May	Bennett
	December 6	Du Barry Was a Lady	Spialek (Bennett, Royal, Paul)
1940			
	January 10	John Henry	Spialek
	February 8	Two for the Show	Spialek, Walker
	April 4	Higher and Higher	Spialek (Walker, Royal, Paul)
	May 12	American Jubilee	Spialek

May 23	Keep Off the Grass	Spialek, Walker
May 28	Louisiana Purchase	Bennett (Lang)
June 4	Walk with Music	(Spialek, Walker)
August 24	The Little Dog Laughed	Spialek
September 11	Hold on to Your Hats	Spialek, Walker
October 1	Boys and Girls Together	Spialek (Bennett, Walker)
October 25	Cabin in the Sky	
October 30	Panama Hattie	Walker (Bennett, Spialek, Royal)
December	Hi Ya, Gentlemen!	Bennett, Spialek, Walker
December 25	Pal Joey	Spialek (Royal)
December 27	All in Fun	

1941

January 23	Lady in the Dark	Weill (Royal)
July	La Belle Helene	(Walker, Spialek)
October 1	Best Foot Forward	Walker, Spialek (Bennett, Royal, Noeltner, Mason)
October 29	Let's Face It!	Spialek, Walker (Royal, Paul)
October 31	High Kickers of 1942	(Spialek, Walker, Royal)
December 1	Sons o' Fun	
December 4	Sunny River	Walker
December 26	Banjo Eyes	

1942

January 9	The Lady Comes Across	
March 28	My Dear Public	Spialek, Walker, Royal
June 3	By Jupiter	Walker
July 4	This Is the Army	(Walker, Spialek, Paul, Lang)
October 5	Let Freedom Sing	Lang
October 8	Count Me In	Bennett (Spialek, Walker)
October 14	Beat the Band	Walker
November	Life of the Party	Spialek, Bennett, Royal

1943

January 7	Something for the Boys	Spialek, Walker (Bennett, Royal, Paul)
March 31	Oklahoma!	Bennett (Salta)
April 1	Ziegfeld Follies of 1943	Walker (Royal, Noeltner, Ginzler)
April 10	Dancing in the Streets	Spialek
June 17	Early to Bed	Walker (Royal, Noeltner)
September 9	My Dear Public	Spialek, Royal
September 16	Bright Lights of 1944	(Bennett, Spialek, Royal)
October 7	One Touch of Venus	Weill (Bennett)
November 5	Artists and Models	Spialek, Walker, Royal
November 11	What's Up?	
November 17	A Connecticut Yankee	Walker (Royal)
December 2	Carmen Jones	Bennett

1944

January 13	Jackpot	Spialek, Bennett (Royal)
January 28	Mexican Hayride	Bennett, Royal
April 8	Follow the Girls	Glover, Paul
April 20	Allah Be Praised!	Walker
May 18	Dream with Music	Bennett, Spialek, Royal
August 21	Song of Norway	(Walker)
October 5	Bloomer Girl	Bennett (Royal)
November 16	Sadie Thompson	Glover
November 22	Rhapsody	Bennett
December 7	Seven Lively Arts	Spialek, Bennett, Royal (Walker, Noeltner)
December 28	On the Town	Kay, Walker, Royal

1945

January 6	Glad to See You	
January 27	Up in Central Park	Walker
March 14	Dark of the Moon	Kay
March 22	The Firebrand of Florence	Weill (Royal)
April 19	Carousel	Walker (Spialek, Bennett, Glover)
May 24	Memphis Bound	Walker (Royal)
May 31	Hollywood Pinafore	Spialek
July 18	Marinka	Spialek
September 27	Carib Song	Royal
October 6	Polonaise	Walker
November 8	The Girl from Nantucket	(Royal)
November 10	Are You with It?	Spialek, Walker, Royal, Glover, Paul
November 22	The Day before Spring	
December 21	Billion Dollar Baby	Lang

1946

January 5	Show Boat	Bennett
January 12	Spring in Brazil	(Walker)
January 21	Nellie Bly	Royal
February 6	Lute Song	
February 13	The Duchess Misbehaves	Walker
March 7	Three to Make Ready	Bennett, Spialek, Royal, Paul
March 30	St. Louis Woman	Royal, Salta, Paul
April 18	Call Me Mister	
April 27	Shootin' Star	Kay
May 16	Annie Get Your Gun	Bennett, Lang, Royal (Noeltner, Spialek, Paul, Walker)
May 31	Around the World	Bennett, Royal
June 6	Windy City	Walker

September 5	A Flag Is Born	(Kay)
October 31	Happy Birthday	Bennett
November 4	Park Avenue	Walker
November 5	Sweet Bye and Bye	Royal (Kay)
December 5	If the Shoe Fits	Bennett (Royal, Spialek, Paul, Glover)
December 26	Beggar's Holiday	(Henderson, Kay)
December 26	Toplitzky of Notre Dame	
December 31	In Gay New Orleans	Bennett

1947

January 9	Street Scene	Weill (Royal)
January 10	Finian's Rainbow	Bennett, Walker
January 21	Sweethearts	Bennett
March 13	Brigadoon	Royal (Noeltner, Lang)
April 3	Barefoot Boy with Cheek	Lang (Bennett)
June 2	Louisiana Lady	Spialek, Bennett
October 2	Music in My Heart	Spialek
October 9	High Button Shoes	Lang
October 10	Allegro	Bennett (Salta, Royal)

1948

January 3	Bonanza Bound	Lang (Bennett)
January 15	Make Mine Manhattan	Royal (Bennett)
January 29	Look Ma, I'm Dancin'!	Walker (Bennett, Ginzler)
April 30	Inside U.S.A.	Bennett (Walker)
May 5	Hold It!	Spialek, Royal
May 6	Sally	Bennett (Lang)
June 3	Sleepy Hollow	Spialek, Royal
September 15	Small Wonder	Royal
September 16	Heaven on Earth	Bennett, Walker
October 2	That's the Ticket!	Walker, Bennett
October 7	Love Life	Weill
October 11	Where's Charley?	Royal, Spialek, Lang
October 19	My Romance	Walker
November 13	As the Girls Go	Royal
December 16	Lend an Ear	
December 30	Kiss Me, Kate	Bennett, Walker (Spialek, Paul)

1949

January 22	All for Love	Walker, Bennett, Royal, Spialek
April 7	South Pacific	Bennett (Walker)
July 15	Miss Liberty	Walker (Ginzler, Bennett, Glover)
October 13	Touch and Go	Walker (Bennett)
October 30	Lost in the Stars	Weill
October 31	Regina	Blitzstein

November 25	Texas, Li'l Darlin'	Bennett
December 8	Gentlemen Prefer Blondes	Walker

1950

January 6	Happy as Larry	Goehr, Cooke
January 17	Alive and Kicking	(Walker)
January 20	Dance Me a Song	Bennett, Walker (Kostal, Ginzler)
February 2	Arms and the Girl	Lang (Bennett)
March 23	Great to Be Alive!	Bennett, Walker
April 24	Peter Pan	Kay
April 27	Tickets, Please!	Royal
May 18	The Liar	
June 28	Michael Todd's Peep Show	Kostal
October 12	Call Me Madam	Walker, Glover
November 24	Guys and Dolls	Royal
December 13	Let's Make an Opera	
December 14	Bless You All	Walker (Ginzler, Kostal, Lang)
December 21	Out of This World	Bennett (Glover)

1951

March 29	The King and I	Bennett (Walker, Spialek, Paul)
April 18	Make a Wish	Lang
April 19	A Tree Grows in Brooklyn	Glover, Bennett (Royal)
May 14	Flahooley	Royal (Noeltner)
June 14	Courtin' Time	Walker
June 21	Seventeen	Royal
July 19	Two on the Aisle	Lang
October 8	Music in the Air	Bennett
November 1	Top Banana	Walker (Ginzler, Henderson)
November 12	Paint Your Wagon	Royal (Bennett, Spialek, Noeltner, Evans)

1952√√√

January 2	Pal Joey	Walker (Ginzler, Kostal)
January 26	A Month of Sundays	Royal
March 4	Paris '90	Bennett
March 21	Three Wishes for Jamie	Bennett (Lang)
April 1	Curtain Going Up	Walker (Ginzler, Kostal, Paul)
May 5	Of Thee I Sing	Walker (Ginzler, Kostal)
May 8	Shuffle Along	(Royal, Evans)
May 16	New Faces of 1952	Royal (Evans, Noeltner)
June 25	Wish You Were Here	Walker (Ginzler)
September 6	Jollyanna	Kay
October 14	Buttrio Square	Walker
October 27	My Darlin' Aida	Spialek
December 15	Two's Company	Walker, Lang

1953

February 11	Hazel Flagg	Walker (Ginzler, Kostal, Mason, Lang, Paul)
February 18	Maggie	Walker (Paul, Bennett, Glover, Lang, Ginzler)
February 25	Wonderful Town	Walker, Ginzler (Kostal, Ramin, Glover, Mason)
May 7	Can-Can	Lang (Noeltner)
May 28	Me and Juliet	Walker (Ginzler, Spialek, Mason)
September 8	Carnival in Flanders	Walker (Ginzler, Spialek, Kostal, Mason)
October 14	Agnes de Mille Dance Theatre	Walker (Spialek, Ginzler, Paul, Kostal)
December 3	Kismet	
December 10	John Murray Anderson's Almanac	Royal (Evans)
December 19	Little Jesse James	Walker (Ginzler)

1954

March 5	The Girl in Pink Tights	Walker (Ginzler, Spialek, Paul, Mason)
March 10	The Threepenny Opera	Weill
April 8	By the Beautiful Sea	Bennett (Glover)
April 20	The Golden Apple	Kay
May 13	The Pajama Game	Walker (Ginzler, Kostal, Glover, Paul)
June 25	Arabian Nights	Glover
September 30	The Boy Friend	Royal (Evans)
October 11	On Your Toes	Walker (Ginzler, Kostal)
October 20	Peter Pan	(Walker, Ginzler)
November 4	Fanny	Lang (Mason, Glover)
November 29	Sandhog	Kay
December 2	Hit the Trail	Walker (Spialek, Ginzler, Glover)
December 30	House of Flowers	Royal (Evans)

1955

January 27	Plain and Fancy	Lang
February 24	Silk Stockings	Walker (Ginzler, Kostal, Spialek)
April 13	Meet the People 1955	Glover
April 18	Ankles Aweigh	Walker (Ginzler, Kostal, Glover)
April 23	Phoenix '55	Burns
May 5	Damn Yankees	Walker (Ginzler, Kostal, Glover)
May 26	Seventh Heaven	(Kostal)
June 20	Almost Crazy	Royal (Evans)
October 22	Reuben Reuben	Blitzstein (Kay, Stegmeyer)
November 10	The Vamp	(Walker)

November 30	Pipe Dream	Bennett (Glover, Lang, Walker, Mason, Noeltner)
December 1	Pleasure Dome	Burns

1956

January 21	The Amazing Adele	Glover
March 15	My Fair Lady	Bennett, Lang (Mason)
March 22	Mr. Wonderful	Royal (Evans)
April 14	Strip for Action	Burns
May 3	The Most Happy Fella	Walker
May 12	Ziegfeld Follies of 1956	
May 22	The Littlest Revue	(Glover)
June 13	Shangri-La	Lang (Bennett)
June 14	New Faces of '56	Royal, Glover
September 6	Catch a Star	
November 15	Li'l Abner	Lang
November 29	Bells Are Ringing	Bennett (Lang, Walker, Glover, Noeltner)
December 1	Candide	Bernstein Kay
December 6	Happy Hunting	Royal (Glover, Walker, Ginzler)

1957

March 1	Ziegfeld Follies of 1957	Bennett, Glover, Stegmeyer, Noeltner (Lang)
April 13	Shinbone Alley	(Kostal, Burns)
April 27	Livin' the Life	Kay, Glover (Burns)
May 14	New Girl in Town	Bennett, Lang
August	Mistress of the Inn	Walker
August 20	Simply Heavenly	
September 26	West Side Story	Ramin, Kostal
October 17	Copper and Brass	Burns
October 26	The Carefree Heart	Walker
October 31	Jamaica	Lang (Matz)
November 6	Rumple	Royal
November 12	Time Remembered	
December 19	The Music Man	Walker (Ginzler, Kostal)

1958

January 23	The Body Beautiful	Royal (Noeltner)
February 4	Oh Captain!	Ginzler, Lang, Glover
February 21	Portofino	Lang
April 3	Say, Darling	Ramin, Ginzler
September 13	At the Grand	
October 11	Goldilocks	Lang (Bennett, Noeltner, Mason)
December 1	Flower Drum Song	Bennett (Glover, Henderson)
December 22	Whoop-Up	Lang

1959

February 5	Redhead	Lang, Bennett
March 9	Juno	Bennett, Kay (Lang)
March 12	Lute Song	Kostal
March 19	First Impressions	Walker (Ginzler)
April 18	Babes in Arms	Walker (Ginzler)
April 23	Destry Rides Again	Lang
May 11	Once upon a Mattress	Kay
May 21	Gypsy	Ramin, Ginzler
October 22	Take Me Along	Lang
November 2	The Girls Against the Boys	Ramin, Ginzler
November 16	The Sound of Music	Bennett
November 23	Fiorello!	Kostal
December 7	Saratoga	Lang
December 12	The Pink Jungle	

1960

February 10	Beg, Borrow or Steal	Matz
March 8	Greenwillow	Walker
April 14	Bye Bye Birdie	Ginzler (Lawrence)
April 20	From A to Z	Tunick
April 28	Christine	Lang
June 9	Meet Me in St. Louis	Lang
September 17	Vintage '60	(Ramin/Ginzler, Matz)
September 29	Irma La Douce	(Ginzler)
October 17	Tenderloin	Kostal
November 3	The Unsinkable Molly Brown	Walker
December 3	Camelot	Bennett, Lang
December 16	Wildcat	Ginzler, Ramin
December 26	Do Re Mi	Henderson (Stegmeyer)

1961

January 16	The Conquering Hero	Ginzler, Ramin
March 2	13 Daughters	Glover, Bennett
April 3	The Happiest Girl in the World	Bennett, Kay
April 13	Carnival	Lang
May 18	Donnybrook!	Ginzler
June 22	Paradise Island	Glover
July	Calamity Jane	Lang
October 3	Sail Away	Kostal
October 10	Milk and Honey	Kay, Sauter
October 12	Let It Ride!	(Henderson, Andrews)
October 14	How to Succeed in Business ...	Ginzler (Lawrence)
October 14	Kicks & Co.	
October 23	Kwamina	Ramin, Kostal
November 2	Kean	Lang

November 10	All in Love	Tunick
November 18	The Gay Life	Walker
December 27	Subways Are for Sleeping	Lang

1962

January 27	A Family Affair	Ginzler (Walker, Ramin)
February 1	New Faces of 1962	Royal
March 15	No Strings	Burns (Matz)
March 19	All American	Ginzler
March 22	I Can Get It for You Wholesale	Ramin
March 31	We Take the Town	Bennett, Kay
April 5	A Thousand Clowns	Walker
May 8	A Funny Thing Happened . . .	Ramin, Kostal
May 19	Bravo Giovanni	Ginzler (Henderson, Walker)
August	An Evening with Carol Burnett	Kostal
August 25	La Belle	Lang
October 3	Stop the World . . .	
October 20	Mr. President	Lang
November 10	Nowhere to Go but Up	Ginzler (Walker, Ramin)
November 17	Little Me	Burns
December 26	The Beauty Part	Walker

1963

January 6	Oliver!	
March 18	Tovarich	Lang
April 15	The Boys from Syracuse	Wilcox
April 15	Sophie	Ramin
April 19	Hot Spot	Henderson, Burns
April 23	She Loves Me	Walker
June 22	Around the World in Eighty Days	Lang
October 3	Here's Love	Walker (Lawrence)
October 17	Jennie	Lang, Bennett
October 24	110 in the Shade	Kay (Stegmeyer)
November 7	The Boys from Syracuse (London)	Burns
November 16	Zenda	Kostal
December 8	The Girl Who Came to Supper	Bennett (Andrews, Lang, Spialek, Stegmeyer)

1964

January 16	Hello, Dolly!	Lang (Andrews)
February 16	Foxy	Kay (Sauter)
February 27	What Makes Sammy Run?	Walker (Evans)
March 26	Funny Girl	Burns (Wilcox, Henderson, Tyler)

April 4	Anyone Can Whistle	Walker
April 4	Cool Off!	Wilcox
April 7	High Spirits	(Henderson)
April 17	Cafe Crown	Kay (Stegmeyer, Andrews)
April 29	To Broadway with Love	Lang (Bennett)
May 5	Ice-Travaganza	Burns
May 26	Fade Out, Fade In	Burns (Wilcox, Tyler)
September 22	Fiddler on the Roof	Walker (Tyler)
October 20	Golden Boy	Burns (Tyler, Wilcox, Lawrence)
October 27	Ben Franklin in Paris	Lang
November 10	Something More!	Burns (Wilcox)
November 23	Bajour	
December 15	I Had a Ball	Lang

1965

January 23	Royal Flush	Wilcox
February 6	Kelly	Kay
February 16	Baker Street	Walker
March 18	Do I Hear a Waltz?	Burns (Wilcox, Tyler)
April 10	Pleasures and Palaces	Lang
April 25	Half a Sixpence	Tyler
May 11	Flora, the Red Menace	Walker
May 16	The Roar of the Greasepaint . . .	Lang (Bennett)
June 26	Mardi Gras	Lang
October 9	Hot September	Lang
October 10	Drat! The Cat!	Kay
October 17	On a Clear Day You Can See Forever	Bennett (Noeltner)
November 4	Xmas in Las Vegas	Walker
November 13	Skyscraper	(Wilcox)
November 22	Man of La Mancha	
November 29	Anya	Walker
December 10	The Yearling	Wilcox

1966

January 29	Sweet Charity	Burns (Wilcox)
March 18	Pousse Café	Wilcox
March 29	It's a Bird . . . It's Superman	Sauter (Walker, Tyler)
May 21	A Time for Singing	Walker
May 24	Mame	Lang (Andrews)
May 31	Annie Get Your Gun	Bennett
July 19	Show Boat	Bennett (Tunick)
October 18	The Apple Tree	Sauter (Lawrence)
November 20	Cabaret	Walker (Tyler)
November 26	Walking Happy	Wilcox

December 5	I Do! I Do!	Lang
December 14	Breakfast at Tiffany's	Burns (Wilcox)
December 15	A Joyful Noise	Stegmeyer

1967

January 19	By Jupiter	(Tunick)
March 28	Sherry!	Lang (Wilcox, Andrews)
April 11	Illya Darling	Burns (Wilcox)
April 26	Hallelujah, Baby!	Matz, Henderson (Tyler)
August	Peg	Lang (Bennett)
September 16	Hellzapoppin	Walker
October 23	Henry, Sweet Henry	Sauter
November	How Do You Do? I Love You	Tunick
December 7	How Now, Dow Jones	Lang
December 9	Mata Hari	Bennett (Spialek, Lang)

1968

January 18	The Happy Time	Walker (Tyler)
January 27	Darling of the Day	Burns (Wilcox, Tyler)
February 4	Golden Rainbow	Andrews (Lawrence)
March 3	Here's Where I Belong	Tunick
April 4	The Education of H*Y*M*A*N K*A*P*L*A*N	Wilcox
April 10	George M!	Lang (Sauter)
April 23	I'm Solomon	Kay (Tunick)
May 2	New Faces of 1968	
October 19	A Mother's Kisses	Andrews, Wilcox
October 20	Her First Roman	Walker (Tyler)
October 23	Maggie Flynn	Lang
November 17	Zorbà	Walker (Tyler)
December 1	Promises, Promises	Tunick
December 11	Ballad for a Firing Squad	Wilcox

1969

January 4	Love Match	Kay
January 22	Celebration	Tyler
February 6	Dear World	Lang (Andrews)
February 26	Georgy	Sauter
March 16	1776	Sauter
March 18	Come Summer	(Tunick)
June 4	Promenade	Sauter
October 23	Jimmy	Andrews (Tunick)
October 30	Angela	Walker
November 5	Rondelay	Lang
November 13	Phil the Fluter	Kostal
December 13	1491	Kostal
December 14	La Strada	Sauter (Lawrence)

	December 18	Coco	Kay (Bennett, Henderson)
1970			
	February 14	Gantry	Tyler
	March 5	Show Me Where the Good Times Are	Lang
	March 15	Purlie	Henderson
	March 26	Minnie's Boys	Burns
	March 29	Look to the Lilies	Wilcox (Matz)
	March 30	Applause	Lang (Andrews)
	October 19	The Rothschilds	Walker
	November 10	Two by Two	Sauter
	December 28	Lovely Ladies, Kind Gentlemen	Lang, Kostal
1971			
	January 15	Ari	Lang
	January 19	No, No, Nanette	Burns, Henderson
	March 6	Prettybelle	Lawrence
	March 27	Lolita, My Love	Sauter
	April 15	70, Girls, 70	Walker
	September 8	Mass	Kay, Tunick
	November 2	The Grass Harp	(Tunick, Bennett)
	December 7	Wild and Wonderful	Henderson
1972			
	March 22	The Selling of the President	Tunick
	April 9	Sugar	Lang
	October 23	Pippin	Burns
	November 19	Ambassador	Lang
1973			
	March 13	Irene	Burns (Tyler, Wilcox)
	March 18	Seesaw	Wilcox (Tunick)
	May 13	Cyrano	Lang (Sauter)
	November 1	Molly	Sauter
	November 13	Gigi	Kostal
	November 24	Gone with the Wind	
1974			
	January 27	Lorelei	Lang, Walker (Bennett)
	March 5	Candide	Kay
	April 11	Music! Music!	Lawrence
	July 28	Sheba	Burns
	October 6	Mack & Mabel	Lang
	October 17	Miss Moffat	
	December 23	Good News	Lang
1975			
	January 7	Shenandoah	Walker
	March 19	Doctor Jazz	Henderson

April 22	Jeeves	Walker
May 13	Rodgers & Hart	Henderson (Bennett, Tyler)
June 1	Chicago	Burns
October 19	A Chorus Line	Tunick, Kay (Lang, Wilcox, Burns)
November 13	A Musical Jubilee	Lang, Kay

1976

February 5	Hans Christian Andersen	Walker
April 25	Rex	Kostal
April 27	So Long, 174th Street	Henderson
May 4	1600 Pennsylvania Avenue	Ramin, Kay
November 13	The Baker's Wife	Walker
December 20	Music Is	Kay (Tyler)

1977

January 22	Hellzapoppin	Burns
April 21	Annie	Lang
October 29	The Act	Burns

1978

February 19	On the Twentieth Century	Kay (Tyler)
February 28	Barbary Coast	Lang
March 1	Timbuktu!	
March 27	Dancin'	Burns
May 9	Ain't Misbehavin'	Henderson
May 10	Angel	Walker
October 31	Bar Mitzvah Boy	Kostal

1979

January 11	The Grand Tour	Lang
February 11	They're Playing Our Song	Burns
April 8	Carmelina	Kay
April 14	Home Again, Home Again	Tyler
May 13	The Utter Glory of Morrisey Hall	
May 31	I Remember Mama	Lang
June 1	A New York Summer	(Lang, Wilcox, Matz)
September 6	Peter Pan	Burns
September 25	Evita	Kay
October 8	Sugar Babies	
October 18	Snow White and the Seven Dwarfs	Lang

1980

March 14	It's Spring	(Lang)
March 30	Swing	Sauter
April 27	Happy New Year	Henderson
April 30	Barnum	(Lang, Tyler, Kay, Ramin)

	June 30	Manhattan Showboat	Lang
	August 25	42nd Street	Lang
	September 14	Charlie and Algernon	Lang
	October 25	One Night Stand	Lang
	November 30	Perfectly Frank	(Henderson)
	December 7	Trixie True Teen Detective	Sauter
1981			
	March 5	Bring Back Birdie	Burns, (Lang, Tyler)
	April 16	Copperfield	Kostal
	November 19	Oh, Brother!	Tyler
1982			
	January 17	The Little Prince and the Aviator	Walker (Tyler)
	March 20	Colette	Wilcox (Tyler)
	March 21	Little Johnny Jones	Sauter
	May 9	Nine	Tunick (Wilcox)
	July 8	Seven Brides for Seven Brothers	Kostal
1983			
	February 13	Merlin	Wilcox
	August 21	La Cage aux Folles	Tyler
	December 14	Peg	(Lang, Wilcox)
1984			
	April 12	Peg	Wilcox
	November 4	The Three Musketeers	Wilcox
1985			
	April 16	Grind	(Tyler)
	July 2	Singin' in the Rain	Wilcox
1986			
	April 10	Big Deal	Burns
	October	Jokers	Wilcox
	November 24	Smile	Ramin
1987			
	December 17	The Wizard of Oz	Wilcox
1989			
	February 26	Jerome Robbins' Broadway	Ramin
	November 2	Meet Me in St. Louis	(Tyler)
1990			
	January 20	Annie 2	(Wilcox)
	November 9	The Christmas Spectacular	(Lang, Tyler, Tunick)
1992			
	February 19	Crazy for You	(Ramin)
1993			
	December 16	The Red Shoes	Ramin
1998			
	April 30	St. Louis Woman	Burns, Henderson

1999			
	January 14	Fosse	Burns
2002			
	April 18	Thoroughly Modern Millie	Burns

SECTION II.
ACKNOWLEDGMENTS

Summer camp visiting day, 1962. All of the kids—and all of the fathers—are swarming toward one of the dads, who happens to be the head coach of the division-champ New York Giants. All except one nine-year-old, that is. I had learned that Ronnie Ramin's dad was the orchestrator of *West Side Story* and *Gypsy*; while I didn't know what an orchestrator was, I knew both cast albums by heart.

Forty-odd years later, I called Sid. As the only survivor among the group of principal orchestrators discussed in this book, Ramin was of primary importance to my research. He helpfully and patiently answered questions about his work, his colleagues, and the work of his colleagues. He also graciously welcomed my occasional calls and helped to explain mysteries as I went along. In assisting my research, he was joined by three men who worked on numerous shows discussed in this book and who were able to fill me in from the inside, as it were. Elliot Lawrence, as musical director of shows orchestrated by Ginzler, Walker, Burns, Lang, and Sauter—and as a contributing orchestrator on many of the shows—was an immense store of knowledge. Don Pippin worked on numerous shows with Lang, plus assorted musicals with Walker, Ginzler, Sauter, Kay, and even Joe Glover. Peter Howard, who worked extensively as musical director, dance arranger, and vocal arranger, spoke of his experiences with Bennett, Walker, Lang, Ramin, and Burns. (During the course of the writing, Peter became ill, and he eventually died in April 2008, while I was doing the final edits on a book to which he was so much looking forward.) Each of these men talked to me repeatedly. If I have succeeded in this book in sounding like I was writing from the standpoint of an orchestra pit in the fifties rather than from a dusty academic archive, it is in good part thanks to the efforts of Sid, Elliot, Don, and Peter. A few others who played an even greater role in the project will be thanked at the very end of this section (as is the custom).

None of the orchestrators other than Sid were alive as I began my research (although during my career as a theatrical manager I worked with both Walker and Wilcox). I was successful, however, in locating the children of the others—or, at least, six of the seven who have surviving offspring. Most had little practical knowledge of precisely what their fathers did—orchestrators worked long and late and around the clock, in their heyday—but they were one and all grateful that somebody was finally directing attention toward their unsung dads. Special thanks, first and foremost, go to Ann Walker Liebgold. An enormous amount of the information in this book comes from the Walker Collection at the Library of Congress; Ann allowed full access, and permitted me to quote liberally from Don's manuscripts and correspondence. Alice Spialek Gruber, similarly, allowed me to use her father's fascinating memoir. Hans must have been quite a character; it is unfortunate that he never finished writing his autobiography, as the full story—with a good deal of editorial prodding—would have made a wonderful book. Irwin Kostal, Jr., too, was most kind in allowing the use of his father's colorful, unpublished memoir. I had a couple of jovial conversations with Roger Lang about the career of his father, Phil Lang; he also was glad to grant permission for quotations and my use of his father's fascinating description of the process of orchestrating *Mame*. (Roger died shortly before publication—at which point his lengthy *New York Times* obituary revealed that he was an architect and preservationist who helped preserve such landmarks as Ellis Island and Boston's Faneuil Hall, without bothering to mention his illustrious father.) I spoke briefly with Kathy Barud, who only had early memories of her somewhat estranged but cherished father, Larry Wilcox. (Oddly enough, she e-mailed me out of the blue—in reference to a column I had written a year earlier—just as I was trying to find information about her father.) Kean McDonald allowed the use of writings by his grandfather Robert Russell Bennett, including material from *The Broadway Sound* (as edited by George Ferencz); he also allowed access to his grandfather's ledger, which listed all of his theatre work from 1946 on. Most illuminating, perhaps, were my discussions with Sheila Kieran, daughter of Red Ginzler. I also interviewed her sister, Myra Kates; between them, Red's long-time collaborator Sid Ramin, and his protégé Jonathan Tunick, I was able to piece together what seems to be the only account of this incredibly talented but virtually anonymous orchestrator.

While the orchestrators are mostly long gone, I was able to talk to most of the surviving composers whose music they arranged. Each kindly took the time to discuss these events of long ago, and all—well, all but two—seemed happy to contribute to this project and help to focus the spotlight on their usually overlooked employees. In alphabetical order, I thank Richard Adler (Walker, Ramin, Kostal, Kay); Jerry Bock (Royal, Kostal, Walker, Sauter), with whom I had numerous conversations, and who graciously went digging through his attic to find partiturs that we feared were lost; Jerry Herman (Lang, Kay, Sauter), who graciously—I'm going to have to stop describing these people as gracious, although that's the word that in so many cases applies—invited further inquiries and gave me complete access to his storage facility; John Kander (Ginzler, Walker, Burns); Hugh Martin, who spoke not only as a composer (with orchestrations by Walker, Bennett, Spialek, and Lang) but as the man who virtually created the art of Broadway vocal arrangement; Mary Rodgers (Kay, Burns), who spoke not only of her experiences as a composer but of her father's relationships with Spialek, Walker, Bennett, Kostal, and Burns; Harvey Schmidt (Kay, Lang, Wilcox), who was always helpful, warm, and insightful; and Charles Strouse (Ginzler, Burns, Lang), who as the first composer I interviewed set the tone with friendly and informative discourse. Stephen Sondheim (Ramin, Kostal, Ginzler, Walker, Burns) offered keen insight and vivid memories, and his intensive musical training gave him a special perspective on the subject. Given his position in our musical theatre world, his interest was most welcome.

I also spoke to several Broadway veterans who—although not composers—offered firsthand observations. Stuart Ostrow (Walker, Bennett, Kay, Sauter, Burns) and Sheldon Harnick (Royal, Kostal, Walker, Sauter) were knowledgeable observers who—unlike many of those interviewed—had a musical understanding of the work of the orchestrator, being dedicated instrumentalists themselves. Samuel "Biff" Liff (Walker, Spialek, Bennett, Lang) provided insight from his experiences as both stage manager—on the original productions of *Gentlemen Prefer Blondes* and *My Fair Lady*—and as associate producer to David Merrick during that showman's golden years. (I worked with Biff back when I was a teenager, and he has remained a constant and appreciated source of information and encouragement for well over thirty years.) Hal Prince, who kindly took time from an especially busy schedule, offered a fascinating conversation from the view of a decidedly nonmusical observer.

Thanks also go to many other interviewees, including copyist Larry Abel; Sam Arlen, son of Harold; musical director/vocal arranger Abba Bogin; Bill Charlap, son of Moose; Emile Charlap, long-time copyist for Ralph Burns; producer Michael Ellis; Marion Evans, who spent a decade on and around Broadway and was able to speak as a contemporary of not only Royal (his teacher) but Bennett, Walker, Burns, Kostal, and others; Frank Fain, son of Sammy; the late Cy Feuer, a musician/arranger who produced shows by Royal, Walker, Ginzler, Burns, and Wilcox; Ernie Harburg, son of Yip; Herb Harris, a percussionist-turned-contractor who worked extensively with Bernstein (and therefore Walker, Ramin, and Kay); Paul Holdenbaum of Chelsea Music; Kay Duke Ingalls, widow of Vernon; Lynn Lane, widow of Burton; Jack Lawrence, who coauthored two musicals with Walker and served with Lang in World War II; John Mauceri, who was musical director for Spialek's reconstruction of *On Your Toes*; John McGlinn, who worked especially closely with Spialek in his final years, on that show and other restorations; John Morris, musical director, composer, and one of Broadway's finest dance arrangers; contractor Seymour "Red" Press, who played reeds in numerous musicals of the era and made himself repeatedly available to me; choreographer Donald Saddler; Joe Soldo, another top reed player; Pat Tolson, who as assistant to Gower Champion sat in on the creation of several important musicals; musical director/dance arranger Fred Werner; orchestrator Harold Wheeler; and producer Allen B. Whitehead, who was integrally involved with Walker in the establishment of the company that became Music Theatre International.

Information and access were provided by Marie Carter and Charles Harmon of the Leonard Bernstein office; Peter L. Felcher and Roberta Staats of the Cole Porter Trust; Duane Camp, for the Luther Henderson estate; Jay Morgenstern and Dave Olsen of Warner/Chappell, who assisted in my (unfortunately unsuccessful) search to find partiturs or archives relating to the early days of Harms, Chappell, and the Dreyfus brothers; Paul McKibbins, who helpfully provided partiturs for two Kander scores (including *Chicago*, which for several reasons was quite important); record producer Didier C. Deutsch; Michael Kerker of ASCAP; Michael Lavine, who has compiled an extensive and important music collection; Craig Tenney of Harold Ober Associates, on behalf of the Agnes de Mille estate; Dean Arthur E. Ostrander of the School of Music, Ithaca College; Anthony Lupinacci of the Shubert Theatre in New Haven, who kindly provided me with elusive tryout dates; Mark York, overseer of the Jerry Herman and Cy Coleman materials; Michael P. Price, of Goodspeed Musicals; Aaron Gandy; Robert Sher; Miles Kreuger; Amy Asch; John Franceschina; and Wayne Shirley, who generously shared his findings on *Porgy and Bess*. Russell Warner and Larry Moore, two orchestrators who spend much of their time restoring lost or partially lost charts by Bennett, Spialek, and other early orchestrators, were also eager to share their expertise.

Special thanks go to Rosanna Bruno of Russell & Volkening, agents for the estate of Lehman Engel, who understood the historical importance of the unpublished interviews that are sitting at Yale and permitted their use—which, I'm sure, is what Lehman would have wanted. I am also grateful to my friends at Oxford University Press, which has now published five of my books. Suzanne Ryan offered firm and unwavering support for this long and unconventional project; Christi Stanforth took my unwieldy manuscript and edited it into a handsome and readable book; and all through the process, Norman Hirschy has been a helpful and constructive sounding board.

George J. Ferencz, a musicologist who is the reigning expert on Russell Bennett—and who was responsible for the publication of Bennett's *The Broadway Sound* (which he edited)—was instrumental in locating the Bennett ledger. This turned out to be a key source of information, and I am exceedingly grateful to Mr. Ferencz. Joseph Weiss, of the Loesser and Styne estates, allowed total access to the scores and business records in the respective archives and acted as a much-appreciated sounding board. My longtime friends Max A. Woodward and Bill Rosenfield both provided encouragement and support. Billy went so far as to read the first third of the manuscript and offer valuable suggestions. As for Max—my kids call him "Theatre Max"—he played the gracious host on my many visits to Washington.

Over the course of this project, I examined thousands of partiturs. Most of these were helpfully congregated in a few archives. Sargent Aborn of Tams-Witmark allowed me to come in and examine whatever materials were in its possession. Finn Byrhard carefully combed through the archives, and did a lot of digging and lifting on my behalf. Dale Kugel, his predecessor, worked at Tams back in the days when the big titles—*My Fair Lady, Bye Bye Birdie, Hello, Dolly!* and the rest—were being prepared for release; he kindly provided me with answers that I couldn't have gotten elsewhere. Brad Lorenz of Samuel French was similarly willing, although a thorough search turned up virtually no partiturs; they all seem to have been lost (or, sad to say, disposed of!) years ago. George Boziwick, chief of the Music Division at the New York Public Library for the Performing Arts, was especially accommodating, going so far as to arrange access to materials that were not quite ready for viewing. The librarians up at Lincoln Center—in both the music and theatre divisions—are too many to name, but their assistance was (as always) appreciated. Suzanne Eggleston Lovejoy of the Irving S. Gilmore Music Library at Yale University was knowledgeable of her collection's holdings, and the staff and working conditions made my trips to New Haven enjoyable. Maryann Chach and Sylvia Wang of the Shubert Archives, too, made the chore of digging through dusty old scores pleasant—and I always find it a positively Belascoesque experience to sit in Daniel Frohman's old offices above the Lyceum.

While my initial focus was on locating partiturs and examining them, I soon realized that the value of this book would be in not only identification but explanation. Thus, I needed to educate myself on the art of orchestration. At just about this time, Freddie Gershon of Music Theatre International opened his warehouse to me—literally so—and permitted me to borrow whatever materials I needed. Karl Gallmeyer, the director of the musical library, went through two floors' worth of metal shelving and found six sets of partiturs, namely, Walker's *The Music Man* and *The Unsinkable Molly Brown*, Ginzler's *How to Succeed* and *A Family Affair*, Bennett's *By the Beautiful Sea*, and Sauter's *The Apple Tree*. Jim Merrilat of MTI also shared his knowledge.

Sitting in my living room for three months with these cartons full of material—reading the scores while listening to the cast albums (and, eventually, without listening to the cast albums), comparing the final versions to the cut materials, and piecing together the orchestration process—allowed me to begin to understand what theatre orchestration truly is. From that point onward, I amassed my own personal collection of copies of partiturs, which by the end of this project had grown to about 30 complete scores plus hundreds of selected songs and overtures. But this working collection started due to Freddie Gershon's generosity and trust, and I am truly appreciative.

A similar hands-on education came courtesy of Jack Viertel, who as soon as he learned about the project invited me to orchestra readings of the musicals produced by City Center Encores! There is no experience comparable to sitting with partiturs in a spacious, well-lit room with perfect acoustics while a group of top New York musicians plays through the charts. Rob Fisher shared his experiences working on the first twelve years of Encores! productions; subsequent Encores! conductors (including Rob Berman and Eric Stern) welcomed me to their rehearsals; and I spent a considerable amount of time with Josh Clayton, the Encores! music man responsible for piecing together disparate scores and parts into readiness for performance.

Within the small world of musical theatre researchers, there are a few of us who keep each other apprised of what we are doing, help to solve each other's mysteries, and generally keep our ears open for information that we know the others are looking for. Principal among these colleagues is Robert Kimball, author, researcher, and artistic consultant to the estates of several composers. Bob, in his various guises, has been instrumental in the rescue and preservation of so many musical theatre materials that he deserves a citation of his own to hang on the wall. Ted Chapin, too, was an early and important supporter of this project, offering insight and encouragement as well as full access to the many resources of the Rodgers & Hammerstein Organization. His efforts and enthusiasm were much appreciated, especially when I was first trying to turn this intriguing idea into a viable project. Tommy Krasker—who in collaboration with Kimball prepared an early catalog of the location of existing materials, their *Catalog of the American Musical*, which was one of the few tools I had in hand when I started this project—was always willing to share his considerable knowledge. Ken Bloom's multivolume tome, *American Song*, has been similarly valuable; so has Ken himself, as he was always quick to put aside his own work to provide information or offer clues. Ken was also of more concrete help by locating live tapes of unrecorded musicals, giving me a chance to hear otherwise vanished orchestrations. Michael Feinstein, too, is a repository of information on matters musical; I still marvel that I could ask him a question about some lost 1930s musical on a Tuesday and receive, by the weekend, a CD copy of an old radio interview that answered my question. (This happened more than once!) Bruce Pomahac enthusiastically shared in each discovery, both as Director of Music for the Rodgers & Hammerstein companies and on his own. Bruce went out of his way to find materials for me and to answer my many questions. All of the above have dedicated many years to finding, preserving, understanding, and sharing bits and pieces of the American musical theatre, and I'm proud to consider them colleagues.

One of my first calls in search of partiturs was to Mark Eden Horowitz at the Music Division of the Library of Congress. His official title is music specialist, but that doesn't begin to describe it. The Music Division has acres and acres of holdings in all disciplines; Mark seems to be one of the main caretakers of most things Broadway -related. But not only caretaker; he knows the collections and—what's more—understands and protects the materials in his charge. Mark served as an amazing guide, helping me to figure out precisely what I was looking for and where to find it. What's more, he would call my attention to things that I didn't realize I was going to need. Like Bob Kimball, Mark deserves a plaque for his unsung services to the legacies of Kern, Rodgers, Berlin, Sondheim, and their brethren. While working at the LOC, I became reacquainted with Elizabeth H. Auman, whose title is donor relations officer. Betty quickly became a strong advocate for this book, so much so that two years into the project she was instrumental in arranging for a much-appreciated research grant from the Ira and Leonore Gershwin Trust. Betty and I remained in continuous contact thereafter. Many thanks to Betty and to Michael Strunsky of the Gershwin Trust.

Jonathan Tunick knows more about orchestrations and orchestrators than anyone; fortunate am I that he made himself available on several occasions over the course of my research. Jonathan talks about writing a book of his own about orchestrations, which will be of immense value. Even so, he generously shared information, insights, and a considerable amount of his time. We are all lucky to have had Jonathan working in the theatre for almost fifty years now, and his input has greatly contributed to what I hope is the authoritative tone of this book.

I met Larry Blank in 1978, when we did a workshop of a musical so bad that we both bailed before it reconvened for Broadway. (All right, it was *Saravà.*) We didn't come across each other again until twenty years later, when he e-mailed about an outspoken review I wrote; he agreed with me, as it happened. We began an occasional electronic correspondence, swapping info about shows we had worked on. He soon mentioned that he was a protégé of Irv Kostal; when he was musical director for *Copperfield*, one of Kostal's final shows, Irv said "You're too good to be a conductor" and started to transform Larry into an orchestrator.

This led to casual conversation about some of the shows Irv ghosted on. Just then, Bruce Pomahac sent over his impressive reconstruction of the original version of *Carousel*, along with preliminary notes on the other Rodgers & Hammerstein musicals. At the same time, I ran into Jonathan Tunick, who once again praised Red Ginzler as the greatest of the great. These concurrent discussions drove home the fact that there was no place to check and verify this information; with all of the hundreds of musical theatre books on the shelves, nobody had ever delved into the subject of orchestration. This awakened the musical comedy detective within me, with the results that now rest in your hands.

I was fairly confident of my ability to compile and write what would become the biographical and show listing sections. I was hesitant about the orchestration section itself; I wondered whether I knew enough to explain the what and how of it. I ultimately managed to learn more about the technical side of orchestration than I anticipated, and was able—four years into the project—to write the "art of orchestration" section I had imagined. But Larry Blank was always available, and over the course of time checked much of the material for accuracy and comprehensibility. Mostly because he was glad that somebody was going to finally write a book on the subject, and happy to help in any way he could. Which was pretty much the attitude of Tunick, Pomahac, Chapin, Kimball, Elliot Lawrence, Peter Howard, and Don Pippin as well.

Finally, this book simply would not have been written without the encouragement and partnership of my wife, Helen Lang Suskin. *The Sound of Broadway Music* was an enormous undertaking, occupying seven years of time and concentration. (Well, partial concentration; while I was compiling the research and figuring it all out, I wrote three other books and about 350 articles and reviews.) The act of amassing thousands of pieces of information, digesting them individually, and figuring out how to piece them together can leave you—well—preoccupied. Once you are in the midst of a puzzle like this, the wheels keep spinning week in and week out; you can't exactly take the pieces off the living room table and put them into the box when company comes, figuratively speaking. Helen has been patient, understanding, and always supportive. If this book is a major accomplishment, it is one that I share with—and that could only have been realized with—Helen by my side.

SECTION III.
SOURCES AND BIBLIOGRAPHY

With the subject of Broadway orchestration being a relatively unmined field, most of the quotations and anecdotes in this book come from personal interviews or unpublished material sitting in dusty archives. It was not my desire to pepper this book with footnote after footnote after footnote, which can quickly become tiring to the reader Even so, I think it might prove useful to provide a generalized guide to the sources.

All quotations from the following people are derived from my interviews with them—on the phone or in person, with follow-up via e-mail—between 2003 and 2008: Jerry Bock, Marion Evans, Sheldon Harnick, Jerry Herman, Peter Howard, John Kander, Elliot Lawrence, Hugh Martin, John Morris, Stuart Ostrow, Don Pippin, Hal Prince, Sid Ramin, Mary Rodgers, Harvey Schmidt, Stephen Sondheim, Charles Strouse, and Jonathan Tunick. Also, Larry Abel, Richard Adler, Larry Blank, Abba Bogin, Mark Bramble, Emile Charlap, Michael Ellis, Cy Feuer, Alice Spialek Gruber, Herb Harris, Myra Ginzler Kates, Sheila Ginzler Kieran, Dale Kugel, Roger Lang, Jack Lawrence, Ann Walker Liebgold, Samuel "Biff" Liff, Phyllis Newman, Seymour "Red" Press, Donald Saddler, David Shire, Joe Soldo, Fred Werner, Harold Wheeler, and Allen B. Whitehead.

The actual words of the orchestrators—in the cases where their words are preserved—have been invaluable. A considerable amount of material has been quoted from the writings of five of the orchestrators, with express permission of their estates (which were glad to have these voices finally heard). Excerpts from "Men of Notes," as well as other writings, correspondence, and interviews by Don Walker, used courtesy of his daughter Alice Walker Liebgold. Excerpts from *The Broadway Sound*, as well as other writings, interviews, and correspondence by Robert Russell Bennett, reprinted by permission of his grandson Kean McDonald.

Excerpts from "A Passing Note" by Hans Spialek used by permission of his daughter Alice Spialek Gruber. Excerpts from "From Ragtime to Riches" by Irwin Kostal used by permission of his son Irwin Kostal, Jr. "Orchestrating *Mame*" as well as other writings and interviews by Philip J. Lang used by permission of his son Roger Philip Lang. Information was also quoted from brief autobiographical notes written by Phil Lang and Ted Royal.

In the late 1970s, Lehman Engel—the legendary musical director-turned-educator—conducted a series of interviews with every important musical theatre personage he could get before a microphone. (A few pointedly refused the offer, including Rodgers and Sondheim; the latter, according to a note in the files, was upset about Engel's public disparagement of *Pacific Overtures*.) These interviews are invaluable in that they give us a chance to hear from some long-departed orchestrators and arrangers. These include Ralph Burns (pages 4, 34, 35, 375), Hershy Kay (pages 48, 53), Buster Davis (pages 133, 337), Herb Harris (page 219), Trude Rittman (page 198), Milton Rosenstock (pages 156, 197, 354, 387), Joe Layton (page 493), Rouben Mamoulian (page 190), Bob Merrill (page 553), Agnes de Mille (pages 197, 317), Morris Stonzek (page 228), Jule Styne (pages

127, 183), and Lehman himself (pages 213, 443). Additionally, we have included several quotes from Engel interviews with Russell Bennett (page 125) and Phil Lang (pages 67, 126, 242, 339, 385). These excerpts are reprinted by the permission of Russell & Volkening as agents for the estate of Lehman Engel.

The most important source material for this book—along with the Bennett, Kostal, Spialek, and Walker memoirs—were the actual partiturs. I also examined unpublished piano-conductor scores, published and unpublished vocal scores, and—for the numerous credits and statistics—an endless array of materials, including programs, souvenir programs, sheet music covers, advertising heralds, newspaper clippings, and liner notes. Additionally, there were many letters, lists, articles, and other documents that were found in the Walker Collection and other archives. It would be cumbersome to list all of this in a bibliography, but without these materials, this book could not exist.

The traditional forms of book research have been upended in recent years by the Internet. There is now so much material available on-line—much of it unavailable elsewhere—that it has become indispensable. However, it must always be kept in mind that the information on the Internet is not especially accurate. The vagaries of Wikipedia, for example, are well known; just about anybody can add information to just about any entry, with accuracy and veracity unpoliced. (Not all of what you read in printed reference books is accurate, for that matter—which is presumably the source of much misinformation on the Web.) The invaluable Internet Broadway Database (www.ibdb.com), a project of the Broadway League, collects and organizes massive amounts of theatrical facts and statistics—a truly Herculean task and a much-appreciated mass of knowledge. However, I note in passing that, when last checked, my personal IBDB listing not only omitted various credits; it credited me with three shows that I never even saw, let alone worked on. So, yes, I did a considerable amount of research on the Web, and I'm a firm believer in the Internet's value to researchers; but I don't necessarily accept every fact as fact.

Due to the nature of this project, more information came from original materials, interviews, and elsewhere than from actual, old-fashioned books. There remains, though, a core group of sources that were consulted and which I am glad to cite.

Banfield, Stephen. *Sondheim's Broadway Musicals.* Ann Arbor: University of Michigan Press, 1993.

Behrman, S. N. "Accoucheur." *New Yorker*, February 6, 1932.

Bennett, Robert Russell. *The Broadway Sound*, edited by George J. Ferencz. Rochester, N.Y.: University of Rochester Press, 1999.

———. *Instrumentally Speaking.* Melville, N.Y.: Belwin-Mills, 1975.

Bloom, Ken. *American Song: The Complete Musical Theatre Companion, 1877–1995*, 2nd ed. New York: Schirmer, 1996.

Bloom, Ken, and Vlastnick, Frank. *Broadway Musicals: The 101 Greatest Shows of All Time.* New York: Black Dog & Leventhal, 2004.

Blum, Daniel, editor. *Theatre World*, vols. 1–4. New York: Daniel C. Blum/Theatre World, 1945–1948.

———. *Theatre World*, vols. 5–13. New York: Greenberg, 1949–1957.

———. *Theatre World*, vols. 14–20. Philadelphia: Chilton, 1958–1964.

Bordman, Gerald. *American Musical Theatre*, 3rd ed. New York: Oxford University Press, 2001.

———. *Days to Be Happy, Years to Be Sad.* New York: Oxford University Press, 1982.

———. *Jerome Kern.* New York: Oxford University Press, 1980.

Chapman, John, editor. *The Best Play Series, 1947–1948* through *1951–1952.* New York: Dodd, Mead, 1948–1952.

Collinson, Francis M. *Orchestration for the Theatre.* London: Bodley Head, 1941.

Drew, David. *Kurt Weill: A Handbook.* Berkeley: University of California Press, 1987.

Duke, Vernon. *Passport to Paris.* Boston: Little, Brown, 1955.

Feinstein, Michael. *Nice Work If You Can Get It: My Life in Rhythm and Rhyme.* New York: Hyperion, 1995.

Fordin, Hugh. *Getting to Know Him.* New York: Random House, 1977.

Gaver, Jack. *Season In Season Out.* New York: Hawthorn, 1966.

Green, Stanley. *Encyclopedia of the Musical Theatre.* New York: Dodd, Mead, 1976.

———. *Ring Bells! Sing Songs!* New York: Arlington House, 1971.

———. *The World of Musical Comedy*, 4th ed. New York: Da Capo, 1984.

Green, Stanley, editor. *Rodgers and Hammerstein Fact Book.* New York: Lynn Farnol Group, 1980.

Hart, Dorothy, and Kimball, Robert, editors. *The Complete Lyrics of Lorenz Hart.* New York: Knopf, 1986.

Horowitz, Mark Eden. *Sondheim on Music.* Lanham, Md.: Scarecrow, 2003.

Hughes, Elinor. *Passing Through to Broadway.* Boston: Waverly House, 1948.

Jablonski, Edward. *Harold Arlen: Rhythm, Rainbows, and Blues.* Boston: Northeastern University Press, 1996.

Kimball, Robert, editor. *The Complete Lyrics of Cole Porter.* New York: Knopf, 1983.

———. *The Complete Lyrics of Ira Gershwin.* New York: Knopf, 1993.

Kimball, Robert, and Emmet, Linda, editors. *The Complete Lyrics of Irving Berlin.* New York: Knopf, 2001.

Kimball, Robert, and Nelson, Steve, editors. *The Complete Lyrics of Frank Loesser.* New York: Knopf, 2003.

Kostal, Irwin. "From Ragtime to Riches." Unpublished, c. 1992.

Krasker, Tommy, and Kimball, Robert. *Catalog of the American Musical.* Washington, D.C.: National Institute for Opera and Musical Theater, 1988.

Lang, Philip J. *Scoring for the Band.* New York: Mills Music, 1950.

Leonard, William Torbert. *Broadway Bound.* Metuchen, N.J.: Scarecrow, 1983.

Mandelbaum, Ken. *Not since "Carrie."* New York: St. Martin's, 1991.

Mantle, Burns, editor. *The Best Plays Series, 1919–1920* through *1923–1924.* Boston: Small, Maynard, 1920–1924.

———. *The Best Plays Series, 1924–1925* through *1946–1947.* New York: Dodd, Mead, 1925–1947.

Mantle, Burns, and Sherwood, Garrison P., editors. *The Best Plays of 1899–1909*. New York: Dodd, Mead, 1944.

———. *The Best Plays of 1909–1919*. New York: Dodd, Mead, 1933.

McNamara, Daniel, editor. *The ASCAP Biographical Dictionary of Composers, Authors & Publishers*. New York: Crowell, 1948.

Meyerson, Harold, and Harburg, Ernie. *Who Put the Rainbow in the Wizard of Oz?* Ann Arbor: University of Michigan Press, 1993.

Nathan, George Jean. *The Theatre Book of the Year, 1941–1942* through *1950–1951*. New York: Knopf, 1943–1951.

New York Theatre Critics' Reviews, vols. 1–30. New York: Critics' Theatre Reviews, 1940–1970.

Norton, Richard C. *A Chronology of the American Musical Theater*. New York: Oxford University Press, 2002.

Prince, Hal. *Contradictions: Notes on Twenty-Six Years in the Theatre*. New York: Dodd, Mead, 1974.

Rigdon, Walter, editor. *Biographical Encyclopedia and Who's Who of the American Theatre*. New York: Heineman, 1966.

Rodgers, Richard. *Musical Stages*. New York: Random House, 1975.

Spialek, Hans. "A Passing Note." Unpublished, c. 1956.

Stewart, John. *Broadway Musicals, 1943–2004*. Jefferson, N.C.: McFarland, 2006.

Stubblebine, Donald J. *Broadway Sheet Music: A Comprehensive Listing, 1918–1993*. Jefferson, N.C.: McFarland, 1996.

Suskin, Steven. *More Opening Nights on Broadway*. New York: Schirmer/Macmillan, 1997.

———. *Opening Night on Broadway*. New York: Schirmer/Macmillan, 1990.

———. *Second Act Trouble*. New York: Applause, 2006.

———. *Show Tunes*, 3rd ed. New York: Oxford University Press, 2000.

Taylor, Theodore. *Jule: The Story of Composer Jule Styne*. New York: Random House, 1979.

Walker, Don. "Men of Notes." Unpublished, c. 1984.

Willis, John, editor. *Theatre World*, vols. 21–46. New York: Crown, 1965–1991.

———. *Theatre World*, vols. 47–54. New York: Applause Theatre Book, 1992–2001.

Willis, John, with Ben Hodges, editors. *Theatre World*, vols. 58–61. New York: Applause Theatre Book, 2004–2007.

Willis, John, with Ben Hodges and Tom Lynch, editors. *Theatre World*, vols. 55–57. New York: Applause Theatre Book, 2002–2003.

Wind, Herbert Warren. "Another Opening, Another Show." *New Yorker*, November 17, 1951.

Zadan, Craig. *Sondheim & Co.*, 2nd ed. New York: Da Capo, 1994.

INDEX

For reasons of length and ease of use, this index has been selectively compiled; with as many as fifty or more pieces of information on the hundreds of pages in this book, a comprehensive index would be unwieldy and unnecessary. The biographical sections for orchestrators and arrangers, and the main entries for each of the productions in the listings, are denoted by boldfaced page numbers. Given the number of pages for some entries, I have also placed in boldface certain mentions that are relatively important, interesting, or simply illuminating. Songs that have undergone specific discussion are duly indexed; those that are simply mentioned in the show listings, however, are not included.